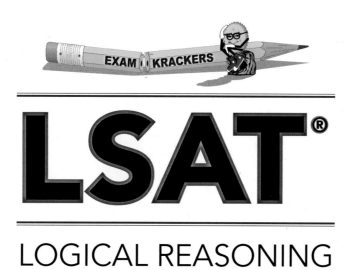

LSAT®

LOGICAL REASONING

by
David Lynch
& the Examkrackers Staff

ISBN 10: 1-893858-53-7
ISBN 13: 978-1-893858-53-4

1st Edition

To purchase additional copies of this or any other book in the Examkrackers LSAT 3-volume set,
call 1-888-572-2536 or fax orders to 1-859-255-0109.

examkrackers.com
osote.com
audioosmosis.com

Printed and bound in China

Acknowledgements

This book is dedicated to my wife, Sophie. You are my best friend and my inspiration, and none of this could have been possible without your unwavering support.

The efforts of many others also made this book possible. Thanks to Steven Horowitz, Roni Sacks, Jonathan Gaynor, Andrew Marx, Chris Barrett, and Steven Voigt for their written contributions. Thanks to my editor, Cullen Thomas. Thanks to my parents and family for their support and editing contributions. Thanks to Chris Thomas for a skilled production job, and thanks of course to Jonathan and Silvia Orsay for creating, building, and fostering the Examkrackers organization.

CONTENTS

LECTURE ② CHAPTER 2: MAIN POINT QUESTIONS

CHAPTER 3: POINT AT ISSUE QUESTIONS

LECTURE ③ CHAPTER 4: FLAW QUESTIONS

LECTURE ④ CHAPTER 5: NECESSARY ASSUMPTION QUESTIONS

LECTURE 5 · CHAPTER 6: WEAKEN QUESTIONS

LECTURE 6 · CHAPTER 7: PARADOX QUESTIONS

LECTURE 7 · CHAPTER 8: SUFFICIENT ASSUMPTION QUESTIONS

LECTURE ⑧ CHAPTER 9: METHOD QUESTIONS

CHAPTER 10: CONFORM QUESTIONS

LECTURE ⑨ CHAPTER 11: PARALLEL REASONING QUESTIONS

LECTURE ⑩ CHAPTER 12: FLAW-DEPENDENT QUESTIONS

LECTURE ⑪ CHAPTER 13 FLAW-INDEPENDENT QUESTIONS

In-Class Examinations

Explanations to the In-Class Examinations

INTRODUCTION

i.1 THE LSAT

If you're reading this book, you're probably getting ready to take the LSAT. Although taking the LSAT is probably less fun than getting a root canal, it's a necessary step in getting into law school.

The LSAT is a hard test. Even though people who take the LSAT are a very intelligent group, 99% of them answer at least **ten** questions incorrectly, and most people miss many more than that.

The good news is that the LSAT is also a very predictable test. Certain patterns of reasoning appear over and over. These patterns of reasoning often trick people the first time—or even the tenth time. But this book will give you everything you need to be able to spot, understand, and master those patterns. If you're willing to put in a lot of hard work and many hours of practice, you *can* raise your LSAT score substantially.

i.1.1 The Structure of the Test

The LSAT has six sections:

> 2 Logical Reasoning sections (These are often called the "Arguments" sections.)
>
> 1 Analytical Reasoning section (This is often called the "Games" section.)
>
> 1 Reading Comprehension section
>
> 1 Unscored section
>
> 1 Writing Sample section

You are given thirty five minutes to complete each section, and (except for the Writing Sample) each one contains 22–28 questions. The Writing Sample is always the final section of the test, but the other five sections may appear in any order.

LSAC uses the unscored section to analyze the questions they plan to use on future versions of the LSAT. You get to pay for the privilege of being their guinea pig! The unscored section is always one of the first three sections of the test.

The unscored may consist of Logical Reasoning, Analytical Reasoning, or Reading Comprehension. Thus, your test may contain a total of three Logical Reasoning sections, or two Analytical Reasoning or Reading Comprehension sections. The person sitting next to you will have a different unscored section from yours, and will see a different order of sections.

Your performance on the unscored sections does not count toward your score. However, there is **absolutely no way** to tell which section is the experimental section, so you must treat each one as if it does count toward your score. While standing in line to take the LSAT, I once overheard a person say that the last time he had taken the test, he "figured out" which section was experimental—so he *skipped* that section. He put his head down and rested his brain. I'll leave it to you to figure out why he was standing in line to take the test again.

Like the unscored section, the Writing Sample does not count toward your score, but your essay is scanned and sent to the schools to which you apply. Some schools read them, while others don't.

The entire test-taking experience will last at least four hours, and could take much longer if there are a lot of people in your testing center.

i.1.2 Scoring

The four scored sections will contain 100 or 101 questions, and the number you answer correctly is called your Raw Score. Using a conversion chart, the Raw Score is then converted into a Scaled Score, which can range from 120–180. This is the score that gets reported to law schools.

Never, ever leave a question blank on the LSAT. Even if you don't have time to finish a section, pick a Guess Letter and fill in that bubble for all the remaining questions.

The LSAT does not differentiate between wrong answers and questions left blank, so you should never leave a question blank. Even if you don't have time to read a question, you still have a 20% chance of getting the question right by guessing randomly.

The LSAT also does not differentiate between hard questions and easy questions. No question is worth more than any other, so spending five minutes on a difficult question is a bad use of your time if you could use that same five minutes to answer three or more easier questions.

Different LSATs vary slightly in difficulty, so the same Raw Score does not always translate to the same Scaled Score. For example, answering 70 questions correctly may yield a score of 159 on some tests but only 157 on other tests. Because the scoring scale is adjusted to compensate for any variations in difficulty, there is no advantage to be gained by taking the test at one time of the year as opposed to another.

The LSAT is designed to produce a range of scores in the shape of a bell curve—lots of people score in the middle, while few people score very high or very low. Nearly 70% of all LSAT-takers score between 140 and 160, but only about 4% of people score below 130 or above 170.

i.1.3 Test Administration

The LSAT is administered four times every year by the Law School Admission Council (LSAC). The four administrations usually occur in early February, early June, early October, and early December. Many law schools require that the LSAT be taken by December for admission the following fall. However, taking the test earlier—in June or October—is often advised.

The registration fee for the LSAT is currently $123. If you meet certain criteria, you may qualify for an LSAC fee waiver. Late registrants must pay an additional $62.

If you haven't already registered for the test, we suggest that you do so as soon as possible. If you wait, the most convenient test center for you may fill up, forcing you to take the LSAT in a less convenient location. In addition, most people find that having a firm deadline for perfecting their LSAT skills helps them to focus their studying and improve their motivation.

Go to **www.lsac.org** to find details about testing dates and locations and to register.

i.1.4 LSDAS

Almost all ABA-approved law schools require that you register for the Law School Data Assembly Service (LSDAS). The LSDAS prepares a report for each law school to which you apply. The report contains information that is important in the law school admission process, including an undergraduate academic summary, copies of all undergraduate, graduate, and law/professional school transcripts, LSAT scores and writing sample copies, and copies of letters of recommendation processed by LSAC

The registration fee for the LSDAS is currently $113. To register for the LSDAS and learn more, visit **www.lsac.org**.

> You need to register well ahead of time for the test. Regular registration ends about a month before the test; there are only a few days after that deadline in which you can register late, and late registration comes with an additional fee.

i.2 THE LOGICAL REASONING SECTION

The Logical Reasoning sections of the LSAT consist of 24–26 multiple choice questions, which you have 35 minutes to complete. Each question asks about a corresponding short passage.

The questions are presented in a rough order of difficulty, so they tend to be more difficult as the section progresses, but questions of all difficulty levels are sprinkled throughout the section. So you should expect to see more challenging questions as you move through the section, but you should not be surprised by difficult questions early on or easy questions toward the end.

i.2.1 What It Tests

The Logical Reasoning section of the LSAT tests three skills:

1. Reading

Each question asks about a corresponding short passage. It is critical that you understand the most important parts of the passage, which vary by question task. Also, the passages and answer choices are *intentionally confusing*, so an ability to analyze complex prose is essential.

2. Reasoning

The questions test your reasoning ability, and reasoning is all about argumentation. You need to know how to analyze, critique, and construct arguments. Most questions ask about flawed arguments, so an ability to spot weaknesses in arguments is particularly important.

> The writers of the LSAT work according to the Convoluted Credo: "Never say in one simple word what you can express in many more complicated words."

3. Time Management

To complete a Logical Reasoning section, you need to spend about 80 seconds on each question. That means you need to read the passage, understand the question, go through every answer choice, and bubble your answer—all in less than one and a half minutes! Of course, you shouldn't budget a specific amount of time per question, as not all questions are equally difficult. The 80-second per question figure is just to show you how tight the time constraints are.

You should know that the Logical Reasoning section does *not* test formal logic, complex logic vocabulary, or knowledge of specific content. The questions are based *only* on what is contained within the corresponding passages, and you won't need anything but the three skills listed above.

i.2.2 Importance to Your Score

It's hard to overstate how important Logical Reasoning is to your LSAT score. There are two scored Logical Reasoning sections of roughly 25 questions each on every LSAT. Since the LSAT has about 100 scored questions overall, that means Logical Reasoning determines *half* of your score!

Because the Logical Reasoning section makes up such a large portion of your overall score, you cannot be successful on the LSAT without being successful on the Logical Reasoning section.

i.3 ARGUMENTS

i.3.1 Elements of an Argument

On the LSAT, an **argument** is not a disagreement or a fight. Instead, it simply refers to someone trying to convince you to believe something.

Most Logical Reasoning passages contain arguments, and every argument has two parts: a **conclusion** and one or more **premises**.

- An argument's **conclusion** is the claim that it attempts to establish. You can think of it as the argument's *point* or the *bottom line*. The conclusion is the central claim that everything else is supposed to support.

- A **premise** is factual evidence that supports an argument's conclusion. Premises explain *why* the reader should accept the truth of the conclusion. While an argument can have only one conclusion, it can have more than one premise.

Here's a simple argument:

> Professor: Beethoven's symphonies are performed more often than those of any other composer. Therefore, Beethoven must be the best composer in the history of music.

What is this argument's conclusion? What is the claim that it attempts to establish? It can't be the first sentence, since that's just a factual observation. The central claim to this argument is that Beethoven must be the best composer. That is the point. The first sentence exists only to support this claim. Therefore, the second sentence is the **conclusion**.

In the sample argument above, the evidence for the conclusion is that Beethoven's symphonies are performed more often than those of any other composer. This statement is a **premise**.

You will learn tools to help you identify the elements of an argument in Lecture 2, and you will continue to apply those tools throughout the course of your study.

> An argument's conclusion does not have to be the final sentence in the passage. It could also appear at the beginning or in the middle.

i.3.2 Be Critical, But Accept the Premises

For every argument on the LSAT, you *must accept that the premises are true.* It doesn't matter how ridiculous they sound or whether you vehemently disagree with them. While taking the test, you must *always* set aside your disbelief and accept the truth of the premises.

On the other hand, the conclusion is up for debate. You are allowed to question whether the conclusion is really true. The person making the argument *believes* the conclusion is true because of the premises he cites—that is, he is not trying to trick or lie to you. But usually the premises, even though they are true, are not enough to completely *prove* that the conclusion is true. It may or may not be, and many questions will ask you to deal with this uncertainty.

For example, *even if* Beethoven's symphonies are performed most often, maybe it's the case that Wagner's operas are performed ten times as often as Beethoven's symphonies. If this is true, then Beethoven isn't the clear-cut choice for best composer in history. He might be the best. Or he might not be.

Dealing with the uncertainty of whether the conclusion is really true depends heavily on spotting flaws in reasoning. Understanding these flaws is an important skill, but you need effective techniques and lots of practice. You'll learn several different methods in Lectures 3 and 4, and you'll practice spotting flaws throughout the rest of the book.

i.3.3 Most LSAT Arguments Are Flawed

A perfect argument does not contain a flaw. Its premises, if true, guarantee that its conclusion is also true. For example, here's a perfect argument:

> Carson always does his laundry every Tuesday. Today is Tuesday. Therefore, Carson will do his laundry today.

If the first two statements are true, then the third is guaranteed to be true.

On the LSAT, most arguments *do* contain a flaw. For example, the argument above about Beethoven is flawed. Even if its premises are true, its conclusion is not guaranteed to be true. Being able to express *why* an argument is flawed is a vital skill on the LSAT, but not every question will require you to do so.

As you learn how to spot flaws in reasoning, you'll start to notice them everywhere, from conversations with friends to news broadcasts.

There are two types of passages that appear in the Logical Reasoning section:

1. **Passages that don't contain an argument**. These passages are simply made up of a collection of facts.

2. **Passages that do contain an argument**. The vast majority of these passages contain a flawed argument, but not every question requires you to be able to describe the flaw in the argument. When a passage contains an argument, there are two types of questions that could be attached to it:

   A. **Flaw-dependent questions**. Answering this kind of question correctly depends on your ability to express the flaw in the argument.

   B. **Flaw-independent questions**. Even though the argument probably contains a flaw, you can ignore it when answering this kind of question.

As you use this book, you will learn which kinds of questions are flaw-dependent and which are flaw-independent.

i.4 THE QUESTIONS

i.4.1 Question Structure

Every Logical Reasoning question consists of three parts: a passage, a question stem, and five answer choices. Here's what a typical question looks like:

> 21. Psychologist: Some astrologers claim that our horoscopes completely determine our personalities, but this claim is false. I concede that identical twins—who are, of course, born at practically the same time—often do have similar personalities. However, birth records were examined to find two individuals who were born 40 years ago on the same day and at exactly the same time—one in a hospital in Toronto and one in a hospital in New York. Personality tests revealed that the personalities of these two individuals are in fact different.
>
> Which one of the following is an assumption on which the psychologist's argument depends?
>
> (A) Astrologers have not subjected their claims to rigorous experimentation.
> (B) The personality differences between the two individuals cannot be explained by the cultural differences between Toronto and New York.
> (C) The geographical difference between Toronto and New York did not result in the two individuals having different horoscopes.
> (D) Complete birth records for the past 40 years were kept at both hospitals.
> (E) Identical twins have identical genetic structures and usually have similar home environments.
>
> Test 28, Section 1, Question 21

PASSAGE

QUESTION STEM

ANSWER CHOICES

This passage has a speaker: the psychologist. Most passages have no speaker at all, and some have two speakers in dialogue. The presence or absence of a speaker has no effect on your approach to a question.

Take a look at each part of a Logical Reasoning question in detail:

1. The Passage

Most LSAT passages contain **arguments**. An argument attempts to establish a *conclusion* based on one or more *premises*, which are the evidence for the conclusion. Questions about arguments often ask you to deal with how well the premises support (or fail to support) the conclusion.

Some LSAT passages are **non-arguments**. Instead of trying to convince you to believe something, they are merely sets of premises (facts). Questions about these passages often ask you to find an implication of the premises or to resolve some sort of contradiction within the premises.

2. The Question Stem

The question stem tells you what you must do with the passage. There are a small number of common tasks that question stems can ask you to perform, and each one can have several variations. Question stems may ask you to

- Recognize the different parts of an argument
- Recognize the assumptions or flaws in a chain of reasoning
- Draw your own reasonable conclusion from a set of premises

- Determine how additional evidence would affect a chain of reasoning
- Find a second situation that matches the major components of a given situation

This book discusses each variation on these tasks in detail, but it's important to recognize that the different tasks are largely rearrangements of the same basic set of skills. We will point out the similarities between different question stems throughout the book.

3. The Answer Choices

Every Logical Reasoning question is accompanied by five answer choices, labeled (A) through (E). Your job is to find the *best* answer.

The *best* answer is not always *perfect*, so you shouldn't be too aggressive as you go through the answer choices. At the same time, the *best* answer is definitely *better* than all of the other choices, so if you think two answer choices are equally good, then you need to reread them more carefully. The four wrong answers are always wrong for specific reasons.

i.5 GENERAL STRATEGY

i.5.1 The Four-Step Approach

The Examkrackers approach allows you to solve every single Logical Reasoning question using the same four-step approach:

1. Identify

First, *identify* the question type by reading the question stem. That way, you know precisely what to look for as you analyze the passage.

For example, passages that contain an argument require a very different analysis than non-argument passages. The only way to know how to analyze a passage is to read the question stem *first*. Note that this is different from how the questions are p resented: the passages come first. *Skip* the passage and go directly to the question stem.

> Always read the question stem before you read the passage.

2. Analyze

Second, *analyze* the passage based on the question type. Depending on the question type, this could include identifying the conclusion, premises, and flaw in reasoning, or it could mean understanding and dissecting a collection of premises.

3. Prephrase

Third, *Prephrase* an answer to the question based on your analysis. Prephrasing means having your own answer in mind *before* attacking the answer choices. That way, you can avoid some of the LSAT's traps and find the correct answer quickly.

Not all questions lend themselves to precise Prephrased answers. Sometimes, Prephrasing means generally knowing what you want and don't want in an answer choice rather than having a particular answer in mind.

> Prephrasing—taking a moment to figure out what the correct answer should say or do before you read the answer choices—is one of the most important habits to form in order to increase your score.

4. Attack

Finally, *attack* the answer choices. Be aggressive and look for reasons to eliminate answer choices instead of simply searching for the right answer.

As you consider each answer choice, realize that you have two options:

1. **Keep it**, if you think it might be right, if you are not sure about it, or if you don't understand it.

2. **Cut it**, if you're sure it's wrong.

Never choose an answer choice without reading all five answers, and never eliminate an answer choice simply because you don't understand it.

i.5.2 The Real Question

One challenge on the Logical Reasoning section of the LSAT is being able to stay focused on what a question is asking you to do as you consider each answer choice. Many students lose track of what they are looking for because they get lost while sorting out what the answer choices mean.

The **Real Question** solves this problem.

The **Real Question** is a short question that encapsulates *precisely* what kind of answer you should look for. Every question type has its own unique Real Question, and you will learn each Real Question as you learn about each new question type.

One of the primary advantages of the Real Question is that it is a simple *yes or no* question. Compare the following:

1. Which one of the following can be properly inferred from the statements above, if they are accurate?

2. Is this guaranteed to be true?

The first question is a typical Inference question stem. This is an *open-ended* question about the *entire set* of answer choices. It asks, "What can you infer?" This question appears to allow for many possible answers, so it makes sorting through the answer choices more difficult. There are also interpretative problems—what exactly does the question mean by *properly inferred*?

The second question is the **Real Question** for Inference questions. Instead of asking about the entire set of answer choices, the Real Question asks about *each* answer choice on its own. The Real Question also has a more direct answer—the answer to the Real Question is *yes* or *no*. The interpretative problems disappear with the Real Question as well. It may not be clear what *properly inferred* means, but *guaranteed to be true* is certainly clear.

The Real Question helps you become more accurate by forcing you to look for precisely what the question demands, and it helps you become more efficient by turning an open-ended search into a yes or no question.

i.5.3 Pacing

Time is tight on the LSAT, so you need to have a pacing plan.

Some test prep companies suggest an overly structured approach to pacing that requires deciding in advance which question types are difficult and making a list of which question types to try first and which to postpone. The problem is that it's hard to tell how hard a question is until you have already invested your time in it, and by then it is too late to decide to skip it. *Every* question type can have hard or easy variations.

As there is no single, reliable factor for determining the difficulty of a question in advance, you shouldn't bother with a hunt-and-peck approach. Still, there are some general pacing principles that you should follow:

1. **Work as quickly as you can *without sacrificing accuracy*.** You have limited time, so you need to work quickly, but it makes no sense to blaze through the section carelessly. You should find a pace at which you can work quickly but comfortably enough to remain accurate. Understand that you may not finish the entire section.

2. **Skip questions that seem to require a lot of time at first glance, and return to them if you have time.** While there is no simple formula for what makes a question difficult, you will develop a sense of what makes a question take

You will learn about Inference questions in Lecture 1.

a long time. In general, if the language is very complex or if the passage or answer choices are very long, then the question might take a long time. If you sense that a question is going to take a long time, *skip it*. There's no reason to spend five minutes on one question when you can spend three minutes on two or three questions.

3. **If you are struggling with a question, guess, circle the question number, and return to it if you have time.** Some questions are very difficult, and sometimes you'll get caught between two or more answer choices. It doesn't make sense to spend three minutes sorting them out. If you are really struggling, choose an answer, and circle the question number. If you have time at the end, you can return to it. If not, then the time you gained for the rest of the questions is well worth it.

> Pick a Guess Letter and choose it as the answer for any question that you don't have enough time for.

i.6 HOW THIS BOOK IS STRUCTURED

i.6.1 Lectures

This book is divided into eleven lectures. The lectures are the fundamental units of the text—you should study them in the order that they are presented, one at a time. After you finish each lecture, you should complete the corresponding exam in the back of the book.

i.6.2 Chapters

Each lecture contains one or more chapters. Each chapter is restricted to an in-depth discussion of a single question type. So, for example, Lecture 8 contains two chapters: Method Questions and Conform Questions.

Every chapter has the same structure. There are seven sections:

1. Identify

In the first section, you learn how to identify the chapter's question type by the question stem. You also learn important terminology for the question type. For example, in Chapter 7: Paradox Questions, you learn exactly what the word *paradox* means on the LSAT.

2. Analyze

Next, you learn how to analyze passages for the chapter's question type. Passages vary by question type, and your approach to analyzing them varies as well.

3. Prephrase

Here, you learn how to Prephrase an answer for the chapter's question type. For some question types, there are techniques to come up with a specific Prephrased answer. For other question types, it isn't useful to come up with a specific Prephrased answer, so you can focus on more general characteristics of the kind of answer you are looking for.

4. Attack

In the attack section, you learn the **Real Question** for the chapter's question type. You also learn about the common distracters, which are wrong answers that the LSAT writers use to distract you from choosing the correct answer.

5. Putting It All Together

After going through each of the preceding four steps in detail, you get to put them all together in this section. This section includes full-length Logical Reasoning questions, exactly like the ones you'll see on the LSAT. For every question, there is a detailed explanation of each step.

6. Variations

There are variations for every question type that come up every so often. In this section, you learn how to spot the variations and how to deal with them.

7. The Big Picture

Each chapter ends with a section devoted to a topic that can apply to many or all Logical Reasoning questions, not just the chapter's question type.

Within each of these sections, there are short drills to test your understanding of the specific topics covered within the section. These drills isolate each of the skills necessary for success on the chapter's question type. By working through the drills and their explanations, you are better prepared to put the entire technique together.

i.6.3 Exams

Every lecture has a corresponding exam in the back of the book. Each exam is like a miniature LSAT. It covers all the question types discussed within the lecture, and it allows you to test your skills while being exposed to many different questions. Each exam is followed by full explanations.

i.6.4 Extra Practice Suggestions

You can find practice and homework regimens specifically tailored for a variety of schedules and intensity levels at www.examkrackers.com.

This book contains hundreds of sample problems, but serious students will want to get as much practice as they can, including taking full-length timed exams. LSAC has published over 5,000 official questions from past tests, which we did not include in this book in order to keep it under $200! You can purchase as many of these past tests as you wish from **www.lsac.org**, and we provide a full list of extra practice drills and ideas for ways to use this official material.

i.6.5 The Use of Color

Colorblind students need not worry. You can still get one hundred percent of the useful information from this book without the colors.

This book uses color to help make important concepts stand out. Of course, we don't expect you to take the LSAT with a fist full of colored pencils. In fact, everything in this book would still be valid and complete if converted into black and white. However, accentuating important categories and concepts with different colors helps you understand them, keep them straight in your mind, and train yourself to pay attention to them as you work through questions.

We use different colors to mean the following:

Green:	Things that are definitely true. For example, since you must accept premises as true, they are written in green when they are listed as part of a discussion.
Blue:	Things that might be true or could change. For example, conclusions, when they are listed as part of a discussion, are written in blue.
Red:	Things that are wrong or forbidden. The names of common distracters are written in red.
Purple:	Used for the Real Question, a central concept in your approach to the Logical Reasoning section.
Orange:	Used for the names of important techniques (Tools) and for the list of steps that constitute the Tool.
Teal:	Used for Conditionals, a special kind of logic used extensively throughout the test.

LECTURE (1) CHAPTER (1)

INFERENCE QUESTIONS

1.1 IDENTIFY

1.1.1 WHAT IS AN INFERENCE?

On the LSAT, the word *inference* has a very specific meaning. An inference is a statement that's guaranteed to be true.

When the LSAT asks you what can be inferred, it is not asking you what is *implied* or *suggested*, or what *might be true*. It is asking you to draw a conclusion that absolutely must be true. That conclusion must be drawn using only

- The information in the passage and

- Valid reasoning

For example, take a look at the following passage:

> Three things are required in order for any fire to start: some kind of fuel, sufficient oxygen, and a source of ignition. Yesterday, there was a fire at the newspaper printing plant downtown.

From this passage, you *cannot* infer that the fuel for the fire was paper. That might be true, but it might not be—there could have been something else that acted as the fuel.

However, you *can* infer that there was some source of ignition for the fire yesterday at the newspaper printing plant downtown. That's guaranteed to be true, because the passage tells you that every fire requires a source of ignition.

Success on Inference questions is largely a matter of separating statements that *might* be true from statements that *must* be true.

Inference questions are very common, as they appear roughly three times per Logical Reasoning section. Some recent tests have included as many as nine Inference questions across the two sections.

1.1.2 Identifying Inference Questions

All **Inference** questions follow the same pattern:

1. **The question stem asks you to choose the statement that is supported by the facts in the passage,** in effect, asking you to draw an inference. If the question specifically asks you to draw a conclusion or to make an inference, then it is an Inference question.

2. **The passage consists only of facts.** The passage contains no argument, conclusion, assumptions, or flaw. Often the question stem directs you to accept the statements as true. This is a sure sign that you have an Inference question. If the question stem indicates that the passage already contains an argument or a conclusion, then you are **not** dealing with an Inference question.

Here are some common Inference question stems:

> From the statements above, which one of the following can be properly inferred?
>
> If all of the statements above are true, which one of the following must be true?
>
> Which one of the following is most strongly supported by the information above?
>
> Which one of the following statements follows logically from the statements above?

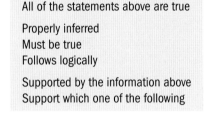

KEY PHRASES
Inference Questions

All of the statements above are true

Properly inferred
Must be true
Follows logically

Supported by the information above
Support which one of the following

All of these ask you to do precisely the same thing: find an inference.

By the way, simply seeing the word "support" in a question stem is not a guarantee that you are looking at an Inference question. You must also pay attention to *what* is supporting *what*. Compare the following question stems:

1. Which one of the following is best supported by the passage?

2. Which one of the following, if true, best supports the passage?

Question 1 requires an answer that is *supported by* the passage, while question 2 requires an answer that *supports* the passage. The difference is the **direction of the support**: if a question stem wants the passage to support an answer, it's an Inference question. On the other hand, if a question stem wants an answer to support the passage, it's NOT an Inference question.

When you see the word "support," notice the direction.

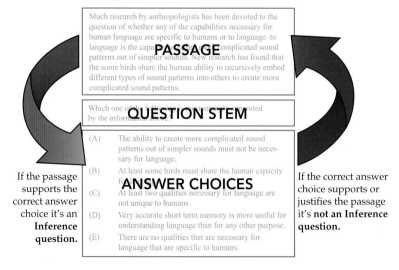

1.1.3 Drill: Identifying Inference Question Stems

Determine whether each of the following is an Inference question stem.

1. If the statements above are true, then which one of the following must also be true?

   Inference question?   ☐ Yes   ☐ No

2. If the statements above are true, then which one of the following can be properly concluded on the basis of them?

   Inference question?   ☐ Yes   ☐ No

3. Which one of the following best expresses the main conclusion of the argument above?

   Inference question?   ☐ Yes   ☐ No

4. Which one of the following, if true, most supports the politician's argument?

   Inference question?   ☐ Yes   ☐ No

5. The statements above, if true, support which one of the following?

   Inference question?   ☐ Yes   ☐ No

6. Which one of the following, if assumed, enables the conclusion of the argument to be properly drawn?

   Inference question?   ☐ Yes   ☐ No

7. Which one of the following most logically follows from the statements above?

   Inference question?   ☐ Yes   ☐ No

8. The conclusion is properly inferred if which one of the following is assumed?

   Inference question?   ☐ Yes   ☐ No

Answers and Explanations

1. **Yes.** The stem asks for something that must be true, which is an inference.

2. **Yes.** The stem asks you to properly draw a conclusion. Properly drawing a conclusion is the same as making an inference.

3. **No.** The question stem tells you that the passage contains a conclusion, which is not true on Inference questions.

4. **No.** The stem asks you to *support the argument* rather than make an inference.

5. **Yes.** The stem asks for what the passage *supports*, which is an inference.

6. **No.** The stem indicates that the passage already contains a conclusion.

7. **Yes.** The stem asks for a logically drawn statement (inference) based on the premises in the passage.

8. **No.** The stem indicates that the passage already contains a conclusion.

1.2 ANALYZE

1.2.1 HOW TO ANALYZE INFERENCE PASSAGES

1. Read each premise literally.

2. Accept that the premises are true but that nothing beyond the premises is necessarily true.

3. Don't look for a conclusion in the passage.

4. Watch out for repeated concepts.

Read each premise literally. As always, accept that the premises are true, but accept *only* what is on the page.

For instance, if the passage says no one is smarter than Sue, then you must accept that no one is *smarter*, though there may be some people who are *as smart as* Sue. Or if the passage says that vehicles powered by fuel cells release only water and heat, you must accept that these vehicles don't release anything else. However, you *don't* have to accept that such vehicles are more environmentally friendly than other vehicles, as this is beyond anything that's in the passage. Read critically to understand and accept the precise meaning of the premises, but do not accept anything more than the precise meaning.

This guiding principle is fundamental to your success in analyzing Inference passages. Unlike most other questions, Inference questions do not tend to require much analysis beyond critical reading.

Be particularly careful with:

1. Words That Express Quantities

Quantity words often play an important role when they appear.

Words that express quantity, such as *all*, *some*, *none*, *many*, *most*, and *at least one*, should be read *literally* according to their precise meanings. If a passage says that *all* lions are fierce, you must accept that there isn't even *one* lion that is not fierce.

Some, *many*, and *at least one* can be deceiving. They all mean *one or more*. The statements "Some dentists don't floss," "Many dentists don't floss," and "At least one dentist doesn't floss" all mean precisely the same thing on the LSAT. Similarly, the words *sometimes* and *often* mean the same thing.

The words *most*, *majority*, and *usually* have more specific meanings than do *some* and *many*. *Most* and *majority* mean more than half. *Usually* means more than half the time.

Some sentences express quantity without using a quantifying word. This occurs most often with statements of rank, such as *best* or *worst*. If a passage says that Jill is the *best* softball player, then *none* of the other players is better than Jill. Again, read such sentences literally.

2. Statements About Opinions

Take a look at this statement:

Technology creates more problems than it solves.

If you read this literally and accept it as true, then it's just a fact: technology creates more problems than it solves. In the real world, you might argue about this, but for an Inference passage, it's a fact. Accept it. How is this next statement different?

Donna believes that technology creates more problems than it solves.

Again, accept this as true. Given this fact, do you have to accept that technology creates more problems than it solves? No! Reading this literally, you only have to accept that Donna *believes* that this is true. Whenever a passage says that someone *says*, *believes*, *thinks*, *argues*, or *claims* something, you only have to accept that the person believes it.

Accept the precise meaning of the premises in the passage. When you get to an answer choice, you will be ready to determine whether that choice can be inferred.

In addition to reading literally, look carefully for **repeated concepts**. If an idea is repeated in more than one statement, you will often be able to use it when you get to Prephrasing.

1.3   PREPHRASE

1.3.1   PREPHRASING INFERENCES

If a passage involves **repeated concepts**, you can often Prephrase your own inference by combining the statements that use the repeated concept. Here are some ways you can do so:

1.   Inferences About An Individual That Is Part Of A Group

Some passages include a general rule that applies to a group, such as *all apes can dance* or *if you're an anarchist, you don't love the government.* These general rules can lead to inferences when a passage tells you that there is an individual who is part of the group. In such cases, you can infer that the individual follows the rule. Here's an example:

- All zebras have stripes.
- Bessie is a zebra.

   What can you infer?

"All zebras have stripes" is a general rule that applies to *all zebras*, as opposed to some or most zebras. "Bessie is a zebra" tells you that Bessie is part of this group, and thus she follows any rule about zebras. If all zebras have stripes, and if Bessie is a zebra, then you can infer that *Bessie has stripes.*

The repeated concept—*zebra*—leads to an inference about Bessie.

2.   Inferences About An Individual That Doesn't Follow A General Rule

Sometimes, a passage with a general rule about a group will tell you about an individual that doesn't follow the rule. If the individual doesn't follow the rule, you can infer that he or she isn't part of the group. Here's an example:

- If an animal is a zebra, then it has stripes.
- Bertha does not have stripes.

   What can you infer?

Here, you have another general rule about zebras. But this time, you're not told about an individual that's part of the group of zebras. Instead, you know there is an individual that does not follow a rule about zebras—Bertha doesn't have stripes. Because *all* zebras follow the general rule about having stripes, and Bertha *does not* follow this rule, you can infer that *Bertha is not a zebra.*

As in the previous example, the repeated concept—in this case, *stripes*—leads to an inference.

Don't worry if you can't come up with your own inference for a passage with repeated concepts. Not all repeated concepts lead to inferences. Suppose a passage says that most gymnasts train for five hours per day and that David is a gymnast. There is a repeated concept—gymnast. But the repeated concept does not lead to an inference. David might train for five hours per day, or he might not.

Repeated concepts can lead to inferences in many more ways than these. If you see a way to combine concepts to produce a good inference, then go ahead and Prephrase the inference. If you can't come up with a Prephrased inference (and you often won't), there are other tools to use for attacking the answers.

> Always try to Prephrase an inference, but be aware that not all Inference questions allow you to do so.

1.3.2 Drill: Prephrasing Inferences

Read each of the following statements and answer the questions.

1. All lottery winners have played the lottery. Jim is a lottery winner.

   a. *What is the repeated concept?* _____

   _____

   b. *Can you Prephrase an inference?* _____

   _____

2. Most people from New York are either Yankees fans or Mets fans. Joey is from New York.

   a. *What is the repeated concept?* _____

   _____

   b. *Can you Prephrase an inference?* _____

   _____

3. Most Americans work forty hours per week, and anyone who works forty hours per week requires at least six hours of sleep every night.

   a. *What is the repeated concept?* _____

   _____

   b. *Can you Prephrase an inference?* _____

   _____

4. Since the beginning of recorded history, every time a new island has been discovered, conflict has followed. Tomorrow, Bob will discover a new island.

   Can you Prephrase an inference? _____

   _____

5. All discoveries are followed by conflict. Tomorrow, Bob will discover a new island.

   Can you Prephrase an inference? _____

   _____

6. All violinists have an excellent sense of pitch. Oscar has a poor sense of pitch.

   Can you Prephrase an inference? _____

   _____

7. Michiko's bank charges her a fee any time her balance falls below $100. Yesterday, her balance was $120. Today, she bought a $50 shirt.

   Can you Prephrase an inference? _____

   _____

8. Michiko's bank charges her a fee any time her balance falls below $100. Yesterday, her balance was $120. Since then, her only transaction was to withdraw $50 to buy a shirt.

   Can you Prephrase an inference? _____

   _____

Answers and Explanations

1. a. **Lottery winner**

   b. **Jim has played the lottery,** since all winners have played, and he is a winner.

2. a. **People from New York**

   b. **You can't Prephrase an inference,** since you know only that *most* New Yorkers like these teams. Joey might be one of the exceptions.

3. a. **People who work forty hours per week**

   b. **Most Americans require at least six hours of sleep every night,** since most Americans work forty hours per week and everyone who does so needs that much sleep.

4. **You can't Prephrase an inference.** You absolutely *cannot* infer that there will be conflict following Bob's discovery. Just because something has happened in the past—even if it has happened *every single time* in the past—does not mean that it will continue to happen in the future. This example does not present a general rule, but rather an observation about history.

5. **Bob's discovery will be followed by conflict.** This is different because you know that *all discoveries are followed by conflict.* It doesn't say *all discoveries in the past*; it says all discoveries. This would include Bob's future discovery.

6. **Oscar is not a violinist.** Since Oscar doesn't follow the general rule that applies to all violinists, he must not be a member of that group.

7. **You can't Prephrase an inference.** You *cannot* infer that she was charged a fee for her balance falling below $100. While she did buy a $50 shirt, she may have deposited another $100 between yesterday and today's shirt purchase.

8. **Michiko's bank will charge her a fee.** Since she didn't do anything with the account between having a $120 balance and buying a $50 shirt, you know for sure that her balance fell below $100. And whenever that happens, she gets hit with a fee.

1.3.3 PREPHRASING WHEN YOU CAN'T COME UP WITH YOUR OWN INFERENCE

There are two types of inferences on the LSAT:

1. Inferences formed by combining multiple statements from the passage

2. Inferences that are mere restatements of part of the passage

You will often Prephrase inferences of the first type by combining statements that use a repeated concept. But often, the passage won't contain repeated concepts or ideas that can be combined. In those cases, the correct answer is often nothing more than a restatement of some part of the passage.

It isn't necessary to Prephrase anything if you don't quickly see some way to combine statements. Instead, just make sure you understand each statement in the passage, and make sure you have read each one literally. This should take no more than a few seconds. After that, attack the answers.

1.4 ATTACK

1.4.1 THE REAL QUESTION

When you attack the answer choices on an Inference question, the **Real Question** is:

Is this guaranteed to be true?

To use the Real Question, look at each answer choice, and after each one, ask yourself whether it is guaranteed to be true. If something is guaranteed to be true, that means you can *prove it* with *evidence from the passage*. Suppose an Inference passage tells you that many chimps enjoy chimichangas. As you attack each answer choice, ask, *"Is this answer guaranteed to be true?"* Here are some examples:

> (A) Chimps enjoy chimichangas more than other apes do.

Is this guaranteed to be true? No. Other apes might like them just as much.

> (B) Most chimps enjoy chimichangas.

Is this guaranteed to be true? No. It's possible that many chimps—but still fewer than half—enjoy chimichangas.

> (C) Many chimps do not enjoy chimichangas.

Is this guaranteed to be true? No. It's possible that all chimps enjoy them.

> (D) Some chimps enjoy traditional burritos.

Is this guaranteed to be true? No. It's possible that chimps only like chimichangas.

> (E) Some animals enjoy chimichangas.

Is this guaranteed to be true? YES! Chimps are animals, and many of them enjoy chimichangas, so of course some animals enjoy chimichangas.

Your success on Logical Reasoning questions often depends on knowing how to ask the **Real Question**. For Inference questions, that means asking, *"Is this guaranteed to be true?"*

> This is the Real Question for Inference questions only. Other question types have different Real Questions.

> **Most** means **more than half**.

> **Many** means **one or more**.

> **Some**, like **many**, is ambiguous. It also means **one or more**.

1.4.2 Drill: Asking the Real Question

Read each of the following short passages and use the Real Question to determine whether the corresponding answer choice is correct.

1. John wakes up at 7 AM every Saturday. Tomorrow is Saturday.

   (A)   John will wake up at 7 AM tomorrow.

   Is it guaranteed that John will wake up at 7 AM tomorrow?

   ☐ Yes   ☐ No

2. Bill goes to the beach every sunny day. Today is cloudy.

   (A)   Bill is not at the beach.

   Is it guaranteed that Bill is not at the beach?

   ☐ Yes   ☐ No

3. No other pain reliever has been shown to be more effective than Zizoyaveck.

   (A)   Zizoyaveck is the most effective pain reliever.

   Is it guaranteed that Zizoyaveck is the most effective pain reliever?

   ☐ Yes   ☐ No

4. Isabella hates any animal with short, dark hair.

   (A)   Isabella dislikes Mike's black domestic shorthair cat.

   Is it guaranteed that Jill dislikes Mike's black domestic shorthair cat?

   ☐ Yes   ☐ No

5. Most apples are delicious. Xavier has a barrel full of apples.

   (A)   Xavier has at least a few delicious apples.

   Is it guaranteed that Xavier has at least a few delicious apples?

   ☐ Yes   ☐ No

6. Most pirates are swashbucklers, and the majority of pirates are parrot owners.

   (A)   At least one parrot owner is a swashbuckler.

   Is it guaranteed that at least one parrot owner is a swashbuckler?

   ☐ Yes   ☐ No

Answers & Explanations

1. **Yes.** Since he wakes up at 7 AM every Saturday, there is no way for him not to wake up at 7 AM tomorrow, if it's a Saturday. So John is guaranteed to wake up at 7 AM tomorrow.

2. **No.** Be careful—you don't know *anything* about what Bill does if it were sunny, he'd be at the beach, but he might also go even when it's cloudy. You just don't know.

3. **No.** Just because something hasn't been explicitly proven doesn't mean it isn't true. For example, no one has proven that Salty (the Examkrackers mascot) doesn't have the ability to predict the future. That doesn't mean that Salty is a prophet. Although no one has shown another pain reliever to be more effective, that doesn't mean that there isn't a more effective one out there.

4. **Yes.** Since Isabella hates *every single* animal with short, dark hair, she has no choice but to dislike Mike's black, short haired cat.

5. **No.** What if Xavier had found a bunch of rotten apples in his back yard and decided to put them in a barrel? Not one of the rotten apples would be delicious. Just because *most* apples are delicious doesn't mean that any given collection of apples will have some delicious ones.

6. **Yes.** If more than half of all pirates are swashbucklers, and more than half of all pirates are parrot owners, there must be at least *some* overlap in the pirate community between the swashbucklers and parrot owners. Imagine there are ten pirates. If more than five (let's say six) are swashbucklers, and more than five (again, just six) own parrots, then at least one of the ten must be both a parrot owner and a swashbuckler.

1.4.3 DISTRACTERS

Distracters are incorrect answer choices designed to distract you and fool you into getting the question wrong.

Here are the four most common distracters for Inference questions. These common distracters can also appear on other question types.

Out of Scope

If something comes up in an answer choice that does not appear at all in the passage, then it is probably **out of scope**. Be careful with this, however, since you can sometimes make inferences about seemingly new concepts by combining facts from the passage.

Suppose the passage states that excessive alcohol consumption can cause brain damage in teenagers. If an answer choice asks whether you can infer that adults suffer similar brain damage from drinking, then that would be **out of scope**, since the passage tells you nothing about adults.

Extreme

Extreme distracters use much stronger language than is warranted by the passage. Some examples of this include: *all, always, none, never, must,* or *certain*. If the passage itself is extreme or leads to extreme inferences, however, an extreme answer choice can be correct.

If a passage says that many baseball players cheat, you cannot infer that *all*—*or even most*—baseball players cheat, since *all* is an **extreme** claim that is stronger than the passage.

Opposite

Opposite distracters are those that change good inferences into bad ones, and if you aren't careful, you could misread them as good inferences.

For example, a passage might say that any great diver can hold his breath for several minutes, and Bob is a great diver. *Bob can hold his breath for several minutes* is a good inference, but an **opposite** distracter would say that *Bob cannot hold his breath for several minutes*. If you miss the *not*, you can easily make a mistake.

Time Mismatch

Statements about the present can lead to inferences about the present but not about the past or future. Likewise, statements about the future lead to inferences about the future, and statements about the past lead to inferences about the past.

Any answer choice that makes an inference about a time period other than one supported by the passage has a **time mismatch**.

Suppose a passage states that it has always been cold in Boston during January. A **time mismatch** distracter might say that it will be cold in Boston next January. The passage only tells you about the past, so you can't predict what might happen in the future.

Extreme language does not guarantee that an answer choice is wrong, but you should inspect it very carefully to determine whether it matches the passage.

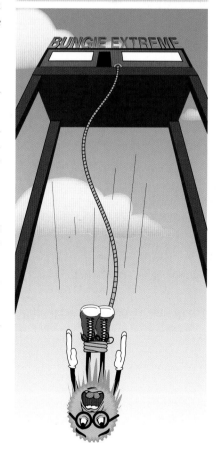

1.4.4 Drill: Distracters

Each of the following questions includes a simple passage and a potential inference. Determine whether the potential inference is a good inference or a distracter. Note that these are not the only possibilities for an answer choice on the LSAT—an answer choice can be wrong for other reasons.

1. Foods that are high in cholesterol exponentially increase the risk of stroke.

   Can you infer that cholesterol is more dangerous for heart health than sodium is?

   (A) Yes.
   (B) No, that's an **out of scope** distracter.
   (C) No, that's an **extreme** distracter.
   (D) No, that's an **opposite** distracter.
   (E) No, that's a **time mismatch** distracter.

2. In every past case, when the economy grew too rapidly, the government responded with increased interest rates to slow economic growth.

   Can you infer that, if the economy is growing more rapidly than ever, the government will soon increase interest rates?

   (A) Yes.
   (B) No, that's an **out of scope** distracter.
   (C) No, that's an **extreme** distracter.
   (D) No, that's an **opposite** distracter.
   (E) No, that's a **time mismatch** distracter.

3. An animal's failure to eat can be caused by loss of appetite, which increases the risk of exacerbation of the very health problem that induced the loss of appetite, a situation that can be fatal.

   Can you infer that, if an unwell animal goes without eating for more than a day, it must have lost its appetite?

   (A) Yes.
   (B) No, that's an **out of scope** distracter.
   (C) No, that's an **extreme** distracter.
   (D) No, that's an **opposite** distracter.
   (E) No, that's a **time mismatch** distracter.

4. Online computer games that have more impressive graphics than their competition will always be successful.

   Can you infer that XeroThero, an online computer game with more impressive graphics than its competition, is likely to be successful?

   (A) Yes.
   (B) No, that's an **out of scope** distracter.
   (C) No, that's an **extreme** distracter.
   (D) No, that's an **opposite** distracter.
   (E) No, that's a **time mismatch** distracter.

5. When a stimulus to a neuron's membrane is not less than the threshold stimulus, an action potential is created. The action potential causes exocytosis, a rapid cellular secretion of neurotransmitters.

   Can you infer that no stimulus greater than the threshold stimulus will result in exocytosis?

   (A) Yes.
   (B) No, that's an **out of scope** distracter.
   (C) No, that's an **extreme** distracter.
   (D) No, that's an **opposite** distracter.
   (E) No, that's a **time mismatch** distracter.

Answers and Explanations

1. **B.** The passage says nothing at all about sodium, which is **out of scope**.

2. **E.** It is not guaranteed that a past pattern will continue in the future, no matter how often it has occurred. This is a **time mismatch**.

3. **C.** Maybe the loss of appetite is to blame, but *must* is **extreme**, since the passage acknowledges that there could be other reasons by saying "can be due to loss of appetite."

4. **A.** The passage states that such games will *always* be successful, so of course this one is likely to be successful.

5. **D.** The passage says such a stimulus *will* result in an action potential and exocytosis, so this is an **opposite distracter**.

1.5 PUTTING IT ALL TOGETHER

Now that you've seen all the parts of the technique in detail, it's time to try a couple of full-length examples:

> 1. Most of the foods we eat contain at least some fats, but certain types of processed foods are especially high in trans fats. Trans fats are known to increase the risk of heart disease.
>
>   Which one of the following can be properly inferred from the passage?

Here's the approach:

1. Identify

This question stem asks you to find a proper inference, so it must be an Inference question. Your job is to find a statement that's guaranteed to be true based on the premises in the passage.

2. Analyze

This passage has three premises:

- Most foods we eat contain at least some fats.

- Certain types of processed foods are high in trans fats.

- Trans fats are known to increase the risk of heart disease.

Make sure to read each of these statements literally. So, for example, you know that *more than half* of the foods we eat contain fats, since that's precisely what *most* means.

There is a repeated concept—*trans fat*—that may lead to an inference.

3. Prephrase

Since there is a repeated concept, see if you can Prephrase an inference.

You know two things about trans fats: certain processed foods are high in them, and they increase the risk of heart disease. Can you infer anything by combining these statements?

Trans fats are known to increase the risk of heart disease is a kind of general rule that governs all foods with trans fats. Certain processed foods are high in trans fats, so these processed foods follow the general rule. These foods must not be good for your heart. Your Prephrased inference is:

> Inference: Certain processed foods can increase the risk of heart disease.

4. Attack

Remember to ask the **Real Question** as you attack each answer choice: *Is this guaranteed to be true?*

> (A)   Trans fats are the primary cause of heart disease.

Choice (A): *Is it guaranteed that trans fats are the primary cause of heart disease?* The passage provides no information about other causes of heart disease, so it's possible that something else is the primary cause. This answer is too **extreme**. *Cut it.*

> (B)   Regularly eating processed foods high in trans fats will cause heart disease.

Choice (B): *Is it guaranteed to be true that regularly eating processed foods high in trans fats will cause heart disease?* Not necessarily. You know only about an increased risk, but that's not the same as a guarantee. This is also **extreme**. *Cut it.*

Did you remember to read the question stem first? This is an important habit to develop right from the beginning.

As you go through the answer choices, look for your Prephrased answer. If you did a good job, the correct answer will be close to what you predicted. However, the ultimate criterion is the Real Question. If an answer choice merits a "yes" to the Real Question, keep it, even if it doesn't match your Prephrased answer.

    (C)   A diet that includes little or no trans fats will prevent heart disease.

Choice (C): *Is it guaranteed to be true that a diet low in trans fats will prevent heart disease?* Not necessarily. The passage tells you nothing about preventing heart disease, so you can't say anything for sure about prevention. Prevention is **out of scope**. *Cut it.*

    (D)   A diet that includes processed foods is likely to increase the risk of heart disease.

Choice (D): *Is it guaranteed to be true that a diet that includes processed foods is likely to increase the risk of heart disease?* Well, the passage does say that certain processed foods are high in these dangerous trans fats. *Keep it.*

    (E)   At least one type of processed food increases the risk of heart disease.

Choice (E): *Is it guaranteed to be true that at least one type of processed food increases the risk of heart disease?* This looks like the Prephrased inference. *Keep it.*

This time, two answer choices remain. When you are down to two, compare them and notice the differences between them. Once you have identified what's different, try to prove your answer with evidence from the passage.

Compare choices (D) and (E). Notice anything different? Both talk about increased risk of heart disease and processed foods, but choice (D) talks about a *diet* whereas choice (E) only talks about processed foods. A *diet* that includes the right amount of processed foods might be perfectly healthy even though certain foods within it are not. Diets are **out of scope**. Also, choice (E) specifies that *at least one* processed food is bad for you, whereas choice (D) just says *processed foods* in general. The passage says only that *certain* processed foods are high in trans fats, so choice (D) is broader than the passage. Choice (D), which looked possible at first, is now definitely wrong.

Choice (E) is the correct answer.

Here's another example:

    2.   Much research by anthropologists has been devoted to the question of whether any of the capabilities necessary for human language are specific to humans or to language. The capacity to formulate many different sounds, for instance, is a skill necessary for using language but not specific to humans, because it is demonstrated by parrots as well. Very accurate short-term memory is required for understanding language but is not specific to it, as it serves many other purposes. One necessary ability hypothesized to be specific to language is the capacity to create more complicated sound patterns out of simpler sounds. New research has found that some birds share the human ability to recursively embed different types of sound patterns into others to create more complicated sound patterns.

       If the above statements are true, which one of the following must also be true?

1. Identify

The question tells you to accept the statements as true, and then it asks you to find a statement that must also be true. This is an Inference question.

2. Analyze

This is a classic Logical Reasoning passage—lots of information, buried in overly complex language. The passage is about whether the capabilities necessary for human language are unique. Three capacities necessary for language are discussed:

- Forming many different sounds (not unique to humans)

- Accurate short-term memory (not unique to language)

- Forming more complicated sounds from simpler ones (not unique to humans)

It's not really important to do much other than make sure you get the gist of the passage here. There are several repeated concepts, but none of them leads to a quick inference that you should Prephrase.

3. Prephrase

Since there's nothing that leads to a quick inference, just make sure you understand each statement. You don't need to memorize the passage. Instead, be ready to go back and check the passage to see whether a given answer choice is guaranteed to be true.

> Don't get stuck on a complex Inference passage. If you're getting bogged down, move on to the answer choices. Once you read a choice, you can return to the passage and focus on the relevant parts.

4. Attack

Always remember the **Real Question**: *Is this guaranteed to be true?*

> (A) The ability to create more complicated sound patterns out of simpler sounds is not necessary for language.

Choice (A): *Is it guaranteed that the ability to create complicated sound patterns is unnecessary for language?* This directly contradicts the passage, which says that the ability to create complicated sound patterns is a *necessary* ability. This is an **opposite distracter**. *Cut it.*

> (B) At least some birds share the human capacity for language.

Choice (B): *Is it guaranteed that some birds share the capacity for language?* The passage says that some birds have certain capacities necessary for language, but that doesn't mean they have the human capacity for language. For example, language could also require reflective thought, which birds might not have. *Cut it.*

> (C) At least two qualities necessary for language are not unique to humans.

Choice (C): *Is it guaranteed that at least two qualities necessary for language are not unique to humans?* The passage discusses three necessary capacities, two of which are not unique to humans. So yes, there are two qualities necessary for language that are not unique to humans. *Keep it.*

> (D) Very accurate short-term memory is more useful for understanding language than for any other purpose.

Choice (D): *Is it guaranteed that accurate short term memory is more useful for language than for any other purpose?* There is no such comparison in the passage. Also, there is no reference to specific purposes for short term memory other than language. Both of these things are **out of scope**. *Cut it.*

> (E) There are no qualities that are necessary for language that are specific to humans.

Choice (E): *Is it guaranteed that there are no qualities necessary for language that are specific to humans?* This answer is **extreme**. We know that *two* qualities necessary for language are not unique to humans, but we don't know that *no* qualities are unique to humans. This is a much stronger, extreme version of choice (C). *Cut it.*

Choice (C) is the correct answer.

1.6 VARIATIONS

1.6.1 BEST SUPPORTED, NOT ALWAYS FULLY SUPPORTED

The majority of Inference questions ask you to find an inference, which is something guaranteed to be true. But on some Inference questions, none of the answer choices is 100% guaranteed. In such cases, the question stem will alert you to the situation, and you should choose the answer that is *best* supported, even though it may not be *fully* supported, by the passage.

The good news is that when there isn't a valid inference in the answer choices, the four incorrect answers are not supported at all—they are nowhere close to correct inferences. You can look out for and eliminate the same distracters that appear on normal Inference questions. The correct answer tends to be very likely, even 99% certain, but not absolutely guaranteed.

Here are some examples of such question stems:

> Which one of the following is best supported by the statements above, if they are true?

> The statements above, if true, provide the strongest support for which one of the following?

These question stems ask for a *supported* statement, not an inference, but in practice, **your approach to these questions is the same as your approach to other Inference questions**. The only difference is that, as you attack the answer choices, remember that the correct answer will either be *guaranteed* to be true (like on a normal Inference question) or *almost guaranteed* to be true. The incorrect answers will not even be close to a valid inference.

Take a look at this example:

> 3. Structuralism has its origins in the linguistic theory of Ferdinand de Saussure. He claimed that the relationship between word and object is arbitrary, and that meaning derives from the relationship between signs, which Saussure defined as a synthesis of word and object. Structuralism is thus primarily concerned with the relationship between signs. Poststructuralist thinkers were also heavily influenced by Saussure, but rejected the notion that meaning could be found in the relationship between signs. Rather, they claimed that words, which they called signifiers, merely produced endless chains of other signifiers.
>
> Which one of the following statements is most strongly supported by the information above?

1. Identify

You're looking for something that is *supported by* the passage. This is an Inference question, but since it is a "best supported" question stem, the correct answer may not be 100% guaranteed. Regardless, you are looking for something that the passage strongly supports.

2. Analyze

This time around, the passage has so much information that it would be a waste of time to list every premise. Don't bother rereading to memorize everything. Instead, just make sure you understand each premise as you go along, and always read literally.

There are several premises that are *claims* here, so they are *opinions*. While you know that Saussure *claimed* that the relationship between word and object is arbitrary, you don't know whether the relationship is *actually* arbitrary.

The passage has several repeated concepts, but there are no obvious inferences.

3. Prephrase

Since there are no obvious inferences that you can Prephrase from the repeated concepts, you will do most of the important work when you attack the answer choices.

4. Attack

To avoid confusion, you should still go ahead and ask the same **Real Question** that you would for any other Inference question. Just don't be too aggressive. If an answer is very likely, but not necessarily true, keep it. You can always come back to it if you have more than one choice remaining after going through them all.

> Use the same Real Question even when an Inference question asks for the "best supported" answer choice.

       (A)   Poststructuralists rejected the notion that the relationship between word and object is arbitrary.

Choice (A): *Is it guaranteed that poststructuralists rejected the notion that the relationship between word and object is arbitrary?* The only thing you know that poststructuralists reject is a claim from structuralism, so you can't say anything about whether they reject the claim from Saussure that the relationship between word and object is arbitrary. This is **out of scope**, and it has *no* support in the passage. *Cut it.*

       (B)   Saussure was one of the first poststructuralist thinkers.

Choice (B): *Is it guaranteed that Saussure was one of the first poststructuralist thinkers?* This has the timeline all messed up. Saussure influenced the poststructuralists, who came after him. This is the **opposite** of a correct inference that Saussure was *not* a poststructuralist. *Cut it.*

       (C)   Both structuralism and poststructuralism are concerned with language.

Choice (C): *Is it guaranteed that both structuralism and poststructuralism are concerned with language?* The passage says that Saussure had a *linguistic* theory that influenced both structuralists and poststructuralists. Since they were both influenced by a *linguistic* theory, they are probably concerned with language. *Keep it.*

       (D)   Structuralism and poststructuralism have less in common than previously believed.

Choice (D): *Is it guaranteed that these two have less in common than previously believed?* The passage says nothing about what was previously believed. This is entirely **out of scope**. The passage provides no support whatsoever for any claim about previous beliefs. *Cut it.*

       (E)   Saussure is often thought of as a poststructuralist.

Choice (E): *Is it guaranteed that Saussure is often thought of as a poststructuralist?* This is a lot like choice (B). It doesn't make sense to say that Saussure is a poststructuralist, since he came before poststructuralism. Also, the passage tells you nothing about what people often think about him. Not only is this an **opposite** distracter, it is also **out of scope**. *Cut it.*

> Sometimes answers are wrong for all sorts of reasons. Of course, all you need is one reason to get rid of an answer.

Choice (C) is the only answer left. Is it a valid inference? Well, it's not 100% guaranteed. These movements could have been influenced by a linguistic theory and yet not have been concerned with language. This can happen in almost any field. For example, a painter might be influenced by musical compositions without producing works that are concerned with music. Still, this answer is *very* likely, and the other answers have no support from the passage at all.

Choice (C) is the correct answer.

1.6.2 Cannot Be True Questions

Inference questions ask you to find what *is guaranteed to be true*, but there are some other questions that ask you what *cannot be true*. You should approach these questions in the same way that you approach Inference questions. The only difference is what counts as a good answer. These Cannot Be True questions are not common. You will probably see no more than one on your test.

Cannot Be True question stems, like Inference question stems, often tell you to accept the truth of the premises in the passage. In addition, they ask you to identify a statement that is certainly false, given these premises. Cannot Be True questions are often phrased in the following ways:

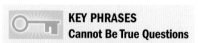

KEY PHRASES
Cannot Be True Questions

All of the statements above are true

Could be true EXCEPT
Must be false
CANNOT be true

> If all of the social critic's statements are true, each of the following could be true EXCEPT:
>
> If all of the statements above are true, then which one of the following must be false?
>
> If all of the statements above are true, which one of the following CANNOT be true?

Any question that asks for something that must be false is a Cannot Be True question.

Try this:

> 4. The highlands of Peru are the only place on Earth where, for thousands of years, large numbers of people have lived at more than ten thousand feet above sea level. Though they live in a land where crops are hard to grow, natural disasters happen regularly, and extreme weather conditions are the rule, the inhabitants of this region have repeatedly created long-lasting, technologically advanced civilizations. One explanation for this seeming paradox is that human civilizations often arise in regions where a great variety of topographic and altitudinal conditions can be found within a relatively small area. In the case of Peru, a traveler making the roughly seventy-five mile journey from mountains to ocean would pass through twenty of the earth's thirty-four primary types of environment.
>
> If all of the statements above are true, which one of the following CANNOT be true?

1. Identify

The question stem tells you to accept the truth of the premises and to find something that can't be true, so this is a Cannot Be True question.

2. Analyze

The passage has three basic premises:

Watch out for quantifying words, especially extreme ones like **only**.

- The highlands of Peru are the only place above ten thousand feet inhabited by large numbers of people for thousands of years.

- The conditions of that area are extreme.

- The success of the highlands' population might be due to the variety of conditions.

There's actually more to the passage than this, but this sums up the gist of it.

If there were an obvious inference you could make by combining statements, you would do so. But in this case, there is not.

3. Prephrase

On Cannot Be True questions, you are looking for what *cannot be true*, or what *must be false*, which is the same thing. The only thing that you can prove to be untrue is something that **directly contradicts** the passage or something that **directly contradicts** a possible inference. For example, you know that there is a place in Peru that is above ten thousand feet. So if an answer said, "The highest point in Peru is nine thousand feet," it would certainly be false. Since you are looking for something that cannot be true, that would be a correct answer.

One of the hardest things about Cannot Be True questions is that, because the correct answer is false, it can feel like you are picking the wrong answer. If you know this in advance, however, you can deal with it.

The key to Cannot Be True questions is getting comfortable with what is true and carefully reading the answer choices. If you can Prephrase a logical combination that must be true, the opposite of your Prephrased answer might turn out to be the correct answer.

Realize also that a correct answer is something that *cannot be true*, which means that every incorrect answer is something that *could be true*. You should get rid of anything that *could* be true, which, on the LSAT, includes things that *must be true*.

> Underlining the question stem may help you avoid getting things backwards on Cannot Be True questions

4. Attack

The **Real Question** for Cannot Be True questions is:

Is this impossible?

Ask yourself this question as you attack each answer choice.

> (A) There are several regions on Earth, more than ten thousand feet above sea level and containing a great variety of topographic and altitudinal conditions, which have for thousands of years been inhabited by large numbers of people.

Choice (A): *Is it impossible that there are several regions above ten thousand feet with successful human populations over long periods of time?* The first sentence says that the highlands of Peru are the *only* such place. If the highlands of Peru are the only place, then there can't be several others. There's only one, and it's in Peru. Since this answer choice is impossible, *keep it.*

> (B) There is on Earth exactly one region, containing more than twenty of the earth's primary types of environment, that has never been inhabited by humans.

Choice (B): *Is it impossible that there is just one such uninhabited region?* You aren't told anything about uninhabited regions. This might be true, so you can't be certain that it's impossible *Cut it.*

> (C) Parts of Peru that have been inhabited for thousands of years are less than ten thousand feet above sea level.

Choice (C): *Is it impossible that there have been successful populations at lower altitudes?* The passage tells you nothing about the regions below ten thousand feet. It is possible. *Cut it.*

> (D) Some regions on Earth, containing fewer than twenty of the earth's thirty-four primary types of environment, have for thousands of years been inhabited by large numbers of people.

Choice (D): *Is it impossible that some regions with less variation have had successful populations?* As in choice (B), you aren't told enough about such regions to say anything one way or the other. *Cut it.*

(E)   Parts of Peru that are less than ten thousand feet
above sea level regularly experience natural
disasters and extreme weather conditions.

Choice (E): *Is it impossible that parts of Peru at lower altitudes also have extreme conditions?* Like choice (C), this refers to regions below ten thousand feet, but the passage says nothing about such regions, so this could be true. *Cut it.*

Since choice (A) is the only answer that is impossible, pick it.

Choice (A) is the correct answer.

1.7   THE BIG PICTURE

1.7.1   EXCEPT QUESTIONS

Throughout the test, you will encounter a few question stems with a word in all capital letters, such as EXCEPT, NOT, LEAST, or something similar. These questions ask you to find the answer choice that *does not* do what you would normally look for on that type of question.

EXCEPT questions can be confusing because there is an extra step of reversal that often leads people to pick the wrong answer. This confusion can be overcome with a tool that takes advantage of the simple fact that the correct answer will always be different from the other four answers. The tool is called the EXCEPT Tool, and it works like this:

1. *Determine from the question stem what the four incorrect answers will do.* For example, on an Inference EXCEPT question, the four incorrect answers will be good inferences. Or on a Weaken EXCEPT question, the four incorrect answers will weaken the conclusion.

2. *Ask the usual Real Question for each choice and mark each choice with the answer to the Real Question.* For example, if you ask, "Is this guaranteed to be true?" and the answer is *yes*, then write a **G** next to the answer choice to show it's guaranteed. If the answer is *no*, then write something else, such as an **N**, a **?**, or nothing at all.

Or, for example, if you are working on a Weaken EXCEPT question, then write a **W** next to each answer choice that weakens the conclusion, and something else next to any answer choice that fails to weaken the conclusion.

3. *The correct answer will be the one that looks different from the rest.* For example, on an Inference EXCEPT question, four of the answer choices will have a **G** written next to them. Pick the one that doesn't.

This tool applies to any EXCEPT question. You can treat EXCEPT questions like the normal version of that question type, but use the EXCEPT Tool to identify the correct answer.

Try this one:

5. Philosopher: Knowledge is a form of belief that has a
specific justification, and it is unlike other justified
beliefs in that it is also a true belief, whereas some
justified beliefs are false. When we claim to know
something, we cannot be certain that we know it, but
only because such certainty would require knowledge
of the conditions required for the possibility of truth,
which we do not currently have.

Each of the following can be logically inferred from
the philosopher's statements EXCEPT:

1. Identify

This question stem asks you to find a logical inference, so it is an Inference question. It also has EXCEPT, so it is an Inference EXCEPT question.

> Weaken questions will be discussed in Lecture 5.

> You may see the word EXCEPT with almost any question type.

2. Analyze

This passage is too complex to bother breaking down every piece of it. Just make sure you understand each sentence. The bulk of the work is going to come when you attack the answer choices.

3. Prephrase

On a normal Inference question, one of the answer choices is a valid inference, so it makes sense to try to predict what it might be. But on an Inference EXCEPT question, four of the answer choices are valid inferences. There's no harm in predicting one or two if they seem obvious to you, but it's unlikely that you could predict all four. Just move on to the answer choices.

For any difficult question or variation, always focus on what is familiar rather than on what is unusual.

4. Attack

Use the **EXCEPT Tool**. Ask yourself the same Real Question that you would normally use for an Inference question: *Is this guaranteed to be true?* Then, put an appropriate mark next to the answer choice.

(A)   Justified beliefs can be false.

Choice (A): *Is this guaranteed to be true?* The first sentence says that some justified beliefs are false. As it is guaranteed to be true, put a *G* next to this answer.

(B)   Knowledge of the conditions required for the possibility of truth is something we will not attain.

Choice (B): *Is this guaranteed to be true?* The answer choice says we won't attain this knowledge, but the passage says only that we don't currently have it. This is a common distracter, a **time mismatch**, and thus it is not guaranteed to be true. Don't put anything next to this answer choice.

(C)   Not all beliefs that have a justification are classified as knowledge.

Choice (C): *Is this guaranteed to be true?* This is supported by the first sentence, which says that knowledge is different from other justified beliefs. Put a *G* next to this answer.

(D)   We cannot be certain of the truth of our claims to know.

Choice (D): *Is this guaranteed to be true?* This is supported by the second sentence, which says we can't be certain that we know something. Put a *G* next to this answer.

(E)   One cannot know whether something is known without knowing the conditions required for the possibility of truth.

Choice (E): *Is this guaranteed to be true?* This must be true, since, according to the second sentence, we can't know the truth of our claims specifically because we don't know about these conditions. Put a *G* next to this answer.

So you should have:

G (A)   Justified beliefs can be false.
(B)   Knowledge of the conditions required for the possibility of truth is something we will not attain.
G (C)   Not all beliefs that have a justification are classified as knowledge.
G (D)   We cannot be certain of the truth of our claims to know.
G (E)   One cannot know whether something is known without knowing the conditions required for the possibility of truth.

Since you are looking for the choice that is different from all the rest, pick answer choice (B).

Choice (B) is the correct answer.

1.7.2   AN IMPORTANT DISTINCTION

Most types of EXCEPT questions are easy to identify. However, there is one case that can be confusing. You must be careful not to mistake Cannot Be True questions for Inference EXCEPT questions, especially since many Cannot Be True question stems contain the word EXCEPT or another word in all capital letters.

> There is a summary of this (and every) question type in the review—Lectures 10 and 11.

Cannot Be True Questions

Correct answer:
  Must be false

Incorrect answers:
  Could be true

Real Question:
  Is this impossible?

Inference EXCEPT Questions

Correct answer:
  Could be false

Incorrect answers:
  Must be true (good inferences)

Real Question:
  Is this guaranteed to be true?

Use the EXCEPT Tool

1.7.3   Drill: Comparing Question Stems

For each question stem, decide whether it is a Cannot Be True question or an Inference EXCEPT question.

1. The statements above provide some support for each of the following EXCEPT:
    ☐ Inference EXCEPT
    ☐ Cannot Be True

2. If all of the statements above are true, then which one of the following CANNOT be true?
    ☐ Inference EXCEPT
    ☐ Cannot Be True

3. Which one of the following CANNOT be logically inferred from the passage?
    ☐ Inference EXCEPT
    ☐ Cannot Be True

4. The information above provides the LEAST support for which one of the following?
    ☐ Inference EXCEPT
    ☐ Cannot Be True

5. If all of the philosopher's statements are true, each of the following could be true EXCEPT:
    ☐ Inference EXCEPT
    ☐ Cannot Be True

6. If the statements above are true, which one of the following must be false?
    ☐ Inference EXCEPT
    ☐ Cannot Be True

Answers and Explanations

1. **Inference EXCEPT.** The question stem indicates that the incorrect choices can be supported by the passage (inferred).

2. **Cannot Be True.** This question stem explicitly matches the name of the question type.

3. **Inference EXCEPT.** The stem indicates that the incorrect choices *can* be inferred.

4. **Inference EXCEPT.** The stem indicates that the incorrect choices will be *more* supported by the passage.

5. **Cannot Be True.** This question stem tells you that the *incorrect* answers could be true, which is the case on Cannot Be True questions.

6. **Cannot Be True.** The phrase "must be false" means the same thing as "cannot be true."

LECTURE ② CHAPTER 2

MAIN POINT QUESTIONS

2.1   IDENTIFY

2.1.1   IDENTIFYING MAIN POINT QUESTIONS

All **Main Point** questions follow the same pattern:

1. **The question stem asks you to choose the statement that matches the argument's conclusion.** Since the correct answer is usually a *rewording* of the conclusion, the question stem asks for what *best* or *most accurately expresses* the main point.

2. **The passage consists of an argument with premises and a conclusion.** The question stem always indicates that the passage contains a conclusion.

Here are some common Main Point question stems:

> Which one of the following most accurately expresses the main conclusion of the argument?

> Which one of the following most accurately expresses the conclusion drawn by the psychologist?

> The author is arguing that

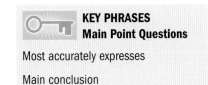

**KEY PHRASES
Main Point Questions**

Most accurately expresses

Main conclusion

These question stems ask for a restatement of the argument's conclusion.

Be careful: Many other question stem types also use the word *conclusion*. Main Point questions differ from other question types in that they ask you to *identify* what the conclusion is instead of asking you to *do something* with the conclusion. Other question types ask you to weaken, strengthen, or otherwise manipulate the passage. Compare the following two question stems:

1. Which one of the following most accurately expresses the main conclusion of the linguist's argument?

2. Which one of the following conclusions can be properly drawn from the statements above, if they are true?

The first question asks you to *identify* a conclusion, so it's a Main Point question. But the second question asks you to *draw* a conclusion (that is, come up with a new one on your own), so it's an Inference question. The word "conclusion" appears in various question types, but only Main Point questions ask you to identify the conclusion in the passage. If a question asks you to *do* something beyond identifying the conclusion, it is **not** a Main Point question.

Main Point questions are a relatively infrequent question type, occurring about twice per test. But finding the main point of an argument is an important skill that you need for almost every question type. The better you become at identifying an argument's conclusion, the more successful you will be throughout the LSAT.

> Being able to quickly and accurately identify the conclusion in *every* argument is vital to raising your LSAT score.

2.1.2 Drill: Identifying Main Point Question Stems

Determine whether each of the following is a Main Point question stem.

1. Which one of the following best expresses the main conclusion of the sociologist's argument?

   Main Point question?   ☐ Yes   ☐ No

2. The statements above, if true, most support which one of the following conclusions?

   Main Point question?   ☐ Yes   ☐ No

3. Which one of the following most accurately expresses the conclusion of the argument?

   Main Point question?   ☐ Yes   ☐ No

4. Which one of the following, if true, most strengthens Linda's conclusion?

   Main Point question?   ☐ Yes   ☐ No

5. The conclusion follows logically if which one of the following is assumed?

   Main Point question?   ☐ Yes   ☐ No

Answers and Explanations

1. **Yes.** The stem asks you to identify the main conclusion.
2. **No.** The stem asks you to draw a conclusion. This is an Inference question.
3. **Yes.** The stem asks you only to identify the conclusion.
4. **No.** The stem asks you to *do* something—to strengthen the conclusion.
5. **No.** The stem asks you to do more than just identify the conclusion.

2.2 ANALYZE

2.2.1 HOW TO ANALYZE MAIN POINT PASSAGES

Your analysis on Main Point questions consists of identifying an argument's parts. You must identify:

> The conclusion can appear anywhere in a passage, not just at the end.

1. The **premises**
2. The **conclusion**

Remember that the conclusion is what the argument sets out to prove, and the premises are evidence for the conclusion.

There are five tools that can help you identify the conclusion and premises:

1. **Indicators**

2. **Facts and opinions**

3. **Suggestions**

4. **Counterarguments**

5. **The Why Tool**

2.2.2 INDICATORS

Indicators are words that often tell you whether something is a conclusion or a premise. There are three types: **conclusion indicators**, **premise indicators**, and **double indicators**. The chart below provides a list of the most common indicators of each type:

Conclusion Indicators	Premise Indicators	Double Indicators
Therefore	After all	Because
So	In fact	Since
Thus	Given that	For
Conclude that	This can be seen from	Due to
Clearly	We know this by	As
This shows that	It has been proven that	
Hence	The fact that	

Almost every argument contains indicators, so you should get into the habit of looking for them in every argument.

2.2.2.1 Conclusion Indicators

Conclusion indicators help you identify the conclusion. If a conclusion indicator begins a sentence, then that sentence is probably the conclusion. Take a look at this argument:

> Developing countries can be hurt by rising interest rates immediately, through increased cost of borrowing. Moreover, such countries are also put at a disadvantage over time, through higher risk spreads. Therefore, developing countries are especially sensitive to sudden increases in interest rates.

The last sentence has a conclusion indicator: *therefore*. This indicator tells you that the last sentence is the conclusion. The other sentences must be premises. You can diagram the argument in the following way:

Turnaround words such as *however*, *but*, and *yet* are not particularly useful in helping you find the conclusion. Stick to the indicators listed here.

> Developing countries can be hurt by interest rates in two ways:
>
> 1. Through increased cost of borrowing
>
> 2. Through higher risk spreads
>
> ---
>
> **Therefore**, developing countries are especially sensitive to sudden increases in interest rates.

You would never take the time to draw a diagram like this on the test, but it is a useful way to organize the information as you begin working through arguments. Green denotes premises, which must be true. Blue denotes the conclusion, which may—or may not—be true. Throughout the book in this kind of diagram the word "Therefore" is always put before the conclusion, even when the word does not appear in the argument, as a reminder of which statement is the conclusion.

2.2.2.2 Premise Indicators

Premise indicators help you identify premises. Take a look at this argument:

> Jane is the coolest girl in the world. After all, Jane has
> an extensive collection of stamps and has memorized
> the ingredients in every major brand of cereal.

After all is a premise indicator, which tells you that the second sentence is a premise. So, the first sentence must be the conclusion: Jane is the coolest girl in the world. Why? Because she has a great stamp collection and knows what's in her cereal, that's why. The argument works like this:

> Jane has an extensive collection of stamps and has memorized the ingredients in every major brand of cereal.
> ....
> **Therefore**, Jane is the coolest girl in the world.

2.2.2.3 Double Indicators

Double indicators point to both a premise and a conclusion. Here's an example:

> Almost anybody can learn to sing, since singing
> requires no instrument other than the human body.

Since is a double indicator. It indicates that the second half of the sentence is a premise, and the first half is the conclusion. This is the argument:

> Singing requires no instrument other than the human body.
> ....
> **Therefore**, almost anybody can learn to sing.

Since and other double indicators are extremely useful, since they help to identify both the conclusion and a premise at the same time.

Double indicators can appear at the beginning of a sentence or in the middle, but they always immediately precede a premise.

Since {premise} *,* {conclusion}.

comma

{Conclusion} *,* *since* {premise}.

comma

Indicators are extremely useful because they help you to identify the conclusion and premises quickly and effectively. However, you must be careful—**you can't rely solely on indicators for analyzing arguments**. There are two reasons why:

1. Some arguments do not contain an indicator.
2. Some arguments use misleading indicators.

Here's how indicators can mislead you:

The LSAT writers try hardest to disguise the conclusion on Main Point questions, so be particularly wary of misleading indicators on this question type.

> Disasters involving mechanical failure on commercial
> airliners, while tragic, invariably lead to greater
> understanding of potential component malfunctions,
> and thus ultimately increase airline safety. Due in part
> to stringent regulatory oversight, no such accident has
> occurred in the last five years. In that time, therefore,
> engineers have had no chance to learn from any new
> catastrophe of this kind. Clearly, commercial airliners
> are no safer today than they were five years ago.

This argument is crawling with conclusion indicators, but there can be only one main point. You would need to use other tools to analyze this argument.

2.2.3 FACTS AND OPINIONS

On the LSAT, you must treat the conclusion as an **opinion**, and you must treat the premises that support the conclusion as **facts**.

As a result, conclusions usually sound like an opinion, and premises usually sound like plain factual evidence. You can often distinguish the conclusion from premises by considering what sounds like a fact and what sounds like an opinion. Consider the following argument:

> Theo: A sure sign of dishonesty in a lawyer is the billing of more than two thousand hours per year. Excluding weekends, two thousand hours per year represents roughly half of a lawyer's waking life.

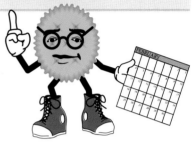

Incidentally, most big firm associates bill more than 2,000 hours per year, even though only 80-90% of their hours are billable.

There aren't any indicators you can use to analyze this argument, but you can look for facts and opinions. Theo clearly believes both of his statements, but do *you* believe them both? Which of the two sentences would you choose to argue with? The second sentence has a simple calculation of hours in a year, and calculations sound like facts. Thus, the second sentence is a premise. The first sentence makes a blanket statement about dishonest lawyers, which makes it sound like an opinion. Therefore, the first sentence is the conclusion. That gives you this diagram:

Excluding weekends, two thousand hours per year represents roughly half of a lawyer's waking life..

- -

Therefore, a sure sign of dishonesty in a lawyer is the billing of more than two thousand hours per year.

Remember, the speaker or author of every LSAT passage believes the statements in the passage. The author never intentionally *lies* to you. However, some statements are opinions that are open to debate, while others are plain factual information. It is often easier to identify the statements that are to be treated as facts, such as

- Calculations
- Statistics
- Matters of historical record
- The results of accepted scientific studies
- The results of simple observation

Such statements are premises. If there is only one statement left after you have identified all the premises, then that remaining statement is the conclusion.

Predictions for the future are usually opinions and thus conclusions.

Unfortunately, **looking for facts and opinions isn't always reliable**, since sometimes *everything* sounds like an opinion. If you encounter a passage in which you can't separate the facts from the opinion, then you can't use this tool to separate the premises from the conclusion.

2.2.4 SUGGESTIONS

Suggestions are usually conclusions. They are similar to opinions, as the best future course of action is usually debatable. Look for words like *should*, *ought to*, and *must*. If you see a sentence that sounds like a recommendation, then it's probably the conclusion.

> Mayor: The taxes in our city are substantially higher than those in nearby cities. We must reform the tax code in order to erase this disparity. A large number of people are moving into our state, and a higher tax burden puts us at a disadvantage if we wish to attract our fair share of new residents.

The mayor has a plan for the future, and this is the conclusion of his argument:

- The taxes in our city are substantially higher than those in nearby cities.

- A higher tax burden puts us at a disadvantage if we wish to attract our fair share of new residents.

Therefore, we must reform the tax code in order to erase this disparity.

2.2.5 Counterarguments

A **counterargument** is an argument directed against an opposing position. These are easy to recognize. When the author of the passage says that another person is wrong or that another viewpoint is mistaken, you are looking at a counterargument.

To identify the conclusion, look at the so-called "wrong" viewpoint and negate it. The negated version is the author's conclusion. This can be slightly tricky, since the author's conclusion is rarely stated directly—you have to construct it yourself.

Here's a sample counterargument:

> Many people believe that all cholesterol is bad for you, but this is not the case. A high level of HDL cholesterol actually protects against heart attacks.

Counterarguments are a fairly reliable sign of a conclusion, but you have to do a little extra work to express the conclusion yourself, since it's usually not written explicitly.

This is a **counterargument** against the viewpoint that all cholesterol is bad for you. Since the conclusion to any counterargument is the negation of the so-called "mistaken" position, this argument's conclusion must be that *not all cholesterol is bad for you*. So you get:

> A high level of HDL cholesterol protects against heart attacks.
>
> **Therefore**, not all cholesterol is bad for you.

Counterarguments like this are very common on the LSAT.

2.2.6 The Why Tool

The Why Tool determines whether a given claim is an argument's conclusion. Here's how it works:

1. Pick out a claim that might be the conclusion.

2. Ask, "Why _____ ?" and insert the potential conclusion into the blank.

3. The rest of the argument should provide evidence to answer the question.

If the rest of the argument provides evidence for the chosen claim, then you have correctly identified the conclusion. If not, you haven't identified the conclusion. If you don't find the conclusion on the first try, use the Why Tool on another claim.

Examine the following argument:

> Apples are much more delicious than oranges. Apples are a better choice than oranges for a snack.

In this argument there are no indicators, and *both* statements sound like opinions, so you can't use indicators or facts and opinions. Here's how to use the Why Tool on this argument:

1. Pick out a claim that might be the conclusion.
   Suppose you think that "Apples are much more delicious than oranges" is the conclusion.

2. Ask, "Why are apples much more delicious than oranges?"
   What's the evidence for the claim that apples are more delicious? There isn't any. The fact that they are a good snack doesn't explain their deliciousness.

So, the first sentence is NOT the conclusion. No problem, just try it the other way around:

1. Pick out a claim that might be the conclusion.
   Try, "Apples are a better choice than oranges for a snack."

2. Ask, "Why are apples a better choice for a snack?"
   Why are they a better snack? They are a better snack *because* they are more delicious! The first sentence answers the question posed by the Why Tool. That means the first sentence is the premise and the second is the conclusion:

> Apples are much more delicious than oranges.
>
> **Therefore**, apples are a better choice than oranges for a snack.

You should not rely on just one of these methods for analyzing arguments. Instead, become comfortable with all five so that you can use whichever is most convenient for each argument you encounter.

The Why Tool **is the most reliable of these tools** for identifying the parts of the argument, since **you can use it on *any* argument**. If you are ever in doubt, or if any of the other tools seem to give contradictory answers, use the Why Tool.

2.2.7 Drill: Using Tools to Find the Conclusion

In each of the following arguments, put brackets around the conclusion, then circle the tool or tools you used to find it. If the conclusion is not explicitly stated (as in a counterargument), you may need to change a few words on the page to make the conclusion.

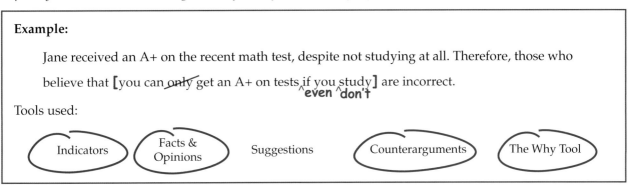

Example:

Jane received an A+ on the recent math test, despite not studying at all. Therefore, those who believe that [you can ~~only~~ get an A+ on tests ^even if you ^don't study] are incorrect.

Tools used:

(Indicators)   (Facts & Opinions)   Suggestions   (Counterarguments)   (The Why Tool)

1. The Himalayas are more beautiful than the Catskills, since the Himalayas are larger.

   Indicators   Facts & Opinions   Suggestions   Counterarguments   The Why Tool

2. Even today, people still believe that time always passes at a constant rate, but they are mistaken. Einstein's theory of special relativity shows us time slows down as you travel at higher speeds.

   Indicators   Facts & Opinions   Suggestions   Counterarguments   The Why Tool

3. Golf is not a sport. After all, it involves no intense physical exertion.

   Indicators   Facts & Opinions   Suggestions   Counterarguments   The Why Tool

4. Modern farmers often cultivate crops that are genetically identical to each other, resulting in entire farms composed of clonal monocultures. To reduce the risk of crop failure, farmers would do well to grow a mixture of different strains of the same crop. Such varied plant populations are less susceptible to disease, since the same vulnerabilities are not shared by every member.

   Indicators   Facts & Opinions   Suggestions   Counterarguments   The Why Tool

5. Children clearly prefer vanilla ice cream, while adults favor chocolate. Last week, Sweety's ice cream shop sold 60 percent of its vanilla ice cream to patrons under the age of 12, while 75 percent of its chocolate ice cream was purchased by adults.

Indicators	Facts & Opinions	Suggestions	Counterarguments	The Why Tool

6. Jon thinks that Kant's categorical imperative is the same as the "golden rule." But the golden rule has nothing to do with one's reasons for acting in a particular way, whereas the categorical imperative is deeply rooted in intentions, so Jon cannot be correct.

Indicators	Facts & Opinions	Suggestions	Counterarguments	The Why Tool

7. The legislative process has often been used by some elected officials to create a particular moral fabric in society. Other lawmakers intentionally avoid imposing ethical decisions upon their constituents, striving instead to improve infrastructure and address other concrete considerations of a functioning civilization. But the ethics of a culture can evolve far faster than the law can. Lawmakers should limit the scope of their legislation to practical issues.

Indicators	Facts & Opinions	Suggestions	Counterarguments	The Why Tool

8. We have not yet found extraterrestrial life, despite centuries of searching. Clearly, scientists will someday concede that we are alone in the universe.

Indicators	Facts & Opinions	Suggestions	Counterarguments	The Why Tool

Answers & Explanations

1. [The conclusion is that the Himalayas are more beautiful than the Catskills.] Indicators, facts & opinions, and the Why Tool are useful for this argument.

2. [The conclusion is that time does not always pass at a constant rate.] Facts & opinions, counterarguments, and the Why Tool are useful for this argument.

3. [The conclusion is that golf is not a sport.] Indicators and the Why Tool are useful for this argument.

4. [The conclusion is that farmers would do well to grow a mixture of different strains of the same crop.] Facts & opinions, suggestions, and the Why Tool are useful for this argument.

5. [The conclusion is that children clearly prefer vanilla ice cream, while adults favor chocolate.] Indicators, facts & opinions, and the Why Tool are useful for this argument.

6. [The conclusion is that Kant's categorical imperative is not the same as the golden rule.] Indicators, counterarguments, and the Why Tool are useful for this argument.

7. [The conclusion is that lawmakers should limit the scope of their legislation to practical issues.] Suggestions and the Why Tool are useful for this argument.

8. [The conclusion is that scientists will someday concede that we are alone in the universe.] Indicators, facts & opinions, and the Why Tool are useful for this argument.

2.3 PREPHRASE

2.3.1 PREPHRASING THE MAIN POINT

Prephrasing on Main Point questions requires nothing more than stating the conclusion. Fortunately, the conclusion is nearly always stated for you already in the argument. All you have to do is find it.

If the conclusion is not explicitly stated (as in a counterargument) you should always Prephrase a specific conclusion. Otherwise, just mark the stated conclusion with brackets so that you can move through the answers quickly and confidently. Don't bother trying to reword, simplify, or paraphrase the conclusion; it's already there on the page for you!

Analyze this argument:

> Some people believe that the only way for a business to be successful is to buy goods at a low cost and sell them at a high cost. But Smartybeanz Coffee, for example, has been wildly successful using a "buy high, sell higher" model. They believe, as do many other companies, that quality can be more important than price.

This is a **counterargument**. Some people believe that "buy low, sell high" is the only way to run a successful business, but they are wrong. Why? Look at Smartybeanz. The argument works like this:

> Smartybeanz has been successful with a "buy high, sell higher" business model.

> **Therefore**, buying goods at a low cost and selling them at a high cost is *not* the only way for a business to be successful.

Your Prephrased conclusion would be:

> Conclusion: Buying goods at a low cost and selling them at a high cost is not the only way for a business to be successful.

Once you have found the conclusion, you can attack the answer choices.

2.4 ATTACK

2.4.1 THE REAL QUESTION

The **Real Question** for Main Point questions is:

Is this the conclusion?

While the Real Question is certainly more important on some other question types, it is still useful for Main Point questions. Compare the following questions:

1. Which one of the following statements most accurately expresses the main point of the politician's argument in the passage above?
2. Is this the conclusion?

The first question is a typical Main Point question stem. While it is understandable, it is not direct. When considering an answer choice, you don't want to have to ask yourself, "Does this most accurately express the main point of the politician's argument in the passage above?"

It's better to look at an answer and ask, *"Is this the conclusion?"* This is the **Real Question**. This simple, direct question reminds you exactly what you should be focusing on, and it trims all the excess fat from the question stem.

> When it is written explicitly, always put brackets around the conclusion of any argument, no matter what the question type.

2.4.2 THE CONCLUSION IN DIFFERENT WORDS

As you ask the **Real Question** for each answer choice, remember that the writers of the LSAT will use different words in the correct answer choice to express the conclusion from the passage. It is unlikely that the correct answer will simply restate the sentence from the passage verbatim. However, if an answer choice *means* the same thing as the conclusion you identified, then that answer choice is correct.

2.4.3 DISTRACTERS

Wrong answers for Main Point questions tend to be one of two kinds of **distracters**:

Premises

Many wrong answers to Main Point questions are premises rather than conclusions. They sound familiar, because they come directly from the argument, but they don't match the conclusion.

Out of Scope

Most of the remaining wrong answers go beyond the scope of the argument in one way or another. These answers make claims that don't appear in the passage.

Most wrong answers to Main Point questions are one of these two common distracters, but any of the common distracters can come up on almost any question type.

2.5 PUTTING IT ALL TOGETHER

It's time to try some examples:

> 1. Essayist: The way science is conducted and regulated can be changed. But we need to determine whether the changes are warranted, taking into account their price. The use of animals in research could end immediately, but only at the cost of abandoning many kinds of research and making others very expensive. The use of recombinant DNA could be drastically curtailed. Many other restrictions could be imposed, complete with a system of fraud police. But such massive interventions would be costly and would change the character of science.
>
> Which one of the following most accurately expresses the main conclusion of the essayist's argument?
>
> Test 28, Section 1, Question 18

Did you remember to read the question stem first?

Here's the approach:

1. Identify

The question stem asks you to identify the main conclusion, so this is a Main Point question.

2. Analyze

This argument has a **suggestion**: "But we need to determine whether…" is a recommended course of action, so it is likely to be the conclusion.

Not convinced? Use **facts and opinions**. All the statements, except for the second sentence, point out things that are possible. It's hard to argue with the idea that such possibilities exist, so those statements are likely to be factual and thus premises. The only opinion left is the second sentence, which is probably the conclusion.

Still not sure? Use The Why Tool.

> 1. Pick out a claim that might be the conclusion.
> The main suspect is "We need to determine whether the changes are warranted, taking into account their price."

2. Ask, "Why do we need to determine whether the changes are warranted, taking into account their price?"

The answer is provided by the rest of the argument: because such changes have such drastic and potentially unwelcome consequences.

All of these tools point to the second sentence as the conclusion. The argument works like this:

- The way science is conducted and regulated can be changed. {A few examples are given.}

- Such massive interventions would be costly and would change the character of science.

Therefore, we need to determine whether the changes are warranted, taking into account their price.

3. Prephrase

Your Prephrased answer is the conclusion, since that's what they're asking about. You're looking for:

> Conclusion: We need to determine whether the changes are warranted, taking into account their price.

The test writers are likely to change the words to make things slightly more challenging. Just look for something that *means* the same thing as this Prephrased answer.

4. Attack

The **Real Question** is: *Is this the conclusion?*

(A) We should not make changes that will alter the character of science.

Choice (A): *Is this the conclusion?* No. The conclusion suggests that we think carefully about changes, but this answer choice suggests that we avoid making changes. That never happened in the argument, so it's **out of scope**. *Cut it.*

(B) If we regulate science more closely, we will change the character of science.

Choice (B): *Is this the conclusion?* No, this answer choice resembles the last sentence in the argument, which is a **premise**. But you're looking for the conclusion. *Cut it.*

(C) The regulation of science and the conducting of science can be changed.

Choice (C): *Is this the conclusion?* No, this is a restatement of the first sentence, which is also a **premise**. *Cut it.*

(D) The imposition of restrictions on the conduct of science would be very costly.

Choice (D): *Is this the conclusion?* No. Like choice (B), this one resembles the last sentence in the argument, which is a **premise**. *Cut it.*

(E) We need to be aware of the impact of change in science before changes are made.

Choice (E): *Is this the conclusion?* This is close to the Prephrased answer. It says we have to think about the consequences of changing science before we act. *Keep it.*

Only choice (E) is left. It's not exactly the same as the second sentence in the passage, but none of the other answer choices come anywhere close to matching the conclusion. Since the question stem asks for the choice that "*most accurately* expresses the main conclusion," it has to be choice (E).

Choice (E) is the correct answer.

Try another one:

2. Literary critic: The author has claimed that the novel is meant merely as an entertaining story, and that it is not meant to be read as an allegorical indictment of the contemporary geopolitical climate. To be sure, the novel provides an entertaining story when read superficially, yet it is hard to believe that none of it is meant to metaphorically address political issues. While it may just be coincidence, many of the characters are strikingly similar in tone and in physical description to major political figures today, and many of the events mirror those that have been at the root of international conflict recently.

Which one of the following most accurately expresses the main point of the literary critic's argument?

Here's the approach:

1. Identify

This question stem asks you to identify the main point, so it's a Main Point question.

2. Analyze

Counterarguments are particularly common on Main Point questions.

The passage contains a **counterargument** against the author's claim that the novel is just a story rather than an allegory. The critic's conclusion must be the negation of the author's claim: the author's novel is *not* just a story; it's an allegory. Why? Many of the characters and events are very similar to real characters and events. So you have:

- Many of the characters are strikingly similar in tone and in physical description to major political figures today.

- Many of the events mirror those that have been at the root of international conflict recently.

Therefore, the novel is an allegorical indictment of the geopolitical climate.

3. Prephrase

Prephrasing here means recognizing the conclusion. You are looking for something like:

Conclusion: The novel is an allegorical indictment of the geopolitical climate.

4. Attack

(A) The story presented by the novel succeeds in its goal of being entertaining.

Choice (A): *Is this the conclusion?* While the critic acknowledges that the novel is entertaining, this is not the conclusion. *Cut it.*

(B) Many of the characters in the novel resemble actual political figures.

Choice (B): *Is this the conclusion?* No, this looks more like a **premise**. *Cut it.*

(C) There is no way to determine the author's true intentions in writing the novel.

Choice (C): *Is this the conclusion?* No. In fact, this appears nowhere in the argument, so it's completely **out of scope**. *Cut it.*

    (D)   All novels can be read both superficially for
               entertainment value or more deeply to uncover
               their moral or political messages.

Choice (D): *Is this the conclusion?* The critic makes no claim whatsoever about *all* novels. He talks only about the author's one novel. This is **extreme** and **out of scope**. *Cut it.*

Should you just choose choice (E)? No way! In the Logical Reasoning section, *never choose an answer without reading it.* Just because you eliminated four answers does not mean that the fifth one is right. You could have misread an answer, and choice (E) could be the worst answer imaginable. Take a second to read it over.

    (E)   The novel is probably intended as an allegory for
               certain contemporary political issues.

Choice (E): *Is this the conclusion?* Yes. You know that the critic makes a counterargument against the author, who claims that the novel *is not* an allegory. So the critic's point had to be that the novel *is* an allegory. This is a good answer.

Choice (E) is the correct answer.

> Always read all five answer choices, even if you quickly eliminate the first four.

2.6 VARIATIONS

2.6.1 COMPLETE QUESTIONS

Complete questions give you an argument with the conclusion omitted from the passage. Your job is to provide the missing conclusion.

You can easily identify a Complete question by the fill-in-the-blank at the end of the passage.

Complete questions have some things in common with Main Point questions. For example, if you see a counterargument, you know how to construct the explicit conclusion to the argument, just as you do for Main Point questions.

Complete questions are also related to Inference questions. The conclusion you provide should take its support from the passage and should not stray from the concepts mentioned on the page. Sometimes you can use **repeated concepts** to predict the conclusion.

These questions are uncommon. Only about half of all tests contain a Complete question.

Here's an example:

KEY PHRASES
Complete Questions

Logically completes
Expresses the conclusion the argument is structured to establish

    3. Many science and medical journals have long practiced
       a thorough peer review system, whereby independent
       experts are invited to evaluate submitted articles before
       they are published. Many professionals, academics, and
       casual readers have long felt assured that the peer review
       process has kept inaccurate or fraudulent papers out
       of respected journals. However, in the past year alone,
       nearly every major journal has been the subject of some
       controversy surrounding articles whose results have
       turned out to be faulty. Therefore, _____.

       Which one of the following most logically completes
       the passage?

1. Identify

All Complete questions look the same: there is a blank at the end of the passage, and you are asked to *complete* the passage.

2. Analyze

Because the argument's conclusion is missing, you can't analyze Complete questions the same way you analyze Main Point questions. That is, you can't put brackets around the conclusion because it's not written in the passage. But you can still analyze the passage. This argument sounds like a counterargument, since a belief that many professionals hold is followed by a *however* statement. The *however* statement is a **premise**, since the conclusion follows the indicator *therefore*. So the argument, without the conclusion filled in, looks like this:

> In the past year alone, nearly every major journal has been the subject of some controversy surrounding articles whose results have turned out to be faulty.
>
> ------
>
> **Therefore**, _____.

3. Prephrase

Prephrasing here means predicting what the conclusion would be. Since the passage appears to be a *counterargument*, there is a good chance that the conclusion is the negation of the opposing viewpoint, which is that peer review has kept inaccurate papers out of respected journals. A *counterargument* would conclude that they are wrong: Peer review has *not* kept inaccurate papers out of respected journals. Why? All that controversy. This makes sense:

> In the past year alone, nearly every major journal has been the subject of some controversy surrounding articles whose results have turned out to be faulty.
>
> ------
>
> **Therefore**, peer review has *not* kept inaccurate papers out of respected journals.

So your Prephrased conclusion is:

> Conclusion: Peer review has not kept inaccurate papers out of respected journals.

4. Attack

You are still looking for an answer choice that contains the conclusion, even though the conclusion wasn't stated in the passage. Since you Prephrased the conclusion, you can use the same **Real Question**.

    (A)   most papers published in scientific and medical journals make false claims

Choice (A): *Is this the conclusion?* No, *most papers make false claims* is an **extreme** statement with no support in the passage. *Cut it.*

    (B)   the peer review process cannot guarantee accuracy in the reviewed articles

Choice (B): *Is this the conclusion?* This is similar to the Prephrased conclusion: that accuracy isn't guaranteed means that peer review has not kept inaccurate papers away. *Keep it.*

    (C)   most faulty results reported in journal articles are fraudulent

Choice (C): *Is this the conclusion?* There's nothing in the passage to support a connection between inaccuracy and fraud. This is **out of scope**. *Cut it.*

    (D)   journals that do not rely on the peer review system are more reliable than those that do

Choice (D): *Is this the conclusion?* There's nothing in the passage about journals that do not use peer review, so there's no basis for comparison. This is **out of scope**. *Cut it.*

(E)   there were no faulty results reported in peer
            reviewed journals more than one year ago

Choice (E): *Is this the conclusion?* There's absolutely no evidence about what happened a year ago, and there's no reason to think that last year was any different from this year. This is **out of scope**. *Cut it.*

Choice (B) is the correct answer.

2.7   THE BIG PICTURE

2.7.1   MARKING THE PASSAGE

Marking the passage allows you to keep track of the conclusion and premises without diagramming the argument. You should mark the premises and conclusion every time an argument appears in a passage. Here's the best way to do it:

1. Put the conclusion in [brackets].

2. Mark the beginning of each premise with a **P**.

To see how marking the passage works, analyze this sample passage:

4. Poison dart frogs owe their toxicity not only to their genome, but also to their diet. They get their poison from eating a particular species of ant in their native Peru. As a result, even frogs born in the wild tend to lose their toxicity in captivity, where owners never feed the frogs their natural diet. Therefore, no one needs to fear handling poison dart frogs in captivity.

Therefore is a conclusion indicator, telling you that the conclusion is *no one needs to fear handling poison dart frogs in captivity*. This is supported by the premise that *frogs lose their toxicity in captivity, where they do not receive their normal diet*. Rather than taking time to rewrite any sentences, you can mark the parts of the argument directly on the passage, using [brackets] and **P**'s. Here's what the marked-up version would look like:

4. Poison dart frogs owe their toxicity not only to their genome, but also to their diet. They get their poison from eating a **P**particular species of ant in their native Peru. As a result,**P**even frogs born in the wild tend to lose their toxicity in captivity, where owners never feed the frogs their natural diet. Therefore, [no one needs to fear handling poison dart frogs in captivity.]

> Marking the passage is simple and fast, yet it is a powerful way to keep yourself focused on the most important things you need in order to answer a question correctly.

Keeping track of the conclusion and premises is important: if you ever lose your place, you never want to be forced to start your analysis over from the beginning. Also, if the answer choices for a question (of any type) throw you off, you can often regain your focus by rereading the conclusion.

NOW MOVE ON TO THE SECOND CHAPTER OF LECTURE 2. WHEN YOU HAVE COMPLETED IT, YOU CAN GET FURTHER PRACTICE WITH MAIN POINT QUESTIONS IN THE CORRESPONDING EXAM AT THE END OF THE BOOK.

LECTURE ② CHAPTER ③

POINT AT ISSUE QUESTIONS

3.1 IDENTIFY

3.1.1 IDENTIFYING POINT AT ISSUE QUESTIONS

Point at Issue questions ask you to identify what two speakers *disagree* about.

There are two characteristics that help you identify a Point at Issue question:

1. **The question stem asks about a disagreement, dispute, or point at issue.**

2. **There are always two speakers in the passage.**

Point at Issue question stems always ask about a disagreement, though the specific terms they use can vary. Here are some of the variations:

> The point at issue between Pedro and Napoleon is whether

> Their dialogue provides the most support for the claim that Jon and Mike disagree over whether

Each of these question stems asks the same thing: what do the speakers disagree about?

Only about ten percent of questions feature two-speaker passages, and roughly half of all two-speaker questions are Point at Issue questions. You should expect to see Point at Issue questions about twice per test.

POINT AT ISSUE QUESTIONS ALWAYS HAVE 2 SPEAKERS

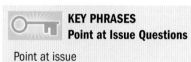

KEY PHRASES
Point at Issue Questions

Point at issue
Disagree

3.2 ANALYZE

3.2.1 HOW TO ANALYZE POINT AT ISSUE QUESTIONS

Analyze Point at Issue questions by identifying which of the first speaker's claims is contradicted by the second speaker.

About half the time, the second speaker will say something that directly contradicts a statement made by the first speaker—an **explicit** disagreement.

The other half of the time, the disagreement is **implicit**, or not stated directly, and you must deduce which statement the second speaker is contradicting.

3.2.2 EXPLICIT DISAGREEMENTS

When you see two statements that say opposite things, circle the statements. Here's an example:

> Takeru: I think we should stop going to Pappy's. Like most restaurants that become trendy, the larger number of patrons every night has stripped the restaurant of its charm and hurt the consistency of the food quality.
>
> Phil: I don't completely agree. The large crowds have definitely affected the atmosphere, but the food quality has become less consistent because the restaurant changed chefs.

In this argument, the speakers agree on a number of things: they both acknowledge the larger crowds, and they concur that the food quality has become less consistent. But Takeru cites the crowds as the cause, while Phil blames the new chef. Thus, they hold contradictory ideas about the *cause* of the poorer food quality.

You should still look for each speaker's conclusion, but their disagreement is not always about their conclusions.

> Takeru: I think we should stop going to Pappy's. Like most restaurants that become trendy, the larger number of patrons every night has stripped the restaurant of its charm and hurt the consistency of the food quality.
>
> Phil: I don't completely agree. The large crowds have definitely affected the atmosphere, but the food quality has become less consistent because the restaurant changed chefs.

3.2.3 IMPLICIT DISAGREEMENTS

If the disagreement is not readily apparent, move through the first speaker's argument claim-by-claim in order to find the disagreement.

In many Point at Issue questions, the second speaker will not explicitly contradict the first. However, there must be *something* the first speaker said that the second disagrees with—after all, it's a Point at Issue question! You have to do some detective work to find the disagreement. Look at each of the first speaker's claims individually and decide whether the second speaker's statements work together to contradict that claim. If the answer is yes, you have found the disagreement. Here's an example:

> Archaeologist: We cannot fully understand the meaning of an uncovered artifact today without understanding what it meant in the context in which it was created and used. Objects should always remain in the place where they are found until they can be adequately studied by experts. By allowing artifacts to be quickly sold on the market, dealers give incentive for looters to grab what they can and sell it for a quick profit, without concern for the potential historical significance of an object.
>
> Dealer: The market that dealers sustain helps get these artifacts into museums around the world, where they can be studied and appreciated. To leave such potentially valuable objects in the unstable parts of the world in which they are often found would expose them to a high probability of being destroyed.

Examine each of the archaeologist's claims and decide which one the dealer is arguing against:

- The archaeologist's first claim is about understanding the meaning of artifacts. The dealer doesn't mention this.

- The archaeologist's second claim is that people should leave objects in the place they were found until they can be studied. The dealer says such action may lead to their destruction. It sounds like the dealer is implying that the objects should **not** be left in their original place. This looks like the point of disagreement.

- The archaeologist's final claim is that dealers create an incentive for looters. The dealer mentions something good that dealers do, but he doesn't argue with the claim about looters.

The two speakers disagree over whether artifacts should be left in place until they can be studied. The archaeologist thinks they should, while the dealer thinks they shouldn't. Circle the statement over which the two speakers are at odds.

Archaeologist: We cannot fully understand the meaning of an uncovered artifact today without understanding what it meant in the context in which it was created and used. Objects should always remain in the place where they are found until they can be adequately studied by experts. By allowing artifacts to be...

In a few cases, the disagreement is implicit, but the second speaker gives you a clue to help you find it. If the second speaker says something like

Your conclusion is unwarranted.

I agree with your overall conclusion, but disagree with one point you make.

You should use this clue to guide you to the statement that the speakers disagree about.

3.3 PREPHRASE

3.3.1 PREPHRASING THE DISAGREEMENT

To Prephrase on a Point at Issue question, *state the disagreement*.

Just as in Main Point questions, the Prephrased answer to at Point at Issue question is nearly always contained in the passage. All you have to do is find it. Just mark the statement that the speakers disagree over so that you can move through the answers quickly and confidently.

Sometimes it helps to express the disagreement in your own words. You can use this phrase for stating the disagreement:

> The speakers disagree over...

Suppose Jeri and Kim agree that candidate X will lose the upcoming election, but Jeri cites inferior fundraising while Kim blames a poor performance in the debate. You can state the disagreement as

> Disagreement: The speakers disagree over the cause of candidate X's predicted loss.

If you don't spot the disagreement right away, don't worry. It's not essential that you have a good Prephrased answer for Point at Issue questions. You can just move on to the answer choices.

> You don't have to write your Prephrased answer down. Just be able to point to it on the page or have it ready in your mind.

3.3.2 Drill: Prephrasing the Disagreement

For each of the following examples, circle the disputed claim or state the disagreement.

1. Ricardo: Soccer is the best sport in the world, since it is more popular than any other sport.

    Rick: That's not true. Baseball is a much better sport. After all, baseball has a much deeper strategic component.

    The speakers disagree over

    _____

    _____

2. Carla: A little-known danger of smoking is the potent carcinogens in cigarette filters. Smokers who can't quit would do well to smoke unfiltered cigarettes.

    Ellen: The filter may be hazardous, but it blocks out ten times more carcinogens than it contributes. No one should smoke unfiltered cigarettes.

    The speakers disagree over

    _____

    _____

3. Lashonda: Life is simpler today than it was a generation ago, since we have new technologies to take over what used to be human tasks. Therefore, people are in general happier than they used to be.

    Irene: Technology complicates life; it doesn't simplify anything. Human tasks require nothing more than human effort, but technology requires a complicated infrastructure.

    The speakers disagree over

    _____

    _____

Answers & Explanations

1. **Soccer is the best sport in the world**: Ricardo believes this claim, whereas Rick thinks baseball is better than soccer. Notice that Rick did not claim that baseball is the best sport in the world.

2. **Smokers who can't quit would do well to smoke unfiltered cigarettes.** Carla thinks some struggling smokers should smoke unfiltered cigarettes, whereas Ellen thinks no one should.

3. **The speakers disagree over whether technology simplifies life.** Lashonda believes that it does, but Irene believes that it does not. Notice that Irene doesn't mention anything about happiness.

3.4 ATTACK

3.4.1 THE REAL QUESTION

The **Real Question** for Point at Issue questions is:

Do the speakers voice disagreement about this?

In order for an answer choice to merit a "yes" to the Real Question, each speaker must have given some indication of (*voiced*) how she or he feels about the statement, AND the two speakers must feel differently about the statement.

If these two conditions are met, then you have found the correct answer—something that the speakers disagree about.

3.4.2 DISTRACTERS

One-sided

This is by far the most common distracter on Point at Issue questions. These answer choices mention something that one of the speakers did not express an opinion on. If you don't know how one of the speakers would feel about an answer choice, then it cannot be right.

Point of Agreement

If both speakers would feel the same way about a statement in an answer choice—whether they *both agree* with the statement, or they *both disagree* with the statement—then the choice cannot be right.

Out of Scope

These distracters bring in additional issues never mentioned by either speaker in the passage.

> An especially tricky type of answer choice is one that both speakers would disagree with. If they both would think a statement is wrong, then they *agree with each other*, so that statement is not the point at issue.

3.4.3 THE SURVEY TOOL

The Survey Tool can help you identify a disagreement in the answer choices.

You will not need to use the Survey Tool on every answer choice, or even on every Point at Issue question. Your Prephrased answer and the Real Question will often be enough to get you to the correct answer. However, this is a useful tool for especially confusing answer choices.

Here's how it works:

1. Create a T-Chart next to the answer choices.

2. Decide whether each speaker agrees or disagrees with the statement in the answer choice. Mark the response in the T-Chart:

    a. If the speaker agrees with the answer choice, put a plus (+).

    b. If the speaker disagrees with the answer choice, put a minus (–).

    c. If the speaker didn't give any information about how he or she would feel about the answer choice, put a question mark (?).

3. The correct answer will have both a plus and a minus next to it.

Note that even one question mark makes an answer choice wrong. In order for the speakers to disagree about a claim, you have to know how they both feel about it. The correct answer requires both a plus and a minus.

Take a look at how the Survey Tool works on a simple example:

1. Arlene: The world is round and beautiful.

    Betty: The world is flat and beautiful.

A	B		
+	+	(A)	The world is beautiful.
?	?	(B)	Pancakes are round
–	–	(C)	The world is ugly.
+	?	(D)	Some round things are beautiful.
–	+	(E)	The world is flat.

Their statements commit Arlene and Betty to disagreeing about which one of the following?

The correct answer is something the speakers disagree about, so there needs to be a plus in one column and a minus in the other column.

Choice (A): Both speakers would agree with this statement that the world is beautiful, so put two plus signs next to this choice.

Choice (B): You have no idea how either speaker feels about pancakes. Put two question marks next to this choice.

Choice (C): Both speakers would disagree with this statement, since they both think the world is beautiful. Put two minuses next to this choice.

Choice (D): Arlene would agree that some round things are beautiful, since she mentioned one beautiful round thing—the world. Put a plus in Arlene's column. But you have no idea how Betty feels about round things, so put a question mark in Betty's column.

Choice (E): Arlene thinks the world is round, so she disagrees with this statement. Put a minus is her column. Betty agrees that the world is flat, so put a plus in her column.

Choice (E) is the only choice with a plus in one column and a minus in the other.

Choice (E) is the correct answer.

You won't use the Survey Tool on every answer choice for every Point at Issue question. It's best used as an additional tool when you aren't sure what to do with one or more answer choices.

3.4.4 Drill: The Survey Tool

Use the Survey Tool by filling out the T-Chart for each of the following short examples. Circle the correct answer.

1. Ramon: English is the hardest of the major languages to learn, since there are exceptions to almost every single grammatical rule. It is no wonder non-native speakers of English have such trouble.

   Taylor: English isn't nearly as difficult to learn as Mandarin. After all, the Mandarin alphabet has thousands of characters: it's a wonder that even native speakers learn how to read and write it.

   Ramon and Taylor are committing to disagreeing about which one of the following?

   R|T

   (A) Mandarin has many characters.
   (B) Mandarin is more difficult than English.

2. David: Our town has had to deal with the smell of the landfill for long enough. Our tax dollars are collected for our own benefit, so the town should pay to take care of the smell.

   Leonard: The landfill certainly has a foul odor, but eliminating the smell is not the most beneficial way to spend our taxes.

   David and Leonard disagree over whether

   D|L

   (A) The landfill smells pleasant.
   (B) The town should pay to eliminate the foul odor.

3. Jolene: Diaspora peoples are ethnic groups that have undergone a geographical spreading. They are remarkable because a community by definition seems to require a fixed, shared land area, yet diaspora peoples retain a true sense of community despite geographical spreading.

   Otto: The true sense of community you refer to does not exist. Community requires proximity, so if diaspora peoples have any sense of community, it is illusory.

   The issue in dispute between Jolene and Otto is whether

   J|O

   (A) Diaspora peoples experience any sense of community.
   (B) The sense of community that diaspora peoples may experience is necessarily illusory.

4. Sharon: Probability is purely theoretical. The predictions it makes do not apply to the real world. For example, it is possible to flip a coin and land on heads one thousand times in a row, even though probability predicts that such an event would almost certainly not happen. We'd be better off ignoring probability altogether.

   Henrietta: Probability doesn't prohibit such unusual events; it merely puts them in perspective. Landing on heads one thousand times in a row is highly unusual, and probability can tell us just how unusual it is. Therefore, we can effectively use probability to understand real world events.

   The point at issue between Sharon and Henrietta is whether

   S|H

   (A) We should continue to use probability.
   (B) Probability prohibits highly unusual events.

Answers and Explanations

1. Ramon and Taylor are committing to disagreeing about which one of the following?

$$\begin{array}{c|c} R & T \\ \hline ? & + \\ & + \end{array}$$

(A) Mandarin has many characters.
(B) Mandarin is more difficult than English.

Choice (B) is correct. Ramon doesn't say anything about characters, so choice (A) can't be the disagreement. He *does* say that English is the most difficult language, while Taylor says that Mandarin is more difficult.

2. David and Leonard disagree over whether

$$\begin{array}{c|c} L & D \\ \hline & + \end{array}$$

(A) The landfill smells pleasant.
(B) The town should pay to eliminate the foul odor.

Choice (B) is correct. They both disagree with the statement that the landfill smells pleasant (so they agree with each other), but they don't agree that the town should pay to eliminate the odor.

3. The issue in dispute between Jolene and Otto is whether

$$\begin{array}{c|c} J & O \\ \hline + & ? \\ + & \end{array}$$

(A) Diaspora peoples experience any sense of community.
(B) The sense of community that diaspora peoples may experience is necessarily illusory.

Choice (B) is correct. Otto doesn't clearly state whether he believes that any sense of community exists. He only says that if a sense exists, it is illusory. They disagree about choice (B) because Jolene thinks there is a true sense of community, but Otto thinks it does not exist.

4. The point at issue between Sharon and Henrietta is whether

$$\begin{array}{c|c} S & H \\ \hline + & \end{array}$$

(A) We should continue to use probability.
(B) Probability prohibits highly unusual events.

Choice (A) is correct. Sharon doesn't address a *prohibition* of highly unusual events. She says probability predicts that certain things *almost certainly* won't happen. They disagree over whether we should use probability.

3.5 PUTTING IT ALL TOGETHER

Take a look at a full example:

2. Bret: Many more bonuses have been given recently to the marketing department than to my design department. I agree that the marketing department has done better work lately, but in my opinion there has not been enough of a difference to justify the huge disparity in bonuses. Therefore the managers deciding the bonus distribution must be biased in favor of the marketing department.

Hart: It's possible that the managers honestly have a higher opinion than you do of the recent work of the marketing department. The bonuses given out have been small, so it doesn't matter much who has received more recently, and you may find that the design department is awarded more bonuses over the next few months.

Bret's and Hart's statements provide the most support for holding that they would disagree about the truth of which one of the following statements?

Here's the approach:

1. Identify

This question has a two-speaker passage, and it asks about a disagreement. This is a Point at Issue question.

2. Analyze

There is no pair of statements that are direct opposites in this passage, so you can't rely on an explicit disagreement. Furthermore, Hart does not indicate exactly which statement he is arguing with. Therefore, move through each of Bret's statements to find the one that Hart offers evidence against.

- Bret's first claim is about the number of bonuses given to each department. Hart doesn't dispute this.

- Bret's next claim is that the difference in work quality does not justify the difference in bonuses. Hart says that *the managers* may disagree, but he does not give *his own* opinion on the subject.

- Bret's final claim is that the managers are biased. All of Hart's statements give evidence that he thinks this *might not* be true. His implied conclusion is that the managers *might not* be biased. This looks like the point of disagreement. Circle it.

> Bret: Many more bonuses have been given recently to the marketing department than to my design department. I agree that the marketing department has done better work lately, but in my opinion there has not been enough of a difference to justify the huge disparity in bonuses. Therefore the managers deciding the bonus distribution must be biased in favor of the marketing department.

3. Prephrase

So what do the speakers disagree about? Since Hart offers a counterargument against Bret's last statement, the disagreement must be over Bret's last statement. A good Prephrased answer is:

> Disagreement: The speakers disagree over whether the managers are biased in favor of the marketing department.

4. Attack

You can use the Survey Tool, or you can just ask the **Real Question**: *Do the speakers voice disagreement about this?* Either way, remember that you must know how *both* speakers feel about an answer choice for it to be correct.

(A)   The marketing department has done better work than the design department lately.

Choice (A): *Do the speakers voice disagreement about this?* Hart doesn't address the quality of work, so you can't know how he feels. Since you must know how *both* speakers feel to know whether they disagree, this can't be right. *Cut it.*

(B)   The disparity in bonus distribution is justified.

Choice (B): *Do the speakers voice disagreement about this?* That's tricky. Bret thinks the decision is biased: perhaps that means it's unjustified as well. Hart doesn't specifically address justification, but he does argue that there may not have been bias. This is a possibility. *Keep it.*

(C)   The bonuses recently given out have been small.

Choice (C): *Do the speakers voice disagreement about this?* You have no idea what Bret thinks about the size of the bonuses. Since you don't know what Bret thinks, this is **one-sided.** *Cut it.*

(D)   The design department will receive more bonuses
          in the near future.

Choice (D): *Do the speakers voice disagreement about this?* This is just like choice (C): Hart believes more bonuses will come, but Bret doesn't address the future. *Cut it.*

(E)   The bosses deciding the bonus distribution have
          definitely been biased.

Choice (E): *Do the speakers voice disagreement about this?* This matches your Prephrased answer, so it looks promising. *Keep it.*

Now that you've seen all the answers, you are down to choices (B) and (E). But (B) is problematic because justification isn't really addressed by *either* speaker. Choice (E) matches the Prephrased answer, which is a strong indication that it's right. Get rid of (B) and choose (E).

Choice (E) is the correct answer.

3.6   VARIATIONS

3.6.1   POINT OF AGREEMENT

Point of Agreement questions are identical to Point at Issue questions, except that they ask you what the speakers **agree** on instead of what they **disagree** on.

You can recognize these questions because they have the same question stem as Point at Issue questions, except that they use the word *agree* instead of *disagree*. This is probably the hardest thing about these questions: when you are reading quickly, you might miss the switch because you will be so used to seeing the word *disagree* in question stems.

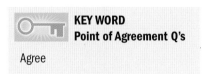

KEY WORD
Point of Agreement Q's

Agree

Your approach to these questions is identical to your approach to Point at Issue questions. Simply reverse your tools to find something the speakers voice agreement over instead of disagreement.

Point of agreement questions are extremely rare. In the past seven years, these questions have appeared on official LSATs only three times.

Here's an example:

3. Dava: Because of the president's impending tax cut,
        wealthy citizens will have more capital available
        to start businesses and create new jobs, which will
        stimulate the economy and reduce the deficit through
        increased tax revenue.

    Elsie: The forthcoming tax cut will have the immediate
        effect of decreasing tax revenue, which will engender
        a drastic reduction in government services. This
        drain on society will deflate the economy and cause
        the loss of jobs, which the government will attempt
        to remedy through increased borrowing and an
        increased deficit.

    On the basis of their statements, Dava and Elsie
    are committed to agreeing about which one of the
    following?

1. Identify

This is a Point of Agreement question, since the question stem asks what the speakers agree about.

2. Analyze

Analyze Point of Agreement questions as you would analyze Point at Issue questions. Look for statements in which the speakers agree with each other.

Both Dava and Elsie mention jobs, the economy, and the deficit. However, they disagree on the future of all three considerations.

The only thing they both agree on is that there will be a tax cut, and it will have a number of results.

3. Prephrase

To Prephrase on a Point of Agreement question, state the agreement.

> Agreement: The speakers agree that there will be a tax cut and that it will have a number of results.

4. Attack

> (A) Wealthy citizens do not rely on government services.

Choice (A): *Do the speakers voice agreement about this?* No, Elsie doesn't mention wealthy citizens, and Dava doesn't mention government services. *Cut it.*

> (B) The president's tax cut will be beneficial to the economy.

Choice (B): *Do the speakers voice agreement about this?* No, Dava thinks this is true, while Elsie thinks it is untrue. They **disagree** over this statement, so it is an **opposite** distracter. *Cut it.*

> (C) Employers' decision whether to create new jobs depends on their available capital.

Choice (C): *Do the speakers voice agreement about this?* No, Elsie doesn't mention the capital available to employers. *Cut it.*

> (D) The size of the deficit will be affected by the president's tax cut.

Choice (D): *Do the speakers voice agreement about this?* Yes. This is a little tricky since Dava thinks the deficit will decrease, while Elsie thinks it will increase, but they both **agree** that it will be *affected*. *Keep it.*

> (E) Government services have not suffered from the enactment of past tax cuts.

Choice (E): *Do the speakers voice agreement about this?* No, no one mentions anything about past tax cuts. This is **out of scope**. *Cut it.*

Choice (D) is the correct answer.

You can also use the Survey Tool on Point of Agreement questions. Instead of looking for an answer choice that merits a plus and a minus, look for one with two plusses.

3.7 THE BIG PICTURE

3.7.1 MARKING THE ANSWER CHOICES

You should have a system for marking answer choices so that you can move through them as quickly and effectively as possible.

Whatever system you use, there should be a distinct mark for each of the following:

1. Possible correct answers
2. Wrong answers
3. Answers you don't understand

For possible correct answers, you can use a check mark. You should simply cross out wrong answers, and you should place a question mark next to answers you don't understand.

For the Point at Issue question above, you might have had:

    (A)   The marketing department has done better work than the design department lately.
✔ (B)   The disparity in bonus distribution is justified.
    (C)   The bonuses recently given out have been small.
    (D)   The design department will receive more bonuses in the near future.
✔ (E)   The bosses deciding the bonus distribution have definitely been biased.

In this situation, you narrowed down the answer choices to (B) and (E). Your next step is to go back and examine the two more closely. Re-read the choices, comparing the language in them to the language in the passage and using any additional tools at your disposal, such as the Survey Tool.

If you don't understand an answer choice, use a question mark. Sometimes, the one you don't understand may be the only answer that could be right:

    (A)
    (B)
? (C) ← If you are in this position, you should
    (D)   pick choice (C), even if you don't fully
    (E)   understand it.

    (A)
    (B)
? (C) ← If you are in this position, you should
    (D)   pick choice (E), since it is a good match
✔ (E) ← for your Prephrased answer and correctly answers the Real Question.

Unless you eliminate all five answer choices or realize you missed something important, resist the urge to go back and re-read the answer choices that you already eliminated. Trust your judgment. Re-reading bad answer choices is a terrible use of your very limited time.

STOP. THIS IS THE END OF LECTURE 2. DO NOT PROCEED TO THE CORRESPONDING EXAM UNTIL INSTRUCTED TO DO SO IN CLASS.

LECTURE ③ CHAPTER ④

FLAW QUESTIONS

4.1 IDENTIFY

4.1.1 IDENTIFYING FLAW QUESTIONS

All **Flaw** questions follow the same pattern:

1. **The question stem asks you to identify an argument's flaw.** This is what distinguishes Flaw questions from every other question type. All Flaw questions ask you to do the same thing: identify the argument's flaw.

2. **The passage contains a flawed argument.** Since Flaw questions ask you to identify the flaw, the passage must have a flawed argument.

Here are some common Flaw question stems:

> The reasoning in the argument is flawed because the argument presumes, without providing justification, that
>
> The reasoning in the argument is most vulnerable to criticism on the grounds that it fails to consider the possibility that
>
> Which one of the following most accurately describes an error in the reasoning above?
>
> A questionable aspect of the reasoning above is that it

Though the language may vary, all of these stems ask you to identify an argument's flaw.

Flaw questions are the most common type of Logical Reasoning question. You can expect to see about eight Flaw questions per LSAT.

KEY PHRASES
Flaw Questions

Describes a flaw

Flawed
Vulnerable to criticism
Questionable
Error in the reasoning

Presumes, without providing justification
Fails to consider the possibility

4.2 ANALYZE

4.2.1 ANALYZING FLAW QUESTIONS

Your analysis of Flaw questions has three steps. Look for:

1. The conclusion

2. The premises

3. The flaw

It may seem somewhat obvious to say that you should look for the flaw as part of your analysis of Flaw questions. But, incredibly, many test-takers ignore this step and move straight to the answer choices. Skipping this step is exactly what LSAC hopes you will do, because they know you are quite likely to answer the question incorrectly if you do.

You should be familiar by now with how to find the premises and conclusion. There are also several techniques you can use to help you find the flaw:

1. Check to see if the flaw is **immediately obvious**.

2. If it's not, look for one of the **common flaws**.

3. If you don't see a common flaw, look for a Concept Shift.

4.2.2 IMMEDIATELY OBVIOUS FLAWS

Sometimes you'll notice the flaw right away. One way to do this is to try to complete this sentence:

> Just because {premise} is true, that doesn't automatically mean that {conclusion} is true, because _____.

Here's an example:

1. A film's budget clearly determines its success. After all, the most successful films of the past two years also had the biggest budgets.

Does anything seem wrong with this argument? You might be thinking that there are many things other than a film's budget that contribute to its success, such as its cast, its marketing, or its quality. You can't conclude that the budget determines success just because there were a couple of successful big-budget films.

You could articulate your criticism of the argument by saying:

> Just because the most successful films of the past two years had the biggest budgets, that doesn't automatically mean that a film's budget determines its success, because there could have been other things that caused their success, such as cast, marketing, or quality—or perhaps the last two years were just an anomaly.

Most correct answer choices to Flaw questions critique the argument by saying that it

- improperly made a connection between two things without enough evidence

- failed to consider some other possibility

So in the case above, you could identify the flaw like this:

> Flaw: The argument presumes, without giving any evidence, that the budget of the last two years' most successful films had some influence on their success.

Or like this:

> Flaw: The argument failed to consider the possibility
> that it was the films' casts, marketing, or quality
> that caused their success.

If you express the flaw in one (or both) of these ways, then you are very likely to find the correct answer choice easily.

4.2.3 COMMON FLAWS

Some flaws show up over and over on the LSAT. Here's one example:

2. Designers of high-end, fashionable furniture have been complaining about the growing trend of discount furniture chains selling items that strongly resemble those of the high-end designers. The designers claim that they have a right to profit from their own creative output if they design an item that people want to own, but that no one will buy their furniture when they can buy very similar-looking pieces for a fraction of the price. However, these designers need look no further than the grocery store, where name brand cereals sell profitably next to cheaper yet nearly identical generic cereals, to see that their concerns are unfounded.

Here's how the argument breaks down:

Brand name cereals sell profitably next to cheaper generic cereals.

....

Therefore, designers of high-end furniture who fear that no one will buy their products with generic options available should not be afraid.

This argument tries to prove its conclusions by using an analogy. However, it's not clear that the cereal market and the designer furniture market are really analogous. Trying to draw an analogy between two things that may not be analogous is one of the most common flaws on the LSAT, and any time you see this situation, you know you will always be able to express the flaw the same way:

> A full list of the common flaws is given in section 4.7.

> Flaw: The argument presumes, without giving any
> evidence, that the cereal market and the designer
> furniture market are analogous in every important
> way.

Or like this:

> Flaw: The argument failed to consider the
> possibility that the cereal market and the designer
> furniture market have important differences,
> such as consumers' heightened sensitivity to price
> differences for more expensive items.

4.2.4 THE CONCEPT SHIFT

A Concept Shift occurs when an argument treats two different concepts as if they were the same concept, or as if one of them led logically to the other. Most often, a Concept Shift occurs between the premises and the conclusion, but a Concept Shift can also occur between premises.

To find a Concept Shift, examine an argument and ask yourself this question:

What two non-identical concepts are intended to be connected?

It's important to remember that the concepts must truly be *different*. There can't be a shift between two identical concepts, even if they are expressed using different words.

Consider this example:

> 3. A reliable form of transportation can take you anywhere you want to go. I want to go to Chicago. Therefore, my 1979 station wagon can take me to Chicago.

What two non-identical concepts does the author try to connect? In this case, the author tries to make a connection between *a reliable form of transportation* and *a 1979 station wagon*. But these two things are certainly not identical. Thus, a Concept Shift occurred in this argument when the author made the switch from talking about a reliable form of transportation to talking about a 1979 station wagon.

This Concept Shift can be expressed like this:

Reliable form of transportation ⚡ 1979 station wagon

This "lightning bolt" notation tells you that the author started off by talking about one concept, then shifted to talking about a different concept, yet treated the two as if they were the same.

In the last example, the Concept Shift occurred between something in the premises and something in the conclusion. That's a common situation, but the Concept Shift can also occur between two premises. Here's the same argument, slightly rearranged:

> 4. A reliable form of transportation can get you anywhere you want to go, and I want to go to Chicago. Fortunately, I have a 1979 station wagon. Therefore, I can get to Chicago.

This version of the argument has the same Concept Shift:

Reliable form of transportation ⚡ 1979 station wagon

This time, it occurred between two premises, but the place in the argument where a Concept Shift occurs is not really important. What's crucial is noticing when the author makes a switch from one concept to another while treating the two concepts as if they were the same.

Here's another argument:

> 5. It is difficult for an appliance manufacturing facility to produce more than a few standard models of any type of appliance. For a manufacturer to remain profitable, each mass-produced appliance has to be manufactured in a way that will appeal to a large consumer base. Therefore, mass-produced appliances are unimaginatively designed.

The indicator *therefore* points to the argument's conclusion: mass-produced appliances are unimaginatively designed. The first two sentences must be premises.

- It is difficult for appliance manufacturing facilities to produce more than a few standard models.

- Each mass-produced appliance has to be manufactured in a way that will appeal to a large consumer base.

Therefore, mass-produced appliances are unimaginatively designed.

Now identify the Concept Shift:

What two non-identical concepts are intended to be connected?

There is supposed to be a connection between appealing to a large consumer base and unimaginative design. But these two concepts are not logically connected, so the author's intended link between them is a Concept Shift:

Broad appeal ⚡ Unimaginative design

The Concept Shift—treating two different concepts as if they were identical—is a very common flaw, but it's not the only kind of flaw an argument may have. Not every flawed argument has a Concept Shift—some have other types of flaws.

Concept Shifts can occur on all kinds of question types, not just Flaw questions. When you find a Concept Shift, draw circles around the two concepts that are intended to be connected.

4.2.5 Drill: Finding the Concept Shift

Mark the conclusion and premises in each of the following arguments and answer the questions that follow.

1. The only way to guarantee success in business is to flood the market with a product so as to create a pseudomonopoly in which consumers believe that a given product is the only available product of its type. Convinced that they have no other choice, consumers will buy the product without comparing its cost to that of similar products. Therefore, the easiest way to become successful in the world of business is to attempt to create a pseudomonopoly.

   What two non-identical concepts are intended to be connected?

   _____

   _____

2. Executive: Recent research indicates that, despite what Western society has believed for decades, stress has no effect on a person's ability to get restful sleep on a regular basis. Even under the most stressful conditions, humans can always sleep peacefully, as long as other relevant conditions are controlled. Employees at our company should have no complaint, therefore, if our workplace remains a high-stress environment.

   What two non-identical concepts are intended to be connected?

   _____

   _____

3. Pizza Princess received thirty complaints in the span of no more than three days about pizzas arriving past the time at which they were promised to arrive at their respective destinations. The delivery manager claimed that the delays were the result of mechanical troubles occurring within their fleet of delivery vehicles. But since no more than one or two delivery vehicles would have mechanical troubles within such a short period of time, these thirty delays must have been caused by something else.

   What two non-identical concepts are intended to be connected?

   _____

   _____

Answers & Explanations

1. **Conclusion:** [Therefore, the easiest way to become successful in the world of business is to attempt to create a pseudomonopoly.]

   Concept Shift: Only way to guarantee success ⚡ Easiest way to become successful. The argument shifts from a discussion about how to guarantee success to the easiest way to become successful. But there might be easier ways than the one that guarantees success.

2. **Conclusion:** [Therefore, employees at our company should have no complaint if our workplace remains a high-stress environment.]

   Concept Shift: Can sleep peacefully ⚡ Should have no complaint. The executive treats the claim that employees can sleep peacefully as if it proves that employees *should have no complaint.* But just because something has no effect on sleep does not mean that there aren't other reasons to complain.

3. **Conclusion:** [These thirty delays must have been caused by something else.]

   Concept Shift: Number of vehicles with mechanical problems ⚡ Number of delays. The possible number of vehicles with mechanical problems is treated as identical to the possible number of delays. But one broken vehicle could cause many delays—these concepts are not identical.

4.2.6 From Concept Shift to Flaw

If you find a Concept Shift in an argument, then you've found the argument's flaw. That's because a flaw is any mistake in logic, and treating two different concepts as if they were the same is certainly a mistake in logic. A Concept Shift is simply one kind of flaw, but it is perhaps the most commonly occurring flaw on the LSAT.

To turn a Concept Shift into an explicit statement of the flaw, construct a sentence about how the assumed connection between the concepts is improper.

Here's an example:

> 6. Psychologist: Amnesia often occurs after an intense stressful emotional episode, but amnesia can also occur without such an episode. Additionally, intense stressful episodes do not always lead to amnesia. From this it is clear that intense stressful emotional episodes do not contribute to the development of amnesia.

It is clear is a conclusion indicator that tells you that the last sentence is the conclusion. The first two sentences are premises:

- Amnesia can occur without intense stressful emotional episodes.
- Intense stressful emotional episodes can occur without amnesia.

Therefore, intense stressful emotional episodes do not contribute to the development of amnesia.

Now identify the Concept Shift:

What two non-identical concepts are intended to be connected?

There is an intended connection between *can occur without* and *do not contribute*. The argument treats these two concepts as identical even though they are different.

So the Concept Shift is:

Can occur without ⚡ Do not contribute

Most correct answer choices to Flaw questions critique the argument by saying that it

· improperly made a connection between two things without enough evidence

· failed to consider some other possibility

To express this Concept Shift as a flaw, all you have to do is express the shift between these two concepts as improper logic:

> Flaw: The argument improperly presumes, without giving evidence, that since stressful emotional episodes <u>can occur without</u> leading to amnesia, they <u>do not contribute</u> to amnesia in any situation.

or

> Flaw: The argument fails to consider the possibility that, even though stressful emotional episodes <u>can occur without</u> leading to amnesia in some cases, they <u>might actually contribute</u> to amnesia in some other cases.

4.3 PREPHRASE

4.3.1 Prephrasing Flaws

To Prephrase on a Flaw question, state the argument's flaw. Don't look at the answer choices until you have identified and expressed the flaw in your own words.

Prephrasing is more powerful on Flaw questions than on any other question type. If you Prephrase well, you are likely to find your Prephrased answer in the answer choices, and it will usually be quite obvious. If you skip this step, then you are very likely to fall for one of the trap answer choices.

The question stem tells you that the argument is flawed, so you know the flaw is there for you to discover. You know that the argument made a logical mistake. The correct answer will not provide you with any new information that you need in order to find the mistake, so there is no need to read the answer choices before you determine what the flaw is.

> Becoming an expert at identifying flaws is one of the most important things you can do to improve your score. It will help you on every flaw-dependent question type.

4.3.2 Drill: Prephrasing Flaws

For each of the following arguments, identify the Concept Shift and Prephrase a flaw.

1. Woodrow Wilson is often praised for his role in World War I, but he deserves as much derision as praise. After all, the national debt roughly tripled during his presidency.

    Concept Shift: _____

    Flaw: _____

    _____

2. In 1993, the United States Congress passed the Brady Bill, aimed primarily at controlling the distribution of firearms. Firearms continue to be a problem, however, so the Brady Bill was unsuccessful.

    Concept Shift: _____

    Flaw: _____

3. Parmenides had a strong influence on Plato, who tried to solve the metaphysical challenges that Parmenides had posed. Therefore, Plato would have been a mediocre philosopher without Parmenides.

    Concept Shift: _____

    Flaw: _____

    _____

4. A work of fiction cannot be properly understood unless one can fully grasp the social and cultural conditions of the time and place in which the work was produced. Therefore, we can never hope to properly understand a work of fiction that was not produced in our own time and place.

    Concept Shift: _____

    Flaw: _____

    _____

Answers & Explanations

1. **Concept Shift: Tripled national debt ⚡ Deserves derision.** The argument intends to connect *tripling the debt* to *deserving derision, but it's possible that Wilson doesn't deserve derision for the debt.*
Flaw: The argument improperly assumes a connection between tripling the national debt and deserving derision.

2. **Concept Shift: Continued problems ⚡ Unsuccessful.** The argument intends to connect *continued problems* with *a lack of success, but the connection is not necessarily there.*
Flaw: The argument improperly assumes that continued problems are indicative of a lack of success.

3. **Concept Shift: Strong influence ⚡ Mediocre without.** *Strong influence* is supposed to lead to *mediocre without,* but just because there was a strong influence on him doesn't mean Plato still couldn't have been great without it.
Flaw: The argument improperly assumes that a strong influence implies mediocrity without such an influence.

4. **Concept Shift: Not fully grasp the social and cultural conditions ⚡ Not in our own time and place.** The argument intends to connect these concepts, but you may be able to fully grasp conditions even if they are not the same as those of your own time.
Flaw: The argument improperly assumes that we can't fully grasp conditions if they are not the same as those of our own time.

4.4   ATTACK

4.4.1   THE REAL QUESTION

The **Real Question** for Flaw questions is:

Is this a flaw in the argument?

The correct answer must not only describe a real flaw, but also describe a flaw *committed by the argument*. If you keep this in mind, you'll be able to avoid the common distracters for Flaw questions.

4.4.2   DISTRACTERS

Flaw questions have two common **distracters**:

Doesn't Match

Most wrong answers to Flaw questions are **doesn't match** distracters. A **doesn't match** distracter describes a real flaw, but it's not the flaw that occurred in the argument that you're working on. Since these are such common wrong answers, you should always consider whether an answer choice matches the argument as soon as you read it. The LSAT writers make these answers tempting because they use fancy language and describe something that really would be a flaw—if it had occurred in the argument in question. They hope to trick test-takers into selecting an incorrect answer choice because it describes a real flaw, but if an answer choice doesn't match what happened in the argument, it's wrong.

Not a Flaw

> These two distracters are especially tempting if you haven't already figured out what the flaw is. Always find and state the flaw before looking at the answer choices in order to avoid falling for one of these traps.

Some answer choices accurately describe something that happened in the argument but that is **not a flaw**. The correct answer must describe an error in the argument's reasoning, so even if an answer matches the argument, if it does not describe a problem in the reasoning, it's a **not a flaw** distracter and incorrect.

You can avoid both of these distracters by relying on the **Real Question**, as it implies two conditions:

1. Since it asks for a *flaw*, the correct answer must be an actual flaw.

2. Since it asks for a flaw *in the argument*, the correct answer must match the argument.

4.4.3   SOME WORDS ON LSAT-SPEAK

The answers to Flaw questions are often vague and intentionally difficult to decipher. The more comfortable you get with LSAT-Speak on Flaw answer choices, the more successful you will be.

Take a look at this argument:

> 7.   Candace: It is unlikely that our perennial garden will produce over fifty flowers this year, since our strongest plants are our lilies, and our lilies will not produce more than thirty flowers.

Candace's argument is flawed in that she assumes that not having fifty lilies means that she won't have fifty flowers. Here are two answer choices, both of which say the same thing:

    (A)   The argument improperly assumes that having less than fifty lilies implies having less than fifty flowers.

    (B)   The argument presupposes, without providing justification, that what is true of one member of a given set is true of the larger set of which that member is just one part.

The first answer is roughly how you might Prephrase the flaw, and the second answer choice is vague and confusing. But they both say the same thing. The primary difference is that the first one refers to terms directly as they are stated in the argument, while the second uses general terms. For example, the first answer choice just says *lilies* where the second says *one member of a given set*. This is typical LSAT-Speak.

There are three ways to combat LSAT-Speak. The first is to realize that every vague, general term in an answer choice must refer to something specific in the argument. To determine whether the choice matches the argument, try to match each general term to something specific in the passage. For choice (B), for example, you would try to identify what the "set" is. The only larger set in the argument is the set of all flowers in the perennial garden. If one of the general terms doesn't match something in the passage, then the choice is incorrect.

The second way to combat LSAT-Speak is to learn the most common vague answer choices. Choice (B) is a common answer choice that describes a **composition flaw**, which you'll learn about later in this lecture. If you learn how common flaws are usually expressed as answers, then you won't need to spend time deciphering answers that describe common flaws.

The third way to combat LSAT-Speak is practice. The more Flaw questions you encounter, the more you'll get used to LSAT-Speak. Just like any other foreign language, LSAT-Speak becomes easier as you practice it.

4.4.4 Drill: The Real Question and Distracters

Each of the following has a simple argument with two potential flaws. Use the Real Question to find the correct answers.

1. If you can speak French fluently, then you are likely to impress your friends. Thus, if you cannot speak French, you will not impress your friends.

   (A)   The argument improperly assumes that most people have the ability to learn French.
   Is this a flaw in the argument?
   ☐ Yes   ☐ No

   (B)   The argument confuses something likely to bring about a certain result with something necessary for that result.
   Is this a flaw in the argument?
   ☐ Yes   ☐ No

2. The well-known "food pyramid" recommends six to eleven servings of bread, rice, cereal, and pasta per day. These foods are all high in carbohydrates, so following the "food pyramid" is likely to cause weight gain.

   (A)   The argument assumes, without justification, that eating foods high in carbohydrates is likely to cause weight gain.
   Is this a flaw in the argument?
   ☐ Yes   ☐ No

   (B)   The argument presupposes that what has not been proven is nevertheless true.
   Is this a flaw in the argument?
   ☐ Yes   ☐ No

3. Experienced gardeners know that zinnias are some of the best flowers to grow in hot climates, since they stand up well to heat. So if you live in a cooler climate, it's probably better not to plant zinnias.

   (A)   The argument presumes, without providing justification, that a plant that survives well in one climate does not survive as well in a different climate.
   Is this a flaw in the argument?
   ☐ Yes   ☐ No

   (B)   The argument fails to consider whether other flowers that thrive in hot climates can withstand cooler temperatures better than zinnias can.
   Is this a flaw in the argument?
   ☐ Yes   ☐ No

4. Accepting responsibility for one's mistakes may be a sign of courage, but any courage it may demonstrate is rarely an enduring virtue, since most people accept responsibility for their mistakes only occasionally.

   (A)   The argument fails to define the critical term "courage."
   Is this a flaw in the argument?
   ☐ Yes   ☐ No

   (B)   The argument presumes, without giving justification, that a personal attribute is present only when displayed.
   Is this a flaw in the argument?
   ☐ Yes   ☐ No

Answers & Explanations

1. Choice (A): *Is this a flaw in the argument?* **No.** The argument makes no such assumption. This is a **doesn't match** distracter.

   Choice (B): *Is this a flaw in the argument?* **Yes.** The argument goes from *likely to impress* to *you can't impress without it*, which is an unjustified logical leap—a flaw.

2. Choice (A): *Is this a flaw in the argument?* **Yes.** The argument concludes that people will gain weight because these foods are high in carbohydrates. But it doesn't provide any justification for why carbohydrates should cause weight gain.

   Choice (B): *Is this a flaw in the argument?* **No.** This is a **doesn't match** distracter.

3. Choice (A): *Is this a flaw in the argument?* **Yes.** The argument assumes that zinnias, which are good in heat, are not good for cooler climates. But there's no reason zinnias couldn't be good in cooler climates as well.

   Choice (B): *Is this a flaw in the argument?* **No.** Although the argument didn't consider other flowers, that's not the reason the argument is flawed. Even if the argument had discussed other flowers, it would still contain the flaw of presuming that since zinnias are good in hot climates, they aren't good in cold climates. So, while this answer choice does match the argument, it's **not a flaw**.

4. Choice (A): *Is this a flaw in the argument?* **No.** Although the argument didn't provide a definition, that's not the reason the argument is flawed. Even if the argument *had* defined "courage," it would still contain the flaw of presuming that a trait isn't permanent just because it's only displayed intermittently. This answer choice matches the argument, but it's **not a flaw**.

   Choice (B): *Is this a flaw in the argument?* **Yes.** The argument jumps from *done occasionally* to *not permanent*.

4.5 PUTTING IT ALL TOGETHER

Now put all this together on some examples.

8. Politician: Many citizens have complained that the curfew imposed to reduce crime unfairly limits the freedom of all citizens based on the actions of a small segment of the population. While I sympathize with my constituents, their complaints are unwarranted. After all, this loss of freedom is like the loss of freedom caused by a traffic accident. Only a few people are responsible for the accident, but the resultant traffic jam slows down everyone on the road.

The politician's argument is most vulnerable to criticism on which one of the following grounds?

Here's the approach:

1. Identify

This question stem asks why the argument is *vulnerable to criticism*, so it's a Flaw question.

2. Analyze

The passage is a *counterargument*. Like all counterarguments, this argument's conclusion is the negation of the opposing position.

The politician argues that the curfew does NOT unfairly limit the freedom of all citizens. In other words, the curfew is fair. Why? The loss of freedom caused by the curfew is like the loss of freedom caused by a traffic accident. *After all* indicates that this is a premise. The argument looks like this:

The loss of freedom caused by the curfew is like the loss of freedom caused by a traffic jam.

Therefore, the curfew is fair.

If you can't see a flaw right away, try looking for a Concept Shift.

What two non-identical concepts are intended to be connected?

The argument tries to draw a connection between *the curfew* and *traffic jams,* but traffic jams are very different from curfews.

So the Concept Shift is:

$$\text{Traffic jams} \nleftrightarrow \text{Curfew}$$

3. Prephrase

To Prephrase a flaw, turn the Concept Shift into a statement about an improper assumption. Here's a Prephrased flaw:

> Flaw: The argument improperly presumes that evidence about <u>traffic jams</u> is relevant to a conclusion about <u>the curfew</u>.

4. Attack

Remember the **Real Question**: *Is this a flaw in the argument?* Also remember that most wrong answers are **doesn't match** distracters, so you usually don't have to consider whether an answer choice is actually a flaw.

> (A)   It makes a generalization about all cases of a certain kind when the evidence supports such a claim only about some cases of that kind.

Choice (A): *Is this a flaw in the argument?* This **doesn't match** the argument, so it can't be the flaw. The argument doesn't make a claim about all cases of anything. The politician is talking about this one loss of freedom resulting from the curfew, not all losses of freedom in the world. *Cut it.*

> (B)   It makes a claim that is too narrow given the evidence advanced to support it.

Choice (B): *Is this a flaw in the argument?* This **doesn't match** the argument either. There's nothing about the conclusion that is *too* narrow. If evidence supports a very strong claim, it supports a weaker claim as well. *Cut it.*

> (C)   It relies on an analogy between two things that are insufficiently alike for the conclusion to be supported.

Choice (C): *Is this a flaw in the argument?* This one, like the other answer choices, is in LSAT-Speak. So try to decode it by matching each general term to something specific in the argument. An analogy is just a comparison between two things, and there is a comparison between a traffic jam and a curfew. What is true of a traffic jam might not be true of a curfew, so yes, the argument does rely on an analogy that it shouldn't. This also matches up well with the Prephrased flaw. *Keep it.*

> (D)   It includes evidence that undermines its conclusion.

Choice (D): *Is this a flaw in the argument?* There doesn't seem to be anything that the argument uses as evidence that undermines the conclusion. Since this **doesn't match** the argument, it can't be a flaw in the argument. *Cut it.*

> (E)   It attempts to divert attention from the point at issue by citing irrelevant evidence.

Choice (E): *Is this a flaw in the argument?* Although it may seem like traffic jams are irrelevant, the analogy is central to the argument. The author uses it as part of a sincere effort to provide evidence for the conclusion, so it's not intended to create a diversion. This answer choice **doesn't match**. *Cut it.*

How to find the flaw in any argument:

1.   Check to see if the flaw is immediately obvious to you.

2.   If it's not, look for one of the common flaws.

3.   If you don't see a common flaw, look for a Concept Shift.

You did not need to consider whether any of the wrong answers were flaws because none of them matched the argument. If you first consider whether an answer matches the argument, you will make your job much easier on Flaw questions.

Choice (C) is the correct answer.

Here's another question:

> 9. Political commentators see recent policies of the government toward Country X as appeasement, pure and simple. This view is fundamentally mistaken, for polls show that most people disagree with the political commentators' assessment of government policies toward Country X.
>
> The reasoning in the argument is questionable because

1. Identify

This question stem asks about *questionable reasoning*, so it's a Flaw question.

2. Analyze

This is another *counterargument*, so the conclusion is summed up in the statement "this view is fundamentally mistaken." Why are the commentators mistaken? Polls show that most people disagree with them. That's the premise. So the argument looks like this:

> Polls show that most people disagree with the commentators who see the recent policies toward Country X as appeasement.
>
> ----------
>
> **Therefore,** the recent policies toward Country X are not appeasement.

In this case, the flaw is pretty obvious. The conclusion is based only on the evidence of what most people think. But there's no evidence to show that most people are correct. Just because most people disagree with the commentators, it doesn't automatically mean the commentators are mistaken, because it's possible that most people don't know what they're talking about.

> *If the flaw is obvious to you, you don't need to look for a Concept Shift.*

3. Prephrase

You can turn this into a statement of the flaw:

> Flaw: The argument fails to consider the possibility that the commentators might be correct even though most people disagree with them.

With this Prephrased flaw, you are ready to attack the answer choices.

4. Attack

Consider first whether each answer choice matches the argument, and you will usually eliminate answers without needing to consider whether they are flaws. To do this, ask the **Real Question**.

> (A) the argument equivocates between two different notions of the term "policies"

Choice (A): *Is this a flaw in the argument?* The argument does not use the term "policies" to mean two different things. Using the same word to mean two different things is called **equivocation**. Answer choices that talk about equivocation are rarely correct, but they often pop up as distracters. This time it **doesn't match**. *Cut it.*

> (B) the political commentators discussed in the passage are not identified

Choice (B): *Is this a flaw in the argument?* This matches the argument: the political commentators really are unidentified. But is that a flaw? No, there's no need to know who these commentators are in order to dispute their claim. This is **not a flaw**. *Cut it.*

> (C) a claim is inferred to be false merely because a
> majority of people believe it to be false

Choice (C): *Is this a flaw in the argument?* The argument does say the commentators' view is wrong just because most people think so, and this is a good match for the Prephrased answer. *Keep it.*

> (D) the claim that the political commentators are
> mistaken is both a premise and a conclusion in
> the argument

Choice (D): *Is this a flaw in the argument?* The conclusion is not identical to the premise, so this **doesn't match**. This references a **circular** flaw, which you'll learn about shortly. It's another type of choice that is rarely correct but is a common distracter. *Cut it.*

> (E) it is assumed that what is true of persons
> individually is true of a country as a whole

Choice (E): *Is this a flaw in the argument?* The argument doesn't shift from individuals to the country as a whole, so this **doesn't match** the argument. *Cut it.*

Choice (C) is the correct answer.

4.6 VARIATIONS

4.6.1 MISINTERPRETATION QUESTIONS

Misinterpretation questions have passages with two speakers, and you are asked to identify how the second speaker misinterprets the first.

KEY WORD
Misinterpretation Q's

Misinterpret

These are just variations on Flaw questions. By misinterpreting the preceding argument, the second speaker presents a flawed response.

Misinterpretation questions are rare. Most tests don't have a single Misinterpretation question.

Here's an example:

> 10. Mayor: Funding for schools in our town has been
> increased by four percent for each of the last four
> years, and our schools are flourishing. This year, we
> may not need to increase our school budget, despite
> recommendations from the superintendent.
>
> Parent: But we need to show continued commitment
> to our children. The best way to show such a
> commitment is to support their education. We should
> not ignore the superintendent's recommendations
> because doing so could send the wrong message to
> our children.
>
> The parent's response to the mayor suggests that the
> parent misinterpreted the mayor to be

1. Identify

This is a Misinterpretation question, since the question stem asks about how the parent *misinterprets* the mayor.

2. Analyze

The second speaker's misinterpretation is always based on a Concept Shift—the second speaker intends to argue about identical concepts as the first speaker, but the second speaker's concepts are different. Your goal is to see where this shift occurs.

You should identify the premises and conclusion for both speakers and look for the Concept Shift between the first and second speaker.

The mayor concludes that we may not need to increase the budget because the schools are flourishing. The parent responds that we should not ignore the superintendent's recommendation to increase the budget because doing so would send a bad message.

But there is a Concept Shift. On any Misinterpretation question, there is always a shift between the speakers.

What two non-identical concepts are intended to be connected?

The parent talks about *ignoring the recommendation to increase the budget* as if it is the same as what the mayor says, but the mayor only said *we may not need to increase the budget.*

Not needing to follow the recommendations is not the same as ignoring them, so there's a Concept Shift:

May not need to increase budget ⚡ Ignore the recommendations to increase budget

3. Prephrase

To Prephrase on a Misinterpretation question, use the Concept Shift to state how the second speaker misinterprets the first.

In this case, the parent wrongly believes that the mayor recommends ignoring the proposed budget increase:

> Misinterpretation: The parent misinterprets the mayor to be saying that we should ignore the proposed budget increase.

It's okay if you don't come up with a good Prephrased answer, however. You can always focus on the **Real Question**.

4. Attack

The **Real Question** for Misinterpretation questions is:

Is this a misinterpretation in the passage?

As on Flaw questions, you are looking for a good match between the answer choice and the argument. The correct answer must describe a real misinterpretation, and it must match what happened in the passage.

(A) maintaining that it is unnecessary to continue to support the needs of the town's children

Choice (A): *Is this a misinterpretation in the passage?* The parent doesn't accuse the mayor of believing it's unnecessary to support the needs of the town's children. This **doesn't match.** *Cut it.*

(B) questioning whether the best way to show a commitment to the town's children is to support their education

Choice (B): *Is this a misinterpretation in the passage?* The parent doesn't address the mayor's position on the best way to show a commitment to the children. This **doesn't match.** *Cut it.*

(C) asserting that the superintendent's recommendation would not provide a substantial enough increase for the school budget

Choice (C): *Is this a misinterpretation in the passage?* No one believes that the mayor is advocating an even greater increase than the superintendent recommends. This is an **opposite** distracter. *Cut it.*

(D)   suggesting that the superintendent's proposal to increase the school budget be ignored

Choice (D): *Is this a misinterpretation in the passage?* This matches the Prephrased answer from above. *Keep it.*

(E)   assuming that the superintendent's budget is motivated by bias

Choice (E): *Is this a misinterpretation in the passage?* No one mentions anything like bias. This is completely **out of scope**. *Cut it.*

Choice (D) is the correct answer.

4.7   THE BIG PICTURE

4.7.1   THE COMMON AND UNCOMMON FLAWS

Some flaws appear all over the LSAT. Others appear often as answer choices but are rarely correct. If you know the **common flaws**, including those that are rarely correct answers, you can move through Logical Reasoning questions much more quickly and effectively.

These common flaws can appear on any flaw-dependent question type, not just on Flaw questions. What follows are some of the most common flaws, in decreasing order of frequency.

> Getting to know these common flaws is important for many different question types. However, not every argument has one of these common flaws, just as not every argument has a Concept Shift.

Necessary vs. Sufficient

Necessary vs. sufficient flaws occur when an argument confuses something that is *needed* for a certain result with something that is *guaranteed* to produce the result. Here's an example:

> A lamp will provide light only if it has a functioning bulb. So if a lamp has a functioning bulb, it will provide light.

The first sentence, a premise, says that a functioning bulb is *necessary* for a lamp to provide light: a lamp must have a functioning bulb in order to provide light. But the conclusion says that a functioning bulb is *sufficient* for a lamp to provide light: if a lamp has a functioning bulb, it will provide light.

But this isn't necessarily true. A lamp may need more than just a functioning bulb—being plugged in might help, for example. If you have a functioning bulb but no electricity, your lamp won't provide much light.

Necessary vs. sufficient flaws can also work the other way around. An argument can conclude that something is necessary merely because it is sufficient. Here's an example:

> Being the child of a United States senator guarantees your acceptance into law school. Therefore, if neither of your parents is a senator, you won't be admitted to law school.

Even if being the child of a senator is *sufficient* to get you into law school, that doesn't mean it's *necessary*. There are plenty of other ways to get into law school. This argument commits a necessary vs. sufficient flaw.

Here are some answer choices that describe such Flaws:

•   The argument confuses a sufficient condition with a required condition.
•   The argument confuses the conditions necessary for X with the conditions sufficient to bring X about.

Causation

An argument with a **causal** flaw argues that one thing caused another because the two things are correlated. Here's a very simple version:

> Children who regularly play video games are more likely to suffer from childhood obesity than those who rarely play video games. Therefore, childhood obesity is caused by playing video games.

The argument takes two correlated events and concludes that one causes the other. The argument concludes that video games *cause* childhood obesity, even though the evidence only supports a claim about a correlation.

The problem with causal arguments is that they ignore possible alternative explanations:

> Take special note of these three problems with causal reasoning. Understanding these will also help you answer several other types of questions.

1. **The causality could have occurred in reverse.** Perhaps obese children are more likely to choose to play video games and less likely to choose other diversions. In other words, perhaps childhood obesity causes children to regularly play video games.

2. **The two things could have a common cause.** Maybe a lack of interest in physically demanding activities causes both an interest in video games *and* childhood obesity.

3. **The correlation could be a mere coincidence.** Lots of things are correlated without being causally related. If you sneezed and it started to rain, you wouldn't feel responsible for the weather.

These three alternative explanations apply to almost any causal argument. Here's what a causal flaw looks like in an LSAT passage:

> A local farmer switched from traditional pesticides to an organic pesticide produced by Bug-gone, Inc. for an eighteen-month period to protect his apple orchard. During that period, the proportion of his crop lost to insects and other pests was less than that of the previous eighteen-month period. Due to this success, the farmer concluded that, at least over a short period of time, the organic pesticide from Bug-gone, Inc. is a more effective protection against pests than traditional pesticides.

The flaw here is identical to the one in the argument about childhood obesity. Two events are correlated:

1. The switch to the organic pesticide

2. The reduced loss to insects

The argument concludes that the switch caused the reduced loss. But there are many other possible explanations.

For example, perhaps it was merely a coincidence that the reduced loss happened at the same time as the switch to the organic pesticide, and the real reason for the reduced loss was a change in weather patterns that resulted in a smaller insect population.

Here are some answer choices that describe a causal flaw:

> Get to know how the LSAT writers translate common flaws into LSAT-speak. Not having to decode the esoteric language while you're taking the test will save you time.

- The argument confuses a mere coincidence with a causal relationship.

- The argument mistakes a correlation between A and B for a causal relation between the two.

- It fails to consider the possible contribution to B of other causes besides A.

If an answer like these appears on a question with a causal flaw, then keep it. If one appears when there is no causal flaw, then cut it—it's a distracter.

Sampling

Sampling flaws occur when an argument relies on a flawed sample or survey. There are two kinds of sampling flaws: unrepresentative groups and flawed methods.

A sampling flaw with an **unrepresentative group** occurs when a sample group does not accurately represent the larger population to which the conclusion refers. Here's an example of a sampling flaw based on an unrepresentative group:

> The Law School Admissions Council recently surveyed all men and women in their twenties who were taking the LSAT. Ninety-nine percent of those who responded said that they were interested in a legal career. Thus, most people in their twenties are interested in a legal career.

Ask people who are taking the LSAT, and you'll find that most of them want to be lawyers. But generalizing about a larger population from such an unrepresentative sample doesn't make sense. On the LSAT, this kind of **sampling flaw** can occur even when the sample is not obviously unrepresentative. Unless the passage provides information indicating that the sample is representative, be critical of the sample.

Here are some common answer choices that describe sampling flaws with unrepresentative groups:

- The argument generalizes from a sample that is unlikely to be representative.
- The argument uses evidence from a small sample that may well be unrepresentative.

Sampling flaws can also be **methodological**. Testing a representative group of people in a flawed way yields flawed results. Consider this:

> A leading research team recently polled millions of fourth graders across the country. When asked which ice cream they prefer—rich, delicious chocolate ice cream or that icky, yellow vanilla stuff—ninety percent responded that they prefer chocolate. As a result, the research team concluded that most fourth graders' favorite ice cream is chocolate.

This test is flawed in at least two ways. First, if you make chocolate sound that much better than vanilla, many people who would otherwise have preferred vanilla will say they prefer chocolate. Second, the study only asks about two flavors, but the team concludes that chocolate is the favorite. Fourth graders whose favorite ice cream is strawberry are ignored.

Here are some common answer choices that describe methodological sampling flaws:

- The behavior of one group of people in the study likely affected the other group of people in the study.
- The argument relies on a flawed study.

Absence of Evidence

An **absence of evidence** flaw occurs when an argument concludes that something is true merely on the grounds that there is no evidence against it. But just because something has no evidence against it doesn't make it true. Here's an example:

> No one has been able to prove that telekinesis is impossible, despite numerous attempts to do so. We must conclude, therefore, that telekinesis is possible.

Telekinesis might be impossible even if there's no evidence to the contrary. In fact, it might never be proven impossible, even if it is impossible. The lack of evidence *against* a claim is not enough to prove that the claim is *true*.

Similarly, a lack of evidence *for* a claim is not enough to prove that it is *false*. The silliness of the following argument should convince you of this:

> Scientists have not published even a single study that demonstrates that Jimmy loves his mother. Therefore, Jimmy does not love his mother.

Here are some common answer choices that describe **absence of evidence** flaws:

- The argument takes for granted that the fact that a claim has not been demonstrated to be false establishes that it is true.

- The argument treats a lack of evidence against Joe as if it exonerated Joe.

False Dichotomy

A **false dichotomy** flaw occurs when an argument proceeds as if there were only two options when other options might exist. For example, an argument might conclude that, because one course of action is unacceptable, a second course of action must be pursued. But there are usually more than just two options. Here's an example of an argument with a **false dichotomy** flaw:

> We could cut costs by buying in larger quantities or by switching to products of lower quality. We must cut costs, and we can't allow the quality of the products to suffer, so we have to buy in larger quantities.

This argument presents two possible options for cutting costs, and concludes that the second must be pursued because the first is unacceptable. But it's possible that there are other ways to cut costs. Perhaps they could lower salaries or be less wasteful.

Here are some common answer choices that describe **false dichotomy** flaws:

- The argument ignores the possibility that there may be other ways to reduce crime.

- The argument presumes, without providing justification, that the given end cannot be achieved without pursuing one of only two options.

Analogy

An analogy flaw can apply to any comparison between two things, no matter how alike they seem. If the two things are not identical, then whatever is different about them might be relevant to the argument.

An **analogy** flaw occurs when an argument relies on a comparison between two things that are similar in some ways but different in other, important ways. Here's an example:

> City X solved its crime problem through its successful "Beat the Streets" program. City Y, where crime is higher than ever, should use the same program.

Does that sound convincing? Suppose City X is Omaha, Nebraska, and City Y is New York. Is a program that works for Omaha the best option for New York? Perhaps not. Even if the cities were more similar, the problem would remain. Just because a property applies to one thing does not mean that property applies to something else.

Here's a passage that has an **analogy** flaw:

> Cheryl has completely memorized all local traffic laws. Therefore, to assert that she sometimes disobeys traffic laws would be like claiming that a trained chemist sometimes violates the laws of chemistry.

This passage depends on the similarity between traffic laws and the laws of chemistry. But there could be a crucial difference between the two—for example, it's possible to disobey traffic laws but impossible to break the laws of chemistry.

Here are some answer choices that describe an **analogy** flaw:

- The argument relies on an analogy between two things that are insufficiently alike in the respects in which they would have to be alike for the conclusion to be supported.

- The argument treats as similar two cases that are different in a critical respect.

- The argument treats two fundamentally different things as essentially the same.

All of these mean the same thing: the argument has an analogy flaw. If you know what an analogy flaw looks like, you'll have no trouble deciding whether these are correct.

Statistics

Be careful with any argument based on statistics. For one, many of them have sampling flaws. They can also have statistical flaws. One common **statistical flaw** is a shift between absolute numbers and proportions. Here's an example:

> There are roughly 70 million Catholics in the United States, whereas there are fewer than one thousand Catholics in Vatican City. Therefore, the United States must be proportionally more Catholic than Vatican City.

This argument makes perfect sense, unless you consider the population of Vatican City—roughly 900 people. There is no way to compare absolute numbers between the United States and Vatican City and make this claim about proportions.

Here are some common answers that describe **statistical** flaws:

- The argument is based on a comparison that inappropriately involves absolute numbers rather than proportions.

- The argument fails to consider the relative sizes of the two populations.

> Another way that the LSAT can talk about proportions is to address the topics of danger and probability. If something is dangerous, a large *proportion* of people who do it get hurt, although that may not translate into a large *number* of injuries if few people try it. If something is probable, then it happens a large proportion of the time, although that again may not translate into a large number.

> If an argument discusses two populations or one population at two different times, you must consider whether the sizes of the groups are comparable in such a way that the conclusion can be properly drawn.

Personal Attacks

Personal attack flaws occur when an argument is directed against an opponent rather than an opposing argument. These flaws usually involve attacks on the character of the opponent. But even the most devious opponents can have good arguments. Attacking a person's character does nothing to weaken that person's argument. Here's an example of a **personal attack**:

> Senator Smith calls for campaign advertising to focus more on the issues and less on opposing candidates' personal lives. But Senator Smith herself ran an advertisement this past election questioning her opponent's personal life, so her request should be ignored.

Instead of addressing Senator Smith's proposal, this argument attacks the senator's own character. But what the senator has done in the past is completely irrelevant to the strength of her proposal.

Here are some common answers that describe **personal attacks**:

- The argument criticizes a characteristic of the person making an argument rather than the argument itself.

- The argument criticizes the scientist's character in order to question his scientific findings.

Composition and Division

A **composition** or **division** flaw occurs when an argument makes a claim about a part based on its whole or a whole based on one of its parts.

If something is true of a part, it is not necessarily true of the whole. An argument that relies on an improper generalization commits a **composition flaw**. Here's an example:

> Played by itself, each individual note from this symphony is emotionally uninspiring. Thus, the symphony as a whole is emotionally uninspiring.

Even if every single note is uninspiring on its own, you can't generalize from the individual notes to the entire symphony. You can never reason from one, many, or even all parts to a whole.

Whenever an argument jumps from parts to a whole, it commits a composition flaw.

The opposite of a composition flaw is a division flaw. A division flaw occurs when an argument assumes that what is true of a whole must be true of its parts:

> The local automobile production plant is over forty years old, and the overall process by which it makes automobiles is very inefficient. Therefore, if one were to inspect each step in the overall process, one would find that none of them is efficient.

This argument is flawed because there could be one or two efficient steps even if the overall process is inefficient. What's true of the overall process is not necessarily true of every single part of the process.

Here are some answer choices that describe composition and division flaws:

- The argument assumes that because something is true of each of the parts of a whole it is true of the whole itself.

- The argument improperly draws an inference about individual members of a community from a premise about the entire community.

A composition flaw is not the same as a sampling flaw. A sampling flaw uses information about a small group to draw a conclusion about a larger group. A composition flaw uses information about individual members of a group to draw a conclusion about the group itself.

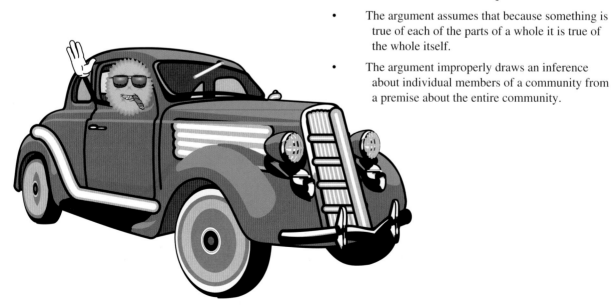

Equivocation

Equivocation flaws occur when an argument uses words ambiguously. Most often, this means that the argument uses two different meanings of the same word. Here's an example:

> People say that the president of this company has not been fiscally responsible. But these people are wrong. The president has in fact taken responsibility for overspending in recent years.

This argument uses the word "responsible" in two different ways. In the first sentence, it means being careful not to overspend. In the third sentence, it means owning up to a mistake. This misleading use of two different meanings of a word is an **equivocation flaw**.

Descriptions of equivocation flaws are rarely correct answers, but they are common incorrect answers.

Here are some common answer choices that describe an **equivocation flaw**:

- The argument confuses two different uses of the term X.

- The argument draws a conclusion based on equivocal language.

- The argument is based on the ambiguity of one of its terms.

> Watch out for answer choices that say, "The argument makes crucial use of a term without properly defining it." This is not the same as equivocation. You don't need to quote the dictionary to be able to make a valid argument. These answers look similar to equivocation flaws, but they are **never** correct.

Circularity

A **circular** argument has a conclusion that is identical to one of its premises. Here is a basic example:

> Alex is the best singer in the class. After all, none of the students sing better than he does.

The conclusion that Alex is the best singer is based on the premise that no one is better. But these two propositions mean precisely the same thing. Since the conclusion is just a restated premise, this argument commits a **circular flaw**.

Like expressions of equivocation flaws, descriptions of circular flaws are common answer choices but not very common *correct* answer choices. Circular flaw answer choices can be elegantly written and confusing at first read, so they are wonderful distracters.

Here are some common **circular flaw** answers:

- The argument presupposes what it sets out to prove.

- The conclusion is no more than a restatement of one of the premises.

4.7.2 Drill: Common Flaws

Write the number of each flawed argument in the box next to the type of flaw it commits and next to the correct, corresponding answer choice.

Flawed Argument		Type of Flaw		Answer Choice
1. John is a weird guy. Therefore, he is not a normal guy.		Necessary vs. sufficient		The argument confuses two different uses of a term.
2. Jeremy accused Sue of eating his jelly doughnut, but it is safe to conclude that she did not, since Sue's hands do not have any jelly or powdered sugar on them, and no one saw her near the doughnut.		Causal		The argument confuses the conditions sufficient to bring about a certain result with what is necessary to produce that result.
3. Jim thinks that cartoon underroos are good luck because every time he wears them, he gets a cookie.		Analogy		The argument confuses a mere coincidence with a causal relationship.
4. Alfina was upset when Ed defended his decision not to invite her to his wedding by saying he invited only his family. After all, she argued, all humans belong to the family *Hominidae*.		Sampling		The reasoning is questionable because its conclusion is based on a comparison that inappropriately involves absolute numbers rather than proportions.
5. The residents of Shelbyville were born over a span of nine decades. Therefore, the students at Hyde Park High School, which is composed entirely of Shelbyville residents, must have been born over a span of nine decades.		Absence of evidence		The argument rejects the possibility that what has not been proven is nevertheless true.
6. Not many people have died of the Ebola virus, whereas many more people have died of more common flu viruses. The fear of Ebola is therefore unwarranted.		Division		The argument treats as similar two cases that are different in a critical respect.
7. If you train hard, you will succeed. In order to be successful, therefore, you have to train hard.		Equivocation		The argument presupposes what it sets out to prove.
8. Ice cream is made all the more delicious by adding hot fudge. We should try hot fudge on lima beans, too.		Circular		The argument assumes that what is true of a whole is also true of its component parts.
9. Bill asked twenty people who worked for Fizzietooth which brand of toothpaste they preferred, and every one said Fizzietooth. He concluded that Fizzietooth is the best toothpaste.		Statistics		The argument improperly relies on a sample that is unrepresentative.

Answers

Flawed Argument	Type of Flaw	Answer Choice
1. John is a weird guy. Therefore, he is not a normal guy.	7 Necessary vs. Sufficient	4 The argument confuses two different uses of a term.
2. Jeremy accused Sue of eating his jelly doughnut, but it is safe to conclude that she did not, since Sue's hands do not have any jelly or powdered sugar on them, and no one saw her near the doughnut.	3 Causal	7 The argument confuses the conditions sufficient to bring about a certain result with what is necessary to produce that result.
3. Jim thinks that cartoon underoos are good luck because every time he wears them, he gets a cookie.	8 Analogy	3 The argument confuses a mere coincidence with a causal relationship.
4. Alfina was upset when Ed defended his decision not to invite her to his wedding by saying he invited only his family. After all, she argued, all humans belong to the family *Hominidae*.	6 Sampling	9 The reasoning is questionable because its conclusion is based on a comparison that inappropriately involves absolute numbers rather than proportions.
5. The residents of Shelbyville were born over a span of nine decades. Therefore, the students at Hyde Park High School, which is composed entirely of Shelbyville residents, must have been born over a span of nine decades.	2 Absence of evidence	2 The argument rejects the possibility that what has not been proven is nevertheless true.
6. Not many people have died of the Ebola virus, whereas many more people have died of more common flu viruses. The fear of Ebola is therefore unwarranted.	5 Division	8 The argument treats two cases that are different in a critical respect.
7. If you train hard, you will succeed. In order to be successful, therefore, you have to train hard.	4 Equivocation	1 The argument presupposes what it sets out to prove.
8. Ice cream is made all the more delicious by adding hot fudge. We should try hot fudge on lima beans, too.	1 Circular	5 The argument assumes that what is true of a whole is also true of its component parts.
9. Bill asked twenty people who worked for Fizzietooth which brand of toothpaste they preferred, and every one said Fizzietooth. He concluded that Fizzietooth is the best toothpaste.	9 Statistics	6 The argument improperly relies on a sample that is unrepresentative.

STOP. THIS IS THE END OF LECTURE 3. DO NOT PROCEED TO THE CORRESPONDING EXAM UNTIL INSTRUCTED TO DO SO IN CLASS.

LECTURE (4) CHAPTER (5)

NECESSARY ASSUMPTION QUESTIONS

5.1 IDENTIFY

5.1.1 WHAT IS A NECESSARY ASSUMPTION?

A **necessary assumption** is an unstated premise on which an argument depends.

This definition has two important parts:

1. *Unstated* premise: A necessary assumption does not appear in the argument.

2. *On which the argument depends*: A necessary assumption must be true in order for the conclusion to follow.

For example, consider this argument:

> The Winston School will hold a singing contest for eighth graders. Since Carol is an excellent singer, she will win the contest.

In order for this conclusion to be true, it must be true that *Carol is an eighth grader.* The argument depends on this premise, yet the premise is never stated in the argument. That makes it a necessary assumption.

Notice that even if it's true that Carol is an eighth grader, she isn't guaranteed to win the contest. So, while this is a *necessary* assumption, it's not *sufficient* to prove that the conclusion is definitely true.

5.1.2 IDENTIFYING NECESSARY ASSUMPTION QUESTIONS

All Necessary Assumption questions follow the same pattern:

1. **The question stem asks you for an assumption that the argument makes or requires.** This is what distinguishes Necessary Assumption questions from all other question types. If a question asks you for an assumption that the argument *makes, requires,* or *depends on,* then you are looking at a Necessary Assumption question.

2. **The passage contains a flawed argument.** Necessary Assumption questions are flaw-dependent, so their passages must contain flawed arguments.

Here are some Necessary Assumption question stems:

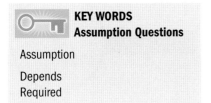

KEY WORDS
Assumption Questions

Assumption

Depends

Required

> Which one of the following is an assumption on which the argument depends?

> Which one of the following is an assumption required by the argument?

> The argument assumes which one of the following?

The word "assumption" in a question stem does not guarantee that you have a Necessary Assumption question. Be sure that the question asks for a *necessary* assumption—one that an argument requires. Compare the following question stems:

1. The conclusion of the argument is properly drawn if which one of the following is assumed?

2. The ethicist's argument depends on which one of the following assumptions?

The first question asks for an assumption but not a *necessary* one. Instead, it asks for an assumption that would help the argument—one that would allow the conclusion to be properly drawn. The second stem asks for an assumption that the argument *depends* on, so it's a Necessary Assumption question stem.

Also, the first question requires an *added* assumption: *if* you assume this, it'll help. The second refers to an assumption that the argument *makes*. Question stems that refer to assumptions made by the author are Necessary Assumption questions.

Necessary Assumption questions appear about four or five times per LSAT.

5.1.3 Drill: Identifying Necessary Assumption Questions

Determine whether each of the following is a Necessary Assumption question stem.

1. Which one of the following is an assumption on which the mayor's argument relies?

    Necessary Assumption question? ☐ Yes ☐ No

2. The argument requires the assumption of which one of the following?

    Necessary Assumption question? ☐ Yes ☐ No

3. The argument's main conclusion follows logically if which one of the following is assumed?

    Necessary Assumption question? ☐ Yes ☐ No

4. An assumption made in the argument above is that

    Necessary Assumption question? ☐ Yes ☐ No

5. Which one of the following is assumed by the conservationist's argument?

    Necessary Assumption question? ☐ Yes ☐ No

6. The conclusion follows logically if which one of the following is added to the premises?

    Necessary Assumption question? ☐ Yes ☐ No

7. Which one of the following, if assumed, allows the astronaut's conclusion to be properly drawn?

    Necessary Assumption question? ☐ Yes ☐ No

Answers & Explanations

1. **Yes.** The stem asks for an assumption that the argument relies upon.

2. **Yes.** The stem asks for an assumption that is required.

3. **No.** The stem asks for an assumption that *would help* the argument, not one that the argument makes.

4. **Yes.** The stem asks for an assumption that the argument makes.

5. **Yes.** The argument assumes it, so it must be a necessary part of the argument.

6. **No.** The stem asks for something to be added, not for an unstated, already present assumption.

7. **No.** The stem asks for an assumption to *help* the argument.

5.2 ANALYZE

5.2.1 ANALYZING NECESSARY ASSUMPTION QUESTIONS

To analyze a Necessary Assumption question, identify:

1. The conclusion
2. The premises
3. The flaw

You should be familiar with this analysis, since it's exactly the same analysis you do for Flaw questions.

> You will carry out this same analysis for many different question types.

> The flaw in Necessary Assumption questions often—but not always—comes in the form of a Concept Shift.

5.3 PREPHRASE

5.3.1 LINKING ASSUMPTIONS AND SHIELDING ASSUMPTIONS

There are two types of necessary assumptions: **linking assumptions** and **shielding assumptions**.

1. **Linking assumptions** provide a link for a Concept Shift. You can often predict the kinds of linking assumptions you're likely to see in the answer choices.

2. **Shielding assumptions** deny a circumstance that would destroy the argument. These can be obscure and unpredictable. It is almost never worth your effort to Prephrase shielding assumptions—there are simply too many possible shielding assumptions for any argument.

Here's how these assumptions work:

> Curator: When a museum exhibits a painting that excites the public imagination, it invariably attracts visitors who would not otherwise have come to the museum. We have just obtained the critically acclaimed *Pale Blue House* by DeCampli, which we plan to exhibit next month. So, when the new display is opened, we can expect to see a rise in museum attendance.

The curator concluded that the museum will receive more visitors, but there was a Concept Shift when she switched from talking about a painting that *excites the public imagination* to *Pale Blue House*. Those two concepts may not be identical—there's no evidence to say that anyone besides the critics cares about the painting.

Excites the public imagination ⚡ Pale Blue House

So you can Prephrase a linking assumption here by simply connecting the two sides of the Concept Shift.

> Necessary Assumption: The curator assumed that Pale Blue House is a painting that excites the public imagination.

> When the flaw comes in the form of a Concept Shift, you can Prephrase a necessary assumption by connecting the two sides of that shift.

This is a **linking assumption**, since it provides a link between the two sides of the Concept Shift. You would expect to see this kind of answer available in the answer choices, and this is the kind of answer you can easily Prephrase.

But you might not expect to see an unusual **shielding assumption**. For example, what would happen to the number of visitors if the mayor hated that painting so much that he erected a police barricade around the museum as soon as the painting was put on display? The curator's prediction about a rise in visitors would certainly be destroyed. In order for her argument to follow, she must assume that the mayor would *not* take that action. Thus, that's another necessary assumption.

Even if the argument's flaw is not a Concept Shift or other common flaw, you should still try to Prephrase based on the particulars of the argument.

Necessary Assumption: The curator assumed that the mayor does not hate the painting so much that he would erect a police barricade around the museum if the painting were displayed.

This is a **shielding assumption**. It is a necessary assumption, since the argument depends on it. But it provides no specific link between the premises and conclusion; it merely denies a circumstance that would destroy the argument.

This should make one thing clear: you can't always predict every possible answer.

To Prephrase on a Necessary Assumption question, identify where a linking assumption might occur. The most obvious place for a linking assumption is between the two sides of a Concept Shift. You don't have to predict exactly how the correct answer choice will be worded. Instead, just state how a linking assumption could connect the two sides of the Concept Shift.

Don't bother trying to Prephrase any shielding assumptions, but be ready for the possibility of one showing up in the answer choices.

5.3.2 NECESSARY ASSUMPTIONS AND COMMON FLAWS

Another tool that will help you Prephrase necessary assumptions is the knowledge that arguments with certain common flaws always have the same necessary assumptions built into them.

Common Flaw	Built-In Assumption
The argument treats something *necessary* to bring about a certain result as if it were *sufficient* to bring about the result.	There are no other things that are *also* necessary to bring about the result.
The argument treats something *sufficient* to bring about a result as if it were *necessary* to bring about the result.	There are no *other* ways the result could occur *without* the sufficient factor.
The argument treats a *correlation* between two things as evidence that one *caused* the other.	There were no other possible causes besides the one cited. The causality did not occur in reverse. The two things did not have a single common cause. The correlation was not a mere coincidence.
The argument draws a conclusion about an overall population based on information from a small *sample* of the population.	The small sample is representative of the overall population. The gathering of information was free of any methodological errors.
The argument treats the *absence of evidence* for one conclusion as if it proves the opposite conclusion is true.	All the possible evidence has been gathered.
The argument shows that one option is impossible and concludes that a certain other option must be chosen (*false dichotomy*).	The two options discussed are the only two possible options.
The argument uses an *analogy* or draws a conclusion about one thing based on information about a different thing.	There are no important differences between the two things that make them not analogous.
The argument uses information about *percentages* to draw a conclusion about absolute *numbers*. The argument uses information about absolute *numbers* to draw a conclusion about *percentages*.	The size of the group has not changed over time. The sizes of the groups being compared are similar.

5.4 ATTACK

5.4.1 THE REAL QUESTION

The **Real Question** for Necessary Assumption questions is:

> *Does the argument depend on this being true?*

This Real Question comes from the definition of a Necessary Assumption. Since the conclusion relies on the truth of a necessary assumption, ask whether the argument depends on the truth of each answer choice. Only one answer choice will be something that the argument *needs* to be true.

The Real Question is especially important for Necessary Assumption questions because it can identify unexpected shielding assumptions. Without the Real Question, you might be tempted to dismiss a necessary shielding assumption.

5.4.2 Drill: The Real Question & Potential Shielding Assumptions

Each of the following contains a short argument with two potential shielding assumptions. Use the Real Question to determine which answer choice is a necessary assumption for each argument.

1. The cottonmouth water moccasin is a deadly poisonous water snake. Even those who merely stand near the waters in which the snake lives should be careful: they might suffer a poisonous bite from a water moccasin that decides to jump out of the water.

   (A) Water moccasins do not dislike leaving the water to bite those nearby.

   Does the argument depend on this being true?

   ☐ Yes ☐ No

   (B) Water moccasins' venom does not lose its poisonous properties when these snakes leave the water.

   Does the argument depend on this being true?

   ☐ Yes ☐ No

2. Thorough planning helps to limit the number of surprises that a business is likely to face. Therefore, if you want to run a successful business, you should always use thorough planning.

   (A) Thorough planning does not occasionally lead to a fatal lack of flexibility for a business.

   Does the argument depend on this being true?

   ☐ Yes ☐ No

   (B) Successful businesses have never failed to have thorough business plans.

   Does the argument depend on this being true?

   ☐ Yes ☐ No

3. Anonymization is a process by which Internet users hide their IP addresses by using free proxy servers. But users need to exercise extreme caution with regard to anonymization: identity thieves can target the proxy servers themselves.

   (A) The proxy servers do not erase all information before identity thieves can access it.

   Does the argument depend on this being true?

   ☐ Yes ☐ No

   (B) Users are not aware of the dangers of identity theft.

   Does the argument depend on this being true?

   ☐ Yes ☐ No

4. The different rainforests of the world are home to vastly different species of animals even though the trees that provide animal habitats are largely the same in each of the world's rainforests. Thus, the species variation must be explained by some factor other than differences in tree species.

   (A) The minimal differences between the trees are unlikely to produce large variations in animal species.

   Does the argument depend on this being true?

   ☐ Yes ☐ No

   (B) The species variation cannot be explained by the ecological conditions of the varied neighboring environments.

   Does the argument depend on this being true?

   ☐ Yes ☐ No

Answers and Explanations

1. (A) **No.** Even if the snakes dislike leaving the water, they still might do it.
   (B) **Yes.** If the venom isn't poisonous out of water, then people can't suffer poisonous bites out of the water.

2. (A) **Yes.** If thorough planning occasionally leads to a fatal lack of flexibility, then you should *not always* use thorough planning. This is a necessary assumption.
   (B) **No.** Even if some successful businesses of the past did not have thorough business plans, a business plan might be essential in the current business world.

3. (A) **Yes.** Identity thieves must be able to access at least some of the information on the proxy servers for there to be a cause for concern.
   (B) **No.** Even if users are aware of the dangers, they may need to be cautious.

4. (A) **Yes.** If the small differences are likely to produce large species variations, then the variations could be explained by the differences in the trees. This is a necessary assumption.
   (B) **No.** If this is the explanation, it's not a problem as long as it has nothing to do with the trees in the rainforest.

Get rid of any answer choice that weakens the argument.

Remember the argument in which the author made a Concept Shift between a *reliable form of transportation* and a *1979 station wagon* (p. 62)? A necessary assumption in that argument is that "not every 1979 station wagon is unreliable." But an **extreme** answer choice would say that "every 1979 station wagon is reliable." That's stronger than what the argument needs, because you don't care about *every* one—just the author's.

5.4.3 DISTRACTERS

The most common wrong answers for Necessary Assumption questions are **out of scope** distracters. If an answer choice has nothing to do with the argument, then the argument probably doesn't require it. Shielding assumptions can sometimes appear to be out of scope, so be careful. Before eliminating an answer choice that introduces brand new concepts, consider whether it is an unexpected shielding assumption.

You should also avoid **extreme** answers, since an argument rarely requires extreme assumptions. The correct answer to a Necessary Assumption question is much more likely to contain the phrase *at least some* than the phrase *every one*.

5.5 PUTTING IT ALL TOGETHER

Here are some examples:

1. At an excavation site once believed to have been first inhabited by refugees during a rebellion in the year 138, several coins were recently found that are known to have been minted in the year 68. On this basis, researchers have concluded that the site was inhabited much earlier than originally believed, closer to the year 68.

   Which one of the following is an assumption on which the argument depends?

Here's the approach:

1. Identify

This question stem asks about an assumption that is necessary, so it's a Necessary Assumption question.

2. Analyze

The word *concluded* in the last sentence is a conclusion indicator. The conclusion is that the site was inhabited much earlier than 138. Why? Coins from 68 were found there. That sounds like a fact, so it's safe to call it a premise.

Coins from 68 were found in an area thought to have been settled in 138.

Therefore, the site is much older than 138.

Next, find the flaw. In this case, the argument's flaw is that the author commits a Concept Shift:

What two non-identical concepts are intended to be connected?

In this case, the author made a connection between the age of the site and the age of the coins found at the site. Since the coins' age is not necessarily the same as the site's age, there's a Concept Shift:

$$\text{The age of coins at the site} \, \nmid \, \text{The age of the site}$$

3. Prephrase

Remember to Prephrase by identifying where a linking assumption is likely to occur. Since you have a Concept Shift, this is all you have to say:

> **Necessary Assumption:** The author assumed there is a connection between the age of the coins at the site and the age of the site.

4. Attack

Use the **Real Question** to spot necessary assumptions: *Does the argument depend on this being true?*

    (A)   More than one group of people inhabited the excavation site.

Choice (A): *Does the argument depend on this being true?* In other words, does the argument need it to be true that more than one group inhabited the site? No. It doesn't matter *how many* groups inhabited the site. The question is *when*. This is **out of scope**. *Cut it.*

    (B)   There is evidence at the excavation site that the inhabitants lived there for several years.

Choice (B): *Does the argument depend on this being true?* No. How long they stayed there is **out of scope**. The only thing that matters is when they first settled. *Cut it.*

    (C)   There were many refugees during the rebellion in the year 138.

Choice (C): *Does the argument depend on this being true?* No. There could have been two refugees or a million—it makes no difference in the argument. This is also **out of scope**. *Cut it.*

    (D)   Emperors and monarchs of the period in question often minted coins to commemorate military victories.

Choice (D): *Does the argument depend on this being true?* Does it matter why the coins were minted? No. Does it matter who minted them? Not really. The only thing that matters is *when* the coins were minted, which you must accept is 68. *Cut it.*

    (E)   There were very few coins from the year 68 still in use by the year 138.

Choice (E): *Does the argument depend on this being true?* That is, does the argument require that few coins from 68 would have survived to 138? The Concept Shift is all about these two dates, so even if you were lost here, you should still choose this one because it's the only answer that isn't out of scope.

In fact, this is a necessary assumption. If coins from 68 were used long after production, they would not be a reliable dating tool. The inhabitants could have settled in 138 bringing their seventy-year-old coins with them. The argument requires that coins have a short shelf-life so that their minting date can be used to figure out the age of the area in which they were found.

Choice (E) is the correct answer.

Here's another example:

2. Any cat owner can report that cat food is certainly not harmful to cats, and a chemical analysis of its contents is even more revealing. While most unhealthy food that people eat is unhealthy because of its amounts of some combination of fat, cholesterol, sugar, and sodium, a typical serving of cat food has very low amounts of each of these elements. Hence cat food must not be unhealthy for humans to eat.

Which one of the following is an assumption required by the argument?

1. Identify

The question stem asks for an assumption that is required, so it's a Necessary Assumption question.

2. Analyze

The conclusion indicator *hence* indicates the conclusion: cat food must not be unhealthy for humans to eat. This is based on the premise that cat food is low in the elements that cause most unhealthy food to be unhealthy.

> Cat food is low in the elements that cause most unhealthy food to be unhealthy.
>
> ---
>
> **Therefore,** cat food must not be unhealthy for humans to eat.

Now find the flaw. As usual, it comes in the form of a Concept Shift:

What two non-identical concepts are intended to be connected?

There are a couple of references to health that are treated as if one leads to the other. In the conclusion, there's *not unhealthy for humans to eat*, but in the premises there's only *low in the elements that cause most unhealthy food to be unhealthy*. These two ideas aren't the same thing.

> The lack of common unhealthy elements ⚡ The healthiness of cat food for humans

3. Prephrase

Prephrase where a linking assumption is likely to occur. Using the Concept Shift, you can predict the following:

> Necessary Assumption: The author assumed there is a connection between the lack of common unhealthy elements and the healthiness of the food for humans.

4. Attack

(A) Anything that is not harmful to cats must be good for humans.

Choice (A): *Does the argument depend on this being true?* This answer is **extreme**. The argument doesn't require that *everything* that cats can eat is good for humans. *Cut it.*

(B) Cat food contains a number of vitamins and minerals that are healthy for humans.

Choice (B): *Does the argument depend on this being true?* The argument only needs cat food not to be unhealthy—kitty kibble need not be a vitamin supplement. *Cut it.*

(C)   Cat food does not contain a significant amount of anthraquinone glycoside, a compound harmless to cats but poisonous to humans.

Choice (C): *Does the argument depend on this being true?* The argument attempts to prove that cat food is not unhealthy for humans. Poison would make it pretty unhealthy. Leave this one in for now—it looks like a necessary **shielding assumption**. *Keep it.*

(D)   Dog food is similarly not unhealthy to eat.

Choice (D): *Does the argument depend on this being true?* The healthiness of dog food is completely irrelevant to whether cat food is healthy. This is **out of scope**. *Cut it.*

(E)   All cat foods are fat-free and cholesterol-free.

Choice (E): *Does the argument depend on this being true?* This is an **extreme** claim. You don't need cat food to be *free* of cholesterol and fat. It just can't have an unhealthy amount of such elements. *Cut it.*

Choice (C) is the correct answer.

> Even though this choice introduces anthraquinone glycoside—something never mentioned in the passage—it is not out of scope because it is directly related to the health of humans, a concept central to the conclusion. This is how many shielding assumptions work.

5.6   VARIATIONS

5.6.1   EVALUATE QUESTIONS

Evaluate questions are rare flaw-dependent questions that ask you to identify what you'd need to know to evaluate the strength of an argument. Since the strength of a flawed argument depends on the truth of its assumptions, Evaluate question really ask you to identify an argument's necessary assumptions.

You should not worry about these questions too much—three quarters of official tests don't contain a single one!

KEY WORD
Evaluate Questions

Evaluating

3. Lawrence Kohlberg argues that there are six identifiable stages of moral development. He says that these six stages must occur in order, and it is not possible to regress from one stage to another. According to Kohlberg, adolescents and young adults tend to enter into a stage of conformity, during which time they seek approval from others. But a recent study of one hundred prison inmates suggests that this stage occurs much later than adolescence. Of the inmates studied, all were over thirty, and none had reached the stage of conformity.

Which one of the following would it be most useful to know in evaluating the findings from the study above?

Here's the approach:

1.   Identify

This question asks you what would be useful to know to *evaluate* the argument. This is an Evaluate question.

2.   Analyze

This is a *counterargument* against one of Kohlberg's claims. Kohlberg says that the stage of conformity occurs during adolescence and young adulthood, but the author argues that this is not true. Why? Look at the evidence from a study of thirty-year-old prison inmates.

None of the many prison inmates over thirty in the study had reached the stage of conformity.

Therefore, the conformity stage occurs much later than adolescence.

Now look for the flaw. This argument has a common flaw. If you recognize a common flaw, there's no need to find a Concept Shift. The argument's evidence is a **sample**, and there are two concerns for any sample: 1) is it representative? and 2) were the sampling methods sound? As to whether the sample is representative, there is serious doubt. The conclusion is about humanity, but the sample is a group of prison inmates. Are prison inmates representative of humanity? Maybe, but maybe not. The argument assumes that these inmates are representative of humanity.

3. Prephrase

To Prephrase on an Evaluate question, identify the necessary assumption as the point to evaluate.

In this case, the argument assumes that the sample of prison inmates is representative of humanity.

> Prephrase: To evaluate this argument, it would be helpful to know whether the sample of inmates is representative of humanity.

> The generic Prephrased answer for Evaluate questions is:
>
> To evaluate this argument, it would be helpful to know whether {the necessary assumption} is true.

4. Attack

The **Real Question** for Evaluate questions is: *Does this address an assumption?* Since evaluating the argument requires determining whether the necessary assumptions are true, the correct answer must address an assumption.

> (A)   the specific ages of the inmates at the prison and their average stage of moral development

Choice (A): *Does this address an assumption?* You already know the applicants are over thirty. Their specific ages make no difference, since the argument is about adolescents and young adults. Neither do their specific stages make a difference, since the argument is about one particular stage. *Cut it.*

> (B)   the extent to which the moral development of prison inmates is representative of the moral development of most humans

Choice (B): *Does this address an assumption?* This is a great match for the Prephrased answer above. You need to know whether this sample is representative. *Keep it.*

> (C)   the conditions under which Kohlberg studied and developed his theory of the six stages of moral development

Choice (C): *Does this address an assumption?* The conditions of Kohlberg's study make no difference. The only concern is the truth of his conclusions. *Cut it.*

> (D)   the reliability of using a sample size of one hundred versus using smaller sample sizes when conducting a study

Choice (D): *Does this address an assumption?* You'd never question a study's validity based on its having too many subjects. Perhaps one might question whether one hundred is *enough*, but there's no reason to worry about one hundred being too many. *Cut it.*

> The answer choices to Evaluate questions can also come in the form of questions. This doesn't affect your approach.

> (E)   the level of general acceptance of the study of prison inmates by social psychologists who research moral development

Choice (E): *Does this address an assumption?* The general acceptance of the study would not help you evaluate the argument, since there are many factors other than validity that determine general acceptance. *Cut it.*

Choice (B) is a good match for the Prephrased answer, and none of the other answers address the argument's assumptions.

Choice (B) is the correct answer.

5.6.2 THE NEGATION TOOL

The Negation Tool helps you decide whether a statement is a necessary assumption.

To apply the Negation Tool to any given answer choice:

1. Negate the answer choice.

2. Ask, "Does this destroy the argument?" If so, then the answer choice is a necessary assumption.

This makes sense: if something is a necessary assumption, then negating it should destroy the argument.

There are two ways a negated statement can destroy an argument:

1. **The statement can imply a conclusion that conflicts with the argument's conclusion.**
   If a statement requires that you draw a conclusion that conflicts with the argument's conclusion, then the statement destroys the argument.

   Suppose Lyn argues that yoga is silly because it involves funny outfits.

   The statement "funny outfits are used only in non-silly activities" would destroy Lyn's argument, since it would require drawing a conclusion that conflicts with Lyn's. Yoga isn't silly.

2. **The statement can imply that the argument's premises cannot be used as evidence for its conclusion.**
   A statement destroys an argument when it implies that an argument's premises cannot be used as evidence for its conclusion. That would mean the argument has no evidence. In order to have an argument, you need both a conclusion and some premises. If the premises are removed, there isn't an argument.

   Suppose James argues that the Yankees are the best baseball team today because Reggie Jackson is a clutch hitter.

   The statement "Reggie Jackson is retired" would destroy the argument, since the premise could no longer be used as evidence for the conclusion. If Reggie Jackson is retired, then his skills cannot be evidence for the Yankees status as the best team in baseball today.

Take a look at this argument:

> Law students who wish to improve the persuasiveness of their oral presentations often work to increase the number of emotionally moving anecdotes contained in their presentations. However, such students should also pay attention to general research skills, since it is impossible to find the best anecdotes without good research skills.

The conclusion is that [law students who wish to improve the persuasiveness of their oral presentations should pay attention to general research skills.] While you would usually proceed by finding the flaw and Prephrasing a necessary assumption, this time try applying the Negation Tool to some answer choices.

> (A) The most skilled researchers do not usually deliver persuasive oral presentations.

1. Negate the answer choice.
   The negated form of this answer is: *the most skilled researchers usually deliver persuasive oral presentations.*

2. Ask, "Does this destroy the argument?"
   The argument isn't about the best researchers—it's about law students, so this negated version is somewhat out of scope. Even if you ignore that, the

negated form of choice (A) helps the argument, if anything. It would suggest that students really should pay attention to research skills, since they are compatible with persuasive presentations. As the negated form of choice (A) certainly does *not* destroy the argument, choice (A) is *not* correct.

> (B) Emotionally moving anecdotes contribute to the persuasiveness of oral presentations.

1. Negate the answer choice.

The negated form of this answer is: *emotionally moving anecdotes do not contribute to the persuasiveness of oral presentations.*

2. Ask, "Does this destroy the argument?"

Does the negated form destroy the argument? Absolutely. If anecdotes have nothing to do with the persuasiveness of a presentation, then there is no reason that students who wish to increase their persuasiveness should be focusing on anecdotes. Since finding anecdotes is the only reason given in the argument for focusing on research skills, the argument no longer has any evidence for why students should care about research. The argument *is* destroyed, which means that the original form of choice (B) *is* indeed a necessary assumption.

The Negation Tool is a useful tool, but it can complicate things because of the added reversals. You should practice using the Negation Tool a lot in your homework in order to become skilled at it, but you should not use the Negation Tool on every answer choice on a timed test. Use it when you come across a confusing or difficult answer choice.

Try the Negation Tool on this example:

> The Negation Tool is like the Survey Tool. It always works for every answer choice on every Necessary Assumption question, but because it's somewhat complex, you shouldn't use it every time. Just save it for when you need it to figure out a difficult choice. Regardless, you should practice it a lot so you get comfortable with it.

3. Psychologist: Some astrologers claim that our horoscopes completely determine our personalities, but this claim is false. I concede that identical twins—who are, of course, born at practically the same time—often do have similar personalities. However, birth records were examined to find two individuals who were born 40 years ago on the same day and at exactly the same time—one in a hospital in Toronto and one in a hospital in New York. Personality tests revealed that the personalities of these two individuals are in fact different.

Which one of the following is an assumption on which the psychologist's argument depends?

Test 28, Section 1, Question 21

1. Identify

The question stem asks for an *assumption* on which the argument *depends*, so it's a Necessary Assumption question.

2. Analyze

This is a *counterargument* against the claim that horoscopes completely determine our personalities. Why don't they? Two 40-year-olds born simultaneously have different personalities.

> Two individuals born at exactly the same time—one in New York and one in Toronto—have different personalities according to a personality test.
> ....
> **Therefore,** horoscopes do not completely determine our personalities.

You'd usually look for the flaw at this point, but forgo that for now to focus on the Negation Tool.

3. Prephrase

Usually you'd Prephrase what you'd expect to see, but again, since the focus is on the Negation Tool, go straight to the answer choices.

4. Attack

This will be a bit unnatural, as you'd never use the Negation Tool for all five answer choices. You'd usually eliminate the answers that are obviously wrong before even thinking about the Negation Tool. But it's good practice, so go ahead and use it on all five of the following answer choices:

> (A) Astrologers have not subjected their claims to rigorous experimentation.

Choice (A):

1. Negate the answer choice.
   The negated form is: Astrologers have subjected their claims to rigorous experimentation.

2. Ask, "Does this *destroy* the argument?"
   No. It's still possible that personalities have nothing to do with horoscopes. *Cut it.*

> (B) The personality differences between the two individuals cannot be explained by the cultural differences between Toronto and New York.

Choice (B):

1. Negate the answer choice.
   The negated form is: The personality differences can be explained by the cultural differences between their cities.

2. Ask, "Does this *destroy* the argument?"
   Quite the opposite. If cultural differences account for personality differences, then personality is *not* based on horoscope alone. This negated version is actually good for the argument. *Cut it.*

> Remember, the conclusion of this argument is: [horoscopes do not completely determine our personalities.]

> (C) The geographical difference between Toronto and New York did not result in the two individuals having different horoscopes.

Choice (C):

1. Negate the answer choice.
   The negated form is: The geographical differences between the individuals resulted in their having different horoscopes.

2. Ask, "Does this *destroy* the argument?"
   If the people have different horoscopes, then they can't be used as evidence for a comparison of the personalities of people with identical horoscopes. The negated form destroys the argument by implying that the argument's premises can't be used as evidence for its conclusion. *Keep it.*

> (D) Complete birth records for the past 40 years were kept at both hospitals.

Choice (D):

1. Negate the answer choice.
   The negated form is: Complete birth records for the past 40 years were not kept at both hospitals.

2. Ask, "Does this *destroy* the argument?"
   Who cares how complete the birth records are? As long as the records for the two individuals in question are accurate, nothing else matters. *Cut it.*

(E)   Identical twins have identical genetic structures
and usually have similar home environments.

Choice (E):

1. Negate the answer choice.
The negated form is: Identical twins don't usually have similar genetics and home environments.

2. Ask, "Does this *destroy* the argument?"
The argument isn't about identical twins, so no. *Cut it.*

Choice (C) is the correct answer.

5.6.3   Drill: The Negation Tool

For each of the following questions, first mark the premises and conclusion in the passage. Then determine which answer choice is a necessary assumption by applying the Negation Tool.

1. Reggie: Our basketball team isn't scoring enough points to win the championship. If we trade to get Nancy, the leading scorer in the league, then we are sure to win this year's championship game.

    (A)   The second-best scorer in the league would not be enough to guarantee a championship.

    Negate the answer: _____

    Does it destroy the argument? _____

    Is it a necessary assumption? _____

    (B)   This year's championship game will not be cancelled.

    Negate the answer: _____

    Does it destroy the argument? _____

    Is it a necessary assumption? _____

2. Most new employees become too bored by long, detailed training programs to pay attention, and as a result, they do not learn the essential skills for the job. The best way to train new employees at any company, therefore, is to give them a 5-minute, upbeat training DVD relaying only the essential skills for the job.

    (A)   New employees are willing to watch training DVDs.

    Negate the answer: _____

    Does it destroy the argument? _____

    Is it a necessary assumption? _____

    (B)   Current employees who have been poorly trained by long, detailed lectures would benefit from the training DVD.

    Negate the answer: _____

    Does it destroy the argument? _____

    Is it a necessary assumption? _____

3. Some of the greatest treasures of world history are buried beneath private property where archaeologists are not allowed to dig. If we care about our culture, we should allow archaeologists to dig wherever they see fit.

    (A)   Archaeologists only want to dig for the greatest treasures of world history.

    Negate the answer: _____

    Does it destroy the argument? _____

    Is it a necessary assumption? _____

    (B)   Allowing archaeologists to dig wherever they see fit will not destroy our culture.

    Negate the answer: _____

    Does it destroy the argument? _____

    Is it a necessary assumption? _____

4. Cable companies have offered increasingly fast high-speed Internet service, currently charging today, for a service that is three times as fast, what they charged three years ago. As a result, slower service will soon disappear.

    (A)   The price of slower service has decreased slightly over recent years.

    Negate the answer: _____

    Does it destroy the argument? _____

    Is it a necessary assumption? _____

    (B)   Consumers do not significantly prefer the low cost of slower service to the performance of faster service.

    Negate the answer: _____

    Does it destroy the argument? _____

    Is it a necessary assumption? _____

Answers & Explanations

1. **Choice (B) is the necessary assumption.**
   Conclusion: [If we trade to get Nancy, then we are sure to win this year's championship game.]
   (A) **Negated:** The second best scorer would be enough.
   Destroys? No, trading for Nancy could still guarantee the championship.
   (B) **Negated:** The championship game will be cancelled.
   Destroys? Yes, Reggie's team can't win a game that isn't played.

2. **Choice (A) is the necessary assumption.**
   Conclusion: [The best way to train new employees at any company is to give them a 5-minute, upbeat training DVD relaying only the essential skills for the job.]
   (A) **Negated:** New employees are not willing to watch training DVDs.
   Destroys? Yes, DVDs can't be the best way to train if new employees won't watch them.
   (B) **Negated:** Current poorly trained employees would not benefit.
   Destroys? No, the argument is about the best way to train new employees.

3. **Choice (B) is the necessary assumption.**
   Conclusion: [If we care about our culture, we should allow archaeologists to dig wherever they see fit.]
   (A) **Negated:** Archaeologists don't only want to dig for the greatest treasures.
   Destroys? No, as long as they uncover great treasures, digging still sounds good.
   (B) **Negated:** Digging will destroy our culture.
   Destroys? Yes, since culture is the explicit concern.

4. **Choice (B) is the necessary assumption.**
   Conclusion: [Slower service will soon disappear.]
   (A) **Negated:** The price of slower service has not decreased.
   Destroys? No, if anything this helps the argument.
   (B) **Negated:** Consumers significantly prefer low cost to performance.
   Destroys? Yes, since this suggests that slower service will stick around.

5.7   THE BIG PICTURE

5.7.1   QUANTITY WORDS AND THEIR NEGATION

Words that express quantity should be understood according to their precise meanings on the LSAT. Negating quantity words can often be a challenge.

Knowing how to negate quantity words helps you tremendously when you need to use the Negation Tool on Necessary Assumption questions. This skill can also help you on other question types when you are analyzing counterarguments.

All and Always

All means every single one, without exceptions. If a passage says that all chemists know the periodic table, then there isn't a single chemist in the world who doesn't know the periodic table.

Suppose you wanted to negate the statement that all chemists know the periodic table. You might be tempted to say no chemists know the periodic table, but you don't need to prove such a strong claim. All you have to do to negate this is find *at least one* chemist who does *not* know the periodic table. Remember, *at least one* means the same as *some*.

Therefore, the negated form of *all* is *some…not*.

> The negated form of *all* is *some…not*.

This discussion also applies to the word *always*. *Always* means *at all times*, so the negated form is *sometimes not*.

None and Never

None means not a single one, without exceptions. So if a passage says that none of Shakespeare's tragedies have happy moments, then there isn't even one Shakespearean tragedy with happy moments.

To negate this claim, you don't need to prove that all Shakespearean tragedies have happy moments. You only need to find *some* tragedies that have happy moments. If you find *some* tragedies that have happy moments, then you have disproved the claim that *none* of Shakespeare's tragedies have happy moments.

The negated form of *none* is *some*.

Therefore, the negated form of *none* is *some*.

This also applies to *never*. Never means not at any time, so the negated form is *sometimes*.

Most

Most means more than half, which could be as little as 51% and as much as all. While there is room for some flexibility, most can never mean half or less than half. So if most teenagers resist their parents, then more than half of them resist their parents.

To negate the claim that most teenagers resist their parents, you have to prove that less than half resist their parents. In other words, you have to prove that most do not resist their parents. If you prove that *most* teenagers do *not* resist their parents, then you disprove the claim that most teenagers resist their parents.

The negated form of *most* is *most... not*.

The negated form of *most* is *most…not*.

Only

Only means that something is true in a single circumstance or for a single type of thing. So if a passage tells you that only legislators can create new laws, then the creation of new laws is the restricted domain of just a single type of person—legislators. There are no other types of people who can make laws.

To negate the claim that *only* legislators can create new laws, you must show that making laws is not restricted to just this one type of person. In other words, if you can show that there is *some other* group of people who can create new laws, then you have disproved the claim that *only* legislators can make new laws.

The negated form of *only* is *some other*. You can also use the phrase *not only*.

Therefore, the negated form of *only* is *some other*. You can also use the phrase *not only*.

Some, Many, At Least One, Sometimes, and Often

Some, many, and at least one are the vaguest of the quantity words. All of them mean one or more. So "some," for example, could mean one, half, most, or all. "Many" would seem to be more than some, but it is too vague to have any specific meaning beyond one or more. At least one is clearer, but all of these mean the same thing.

The negated form of *some, many*, and *at least one* is *no* or *none*.

So if a passage says that some patients experience nausea, then one or more patients experience nausea. It could be that all or most patients do, or it could be that only one patient does. Some is vague. To disprove this claim, you must prove that there is not even one patient who experiences nausea. If you can show that no patients experience nausea, then you have disproved the claim that some patients experience nausea.

The negated form of *some, many*, and *at least one* is *no* or *none*.

Sometimes and *often* work in much the same way. Their meanings are identical and vague, and the negated form of each is *never*.

CHAPTER 5: NECESSARY ASSUMPTION QUESTIONS • 99

SUMMARY OF NEGATED QUANTITY WORDS	
Original Statement	Negated Version
All musicians are kind.	Some musicians are not kind.
Most musicians are kind.	Most musicians are not kind.
Some musicians are kind.	No musicians are kind.
Some musicians are not kind.	All musicians are kind.
Most musicians are not kind.	Most musicians are kind.
No musicians are kind.	Some musicians are kind.
Only musicians are kind	Some other types of people besides musicians are kind.
Musicians are always kind.	Musicians are sometimes not kind.
Musicians are usually kind.	Musicians are usually not kind.
Musicians are sometimes kind.	Musicians are never kind.
Musicians are sometimes not kind.	Musicians are always kind.
Musicians are usually not kind.	Musicians are usually kind.
Musicians are never kind.	Musicians are sometimes kind.

5.7.2 Drill: Negating Quantity Statements

Negate each of the following statements.

1. Some video games are meant to reflect real-world events.

   Negated: _____

   _____

2. All gasoline-powered engines harm the environment.

   Negated: _____

   _____

3. Most college students work part-time jobs.

   Negated: _____

   _____

4. Boston is often hot in the summer.

   Negated: _____

   _____

5. Many people have been on road trips.

   Negated: _____

   _____

6. None of the 1927 New York Yankees hit over 50 home runs.

   Negated: _____

   _____

7. Art is sometimes ugly.

   Negated: _____

   _____

8. Some engineers don't know calculus.

   Negated: _____

   _____

9. Most resorts are not all-inclusive.

   Negated: _____

   _____

10. At least one lender does not evaluate borrowers based on credit score.

    Negated: _____

    _____

11. Only poets appreciate the true beauty of words.

    Negated: _____

    _____

Answers

1. No video games are meant to reflect real-world events.

2. Some gasoline-powered engines do not harm the environment.

3. Most college students do not work part-time jobs.

4. Boston is never hot in the summer.

5. No one has been on a road trip.

6. Some of the 1927 New York Yankees hit over 50 home runs.

7. Art is never ugly.

8. All engineers know calculus.

9. Most resorts are all-inclusive.

10. All lenders evaluate borrowers based on credit score.

11. Some other people besides poets (or not only poets) appreciate the true beauty of words.

STOP. THIS IS THE END OF LECTURE 4. DO NOT PROCEED TO THE CORRESPONDING EXAM UNTIL INSTRUCTED TO DO SO IN CLASS.

LECTURE (5) CHAPTER (6)

WEAKEN QUESTIONS

6.1 IDENTIFY

6.1.1 IDENTIFYING WEAKEN QUESTIONS

All Weaken questions follow the same pattern:

1. **The question stem asks you to choose the statement that most weakens the argument.** This is what distinguishes Weaken questions from every other question type. The question asks you to find what would *weaken* the argument. The LSAT writers say this in various ways, such as *undermine, cast doubt upon,* or *counter.* But all of these mean the same thing: your job is to find the answer that is the best at making the argument less convincing.

2. **The question stem requires that you accept the truth of the answer choices.** The question stem usually does this by including the phrase *if true,* as in, "Which one of the following, *if true,* most weakens the argument?" This is significant—since you must accept the truth of the answer choices, you should never eliminate an answer choice just because it seems implausible. You must accept that even the most implausible of answer choices is true. Your job is to determine, given the truth of the answer choices, which answer choice most weakens the argument.

3. **The passage contains a flawed argument.** Weaken questions are flaw-dependent, which means that your analysis depends on understanding how the argument goes wrong. The passage for every Weaken question has a flawed argument.

You should also note that the question asks for the *best* answer—the one that weakens the argument the *most.* The correct answer need not destroy the argument. It must only weaken the argument more than the other answer choices do.

Here are some Weaken question stems:

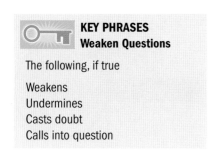

KEY PHRASES
Weaken Questions

The following, if true

Weakens
Undermines
Casts doubt
Calls into question

Which one of the following, if true, most seriously weakens the argument?

Which one of the following statements, if true, would most seriously undermine the conclusion above?

Which one of the following, if true, casts the most doubt on the scholar's interpretation?

You should expect to see about five Weaken questions per test.

6.1.2 WEAKEN, NOT DESTROY

Weaken questions ask for the answer that does the best job of weakening the argument. The correct answer need not *destroy* the argument. It only needs to be the one that weakens the argument the most.

6.2 ANALYZE

6.2.1 ANALYZING WEAKEN QUESTIONS

Weaken questions are flaw-dependent questions, which means you analyze them just as you analyze any other flaw-dependent question. Look for:

1. The conclusion

2. The premises

3. The flaw

None of this is any different from your approach to Necessary Assumption or Flaw questions.

All flaw-dependent questions require the same analysis.

Here's a passage to refresh your analysis skills:

Using theoretical mathematics, physicists have predicted the existence of axions—subatomic particles that have less than one millionth of the mass of an electron. Because axions are too small to be seen by any microscope that could ever be invented, scientists will never be able to provide direct evidence that these particles exist.

Because is a **double indicator**, showing you both the conclusion and a premise. Here's how the argument works:

Axions are too small to be seen by any microscope that could ever be invented.

Therefore, scientists will never provide evidence that these particles exist.

The next step is to find the flaw. In this case, the author committed a flaw when she attempted to connect two concepts that are not necessarily the same. In other words, she committed a Concept Shift:

What two non-identical concepts are intended to be connected?

Scientists will never provide direct evidence is intended to follow from *too small to be seen.*

So there's a Concept Shift:

Too small to be seen ⚡ Scientists will never provide direct evidence

6.3 PREPHRASE

6.3.1 PREPHRASING ON WEAKEN QUESTIONS

The first step in your Prephrasing is to think about **what** the correct answer will **do**. The correct answer to a Weaken question will *suggest* (not prove) that the conclusion is untrue.

The next step in your Prephrasing is to decide **how** the correct answer will do it. The correct answer to a Weaken question attacks a weakness already present in the argument. Therefore, the most effective Prephrasing strategy is to find the weaknesses (flaws) in the argument and predict how an answer might attack them.

You don't need to Prephrase a specific attack on the argument. Instead, you should Prephrase what kind of attack the answer is likely to make.

Try Prephrasing on the argument about axions above. The analysis provides the point of attack: since the weakness in this argument is the Concept Shift, that's what you should attack.

The argument assumes that, because something is too small to be seen, one can never provide direct evidence for it. But if you were to find a reason not to believe this, then the argument would be much weaker. Instead of Prephrasing a specific way to attack the argument, you can Prephrase the type of answer you might expect to see:

> Prephrase: The correct answer will likely undermine
> the connection between "too small to be seen" and
> "can never provide direct evidence of it."

This is a good Prephrased answer for a Weaken question. It is specific enough to help you as you attack the answer choices, but it is general enough to be flexible and allow for various possibilities.

If there is a specific attack that you might expect to see in an answer choice, you can Prephrase that as well. Just realize that there are always other ways to weaken the argument. For this argument, you might have Prephrased a more specific answer:

> Prephrase: There are ways to provide evidence of
> things smaller than what any microscope can see,
> such as bubble chambers or other instruments.

This is a likely answer. It doesn't destroy the argument—just because you can measure some very small things doesn't mean you can provide direct evidence of the existence of axions. But it does make the argument much less convincing.

6.3.2 HOW TO WEAKEN AN ARGUMENT

The correct answer to a Weaken question provides a reason why the conclusion might be false *even if all of the premises are true*. This is no surprise. You must accept the truth of the premises, and the correct answer to a Weaken question never directly attacks or contradicts the conclusion, but it must provide a reason to doubt the conclusion even if all the premises are true.

There are a number of common ways that answer choices can weaken an argument:

1. **Some answer choices weaken the argument by showing that something the argument failed to consider is actually true.** One major difference between Weaken questions and Flaw questions is that, while Flaw questions just *describe* what went wrong in the argument, Weaken questions bring in a *new piece of information* that has an effect on the argument. That new piece of information is often something that you predicted yourself when you stated the argument's flaw.

> The correct answer to a Weaken question suggests that the conclusion is untrue even though all the premises are true.

> The correct answer choice will introduce a brand new piece of information. There could be more than one possible new piece of information that weakens an argument, so don't get too specific or inflexible in your Prephrased answer. The correct answer may match your prediction, but it may not. Always rely on the Real Question.

For example, imagine that a politician concluded that an arsenic pollution policy should be abandoned because it had failed to produce the desired results over the past year. You might express one flaw the politician committed like this:

> Flaw: The argument failed to consider the possibility that arsenic pollution takes longer than a year to dissipate from a particular environment.

That's a good description of a flaw, but it also gives you an idea of a likely weakening answer choice. One good weakening answer choice might say that arsenic takes seven to ten years to significantly decline in any particular ecosystem. This shows that something the politician failed to consider is actually true, and it gives you a reason to believe that maybe it's *not* a good idea to abandon the pollution policy just yet.

Be on the lookout for choices that say the same thing in a more subtle way. For example, what if an answer choice says that arsenic gets concentrated in animals higher on the food chain, and environmental levels only decrease when apex predators die? While this doesn't directly say anything about the *time* this process takes, it's reasonable to assume that the process could take longer than a year. So this would still be a good weakening answer choice, although more difficult to see.

Knowing your common flaws is crucial on all kinds of questions, not just Flaw questions.

KNOW THE COMMON FLAWS

2. **Some answer choices weaken the argument by attacking a common flaw.** You saw in the last chapter that every argument with a common flaw has some predictable necessary assumptions built in. By the same token, every argument with a common flaw can be weakened in some predictable ways.

Common Flaw	How to Weaken
The argument treats something *necessary* to bring about a certain result as if it were *sufficient* to bring about the result.	Show that there is something else *also* necessary to bring about the result.
The argument treats something *sufficient* to bring about a result as if it were *necessary* to bring about the result.	Show that there is *another* way the result can occur *without* the sufficient factor.
The argument treats a *correlation* between two things as evidence that one *caused* the other.	Show another cause besides the one cited. Show that the causality could have occurred in reverse. Show that the two things had a single common cause. Show that the correlation was a mere coincidence.
The argument draws a conclusion about an overall population based on information from a small *sample* of the population.	Show how the small sample is unrepresentative of the overall population. Show a methodological error in the gathering of information.
The argument treats the *absence of evidence* for one conclusion as if it proves the opposite conclusion is true.	Show that not all the possible evidence has been gathered.

The argument shows that one option is impossible and concludes that a certain other option must be chosen (*false dichotomy*).	Describe a third option.
The argument uses an *analogy* or draws a conclusion about one thing based on information about a different thing.	Show an important difference between the two things that makes them not analogous.
The argument uses information about *percentages* to draw a conclusion about absolute *numbers*. The argument uses information about absolute *numbers* to draw a conclusion about *percentages*.	Show that the size of the group has changed over time. Show that the groups being compared have very different sizes.

3. **Some answer choices weaken the argument by making the premises irrelevant to the conclusion.** The premises are supposed to be the evidence for the conclusion. But an answer choice can make the premises irrelevant so that they no longer act as evidence for the conclusion. Take a look at this argument:

> Studies show that introducing Arcos E as an ingredient to toothpaste always improves the quality of the toothpaste. Therefore, the new version of ArcExcellent with Arcos E must be a better toothpaste than the old version.

Suppose an answer choice says that ArcExcellent has always contained Arcos E as an ingredient. If that were true, then the studies about *introducing* Arcos E as an ingredient would be completely irrelevant. The new version doesn't *introduce* Arcos E.

Any answer that makes the premises irrelevant to the conclusion weakens the argument. One common way for an answer choice to do this is to **prove or illustrate that the two sides of the Concept Shift are not actually the same.** This takes away the author's logical flow from premises to conclusion, and thus weakens the argument.

Since the Concept Shift is such a common flaw, this is a common feature in correct answer choices to Weaken questions.

4. **Some answer choices weaken the argument by introducing entirely new considerations that have little to do with any linking assumptions.** Weaken questions, like Necessary Assumption questions, can have very unusual correct answers. If an answer choice introduces entirely new considerations, that doesn't make it incorrect. If the new considerations give you reason to think the conclusion might be false, then they weaken the argument. Take a look at this argument:

> Keenan: My new computer has the best hard drive, the best processor, and the best memory available on the market today. There is no hardware component in my computer that isn't the best available component of its kind. Therefore, my computer is a great computer.

An answer choice might weaken this argument by introducing an entirely new consideration that doesn't directly attack any linking assumption. For example, even if you accept that Keenan's computer has the best available component for every piece it contains, an answer choice could weaken the argument by saying that Keenan's computer lacks a power supply, which is necessary for a computer to run. Such an answer choice would definitely provide a reason to think that Keenan's computer is not so great. After all, the computer doesn't even run.

6.4   ATTACK

6.4.1   The Real Question

The **Real Question** for Weaken Questions is:

> *Does this suggest that the conclusion is untrue?*

First, notice that the **Real Question** uses the word *suggest*, not the word *prove*. This is because the correct answer will weaken the argument, not destroy it.

Second, you should always adapt the **Real Question** to fit the particular passage you are working on. Instead of *"the conclusion is untrue"*, substitute the negation of the conclusion into the **Real Question**.

For example, if the conclusion of an argument states

> [**Therefore**, the insurance company is legally
> obligated to pay Ms. Kuan]

You should adapt the **Real Question** to be: *Does this suggest that the insurance company is NOT legally obligated to pay Ms. Kuan?*

6.4.2   Distracters

Reliable Distracters

Opposite

Wrong answers to Weaken questions often *strengthen* rather than *weaken* the argument. If an answer choice strengthens the argument on a Weaken question, then it's definitely wrong, and you can confidently eliminate it.

Extreme

Extreme answers are actually *good* for Weaken questions. If there's a really strong blanket statement that can weaken almost anything, it can probably weaken the argument at hand.

Suppose Bill argues that coffee causes him to get jumpy because he's always jumpy after a cup of coffee. Here's an extreme possible answer choice:

> (C)   No events in the universe are causally connected
> in any way, and anything that appears to be a
> causal relationship is a mere coincidence.

This is an unbelievably extreme answer choice! But that doesn't make it wrong. In fact, if this is true, it most certainly weakens Bill's argument because Bill argues for causation when causation doesn't exist. You should not automatically avoid extreme answers to Weaken questions: they are often correct.

Less Reliable Distracter

Out of Scope

Choices that have nothing to do with the conclusion or the argument's chain of logic are **out of scope**. However, you have to be very careful with answers that appear out of scope on Weaken questions. If you dismiss answers too quickly because they seem irrelevant, you may end up eliminating the correct answer.

Suppose Ira argues that the local paper mill is responsible for pollution in a nearby river because it is the only company located near the river capable of producing such pollution. Here's a seemingly out of scope possible weaken answer choice:

> (A)   Toxico, which is located one thousand miles from
> any river, transports its waste and dumps it into
> numerous bodies of water.

Ira's argument has nothing to do with Toxico, and Ira focuses only on local businesses. At the same time, this definitely weakens the argument. If Toxico is dumping its own waste into the river near the paper mill, then the paper mill might not be responsible for the pollution.

You should not quickly eliminate answer choices just because they seem to be out of scope. Ask yourself first whether they impact the conclusion in some way.

> Every answer choice, including the correct one, introduces brand new information that never appeared in the passage.

6.5 PUTTING IT ALL TOGETHER

Here are some examples:

1. The number of codfish in the North Atlantic has declined substantially as the population of harp seals has increased from two million to more than three million. Some blame the seal for the shrinking cod population, but cod plays a negligible role in the seal's diet. It is therefore unlikely that the increase in the seal population has contributed significantly to the decline in the cod population.

   Which one of the following, if true, most seriously weakens the argument?
   Test 28, Section 1, Question 5

Here's the approach:

1. Identify

This question stem asks for what most seriously *weakens* the argument, so this is a Weaken question.

2. Analyze

Therefore indicates that the last sentence is the conclusion, which makes sense because this is a *counterargument* against those who blame seals for the decrease in cod. Why aren't seals responsible? They don't eat much cod.

> Cod plays a negligible role in a seal's diet.
>
> **Therefore,** seals are not responsible for the decrease in the cod population.

Now find the flaw. In this case, perhaps the easiest way to see the problem in this argument is to notice the Concept Shift:

What two non-identical concepts are intended to be connected?

The argument intends to connect *not responsible* to whether the seals *eat the cod*.

Here's the Concept Shift:

Don't eat the cod ⚡ Not responsible for the cod decrease

3. Prephrase

The correct answer will suggest that the conclusion is untrue—specifically, that the seals *are* responsible for the shrinking cod population.

The argument assumes that there is a connection between not eating and not being responsible, but there could be ways other than eating the cod for which the seals could be responsible. You should expect an answer to attack this assumed connection.

> Prephrase: The correct answer will likely undermine the connection between "not eating the cod" and "not being responsible for the cod decrease."

> Remember, you don't need to get too specific with *what* the correct answer will say. Just try to predict *how* it will suggest the conclusion is untrue.

One way an answer choice could do this is by providing a different reason for why seals might be responsible for the decrease in cod.

4. Attack

(A)   People who fish for cod commercially are inconvenienced by the presence of large numbers of seals near traditional fishing grounds.

Choice (A): *Does this suggest that the seals are responsible for the shrinking cod population?* No, it doesn't matter that people are inconvenienced by seals. The question is whether seals have anything to do with cod population. People are **out of scope**. *Cut it.*

(B)   Water pollution poses a more serious threat to cod than to the harp seal.

Choice (B): *Does this suggest that the seals are responsible for the shrinking cod population?* If water pollution is worse for cod than for seals, that's all the more reason to accept that seals are not the problem. If anything, this *strengthens* the argument, so it's an **opposite** distracter. *Cut it.*

(C)   The harp seal thrives in water that is too cold to support a dense population of cod.

Choice (C): *Does this suggest that the seals are responsible for the shrinking cod population?* Like choice (B), this *strengthens* the argument. It says that a change in water temperature is responsible for the increased seal population, which suggests that the temperature, not the seals, is affecting the cod population. This is an **opposite** distracter. *Cut it.*

(D)   Cod feed almost exclusively on capelin, a fish that is a staple of the harp seal's diet.

> This choice is a good example of how something never mentioned in the passage is not out of scope because it impacts the logic of the argument.

Choice (D): *Does this suggest that the seals are responsible for the shrinking cod population?* If this is true, then cod and seals have the same diet, and the passage suggests that there are way too many seals around. If that's true, then the link between eating the cod and responsibility becomes an issue. Instead of eating the cod, the seals could eat all of the cod's food, thereby causing a decrease in cod. This definitely weakens the argument, even though "capelin" is entirely new. *Keep it.*

(E)   The cod population in the North Atlantic began to decline before the harp seal population began to increase.

Choice (E): *Does this suggest that the seals are responsible for the shrinking cod population?* This also *strengthens* the argument. If the problem began before the seals arrived, then it's less likely to be the seals' fault. This is an **opposite** distracter. *Cut it.*

Choice (D) is the only one left, and (D) does its job: it suggests that the argument's conclusion is untrue.

Choice (D) is the correct answer.

2.   Dean: Collectively, the athletic programs of American colleges bring in about four billion dollars per year from all direct revenue sources: television and radio contracts, ticket and merchandise sales, licensing, and donations earmarked for athletic programs. Unfortunately, the same athletic programs collectively cost schools about five billion dollars per year to operate. Thus, colleges are losing money overall because of their athletic programs.

Which one of the following, if true, most undermines the dean's argument?

1. Identify

The question stem asks for something that *undermines* the argument, so it's a Weaken question.

2. Analyze

The conclusion indicator *thus* indicates that the last sentence is the conclusion. Why are colleges losing money on their athletic programs? They cost more to operate than they make in direct revenue.

> Athletic programs cost more to operate than they make from direct revenue sources.
> ....
> **Therefore,** colleges are losing money overall on their athletic programs.

Now find the flaw. As with every argument, it can be expressed in several ways, but perhaps the most obvious in this case is to point out what the dean failed to consider:

> Flaw: The argument failed to consider any <u>indirect</u> revenue sources generated by college athletic programs.

3. Prephrase

The correct answer will suggest that the conclusion is untrue—specifically, that colleges are *not* losing money overall because of their athletic programs.

It will most likely do this by specifically naming some indirect revenue generated by college sports.

> Prephrase: The correct answer will likely name some indirect revenue source generated by college athletic programs.

> **Remember to use all your tools to help you find flaws:**
> · Common flaws
> · Something the author failed to consider
> · Unjustified assumptions
> · The Concept Shift

4. Attack

Remember to adapt the **Real Question** to fit the conclusion.

> (A) Television ratings for the major college championship games have declined in recent years.

Choice (A): *Does this suggest that colleges are NOT losing money overall because of their athletic programs?* No. If anything, this answer *strengthens* the argument. The money was tight to begin with, and now ratings are down. *Cut it.*

> (B) College athletic programs that run at a deficit can put financial strain on the academic programs of their schools.

Choice (B): *Does this suggest that colleges are NOT losing money overall because of their athletic programs?* This talks about the consequences of the problem, but the issue is whether the problem actually exists. Are colleges losing money on sports programs? This answer provides nothing to address this issue. *Cut it.*

> (C) Entertainment analysts predict no major change in the current popularity of college sports.

Choice (C): *Does this suggest that colleges are NOT losing money overall because of their athletic programs?* Nothing is going to change. Okay, so what? This has nothing to do with whether colleges are making or losing money on their programs. *Cut it.*

> (D) College athletic programs often motivate alumni to make general donations to their schools.

Choice (D): *Does this suggest that colleges are NOT losing money overall because of their athletic programs?* If alumni donate money to general funds, then that money is not counted as a *direct* source of revenue for college sports. But if sports motivate alumni to make such donations often enough, then colleges might break even or even make money overall from this *indirect* source of revenue. This definitely could weaken the argument that sports cost colleges money. *Keep it.*

(E)   In many sports, college team jerseys are more
        popular than professional team jerseys.

Choice (E): *Does this suggest that colleges are NOT losing money overall because of their athletic programs?* College team jerseys might be popular, but the argument already tells you that jersey sales just won't cut it—direct revenue is less than operating costs. This doesn't do anything for the argument. *Cut it.*

Choice (D) is the correct answer.

6.6   VARIATIONS

6.6.1   STRENGTHEN QUESTIONS

Strengthen questions are just like Weaken questions, and you should approach Strengthen and Weaken questions in the same way. The only difference is the kind of answer you should look for. For Strengthen questions, the correct answer is the one that most strengthens the argument in the passage.

6.6.1.1   Identifying Strengthen Questions

Strengthen question stems ask for an answer that strengthens the argument in the passage. Here are some of the more common variations:

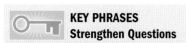

KEY PHRASES
Strengthen Questions

The following, if true

Strengthens
Provides the most support

> Which one of the following, if true, most strengthens
> the argument?

> Which one of the following, if true, would provide
> the most support for the physician's assertion?

If you are looking only at the key word *support*, you could confuse certain Strengthen questions with Inference questions. Remember that a Strengthen question asks for the *answer* that best supports the *passage*, whereas an Inference questions looks for the *passage* to support the correct *answer*.

6.6.1.2   Analyzing Strengthen Questions

Your analysis of Strengthen questions is identical to your analysis of Weaken questions. Look for:

1. The conclusion
2. The premises
3. The flaw

6.6.1.3   Prephrasing on Strengthen Questions

Just as on Weaken questions, the first step in your Prephrasing is to decide what the correct answer will do. The correct answer to a Strengthen question will *suggest* (not prove) that the conclusion is **indeed true**.

The next step in your Prephrasing is to decide **how** the correct answer will do it. You should still focus on the weaknesses in the passage—the Concept Shift, necessary assumption, or flaw—but this time, determine how an answer choice could defend against the weakness. For example, the correct answer choice could provide explicit proof that a necessary assumption is true, or it could explicitly connect the two sides of a Concept Shift.

6.6.1.4 The Real Question for Strengthen Questions

The **Real Question** for Strengthen questions is:

Does this suggest that the conclusion is indeed true?

This is the point where Strengthen questions differ from Weaken questions. But all the other rules regarding answer choices—which distracters are in play and which you should ignore—still apply. The only thing that changes is the **Real Question**.

6.6.1.5 Strengthen Question Practice

Here are a couple of examples.

> 3. Investigators have not determined what caused hundreds of dolphins to leave their deep water habitat and become stranded in shallow water off the northern coast of Zanzibar. However, they have ruled out the possibility that sonar from ships or submarines was responsible for disorienting the dolphins, as no sonar-capable vessels were within six hundred miles of the location at the time.
>
> Which one of the following, if true, lends the most support to the investigators' conclusion?

> You can also use the chart on pages 104-105 to help you *strengthen* arguments with common flaws. Instead of showing one of those possible flaws is true, just look for an answer choice that *rules out* one of those flaws.

1. Identify

The question asks for an answer choice that supports the conclusion in the passage, so this is a Strengthen question.

2. Analyze

The only thing that sounds like it might be the conclusion is *they have ruled out the possibility that sonar from ships or submarines was responsible for disorienting the dolphins.* To make sure, try the **Why Tool**. Why have they ruled out the possibility that sonar from ships was responsible? The passage provides an answer: because no sonar-capable vessels were within six hundred miles. That sounds like a premise.

No sonar-capable vessels were within six hundred miles at the time.

Therefore, sonar from ships or submarines was not responsible for disorienting the dolphins.

Now find the flaw. In this case, the problem with the argument occurred when the author tried to equate two different concepts:

What two non-identical concepts are intended to be connected?

The argument intends to connect *not responsible* to *not within six hundred miles.*

This is the **Concept Shift**:

Not within six hundred miles ⚡ Not responsible

3. Prephrase

The correct answer will suggest that the sonar was *indeed* not responsible.

The **Concept Shift** is a weakness in the argument, so it's the best place to start when you want to strengthen an argument. There is an assumed connection between being farther than six hundred miles away and not being responsible. But is six hundred miles really far enough away? The sun is more than six hundred miles away, but it certainly has an effect on us. The weakness here is that six hundred miles might not be enough. To strengthen this argument, you'd expect to see a reason why six hundred miles really is enough.

> Prephrase: The correct answer will likely strengthen the connection between "not within six hundred miles" and "not responsible."

4. Attack

      (A)   Only submarines are equipped with sufficiently powerful sonar instruments to cause marine mammal strandings.

Choice (A): *Does this suggest that the sonar was indeed not responsible?* No, it doesn't help the argument at all. *Cut it.*

      (B)   There are few documented cases of dolphins being stranded as a result of sonar use.

Choice (B): *Does this suggest that the sonar was indeed not responsible?* The argument is all about the cause of this dolphin problem. The fact that it's a rare occurrence is completely irrelevant. *Cut it.*

      (C)   Several local residents often have ships in the waters to the north of Zanzibar.

Choice (C): *Does this suggest that the sonar was indeed not responsible?* There are nearby ships, yes. But these ships, if they are within six hundred miles, are not sonar-capable according to the passage. Since you must accept that this is true, then the nearby presence of these ships has no effect on the argument about whether sonar from ships is responsible. *Cut it.*

      (D)   Sonar signals are usually too weak to be perceived by most marine mammals more than five hundred miles away.

> This doesn't *guarantee* the conclusion is true (it uses words like *usually* and *most*), but it does *suggest* that the conclusion is true. That's what you're looking for.

Choice (D): *Does this suggest that the sonar was indeed not responsible?* If sonar signals are too weak to be perceived from more than five hundred miles away, then the sonar from the nearest sonar-capable ships six hundred miles away is unlikely to have affected the dolphins. This strengthens the link between the distance and the claim that sonar from ships was not responsible. *Keep it.*

      (E)   Investigators have ruled out the possibility that a sudden change in water temperature caused the dolphins to become disoriented.

Choice (E): *Does this suggest that the sonar was indeed not responsible?* So the water temperature is not to blame. That doesn't strengthen the claim that sonar from ships is blameless. *Cut it.*

Choice (D) is the correct answer.

    4. The executives at the Lazar corporation recently carried out the annual employee performance review. One goal of the review was to determine whether the company's associates are underperforming relative to their salaries. The executives determined that the company is overpaying its associates relative to the quantity of output expected from an average associate, and that the ratio of productivity to pay for associates must increase in order to avoid wasted revenue. As a result, the executives concluded that the only way to rectify the situation is to reduce the salary of associates at Lazar.

        Which one of the following, if true, most strengthens the executives' conclusion?

1. Identify

The question asks for an answer choice that strengthens the executives' position, so this is a Strengthen question.

2. Analyze

They concluded is a conclusion indicator, so the last sentence is the conclusion. Why is the only way to solve the problem to reduce salaries? Associates are being paid more than they should be based on productivity.

> Associates are being paid more than they should be based on productivity.
>
> **Therefore,** the only way to solve the problem is to reduce associates' salary.

Now find the flaw. This time around, there is an **extreme** claim in the conclusion, which is in itself a weakness. The conclusion says that the *only* way to solve the problem is to change what the company pays associates. If there is even one other way to solve the problem, then this argument falls apart.

You can also look at this as a **false dichotomy** flaw. There's a problem for which the argument says there is only one solution. The argument assumes that there are only two possibilities: continuing to have the problem or reducing salaries. But there are many other possibilities the executives failed to consider, such as increasing employee productivity at the same salary.

> When an argument has a false dichotomy flaw, you can weaken the argument by *showing* the existence of a third option, or strengthen the argument by *ruling out* the existence of some third option.

3. Prephrase

The correct answer will suggest that the salary reduction is *indeed* the only solution.

The argument's weakness is in its extreme conclusion: the *only* way to solve the problem. To strengthen such an extreme claim, it's helpful to <u>eliminate</u> other possible solutions to the problem. That's the kind of answer you should expect to see.

> Prephrase: The correct answer will likely strengthen the extreme claim "only" by eliminating other possible ways the problem could be solved.

4. Attack

    (A)   The associates are currently working the maximum allowable hours without overtime under the law.

Choice (A): *Does this suggest that the salary reduction is indeed the only solution?* This might appear irrelevant, but does it eliminate other possible ways the problem could be solved? One solution might have been to make the associates work more hours for the same pay, thereby increasing productivity per dollar. But choice (A) denies that possibility, as the associates already work the maximum number of hours. This is a tricky one, but a keeper. *Keep it.*

    (B)   The associates are paid at about the same rate as their peers at other companies.

Choice (B): *Does this suggest that the salary reduction is indeed the only solution?* No, this doesn't strengthen the claim about solving the problem. Maybe other companies have more productive associates, or maybe they don't. Either way, this has nothing to do with the problem at hand. *Cut it.*

    (C)   Under the current contract, the associates' pay structure does not allow for a reduction.

Choice (C): *Does this suggest that the salary reduction is indeed the only solution?* If anything, this weakens the argument. The contract says that associates can't be paid less, so, without renegotiating the contract, cutting their salaries can't be the solution. In any case, this answer choice doesn't help the argument that a salary cut is the *only* solution. *Cut it.*

    (D)   Many associates at Lazar have recently left the company to pursue higher-paying jobs elsewhere.

Choice (D): *Does this suggest that the salary reduction is indeed the only solution?* Again, this isn't good for the argument. If associates are leaving to take higher-paying jobs already, cutting pay might cause more problems than it would solve. *Cut it.*

(E)   The ratio of productivity to pay for associates is
        at a historical low for Lazar, whereas associates'
        pay is higher than ever.

Choice (E): *Does this suggest that the salary reduction is indeed the only solution?* This just repeats the problem, but it doesn't strengthen the argument. Yes, productivity is low and costs are high. This doesn't mean the *only* solution is to cut salaries. *Cut it.*

Choice (A) is the correct answer.

6.6.2   Weaken and Strengthen EXCEPT Questions

Weaken and Strengthen EXCEPT questions are no different from any other EXCEPT questions: you should use the Except Tool to choose the correct answer. But Weaken and Strengthen EXCEPT questions prove to be more challenging for students who wrongly assume that they should look for the *opposite* of what the question stem would usually require. This is not the case:

1. On Weaken EXCEPT questions, the correct answer does *not* have to strengthen the argument. It only has to *not weaken* the argument.

2. On Strengthen EXCEPT questions, the correct answer does *not* have to weaken the argument. It only has to *not strengthen* the argument.

> Strengthen and Weaken EXCEPT questions are the most common types of EXCEPT questions.

If an answer choice is completely irrelevant to the argument, then it is a good answer for both Weaken EXCEPT and Strengthen EXCEPT questions. The correct answer *can* be the opposite of the question stem (something that strengthens on a Weaken question), but it need not be.

Remember to use the Except Tool. Ask the standard **Real Question** for the question type, and put a mark next to each answer choice depending on your answer to the **Real Question**.

Here's an example:

5. Researchers performed brain scans on two groups of seven-year-old children. They compared the brains of a highly intelligent group, as determined by a standard I.Q. test, to those of a control group composed of children of average intelligence. The researchers were surprised to find that the cortex, a region of the brain previously thought to be instrumental in many intelligent thought processes because it is packed with neurons, was thinner in the intelligent children than in the children from the control group. They concluded that the cortex must not be a relevant part of intelligent thought processes.

    Each one of the following, if true, strengthens the conclusion of the researchers EXCEPT:

Here's the approach:

1. Identify

The question asks for an answer that strengthens the argument, so it's a Strengthen question. But it has an EXCEPT at the end, so it's a Strengthen EXCEPT question.

2. Analyze

They concluded is a **conclusion** indicator, telling you that the last sentence is the conclusion. Why is the cortex not a relevant part of intelligent thought processes? It is thinner in intelligent children than in normal children; that's why.

> According to brain scans in a recent study, intelligent children have a thinner cortex than do normal children.

Therefore, the cortex is not a relevant part of intelligent thought processes.

But this argument is definitely flawed. One flaw can be expressed by pointing out a Concept Shift. The thickness of the cortex does not necessarily indicate whether it is used in any thought process. The Concept Shift is:

Thinner in intelligent children ⚡ Not a relevant part of intelligent thought processes

There's a second important flaw here, and it's a common flaw: this is a study based on a particular sample, but the passage provides no evidence to show that the sample was representative of all children and that the study was free of methodological errors.

3. Prephrase

The argument has two sets of weaknesses. The first is the set of weaknesses associated with the Concept Shift. Size may or may not have anything to do with whether something is used in intelligent thought processes. You should expect to see answers that strengthen this assumed connection.

The second set of weaknesses concerns the sample. Is the group representative? Are the methods sound? Some answers may address these concerns.

Ultimately, since this is a Strengthen EXCEPT question, you are looking for an answer that does NOT strengthen the argument.

> The arguments in Strengthen and Weaken EXCEPT questions often have several flaws, so try to find at least two before moving on.

4. Attack

To use the Except Tool, ask the usual **Real Question** and put an appropriate mark next to the answer choice depending on your answer. The correct answer will look different from all the rest.

> (A) The cortices of the intelligent children did not have a much larger surface area than the cortices of the children from the control group.

Choice (A): *Does this suggest that the cortex is indeed irrelevant?* This eliminates a possible objection: perhaps the cortex's surface area rather than its thickness is what makes children intelligent. But if choice (A) is true, then surface area is not a concern. Since (A) eliminates this concern, it strengthens the argument. *Put an S next to this choice.*

> (B) Previous studies suggesting a link between the cortex and intelligent thought processes have recently been discredited due to flawed methods.

Choice (B): *Does this suggest that the cortex is indeed irrelevant?* If the studies that suggested a link between the cortex and intelligent thought were flawed, then that's all the more reason to believe the study from the passage. This strengthens the argument. *Put an S.*

> (C) The cortices of the intelligent children did not have a greater concentration of neurons than the cortices of the children from the control group.

Choice (C): *Does this suggest that the cortex is indeed irrelevant?* Like choice (A), this eliminates a potential cause for concern. If the important difference between cortices is not size but number of neurons, and if the intelligent children had more neurons, then the cortex might be responsible for some intelligent thought. But choice (C) denies this possibility and thereby strengthens the argument. *Put an S.*

> (D) Brain scans measuring the size of a given part of the brain are generally a reliable indicator of the frequency of use for that brain part.

Choice (D): *Does this suggest that the cortex is indeed irrelevant?* This at least partially eliminates the concern that the study's methods might have been flawed, so it makes the conclusion stronger. *Put an* S.

(E) The researchers' study has been submitted to a leading scientific journal and is under review, but the study has not yet been accepted for publication.

Choice (E): *Does this suggest that the cortex is indeed irrelevant?* It doesn't make a difference whether the research has been published yet or not. It makes the argument neither stronger nor weaker. Since this doesn't suggest anything about the cortex, *Don't put anything next to this choice.*

Here's what you should have:

S (A) The cortices of the intelligent children did not have a much larger surface area than the cortices of the children from the control group.

S (B) Previous studies suggesting a link between the cortex and intelligent thought processes have recently been discredited due to flawed methods.

S (C) The cortices of the intelligent children did not have a greater concentration of neurons than the cortices of the children from the control group.

S (D) Brain scans measuring the size of a given part of the brain are generally a reliable indicator of the frequency of use for that brain part.

(E) The researchers' study has been submitted to a leading scientific journal and is under review, but the study has not yet been accepted for publication.

Since choice (E) looks different from all the rest, pick it.

Choice (E) is the correct answer.

6.7   THE BIG PICTURE

6.7.1   FLAW-DEPENDENT QUESTIONS

All flaw-dependent questions are closely related, and they require almost identical strategies.

So far, you have seen the following flaw-dependent question types:

- **Flaw** and its variation, Misinterpretation

- **Weaken** and its variation, Strengthen

- **Necessary Assumption** and its variation, Evaluate

The flaw-dependent questions still to come are Sufficient Assumption, Justify, and Parallel Flaw questions.

You have probably noticed by now that these are all very similar. While the things you are looking for in the answer choices may differ, your analysis of the passage will not. You should always look for:

1. The conclusion

2. The premises

3. The flaw

Here's a sample passage for a flaw-dependent question:

> 6. Commissioner: I have been incorrectly criticized for having made my decision on the power plant issue prematurely. I based my decision on the report prepared by the neighborhood association and, although I have not studied it thoroughly, I am sure that the information it contains is accurate. Moreover, you may recall that when I received input from the neighborhood association on jail relocation, I agreed with its recommendation.
>
> Test 26, Section 2, Question 17

You can analyze this passage without knowing the specific question type, since all flaw-dependent questions require the same analysis.

The first sentence has a counterargument, which tells you that the commissioner's conclusion is the negation of the one she's arguing against. After you isolate the conclusion and premises, you can find the underlying flaws and assumptions. Here's how the argument works:

The similarity between different question types is great news for you, because you don't have to learn a whole new set of skills for each different type, and making improvements in one area can help you across the entire test.

- I based my decision on the neighborhood association's report.

- I am sure its information is accurate (although I haven't studied it thoroughly).

- I agreed with past recommendations of the neighborhood association.

Therefore, I did not make my decision on the power plant issue prematurely.

This argument has several Concept Shifts going on. First, the commissioner tries to establish a connection between the decision being based on the report and not being premature. Those aren't identical.

Based on the association's report ⚡ Not premature

Another Concept Shift is between the jail relocation decision and the power plant decision. The commissioner seems to think one is relevant to the other, but there may be important differences, and it's questionable whether the jail decision makes any difference in this case.

Jail relocation decision ⚡ Power plant decision

Finally, you may have noticed another pretty obvious flaw committed by the commissioner. She feels confident that the report is accurate, even though she barely studied it. That seems questionable.

Having completed this analysis, you are ready for any flaw-dependent question.

- For a Necessary Assumption question, you would look for an answer that links the two sides of either of the Concept Shifts above.

- For a Flaw question, you would look for an answer that describes one of the flaws.

- For a Weaken question, you would look for an answer that attacks a necessary assumption and suggests that the commissioner's decision *was* premature.

- For a Strengthen question, you would look for an answer that makes you more likely to accept a necessary assumption and suggests that the commissioner's decision was indeed *not* premature.

What you look for differs according to the question type, but your initial analysis is always the same. Try to put that analysis to work on these flaw-dependent questions.

6.7.2 Drill: Flaw-Dependent Questions

Complete each of the following flaw-dependent questions.

> Commissioner: I have been incorrectly criticized for having made my decision on the power plant issue prematurely. I based my decision on the report prepared by the neighborhood association and, although I have not studied it thoroughly, I am sure that the information it contains is accurate. Moreover, you may recall that when I received input from the neighborhood association on jail relocation, I agreed with its recommendation.

1. The commissioner's argument depends on which one of the following assumptions?

   Question type? _____

   Real Question? _____

   _____

   (A) The neighborhood association's information is not prejudiced toward any particular outcome.
   (B) No other government officials will be called upon for an opinion on the power plant issue.
   (C) The association's recommendation on jail relocation was ultimately implemented.
   (D) Given more time, more information about the power plant issue could not be assembled.
   (E) The power plant will not significantly affect inmates at the relocated jail.

2. The commissioner's argument is LEAST vulnerable to which one of the following criticisms?

   Question type? _____

   Real Question? _____

   _____

   (A) It takes for granted that the association's information is not distorted by bias.
   (B) It draws a conclusion about the recommendations of the association from incomplete recollections.
   (C) It takes for granted that the association's report is the only direct evidence that needed to be considered.
   (D) It hastily concludes that the association's report is accurate, without having studied it in detail.
   (E) It takes for granted that agreeing with the association's past recommendation helps to justify agreeing with its current recommendation.

   Test 26, Section 2, Question 17

3. Which one of the following, if true, most weakens the commissioner's argument?

   Question type? _____

   Real Question? _____

   _____

   (A) If the commissioner's decision is implemented, nearly 40 employees at the power plant will lose their jobs.
   (B) A local newspaper has published an editorial that strongly disagrees with the commissioner's decision.
   (C) Several previous commissioners displayed a pattern of premature decision-making.
   (D) A respected group of experts on the power plant is expected to release a detailed report on the issue within the next few days.
   (E) Those who agree with the commissioner's decision will likely profit from its outcome.

4. Which one of the following, if true, provides the strongest support for the commissioner's argument?

   Question type? _____

   Real Question? _____

   _____

   (A) The commissioner rarely studies any report thoroughly, yet has made hundreds of decisions.
   (B) Few members of the neighborhood association have any expertise regarding the power plant.
   (C) None of the association's numerous previous reports contained any significant inaccuracies.
   (D) Most power plants prove to be major contributors to their local economies.
   (E) The commissioner still agrees with the association's recommendation on jail relocation.

Answers & Explanations

1. Necessary Assumption question

Does the argument depend on this being true?
Choice (A) is the correct answer.

Choice (A): Yes. In order to make a non-premature decision, the commissioner needs to be using objective information. This links the Concept Shift between basing the decision on the report and it not being premature.

Choice (B): No. Other government officials' opinions are irrelevant and **out of scope**.

Choice (C): No. Knowing whether their recommendation was implemented does not tell you whether it was a well-informed or premature decision.

Choice (D): No. Use the Negation Tool. Even if it were possible to gather a few more details, does that destroy the commissioner's conclusion that her decision was not premature? No. You could still make a well-informed decision with only 98% of the information.

Choice (E): No. What happens to the inmates has nothing to do with whether the decision was premature or not. This is **out of scope**.

2. Flaw EXCEPT question

Is this a flaw in the argument?
Choice (B) is the correct answer.

Use the EXCEPT Tool.

Choice (A): The commissioner did assume this, and this is a flaw. Put an **F**.

Choice (B): Even though she said, "You may recall," this does not mean she has incomplete recollections. This **doesn't match** the argument. Don't put an **F**.

Choice (C): This matches the first identified Concept Shift. Put an **F**.

Choice (D): This is another flaw identified beforehand. Put an **F**.

Choice (E): This matches the second identified Concept Shift. Put an **F**.

Choice (B) is correct since it is different from all the rest.

3. Weaken question

Does this suggest that the commissioner's decision WAS premature?
Choice (D) is the correct answer.

Choice (A): No. Too bad for the employees, but it still could have been a well-informed decision.

Choice (B): No. You already know that some people have criticized the decision, so this choice doesn't tell you anything new.

Choice (C): No. Past commissioners are completely **out of scope**.

Choice (D): Yes. This seems like the kind of information the commissioner should have waited for before making her decision.

Choice (E): No. Just because someone will get rich doesn't mean it was a premature decision.

4. Strengthen question

Does this suggest that the commissioner's decision was NOT premature?
Choice (C) is the correct answer.

Choice (A): No. What if all those hundreds of decisions were premature too? This could just be the latest premature decision.

Choice (B): No. This would actually weaken the argument, so it's an **opposite** distracter.

Choice (C): Yes. This boosts the credibility of the report and thus that of any decisions based on it.

Choice (D): No. This gives you no information at all about the decision-making process.

Choice (E): No. You know that the commissioner agreed at the time. Just because she still agrees doesn't really have any bearing on the current decision.

STOP. THIS IS THE END OF LECTURE 5. DO NOT PROCEED TO THE CORRESPONDING EXAM UNTIL INSTRUCTED TO DO SO IN CLASS.

LECTURE (6) CHAPTER (7)

PARADOX QUESTIONS

7.1 IDENTIFY

7.1.1 WHAT IS A PARADOX?

A **paradox** is a set of two apparently contradictory facts.

People use the word *paradox* to mean all kinds of things in everyday life, but *paradox* has a precise meaning on the LSAT. A paradox isn't something ironic, strange, impossible, or unfortunate—it's a set of two apparently contradictory facts. That's it.

Here's an example of a paradox: Jane runs faster than anyone in her family, yet she is one of the ten slowest human beings on the planet. If you accept both of these statements as true, then the statement that Jane is the fastest in her family appears to contradict the statement that she is among the ten slowest people on the planet. Since this is a set of two apparently contradictory facts, it is a paradox. Here's a diagram for the paradox:

Fact₁: Jane runs faster than anyone else in her family.

Fact₂: Jane is one of the ten slowest human beings on the planet.

These are written in green because they are premises, which you must accept as true.

On Paradox questions, your job is to resolve the paradox. You must find an answer to explain how *both* facts could simultaneously be true. You can do this with Jane's paradox. How could she be the fastest person in her family if she is, at best, the tenth-slowest person on the planet? There's only one way it works out: the rest of her family is even slower. She must have a very slow family.

Jane's paradox, when you think about it, isn't that weird at all. Sometimes paradoxes on the LSAT have simple resolutions, and sometimes they are more complicated. Every paradox, however, is a set of two apparently contradictory facts that you must resolve.

7.1.2 IDENTIFYING PARADOX QUESTIONS

All **Paradox** questions follow the same pattern:

1. **The question stem asks you to resolve a paradox.** No other question type asks you to *resolve* or *reconcile* anything, but every Paradox question asks you to do so. This is one way to distinguish Paradox questions from every other question type.

2. **The question stem requires that you accept the truth of the answer choices.** Even if the answer choices are odd or unlikely, you must accept that they are true. If an answer reconciles the contradictory facts in the passage, then it is a good answer, regardless of how unlikely it seems. As a result, you should never eliminate an answer choice just because you doubt it could be true.

3. **The passage contains a paradox.** Every passage for a Paradox question has two contradictory facts. Paradoxes rarely appear in the passages for most other question types, but they always appear on Paradox questions.

Here are some Paradox question stems:

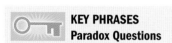

KEY PHRASES
Paradox Questions

The following, if true

Resolve
Reconcile

Apparent paradox
Apparent discrepancy

> Which one of the following, if true, most helps to resolve the apparent discrepancy above?

> Which one of the following, if true, contributes to a resolution of the apparent paradox?

Which one of the following, if true, most helps to reconcile the activist's two claims?

Each of these asks you to resolve a paradox. You should also note that they also ask what does *most* to resolve the paradox. The correct answer isn't always a perfect resolution. Sometimes it's just the best resolution among the possible choices.

Paradox questions appear roughly three or four times per test.

7.2 ANALYZE

7.2.1 ANALYZING PARADOX QUESTIONS

To analyze the passage on a Paradox question, identify the paradox. In other words, find the two apparently contradictory facts in the passage.

Turnaround words can help you identify the paradox. A **turnaround word** is a word that indicates a change in the direction of a sentence or passage. Here are some of the more common turnaround words:

- However
- Yet
- But
- Despite
- Though
- Nevertheless
- Unlike

Turnaround words usually appear immediately before one of the facts in the paradox. Often, they immediately follow the first fact. They always indicate a change of direction, and this change of direction indicates that two the statements conflict. Nearly every passage with a paradox has a turnaround word, so you can almost always rely on them.

For passages without turnaround words, look for inconsistencies. If two statements fight against one another, they probably form the paradox.

Here's a sample Paradox passage:

> 1. Every member of the city council has unequivocally pledged support for education, both in speeches and action. In fact, over the last five years every proposal to increase spending for education has passed. The city has greatly benefited from the council's focus on education. Yet not one member of the city council supports the most recent proposal to increase education spending.

Yet functions as a turnaround word, and comes before the second of the facts that make up the paradox. What fact fights against the claim that not one member supports the recent proposal? The fact that every council member has pledged unequivocal support for education. So the paradox works like this:

Fact$_1$: Every member of the city council has pledged unequivocal support for education.

Fact$_2$: Not one member supports the most recent proposal to increase education spending.

That's the end of your analysis.

Of course, you won't ever write out the paradox. Instead, you can mark the paradox in the passage by circling each of the contradictory statements. For the example above, you would do this:

> 1. Every member of the city council has unequivocally pledged support for education, both in speeches and action. In fact, over the last five years every proposal to increase spending for education has passed. The city has greatly benefited from the council's focus on education. Yet not one member of the city council supports the most recent proposal to increase education spending.

7.2.2 Drill: Identifying Paradoxes

Circle the two apparently contradictory facts in each of the following passages.

1. Most people think that, if a person has few or no cavities, then that person must have good dental hygiene. After all, regular brushing and flossing is known to reduce the incidence of cavities. Some people, however, who have few or no cavities rarely brush or floss their teeth.

2. Percussionists, if they want to become professional musicians, must learn to play many different instruments. Fortunately, some of these instruments are closely related. For example, a marimba and a xylophone are both sets of tuned bars played with mallets, and they are nearly identical except for their size. Despite the similarities, some percussionists are skilled at one but not the other of these two instruments.

3. A car with low mileage is more reliable than a car with high mileage. This is because the more a car is used, the more it breaks down. Nevertheless, used car buyers should avoid any car with unusually low mileage for its age.

4. Graduate schools offer deferred admission for those who wish to wait a year between being admitted and enrolling. Those who apply for a deferral must commit to their school, which ensures that deferring students will not apply elsewhere the following year. This is good for schools, since they can admit fewer students and be confident that they can fill their incoming class. Despite this benefit, schools are often unwilling to grant deferrals.

Answers & Explanations

1. Fact$_1$: Regular brushing and flossing is known to reduce the incidence of cavities.

   Fact$_2$: Some people who have few or no cavities rarely brush or floss their teeth.

   However is a turnaround word, which tells you that the last sentence is one fact in the paradox. The sentence immediately before it fights against it, so that is the other fact.

2. Fact$_1$: A marimba and a xylophone are nearly identical.

   Fact$_2$: Some percussionists are skilled at one but not the other.

   Despite is a turnaround word, which tells you the last sentence is one fact in the paradox. It also hints at the other fact by saying "despite *the similarities*," so the statement about similarities is the other fact.

3. Fact$_1$: A car with low mileage is more reliable.

   Fact$_2$: Used car buyers should avoid any car with unusually low mileage

   Nevertheless is a turnaround word, which tells you one of the facts. The first sentence fights against this last sentence.

4. Fact$_1$: Deferring students is good for schools.

   Fact$_2$: Schools are often unwilling to grant deferrals.

   Despite is a turnaround word, which tells you one of the facts. As in the second example, it also hints at the other fact: "Despite *this benefit*...." The benefit must be the other fact in the paradox.

7.3   PREPHRASE

7.3.1   PREPHRASING RESOLUTIONS

Prephrasing is not a major part of Paradox question strategy, since you can rarely Prephrase the specific correct answer. As a result, all you have to do is make sure that you know what the correct answer must do.

> The correct answer will introduce entirely new information and is often unpredictable. Don't try to get too specific with your Prephrased answer.

That said, if there is an obvious way to explain the facts, feel free to Prephrase a particular explanation, knowing that the correct answer may or may not match your prediction.

The correct answer to a Paradox question should explain how *both* facts could *simultaneously be true*. For any given Paradox question, then, just remind yourself of the facts that must be explained.

For example, in the passage above, you saw this contradiction:

> Fact$_1$: Every member of the city council has pledged unequivocal support for education.

> Fact$_2$: Not one member supports the most recent proposal to increase education spending.

To Prephrase, make sure you know what the correct answer must do:

> Prephrase: The correct answer must explain how it could be true that everyone on the city council pledges unequivocal support for education even though not one of them supports the most recent educational spending increase.

That's all there is to Prephrasing. The general form of this is:

> Prephrase: The correct answer must explain how it could be true that [Fact$_1$] even though [Fact$_2$].

Once you know what the correct answer must do, you can attack the answer choices.

7.4 ATTACK

7.4.1 THE REAL QUESTION

The **Real Question** for Paradox questions:

Does this explain how both facts could be true?

If an answer explains how one fact could be true but not how the other could simultaneously be true, then it is wrong, and you should cut it.

Sometimes, the correct answer is wacky. You might never predict certain answers, or you might think they are implausible. Neither of these is a consideration. You must assume that the answer choices are true, and your job is to determine whether they explain how both facts could be true.

7.4.2 EXPLAIN BOTH, NOT ADDRESS BOTH

The correct answer to a Paradox question must *explain* how both facts can be true, but it need not *mention* or *address* both facts.

Here's a sample passage:

> Teams usually look for the tallest basketball players available, since height can be a great advantage. But a team full of the tallest basketball players is unlikely to be successful.

The **turnaround word** *but* helps you identify the contradiction:

Fact$_1$: Height can be a great advantage in basketball.

Fact$_2$: A team full of the tallest basketball players is unlikely to be successful.

If you are trying to resolve this paradox, then the correct answer must explain how a team full of tall players isn't successful even though height can be a great advantage. But it doesn't need to *mention* or *address* both of these facts. Here's a potential explanation:

> (A)   A successful team requires speed, a characteristic that the tallest players tend to lack.

This *explains* how, even though height can be a great advantage, a team full of the tallest players is unlikely to be successful. It doesn't *mention* the first fact, or *address* how height can be an advantage, but that's okay—it doesn't have to. It must only explain how both facts can be true, which it does, so it is a good answer.

7.4.3 DISTRACTERS

Three distracters commonly appear on Paradox questions:

Incomplete

The most common distracters for Paradox questions are **incomplete** answers. These answers explain how *one* but not *both* facts could be true. In the example about basketball above, an example of an incomplete distracter might be:

> (B)   Taller players suffer fewer blocked shots than shorter players.

This explains how it could be true that height is an advantage, but it doesn't explain how a tall team would be unsuccessful. So it's incomplete.

Out of Scope

Out of scope answers explain neither fact. You should be careful, however, about dismissing an answer as out of scope simply because it's unusual. Some correct answers are weird, but they provide the necessary explanation. If an answer explains neither fact, however, it is out of scope. An example of such a distracter for the para-

> Because you must accept as true everything in the passage, any choice that contradicts the passage is wrong.

dox above might be:

(C)   Players of average height tend to run no faster
than players of average skill.

This information about players of average height is completely out of scope. It doesn't explain either fact in the least.

Opposite

Opposite answers exacerbate the paradox, making it harder to believe that both facts could simultaneously be true. An example of an opposite answer for the basketball passage might be:

(D)   The tallest players tend to get the most rebounds,
which are necessary for any successful team.

This makes it even harder to believe that a team of the tallest players wouldn't be good. The tallest players get the most rebounds, and successful teams need rebounds. So why wouldn't a team full of the tallest players be successful? This choice certainly doesn't provide an explanation. It only makes things worse.

7.5   PUTTING IT ALL TOGETHER

Try these complete examples:

1. Complaints to the federal standards board about offensive content on nationally syndicated radio were down last year by more than fifty percent relative to the year before. However, one independent media watchdog group conducted a comprehensive study that found there was no decrease in the amount of offensive content broadcast last year on nationally syndicated radio.

    Which one of the following, if true, does the most to reconcile the apparent discrepancy above?

Here's the approach:

1. Identify

This question stem asks you to reconcile an apparent contradiction, so this is a Paradox question.

2. Analyze

To analyze, find the two apparently contradictory facts. The turnaround word *however* helps, but the analysis is pretty straightforward since there are only two facts in the passage anyway. Therefore, the apparent contradiction is:

Fact$_1$: Complaints about offensive content were down last year compared to the year before.

Fact$_2$: There was no decrease in the amount of offensive content.

3. Prephrase

To Prephrase on Paradox questions, know what the correct answer must do. The correct answer must always explain how both facts could simultaneously be true. In this case, that means:

Prephrase: The correct answer must explain how it could be true that complaints about offensive content were down last year **even though** there was no decrease in the amount of offensive content.

If you know what the correct answer must do, you'll find it more easily.

4. Attack

Remember the **Real Question**: *Does this explain how both facts could be true?* Also remember that the correct answer does not need to *address* both facts, only to explain how they could both be true.

> (A) The number of complaints filed last year regarding profanity on the radio was roughly equal to the number filed regarding inappropriately violent content.

Choice (A): *Does this explain how both facts could be true?* No, it doesn't explain why the number of complaints decreased at all. In fact, it doesn't explain anything, so it's entirely **out of scope**. *Cut it.*

> (B) Many listeners who complained two years ago have chosen to stop listening to the offensive programs.

Choice (B): *Does this explain how both facts could be true?* If listeners who used to complain no longer listen, then it would make sense that complaints would decrease even if the content remained the same. The complainers are no longer listening, so they no longer complain. This explains how both facts could simultaneously be true. *Keep it.*

> (C) Federal regulations relating to offensive content are less strict than they were a generation ago.

Choice (C): *Does this explain how both facts could be true?* Federal standards are completely **out of scope**, particularly those of another generation. The passage is about this year's complaints and the amount of offensive content, not the regulation of offensive content. *Cut it.*

> (D) Audiences are more sensitive to offensive content than ever before.

Choice (D): *Does this explain how both facts could be true?* This is an **opposite** distracter since it exacerbates the problem. If audiences are more sensitive, then you'd expect even *more* complaints. *Cut it.*

> (E) There has been a similar decrease in the number of complaints about offensive content on television.

Choice (E): *Does this explain how both facts could be true?* This is completely **out of scope**. Television doesn't matter, since the passage is all about complaints about the radio. This explains nothing. *Cut it.*

Choice (B) is the correct answer.

Try another question:

> 2. Many British people go to Hungary for dental work because many dental procedures have become too expensive in Britain. However, on average, they spend more per dental appointment in Hungary than in Britain.
>
> Which one of the following, if true, most helps explain the apparent contradiction described above?

Here's the approach:

1. Identify

This question stem asks you to explain an apparent contradiction, so it's a Paradox question.

2. Analyze

Find the two apparently contradictory facts. There is a turnaround word, *however*, which tells you that the second sentence is one of the facts you're looking for. What conflicts with the fact that British people spend more per appointment in Hungary? The fact that they go to Hungary for cheap dental work. The apparent contradiction is:

Fact₁: British people go to Hungary for its inexpensive dental work.

Fact₂: British people spend more per appointment for dental work in Hungary.

3. Prephrase

Again, all you have to do to Prephrase is know what the correct answer must do. If you immediately think of a possible explanation, that's fine, but you don't have to. In this case, this is what you should come up with:

> Prephrase: The correct answer must explain how it could be true that British people go to Hungary for its inexpensive dental work **even though** they spend more per appointment for dental work in Hungary.

Now you're ready to attack the answers.

4. Attack

Always ask the **Real Question**: *Does this explain how both facts could be true?*

(A)   British people spend a smaller portion of their income on dental work than do Hungarians.

Choice (A): *Does this explain how both facts could be true?* No. The paradox has nothing to do with a comparison between British people and Hungarians, so this is **out of scope**. *Cut it.*

(B)   Obtaining the credentials required for practicing dentistry in Britain costs much more than obtaining the required credentials in Hungary.

Choice (B): *Does this explain how both facts could be true?* This explains why dental work would be more expensive in Britain, but it doesn't explain why British people would spend more per appointment in Hungary. So this answer is **incomplete**. *Cut it.*

(C)   British dentists are no more skilled than are Hungarian dentists at carrying out most dental procedures.

Choice (C): *Does this explain how both facts could be true?* This explains why it wouldn't be a problem to go to Hungary for dental work, but it still doesn't explain the difference in cost per appointment. So like choice (B), this one is **incomplete**. *Cut it.*

(D)   Round-trip travel from Britain to Hungary is not very expensive when booked far enough in advance.

Choice (D): *Does this explain how both facts could be true?* This answer is just like choice (C). If the airfare is cheap, that would explain why it isn't a problem to go to Hungary, but this has nothing to do with why the cost per appointment is high. This is **incomplete**. *Cut it.*

(E)   British people are more likely to travel to Hungary for more significant dental procedures, which also tend to be more expensive.

Choice (E): *Does this explain how both facts could be true?* If British people go to Hungary for the more expensive procedures, then that would explain why the price per appointment is higher even if comparable procedures cost less in Hungary than in Britain. *Keep it.*

Choice (E) is the correct answer.

7.6 VARIATIONS

7.6.1 EXPLAIN QUESTIONS

Explain questions are very similar to Paradox questions. The difference is that in these there is only *one* fact to be explained, rather than two contradictory facts. Since you don't have to juggle two facts at a time, Explain questions are often easier than Paradox questions.

Explain question stems always use the word *explain* or *explanation*. They refer you to the passage and ask you to explain some particular fact or phenomenon. Here are some Explain question stems:

> Which one of the following, if true, most helps to explain the viewpoint of the economists described above?

> Which one of the following, if true, contributes most to an explanation of the patterns of erosion described above?

KEY PHRASES
Explain Questions

The following, if true

Most helps to explain
Contributes most to an explanation

Described above

Note that all of these ask about a specific part of the passage, and they all use the phrase "described above." Both of these characteristics are typical of Explain questions.

Your approach to Explain questions should be the same as your approach to Paradox questions, except that you are dealing with one fact rather than two throughout the process.

Explain questions aren't very common. They only appear on about half of all tests.

Try this one:

> 3. All newborn mammals grow quickly, but seals grow at an amazing rate, even for mammals. Some even grow three pounds per day during the first three weeks of their life, roughly quadrupling their weight in less than a month.
>
> Which one of the following, if true, contributes most to an explanation of the growth of newborn seals described above?

Here's the approach:

1. Identify

This question stem asks you to explain a single fact—the growth of baby seals. That's how you know it's an Explain question rather than a Paradox question.

2. Analyze

All you have to explain is the unusual growth of the baby seals. For Explain questions, just make sure you understand what you have to explain. Fortunately, the question stem will always explicitly tell you what you have to explain.

> Fact: Baby seals grow at an amazing rate, even for mammals.

3. Prephrase

On Explain questions, there's no need to Prephrase a particular explanation of the fact from the passage. Just know what the correct answer must do.

> Prephrase: The correct answer must explain how baby seals grow at an amazing rate, even for mammals.

Solving Explain questions is a little like using the Why Tool. Ask yourself, "Why {fact from the passage}?" The correct answer must provide a supporting explanation.

4. Attack

The **Real Question** for Explain questions is:

Does this explain the fact from the passage?

> (A)   Baby seals are very active, particularly compared
> to other mammals.

Choice (A): *Does this explain the fact from the passage?* No, if baby seals were very active, you wouldn't expect them to gain significantly more weight. They'd probably be especially light. This is an **opposite** answer. *Cut it.*

> (B)   Most mammals live on land, whereas seals live
> most of their lives in the water.

Choice (B): *Does this explain the fact from the passage?* There's no reason that living in water should make any difference for the weight of the seal. This doesn't explain the unusual weight gain. *Cut it.*

> (C)   Seal milk, which is the staple of a baby seal's
> diet, is extremely high in fat and calories
> compared to milk of other mammals.

Choice (C): *Does this explain the fact from the passage?* If seal milk is extremely high in fat and calories compared to the milk of other mammals, then baby seals would likely gain more weight than other mammals. This definitely explains the baby seal weight. *Keep it.*

> (D)   The growth of baby seals slows dramatically after
> the first two months of their lives.

Choice (D): *Does this explain the fact from the passage?* This doesn't provide any explanation for the rapid seal growth. Whether they slow down is completely irrelevant to why they gain so much weight. This is **out of scope**. *Cut it.*

> (E)   Adult seals eat more calories per pound of body
> weight than do most mammals.

Choice (E): *Does this explain the fact from the passage?* What adult seals do is irrelevant to baby seal weight. This is **out of scope**. *Cut it.*

Choice (C) is the correct answer.

7.7   THE BIG PICTURE

7.7.1   INTRODUCTION TO CONDITIONAL STATEMENTS

Conditional statements are a special kind of logic that appears throughout the LSAT. Conditional statements express a rule that only applies under certain conditions. Compare the following statements:

- Gerald isn't allowed to vote.

- If Gerald isn't registered, then he isn't allowed to vote.

The first statement is an unconditional rule: Gerald cannot vote, no matter what. It applies all the time. But the second statement is *conditional*: **IF** Gerald isn't registered, then he can't vote. You can make a judgment about his voting ability only in the case when you know he isn't registered.

Conditional statements can appear on any Logical Reasoning question, and they can be very challenging to work with. However, mastering them is one of the single most important things you can do to increase your LSAT score.

7.7.2 THE BASIC CONDITIONAL STATEMENT

The basic conditional statement is a sentence with the words *if* and *then*. Any time you see a sentence with *if* and *then*, you should always symbolize it using an arrow. Write the *if* part of the sentence on the left side of the arrow, and the *then* part of the sentence on the right side of the arrow. Feel free to use abbreviations to save time.

For example:

> If you are in California, then you are in the United States.

This can be correctly symbolized like this:

$$CA \longrightarrow US$$

In English, sentences can be rearranged—or even have words left out of them—without changing their meaning. You can see that the following three sentences all mean precisely the same thing:

> If you are in California, then you are in the United States.

> If you are in California, you are in the United States.

> You are in the United States if you are in California.

Since all three sentences mean the same thing, they should all be symbolized precisely the same way: with the *if* part of the sentence on the left, and the *then* part (even when the word *then* is missing) on the right. It doesn't matter whether the *if* part appears at the beginning or the end of the sentence.

Conditional symbols should always be read left to right. Never go backwards or against the arrow.

Notice that the two sides of the symbol tell you nothing about time. It is **not** true that the left side always occurs earlier in time than the right side. A sentence that says, "If you are in law school, then you must have taken the LSAT," would be symbolized

$$\text{Law school} \longrightarrow \text{LSAT}$$

Law school is on the left side of the conditional, but it occurred *after* the person took the LSAT. Conditional symbols have nothing to do with *before* and *after*.

7.7.3 NECESSARY AND SUFFICIENT

You can also understand the symbol in terms of **sufficient** and **necessary conditions**.

- A sufficient condition is enough, in itself, to <u>guarantee</u> a given result.
- A necessary condition <u>is required</u> for a given result.

The left side of any conditional statement is a **sufficient condition**. When the left side of a conditional statement is true, then it <u>guarantees</u> that the right side is true. Being in California <u>guarantees</u> that you are in the United States.

The right side of any conditional statement shows a **necessary condition**. The right side of the conditional <u>is required</u> in order for the left side to be true. Being in the United States <u>is required</u> in order for you to be in California.

7.7.4 THE CONTRAPOSITIVE

For every conditional statement, you can create a **contrapositive**, which is a way to write precisely the same information in another form. This might seem like a waste of time, but it is often useful on the LSAT. In fact, the contrapositives are so useful that not understanding them could easily lower your LSAT score by **ten points**!

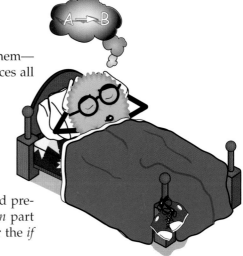

It's hard to overstate the importance of mastering conditional logic. Keep reviewing this material until you know it in your sleep. This is one of the single most important things you can do to improve your LSAT score.

Writing the contrapositive should be your automatic, knee-jerk, instantaneous reflex response every time you write a conditional. Every *if-then* sentence should produce a pair of symbols: the original conditional symbol and its contrapositive.

The rule is:

> To make the contrapositive,
> Switch and Negate.

That is, reverse the order of the two parts, and negate **both** of them using the "~" symbol, which means *not*.

To continue with the California example, the original conditional symbol was

$$CA \longrightarrow US$$

Thus, switching and negating produces

$$\sim US \longrightarrow \sim CA$$

If you turn this symbol back into a sentence, it reads

> If you are not in the United States, then you are not in California.

This makes a lot of sense. If you are outside the U.S., there is clearly no way you could be in California.

When making contrapositives, be sure not to make these common mistakes:

This mistake	Produces this symbol	Which means	Which is wrong because
Going backwards	$CA \longleftarrow US$	If you are in the United States, you are in California.	You could be in Florida.
Switching without negating	$US \longrightarrow CA$	If you are in the United States, you are in California.	You could be in Ohio.
Negating without switching	$\sim CA \longrightarrow \sim US$	If you are not in California, you are not in the United States.	You could be in New York.

So, never go backwards (against the arrow), and stick to Switch and Negate. This way, you'll never go wrong.

7.7.5 Drill: Basic Conditionals and Contrapositives

Using abbreviations, symbolize each of the following conditional statements and its contrapositive.

1. If it's Tuesday, then it's enchilada night.

    Symbolization: _____

    Contrapositive: _____

2. If you don't vacuum, your house won't be clean.

    Symbolization: _____

    Contrapositive: _____

3. You don't get a medal if you lose.

    Symbolization: _____

    Contrapositive: _____

Answers

1. Symbolization: T ⟶ EN
   Contrapositive: ~EN ⟶ ~T
2. Symbolization: ~V ⟶ ~C
   Contrapositive: C ⟶ V
3. Symbolization: L ⟶ ~M
   Contrapositive: M ⟶ ~L

The *if* part of the sentence always goes on the left side of the conditional symbol, even if it appeared on the right side of the sentence.

7.7.6 VARIATIONS ON THE BASIC CONDITIONAL

The LSAT writers often dress up the basic conditional statement in complicated language. Learning to understand each of these syntactic variations inside and out is one of the most important things you can do to increase your LSAT score.

7.7.6.1 Only If

One common trick used by the LSAT writers is the phrase *only if*.

> The car will start only if you put gas in it.

You may be tempted to write "Gas ⟶ Start," but that is not a correct representation of the statement. That symbol means "If you put gas in the car, then it will start," which is not necessarily true. Yes, gas is needed, but there are many other things required to make the car start, such as spark plugs, a battery, and a key. Without those, gas won't do much good.

The easiest way to deal with *only if* is to cross out the phrase and write an arrow in its place. Whatever immediately follows the arrow always goes on the right hand side of the conditional symbol. The correct way to write the conditional is:

$$\overrightarrow{}$$

> The car will start ~~only if~~ you put gas in it.
>
> Start ⟶ Gas
> ~Gas ⟶ ~Start

This says that if you see that the car has started, that <u>guarantees</u> you'll find gas in the tank. Also, if you don't put gas in the tank, that <u>guarantees</u> the car won't start.

> If you see
> *only if,*
> cross it out and write
> an arrow in its place.

"If" and "only if" are completely different animals. The "if" part of a sentence always goes on the left, but the part of a sentence following "only if" always goes on the right. Ignore the fact that they contain the same word, treat them as completely different, and replace the phrase "only if" with an arrow.

7.7.6.2 Unless

The word *unless* is also commonly found in conditional statements, and it is a little tricky:

> You cannot be a professional musician unless you practice.

Test-takers often make a lot of mistakes with *unless*, but you don't have to. **The easiest way to deal with *unless* is to cross it out and write *if not* in its place.** This may produce some funky grammar, but don't worry. Whatever immediately follows the *if* should be written on the left side of the conditional symbol.

> **if not**
> You cannot be a professional musician ~~unless~~ you practice.
>
> ~Practice ⟶ ~PM
> PM ⟶ Practice

This makes sense: If you don't practice, then you're guaranteed not to be a professional musician. If you are a professional musician, you must have practiced.

> If you see
> *unless,*
> cross it out and write
> "if not" in its place.

7.7.6.3   *All, Every, Always, Whenever*

These words can also be included in conditional statements. For example:

> All fish can swim.
>
> Every fish can swim.
>
> Fish can always swim.
>
> Whenever you see a fish, you know it can swim.

These are pretty simple to symbolize. Whatever follows *all* or *every* goes on the left side of the conditional symbol.

$$\text{Fish} \longrightarrow \text{Swim}$$
$$\sim\text{Swim} \longrightarrow \sim\text{Fish}$$

You shouldn't write "Swim $\longrightarrow$ Fish" because there are some things that can swim but that are not fish, such as whales and people and penguins.

7.7.6.4   *No, None, Never*

No, *none*, and *never* are only slightly trickier.

> No dogs have six legs.
>
> None of the dogs has six legs.
>
> Dogs never have six legs.

> To symbolize a conditional with
> *no, none,* or *never,*
> **make sure the "~" is always to the right of the arrow.**

$$\text{Dog} \longrightarrow \sim6 \text{ Legs}$$
$$6 \text{ Legs} \longrightarrow \sim\text{Dog}$$

If you see a dog, you know it won't have six legs, and if you see a six-legged creature, you know it's not a dog (and you should probably go get the bug spray). Be careful not to say "~Dog $\longrightarrow$ 6 Legs" because there are some animals that are not dogs but that don't have six legs—cats, for example.

7.7.6.5   *Requires*

Some sentences refer to something *requiring* something else, or another language variation that means the same thing. This goes back to sufficient and necessary conditions.

> A functioning government requires a steady source of tax revenue.

> To symbolize a conditional with
> *requires,*
> put the thing that <u>is required</u> on the right side.

Be careful not to get confused here. Although *a functioning government* requires something, *a functioning government* is not the thing that <u>is required</u>. What <u>is required</u> is the *steady source of tax revenue*, so that goes on the right-hand side.

$$\text{FG} \longrightarrow \text{Tax}$$
$$\sim\text{Tax} \longrightarrow \sim\text{FG}$$

7.7.6.6   A*ND* and O*R*

Some conditional statements include the word *and* or *or*, which you can simply write as part of the conditional symbol. For example:

If you make a cake, you must use flour and sugar.

Cake → Flour AND Sugar
~Flour OR ~Sugar → ~Cake

The original conditional symbol is straightforward enough, but something interesting happened in the contrapositive: When negated, the and became an or. Upon examination, this makes sense. If you leave out flour, or if you leave out sugar, your result will not be a cake. You don't need to leave out both; simply omitting one of them will guarantee a non-cake result.

Here's another example:

If you unplug the TV or pour water into it, it will not work.

Unplug OR Water → ~Work
Work → ~Unplug AND ~Water

It happened again. This time, the negated or became an and. It makes sense to say that if you see a working TV, you can be sure that it is both plugged in and water free.

Another example:

If you play pro football without a helmet, you will get hurt.

Football AND ~Helmet → Hurt
~Hurt → ~Football OR Helmet

The contrapositive says that if you didn't get hurt, then you either didn't play pro football, or you wore a helmet.

> **When negated,**
> AND **becomes** OR,
> OR **becomes** AND.

Recall that dealing with the word *unless* entails changing it to *if not*. The word *not* introduces a negation, so pay close attention to conditionals that contain both *unless* and *and* or *or*. If the *not* applies to one of these words, then you have to change it. For example:

if not
You cannot go to Hawaii ~~unless~~ you take a plane or a boat.

~Plane AND ~Boat → ~Hawaii
Hawaii → Plane OR Boat

Another related situation is the word *nor*. It means the same thing as "not or." Since it involves negating an or, the result will be an and.

If you are afraid of animals, you will visit neither the zoo nor the circus.

Afraid → ~Zoo AND ~Circus
Zoo OR Circus → ~Afraid

> **Neither A nor B**
> **means**
> **Not A** AND **not B.**

7.7.6.7   When a Conditional Rule Applies

Recall the football example:

$$\text{Football AND } \sim\text{Helmet} \longrightarrow \text{Hurt}$$
$$\sim\text{Hurt} \longrightarrow \sim\text{Football OR Helmet}$$

If you see someone who *is* hurt, what can this rule tell you?

The answer is: nothing at all. If the left-hand side of a conditional statement doesn't apply, then don't even bother looking at the right-hand side. You can't go backwards against the arrow and start making statements about football. Maybe the person fell down the stairs. Or had a car accident. Or maybe he *did* play football but wore a helmet and hurt his knee. The scenario of someone who is hurt is simply not addressed within the realm of the conditional. All conditional rules apply only under certain conditions, and if those conditions aren't met, then the rule doesn't matter.

7.7.6.8   Drill: Symbolizing Conditional Statements

Using abbreviations, symbolize each of the following conditional statements and its contrapositive.

1. If you put a CD in the microwave, it will explode.

    _____

    _____

2. Only if you go to Japan can you truly experience Japanese culture.

    _____

    _____

3. Unless you tell me about a better restaurant, I'm going to MegaBurger.

    _____

    _____

4. Ubiquicorp will proceed with the project only if it receives regulatory approval.

    _____

    _____

5. Whenever I take KoldBGon, it cures my cold.

    _____

    _____

6. Only if it's a weekend or over 70 degrees will Sagitha walk to the store.

    _____

    _____

7. No member of Jerry's family eats broccoli.

    _____

    _____

8. If you enjoy Frisbee, then you must be a college student or a dog.

    _____

    _____

9. Joe will wash the dishes if Mary clears the table.

    _____

    _____

10. Climbing to the top of Mt. Everest necessitates a strong rope.

    _____

    _____

11. The machine won't give you a soda unless you put enough money in.

    _____

    _____

7.7.7 Linking Conditional Statements

7.7.7.1 The Conditional Chain

If you are presented with more than one conditional statement, there is a good chance that you will be able to link them, especially in the Logical Reasoning section. **In order to be able to link conditional symbols, you must find something <u>identical</u> on the left side of one symbol and on the right side of another symbol.** It's important to note that A and ~A are not identical, since one is negated but the other isn't.

When you find identical elements on the left and the right of two different conditional symbols, you can put them together to create a conditional **chain**. To make the chain, put the thing that's identical in the middle of the chain, and rewrite the other conditional symbols around it. For example:

Conditional 1: A → F
~F → ~A

Conditional 2: F → ~M
M → ~F

You'll notice that F is on the right side of conditional 1, and an identical F is on the left side of conditional 2. That means you can put F in the middle of the chain:

Chain 1: A → F → ~M

You'll also notice that ~F is on the left side of conditional 1, and an identical ~F is on the right side of conditional 2. That means you could also put ~F in the middle of another chain:

Chain 2: M → ~F → ~A

Sharp-eyed readers will have noticed that the second chain looks a lot like the first chain, only backwards and with everything negated. That's because the second chain is the **contrapositive** of the first chain. No matter how long a chain is, you will always be able to make the contrapositive of it if you **switch** the entire order backwards **and negate** everything.

Thus, every chain should be written as two symbols: the original chain and its contrapositive. If you want to search through your original conditional symbols to find the identical elements that make up the contrapositive chain, that's perfectly valid. However, it's usually faster and simpler to just complete one chain and then **switch and negate** it to create the contrapositive.

7.7.7.2   Chains with AND and OR

Sometimes you can create a chain using conditionals that contain and and or. Consider the following:

$$\text{Conditional 1:} \quad B \longrightarrow G \text{ AND } R$$
$$\sim R \text{ OR } \sim G \longrightarrow \sim B$$

$$\text{Conditional 2:} \quad G \longrightarrow \sim N$$
$$N \longrightarrow \sim G$$

If you know B is true, that guarantees both G and R. Furthermore, G *alone* is enough to guarantee ~N. So you know that if B is true, it will eventually guarantee ~N. Thus, these two conditionals can be linked together to make a branching chain:

$$\text{Chain:} \quad B \longrightarrow G \text{ AND } R$$
$$\searrow$$
$$\sim N$$

What about the contrapositive? Well, think about the original conditional symbols. If N is true, that guarantees ~G. And either ~G or ~R is enough to guarantee ~B. So it is possible to link the contrapositives as well, and this also shows you how to make the contrapositive of a branched chain.

$$\text{Contrapositive:} \quad \sim R \text{ OR } \sim G \longrightarrow \sim B$$
$$\nearrow$$
$$N$$

However, you can't *always* link conditionals that contain and and or. Think about this situation:

$$\text{Conditional 1:} \quad X \longrightarrow L$$
$$\sim L \longrightarrow \sim X$$

$$\text{Conditional 2:} \quad C \text{ AND } L \longrightarrow H$$
$$\sim H \longrightarrow \sim C \text{ OR } \sim L$$

There is an L on the right-hand side of conditional 1 and an identical L on the left-hand side of conditional 2. If X is true, that guarantees L is true, but L alone is **_NOT_** enough to guarantee that H is true—you would also need C, which you may or may not have. Therefore, you can't make a chain.

Similarly, if you know you have ~H, then you are guaranteed to have either ~C or ~L, but *you don't know which one*. That means you can't say for sure whether you will get ~X. Therefore, you also can't link the contrapositives.

> You can make a chain only when:
> AND is on the right side,
> OR is on the left side.

7.7.7.3   How To Use a Chain

Chains can be tremendously useful tools because they can consolidate a lot of complex information into a single compact symbol, but it's important to understand how they work. Imagine you have constructed the following chain:

$$\text{Chain:} \quad L \longrightarrow M \longrightarrow N \longrightarrow O \longrightarrow P$$
$$\sim P \longrightarrow \sim O \longrightarrow \sim N \longrightarrow \sim M \longrightarrow \sim L$$

Whenever you know that one part of the chain is true, then you know that everything to the <u>right</u> of it is also true. For example, if M is true, then N, O, and P are also true.

Don't make the mistake of going backwards against the arrow. Many questions, especially in the Logical Reasoning section, will try to trick you by tempting you to go backwards along the chain. For example, a question may tell you that ~L is true and ask what you can say about the other parts of the chain. The answer is: nothing. You have no information about the other parts of the chain because you can't go backwards.

7.7.7.4 When To Make Chains

No matter what it is, you should only do something on the LSAT if it's a good use of your time. That is, it should be leading to your getting points faster and with a higher degree of success than anything else you could be doing.

When you see a passage in the Logical Reasoning section that contains a lot of conditional language and repeated elements that can be linked together in a chain, it's almost always a good use of your time to create a conditional chain. The LSAT writers love to test your ability to make contrapositives and link conditionals.

Sometimes in the Analytical Reasoning section, and on rare occasions in the Logical Reasoning section, it's not a good use of your time to make chains. Such occasions would be when:

- Making a chain is likely to confuse you, lead to mistakes, or take an extraordinarily long time. This can be true when there are a large number of ANDs and ORs.

- The correct answer does not depend on making a chain. This can be hard to predict, but sometimes a glance at the answer choices tells you that the question is focused elsewhere.

That being said, it pays to get as fast and accurate as you can at making chains. In the end, this skill is likely to bring you more points.

7.7.7.5 Drill: Linking Conditionals

Symbolize each pair of conditional statements and link them if possible.

1. If A is polished, then B must be polished.

   C will be polished only if A is polished.

   _____

   _____

   _____

2. F will be honored unless D is honored.

   Every time D is honored, E must be honored.

   _____

   _____

   _____

3. No G will be repaired when an H is repaired.

   Only if a J is repaired may a G be repaired.

   _____

   _____

   _____

4. Unless L is not elected, K will be elected.

   N will be elected if M or K is elected.

   _____

   _____

   _____

5. R will be cultivated if O and Q are cultivated.

   Only if O is cultivated will P be cultivated.

   _____

   _____

   _____

6. The study of T requires the study of S and V.

   Unless W is studied, S cannot be studied.

   _____

   _____

   _____

Answers

1. First conditional: $A \longrightarrow B$

    $\sim B \longrightarrow \sim A$

    Second conditional: $C \longrightarrow A$

    $\sim A \longrightarrow \sim C$

    Linked chain: $C \longrightarrow A \longrightarrow B$

    $\sim B \longrightarrow \sim A \longrightarrow \sim C$

2. First conditional: $\sim D \longrightarrow F$

    $\sim F \longrightarrow D$

    Second conditional: $D \longrightarrow E$

    $\sim E \longrightarrow \sim D$

    Linked chain: $\sim F \longrightarrow D \longrightarrow E$

    $\sim E \longrightarrow \sim D \longrightarrow F$

3. First conditional: $H \longrightarrow \sim G$

    $G \longrightarrow \sim H$

    Second conditional: $G \longrightarrow J$

    $\sim J \longrightarrow \sim G$

    Linked chain: Not possible

4. First conditional: $L \longrightarrow K$

    $\sim K \longrightarrow \sim L$

    Second conditional: $M \text{ OR } K \longrightarrow N$

    $\sim N \longrightarrow \sim K \text{ AND } \sim M$

    Linked chain: $M \text{ OR } K \longrightarrow N$
    $$\nearrow$$
    $$L$$
    $\sim N \longrightarrow \sim K \text{ AND } \sim M$
    $$\searrow$$
    $$\sim L$$

5. First conditional: $O \text{ AND } Q \longrightarrow R$

    $\sim R \longrightarrow \sim O \text{ OR } \sim Q$

    Second conditional: $P \longrightarrow O$

    $\sim O \longrightarrow \sim P$

    Linked chain: Not possible

6. First conditional: $T \longrightarrow S \text{ AND } V$

    $\sim V \text{ OR } \sim S \longrightarrow \sim T$

    Second conditional: $\sim W \longrightarrow \sim S$

    $S \longrightarrow W$

    Linked chain: $\sim V \text{ OR } \sim S \longrightarrow \sim T$
    $$\nearrow$$
    $$\sim W$$
    $T \longrightarrow S \text{ AND } V$
    $$\searrow$$
    $$W$$

7.7.8 CONDITIONALS WITHIN LOGICAL REASONING QUESTIONS

Conditional statements in the Logical Reasoning section appear most often in Inference questions, although they also frequently appear in Sufficient Assumption and Parallel questions.

When symbolizing conditional statements from Logical Reasoning passages, you don't want to leave out important information, but you also don't want to waste time by rewriting entire sentences. The best solution is to get comfortable creating acronyms for complex ideas. For example, if the passage contained a conditional statement that began

> If a country has experienced sustained economic
> growth for over a year…

It would best be symbolized as

$$\text{ESEGOY} \longrightarrow \text{…}$$

(which stands for Experienced Sustained Economic Growth for Over a Year.) Even though this looks ugly, it's the best compromise between dangerous oversimplification and wasting time.

Here are a few examples of questions that demand a strong grasp of conditional statements.

4. Manager: An employee can neither be promoted nor avoid monetary penalties if that employee is known by his or her employer to have stolen significant company resources. Several senior employees at this company have just now been shown to have carried out a plot that enabled them to steal significant company resources. These employees will therefore not be promoted.

If the manager's statements are all true, which one of the following statements must also be true?

Here's the approach:

1. Identify

This question stem asks you to find something that must be true, so this is an Inference question.

2. Analyze

To analyze an Inference passage, you just have to understand the premises. In this case, the passage contains a conditional statement and some other information, so the best way to understand it is to symbolize it. The first sentence can be symbolized by creating acronyms for the important ideas and constructing a conditional symbol.

> Remember, *neither A nor B* means *not A AND not B*.

An employee can neither be <u>P</u>romoted nor <u>A</u>void <u>M</u>onetary <u>P</u>enalties if that employee is <u>K</u>nown <u>B</u>y his or her <u>E</u>mployer to have <u>S</u>tolen <u>S</u>ignificant company <u>R</u>esources:

$$\text{KBESSR} \longrightarrow \sim\!P \text{ and } \sim\!AMP$$
$$P \text{ or } AMP \longrightarrow \sim\!\text{KBESSR}$$

In the rest of the passage, the manager tells you some things that are definitely true. You can place check marks over the things that you are told are true and follow the conditional symbol to infer other things that must also be true. In this case, you know that there are some employees who are known to have stolen resources, so that triggers the first conditional. You therefore know that both things on the right-hand side of the symbol must also be true.

$$\overset{\checkmark}{\text{KBESSR}} \longrightarrow \overset{\checkmark}{\sim\!P} \text{ and } \overset{\checkmark}{\sim\!AMP}$$
$$P \text{ OR } AMP \longrightarrow \sim\!\text{KBESSR}$$

> When you know something is definitely true, write a check mark above it and follow the conditional chain to see what else you can infer.

3. Prephrase

When following your conditional symbol allows you to infer other things that must be true, those other things are very likely to be the correct answer. In this case, the passage already says that the employees won't be promoted, but you figured out on your own that they also won't avoid monetary penalties. This is a great Prephrased inference.

Inference: The senior employees will not avoid monetary penalties.

4. Attack

Remember the **Real Question** for Inference questions: *Is this guaranteed to be true?* Take a look at these answer choices:

(A) The senior employees initially benefited from the plot that resulted in the theft.

Choice (A): *Is it guaranteed that the senior employees initially benefited from the plot that resulted in the theft?* The passage contains no information about anyone initially benefiting from anything, so this choice is **out of scope**. *Cut it.*

(B)   If there had been no plot, the senior employees
would be promoted.

Choice (B): *Is it guaranteed that if there had been no plot, the senior employees would be promoted?* This choice, like many choices in this style of question, is a conditional statement itself. The best approach is to see if it matches the conditionals from the passage. The choice can be symbolized

$$\sim Plot \longrightarrow P$$

This doesn't match the conditionals from the passage. First, none of the original conditionals mentions what happens when there is no plot, so that's **out of scope**. Second, even if you assume that no plot means the employees would not have been known to have stolen resources, you can't go **backwards** and infer that they would have been promoted. *Cut it.*

(C)   The senior employees cannot escape monetary
penalties.

Choice (C): *Is it guaranteed that the senior employees cannot escape monetary penalties?* Yes. This is a perfect match for the Prephrased answer, and it conforms perfectly with the passage's conditional statements. *Keep it.*

(D)   Some employees who are involved in thieving
plots avoid detection and penalties.

Choice (D): *Is it guaranteed that some employees who are involved in thieving plots avoid detection and penalties?* The conditionals in the passage tell you only what happens when someone is *known by his or her employer* to have stolen things. Thus you can't draw any conclusions about someone who has simply stolen things. That situation is **out of scope**. This underscores the importance of retaining all the details from the passage in your conditional symbols. *Cut it.*

(E)   No employee receives monetary penalties unless
he or she is known to have stolen significant
company resources.

Choice (E): *Is it guaranteed that no employee is assessed monetary penalties unless he or she is known to have stolen significant company resources?* Here's another conditional statement in the answer choice. Symbolize it by crossing out the *unless* and writing *if not.*

$$\sim KBESSR \longrightarrow AMP$$

(The **A** in **AMP** means *avoid*, which is the same as *not receiving*.) This choice again gets things **backwards**. *Cut it.*

Choice (C) is the correct answer.

Try another one:

5. Ornithologist: The following things are known about bird species Q. Individuals with feathery plumes always have striped wings but never have yellow feet. Individuals with curved beaks always have yellow feet, and individuals with trilled calls always have curved beaks. A specimen of bird Q in my sanctuary has striped wings and a curved beak.

    From the ornithologist's statements, which one of the following can be properly inferred about the specimen of bird Q in the ornithologist's sanctuary?

Here's the approach:

1. Identify

This question stem asks you to find something that can be properly inferred, so this is an Inference question.

Some Logical Reasoning questions, like this one, start to resemble an Analytical Reasoning game! You should always diagram these.

2. Analyze

Like the last passage, this one provides you with a set of conditional statements and some facts that are known to be true. Start your analysis by symbolizing the conditional statements.

> Individuals with <u>F</u>eathery <u>P</u>lumes always have <u>S</u>triped <u>W</u>ings but never have <u>Y</u>ellow <u>F</u>eet:
>
> $$FP \longrightarrow SW \text{ AND } {\sim}YF$$
> $${\sim}SW \text{ OR } YF \longrightarrow {\sim}FP$$

> Individuals with <u>C</u>urved <u>B</u>eaks always have <u>Y</u>ellow <u>F</u>eet:
>
> $$CB \longrightarrow YF$$
> $${\sim}YF \longrightarrow {\sim}CB$$

> Individuals with <u>T</u>rilled <u>C</u>alls always have <u>C</u>urved <u>B</u>eaks:
>
> $$TC \longrightarrow CB$$
> $${\sim}CB \longrightarrow {\sim}TC$$

The first thing you should notice is that these conditionals can be linked together into a chain, and it is very likely that the correct answer will depend on creating this chain:

$$FP \longrightarrow {\sim}YF \text{ and } SW$$
$$\searrow$$
$${\sim}CB \longrightarrow {\sim}TC$$
$${\sim}SW \text{ or } YF \longrightarrow {\sim}FP$$
$$\nearrow$$
$$TC \longrightarrow CB$$

In the last sentence of the passage, the ornithologist tells you some things that are definitely true about this one specimen. Again, you can place check marks over the things that you are told are true and follow the conditional symbol to infer other things that must also be true about that specimen. In this case, you're told that the specimen has striped wings and a curved beak. This leads to a couple of new inferences:

$$FP \longrightarrow {\sim}YF \text{ and } \overset{\checkmark}{SW}$$
$$\searrow$$
$${\sim}CB \longrightarrow {\sim}TC$$
$${\sim}SW \text{ or } \overset{\checkmark}{YF} \longrightarrow \overset{\checkmark}{{\sim}FP}$$
$$\overset{\checkmark\nearrow}{}$$
$$TC \longrightarrow \overset{\checkmark}{CB}$$

> Don't go backwards and attempt to infer anything from **SW**.

3. Prephrase

In this case, you are able to infer that the specimen also has yellow feet and no feathery plume. This makes a great Prephrased answer:

> Inference: The specimen has yellow feet and no feathery plume.

4. Attack

The **Real Question** for Inference questions is: *Is this guaranteed to be true?* Take a look at these answer choices:

> (A)   It has yellow feet and a trilled call.

Choice (A): *Is it guaranteed that it has yellow feet and a trilled call?* The information in this passage makes it impossible to infer anything about whether or not it has a trilled call. *Cut it.*

(B) It has yellow feet but lacks a trilled call.

Choice (B): *Is it guaranteed that it has yellow feet but lacks a trilled call?* Again, you can't infer anything about a trilled call. *Cut it.*

(C) It has yellow feet but lacks a feathery plume.

Choice (C): *Is it guaranteed that it has yellow feet but lacks a feathery plume?* Yes. This is a perfect match for the Prephrased answer, and it conforms perfectly with the passage's conditional statements. *Keep it.*

(D) It has a feathery plume and a trilled call.

Choice (D): *Is it guaranteed that it has a feathery plume and a trilled call?* Same problem. You don't know anything about a trilled call. *Cut it.*

(E) It lacks both yellow feet and a feathery plume.

Choice (E): *Is it guaranteed that it lacks both yellow feet and a feathery plume?* You inferred that the bird *has* yellow feet, so this is an **opposite** distracter. *Cut it.*

Choice (C) is the correct answer.

Here's a final example:

6. All accomplished musicians are both personally driven and well studied, attributes missing from many musicians who are not accomplished. Additionally, although only those who are accomplished possess technical virtuosity, no musicians who are well studied ignore the history of their genre.

If all of the statements above are true, which one of the following must be true?

Here's the approach:

1. Identify

This question stem asks you to find something that must be true, so this is an Inference question.

2. Analyze

> Any statement that talks about *some, many, most, sometimes, often,* or other similar "halfway" situations cannot be symbolized as a conditional.

This passage is composed entirely of conditional statements. Start your analysis by symbolizing them:

All Accomplished Musicians are both Personally Driven and Well Studied, attributes missing from many musicians who are not accomplished:

$$AM \longrightarrow PD \text{ AND } WS$$
$$\sim PD \text{ OR } \sim WS \longrightarrow \sim AM$$

It's easy to see how the first half of this sentence becomes a conditional symbol, but what about the second half? Conditional statements are always "all or nothing" situations. Any statement that talks about *some, many, most, sometimes, often,* or other similar "halfway" situations cannot be symbolized as a conditional. Thus, ignore the second half of this sentence, since it's likely that you'll be able to answer the question without it. Here's the next conditional:

Only those who are Accomplished possess Technical Virtuosity:

$$TV \longrightarrow AM$$
$$\sim AM \longrightarrow \sim TV$$

Treat the phrase *only those* like *only if*: cross it out and write an arrow in its place. The sentence is still talking about musicians, so even though that word is missing, you can continue to use the **AM** symbol.

No musicians who are <u>W</u>ell <u>S</u>tudied <u>I</u>gnore the
<u>H</u>istory of their <u>G</u>enre:

$$WS \longrightarrow \sim IHG$$
$$IHG \longrightarrow \sim WS$$

Remember, when you see "no," the "~" always goes on the right-hand side.

Not surprisingly, these conditionals can be linked together into a chain, and it is again very likely that the correct answer will depend on your creating this chain:

$$TV \longrightarrow AM \longrightarrow WS \text{ and } PD$$
$$\searrow$$
$$\sim IHG$$

$$\sim PD \text{ or } \sim WS \longrightarrow \sim AM \longrightarrow \sim TV$$
$$\nearrow$$
$$IHG$$

This passage, unlike the last two, does not contain any statement telling you about things that are definitely true. Thus, there is nothing more you can do in your analysis.

3. Prephrase

In this case, you are unable to infer anything that is definitely true—all your symbols are still in the realm of conditional statements. This is relatively common. In such cases, all the answer choices will also be conditional statements, and you will have to look for the one that matches your symbols.

When there are long chains involved, the correct answer often links two extreme ends of the chain. For example, in this case $TV \longrightarrow PD$ would be a valid inference and a likely correct answer. However, there are a number of different ways to link the ends of these branching chains, so don't bother trying to Prephrase every one. Just move on and attack the answer choices.

4. Attack

The **Real Question** for Inference questions is: *Is this guaranteed to be true?* Take a look at these answer choices:

(A)   No well-studied musicians who are not
         accomplished are personally driven.

Choice (A): *Is it guaranteed that no well-studied musicians who are not accomplished are personally driven?* Symbolize this conditional answer choice and see if it matches your symbols. Remember, the "no" means to put the "~" on the right-hand side.

$$WS \text{ AND } \sim AM \longrightarrow \sim PD$$

This is all mixed up and does not match your symbols. *Cut it.*

(B)   All musicians who are personally driven but not
         accomplished are well studied.

Choice (B): *Is it guaranteed that all musicians who are personally driven but not accomplished are well studied?* This conditional can be symbolized as

$$PD \text{ AND } \sim AM \longrightarrow WS$$

Again, this is all mixed up and does not match your symbols. *Cut it.*

(C)   All musicians who are not personally driven
         ignore the history of their genre.

Choice (C): *Is it guaranteed that all musicians who are not personally driven ignore the history of their genre?* This choice can be symbolized as

$$\sim PD \longrightarrow IHG$$

> You can write down the symbol for each answer choice, or save time by simply checking to see whether it follows along with your symbols from the passage.

Linked chains from the passage:

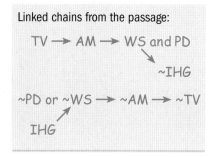

The chain you constructed does not allow you to make a connection between these two ideas. *Cut it.*

(D)   All musicians who do not ignore the history of their genre are accomplished.

Choice (D): *Is it guaranteed that all musicians who do not ignore the history of their genre are accomplished?* Symbolize this conditional as

$$\sim IHG \longrightarrow AM$$

This goes **backwards** against the arrows. *Cut it.*

(E)   No musicians who possess technical virtuosity ignore the history of their genre.

Choice (E): *Is it guaranteed that no musicians who possess technical virtuosity ignore the history of their genre?* Again, the "no" means that the "~" goes on the right. This conditional can be symbolized as

$$TV \longrightarrow \sim IHG$$

This matches your original symbols perfectly, and, as predicted, follows the chain from one extreme to the other. *Keep it.*

Choice (E) is the correct answer.

STOP. THIS IS THE END OF LECTURE 6. DO NOT PROCEED TO THE CORRESPONDING EXAM UNTIL INSTRUCTED TO DO SO IN CLASS.

LECTURE 7 | CHAPTER 8

SUFFICIENT ASSUMPTION QUESTIONS

8.1 IDENTIFY

8.1.1 WHAT IS A SUFFICIENT ASSUMPTION?

A **sufficient assumption** is an unstated premise that, if added to the premises of an argument, *guarantees* that the argument's conclusion is true.

For example, recall this argument, which you first saw in the Necessary Assumption chapter:

> The Winston School will hold a singing contest for eighth graders. Since Carol is an excellent singer, she will win the contest.

You saw before that a necessary assumption is: *Carol is an eighth grader,* but this isn't enough to guarantee that the conclusion is definitely true. Even if she's an eighth grader, she might win, or she might not.

But a sufficient assumption, if added to the premises, guarantees that Carol will win. Here's an example of something that guarantees the conclusion: *Carol will be the only person to enter the contest.* If this is true, then there is no way she can fail to win, since there is no one else that could beat her. So this is a **sufficient assumption**.

Notice that, while Carol is guaranteed to win if she is the only person who enters, this isn't the only way she could win. If she sings well, she could still win even if there are other people in the contest. So, while this is a *sufficient* assumption, it's not *necessary* in order for the conclusion to be true.

8.1.2 IDENTIFYING A SUFFICIENT ASSUMPTION QUESTION

All **Sufficient Assumption** questions follow the same pattern:

1. **The question stem asks you to choose a statement that makes the argument perfect.** This is what makes Sufficient Assumption questions different

from every other question type. The correct answer eliminates all the flaws in the argument. If you add the correct answer to the premises, the conclusion follows by necessity. In other words, the question asks for a sufficient assumption.

2. **The question stem asks you to assume the truth of each answer choice.** The question stem always includes an indication that you should *assume* the truth of the answer choices, as in, "Which one of the following, *if assumed*, allows the conclusion to be properly drawn?" You must accept the truth of the answer choices.

3. **The passage contains a flawed argument.** Since Sufficient Assumption questions are flaw-dependent, their passages must contain flawed arguments.

Note that the question stem *never* asks for the *best* answer or the one that *most* allows the conclusion to be properly drawn. The correct answer is the *only* answer that allows the conclusion to be properly drawn. In other words, the correct answer is perfectly correct, and all of the other answers are indisputably *wrong*, not just worse.

Here are some Sufficient Assumption question stems:

> The conclusion of the argument follows logically if which one of the following is assumed?

> Which one of the following, if assumed, would allow the conclusion to be properly drawn?

> Which one of the following, if assumed, enables the argument's conclusion to be properly inferred?

Remember that Sufficient Assumption questions are different from Necessary Assumption questions. Sufficient Assumption questions ask for an assumption that *guarantees* the conclusion, but Necessary Assumption questions ask for an assumption that *is required* by the argument.

You should expect to see about three Sufficient Assumption questions per test.

8.1.3 Drill: Identifying Sufficient Assumption Questions

Determine whether each of the following question stems belongs to a Sufficient Assumption question or a Necessary Assumption question.

1. Which one of the following is an assumption on which the politician's argument depends?

   ☐ Sufficient Assumption   ☐ Necessary Assumption

2. Which one of the following, if assumed, allows the scientist's conclusion to be properly drawn?

   ☐ Sufficient Assumption   ☐ Necessary Assumption

3. An assumption made in the argument above is that

   ☐ Sufficient Assumption   ☐ Necessary Assumption

4. The argument's conclusion follows logically if which one of the following is assumed?

   ☐ Sufficient Assumption   ☐ Necessary Assumption

5. Which one of the following is an assumption on which the argument relies?

   ☐ Sufficient Assumption   ☐ Necessary Assumption

Answers & Explanations

1. **Necessary Assumption.** The stem asks for an assumption the argument *depends upon or requires*.

2. **Sufficient Assumption.** The stem asks for an assumption that allows the conclusion to be properly *drawn*.

3. **Necessary Assumption.** The stem asks for an assumption *made* rather than an assumption that could be *added* to guarantee the conclusion.

4. **Sufficient Assumption.** The stem asks for an assumption that would allow the conclusion to *follow logically*.

5. **Necessary Assumption.** The stem asks for an assumption that the argument *relies on or requires*.

8.2 ANALYZE

8.2.1 ANALYZING SUFFICIENT ASSUMPTION QUESTIONS

Sufficient Assumption questions are flaw-dependent, so you should analyze them just as you would analyze any other flaw-dependent question type. Look for:

1. The conclusion
2. The premises
3. The flaw

Recognizing common flaws is not as useful on Sufficient Assumption questions as it is on other flaw-dependent question types, such as Weaken, Flaw, or Necessary Assumption questions. But the Concept Shift is more important on Sufficient Assumption questions than on any other question type, since the flaw in the passage almost always occurs in the form of a Concept Shift, and the correct answer usually provides a link for the Concept Shift.

> Exact wording is always important throughout the LSAT, but it's even more so on Sufficient Assumption questions. They are almost mathematical in their adherence to the phrases in the passage.

8.3 PREPHRASE

8.3.1 PREPHRASING A SUFFICIENT ASSUMPTION

Prephrasing on Sufficient Assumption questions means stating the link the answer should make to guarantee the conclusion.

Here's a Sufficient Assumption passage:

1. The promoters of the recent film festival boasted that their festival featured films from a variety of different genres. But the ten featured films were all produced by the same production company, so the promoters were wrong.

This is a classic counterargument, so the conclusion is the negation of the opponent's position. The argument works like this:

> The ten featured films at the film festival were all produced by the same production company.
>
> **Therefore**, the festival did not feature films from a variety of genres.

This argument is flawed. It intends to connect *produced by the same production company* to *not a variety of genres*. But these concepts are non-identical, so the flaw in this case is a Concept Shift:

Same production company ⚡ Not a variety of genres

Here's where Prephrasing comes in. The best way to guarantee this argument's conclusion is to link the two sides of the Concept Shift by coming up with a statement that makes them identical. For example, if films produced by the same production company are always of the same genre, then the argument no longer has a Concept Shift because the two different concepts have suddenly been made identical. So one Prephrased sufficient assumption might be:

> Sufficient Assumption: Films produced by the same production company are always films of the same genre.

If this is added as a premise, the argument then becomes:

- The ten featured films at the film festival were all produced by the same production company.
- Films produced by the same production company are always films of the same genre.

Therefore, the festival did not feature films from a variety of genres.

This new argument is perfect. If you accept the premises (which you must do on the LSAT , even if you disagree with them), then the conclusion is guaranteed to be true. Thus, the new premise is a sufficient assumption.

This kind of Prephrased answer is very likely to be the correct answer, and the process makes sense if you think about it. The reason the original argument was flawed was that it tried to link two concepts that were not necessarily identical. If you step in with a new statement that says those two concepts *are* identical, then the flaw disappears and the argument becomes perfect.

8.3.2 Drill: Prephrasing Sufficient Assumptions

Identify the Concept Shift and Prephrase a sufficient assumption for each of the following passages.

1. Every electric company produces electricity by using either renewable or non-renewable resources. It follows that Newgenerate, Inc. produces electricity by using either renewable or non-renewable resources.

    Concept Shift: _____

    _____

    Sufficient Assumption:_____

    _____

2. The government requires that all non-profits operated exclusively for the promotion of social welfare serve the general community rather than some particular subset of the community. Therefore, the National Reform Association is required to serve more than a select group of individuals and corporations.

    Concept Shift: _____

    _____

    Sufficient Assumption:_____

    _____

3. No principle of theoretical physics can be empirically tested. Thus, we can never know whether a given principle of theoretical physics is true.

    Concept Shift: _____

    _____

    Sufficient Assumption:_____

    _____

4. If the highway maintenance budget is reduced, then the state's major roads will fall into disrepair. But if the state's major roads fall into disrepair, then commuters will be inconvenienced by longer commutes. Since the governor has signed legislation reducing the highway maintenance budget, commuter complaints to the governor's office will increase.

    Concept Shift: _____

    _____

    Sufficient Assumption:_____

    _____

Answers & Explanations

1. Concept Shift: **Electric company ⚡ Newgenerate, Inc.** The claim about every electric company is intended to be connected to Newgenerate, Inc., but Newgenerate, Inc. may not be an electric company.

    Sufficient Assumption: **Newgenerate, Inc. is an electric company.** If Newgenerate, Inc. is an electric company, then the conclusion is guaranteed. Since it is an electric company, and since all electric companies produce electricity in one of two ways, then it produces electricity in one of these two ways.

2. Concept Shift: **Non-profits operated for the promotion of social welfare ⚡ National Reform Association.** The claim about these non-profits is supposed to be connected to the NRA, but these concepts are not identical.

    Sufficient Assumption: **The National Reform Association is a non-profit operated for the promotion of social welfare.** If the NRA is such a non-profit, then the conclusion is guaranteed, since the NRA would have to follow all the rules for such non-profits.

3. Concept Shift: **Whether something can be empirically tested** ⚡ **Whether we can know if something is true.**
The argument intends to connect testability with knowing the truth, but these concepts are not necessarily the same.

Sufficient Assumption: **If something cannot be empirically tested, then we can never know if it's true.** If this is true, then we can't know whether the principles of theoretical physics are true, as they can't be tested. Adding this to the premises guarantees the truth of the conclusion.

4. Concept Shift: **Commuters will be inconvenienced** ⚡ **Complaints to the governor's office will increase.** The argument does a good job establishing that commuters will be inconvenienced, but there's no guarantee that complaints to the governor will increase. Perhaps people will complain to the mayor instead, or maybe they're already so jaded that they'll take it in stride.

Sufficient Assumption: **If commuters are inconvenienced by increased commutes, they will increase their complaints to the governor's office.** Adding this to the premises would guarantee the conclusion that the complaints will increase.

8.4 ATTACK

8.4.1 THE REAL QUESTION

The **Real Question** for Sufficient Assumption questions is:

Does this guarantee the conclusion?

If an answer choice doesn't guarantee the conclusion when added to the premises, then it is not a sufficient assumption.

It is not enough for an answer choice to *help* the argument, as it would be on a Strengthen question, nor is it enough for an answer to be *required* by the argument, as it would be on a Necessary Assumption question—the correct answer must *guarantee* the conclusion.

8.4.2 THE NEW CONCEPT TOOL

You can use the New Concept Tool on any Sufficient Assumption question that has an entirely new concept in the conclusion. If you spot a new concept as you analyze the passage, then use the New Concept Tool.

To use the New Concept Tool:

1. Find the new concept that appears only in the conclusion.

2. Quickly read through the answer choices to eliminate any answer choice that does not address the new concept.

Usually, if there is a new concept in the conclusion, you can eliminate two or three answers immediately without even using the **Real Question**.

Take a look at this passage:

2. Astronomers learn about the history of the universe by looking into distant regions of space. Because light takes so long to cover the distance between Earth and these distant regions, astronomers observe space as it was in the past, not as it is today. But astronomers cannot observe the moment at which the universe was born, so they should not hypothesize about the origin of the universe.

Which one of the following, if assumed, enables the argument's conclusion to be properly drawn?

You can use the New Concept Tool to eliminate some answer choices before getting too deep into analysis and Prephrasing. Sometimes you can eliminate all four incorrect choices with this tool alone!

The conclusion indicator *so* tells you the conclusion: astronomers should not hypothesize about the origin of the universe. But *hypothesizing about the origin of the universe* is entirely new to the passage. The argument provides no evidence or premises that have anything to do with what it takes to hypothesize about the origin of the universe. In order to guarantee this conclusion, the argument needs an additional premise that addresses hypothesizing about the origin of the universe.

Here are some possible answer choices:

(A)   Astronomers should hypothesize about the origin of the universe if they can observe the moment at which the universe was born.

(B)   With advancements in observational instruments, astronomers should be able to observe the moment at which the universe was born within a few decades.

(C)   Astronomers can never be certain of the history of the universe.

(D)   One should not hypothesize about something's origins unless one can observe the moment at which the thing was created.

(E)   One cannot observe the moment at which something was created unless one is present at that moment in time.

The new concept that appears only in the conclusion is *hypothesizing about the origin of the universe*. This MUST be addressed by the correct answer. Note that the concept must be *addressed*, not necessarily *directly mentioned*.

Which answer choices can you eliminate using the New Concept Tool?

Choices (B), (C), and (E) do not address any kind of hypothesizing. They can provide no support for any claim about hypothesizing. Therefore, you can eliminate them without a second thought—they are definitely wrong.

The tricky answer, of course, is choice (D). It doesn't directly mention hypothesizing about the origin *of the universe*, but it addresses hypothesizing more generally. Since hypothesizing about the origin of the universe counts as hypothesizing about something, you should leave this in.

From here, you would proceed using other tools, such as the Real Question, but because you are down to only two answer choices, you are in a great position to find the correct answer very quickly.

8.4.3 Drill: The New Concept Tool

Analyze each passage by marking the premises and conclusion. Then circle the new concept in the conclusion and eliminate the answer choice that does not address the new concept.

1. Muzio won this year's state spelling bee by beating Ernesto, who had won the event twice before. It follows that Muzio practiced spelling regularly.

   (A) Ernesto would have won the state spelling bee if Muzio had not entered.
   (B) Muzio could only have beaten a two-time winner of the spelling bee if he practiced regularly.

2. Environmental activists have successfully lobbied for a bill protecting wildlife in our nation's arctic refuge. The bill will soon be voted upon by the Senate, but it will almost certainly fail to pass. Every senior senator who has spoken out about the bill has opposed it.

   (A) Any bill opposed by senior senators is almost certain not to pass.
   (B) Junior senators are less allied with environmental activists than are senior senators.

3. Resident: Our condominium association ought to protect the right to plant any variety of shrubbery. After all, though the association has outlawed all unsanctioned shrubberies, botanical diversity only adds to the beauty and thus to the value of our properties.

   (A) Outlawing unsanctioned shrubberies does not add botanical diversity.
   (B) The condominium association ought to protect any right that could add to the value of the properties.

4. Banks have an obligation to be sure that those to whom they lend money are who they say they are, rather than identity thieves under assumed identities. Therefore, banks that provide loans to identity thieves under assumed identities are as much to blame for the ramifications of the loans as the identity thieves themselves.

   (A) Any institution that has an obligation to verify the identities of its customers is as much to blame for customers with assumed identities as the deceitful customers themselves.
   (B) Any institution that knowingly provides loans to identity thieves must not have an obligation to verify the identities of its customers.

Answers & Explanations

1. New Concept: **Practiced spelling regularly**
Correct Answer: (B). Because choice (A) doesn't address regular practice at all, it must be wrong.

2. New Concept: **Fail to pass**
Correct Answer: (A). Choice (B) doesn't mention anything about passing, but choice (A) explains why it won't pass.

3. New Concept: **Ought to protect the right**
Correct Answer: (B). Choice (A) doesn't address what the condominium association should or should not do, but choice (B) does.

4. New Concept: **As much to blame for ramifications**
Correct Answer: (A). Choice (B) doesn't address blame at all, but choice (A) does.

8.4.4 DISTRACTERS

Sufficient Assumption questions have three common distracters:

Necessary Assumption Distracters

Some incorrect answers to Sufficient Assumption questions would be correct answers for Necessary Assumption questions. Remember: just because something is an *assumption* does not mean that it is a *sufficient assumption*.

Opposites

A sufficient assumption guarantees an argument's conclusion, but some incorrect answers to Sufficient Assumption questions actually *weaken* the argument. If an answer choice makes the argument weaker, then it's definitely wrong.

Reversals

Many correct answers to Sufficient Assumption questions are conditionals, but often there will be two nearly identical conditionals in the answer choices. In such a case, the wrong answer is usually the reversed form of the correct conditional.

For example, suppose an argument says:

> Company Blue had higher ticket sales than any ballet company in its region.
>
> **Therefore,** Company Blue must have been awarded the Winschell Prize.

A good sufficient assumption would be: "If a ballet company has higher ticket sales than any other company in its region, then it is awarded the Winschell Prize."

A **reversal** would be, "If a ballet company is awarded the Winschell Prize, then it has higher ticket sales than any other company in its region."

To avoid picking reversal distracters, remember the correct direction for a conditional answer choice:

> The right direction for a conditional answer choice to a Sufficient Assumption question is:
>
> If the premises are true → then the conclusion is true.

8.5 PUTTING IT ALL TOGETHER

Here are some examples:

3. To truly understand modern interpretive dance is to be more in touch with one's emotions than those that do not understand modern interpretive dance. Many people do not understand modern interpretive dance. Therefore, those that enjoy modern interpretive dance are more in touch with their emotions than many people.

The conclusion is logically valid if which one of the following is assumed?

(A) Many people enjoy modern interpretive dance.
(B) Those that truly understand modern interpretive dance enjoy modern interpretive dance.
(C) Those that enjoy modern interpretive dance are very in touch with their emotions.
(D) Those that enjoy modern interpretive dance truly understand modern interpretive dance.
(E) Many people understand modern interpretive dance.

Here's the approach:

1. Identify

This question stem asks for an assumption that would make the conclusion *follow logically*. In other words, it's looking for something that would guarantee the conclusion—a sufficient assumption.

2. Analyze

Therefore is a conclusion indicator, which tells you that the last sentence is the conclusion. The other two sentences are premises. Here's how the argument works:

- Those that understand modern interpretative dance are more in touch with their emotions than those who do not understand it.

- Many people do not understand modern interpretative dance.

  Therefore, those that enjoy modern interpretive dance are more in touch with their emotions than many people.

Find the flaw. In this case (like on most Sufficient Assumption questions) the flaw is a Concept Shift:

What two non-identical concepts are intended to be connected?

The author makes a shift from talking about *understanding* modern interpretive dance to talking about *enjoying* modern interpretative dance.

But just because people understand something does not mean they enjoy it, so there's a Concept Shift:

$$\text{Understand} \nrightarrow \text{Enjoy}$$

As it stands, the premises support the claim that those who *understand* modern interpretative dance are more in touch with their emotions than many people. To guarantee the truth of the author's conclusion, you need to connect *understanding* to *enjoying*.

3. Prephrase

You can usually Prephrase a sufficient assumption from the Concept Shift, and this question is no exception. The correct answer will most likely make the link between understanding and enjoying interpretative dance. A good Prephrased answer is:

> Sufficient Assumption: Those who enjoy
> interpretative dance understand it.

You might be tempted to phrase things the other way around—those who understand it enjoy it. But if that were added to the premises, then it could still be the case that there are a lot of people out there who enjoy it but don't understand it, and in that case you wouldn't be able to say that those people are more in touch with their emotions.

By Prephrasing this particular assumption you create a chain of logic in the premises that results in the conclusion following logically.

4. Attack

Before you attack the answers, you can quickly use the New Concept Tool if there is an entirely new concept in the conclusion that appears nowhere else in the argument. In this case enjoying interpretative dance is entirely new, so you can immediately eliminate any answer that doesn't address enjoying. This time around, that just gets rid of choice (E), but now there are only four answers to worry about. It's time to attack.

Use the **Real Question** to spot sufficient assumptions: *Does this guarantee the conclusion?*

> (A)   Many people enjoy modern interpretive dance.

Choice (A): *Does this guarantee the conclusion?* Even if many people enjoy modern interpretative dance, they might not understand it—this doesn't provide the link between the premises and conclusion. *Cut it.*

> (B)   Those that truly understand modern interpretive
>   dance enjoy modern interpretive dance.

Choice (B): *Does this guarantee the conclusion?* This seems to provide a link between enjoying and understanding, so hold onto it for now. *Keep it.*

(C)   Those that enjoy modern interpretive dance are
       very in touch with their emotions.

Choice (C): *Does this guarantee the conclusion?* This doesn't guarantee that those who enjoy interpretative dance are *more* in touch with their emotions, and it doesn't provide the link between understanding and enjoying. *Cut it.*

(D)   Those that enjoy modern interpretive dance truly
       understand modern interpretive dance.

Choice (D): *Does this guarantee the conclusion?* This is very similar to choice (B), but the concepts are reversed. You'll have to compare the answers to see which is right, but leave this in for now. *Keep it.*

Choice (E) was eliminated with the New Concept Tool, so you don't even have to worry about it.

You've narrowed it down to choices (B) and (D). Choice (D) matches the Prephrased answer, which is good. If choice (B) is added to the premises, then there could be people who enjoy but don't understand interpretative dance. If they don't understand interpretative dance, then there isn't any reason to believe that they are especially in touch with their emotions. Choice (B) doesn't guarantee the conclusion. It's just a **reversal**. That leaves you with choice (D).

Choice (D) is the correct answer.

> The correct answer choice is often extreme and mathematically precise in matching its language to the passage. That's because it's hard to guarantee that an argument is perfect, so the correct answer must go to extreme lengths.

4. We ought to pay attention only to the intrinsic properties of a work of art. Its other, extrinsic properties are irrelevant to our aesthetic interactions with it. For example, when we look at a painting we should consider only what is directly presented in our experience of it. What is really aesthetically relevant, therefore, is not what a painting symbolizes, but what it directly presents to experience.

    The conclusion follows logically if which one of the following is added to the premises?

    (A)   What an artwork symbolizes involves only
          extrinsic properties of that work.
    (B)   There are certain properties of our experiences of
          artworks that can be distinguished as symbolic
          properties.
    (C)   Only an artwork's intrinsic properties are relevant
          to our aesthetic interactions with it.
    (D)   It is possible in theory for an artwork to
          symbolize nothing.
    (E)   An intrinsic property of an artwork is one that
          relates the work to itself.

    Test 28, Section 1, Question 24

1. Identify

The question stem asks you for something that will allow the conclusion to follow logically, so it's a Sufficient Assumption question.

2. Analyze

The conclusion indicator *therefore* tells you the conclusion: [what is really aesthetically relevant is not what a painting symbolizes, but what it directly presents to experience.] The rest of the argument is a bunch of premises, and they are a bit confusing. Here's how the argument works:

- We ought to pay attention only to intrinsic properties of art, which are the only aesthetically relevant aspects of art.

- Extrinsic properties are aesthetically irrelevant.

- We should only consider what is directly presented to our experience when we look at a painting.

Therefore, what is aesthetically relevant is not what a painting symbolizes, but what it directly presents to experience.

This is an argument that takes a few moments to understand—so take a few moments to understand it. What is directly presented to experience must be an intrinsic property, since the argument thinks it should be considered. So half the conclusion is well established: what is aesthetically relevant is what a painting directly presents to experience. The problem is that the premises don't say anything about symbolizing.

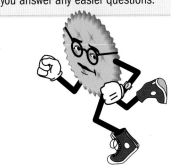

Pacing note: if you ran into a question like this on your test and could see right away that you'd struggle with it, then you'd want to postpone it until after you answer any easier questions.

Now find the flaw, in the form of a Concept Shift:

What two non-identical concepts are intended to be connected?

Symbolizing is judged to be aesthetically irrelevant, so there's an intended connection between *symbolizing* and *extrinsic properties*, since the argument has established that extrinsic properties are aesthetically irrelevant.

Thus, the Concept Shift is:

Extrinsic properties ⚡ What a painting symbolizes

3. Prephrase

The premises provide no information about what a painting symbolizes. Symbols might be extrinsic or intrinsic, but the argument needs them to be extrinsic to say that they are aesthetically irrelevant. So a good Prephrased answer might be:

Sufficient Assumption: What a painting symbolizes is extrinsic.

4. Attack

Again, you can use the New Concept Tool, since symbolizing is entirely new to the conclusion. The correct answer must provide information about symbolizing. Using the New Concept Tool, you can eliminate choices (C) and (E). So you are down to just three answer choices.

(A)   What an artwork symbolizes involves only extrinsic properties of that work.

Choice (A): *Does this guarantee the conclusion?* This answer is a great match for the Prephrased answer, and it provides the link between symbolizing and extrinsic. *Keep it.*

(B)   There are certain properties of our experiences of artworks that can be distinguished as symbolic properties.

Choice (B): *Does this guarantee the conclusion?* You are looking for something that guarantees the conclusion, but this doesn't do much for the argument. Symbolic properties exist, but that's not useful. *Cut it.*

Choice (C) was already cut using the New Concept Tool.

(D)   It is possible in theory for an artwork to symbolize nothing.

Choice (D): *Does this guarantee the conclusion?* Like choice (B), this is not very useful for anything. So what if art can symbolize nothing? That doesn't help link symbolizing to extrinsic properties. *Cut it.*

Choice (E) was already cut using the New Concept Tool.

Choice (A) is the correct answer.

8.6 VARIATIONS

8.6.1 JUSTIFY QUESTIONS

Justify questions are closely related to Sufficient Assumption questions. Just as before, your job is to add a new piece of information to the argument that bridges the Concept Shift and eliminates the argument's flaws. You should use the same analysis techniques and look for the same thing in the correct answer. There are only a few minor differences:

- Both question types tell you to accept the answer choices as true, but Sufficient Assumption questions usually use the phrase *if assumed*, whereas Justify questions use the phrases *if accepted, if valid,* or *if established*.

- Both question types tell you to make the conclusion guaranteed, but Sufficient Assumption questions usually use the phrases *properly drawn* or *logically follows*, whereas Justify questions almost always use the word *justified* (or sometimes *supported*).

- Sufficient Assumption questions don't ask you for the *best* answer, but Justify questions do. They ask you to find the choice that *most helps* to justify or that provides the *strongest* justification.

- Justify questions almost universally ask you to find a *principle* that justifies the conclusion. This is probably the easiest way to spot Justify questions. On the LSAT, a principle is a general rule, so the answer choices for Justify questions often use more general language than they do on Sufficient Assumption questions, and more general language than is used in the passage. For example, the passage may talk about a specific decision made in a particular courtroom, but the correct answer may be a broad rule about *all* cases of a certain type.

 **KEY PHRASES**
Justify Questions

Following principles

If valid

If established

Most helps to justify

Provides the strongest justification

Here are some common Justify question stems:

> Which one of the following principles, if valid, most helps to justify the reasoning above?

> Which one of the following generalizations, if established, would most help to justify the pacifist's reasoning?

If a question asks for a principle that helps you to justify or support a conclusion or an argument's reasoning, then it is a Justify question, and you should treat it just like a Sufficient Assumption question.

Here are some examples:

5. A journalist undertook to determine whether the hiring policies of local retailers were unfairly discriminatory. Two retailers in particular had failed to hire any men in more than a year. The first retailer offered a wide variety of merchandise and attracted all kinds of customers, who showed no preference with respect to the gender of the staff. The second retailer specialized in women's beauty products and served customers who generally felt more comfortable dealing with female staff. The journalist judged that the first retailer, and not the second, had unfairly discriminatory hiring practices.

Which one of the following principles, if established, provides the most justification for the journalist's judgment?

(A) Larger retailers have a responsibility to maintain fair hiring practices, while small retailers may not have the ability to attract a diverse staff.

(B) A store that does not hire any members of a certain group is not unfairly discriminatory in its hiring practices if it does not receive many job applications from people in that group.

(C) A company can be deemed discriminatory only if it does not hire any members of a particular group over a substantial period of time.

(D) It is evidence of unfair discrimination if any retail store has a gender distribution of employees different from the gender distribution of the entire population.

(E) It is unfairly discriminatory for a company to hire one group of people to the exclusion of others, except when its customers demonstrate a partiality toward the preferentially hired group.

1. Identify

The question stem asks you for a *principle* that can *justify* the judgment, so this is a Justify question.

> The differences between Sufficient Assumption and Justify questions are cosmetic. Your job is the same on both.

2. Analyze

You should treat the journalist's judgment as the conclusion, since that's what you're asked to justify. The evidence is the set of facts in the passage. Here's how the argument works:

• Both retailers failed to hire men in over a year.

• The first retailer offered a wide variety of merchandise and attracted all kinds of customers, who showed no preference with respect to the gender of the staff.

• The second retailer specialized in women's beauty products and served customers who generally felt more comfortable dealing with female staff.

Therefore, the first retailer, but not the second, had unfairly discriminatory hiring practices.

The argument provides no evidence for what counts as unfairly discriminatory. This is an entirely new concept. There's a big shift between the characteristics of the first retailer and *unfairly discriminatory*.

Just as in Sufficient Assumption questions, the flaw in Justify questions typically comes in the form of a Concept Shift:

What two non-identical concepts are intended to be connected?

The set of characteristics describing the first retailer is intended to be connected to *unfairly discriminatory*.

Thus, the Concept Shift is:

The characteristics of the first retailer ⚡ Unfairly discriminatory

3. Prephrase

Since there are a bunch of differences between the two retailers, there are a bunch of different ways to make the link between the characteristics of the first retailer and unfairly discriminatory. You don't have to Prephrase any particular principle. What you need is anything that links the characteristics of the first retailer to unfairly discriminatory but does not make that link for the second retailer.

4. Attack

You can use the New Concept Tool, since *unfairly discriminatory* is entirely new and appears in the conclusion. The correct answer must address unfair discrimination. Choice (A) doesn't address discrimination at all, and choice (C) doesn't address *unfair* discrimination. You can get rid of those right away.

Now attack the answers using the same **Real Question** you use for Sufficient Assumption questions: *Does this guarantee the conclusion?*

Choice (A) was cut using the New Concept Tool.

> (B)   A store that does not hire any members of a certain group is not unfairly discriminatory in its hiring practices if it does not receive many job applications from people in that group.

Choice (B): *Does this guarantee the conclusion?* The argument provides no information whatsoever about the applicants for jobs at the stores. This is entirely **out of scope**. *Cut it.*

Choice (C) was cut using the New Concept Tool.

> (D)   It is evidence of unfair discrimination if any retail store has a gender distribution of employees different from the gender distribution of the entire population.

Choice (D): *Does this guarantee the conclusion?* If this is the principle, then both retailers unfairly discriminated. This doesn't guarantee the conclusion that the first retailer is to blame and the second isn't. *Cut it.*

> (E)   It is unfairly discriminatory for a company to hire one group of people to the exclusion of others, except when its customers demonstrate a partiality toward the preferentially hired group.

Choice (E): *Does this guarantee the conclusion?* This says that any company that hires one group over another is discriminatory except when the customers prefer the hired group. The second retailer's customers prefer women, but the first retailer's customers show no preference. This justifies the conclusion that the first but not the second retailer was unfairly discriminatory. *Keep it.*

Choice (E) is the correct answer.

The New Concept Tool also works for Justify questions, but don't use it on anything other than Sufficient Assumption and Justify questions.

Try another example:

6. Larry: I allowed you to use my phone to make a five-
minute long-distance call just last week, so in fairness
you should let me use your phone to make a long-
distance call now. The battery on my phone is empty,
and I only need to make a single five minute call.

Donyell: But your phone service has unlimited long-
distance calling for no extra fee, while long-distance
calls are expensive from my phone, so I'm not
obligated to let you use my phone.

Which one of the following principles, if valid,
provides the strongest justification for Donyell's
claim?

(A) One is not obligated to return a favor if doing so
would entail a greater cost than the initial favor.

(B) One is never obligated to return favors to those
who would not do the same if put in the same
position.

(C) One is not obligated to return a favor unless it is
urgently necessary.

(D) Whenever a requested favor is similar to a favor
previously afforded, the request should be
granted.

(E) One should grant any favor requested by a friend
that is not too costly, regardless of the reason for
the request.

> Justify questions often feature general language in the answer choices. You have to match each general concept to something specific in the passage.

1. Identify

The question stem asks you for a *principle* to *justify* Donyell's claim, so this is a Justify
question.

2. Analyze

This is a two-speaker passage, which can occur on almost any question type. In this
case, you should focus on Donyell's argument, since that's what the question is all
about. You should of course read Larry's argument, but you shouldn't waste your
time with a detailed analysis.

Donyell has a counterargument, and she directly states her conclusion in the last
sentence:

- Larry's phone service has unlimited long-distance calling
for no extra fee.

- Long-distance calls are expensive from Donyell's phone.

Therefore, Donyell is not obligated to let Larry use her phone.

Donyell's argument is flawed. Just because it would cost more doesn't mean that
Donyell isn't obligated to return the favor. So there's a Concept Shift.

What two non-identical concepts are intended to be connected?

The *higher cost* is intended to lead to *not obligated*.

Thus, the Concept Shift is:

Higher cost ⚡ Not obligated

3. Prephrase

The correct answer needs to justify the connection between the higher cost and what
Donyell isn't obligated to do. You should expect something like this:

Justification: Donyell is not obligated to return the
favor if it costs more than the original favor.

> Your Prephrased answer may not use such general language, but that's okay. Just be ready to match your answer to the more general language in the answer choices.

4. Attack

You can use the New Concept Tool, since *not obligated* is new to the conclusion. The correct answer needs to provide some basis for making a claim about obligation. Choices (D) and (E) do not address obligation at all, so you can eliminate them up front.

> (A) One is not obligated to return a favor if doing so would entail a greater cost than the initial favor.

Choice (A): *Does this guarantee the conclusion?* Yes, since Donyell's returning the favor would cost more than the initial favor, this justifies her lack of obligation. *Keep it.*

> (B) One is never obligated to return favors to those who would not do the same if put in the same position.

Choice (B): *Does this guarantee the conclusion?* The passage provides no evidence that Larry wouldn't have returned the favor in Donyell's position, so this is completely **out of scope**. *Cut it.*

> (C) One is not obligated to return a favor unless it is urgently necessary.

Choice (C): *Does this guarantee the conclusion?* The passage doesn't reveal whether the favor is urgently necessary, so it's unclear whether there's an obligation with this one. Since it's unclear, the conclusion is not guaranteed. *Cut it.*

Choices (D) and (E) were already cut using the New Concept Tool.

Choice (A) is the correct answer.

8.7 THE BIG PICTURE

You can solve some Logical Reasoning questions more easily by diagramming them. Diagramming is especially useful when the passage has more than one conditional or quantifying statement.

The most common question types on which you may find diagramming useful are Inference, Sufficient Assumption, and Parallel Reasoning questions (which you'll learn about in Lecture 9).

Here are some general principles for diagramming:

> Each test features only a few questions that you really need to diagram. If a passage has only one conditional or quantity statement, or if it doesn't look like you can make any links, make sure it's really necessary before you start diagramming things.

- **Avoid abstraction.** Abbreviations are useful, but don't use meaningless symbols for what you can express more clearly with initials or in a word or two.

  Example: If it rains, it will be wet.

Not:	A → B
But instead:	Rain → Wet

- **Be consistent.** If a concept appears in more than one statement, diagram it in the same way.

  Example: All pictures are taken with a camera, and all cameras have batteries.

Not:	Picture → Camera; Cam. → Batt.
But instead:	Picture → Camera; Camera → Batt.

- **Always symbolize the contrapositive** when you symbolize a conditional.

  Example: No scientists are teenagers.

Not just:	Scientist → ~Teenager
But instead:	Scientist → ~Teenager
	Teenager → ~Scientist

8.7.1 DIAGRAMMING WITH CONDITIONALS

If a passage has more than one conditional, a diagram of the conditionals might be useful. Don't start drawing conditionals as soon as you see one in a passage. Keep reading and notice whether there are several conditionals and whether they can be linked. If it appears they can be linked, then start making the chains right away. That is, add the second conditional to the first immediately instead of drawing two separate symbols and then combining them later.

Here are some examples:

> 7. All of the highest-grossing movies last year were sequels. No sequel can be truly original, and truly original movies are always influential.
>
> If the above statements are true, which one of the following must be true?

> Conditional statements in the Logical Reasoning section appear most often in Inference passages, although they also frequently appear in passages for Sufficient Assumption and Parallel questions.

1. Identify

The question stem asks you for something that *must be true*, so this is an Inference question.

2. Analyze

As this is an Inference question, the passage is just a set of premises. This time, the premises are three conditionals. Here's how you would diagram them:

All of the highest-grossing movies last year were sequels.

$$\text{High G} \longrightarrow \text{Seq}$$
$$\sim\text{Seq} \longrightarrow \sim\text{High G}$$

No sequel can be truly original.

You can connect this conditional directly to the first one to begin to form a chain.

$$\text{High G} \longrightarrow \text{Seq} \longrightarrow \sim\text{Orig}$$
$$\text{Orig} \longrightarrow \sim\text{Seq} \longrightarrow \sim\text{High G}$$

Truly original movies are always influential.

This next conditional does *not* fit onto the beginning or end of the chain. You could create a branched chain, but it is usually better to symbolize such statements separately.

$$\text{Orig} \longrightarrow \text{Influ}$$
$$\sim\text{Influ} \longrightarrow \sim \text{Orig}$$

So somewhere in the blank space in your test booklet, you would have all the important information from the passage symbolized like this:

$$\text{High G} \longrightarrow \text{Seq} \longrightarrow \sim\text{Orig} \qquad \text{Orig} \longrightarrow \text{Influ}$$
$$\text{Orig} \longrightarrow \sim\text{Seq} \longrightarrow \sim\text{High G} \qquad \sim\text{Influ} \longrightarrow \sim \text{Orig}$$

3. Prephrase

When an Inference passage allows you to build a chain, the correct answer often consists of something that follows the chain. That is, it starts on the left end of the chain and concludes at the right end. Be careful not to pick something that goes backwards.

High G → Seq → ~Orig
Orig → ~Seq → ~High G

Orig → Influ
~Influ → ~ Orig

4. Attack

For Inference questions, the **Real Question** is: *Is this guaranteed to be true?*

(A)   Truly original movies are never very profitable
for their production companies.

Choice (A): *Is this guaranteed to be true?* Nothing in the passage says anything about profit, so this is completely **out of scope**. *Cut it.*

(B)   No truly original movie was among the highest-grossing movies last year.

Choice (B): *Is this guaranteed to be true?* This answer choice says Original → ~High G, which follows the chain perfectly. *Keep it.*

(C)   None of the highest-grossing movies last year was a critical success.

Choice (C): *Is this guaranteed to be true?* There's nothing in the passage about critical success, so this is **out of scope**. *Cut it.*

(D)   None of the highest-grossing movies last year was influential.

Choices (D): *Is this guaranteed to be true?* If you know a movie was one of the highest grossers, the chain allows you to conclude that it was a sequel and not original, but there is no connection that allows you to jump over to the other conditional and make any conclusions about its influence. *Cut it.*

(E)   The lowest-grossing movie last year was truly original.

Choice (E): *Is this guaranteed to be true?* This choice attempts to go **backwards** along the chain from ~High G to Orig. That's not allowed. *Cut it.*

Choice (B) is the correct answer.

Here is another example:

8. If the hamburgers are undercooked, then they should be put back on the grill. If they are overcooked, they should be thrown out. And they are bound to be either undercooked or overcooked.

If the statements above are true, which one of the following must also be true?

1. Identify

This question stem also asks you for something that *must be true*, so it's an Inference question.

2. Analyze

This inference passage has two conditionals and an "either...or" statement. Here's how you should diagram them:

If the hamburgers are undercooked, then they should be put back on the grill.

Under → Grill
~Grill → ~Under

If they are overcooked, they should be thrown out.

Over → Toss
~Toss → ~Over

They are bound to be either undercooked or overcooked.

This statement looks weird, but if you think about it, it's also a conditional. By telling you that the burgers must be one or the other, the statement is saying that *IF* they are not one, *THEN* they are the other.

$$\sim\!\text{Under} \longrightarrow \text{Over}$$
$$\sim\!\text{Over} \longrightarrow \text{Under}$$

> An either/or statement is really a conditional in disguise. "Either X or Y" means:
>
> $$\sim\!X \longrightarrow Y$$
> $$\sim\!Y \longrightarrow X$$

With the addition of this third conditional symbol, it now becomes clear that you can link all three together in a long chain:

$$\sim\!\text{Grill} \longrightarrow \sim\!\text{Under} \longrightarrow \text{Over} \longrightarrow \text{Toss}$$
$$\sim\!\text{Toss} \longrightarrow \sim\!\text{Over} \longrightarrow \text{Under} \longrightarrow \text{Grill}$$

This chain contains all the information in the passage, so you can ignore anything else on the page and simply focus on this.

3. Prephrase

Since this passage allows for a chain to be formed, expect the correct answer choice to follow the chain. It may begin at the far left or somewhere in the middle, but it will finish at the right-hand end of the chain.

4. Attack

(A)   The hamburgers should be carefully cooked to avoid either overcooking or undercooking them.

Choice (A): *Is this guaranteed to be true?* The passage doesn't allow for this—it says the burgers *will* be overcooked or undercooked. *Cut it.*

(B)   The hamburgers should be put back on the grill only if it will not cause them to be overcooked.

Choice (B): *Is this guaranteed to be true?* There is nothing about avoiding overcooking in the passage. *Cut it.*

(C)   The hamburgers should be put back on the grill if doing so will help avoid undercooked hamburgers.

Choice (C): *Is this guaranteed to be true?* The passage provides no reasoning for *why* the burgers should go on the grill. If they're undercooked, put them on the grill. That's it. *Cut it.*

(D)   If the hamburgers are not overcooked, they should be thrown out.

Choices (D): *Is this guaranteed to be true?* If the burgers are not overcooked, then the chain tells us they should be put on the grill, not thrown out. This is wrong. *Cut it.*

(E)   If the hamburgers are not undercooked, they should be thrown out.

Choice (E): *Is this guaranteed to be true?* This choice follows the chain perfectly. *Keep it.*

Choice (E) is the correct answer.

The last two examples were both Inference questions, and you were asked to draw a valid conclusion of your own. Many Sufficient Assumption questions are also diagrammable, but they work slightly differently. Sufficient Assumption questions contain a conclusion, but the conclusion is always insufficiently supported by the premises. Your job is to fill in the missing piece that will guarantee that the conclusion is true. In the context of diagrammable arguments, this usually means adding a missing link in a conditional chain.

Your strategy in these cases is to *separately* diagram both the premises and the conclusion, and determine the missing link. It's very important to keep the premises apart from the conclusion—keep them above the line, while the conclusion goes below the line. Here's an example:

9. Nothing that resists change is in its simplest state, and anything that satisfies people is in its simplest state. So nothing that satisfies people is a bureaucracy.

The conclusion above follows logically if which one of the following is assumed?

(A)   All bureaucracies are in their simplest state.
(B)   All bureaucracies resist change.
(C)   Anything in its simplest state satisfies people.
(D)   No bureaucracies resist change.
(E)   Nothing that resists change satisfies people.

1. Identify

The question stem asks for something that would make the conclusion *follow logically*, so this is a Sufficient Assumption question.

2. Analyze

The passage is made up of conditional statements. Thus, the approach is to *separately* diagram both the premises and the conclusion and determine the missing link. Here are the first two conditionals:

Nothing that <u>R</u>esists <u>C</u>hange is in its <u>S</u>implest <u>S</u>tate, and anything that <u>S</u>atisfies <u>P</u>eople is in its <u>S</u>implest <u>S</u>tate.

$$RC \longrightarrow \sim SS$$
$$SS \longrightarrow \sim RC$$
$$SP \longrightarrow SS$$
$$\sim SS \longrightarrow \sim SP$$

These conditionals can be combined into a chain:

$$RC \longrightarrow \sim SS \longrightarrow \sim SP$$
$$SP \longrightarrow SS \longrightarrow \sim RC$$

Next, symbolize the conclusion of the argument. Be sure to keep it separate from the premises:

So nothing that <u>S</u>atisfies <u>P</u>eople is a <u>B</u>ureaucracy.

$$SP \longrightarrow \sim B$$
$$B \longrightarrow \sim SP$$

> Your diagram for a Sufficient Assumption question looks different from your diagram for an Inference question. You must keep the premises and conclusion separate since the premises contain good logic but the conclusion is questionable. You don't want them to mix.

Finally, take a look at the difference between the premises and conclusion and look for the missing link:

Premises: $RC \longrightarrow \sim SS \longrightarrow \sim SP$
$SP \longrightarrow SS \longrightarrow \sim RC$
_____
Conclusion: $SP \longrightarrow \sim B$
$B \longrightarrow \sim SP$

In this case, notice that *bureaucracy* is a new concept that appears only in the conclusion. That means that your job is to find a way to link the new concept of bureaucracy to the existing chain in the premises.

3. Prephrase

How can you find a way to link B to the premise chain?

First, notice that one of the conditionals in the premises starts with SP, and one of the conditionals in the conclusion also starts with SP. This is a good place to start. If you can find a way to add a link to the premise chain that will enable you to start with SP on the left and end with ~B on the right, then you will have guaranteed the conclusion. Since the LSAT writers love long chains, the most likely place they will add the link is at the end of the chain.

Premises: RC → ~SS → ~SP — missing link
SP → SS → (~RC → ~B)

Conclusion: SP → ~B
B → ~SP

Similarly, you can look at the contrapositives. One of the conditionals in the premises ends with ~SP, and one of the conditionals in the conclusion also ends with ~SP. If you can find a way to add a link to the premise chain that will enable you to start with B and end with ~SP, then you will have again guaranteed the conclusion. And again, the most likely place for the correct answer to do this is at one end of the chain:

Premises: (B → RC) → ~SS → ~SP — missing links
SP → SS → (~RC → ~B)

Conclusion: SP → ~B
B → ~SP

You are now equipped with a very good Prephrased answer:

Sufficient Assumption: The correct answer choice
will contain one of the identified missing links.

4. Attack

As is true of any other Sufficient Assumption question that contains a new concept in the conclusion, you can use the New Concept Tool to eliminate any answer choice that does not address the new concept. In this example, you can eliminate any answer choice that does not mention bureaucracy. This gets rid of choices (C) and (E).

(A)   All bureaucracies are in their simplest state.

Choice (A): *Does this guarantee the conclusion?* This says B → SS, but you're looking for B → ~SS. *Cut it.*

(B)   All bureaucracies resist change.

Choice (B): *Does this guarantee the conclusion?* This says B → RC, which is exactly the link you are looking for. *Keep it.*

Choice (C) was already cut using the New Concept Tool.

(D)   No bureaucracies resist change.

Choice (D): *Does this guarantee the conclusion?* This says B → ~RC, but you're looking for B → RC. *Cut it.*

Choice (E) was already cut using the New Concept Tool.

Choice (B) is the correct answer.

8.7.2 DIAGRAMMING QUANTIFYING STATEMENTS

Remember, conditional statements are always "all or nothing" situations. Any statement that talks about *some, many, most, sometimes, often,* or other similar "halfway" situations cannot be symbolized as a conditional.

However, you can use *other* symbols to diagram these quantifying relationships. Furthermore, you can combine quantifying symbols and conditional symbols to make deductions.

8.7.2.1 *Some*

As you learned previously, the LSAT uses a variety of different terms that all mean *some*. These phrases include

- Some
- Many
- At least one
- A few

- Several
- Sometimes
- Often
- Frequently

When you see one of these words or phrases, symbolize it with a dotted line. For example:

Some operas are French.

The dotted line works in both directions. It tells you that some operas are French, and that some French things are operas.

8.7.2.2 *Most*

The LSAT uses the word *most* to mean something more specific than *some*. *Most* means *a majority* or *more than half*. There are a variety of different terms that all mean the same thing, including

- Most
- Majority
- More than half

- Nearly all
- Usually
- Almost always

When you see one of these words or phrases, again symbolize it with a dotted line. In addition to the dotted line, write the word *most* above or below the appropriate word. For example:

Most infants have hair.

This symbol tells you that most infants have hair, and that <u>some</u> (not most) things that have hair are infants.

It's important to put the word *most* in the right place. If you had made a mistake in the previous example by writing this symbol:

Infants
·
·
·
most
Have hair

WRONG

Then your symbol would mean, "Most of those who have hair are infants." This is not what the original statement said, and not correct.

(sidebar) Never try to negate or make the contrapositive of a quantity statement.

(sidebar) Write the word "most" next to the thing it modifies in the sentence, regardless of whether it's at the top or the bottom of the diagram.

8.7.2.3 Combining Quantity Symbols

You <u>cannot</u> make any deductions from two *some* statements alone.

For example, consider the following two statements:

Some fruits are apples.

Some fruits are oranges.

You can correctly symbolize the two statements like this:

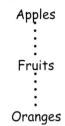

Apples
⋮
Fruits
⋮
Oranges

But you cannot make any deductions across two dotted lines. That is, you cannot deduce that some apples are oranges.

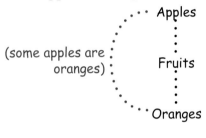

(some apples are oranges)   Apples ⋮ Fruits ⋮ Oranges

WRONG

You <u>can</u> make deductions from two *most* statements, if they are arranged properly. This is called the Most-Most Overlap. Think about this situation.

Most cars use gasoline.

Most cars have CD players.

You can symbolize the two statements like this:

Use gasoline
⋮
most
Cars
most
⋮
Have CD players

And in this case, you can deduce that there are <u>some</u> things that both use gasoline and have CD players.

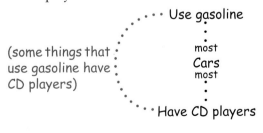

(some things that use gasoline have CD players)   Use gasoline ⋮ most Cars most ⋮ Have CD players

VALID DEDUCTION

Remember, the dotted line works in both directions: some things that have CD players use gasoline, and some things that use gasoline have CD players.

However, in order to be able to make a deduction, you have to make sure that both *mosts* are attached to the same word. Think about this example:

Most infants have hair.

A majority of those who have hair can drive.

You can correctly symbolize the two statements like this:

But in this case, you cannot deduce that some infants can drive.

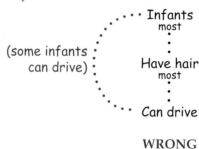

WRONG

Thus, the general rule is that **you cannot connect two quantity statements, except in the case of the Most-Most Overlap**.

8.7.2.4   Combining Quantity Symbols with Conditional Symbols

It is sometimes possible to make deductions by combining quantity statements with conditional statements. In order to do so, the quantity symbol must be initially connected to the *left-hand side* of the conditional symbol. Take a look at this example:

Wild fruits are often yellow.

All wild fruits contain seeds.

The correct symbolization of these statements is:

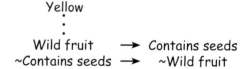

When you make the contrapositive of the conditional statement, don't bother trying to incorporate the quantity symbol. It's impossible to make any deductions like that.

But you can make another deduction in this case. Since the *some* symbol is initially connected to the *left-hand side* of the conditional symbol, you can deduce that it also connects to the *right-hand side*, like this:

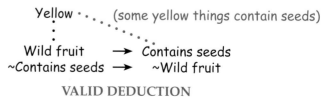

VALID DEDUCTION

There are only two ways you can make a deduction using quantity statements: when you have the Most-Most Overlap, and when you have a quantity statement properly connected to the left-hand side of a conditional statement.

On the other hand, you **cannot** make a deduction when the quantity symbol initially connects to the *right-hand side* of the conditional. That's akin to going backwards against the arrow of a conditional, which is of course not allowed. For example:

A few mammals have wings.

All cats are mammals.

The correct symbolization of these statements is:

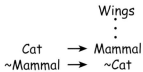

But you cannot deduce that some cats have wings.

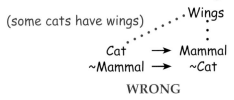

WRONG

> When you make the contrapositive of the conditional statement, don't bother trying to incorporate the quantity symbol. It's impossible to make any deductions like that.

8.7.3 EXAMPLES

Here's an example of a question involving quantity statements:

10. Most serious students are happy students, and most serious students go to graduate school. Furthermore, all students who go to graduate school are overworked.

    Which one of the following can be properly inferred from the statements above?

Test 41, Section 3, Question 25

1. Identify

The question stem asks you for something that can be *properly inferred* from the passage, so this is an Inference question.

2. Analyze

Since this is an Inference question, the passage is just a set of premises. This time, the premises are a mixture of conditional and quantity statements, so it makes sense to diagram them. Here's how you would do that:

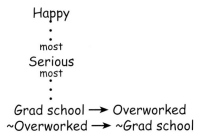

3. Prephrase

There are several Prephrased inferences you can make here. First, you have a Most-Most Overlap, so you can infer that some happy students go to grad school. After making this deduction, because both of the *some* symbols are initially connected to the *left-hand side* of the conditional symbol, you can deduce that they both also connect to the *right-hand side*. So here are all the inferences you can draw in this situation:

Inferences: Some happy students go to grad school.
Some happy students are overworked.
Most serious students are overworked.

4. Attack

For Inference questions, the **Real Question** is: *Is this guaranteed to be true?*

(A)   Most overworked students are happy students.

Choice (A): *Is this guaranteed to be true?* You can say that *some* overworked students are happy students, but not *most*. This is **extreme**. *Cut it.*

(B)   Some happy students are overworked.

Choice (B): *Is this guaranteed to be true?* This is a perfect match for the Prephrased inference. *Keep it.*

(C)   All overworked students are serious students.

Choice (C): *Is this guaranteed to be true?* This doesn't match the diagram. *Cut it.*

(D)   Some unhappy students go to graduate school.

Choices (D): *Is this guaranteed to be true?* You can never make contrapositives using quantity statements, so you cannot say anything at all about *un*happy students. This is completely **out of scope**. *Cut it.*

(E)   All serious students are overworked.

Choice (E): *Is this guaranteed to be true?* You can say that *most* serious students are overworked, but not *all*. This is **extreme**. *Cut it.*

Choice (B) is the correct answer.

Here's another example:

11.   Most automobile companies are foreign companies, even though very few foreign companies are automobile companies. It follows that some companies that have domestic production plants are foreign companies.

Which one of the following, if assumed, enables the argument's conclusion to be properly drawn?

(A)   Most companies that have domestic production plants are automobile companies.
(B)   Some automobile companies are not foreign companies.
(C)   Most automobile companies have domestic production plants.
(D)   Many foreign companies are automobile companies.
(E)   Many automobile companies have domestic production plants.

1. Identify

The question asks for an assumption that would enable the conclusion to be *properly drawn*, so it's a Sufficient Assumption question.

2. Analyze

Since this is a Sufficient Assumption question, you are looking for the conclusion, premises, and Concept Shift. The last sentence is the conclusion, as it has a conclusion indicator. The rest of the argument is premises. Because these statements all contain quantity words, you should separately diagram the premises and conclusion.

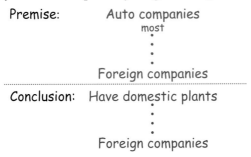

As you can see, the concept of having a domestic production plant is a brand new idea that appears only in the conclusion. Thus, the Concept Shift in this argument is between *automobile companies* and *having domestic production plants*. You'll need to find some way to link these two ideas.

$$\text{Automobile companies} \lightning \text{Having domestic production plants}$$

3. Prephrase

You need to find an answer choice that provides a link between the two sides of the Concept Shift. However, just linking *automobile companies* and *having domestic production plants* is not enough. The link needs to be formed in such a way that guarantees the additional link in the conclusion. You have to be able to deduce a link between *foreign companies* and *having domestic production plants*. As you know, there are only two ways that you can make deductions using quantity statements: when you have the Most-Most Overlap, and when you have a properly arranged conditional statement.

> Use this "missing links" technique on Sufficient Assumption questions.

So there are two Prephrased answers that would allow the argument's conclusion to be properly drawn:

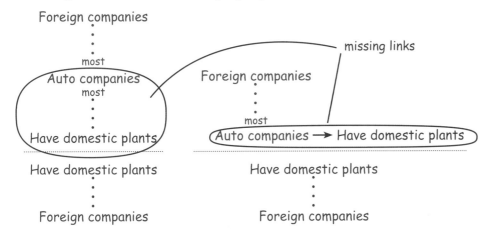

So you can Prephrase two possible answers:

Sufficient Assumption: Most automobile companies have domestic production plants.

All automobile companies have domestic production plants.

4. Attack

Since this is a Sufficient Assumption question with a new concept in the conclusion, you can use the New Concept Tool. If an answer doesn't address domestic production plants, you can get rid of it. That eliminates choices (B) and (D) right away.

For Sufficient Assumption questions, the **Real Question** is: *Does this guarantee the conclusion?*

(A)   Most companies that have domestic production
         plants are automobile companies.

Choice (A): *Does this guarantee the conclusion?* This comes close to the Prephrased answer, but the *most* is in the wrong place. This does not allow you to use the Most-Most Overlap, so this doesn't guarantee the conclusion. *Cut it.*

Choice (B) was eliminated using the New Concept Tool.

(C)   Most automobile companies have domestic
         production plants.

Choice (C): *Does this guarantee the conclusion?* This matches perfectly with the Prephrased answer, and it allows you to use the Most-Most Overlap, which guarantees the conclusion. *Keep it.*

Choice (D) was eliminated using the New Concept Tool.

(E)   Many automobile companies have domestic
         production plants.

Choice (E): *Does this guarantee the conclusion? Many* means the same thing as *some,* which does not allow you to make any deductions and does not guarantee the conclusion will be true. *Cut it.*

Choice (C) is the correct answer.

Again, there are only a few questions per test where you'll need to use this diagramming technique, but if you're aiming for a top score, you should practice this as much as possible, since it's fairly complex.

STOP. THIS IS THE END OF LECTURE 7. DO NOT PROCEED TO THE CORRESPONDING EXAM UNTIL INSTRUCTED TO DO SO IN CLASS.

LECTURE (8) CHAPTER (9)

METHOD QUESTIONS

9.1 IDENTIFY

9.1.1 IDENTIFYING METHOD QUESTIONS

All **Method** questions follow the same pattern:

1. **The passage contains an argument.** Since Method questions are all about reasoning, they always refer to arguments. As a result, every Method question has an argument-based passage.

2. **The question asks you to describe *how* the argument reaches its conclusion.** This is what distinguishes Method questions from every other question type. Method questions ask you to identify the *reasoning* behind an argument—how the argument proceeds from premises to conclusion.

3. **The question does not require that you consider the strength of the argument's reasoning.** Method questions are flaw-independent, which means you don't have to consider whether the argument in the passage is flawed. You shouldn't waste your time evaluating the strength of the argument's reasoning.

Here are some examples of Method question stems:

> The argument proceeds by
>
> The specialist's argument does which one of the following?
>
> Which one of the following is an argumentative strategy employed in the argument?
>
> Which one of the following most accurately describes a technique used in the banker's argument?

KEY PHRASES
Method Questions

Proceeds by

Argumentative strategy
Technique
Method

All of these ask you to describe the *reasoning* behind the argument. Any question that asks you to describe a *method*, *technique*, or *strategy* of reasoning is a Method question.

Method questions appear roughly once or twice per test.

9.2 ANALYZE

9.2.1 ANALYZING METHOD QUESTIONS

Method questions have an argument in the passage, but they are flaw-independent questions. As a result, you should analyze Method questions by identifying:

1. The conclusion

2. The premises

Don't look for flaws on Method questions.

Since you've already had plenty of practice analyzing arguments for conclusions and premises, it's time to talk about Prephrasing.

9.3 PREPHRASE

9.3.1 PREPHRASING THE METHOD

Prephrasing on Method questions means telling the general story of the argument, divorced from the details.

Suppose June argues that, because every dentist she knows recommends Superbrite toothpaste, Superbrite must be the best toothpaste. June's conclusion is that Superbrite is the best, based on the premise that every dentist she knows recommends Superbrite.

For a Method question, the details of the argument do not matter. You shouldn't care that the item in question is *Superbrite toothpaste* or that the authority that June cites is a bunch of *dentists*. To Prephrase on a Method question, you should tell the general story without those details. Here's an example of a Prephrased method to June's argument:

> Method: The argument concludes that one product is the best based on an appeal to a set of authorities on that product.

Reading this, you wouldn't know that the product was toothpaste or that the authorities were dentists. However, this is precisely the kind of correct answer you should expect on a Method question, so it is precisely the kind of Prephrased answer you want to have.

9.3.2 Drill: The Method

Prephrase the method of argument used in each of the following passages.

1. Computer software viruses are a serious threat. Like the viruses that harm people, they spread and replicate inside a host. We can protect our bodies from viruses with vaccines that teach the body to detect and neutralize these biological threats. It is reasonable to conclude, then, that the best way to protect computers is to program them to recognize and attack hostile viruses.

   What is a technique of reasoning used in the argument?

   _____

   _____

   _____

   _____

2. Gary: The police department's new crime fighting strategies are not making this city any safer. Despite all of the new policies and methods, the annual number of crimes in the city is the same as it was before these changes took effect.

   Joan: The statistic you cite does not tell the whole story. Prior to the department's efforts, many people had moved away from the city. Because of these new strategies, many former residents have returned, resulting in a substantial increase in the population without an accompanying rise in the incidence of crime.

   Joan responds to Gary's argument by

   _____

   _____

   _____

   _____

3. Karen: A great deal of air pollution is created by gasoline-powered engines. Soon, more people will be using hybrid vehicles that consume far less gasoline for every mile they travel. As hybrid vehicle use increases, automobile-related pollution will decrease.

Steve: Don't be so sure that drivers of hybrid vehicles won't start driving more. Your conclusion depends on driving habits remaining the same, but who is to say that people won't start driving more once they are paying less to operate their vehicles on a per-mile basis.

In response to Karen's argument, Steve does which one of the following?

_____

_____

_____

_____

4. Many people in the Bainbrook community have reported problems with the reception on one cable television channel. It has been suggested that the problem is a result of a damaged junction box. However, such damage would affect the internet service that the cable system also provides. No one has complained about any internet service disruptions. Therefore, we should investigate the possibility of a faulty signal at the source of the channel's transmission.

The argument proceeds by

_____

_____

_____

_____

Answers

1. This argument reaches its conclusion by **drawing an analogy** between computer viruses and biological viruses.

2. Joan reaches her conclusion by **introducing additional considerations that point to a different conclusion** from Gary's.

3. Steve reaches his conclusion by **questioning an assumption** inherent in Karen's argument.

4. This argument concludes that one particular cause of the reception problem should be investigated by **ruling out an alternative possible cause.**

9.4 ATTACK

9.4.1 THE REAL QUESTION

The **Real Question** for Method Questions is:

Does this match the argument?

If an answer choice describes what the argument actually does, then it's a good answer. Otherwise, get rid of it.

The **Real Question** reflects the similarity between Method and Flaw questions. Method questions are just like Flaw questions in that the correct answer describes the argument using vague language. For both Method and Flaw questions, if an answer choice doesn't match the argument, it's wrong. The only difference is that a Flaw question describes an argument's *flawed* reasoning, whereas a Method question describes reasoning with no attention to an argument's flaw.

> You don't need to worry about a list of different kinds of distracters for Method questions. Every incorrect answer fails to match the passage. Every correct answer matches.

9.5 PUTTING IT ALL TOGETHER

Here's an example:

1. Lloyd: The skepticism surrounding the results of the report is unwarranted. Several well-respected academics put considerable time and effort into the published version, so it's highly doubtful that there would be any calculation errors in it.

    Jesse: But even a brief glance at the report reveals several typographical and formatting errors, so some skepticism towards the calculations is warranted.

    Jesse responds to Lloyd's argument by

Here's the approach:

1. Identify

This question asks *how* Jesse responds, so it's asking about Jesse's *method*. This is a Method question.

2. Analyze

In this case, there are two speakers, but the question is about Jesse. Jesse's argument has an indicator, *so*, which points to his conclusion that some skepticism towards the calculations is warranted. Why? Because the report contains typographical and formatting errors. Here's the argument:

> Even a brief glance at the report reveals several typographical and formatting errors.
> ....
> **Therefore**, some skepticism towards the calculations is warranted.

3. Prephrase

To Prephrase on a Method question, tell the general story of the argument. How does Jesse establish his conclusion? He cites evidence of careless errors in the report. These careless errors don't imply that anything in the report is necessarily wrong, but they do call into question the quality of the report. Here's a good Prephrased answer:

> Method: Jesse responds by citing evidence that calls into question the quality of the report.

4. Attack

Remember the **Real Question** for Method Questions: *Does this match the argument?*

(A) citing more authoritative reports with contradictory results

Choice (A): *Does this match the argument?* Jesse doesn't cite any reports other than the one Lloyd is talking about. *Cut it.*

(B) providing evidence that weakens the claim that the calculations could not have been flawed

Choice (B): *Does this match the argument?* Jesse provides evidence that questions the *quality* of the report, so that would weaken the claim that the calculations could not have been flawed. *Keep it.*

(C) proving that the authors of the report did not put much time into it

Choice (C): *Does this match the argument?* Jess doesn't *prove* anything, and he doesn't even mention the time the authors put into the report. *Cut it.*

(D)   questioning whether the authors of the report are
          truly well respected

Choice (D): *Does this match the argument?* Jesse never questions the authors' credentials, so this can't be right. *Cut it.*

(E)   pointing out errors in the calculations in the
          published version of the report

Choice (E): *Does this match the argument?* Jesse points out errors, but not errors in the calculations themselves. This answer is tricky, but it doesn't match the argument. *Cut it.*

Choice (B) is the correct answer.

9.6   VARIATIONS

9.6.1   ROLE QUESTIONS

Role questions are Method questions that ask you about only **one claim** within an argument. They ask what *role* a claim plays within an argument. Since arguments are made up of premises and conclusions, most claims are either premises or conclusions.

Role questions usually appear about once or twice per test, although the December 2003 LSAT had five of them.

Role questions are easy to identify because they always repeat the claim they're asking you about within the question stem. Here are some typical Role question stems:

> Which one of the following most accurately describes the role played in the argument by the assertion that the Tunguska event was probably due to a meteoroid impact?

> The claim that the decaying algal biomass will deplete the oxygen in the pond water figures in the argument in which one of the following ways?

KEY PHRASES
Role Questions

Describes the role played
The claim that...figures in the argument in which way

These questions present the claim they're asking about within the question stem, and they ask about that claim's role within the argument.

In terms of your approach, the difference between Method and Role questions is that, for the latter, you are only focusing on one claim. When you Prephrase, you are looking to explain the role of just one claim in the argument.

9.6.1.1   Subsidiary Conclusions

Some arguments contain a **subsidiary conclusion,** also referred to as an **intermediate conclusion**. A subsidiary conclusion, just like any other conclusion, is based on evidence and often features conclusion indicators. However, it is not the main conclusion of the argument. The main conclusion uses the subsidiary conclusion as its own premise—the subsidiary conclusion acts as evidence to support the main conclusion.

Role questions sometimes ask you about subsidiary conclusions, but they rarely use this concept as a distracter. In the past twelve years, when an answer choice says something to the effect of "The claim acts as a subsidiary conclusion that supports the argument's main conclusion," it has been the correct answer about 80% of the time. If you see an answer choice that mentions a subsidiary conclusion, check carefully and remember that it's very likely to be correct.

Subsidiary conclusions can also appear in the passages for other question types, making it harder to find the main conclusion. That's why you need to get very good at using all the techniques for finding the conclusion as discussed in Lecture 2.

Here's a sample Role question:

2. Physician: Dr. Retzler's claim that people can lose weight eating anything they want, so long as it doesn't contain carbohydrates, is completely unfounded. His literature has failed to prove that excess calories ingested from fat are not stored as fat in the absence of carbohydrates. Studies following people on his diet have found that all of their weight loss can be accounted for by calorie reduction alone. Many global epidemiological studies empirically contradict the results that his writings would predict for populations with high-carbohydrate diets. And people who would assume that Dr. Retzler's claims must be reasonable simply because he is a doctor should remember that he has become very rich marketing his diet.

Which one of the following best describes the role played in the physician's argument by the claim that Dr. Retzler has become very rich marketing his diet?

1. Identify

This is a Role question because it asks about the role played by the claim that Dr. Retzler has become very rich marketing his diet.

2. Analyze

The physician's argument is a *counterargument* against Retzler's claim. So the physician's conclusion must be that [people can't lose weight eating anything they want.] His premises include the results of several studies, but the specifics are not important.

The last sentence, the claim the question is focused on, is a little tricky. It's not the conclusion, and it doesn't look like it directly supports the conclusion as a premise either. In this sentence, the physician addresses people's assumptions directly and counters them. The function of the claim "he has become very rich" is to respond to those who might think Retzler's claims are reasonable. In other words, the physician is saying Dr. Retzler's monetary motivations should lead people to view his diet plan with suspicion.

3. Prephrase

Role questions are great questions to Prephrase on. You should always come up with a general description of the role played by the claim in the question stem. Some common roles are:

- The main conclusion
- A premise
- A counterexample
- A concession
- An illustration
- A subsidiary conclusion

In this example, the claim in question isn't the conclusion, and it isn't a premise. Instead, it's a way to respond to those who might think differently than the physician does. He is trying to argue against the opposition by pointing out that Retzler is motivated by money. So ultimately, the claim is a reason to question Retzler's credibility.

4. Attack

The **Real Question** for Role questions is:

Does this match the claim?

(A)   It is evidence that contradicts the claim the
         physician's argument is attempting to refute.

Choice (A): *Does this match the claim?* The fact that Retzler makes a lot of cash doesn't *contradict* anything. Since there's no contradiction, this doesn't match the claim. *Cut it.*

(B)   It suggests a basis for bias in the claim the
         physician's argument is attempting to refute.

Choice (B): *Does this match the claim?* The answer says that the last sentence is suggesting bias. Is the physician trying to say that Retzler would be biased because of the money? Maybe. *Keep it.*

(C)   It is the assertion the physician's argument is
         designed to prove.

Choice (C): *Does this match the claim?* This choice sounds like it's describes a conclusion. The last sentence isn't an assertion the physician is trying to prove. It's a reason not to trust Retzler. *Cut it.*

(D)   It suggests an alternative explanation for the
         results of the diet the physician is calling into
         question.

Choice (D): *Does this match the claim?* This is about an alternative explanation for the results of the diet, but the actual results recorded support the physician's claim that the diet is no good. There's no need for alternative explanations. *Cut it.*

(E)   It is an assumption from which the physician
         concludes that Dr. Retzler's diet claim is flawed.

Choice (E): *Does this match the claim?* The last sentence is not an assumption, since the physician comes right out and says it. An assumption is *unstated. Cut it.*

Choice (B) is the correct answer.

> On a Role question, *never* pick an answer choice that says something is an assumption.

9.7   THE BIG PICTURE

9.7.1   FLAW-INDEPENDENCE

Flaw-independent questions are not as closely related to each other as flaw-dependent questions are. Some flaw-independent questions have argument-based passages, and some have nothing more than a set of premises.

So far, you have seen the following flaw-independent question types with argument-based passages:

- **Main Point** and its variation, Complete
- **Point at Issue** and its variation, Point of Agreement
- **Method** and its variation, Role

> The flaw-independent questions still to come are Conform and Parallel Reasoning questions.

The similarity between these is that, even though the passage is argument-based, it is never important to evaluate the reasoning and find flaws. For most of these, finding the conclusion and premises is all you need to do.

You've also seen a few flaw-independent questions without argument-based passages:

- **Inference** and its variation, Cannot Be True
- **Paradox** and its variation, Explain

For these, you should never look for the conclusion—there isn't one. Your job is to work the set of premises in the argument. What you do with them varies by question type.

9.7.2 Drill: Practicing Flaw-independent Questions

Complete each of the following flaw-independent questions.

Questions 1-4

Anwar: Students have had nothing but criticism for the mural in the school's cafeteria ever since it was put up. But the vast majority of high school students are not in a position to judge fine art, so their response does not take away from the quality of the mural. Therefore, there is no reason to take down the mural.

Reuben: You are probably right about the relationship between the students' response and the quality of the mural. But if a mural is to be displayed in a school cafeteria, it ought to be good for the students. And surveying student opinion is ultimately the only way to judge whether the students feel the mural is good for them. If the students dislike the mural as much as you say, then the mural should be taken down.

1. Anwar's and Reuben's statements commit them to disagreeing about which one of the following principles?

    Question type? _____

    Real Question? _____

    _____

    (A) In determining whether the mural should be removed from the cafeteria, the quality of the mural itself should be a central consideration.
    (B) People's opinion of a work of art is an important consideration in establishing the work's quality.
    (C) Murals displayed in public places should at least have enough quality to be good for their viewers.
    (D) The mural cannot be good for the students by remaining in the cafeteria unless the mural is of high quality.
    (E) The only reason for removing a work of art displayed in a public space would be that most people have nothing but criticism for the work.

2. Which one of the following best expresses the main point of Reuben's argument?

    Question type? _____

    Real Question? _____

    _____

    (A) What the students say about the mural should be a central concern.
    (B) Anwar is probably right about the relationship between the students' responses and the quality of the mural.
    (C) There is no reason to take down the mural.
    (D) If a work of art is to be displayed in a particular place, it ought to be good for the people who frequent that place.
    (E) The mural hanging in the cafeteria should be removed.

3. Reuben responds to Anwar's position by

    Question type? _____

    Real Question? _____

    _____

    (A) disputing the evidence on which the opposing argument is based
    (B) denying the relevance of an analogy central to the claim being opposed
    (C) suggesting a different set of criteria for deciding whether to take a given course of action
    (D) redefining a term in a way that is favorable to his own conclusion
    (E) attacking his opponent's character rather than the claims presented

4. The claim that Anwar is probably right about the relationship between the students' responses and the quality of the mural plays which one of the following roles in Reuben's argument?

    Question type? _____

    Real Question? _____

    _____

    (A) It is a subsidiary conclusion that acts as a premise for the main conclusion.
    (B) It is a presupposition upon which the argument is explicitly based.
    (C) It is the claim that the argument as a whole is structured to support.
    (D) It is a concession that the argument treats as irrelevant to the issue in question.
    (E) It is a statement indicating that Reuben agrees with Anwar's overall conclusion.

Questions 5-7

The most common commercial weed killers eliminate weeds from grass lawns by limiting the production of an enzyme involved in plant metabolism. Though grass uses the same enzyme in the same way, these weed killers do not eliminate grass.

5. Which one of the following, if true, most helps resolve the apparent paradox?

Question type? _____

Real Question? _____

_____

(A) Most common lawn weeds are more resilient than grass.
(B) Grass produces much more of the inhibited enzyme than it needs.
(C) Several herbicides eliminate both weeds and grass, though by a different mechanism.
(D) Consumers who purchase the weed killer do not want to damage the grass in their lawns.
(E) The enzyme targeted by the weed killer is used by plants in the synthesis of amino acids.

6. If the statements above are true, then which one of the following must also be true on the basis of them?

Question type? _____

Real Question? _____

_____

(A) Commercial weed killers were developed to target weeds without killing grass.
(B) At least one commercial weed killer is harmful to human health.
(C) The most common commercial weed killers have no effect on grass.
(D) Grass and weeds use at least one identical enzyme involved in plant metabolism.
(E) All plants use the same metabolic enzyme in the same way.

7. If the statements above are true, then which one of the follow CANNOT be true?

Question type? _____

Real Question? _____

_____

(A) Many common commercial weed killers eliminate grass when used properly.
(B) Manipulation of a plant's metabolic enzymes always kills the plant.
(C) No common commercial weed killers eliminate grass when used properly.
(D) Commercial weed killers were developed to target weeds without killing grass.
(E) At least one commercial weed killer is harmful to human health.

Answers & Explanations

1. Point at Issue question
Do the speakers voice disagreement about this?
Choice (A) is the correct answer.
Choice (A): Yes. Anwar thinks that student concerns should not determine whether the mural stays, and Reuben thinks that what the students think should be the primary consideration.
Choice (B): No. They agree about choice (B)—they both think it's incorrect.
Choice (C): No. Anwar says nothing about what is good for viewers. This is one-sided.
Choice (D): No. Again, Anwar says nothing about what is good for students. This is one-sided.
Choice (E): No. Anwar doesn't mention what should cause artwork to be removed, and Reuben doesn't mention whether there could be other reasons.

2. Main Point question
Is this Reuben's conclusion?
Choice (E) is the correct answer.
Choice (A): No. This is a premise for the conclusion that the mural should be taken down.
Choice (B): No. Reuben's conclusion is about the fate of the mural, not its quality.
Choice (C): No. This is Anwar's conclusion, which is the opposite of Reuben's.
Choice (D): No. This is another premise.
Choice (E): Yes. This is a suggested course of action, and the rest of the argument provides support for why Reuben believes this statement.

3. Method question
Does this match the argument?
Choice (C) is the correct answer.
Choice (A): No. Anwar's evidence is that the students have criticized the mural and that they can't judge fine art. Reuben doesn't dispute this.

Choice (B): No. There is no analogy in either argument.

Choice (C): Yes. Reuben suggests that student opinion, rather than the quality of the mural, should be the criterion.

Choice (D): No. There is no term that gets redefined.

Choice (E): No. Reuben makes no attack on Anwar's character.

4. **Role question**

Does this match the claim?

Choice (D) is the correct answer.

Choice (A): No. The main conclusion is based on a discussion of what is good for students, not the quality of the mural.

Choice (B): No. *Presupposition* means *assumption*, which this is definitely not.

Choice (C): No. This is not the conclusion of Reuben's argument.

Choice (D): Yes. Reuben concedes that Anwar is probably right about the students, but he doesn't think that it is relevant to whether the mural should be taken down.

Choice (E): No. Reuben disagrees with Anwar's overall conclusion, since he believes the mural should be taken down.

5. **Paradox question**

Does this explain how both facts could be true?

Choice (B) is the correct answer.

Choice (A): No. If this were true, it would make the paradox worse. This is an **opposite** distracter.

Choice (B): Yes. If grass produces much more of the enzyme than it needs, it could survive even as the weed killer limits the production of the enzyme.

Choice (C): No. The argument is not concerned with those herbicides that kill grass. This is **out of scope**.

Choice (D): No. This explains *why* such weed killers exist, but not *how* they could kill weeds without killing grass.

Choice (E): No. This gives you more information about how the enzyme works, but doesn't explain why grass is not killed.

6. **Inference question**

Is this guaranteed to be true?

Choice (D) is the correct answer.

Choice (A): No. The passage mentions nothing about *why* they were developed.

Choice (B): No. The passage never mentions human health. This is completely **out of scope**.

Choice (C): No. You know those weed killers "do not eliminate grass," but you don't know that they "have no effect." Maybe they make the grass grow faster or turn it purple.

Choice (D): Yes. The passage says that grass uses the same enzyme in the same way as weeds, so they must have at least one identical enzyme involved in plant metabolism.

Choice (E): No. This is **extreme**. There is not enough information in the passage to be able to draw a conclusion about *all* plants.

7. **Cannot Be True question**

Is this impossible?

Choice (D) is the correct answer.

Choice (A): No. The passage tells you about the *most common* commercial weed killers, but you can't say anything for sure about other common weed killers.

Choice (B): Yes. The passage provides an example in which the manipulation of a metabolic enzyme in grass does *not* kill the plant, so this choice cannot be true.

Choice (C): No. Again, the passage tells you about *the most common* commercial weed killers, but you can't say anything for sure about other common weed killers.

Choice (D): No. The passage mentions nothing about *why* they were developed, so you can't say for sure that this is impossible.

Choice (E): No. The passage never mentions human health. This is completely **out of scope**.

NOW MOVE ON TO THE SECOND CHAPTER OF LECTURE 8. WHEN YOU HAVE COMPLETED IT, YOU CAN GET FURTHER PRACTICE WITH METHOD QUESTIONS IN THE CORRESPONDING EXAM AT THE END OF THE BOOK.

LECTURE (8) CHAPTER (10)

CONFORM QUESTIONS

10.1 IDENTIFY

10.1.1 WHAT IS A PRINCIPLE?

On the LSAT, a "principle" is a general rule. Most principles on the LSAT tell you either

- a rule of conduct in a particular circumstance, or

- how something should be judged, if it meets certain criteria.

The following examples would be considered principles on the LSAT:

> Every new law passed by public referendum should be given a sixty-day trial period in which it cannot be repealed.

> If a new car that has not been in an accident breaks down after less than five thousand miles, it is a lemon.

The first example provides a rule of conduct in a particular circumstance—that of new laws passed by public referendum. The second says how a car should be judged if it meets certain criteria.

10.1.2 WHAT IS A CONFORM QUESTION?

Conform questions are all about matching. They ask you to match a *general rule* (a principle) to a *specific example* in which that rule is followed.

General rule	Match	Example in which the rule is followed

Conform questions are flaw-independent and come in two closely related versions. Sometimes, the specific example is in the passage, and you have to extract the general rule from the example and find the answer choice in which it is correctly expressed. In such cases, you are essentially being asked to **state the principle**.

In the other version of Conform questions, the general rule is already stated for you in the passage, and you have to find the matching example in the answer choices in which the rule is followed. In such cases, your job is to **apply the principle**.

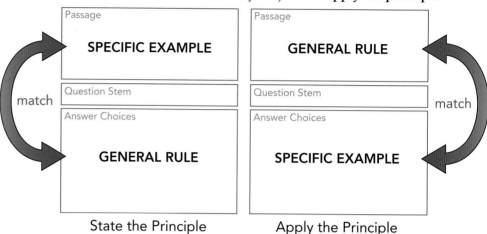

Although these two versions of Conform questions seem to be opposites, they are very closely related, and you can use the same basic techniques to answer both of them.

10.1.3 IDENTIFYING CONFORM QUESTIONS

Conform question stems look slightly different depending on whether they're asking you to state the principle or apply the principle.

1. State the Principle

When a Conform question asks you to **state the principle**, the question stem does the following things:

- It tells you the passage contains a *situation*, an *example*, an *argument*, or *reasoning*.

- It tells you the answer choices contain *principles*, *generalizations*, or *propositions*.

- It asks you to find the principle that *conforms to, is illustrated by,* or *underlies* the situation.

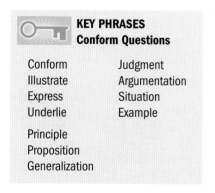

Here are some examples:

> Which one of the following most closely conforms to the principle illustrated by the situation described above?

> The examples presented above best illustrate which one of the following propositions?

> Which one of the following generalizations most accurately expresses the principle underlying the argumentation above?

All of these ask about a principle behind the passage. Your job is to state the principle that matches the example in the passage.

2. Apply the Principle

When a Conform question asks you to **apply the principle**, the question stem does the following things:

- It tells you the passage states a *principle* or a *generalization*.
- It tells you the answer choices contain *examples, situations,* or *judgments*.
- It asks you to find the example that *conforms to, illustrates, is an application of,* or *corresponds to* the principle.

Here are some examples:

> Which one of the following conforms most closely to the principle stated above?

> Which one of the following judgments best illustrates the proposition above?

> Which one of the following situations most closely conforms to the principle cited above?

All of these ask for an example that matches the principle already stated in the passage.

Conform questions occur roughly three times per test.

10.1.4   The Difference Between Conform And Justify Questions

Both Conform and Justify questions usually use the word *principle* in the question stem, but they are very different types of questions. Justify questions ask you to *manipulate* the logic of the argument. The passage contains an insufficiently proven conclusion, and you must provide a new piece of information that makes the logic better. A large part of your strategy is to discover the flaw in the argument.

Conform questions, on the other hand, are all about *matching*. The passage and the correct answer choice must both follow the same general rule, but you are not asked to supply any additional information to make any logic work. You don't need to look for a flaw.

10.1.5 Drill: Identifying Conform Questions

Determine whether each of the following question stems is a Justify question or a Conform question.

1. The clerk's reasoning most closely conforms to which one of the following generalizations?
   ☐ Justify   ☐ Conform

2. Which one of the following principles, if valid, provides the most support for the clairvoyant's inference?
   ☐ Justify   ☐ Conform

3. Which one of the following conforms most closely to the principle stated by the molecular biologist?
   ☐ Justify   ☐ Conform

4. Which one of the following principles, if valid, most helps to justify the reasoning above?
   ☐ Justify   ☐ Conform

5. Which one of the following principles is best illustrated by the statements above?
   ☐ Justify   ☐ Conform

6. Which one of the following is an application of the legal principle above?
   ☐ Justify   ☐ Conform

7. The principle that Noriko invokes, if established, would justify which one of the following judgments?
   ☐ Justify   ☐ Conform

8. Which one of the following principles, if valid, justifies the technician's argument?
   ☐ Justify   ☐ Conform

9. Which one of the following principles, if established, would provide the strongest support for the conductor's argument?
   ☐ Justify   ☐ Conform

Answers & Explanations

1. **Conform.** The question stem asks you to *identify* the principle in the passage.

2. **Justify.** The question stem asks you to use one of the answer choices to improve the clairvoyant's reasoning.

3. **Conform.** The question stem asks you to *apply* the principle in the passage to a situation in the answer choices.

4. **Justify.** The question stem asks you to use one of the answer choices to improve the reasoning in the passage.

5. **Conform.** The question stem asks you to *identify* the principle in the passage.

6. **Conform.** The question stem asks you to *apply* the principle in the passage to a situation in the answer choices.

7. **Conform.** This one is quite tricky since it actually contains the word *justify*. However, the question stem asks you to *apply* the principle in the passage to a situation in the answer choices. It does not ask you to *improve* the reasoning in the passage using one of the answer choices. That makes it a Conform question.

8. **Justify.** The question stem asks you to use one of the answer choices to improve the technician's reasoning.

9. **Justify.** The question stem asks you to use one of the answer choices to improve the conductor's reasoning.

10.2 ANALYZE

10.2.1 ANALYZING CONFORM QUESTIONS

Your analysis of Conform questions varies depending on whether the question asks you to state the principle or apply the principle.

1. State the Principle

If the question asks you to state the principle, then the passage is usually a situation—a set of circumstances or events. As far as analysis is concerned, there isn't much you should do with a situation other than understanding what's going on—it's a lot like a passage for an Inference question. The majority of your work comes when you Prephrase and attack the answers.

All Conform questions are flaw-independent.

In a few cases in which a Conform question asks you to state the principle, the passage actually contains an argument. If there is an argument, you should analyze it for its conclusion and premises, but don't bother with flaws or assumptions. Conform questions are flaw-independent.

Here's a sample passage for a question that asks you to state the principle:

> During the last decades of the twentieth century, businesses began to switch from conventional bookkeeping to computerized bookkeeping. They were attracted to the reduced errors and costs associated with computerized bookkeeping. But computerized bookkeeping is not error-free, and further cost-cutting is always desirable, so businesses should remain alert for newly developed forms of bookkeeping.
>
> The situation described above most closely conforms to which one of the following principles?

All you'd have to do for your analysis of this passage is to understand what's going on: businesses have switched methods to cut costs, and they should remain open to switching again.

2. Apply the Principle

If a Conform question asks you to apply the principle, then your first job is to find the principle in the passage. Sometimes, the passage is nothing more than a one-sentence principle. That makes your job very easy. Other times, there's a lot of fluff around the principle. For these passages, sift through the fluff and find the statement that sounds like a general rule, since you need to know the principle in order to apply it.

Here's a sample passage for a question that asks you to apply the principle:

> Architect: A structure is effective if it is beautiful and its form fits its function. But a structure is ineffective if it is ugly or uses bad materials.
>
> Which one of the following judgments most closely corresponds to the principle cited above?

This passage is typical of Conform questions that ask you to apply a principle. The passage is nothing more than a statement of a general rule. In this case, the principle has two parts that determine whether a structure is effective or ineffective.

10.3 PREPHRASE

10.3.1 PREPHRASING ON CONFORM QUESTIONS

Your Prephrasing also varies according to whether the question asks you to state the principle or apply it.

1. State the Principle

When you are asked to state the principle, Prephrasing is important and effective. To Prephrase on such questions, tell the *general story* of the situation in the passage. Prephrasing on these questions is a lot like Prephrasing on Method questions, except that the passage is usually not based on an argument. Just like Method questions, these questions require a good Prephrased answer that doesn't focus on the details of the passage.

> The way in which you Prephrase for a Conform question depends on whether you're asked to state or apply the principle.

Go ahead and revisit the passage from earlier on:

> During the last decades of the twentieth century, businesses began to switch from conventional bookkeeping to computerized bookkeeping. They were attracted to the reduced errors and costs associated with computerized bookkeeping. But computerized bookkeeping is not error-free, and further cost-cutting is always desirable, so businesses should remain alert for newly developed forms of bookkeeping.
>
> The situation described above most closely conforms to which one of the following principles?

To Prephrase the principle underlying this passage, you should tell the *general* story. This situation describes how businesses switched bookkeeping methods to reduce errors and costs, and it explains how the problems of errors and cost have not been completely solved, so businesses should switch again if the opportunity arises. The passage talks about computerized versus conventional bookkeeping, but details like these aren't too important. Here's a good Prephrased principle:

> Principle: When an improvement on a process does not completely solve its problems, businesses should continue to look for better solutions.

This is the general story, and it removes the details about bookkeeping, the time period in question, and computers. This is the kind of Prephrased answer you should aim for when you are asked to state the principle. Don't go out of your way to be abstract, however—if your Prephrased principle includes some details from the passage, that's just fine. The correct answer often includes some details as well.

2. Apply the Principle

Prephrasing is simpler when you are asked to apply the principle. All you have to do is take an inventory of the specific concepts you need to see in the correct answer. Those concepts are the circumstances and the outcome. The correct answer must:

1. **Match the circumstances**. All principles apply only under certain circumstances or when certain criteria are met. If an answer choice talks about anything outside the applicable circumstances, then it can't be right.

2. **Match the outcome**. In a principle, the outcome is the judgment or the suggested course of action. If an answer choice has the right circumstances but the wrong outcome, then it's wrong.

Here's the passage from above:

> Architect: A structure is effective if it is beautiful and its form fits its function. But a structure is ineffective if it is ugly or uses bad materials.
>
> Which one of the following judgments most closely corresponds to the principle cited above?

Sometimes a principle's circumstances and outcome start to resemble a conditional statement, but you should *never* try to create the contrapositive of a principle.

To apply this principle, you need **circumstances** that describe a *structure* and its *beauty*, *function*, or *materials*. Then you'd look for an **outcome** that judges the structure to be either *effective* or *ineffective*.

An answer choice that describes a painting, for example, would be incorrect, since it doesn't match the circumstances—this principle concerns structures, not paintings. An answer choice that advocated tearing down an ugly structure would be incorrect since it doesn't match the outcome—this principle concerns judging something to be effective or ineffective, not what should be done about it.

10.4 ATTACK

10.4.1 THE REAL QUESTION

The **Real Question** for all Conform questions is:

> *Does this match the principle in the passage?*

The Real Question doesn't change, no matter whether you are stating or applying the principle. In the end, these two tasks amount to the same thing: can you match a principle to a situation?

For questions that ask you to state the principle, you should look for an answer that matches the *underlying principle in the passage*—the one that you Prephrased before attacking the answer choices. If an answer choice matches the underlying principle, hold onto it.

For questions that ask you to apply the principle, you should look for an answer that matches the *explicit* principle from the passage. For these questions, the answer choices are examples of situations. Find the answer choice whose example matches both the circumstances and the outcome of the principle stated in the passage.

10.4.2 ALL CONFORM QUESTIONS ARE THE SAME

Despite their apparent differences, both flavors of Conform questions are ultimately the same: your job is to match a principle to a situation. How similar are they? Any question that asks you to state the principle could easily be turned into a question asking you to apply the principle just by turning things upside down a bit. Here are two examples:

1. When doctors cannot diagnose a patient with severe symptoms, they sometimes turn to exploratory surgeries, hoping to find a clue for a diagnosis. But these surgeries can have serious enough side effects that they are worse than not diagnosing the patient at all.

    The situation above most closely conforms to which one of the following principles?

    (A) Attempted solutions carried out in good faith can sometimes be worse than the problems they are intended to solve.

    (B) Sometimes the benefits of a possible course of action outweigh its costs, despite the severity of the costs.

2. Attempted solutions carried out in good faith can sometimes be worse than the problems they are intended to solve.

    Which one of the following best illustrates the proposition above?

    (A) When lawyers are aware of a client's guilt, they are often put in a position of advocating for someone they would otherwise have wanted in prison. While most lawyers uphold their ethical standards and provide a zealous defense, others cannot help being less passionate in their defense.

    (B) When doctors cannot diagnose a patient with severe symptoms, they sometimes turn to exploratory surgeries, hoping to find a clue for a diagnosis. But these surgeries can have serious enough side effects that they are worse than not diagnosing the patient at all.

The first question above asks you to state the principle, and the second asks you to apply it. But in both cases, asking the **Real Question** gets you to the right answer. When considering an answer, always ask: *Does this match the principle in the passage?*

> Use the same Real Question for all types of Conform questions.

For the first question, choice (A) matches the passage, since the surgery is sometimes worse than the illness. Choice (B) doesn't match, since it says the benefits outweigh the costs, which is the opposite of the principle in the passage. **Choice (A) is the correct answer.**

The second question is identical—it's just flipped upside-down. The correct answer is of course choice (B), since the principle is a match for the situation even if you change the task. Choice (A) doesn't match since it doesn't have a problem/solution framework. **Choice (B) is the correct answer.**

Of course, the correct answer is less important than the underlying message of these examples: all Conform questions are really asking you to do the same thing.

10.5 PUTTING IT ALL TOGETHER

1. Bert: I enjoyed some aspects of the movie, but the dialogue was terribly written. The writers clearly are untalented and uncreative, and the movie was ruined as a result.

    Rupinder: Your one attempt to write a movie was an abject failure. You should not be so critical of the output of others in a field in which you have no talent or expertise.

    Of the following, which one most closely conforms to the principle stated by Rupinder?

1. Identify

This is a Conform question, since it asks for something that conforms to Rupinder's principle. Since it asks about a principle *stated* by Rupinder, there must be a principle in the passage, and you have to apply it.

2. Analyze

Rupinder states only one principle: "You should not be so critical of the output of others in a field in which you have no talent or expertise."

Of course, Rupinder is talking only to Bert here. But this is a general rule that could apply to other situations—it's a principle. That's it for the analysis.

3. Prephrase

To Prephrase when you are applying a principle, you need to identify the **circumstance** and the **outcome**.

Based on the principle, the correct answer must have circumstances in which someone has a *lack of talent or expertise*. The outcome is that the person *should not be critical*. If nothing about being critical appears, or if talent or expertise is not questioned, then the answer is incorrect. This helps you move through the answers quickly and effectively.

4. Attack

Remember the two things you are looking for: there needs to be someone who *should not be critical*, and there needs to be a lack of *talent or expertise*.

> (A) Bosses should not conclude that any particular employees are undeserving of a raise without first getting to know those employees.

Choice (A): *Does this match the principle in the passage?* This doesn't include any questioning of talent or expertise, so it doesn't match the principle in the passage. *Cut it.*

> (B) Gene should not claim that "Air" is the worst play ever produced, as Gene has not seen every play.

Choice (B): *Does this match the principle in the passage?* This doesn't include talent or expertise either. Not seeing *every* play is not the same as lacking expertise: it's not even possible to see every play. *Cut it.*

> (C) Movie producers should not hire unproven writers, because those writers can often ruin a good movie.

Choice (C): *Does this match the principle in the passage?* This doesn't have anyone who is critical of anyone else, so it doesn't match. *Cut it.*

> (D) Most viewers should not so readily mock the poor singing performances of the contestants on a popular show, as most viewers have no singing ability.

Choice (D): *Does this match the principle in the passage?* This has *mocking*, which might match being *critical*, and *no singing ability* is a good match for *no talent*, so this is a good match for the principle in the passage. *Keep it.*

> (E) Audiences attending athletic events should not boo athletes performing poorly, because those athletes are usually giving their best effort.

Choice (E): *Does this match the principle in the passage?* This has people who are *critical*, but there is no question of *talent or expertise*. *Cut it.*

The only answer that includes both important aspects of the principle, being *critical* and a lack of *talent or expertise*, is choice (D).

Choice (D) is the correct answer.

Every incorrect answer in this example was missing a key concept from either the circumstances or the outcome.

Here's another example:

2. Bankruptcy is based on laws that allow for a compromise between a debtor and a set of creditors through which the debtor agrees to pay creditors as much as possible in an orderly manner. The creditors inevitably lose money that they might otherwise have earned on the loans they provide. But creditors are often happy to see their most delinquent debtors file for bankruptcy, since these debtors are not otherwise likely to pay the creditors at all. Debtors, too, prefer bankruptcy to other options that the law might provide.

The situation described above most closely conforms to which one of the following principles?

1. Identify

This is a Conform question, since it asks for a principle that conforms to the situation. In this case, your job is to state the principle illustrated in the passage.

2. Analyze

To analyze the passage, just make sure you understand the situation. In this case, the passage is about how bankruptcy affects both creditors and debtors. Creditors are often happy when a delinquent debtor files for bankruptcy, and debtors prefer it to other options as well.

3. Prephrase

Your job is to tell the *general* story of the situation in the passage. In this case, there are debtors and creditors dealing with bankruptcy laws. Both sides, it turns out, are often happy to deal with bankruptcy, despite its costs. That's the general story:

> Principle: **In the case of delinquent debtors, bankruptcy is something that can make both sides happy.**

This includes some of the specifics, but it captures the general story of the passage in one concise principle. Again, don't try too hard to be overly abstract with your Prephrased principle: there's no reason to be more abstract than the writers of the LSAT.

4. Attack

(A) Debtors should compromise with creditors as much as possible to avoid protracted battles in court.

Choice (A): *Does this match the principle in the passage?* This answer is one-sided, focusing on the debtors. But the passage is about how both sides like bankruptcy, so this isn't a good match. *Cut it.*

(B) Creditors should support only those laws with which they are as satisfied as their debtors.

Choice (B): *Does this match the principle in the passage?* This has the same kind of problem as choice (A)—where's the other side? *Cut it.*

(C) The government should not design its laws in such a way as to serve all parties' interests, since doing so results in weaker laws.

Choice (C): *Does this match the principle in the passage?* This says the government shouldn't try to please everyone, but that's *exactly* what happens in the passage. This is an **opposite** distracter.

> As on Method questions, every answer either matches the principle or it doesn't.

(D)   The government can design laws that balance the
needs of creditors and debtors.

Choice (D): *Does this match the principle in the passage?* This answer says that the government can design laws that make everyone happy, and that's exactly what happens in the passage, so this is a good match. *Keep it.*

(E)   The most effective way to ensure easy credit is to
cater to the needs of creditors.

Choice (E): *Does this match the principle in the passage?* This answer, like choices (A) and (B), is about one side of the story—the creditors' needs. But the passage had a happy compromise for both sides. *Cut it.*

Choice (D) is the correct answer.

10.6 VARIATIONS

10.6.1 APPLYING THE UNSTATED PRINCIPLE

There is actually a third type of Conform question that is basically a combination of the other two types. These questions require you to both state *and* apply a principle.

These questions do not directly tell you the principle, either in the passage or in the answer choices. The question stem asks you to *apply* a principle *illustrated* rather than stated by the passage. Here's a sample question stem:

Which one of the following judgments best illustrates
the principle illustrated by the argument above?

This question asks you to find the principle illustrated by the situation in passage and then apply that principle to a *new* situation.

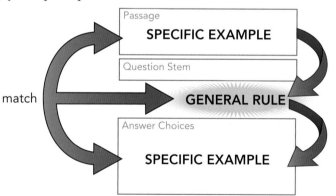

Apply the Unstated Principle

Questions that ask you to apply an unstated principle are often difficult and time-consuming. They're also relatively rare, but the LSAT writers appear to be using them with increasing frequency.

Try this one:

3.   Marathon runners train in order to compete in a full marathon, a grueling race of over 26 miles. Proper training is essential, and serious runners know that a strong work ethic during training leads to success in competition. But the benefit that an hour of training yields tends to decrease as the regimen extends beyond the four-hour mark per day.

Which one of the following conforms most closely to the principle illustrated by the statements above?

Together with the answer choices, this question is incredibly long! The time it takes simply to read it makes this a huge time investment. But if you're aiming for a top score, you should be ready to deal with some questions like this.

1. Identify

This is a Conform question, since it asks for a situation that conforms to a principle in the passage. But the principle isn't *stated* in the passage. It's illustrated by the passage. This makes it more challenging.

If it isn't clear whether the principle is stated in the answer choices, skimming the first sentence of one or two should do the trick. The answers are obviously situations, not principles.

2. Analyze

You should analyze the passage as you would analyze any other passage for which you are asked to state the principle. Your job is to understand what's going on.

This is about marathon runners and their training programs. They need to train hard, but after a certain point, each hour they train becomes less valuable.

3. Prephrase

When you are asked to state the principle, you Prephrase by telling a general story about what happened in the passage. This might be something like:

> Principle: Training hard is important, but after enough hours, training becomes less valuable.

There's an extra step when you have to apply the principle, as you do on this question. Take the Prephrased principle, and determine the circumstances and the outcome you should see in the correct answer.

The correct answer needs to have circumstances in which *work is valuable,* but it needs to have an outcome that describes *diminishing returns* after some point.

4. Attack

The same **Real Question** applies: *Does this match the principle in the passage?* Remember that you are looking for *the importance of work* and *diminishing returns.*

> (A)   In order to become great composers, aspiring composers practice their composition techniques. Regimented practice is important, and those composers who practice their techniques regularly are more likely to become great.

Choice (A): *Does this match the principle in the passage?* This includes hard work, but there are no diminishing returns for aspiring composers. *Cut it.*

> (B)   Young politicians work hard to become leaders, and they need to develop relationships with experienced politicians. But during a conversation with an experienced politician, the chances of developing a good relationship decrease over time from the beginning of the conversation.

Choice (B): *Does this match the principle in the passage?* This has an element of hard work and diminishing returns for young politicians. This could be a match. *Keep it.*

(C)   To be a good teacher, one must learn a subject in tremendous depth. It is usually true that those who study harder become better teachers. The amount of effective study that can be done in one day is limited, however, and after five consecutive hours of study, any additional study becomes decreasingly useful.

Choice (C): *Does this match the principle in the passage?* This has hard work and diminishing returns for those studying to be teachers, so this also could be a good match. *Keep it.*

(D)   Young chefs aspire to become executive chefs. And it is usually the case that the more work a chef puts into the development of recipes, the more likely the chef is to become an executive chef. Increasing the amount of time spent developing recipes only increases a young chef's chances of being successful.

Choice (D): *Does this match the principle in the passage?* This also has hard work, but the chef's returns on the hard work never diminish. *Cut it.*

This choice is a **topic trap.** That's a common distracter on this type of question. Matching the principle doesn't mean matching the topic.

(E)   To become great sprinters, runners must eat a healthy diet. The right diet can provide the right fuel during a race. Most of the time, sprinters focus on consuming a high volume of proteins, but any component of a diet can be dangerous if consumed excessively.

Choice (E): *Does this match the principle in the passage?* This doesn't have hard work—a healthy diet doesn't fit the mold. Also, the diminishing returns of excessive eating apply to everyone and every component of any diet, not just to sprinters who are training. Don't fall for the trap of picking this choice just because it talks about a topic similar to the one in the passage. *Cut it.*

It's now down to two answer choices, which is a place many students find themselves from time to time.

So what are you supposed to do? One of the most useful tools to use when you're down to two answer choices is to *compare* them to find out what's different about each one. So reread answer choices, and focus on the differences.

Of course, these topics are different, but the topics don't matter. There's a more important difference: in choice (B), the diminishing returns begin as soon as the politician starts. In choice (C), the diminishing returns occur after some time at work. Which do you want? Well, look at the passage. There, the diminishing returns began after four hours of training. So (C) is a better match.

Choice (C) is the correct answer.

10.7 THE BIG PICTURE

10.7.1 Section Strategy
Your strategy for approaching the Logical Reasoning section can affect your score in a big way. In the introduction, you learned three general principles for section strategy:

High accuracy means missing no more than one out of every six or seven questions you attempt.

1. **Work as quickly as you can _without sacrificing accuracy._** This principle hasn't changed. You should still aim to work as quickly as you can work while remaining as accurate as possible. You may not finish the entire section, but you can get a great score even without finishing the section if you can maintain a high level of accuracy.

2. **Skip questions that seem to require a lot of time at first glance, and return to them if you have time.** You've now seen enough questions to know which ones tend to take more time and which ones you can usually work through quickly. This shouldn't be based entirely on question type, but there are some questions—like those unstated principle questions—that are best left for the end. If a passage is very long, filled with conditionals, regarding a difficult topic, or if it immediately looks challenging, put it off. It makes no sense to spend two or three minutes struggling with a difficult question when you can spend the same amount of time answering two easier questions correctly.

3. **If you are struggling with a question, guess, circle the question number, and return to it if you have time.** Don't stagnate! Keep moving, even if it means guessing and moving on. Time is simply too tight to be wasted by vacillating between answer choices. If you've been looking at a question for a long time and haven't made up your mind, guess and move on. You will rarely have time to return to questions like these, but you should circle the question number just in case you do.

10.7.2 Drill: Two Questions, 60 Seconds

Use your timer and give yourself 60 seconds in each of the following scenarios to answer ONE of the questions. Choose which question you are more likely to answer correctly and work that question.

Scenario 1

Option I

1. Literary critic: All great gothic novels incorporate both psychological and physical terror into their plots. And no great gothic novel fails to be influenced by the desire to induce a kind of pleasing terror in its readers. Hence, any gothic novel that desires to induce a pleasing terror in its readers incorporates both psychological and physical terror into its plot.

The flawed pattern of reasoning in which one of the following most closely parallels that in the literary critic's argument?

(A) Romance novels always focus on the romantic love between two people, and no romance novel fails to end positively. Therefore, if a novel focuses on the romantic love between two people and ends positively, it is a romance novel.

(B) Without compassion, a politician cannot lead honorably. Without honor, a politician cannot lead effectively. It follows that a great politician is compassionate and honorable.

(C) The best instances of Romanesque architecture have round arches, and no great instance of Romanesque architecture is without a groin vault. Therefore, without round arches and a groin vault, an example of Romanesque architecture cannot be great.

(D) Any baroque concerto that fails to include a solemn middle movement must have a triumphant end, since the great baroque concertos never fail to include both a solemn middle and a triumphant ending.

(E) Clearly, any public intellectual that cares deeply about social injustice will try to do something about it. After all, any worthy public intellectual cares deeply about social injustice, and no worthy public intellectual does nothing about the social injustice he cares about.

Option II

2. The problem of profanity infiltrating our everyday language at an increasing pace is indisputable. This is clear from an inspection of the record of a Senate floor discussion last month in which none other than the vice president used an especially profane term while arguing a point with a colleague.

Which one of the following most accurately describes a flaw in the argument?

(A) It fails to propose any solutions to the problematic issue it raises.

(B) It presumes, without providing justification, that the vice president is the only elected official to have used profanity on record.

(C) It presumes, without providing justification, that the use of profanity by high-ranking members of government causes others to use profanity.

(D) It relies on an isolated example to make a point about a general trend.

(E) It does not relate the context in which the vice president used the profane term.

Scenario 2

Option I

3. Many casual weight-lifters have large biceps but relatively undeveloped back muscles. Yet almost no weight-lifters have well-developed back muscles and undeveloped biceps.

   Which one of the following would most contribute to an explanation of the observation?

   (A) There are many more casual weight-lifters than professional body builders.

   (B) Most exercises that develop the back muscles help develop the biceps as well.

   (C) The back muscles are typically much larger than the biceps.

   (D) Knowledgeable weight-lifters are aware of the importance of a well-balanced workout.

   (E) Back muscles are considered essential for overall body stability.

Option II

4. Historian: Whenever people think of Henry Ford, they tend to think of the assembly line, often crediting him with its invention. But sequential production techniques, which we know as the assembly line, predate the Ford Motor Company by at least a century. Ford's great innovation, of course, was not the assembly line itself but instead the application of power to sequential production. As a result of Ford's combination of sequential production and direct-current power, the world saw the first widely affordable automobiles in 1919.

   The historian's statements above, if true, most strongly support which one of the following conclusions?

   (A) Henry Ford's sequential production techniques were not nearly as innovative as they are generally thought to be.

   (B) The Ford Motor Company's innovation inspired other automobile manufacturers to use electrical power with sequential production techniques.

   (C) Without direct-current power, Ford could not have combined electricity and sequential production techniques to create the modern assembly line.

   (D) The inventor of sequential production techniques is less well known than Henry Ford because Ford's achievement was more important to the development of modern technology.

   (E) There were no widely affordable automobiles during the first decade of the twentieth century.

Scenario 3

Option I

5. Philosopher: Critics of utilitarianism and related
    consequentialist theories have argued that
    they cannot provide a coherent theory of right
    action because they require an impossible set of
    calculations. They say that, using the utilitarian
    calculus, one cannot possibly determine which of an
    infinite set of possible actions provides the optimal
    utility in any given situation. But one can certainly
    compare any two choices and decide which of them
    is preferable, and this process can be repeated many
    times successfully. Thus, critics are wrong when
    they say that optimal utility is incalculable.

    The reasoning in the argument above is flawed in that

    (A)   It fails to consider the possibility that not all
          utilitarian or consequentialist theories suggest that
          optimal utility is required for right action.
    (B)   It improperly relies on the assumption that a
          utilitarian calculus requires repeated iterations of
          a decision procedure.
    (C)   It fails to distinguish between calculating the utility
          of actions versus calculating the utility of rules
          for governing action.
    (D)   It confuses what is the best of an infinite set of
          options with what is the best of a limited set of
          options.
    (E)   It confuses what is necessary for a successful
          utilitarian calculus to work with what is sufficient
          for it work.

Option II

6. Justin beat all seven of the other competitors in the race
    by over three seconds, with the second-place racer several
    meters behind. However, the wind helped improve his
    time by blowing in the direction that the runners were
    running. Hence Justin cannot claim a fair victory over his
    opponents.

    The argument is flawed because it

    (A)   neglects to consider the effect of air resistance in
          limiting a runner's speed
    (B)   presumes, without providing justification, that
          the recorded time for each of the runners was
          accurate
    (C)   fails to consider whether or not the wind improved
          Justin's time by more than three seconds
    (D)   overlooks the possibility that Justin may have won
          races against the same opponents before
    (E)   distinguishes one member of a group on the basis
          of something that applies equally to all members
          of the group

Scenario 4

Option I

7. It is difficult to grow cacti in a humid climate. It is difficult to raise orange trees in a cold climate. In most parts of a certain country, it is either easy to grow cacti or easy to raise orange trees.

   If the statements above are true, which one of the following must be false?

   (A) Half of the country is both humid and cold.
   (B) Most of the country is hot.
   (C) Some parts of the country are neither cold nor humid.
   (D) It is not possible to raise cacti in the country.
   (E) Most parts of the country are humid.

   Test 42, Section 4, Question 25

Option II

8. Skeletal remains of early humans indicate clearly that our ancestors had fewer dental problems than we have. So, most likely, the diet of early humans was very different from ours.

   Which one of the following, if true, most strengthens the argument?

   (A) A healthy diet leads to healthy teeth.
   (B) Skeletal remains indicate that some early humans had a significant number of cavities.
   (C) The diet of early humans was at least as varied as is our diet.
   (D) Early humans had a shorter average life span than we do, and the most serious dental problems now tend to develop late in life.
   (E) Diet is by far the most significant factor contributing to dental health.

   Test 40, Section 1, Question 6

Answers

Scenario 1:
Most people find question 2 easier to approach. Question 1 is longer and filled with conditional language, and each answer choice contains a full argument in itself. Parallel Flaw questions like question 1 are often very time-consuming. Question 2 is shorter and uses more conversational language.

Scenario 2:
Most people find question 3 easier to approach. Question 3 is much shorter and does not present any strange topics or logical constructions. Paradox questions like question 3 are usually among the easier question types.

Scenario 3:
Most people find question 6 easier to approach. Although both are Flaw questions, question 5 is longer and filled with difficult philosophical concepts. Question 6 is much shorter and uses more conversational language.

Scenario 4:
Most people find question 8 easier to approach. Both questions are relatively short, but question 7 is filled with conditional and quantifying statements, while question 8 is more straightforward and deals with approachable topics.

1. E
2. D
3. B
4. E
5. D
6. E
7. A
8. E

STOP. THIS IS THE END OF LECTURE 8. DO NOT PROCEED TO THE CORRESPONDING EXAM UNTIL INSTRUCTED TO DO SO IN CLASS.

LECTURE **9** CHAPTER **11**

PARALLEL REASONING QUESTIONS

11.1 IDENTIFY

11.1.1 WHAT IS PARALLEL REASONING?

Two arguments have *parallel reasoning* if they use identical methods of reasoning to proceed from premises to conclusion.

Here are two arguments that have parallel reasoning:

If someone is Greek, then he is European.	The Yomooza T28 is a cellular phone.
Stephanos is Greek.	All cellular phones have rechargeable batteries.
Therefore, Stephanos is European.	**Therefore**, the Yomooza T28 has a rechargeable battery.

Both of these arguments have the same method of reasoning. They each properly combine a conditional statement with a fact to reach their conclusion. Since they have the same method of reasoning, they have parallel reasoning.

You should note that there are some characteristics that these two arguments don't share. These are three characteristics that are NOT part of parallel reasoning:

1. **The Topic.** The topic of an argument has absolutely nothing to do with parallel reasoning. Topic should not factor into your consideration of whether two arguments are parallel.

2. **The Order.** The order in which the premises and conclusion are presented also has nothing to do with parallel reasoning. The two arguments above are a good example of this.

3. **The Wording.** Two arguments do not have to have identical wording to have parallel reasoning. In the example above, the conditional statements are worded differently, but they are still conditional statements.

11.1.2 IDENTIFYING PARALLEL REASONING QUESTIONS

All Parallel Reasoning questions follow the same pattern:

1. **The question stem asks you to choose the answer choice that** *parallels the reasoning* **in the passage.** Your job is to find the answer choice that is the closest match for the *reasoning* in the passage. This is what distinguishes Parallel Reasoning questions from every other question type. You have to find the best match in the answer choices for the reasoning in the passage.

2. **The passage contains an argument.** Parallel Reasoning questions are about *reasoning*, so the passage always contains an argument.

3. **Each of the answer choices is an argument.** Parallel Reasoning questions are unique in that each answer choice is an argument. That means that, between the passage and the answer choices, every Parallel Reasoning question consists of six arguments! This tends to make these questions longer and more time-consuming than most others.

KEY PHRASES
Parallel Reasoning Q's

Pattern of reasoning

Most similar
Most closely parallel

Here are some Parallel Reasoning question stems:

> If all of the social critic's statements are true, each of the following could be true EXCEPT:

> If all of the statements above are true, then which one of the following must be false?

> If all of the statements above are true, which one of the following CANNOT be true?

All of these ask you to identify an argument with the same pattern of reasoning as the argument in the passage.

Identifying Parallel Reasoning questions is especially important because of how time consuming they are. It's usually a good idea to save Parallel Reasoning questions for last, since you can often tackle two other questions in the time it takes you to deal with one Parallel Reasoning question.

That's roughly where the standard advice from most test preparation companies ends: Parallel Reasoning questions are time-consuming, so save them for the end. Fortunately, there's a *lot* more to say, and there are many ways to make Parallel Reasoning questions much more manageable.

Parallel Reasoning and Parallel Flaw questions appear about four times per test.

11.2 ANALYZE

11.2.1 ANALYZING PARALLEL REASONING QUESTIONS

The passage for a Parallel Reasoning question contains an argument, but these questions are flaw-independent, so you should identify the conclusion and premises as usual, but you can ignore the flaw. In addition, you can quickly and effectively deal with Parallel Reasoning questions by taking note of two things—the Parallel Pair:

1. Number and Types of Premises. Count how many premises there are, since the correct answer will always have the same number of premises as the argument in the passage.

   You should also look at the *types* of premises. It's not necessarily to get technical here. If the premises in the passage are conditionals, then you should see conditional premises in the correct answer. If there are quantity statements, or extreme statements like *must*, take note of those.

2. Type of Conclusion. Take note of the conclusion—is it a conditional, a recommendation, a prediction, a quantity statement, a counterargument, or an extreme statement? Whatever it is, the correct answer will need to have a

conclusion of the same type. It's not essential that you have a technical name for the type of conclusion. Just make sure that you have a feeling for the type of conclusion it is.

Take a look at how this works in an argument:

> 1. Politician: A government should tax a service if it is not essential for citizens. Public transportation is not essential for a government's citizens, so the government should tax public transportation.

Also notice words like *not*, *and*, and *or* as part of the Parallel Pair.

The argument works like this:

- A government should tax a service if it is not essential for citizens.

- Public transportation is not essential for a government's citizens.

Therefore, the government should tax public transportation.

Here's what you should find for the Parallel Pair:

1. Number and Types of Premises
   There are *two* premises. The first is a conditional, and the second states that there is something that matches the conditional.

2. Type of Conclusion
   The conclusion is a *should* statement—a prescriptive claim.

That's it. If you can find that much, you can find the correct answers to Parallel Reasoning questions. If you characterized things a little differently than what appears above, don't worry. As long as you look at the answer choices the same way you look at the passage, you'll be able to find the right answer.

11.2.2 Drill: The Parallel Pair

Analyze each of the following arguments, looking for the Parallel Pair.

1. Sweet Pickles is the horse most likely to win the upcoming race. After all, Sweet Pickles has won every race he has ever run in.

   (A) Number and Types of Premises:

   _____

   _____

   (B) Type of Conclusion:

   _____

   _____

2. All great impressionist paintings show effective use of color. This painting doesn't show effective use of color, so it's not a great impressionist painting.

   (A) Number and Types of Premises:

   _____

   _____

   (B) Type of Conclusion:

   _____

   _____

3. Most police officers regularly carry a weapon, and more than half of all police officers do not regularly wear a traditional police uniform. Therefore, at least one police officer regularly carries a weapon without wearing a traditional police uniform.

   (A) Number and Types of Premises:

   _____

   _____

   (B) Type of Conclusion:

   _____

   _____

Answers & Explanations

1. (A) There's one premise, and it's about *past performance*.

   (B) The conclusion is a prediction.

2. (A) There are two premises: a *conditional* and an *observation*.

   (B) The conclusion is a statement about the same thing as the second premise.

3. (A) There are two premises, both of which are *most* statements.

   (B) The conclusion is an *at least one* statement, which is the same as a *some* statement.

11.3 PREPHRASE

11.3.1 PREPHRASING ON PARALLEL REASONING QUESTIONS

There is an unlimited number of arguments that could have reasoning parallel to the reasoning in the passage, so there is no way you can predict the exact argument in the correct answer choice. But you can predict its features.

To Prephrase on Parallel Reasoning questions, all you have to do is remember the Parallel Pair from your analysis. The correct answer should have all the characteristics you identify as the Parallel Pair.

For example, you saw this argument above:

- A government should tax a service if it is not essential for citizens.
- Public transportation is not essential for a government's citizens.

Therefore, the government should tax public transportation.

In your analysis, you would identify the Parallel Pair, which you saw above. Your Prephrased answer would simply be a statement of what the correct answer must have:

> Prephrase: The correct answer must have two premises (including one conditional), and the conclusion must be a should statement.

That's it for Prephrasing. If some aspects of the Parallel Pair are too cumbersome to keep track of, then you can focus on the easier ones first. In any case, this is all you have to do.

Never try to predict the exact argument in the correct answer.

11.4 ATTACK

11.4.1 THE REAL QUESTION

Attacking the answers for Parallel Reasoning questions is all about matching the Parallel Pair. You can go quickly through the answers if you are looking only for the Parallel Pair.

The **Real Question** for Parallel Reasoning questions is this:

> *Does this match the Parallel Pair from the passage?*

If an answer matches the Parallel Pair, Keep it. If not, Cut it. It's that simple.

Try this on some answer choices, using the Prephrased answer from above. Remember, this is what you're looking for:

> Prephrase: The correct answer must have two premises (including one conditional), and the conclusion must be a should statement.

Here are some answer choices. Try to match the Parallel Pair, using the **Real Question**.

    (A)   A sports agent should represent a given athlete only if that athlete is a great athlete. If an athlete is great, the athlete can get a lucrative contract. Therefore, a sports agent should only represent those athletes who can get lucrative contracts.

Choice (A): *Does this match the Parallel Pair from the passage?* The Parallel Pair included only one conditional premise, but this has two conditionals. This doesn't match the Parallel Pair. *Cut it.*

    (B)   Most Baroque music is characterized by fast-moving melodic lines and relatively simple harmonies, compared to the music of the Classical period. Since this piece does not have fast-moving melodic lines, it is probably not Baroque.

Choice (B): *Does this match the Parallel Pair from the passage?* There are no conditional statements here. Instead, there is a *most* statement, but that doesn't match the Parallel Pair. *Cut it.*

    (C)   If a pesticide is harmful to the environment, it should not be used. Tweezle should not be used as a pesticide, so it must be harmful to the environment.

Choice (C): *Does this match the Parallel Pair from the passage?* This has two premises, including one conditional. But the conclusion isn't a *should* statement—it's a *must* statement. So this doesn't match either. *Cut it.*

    (D)   Dog owners should not spay or neuter their pets if they do not plan to use their dogs for breeding. Yoomi does not plan to use her dogs for breeding, so she should spay or neuter her pets.

Choice (D): *Does this match the Parallel Pair from the passage?* This has two premises, including one conditional. The conclusion is a *should* statement. This is a good match. *Keep it.*

    (E)   A government should tax products that are dangerous to the health of its citizens. Therefore, if a product is dangerous to the health of citizens, the government should tax it.

Choice (E): *Does this match the Parallel Pair from the passage?* This has a similar topic as the original argument, but this is meaningless on Parallel Reasoning questions. Just focus on the Parallel Pair. This has only one premise, so it's definitely out. *Cut it.*

Choice (D) is the correct answer.

You can often skim the answer choices, just looking for deviations from the Parallel Pair, instead of getting too caught up in following the logic of the choices. This can save a lot of time.

11.4.2 Drill: Matching the Parallel Pair

Each of the following has a description of Parallel Pair and two arguments. Choose the argument that matches the Parallel Pair.

1. Number and Types of Premises: One conditional premise.

    Type of Conclusion: Conditional conclusion.

    (A) Most antibiotics can become ineffective when they are improperly taken. Therefore, most people who take antibiotics improperly rarely see the full benefits of their treatment.

    (B) If someone cannot distinguish blue from black, that person is considered colorblind. Thus, anyone who is not considered colorblind must be able to distinguish blue from black.

2. Number and Types of Premises: Two premises: an either/or statement and a denial.

    Type of Conclusion: A must statement.

    (A) This alleged criminal must be correctly accused. After all, this alleged criminal is not incorrectly accused, and all alleged criminals are either correctly or incorrectly accused.

    (B) All neighborhoods in this town are either wealthy or poor. This neighborhood is probably not poor, so there is an excellent chance that it is wealthy.

3. Number and Types of Premises: Two premises: one conditional and one fact.

    Type of Conclusion: A must statement.

    (A) If over three percent of a nation's adult citizens open new savings accounts in a given year, then the economy is strong. Thus, the economy in country D must be strong, since four percent of country D's adult citizens opened new savings accounts this year.

    (B) If oil prices increase, spending decreases, and if spending decreases, the economy suffers. Since oil prices are increasing, it must be true that the economy will suffer.

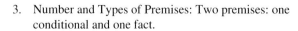

Answers & Explanations

1. **Choice (B) is correct.** Choice (A) has *most* statements, not conditionals.

2. **Choice (A) is correct.** Choice (B) has a conclusion with high probability, but the conclusion should be a *must* statement

3. **Choice (A) is correct.** Choice (B) has an extra conditional premise.

11.4.3 BEYOND THE PARALLEL PAIR

The vast majority of the time, the Parallel Pair can get you the correct answer right away. Four answers won't match the Parallel Pair, and one will. Choose the match.

But sometimes matching the Parallel Pair leaves you with two answer choices. In that case:

1. Compare the answer choices you have left and isolate a difference.

2. Check the argument from the passage to see, based on the isolated difference, which answer is a better match.

There will always be a difference between the two answers you are left with after using the Parallel Pair. If you can isolate the difference, then you can use it to choose the correct answer.

Here are two arguments that do *not* have parallel reasoning, but yet they pass the test of the Parallel Pair. What is the difference between them?

*   Number and Type of Premises: Two premises: one conditional and one fact.

*   Type of Conclusion: A statement about the past.

Example 1

*   If we rented *The Amazing*, we were going to buy popcorn.

*   We bought popcorn.

Therefore, we rented *The Amazing*.

Example 2

*   If June went to the park, she was going to walk her dog.

*   June went to the park.

Therefore, she walked her dog.

These arguments would match using the Parallel Pair: they both have two premises of the same type and a conclusion of the same type.

So what's the difference? The difference is that the first example uses the conditional backwards—it doesn't make a proper inference! The second example uses the conditional properly. Once you isolate a difference between two answer choices in this way, you can look at the argument in the passage and ask whether it properly or improperly uses a conditional. In this case, example 2 would almost certainly be correct—the vast majority of Parallel Reasoning questions do not have flawed reasoning.

11.4.4 DISTRACTERS

There are two types of distracters that are especially common on Parallel Reasoning questions:

Topic Trap

Some answer choices have topics that are similar to the topic in the passage. The writers of the LSAT hope that test-takers will be distracted by the similarities in topics and overlook the differences in reasoning. Never choose an answer based on topic.

Word Trap

Some answer choices will use identical words and phrases as the passage. Again, the LSAT writers hope that they can distract you with identical words and force you to ignore the differences in reasoning. Don't choose an answer choice based on identical wording.

In addition to the traps that try to make you pick the wrong answer, there is another common trap the test writers use *to try to get you to eliminate the correct answer*:

Mixed-Up Order

Often, the correct answer contains the same components of reasoning as the passage, but presented in a different order. Don't be bothered by this. Order makes no difference when you are dealing with Parallel Reasoning questions. If you see an answer choice with the same reasoning in a mixed-up order, *Keep it*.

11.5 PUTTING IT ALL TOGETHER

Here are some examples of Parallel Reasoning questions:

> 2. Alvin claimed that he went to the ceremony to show support for the honoree. If this were true, though, he would have made an effort to talk to the honoree, which he did not. So he must have had another motive for attending the ceremony.
>
> Which one of the following most closely parallels the reasoning in the passage above?

1. Identify

This question asks you to choose the answer that most closely parallels the reasoning in the passage, so this is a Parallel Reasoning question.

2. Analyze

Here's how the argument works:

- Alvin claimed that he went to show support for the honoree.
- If he went to show support, he would have tried to talk to the honoree.
- He did not.

Therefore, he must have had another motive.

Here's what you should find for the **Parallel Pair**:

1. Number and Types of Premises
   There are *three* premises: a *claim*, a *conditional* associated with the claim, and an *observation*.

2. Type of Conclusion
   The conclusion is a *denial* of the original claim: it says there must have been some other reason.

3. Prephrase

Your Prephrased answer should be a statement of what the correct answer must have:

> Prephrase: The correct answer must have three premises: a claim, a conditional, and an observation. The correct answer must have a conclusion that denies the original claim by saying something like, "It must have been something else."

That's it. It's time to attack the answer choices.

4. Attack

Try to match the Parallel Pair.

> (A)   Zan said he went to the grocery store to buy some ham. If this were true, he would have returned with some ham, which he did. So this was probably his reason for going to the grocery store.

Choice (A): *Does this match the Parallel Pair from the passage?* The premises are a good match, but the conclusion is not. The conclusion doesn't deny the original claim. Instead, it affirms the original claim. *Cut it.*

> (B)   Tracy said she borrowed the book because a friend recommended it to her. However, she also read a positive review of the book in the newspaper. So she had at least two reasons for borrowing the book.

Choice (B): *Does this match the Parallel Pair from the passage?* This has no *conditional* statement. That means it doesn't match the premises from the passage. *Cut it.*

> (C)   Del said he made the sculpture to display on his mantle. However, since he does not have a mantle, this is impossible. So he must have had another motive for making the sculpture.

Choice (C): *Does this match the Parallel Pair from the passage?* This also has no *conditional* statement. For the same reason you eliminated choice (B), you can get rid of it. *Cut it.*

> (D)   Doug said he called his wife to ask how her trip was going. However, he also asked whether there were any errands he needed to run and whether she needed him to pick her up from the airport. So he must have had several reasons for calling his wife.

If there are conditional statements in the passage, looking for the same number of conditional statements in the answers can be a very fast way to eliminate a few choices.

Choice (D): *Does this match the Parallel Pair from the passage?* This also has no *conditional* statement, so it's also out. *Cut it.*

> (E)   Vince said he joined the team to get in shape. However, if this were true, he would have exerted himself during practices, which he failed to do. So he must have had another reason for joining the team.

Choice (E): *Does this match the Parallel Pair from the passage?* This has the right number and types of premises. It also has the right type of conclusion. *Keep it.*

See how fast that works? On this one, you can eliminate *three* answer choices just by looking for a conditional statement!

Choice (E) is the correct answer.

Here's another one:

3. Having a long time off from work can sometimes be detrimental to the quality of one's work by negatively impacting work ethic, but more often the rest and recuperation is helpful. Therefore it is likely that Tim's work will be better upon his return from his long vacation.

The reasoning in which one of the following arguments is most similar to that in the argument above?

1. Identify

This question stem is asking about *most similar reasoning*, so it's a Parallel Reasoning question.

2. Analyze

Here's how the argument works:

> Having a long time off can sometimes be detrimental, but it is more often helpful.
> ....
> **Therefore**, Tom's long time off is probably helpful.

Here's what you should find for the **Parallel Pair**:

1. **Number and Types of Premises**
   There is only *one* premise. It says something is sometimes bad, but more often good.

2. **Type of Conclusion**
   The conclusion brings in a *person*, saying that what the person does will be good.

> You can describe the Parallel Pair in a way that makes sense to you—don't worry about getting too technical. You'll have to practice to settle on the right level of detail.

3. Prephrase

Your Prephrased answer should be a statement of what the correct answer must have:

> Prephrase: The correct answer must have one premise: a claim that something is sometimes bad, but more often good. The correct answer must have a conclusion that brings in a person, saying what the person does will be good.

4. Attack

(A) Installing new computers can sometimes be detrimental to office efficiency as workers need to learn to use the new machines, but it can also be helpful if the new computers are superior to the ones they are replacing. Therefore, Manu's decision to install new computers in the office is justified if they are sufficiently superior to the old computers.

Choice (A): *Does this match the Parallel Pair from the passage?* This has a *conditional* statement in the conclusion, but there were no conditionals in the passage. *Cut it.*

(B) Many shows on television are of very low quality in terms of both their writing and acting, but most shows are fairly entertaining or informative. Therefore, Tony should buy a television.

Choice (B): *Does this match the Parallel Pair from the passage?* This has a conclusion with a *recommendation*, but there were no recommendations in the passage. *Cut it.*

(C) Taking a plane on cross-country trips can sometimes be slower than driving, due to flight delays and layovers, but more often it is much faster. Therefore, Bruce will probably arrive at his cross-country destination faster if he takes a plane rather than a car.

Choice (C): *Does this match the Parallel Pair from the passage?* This says that planes are *sometimes bad, but more often good*. It has Bruce taking a plane, and it says that Bruce will probably be better off. This seems to be a good match, so leave it in. *Keep it.*

(D) Fugues are sometimes interesting in their polyphonic melding of separate but similar melodies, but they are always difficult to play. Therefore, it is likely that the fugue that Rasho composed is interesting.

Choice (D): *Does this match the Parallel Pair from the passage?* This has an *always* statement in the premise. This is an **extreme** claim, but the passage has no such extreme claim. *Cut it.*

(E) Athlete's foot sometimes goes away on its own after a few days, but it sometimes persists for months. Therefore, Greg's case of athlete's foot will probably require medication.

> Extreme claims can appear in the correct answer for a Parallel Reasoning question. The key is to watch out for them in the passage first. If there is an extreme claim in the passage, one will appear in the correct answer. If the passage doesn't have an extreme claim, the correct answer won't have one either.

Choice (E): *Does this match the Parallel Pair from the passage?* This introduces a *new concept* in its conclusion, namely medication. But in the passage, the conclusion only introduces a new person, Tim. The conclusion has no new concepts. *Cut it.*

Choice (C) is the correct answer.

11.6 VARIATIONS

11.6.1 PARALLEL FLAW QUESTIONS

Parallel Flaw are very similar to Parallel Reasoning questions, since you are again asked to find an argument in the answer choices that has reasoning parallel to that in the original argument. But these questions are different from Parallel Reasoning questions in a few ways:

1. **Parallel Flaw question stems indicate that the passage has flawed reasoning.** This is the easiest way to distinguish Parallel Flaw from Parallel Reasoning questions quickly. Parallel Flaw question stems always use words such as *flawed reasoning* to indicate that the passage has flawed reasoning.

2. **Parallel Flaw questions are flaw-dependent.** Every Parallel Flaw question has a passage with a flawed argument. Since your job is to parallel the flawed reasoning from the passage, you must be aware of the flaw in the passage.

3. **Parallel Flaw questions give you additional tools to use when attacking the answer choices.** You can use a *Prephrased flaw* to find the correct answer to Parallel Flaw questions. For example, if the argument from the passage has a causal flaw, then the correct answer must also have a causal flaw.

Here's some specific advice on each part of your strategy on Parallel Flaw questions:

1. Identify

Parallel Flaw question stems are just like Parallel Reasoning question stems. The only difference is that Parallel Flaw questions always refer to *flawed* reasoning. Here are some Parallel Flaw question stems:

> The flawed reasoning in the argument above is most similar to that in which one of the following?

> Which one of the following employs a flawed argumentative strategy that is most closely parallel to the flawed argumentative strategy above?

> The questionable pattern of reasoning in the argument above is most similar to that in which one of the following?

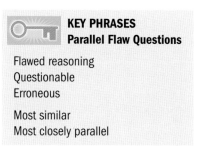

KEY PHRASES
Parallel Flaw Questions

Flawed reasoning
Questionable
Erroneous

Most similar
Most closely parallel

All of these ask you to parallel the flawed reasoning from the passage.

2. Analyze

Your analysis of Parallel Flaw questions is different from your analysis of Parallel Reasoning questions. You should identify:

1. The premises
2. The conclusion
3. The flaw

Since Parallel Flaw questions are all about the flaw in the passage, you must identify it. This is different from your approach to Parallel Reasoning questions, but it works to your advantage: by taking advantage of the flaw you can usually Prephrase and attack Parallel Flaw questions much more quickly than you can Parallel Reasoning questions.

Parallel Flaw questions use **common flaws** more often than any other question type. This is one more reason to know your common flaws: if you know the common flaws, you can spot them quickly in Parallel Flaw passages and attack the answers.

You should *not* bother to analyze for the Parallel Pair on Parallel Flaw questions—just finding the flaw is almost always enough to get you the correct answer. But if the flaw is not enough, or if you are unable to find the flaw on a given question, you can always revert back to treating a Parallel Flaw question just like a Parallel Reasoning question and use the Parallel Pair. However, this is a slower approach.

3. Prephrase

Prephrasing on Parallel Flaw questions consists of knowing what flaw you are looking for. For example, if the argument from the passage has a necessary vs. sufficient flaw, your Prephrased answer would describe what the correct answer must have:

> Prephrase: The correct answer must have a necessary vs. sufficient flaw.

Again, avoid Prephrasing a specific argument.

That's it. Don't be deceived by how fast this process is: it is very important. Parallel Flaw questions are among the best questions to Prephrase on. If you know what kind of Flaw you are looking for, you are likely to find the correct answer quickly.

4. Attack

Attacking the answers on Parallel Flaw questions means looking for the same flaw as the one in the passage. As a result, the **Real Question** is different.

The **Real Question** for Parallel Flaw questions is:

> *Does this match the flaw in the passage?*

If you don't get down to one answer choice using the flaw, you can of course use the Parallel Pair to supplement your approach. But finding the flaw is a more efficient way to deal with Parallel Flaw questions, so that should be your primary point of attack.

Try this example:

4. The student body at Walton High School participates in a variety of extracurricular activities. Umair is a student at Walton High School, so he must participate in a variety of extracurricular activities.

The flawed reasoning in which one of the following is most similar to that in the argument above?

1. Identify

The question asks for *flawed reasoning* similar to the passage, so it's a Parallel Flaw question.

2. Analyze

Here's how the argument works:

- Walton High School students participate in a variety of extracurricular activities.
- Umair is a student at Walton High School.

Therefore, Umair participates in a variety of extracurricular activities.

After identifying the premises and conclusion, you need to identify the argument's flaw. You should start by looking for common flaws. Does this argument have a common flaw? It says that Umair does something because he is a member of a larger group that does something. This reasoning has a **division flaw**—it assumes that what is true of the whole (student body) must also be true of its parts (individual students). If you didn't see the flaw, you could catch it using Concept Shift between Umair and the student body.

A **division flaw** occurs when an argument assumes that what is true of a whole must be true of its parts.

3. Prephrase

To Prephrase on Parallel Flaw questions, just state what the correct answer must have. The correct answer must always have the same flaw as the passage, which is usually a common flaw:

Prephrase: The correct answer must have a division flaw.

You must know your common flaws. If you can spot them quickly, Parallel Flaw questions will be much easier.

4. Attack

You are looking for a division flaw.

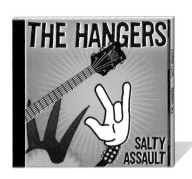

(A) The songs on The Hangers' new album represent a greater variety of distinct styles than the songs on their previous album. Therefore, their new album is the superior album.

Choice (A): *Does this match the flaw in the passage?* This does not have a division flaw—there is no whole-to-part problem. *Cut it.*

(B) The actors in the theater production of *Glue* come from a varied range of acting backgrounds. Meyer is an actor in the theater production of *Glue*, so he must have an acting background different from that of some of the other actors in the production.

Choice (B): *Does this match the flaw in the passage?* This looks like a division flaw, since it makes a statement about the group and then a statement about the individual. *Keep it.*

(C)   The players on the Meltdowns have many
        valuable skills. Carl is a player on the
        Meltdowns, so he must be better than the players
        on the Jets.

Choice (C): *Does this match the flaw in the passage?* This is not a division flaw. It brings in a comparison to an entirely different team than the original one being discussed. *Cut it.*

(D)   The employees at this firm have a wide variety of
        abilities. Hitesh is an employee at this firm, so
        he must have a wide variety of abilities.

Choice (D): *Does this match the flaw in the passage?* Like choice (B), this seems like it might have some division issues. *Keep it.*

(E)   The mechanics on staff at AutoMan have a wide
        variety of tools at their disposal. Frank is a
        mechanic at CarGuy, so he must not have as
        many different tools at his disposal.

Choice (E): *Does this match the flaw in the passage?* This is not a division flaw. Like choice (C), it brings in extra stuff, this time another car company. *Cut it.*

If you find yourself down to two, you should look carefully at what you are left with—there's a difference that makes one of them incorrect.

Choice (B) says the actors come from varied backgrounds, so Meyer must come from a background different than some of the other actors. Wait a minute…that sounds pretty reasonable. In fact, this argument is actually *valid*. If there is more than one background in the company, Meyer must have a different background than somebody else. If the reasoning here isn't flawed, then it can't be the correct answer to a Parallel Flaw question. Choice (B) is out.

> The correct answer to Parallel Flaw questions *always* has flawed reasoning.

Choice (D), however, is genuinely flawed. Just because the firm *as a whole* has a wide variety of abilities does not mean that any *individual* has a wide variety of abilities. In fact, every single employee might have a single, unique skill. Choice (D) has a division flaw.

Choice (D) is the correct answer.

Here's another example:

5. Many hot, clear mornings are not followed by afternoon thunderstorms, and many thunderstorms occur following weather that is not hot and clear. Therefore, this afternoon's thunderstorm must not have been caused by the hot, clear weather this morning.

Which one of the following contains flawed reasoning most similar to that in the argument above?

1. Identify

Flawed reasoning and *most similar* tell you that you are looking at a Parallel Flaw question.

2. Analyze

Here's how this argument works:

- Many hot, clear mornings are not followed by afternoon thunderstorms.
- Many thunderstorms occur following weather that is not hot and clear.

Therefore, this afternoon's thunderstorm must not have been caused by the hot, clear weather this morning.

As this is a Parallel Flaw question, you should try to identify the flaw, but this time around it doesn't seem to be a **common flaw**, at least not one that is easily recognizable. You have two options at this point, each of which would work well: 1) look for the flaw anyway (either through the Concept Shift or some other method) and use that throughout the answers, or 2) treat this as a Parallel Reasoning question and work through the answers using the tools for that question type.

Since it's worth seeing how similar these question types really are, try to use the latter approach this time around. But remember that either approach can get you the correct answer.

If you treat this like a Parallel Reasoning question, you should find the Parallel Pair.

1. Number and Types of Premises
    There are *two* premises. They are both *many* statements about how one event can occur *without* another.

2. Type of Conclusion
    The conclusion is a *must not* statement, which is extreme.

3. Prephrase

Your Prephrased answer should be a statement of what the correct answer must have:

> Prephrase: The correct answer must have two premises, both of which need to be many statements about how one event can occur without another event. The conclusion must be a must not statement.

4. Attack

Since you are treating this like a Parallel Reasoning question, use the same **Real Question**: *Does this match the Parallel Pair in the passage?*

(A)   Many currency appreciations do not precede recessions, and many recessions occur when there has been no recent currency appreciation. Therefore, the current recession must not have been caused by a currency appreciation.

Choice (A): *Does this match the Parallel Pair in the passage?* This has two *many* statements as premises, both of which are about events occurring without one another. The conclusion is a *must not* statement. This is a good match. *Keep it.*

(B)   Many shifts of tectonic plates do not result in earthquakes, but all earthquakes are the result of shifts in tectonic plates. Therefore, the recent earthquake must have been caused by shifts in tectonic plates.

Choice (B): *Does this match the Parallel Pair in the passage?* This has a *many* statement and an *all* statement. But the passage doesn't have an *all* statement, so this is a bad match. *Cut it.*

(C)   Many blackouts are caused by downed power lines, and many blackouts are caused by computer malfunctions at power distribution control centers. Therefore, the recent blackout must have been caused by a downed power line.

Choice (C): *Does this match the Parallel Pair in the passage?* This has two *many* statements as premises, but they are not about events that occur without one another. So this is also a bad match. *Cut it.*

(D)   Many fires are the result of electrical short circuit, and many electrical short circuits cause fires. Therefore, the fire could have been caused by an electrical malfunction.

You can use the same tools for Parallel Reasoning questions on Parallel Flaw questions because Parallel Flaw questions are just a variation on the other. If the flaw is obvious, it's usually easier to focus on the flaw. But when the flaw is not obvious, you can still find the answer using your other tools.

Choice (D): *Does this match the Parallel Pair in the passage?* This has two *many* statements as premises, but the conclusion is a *could* statement rather than a *must* statement. *Cut it.*

> (E)   Many unsafe tools are not power tools, but all
>   power tools are somewhat unsafe. Therefore, the
>   tools on sale must not be safe.

Choice (E): *Does this match the Parallel Pair in the passage?* This, like choice (B), includes an *all* statement, so it's definitely wrong. *Cut it.*

Choice (A) is the correct answer.

11.7 THE BIG PICTURE

You have probably noticed that many different types of Logical Reasoning questions call for the same kinds of skills. For example, you know that finding premises and the conclusion is crucial for many different types of questions.

Another skill that you have already been practicing on many different types of questions is the skill of *matching*. Here is a list of all the different kinds of questions in which matching is important.

Question Type	Your Goal
Main Point	Your goal is to find the answer choice that <u>matches</u> the conclusion that was stated in the passage
Flaw	Your goal is to find the answer choice that <u>matches</u> the flaw that occurred in the passage
Misinterpretation	Your goal is to find the answer choice that <u>matches</u> the misinterpretation that occurred in the passage
Method	Your goal is to find the answer choice that <u>matches</u> the method of reasoning that was used in the passage
Role	Your goal is to find the answer choice that <u>matches</u> the role of one particular claim as it was used in the passage
Conform	Your goal is to find the answer choice that <u>matches</u> the principle that was stated or illustrated in the passage
Parallel Reasoning	Your goal is to find the answer choice that <u>matches</u> the method of reasoning that was used in the passage
Parallel Flaw	Your goal is to find the answer choice that <u>matches</u> the method of reasoning (including the flaw) that was used in the passage

The best test-takers see parallels, connections, and repeated patterns throughout the test, rather than just a collection of isolated question types.

On the LSAT, matching two things can take several forms.

The easiest kind of matching is when you are simply looking for a sentence that repeats or restates another sentence, such as in Main Point questions.

A more complicated kind of matching occurs when you have to look for a sentence that describes a specific situation in more general or abstract terms, such as in Method questions.

The most complicated kind of matching is when you have to find a situation that contains the same underlying structure as a completely different situation, such as in Parallel questions.

However, these are all just different versions of the same skill. As you practice the different types of questions that involve matching, notice how the LSAT writers ask you to use this skill, and think about how the skill you are building can be transferred to other question types.

STOP. THIS IS THE END OF LECTURE 9. DO NOT PROCEED TO THE CORRESPONDING EXAM UNTIL INSTRUCTED TO DO SO IN CLASS.

Copyright © 2007 Examkrackers, Inc.

REVIEW OF FLAW-DEPENDENT QUESTION TYPES

12.1 THE FLAW-DEPENDENT QUESTION TYPES

By now, you have seen everything that the LSAT writers can throw at you in the Logical Reasoning section. You have seen that some passages contain arguments, while others do not. You learned that when a passage does contain an argument, it is sometimes unnecessary to notice the flaw in the reasoning, but many question types cannot be correctly answered unless you have a firm grasp of exactly where the argument went wrong. These question types are called flaw-dependent questions.

Here's a list of all the flaw-dependent question types:

- **Flaw** and its variation, Misinterpretation

- **Weaken** and its variation, Strengthen

- **Necessary Assumption** and its variation, Evaluate

- **Sufficient Assumption** and its variation, Justify

- **Parallel Flaw**

12.2 THE COMMON FEATURES OF FLAW-DEPENDENT QUESTIONS

Although these different question types call on you to use your skills in different ways, the one thing they all have in common is that you need to know exactly what the flaw in the argument is before you move on to the answer choices.

You have several tools at your disposal to help you find the flaw in an argument. Throughout this book, you have seen the words *flaw*, *concept shift*, and *assumption* all used to describe very similar ideas. In a way, they are all exactly the same thing. They all describe, in slightly different ways, how an argument goes wrong.

Here is a review of these ideas and the tools you can use to find the flaw.

12.2.1 COMMON FLAWS

Some flawed patterns of reasoning appear over and over on the LSAT. That's because people use them over and over in real life without noticing it. Train yourself to recognize these common flaws, and you'll have more success on the LSAT and in winning arguments with your friends.

Common Flaw	Description
Necessary vs. Sufficient	• Some things are needed (*necessary*) to bring about a certain outcome, but they might not be the only thing needed. • Some things can, by themselves, guarantee that a certain outcome will occur (they are *sufficient*), but there might be other ways the same outcome could also occur. Don't confuse the two.
Correlation vs. Causation (Causal)	It is very common for two trends to match or for two things to occur at or close to the same time (*correlation*), but that doesn't mean that one *caused* the other. Instead of A causing B, perhaps: • B caused A. • C caused both A and B. • It was just a random coincidence.
Sampling	It is possible to draw a valid conclusion about a large group of people or things based on what you know about a small group. However, in order to do so: • The small group must be *representative* of the large group. • The way in which you draw your conclusion about the small group must be free of *methodological* errors (e.g. biased questions). If these criteria are not followed, then there is a sampling flaw.
Analogy	It is possible to use an analogy between two things to draw a valid conclusion. However, in order to do so, the two things must actually be *analogous* in every way that could be important to the argument.
Absence of Evidence	Something can still be true even if there is no evidence to prove it. Don't make the mistake of thinking that, if there is no evidence to show that X is true, then the opposite of X must be true. Perhaps no one has bothered to gather any evidence yet.
False Dichotomy	A *false dichotomy* flaw occurs when someone assumes that there are only two possible choices, when in fact there could be more than two. If someone says, "We can't use plan A, so we have to go with plan B," you should ask, "What about plan C?"
Composition and Division	• A *composition* flaw occurs when someone assumes that a characteristic that is true for every member of a group must also be true for the group itself. • A *division* flaw occurs when someone assumes that a characteristic that is true for a group as a whole must also be true for every member of the group.
Statistics	When comparing two groups, you need to know something about the relative *size* of each group. Otherwise it is very misleading to • use *percentages* to draw a conclusion about *numbers*. • use *numbers* to draw a conclusion about *percentages*. Things like probability and safety are just a subtle way of talking about percentages.
Personal Attack	Attacking a person's *character* is a logically flawed way of arguing against that person's *conclusion*. Address the issue, not the person.

Appeal to Authority	Some arguments use evidence such as "Theory Z must be true because Ms. R says it's true." In cases like this, you have to make sure that Ms. R's opinion really means anything. Is she a credible authority on the topic? Could her opinion be biased in any way?
Equivocation	It's a logical flaw to base an argument on switching between *two different meanings* of the same word. This is not the same as failing to define a word. Failing to provide the definition of something is **not** a logical flaw.
Circularity	If someone's conclusion is just a restatement of one of the premises, then the argument is *circular*. That's a flaw.

12.2.2 THE CONCEPT SHIFT

The Concept Shift is the most common flaw of all. Simply put, if an argument bases its premises on one concept but draws a conclusion about a different concept, then it has committed a logical flaw. The same can be said if the shift occurs between two premises.

To spot the Concept Shift, look for a place where the argument uses two different concepts, one of which is intended to lead to the other. You can ask yourself the following question:

What two non-identical concepts are intended to be connected?

It's important to note that the two sides of the shift must be truly different concepts, not just the same concept expressed in different words. There can't be a shift between identical concepts.

12.2.3 ANOTHER WAY TO FIND THE FLAW

Sometimes an argument doesn't contain a common flaw and doesn't contain an immediately obvious Concept Shift. You should still make every effort to express how the argument went wrong before you start looking at the answer choices. It often helps to construct the following sentence and try to complete it:

just because

> Just because {premise} is true, that doesn't
> automatically mean that {conclusion} is true,
> because _____.

12.2.4 NECESSARY ASSUMPTIONS

A necessary assumption is something left out of the argument that needs to be true in order for the argument to be valid. When constructing the argument, the author assumed that certain questionable things were true but didn't provide any evidence to show they were actually true. That's bad logical reasoning—that's a flaw.

Sometimes you can immediately spot the assumptions made in an argument. It's also helpful to know the assumptions built in to all of the common flaws. For example, take a look at this argument:

> Elena fell asleep in her armchair while smoking a
> cigarette. Five minutes after she fell asleep, a fire
> started in her house. Therefore, Elena's still-burning
> cigarette must have caused the fire.

The author confuses a *correlation* (her falling asleep happened at the same time as the fire) with *causation* (the cigarette caused the fire). A necessary assumption in this case—and in every causal flaw—is that there was no other possible cause for the fire, such as faulty wiring.

12.2.5 Flaws, Concept Shifts, & Assumptions Are All the Same

Don't feel overwhelmed. These three ideas are all really the same. They are all just different ways to express how an argument goes wrong, and once you've discovered the author's mistake, you are well prepared to find the correct answer, no matter how you express that mistake. Take a look at this example:

> Ivana is the best-liked student at Moeller High School. This is evident from the fact that she received more votes than any candidate in school history in the recent student council election.

You can probably see where this argument went wrong. Here are several ways to express the argument's problem:

Concept Shift: The author's evidence concerns *how many votes* she received, but the conclusion is about *how well-liked* she is. The Concept Shift is:

How many votes ⚡ How well-liked

Necessary assumption: The author assumed that the number of votes a candidate receives is influenced by how well-liked that candidate is.

Flaw: The author failed to consider that the number of votes a candidate receives may not be influenced by how well-liked that candidate is.

As you can see, these all address the same problem. This argument has a second problem, which can also be expressed in these three ways:

Concept Shift: The author's evidence concerns how she compares to other candidates *in the election*, but the conclusion is about how she compares to students *in the entire school*. The Concept Shift is:

Comparison to other candidates ⚡ Comparison to all students

Necessary assumption: The author assumed that a comparison to the other candidates in a student council election can be used to draw a comparison to all students.

Flaw: The author failed to consider that a comparison to the other candidates in a student council election may not be a good way to draw a comparison to all students.

Again, these are three ways of expressing the same problem in the argument.

12.3.6 All Flaw-Dependent Questions Merit the Same Analysis

Your analysis of every flaw-dependent question type is the same:

Find the premises and conclusion. Then use these to find the flaw.

After that, what you do with the flaw varies depending on the question type. But the good news is that since you are using the same approach on so many different question types, you should become very well-practiced at this process. Since the LSAT writers use the same flaws over and over again, lots of practice should lead you to high speed and accuracy in this process.

> You don't have to express every flaw in every possible way. Once you see where an argument goes wrong, you're ready to move on.

12.3 A REVIEW OF EACH QUESTION TYPE

12.3.1 FLAW QUESTIONS

Flaw questions are the most common type of Logical Reasoning question. Most tests have about eight Flaw questions.

1. Identify

Flaw question stems ask you to identify the argument's flaw.

Here are some common Flaw question stems:

> The reasoning in the argument is flawed because the argument presumes, without providing justification, that

> The reasoning in the argument is most vulnerable to criticism on the grounds that it fails to consider the possibility that

> Which one of the following most accurately describes an error in the reasoning above?

> A questionable aspect of the reasoning above is that it

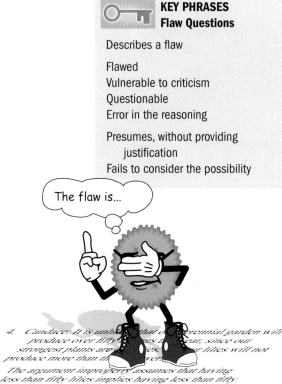

**KEY PHRASES
Flaw Questions**

Describes a flaw

Flawed
Vulnerable to criticism
Questionable
Error in the reasoning

Presumes, without providing justification
Fails to consider the possibility

The flaw is...

2. Analyze

To analyze a Flaw passage, look for:

- The conclusion
- The premises
- The flaw

3. Prephrase

To Prephrase on a Flaw question, state the argument's flaw. You can state the flaw in several ways:

- State the flaw immediately, if it's a common flaw or if the flaw is obvious without the Concept Shift.

- Look for the Concept Shift and turn it into a statement of a flaw.

> You never want to look at the answer choices without expressing the flaw yourself.

Either way, Prephrasing is more powerful on Flaw questions than on any other question type. If you Prephrase well, you are likely to find your Prephrased answer in the answer choices.

4. Attack

The Real Question for Flaw questions is:

Is this a flaw in the argument?

The correct answer has to describe something the argument actually did (*in the argument*) and something that's actually an error in reasoning (*a flaw*). If you keep this in mind, you'll be able to avoid the common distracters for Flaw questions.

Flaw questions have two common distracters:

- **Doesn't match** the argument
- **Not a flaw**

12.3.2 WEAKEN QUESTIONS

Weaken questions are a very common type of Logical Reasoning question. Most tests have about five Weaken questions.

1. Identify

Weaken question stems require that you accept the truth of the answer choices, and they ask you to choose the statement that most weakens the argument.

Here are some Weaken question stems:

> Which one of the following, if true, most seriously weakens the argument?
>
> Which one of the following statements, if true, would most seriously undermine the conclusion above?
>
> Which one of the following, if true, casts the most doubt on the scholar's interpretation?
>
> Which one of the following statements, if true, most calls into question the critic's argument?

2. Analyze

To analyze a Weaken passage, look for:

- The conclusion
- The premises
- The flaw

3. Prephrase

The correct answer to a Weaken question will *suggest* (not prove) that the conclusion is untrue.

It does so by attacking a weakness already present in the argument. You don't need to Prephrase a specific attack on the argument. Instead, you should Prephrase what kind of attack the answer is likely to make. For example, you could predict that the correct answer will undermine the argument's assumption that the population of the city remained the same over the time period in question, but you don't need to predict exactly what information the answer choice will use in order to do so.

4. Attack

The Real Question for Weaken Questions is:

> *Does this suggest that the conclusion is untrue?*

You should always adapt the Real Question to fit the particular passage you are working on. Instead of "the conclusion is untrue," substitute the negation of the conclusion into the Real Question. For example, if an argument's conclusion is that a certain report is biased, you should adapt the Real Question to be, *"Does this suggest that the report is NOT biased?"*

Look for these distracters on Weaken questions:

Opposite

Wrong answers to Weaken questions often strengthen rather than weaken the argument.

Out of Scope

You have to be very careful with answers that appear out of scope on Weaken questions because answers that introduce new considerations can weaken the argument and are often correct.

12.3.3 STRENGTHEN QUESTIONS

Strengthen questions are just like Weaken questions, and you should approach Strengthen and Weaken questions in the same way. The only difference is the kind of answer you should look for. For Strengthen questions, the correct answer is the one that most strengthens the argument in the passage.

There are about four Strengthen questions on each test.

1. Identify

Strengthen question stems tell you to accept the truth of the answer choices and ask for an answer that strengthens the argument in the passage.

Here are some of the more common variations:

> Which one of the following, if true, most strengthens the argument?

> Which one of the following, if true, would provide the most support for the physician's assertion?

KEY PHRASES
Strengthen Questions

The following, if true

Strengthens
Provides the most support

Because both Inference and Strengthen question stems can contain the word *support*, you have to be careful not to confuse the two. Remember that a Strengthen question asks for the answer that best supports the passage, whereas an Inference question looks for the passage to support a certain answer.

2. Analyze

To analyze a Strengthen passage, look for:

* The conclusion
* The premises
* The flaw

3. Prephrase

The correct answer to a Strengthen question will *suggest* (not prove) that the conclusion is indeed true.

It does so by defending a weak point present in the argument. You don't need to Prephrase a specific strengthening statement. Instead, you should Prephrase what kind of defense the answer is likely to make. For example, the correct answer choice could provide explicit proof that a necessary assumption is true or rule out a possible alternative cause.

4. Attack

The Real Question for Strengthen questions is:

> *Does this suggest that the conclusion is indeed true?*

Look for these distracters on Strengthen questions:

Opposite

Wrong answers to Strengthen questions often weaken rather than strengthen the argument.

Out of Scope

You have to be very careful with answers that appear out of scope on Strengthen questions because answers that introduce new considerations can strengthen the argument and are often correct.

12.3.4 NECESSARY ASSUMPTION QUESTIONS

A necessary assumption is an

- **Unstated premise:** A necessary assumption does not appear in the argument.

- **On which the argument depends:** A necessary assumption must be true in order for the conclusion to logically follow.

There are about five Necessary Assumption questions on each test.

1. Identify

Necessary Assumption question stems ask you for an assumption that an argument makes or requires. The language can vary: sometimes the LSAT uses *presupposition* instead of *assumption*. Sometimes the question says *relies on* or *depends on* instead of *requires*.

Here are some common Necessary Assumption question stems:

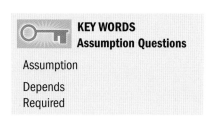

KEY WORDS
Assumption Questions

Assumption

Depends

Required

> Which one of the following is an assumption on which the conclusion depends?
>
> Which one of the following is an assumption on which the argument relies?
>
> The argument above depends on assuming which one of the following?
>
> The argument assumes which one of the following?

Be careful not to confuse Necessary Assumption questions with Sufficient Assumption questions, which ask you to choose the answer choice that would allow the conclusion to be properly drawn.

2. Analyze

To analyze a Necessary Assumption passage, look for:

- The conclusion

- The premises

- The flaw

3. Prephrase

To Prephrase on a Necessary Assumption question, identify where a linking assumption might occur. Linking assumptions simply state that the two sides of a Concept Shift are connected. You can often predict the kinds of linking assumptions you're likely to see in the answer choices.

Shielding assumptions, which deny a circumstance that would destroy the argument, can be obscure and unpredictable, so it is almost never worth your effort to Prephrase shielding assumptions—there are simply too many possible shielding assumptions for any argument.

4. Attack

The Real Question for Necessary Assumption questions is:

> *Does the argument depend on this being true?*

The Real Question is especially important for Necessary Assumption questions because it can identify unexpected shielding assumptions. Without the Real Question, you might be tempted to dismiss a necessary shielding assumption.

Out of Scope

The most common wrong answers for Necessary Assumption questions are **out of scope**. If an answer choice has nothing to do with the argument, then the argument probably doesn't require it.

Extreme

You should also avoid **extreme** answers, since an argument rarely requires extreme assumptions. The correct answer to a Necessary Assumption question is much more likely to have the phrase *at least some* than the phrase *every one*.

The Negation Tool is a powerful tool that can help you to decide whether to cut or keep an answer choice. To apply the Negation Tool to any given answer choice:

1. Negate the answer choice.

2. Ask, "Does this destroy the argument?" If so, then the answer choice is a necessary assumption.

12.3.5 EVALUATE QUESTIONS

Evaluate questions ask you to identify what you'd need to know in order to evaluate the strength of an argument. Since the strength of a flawed argument depends on the truth of its assumptions, Evaluate questions are really asking you to identify an argument's necessary assumptions.

Evaluate questions are rare. Three quarters of official tests don't contain a single one.

1. Identify

Evaluate question stems ask you to choose the piece of information that it would be helpful to know in order to evaluate the argument. Sometimes each answer choice is a question.

Here are a few typical Evaluate question stems:

> It would be most important to determine which one of the following in evaluating the argument?

> The answer to which one of the following questions would most help in evaluating the columnist's argument?

KEY WORD
Evaluate Questions

Evaluating

2. Analyze

To analyze an Evaluate passage, look for:

- The conclusion
- The premises
- The flaw

3. Prephrase

To Prephrase on an Evaluate question, express the flaw or Concept Shift in terms of a necessary assumption, and use that as the point to evaluate.

4. Attack

The Real Question for Evaluate questions is:

Does this address an assumption?

Because evaluating any argument requires determining whether its necessary assumptions are true, the correct answer must address an assumption.

12.3.6 SUFFICIENT ASSUMPTION QUESTIONS

A sufficient assumption is an unstated premise that, if added to the premises of an argument, guarantees that the argument's conclusion is true.

You should expect to see about three Sufficient Assumption questions per test.

1. Identify

Sufficient Assumption question stems tell you to assume the truth of each answer choice, then ask you to choose a statement that makes the argument perfect. The correct answer eliminates all the flaws in the argument. If you add the correct answer to the premises, the conclusion follows by necessity.

Here are some Sufficient Assumption question stems:

> The conclusion of the argument follows logically if which one of the following is assumed?
>
> Which one of the following, if assumed, would allow the conclusion to be properly drawn?
>
> Which one of the following, if assumed, enables the argument's conclusion to be properly inferred?

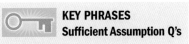

**KEY PHRASES
Sufficient Assumption Q's**

If assumed

The conclusion drawn above

Follows logically
Properly drawn
Logically inferred

Remember that Sufficient Assumption questions are different from Necessary Assumption questions. Sufficient Assumption questions ask for an assumption that *guarantees* the conclusion, but Necessary Assumption questions ask for an assumption that *is required* by the argument.

2. Analyze

To analyze a Sufficient Assumption passage, look for:

- The conclusion
- The premises
- The flaw

It's usually best to express the flaw in terms of a Concept Shift. The Concept Shift is more powerful on Sufficient Assumption questions than on any other question type, since the correct answer usually makes a strong link between the two sides of the shift.

If a Sufficient Assumption question can be diagrammed, make sure to keep the premises and conclusion separate. Then use the "missing links" technique.

3. Prephrase

Prephrasing on Sufficient Assumption questions means stating the link the answer should make to guarantee the conclusion. The best way to guarantee any argument's conclusion is to link the two sides of the Concept Shift by coming up with a statement that makes them identical.

4. Attack

The Real Question for Sufficient Assumption questions is:

> *Does this guarantee the conclusion?*

You can use the New Concept Tool on any Sufficient Assumption question that has an entirely new concept in the conclusion. To use the New Concept Tool:

1. Find the new concept that appears only in the conclusion.
2. Quickly read through the answer choices to eliminate any answer choice that does not address the new concept.

Sufficient Assumption questions have three common distracters:

Necessary Assumptions

Some incorrect answers to Sufficient Assumption questions would be correct answers for Necessary Assumption questions.

Opposites

A sufficient assumption guarantees an argument's conclusion, but some incorrect answers to Sufficient Assumption questions actually weaken the argument.

Reversals

Many correct answers to Sufficient Assumption questions are conditionals, but you have to make sure the direction of the conditional isn't reversed. The right direction for a conditional answer choice to a Sufficient Assumption question is: If premises are true → then conclusion is true.

12.3.7 JUSTIFY QUESTIONS

Justify questions are just like Sufficient Assumption questions. You should use the same techniques and look for the same thing in the correct answer. The only difference is the question stem.

Most tests contain about two Justify questions.

1. Identify

Justify questions ask for a principle or general rule that could justify the reasoning in the argument.

Here are some of the more common variations:

> Which one of the following principles, if valid, most helps to justify the conclusion drawn in the argument above?

> Which one of the following principles, if established, most justifies the reasoning above?

> Which one of the following principles, if accepted, provides the strongest support for the reasoning above?

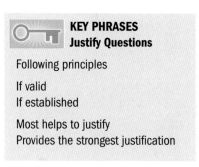

KEY PHRASES
Justify Questions

Following principles

If valid
If established

Most helps to justify
Provides the strongest justification

If a question asks you to justify a conclusion or an argument's reasoning, then you should treat it like a Sufficient Assumption question in every way.

12.3.8 PARALLEL FLAW QUESTIONS

Parallel Flaw questions require you to find the answer choice that uses that same flawed reasoning that was used in the passage. You're looking for a good match.

You should expect to see two Parallel Flaw questions on your test.

1. Identify

On Parallel Flaw questions, each of the answer choices is an argument. The question stem asks you to choose the answer choice that has the same flawed reasoning as that in the passage. Parallel Flaw question stems always use words such as *flawed reasoning* to indicate that the passage has flawed reasoning.

Here are some Parallel Flaw question stems:

> Which one of the following is most closely parallel in its flawed reasoning to the flawed reasoning in the argument above?

> Which one of the following employs a flawed argumentative strategy that is most closely parallel to the flawed argumentative strategy in the advertisement above?

> Which one of the following uses flawed reasoning most similar to that used in the argument above?

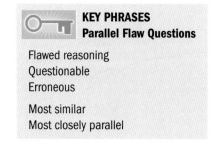

KEY PHRASES
Parallel Flaw Questions

Flawed reasoning
Questionable
Erroneous

Most similar
Most closely parallel

2. Analyze

To analyze a Parallel Flaw passage, look for:

- The conclusion

- The premises

- The flaw

Parallel Flaw questions use common flaws more often than any other question type, so stay alert for them.

3. Prephrase

Prephrasing on Parallel Flaw questions consists of knowing which flaw you are looking for. For example, if the argument from the passage has a necessary vs. sufficient flaw, your Prephrased answer would state that the correct answer must also have a necessary vs. sufficient flaw.

4. Attack

Attacking the answers on Parallel Flaw questions means looking for the same flaw as the one in the passage. The Real Question for Parallel Flaw questions is:

Does this match the flaw from the passage?

12.3.9 MISINTERPRETATION QUESTIONS

Misinterpretation questions are rare. Most tests don't have a single Misinterpretation question.

1. Identify

Misinterpretation questions have passages with two speakers, and you are asked to identify how the second speaker misinterprets the first:

Here's a typical Misinterpretation question stem:

> The parent's response to the mayor suggests that the
> parent misinterpreted the mayor to be

2. Analyze

The second speaker's misinterpretation is always based on a Concept Shift—the second speaker intends to argue about identical concepts as the first speaker, but the second speaker's concepts are different. Your goal is to see where the shift occurs.

To analyze a Misinterpretation passage, look for:

- The conclusion

- The premises

- The Concept Shift

3. Prephrase

To Prephrase on a Misinterpretation question, use the Concept Shift to state how the second speaker misinterprets the first.

4. Attack

The Real Question for Misinterpretation questions is:

Is this a misinterpretation in the passage?

The most common type of distracter is an answer choice that **doesn't match** the Concept Shift in the passage.

12.4 Drill: Identifying Question Types

Look at each question stem and determine which question type it represents. Not all of the stems are flaw-dependent questions.

1. The conclusion drawn in the argument above follows logically if which one of the following is assumed?

   _____

2. The reasoning in the argument above is flawed in that it

   _____

3. Which one of the following is an assumption on which the argument depends?

   _____

4. Which one of the following principles, if established, does the most to justify the conclusion of the essayist's argument?

   _____

5. The conclusion drawn by the editorial follows logically if it is assumed that what is called "environment" usually

   _____

6. Which one of the following propositions is best illustrated by the statements above?

   _____

7. The conclusion of the argument follows logically if which one of the following is assumed?

   _____

8. Which one of the following principles most helps to justify Shaw's argumentation?

   _____

9. Each of the following, if true, supports the activist's claim EXCEPT:

   _____

10. The argument above exhibits an erroneous pattern of reasoning most similar to that exhibited by which one of the following?

    _____

11. Which one of the following, if true, provides the most support for the argument?

    _____

12. In drawing her conclusion, the educator made which one of the following assumptions?

    _____

13. Which one of the following, if true, most strengthens the argument above?

    _____

14. The priest's response can best be explained on the assumption that he has misinterpreted the rabbi to mean which one of the following?

    _____

15. Which one of the following most closely conforms to the principle illustrated by the passage above?

    _____

16. Which one of the following, if true, most calls into question the columnist's argument?

    _____

17. The answer to which one of the following questions would most help in evaluating the columnist's argument?

    _____

18. Which one of the following is an assumption on which the argument depends?

    _____

19. The cardiologist's argument is most vulnerable to criticism on the grounds that it

    _____

20. Which one of the following is an assumption required by the scientist's argument?

    _____

21. Which one of the following most accurately describes a flaw in the reasoning above?

    _____

22. Which one of the following, if true, would most seriously weaken the argument?

    _____

23. The flawed pattern of reasoning in the argument above is most similar to that in which one of the following?

    _____

24. Each of the following, if true, helps to support the social critic's hypothesis EXCEPT:

    _____

25. Which one of the following is most strongly supported by the statements above?

    _____

26. Which one of the following, if true, most weakens the argument?

    _____

27. The industry spokesperson's statements, if true, most strongly support which one of the following?

    _____

28. Each of the following, if true, weakens the argument EXCEPT:

    _____

29. A questionable technique used in the criminologist's argument is to

    _____

30. Which one of the following principles, if valid, most helps to justify the local citizen's reasoning?

    _____

Answers

1. Sufficient Assumption	11. Strengthen	21. Flaw
2. Flaw	12. Necessary Assumption	22. Weaken
3. Necessary Assumption	13. Strengthen	23. Parallel Flaw
4. Justify	14. Misinterpretation	24. Strengthen
5. Sufficient Assumption	15. Conform	25. Inference
6. Conform	16. Weaken	26. Weaken
7. Sufficient Assumption	17. Evaluate	27. Inference
8. Justify	18. Necessary Assumption	28. Weaken
9. Strengthen	19. Flaw	29. Flaw
10. Parallel Flaw	20. Necessary Assumption	30. Justify

12.5 A LIST OF REAL QUESTIONS

These are the Real Questions for all the flaw-dependent question types.

Flaw	*Is this a flaw in the argument?*
Weaken	*Does this suggest that the conclusion is untrue?*
Necessary Assumption	*Does the argument depend on this being true?*
Strengthen	*Does this suggest that the conclusion is indeed true?*
Sufficient Assumption	*Does this guarantee the conclusion?*
Justify	*Does this guarantee the conclusion?*
Parallel Flaw	*Does this match the flaw in the passage?*
Evaluate	*Does this address an assumption?*
Misinterpretation	*Is this a misinterpretation in the passage?*

12.6 Drill: Putting It All Together

Read and analyze the following passage. The passage is followed by seven flaw-dependent questions and 18 answer choices. Some answer choices correctly answer more than one question, while others do not correctly answer any question. Some questions are correctly answered by more than one choice.

> Burns: The chemicals released by our factory into the river do not damage wildlife. This is clear from the results of a research study we commissioned to investigate the effects of the chemicals, which found that the fish in the river grow faster and produce more young than do fish in a nearby lake that does not contain any industrial chemicals.

1. Which answer choice or choices accurately describe a flaw in the reasoning above?

   _____

2. Which answer choice or choices, if true, would weaken the argument?

   _____

3. Which answer choice or choices, if true, would strengthen the argument?

   _____

4. The answer to which question or questions would help in evaluating Burns's argument?

   _____

5. Which answer choice or choices are an assumption on which the argument depends?

   _____

6. The conclusion drawn in the argument follows logically if which answer choice or choices are assumed?

   _____

7. The argument exhibits a flawed pattern of reasoning parallel to that exhibited by which answer choice or choices?

   _____

(A) The population of frogs that live in the river has increased substantially over the last five years.

(B) The argument presumes, without providing justification, that the fact that the company commissioned the research did not cause the research to be affected by bias.

(C) Did the company study the effects of the chemicals before it began to release them into the river?

(D) The fact that the lake drains into the river allows the two fish populations to share some of the same food sources.

(E) The students in our high school do not cheat, a conclusion supported by a student newspaper study that found that far fewer ninth grade students in this high school work on class assignments in groups than do students at a rival high school.

(F) Nearly all the people who live near the factory grow to a shorter height than the national average.

(G) The company has also commissioned a study to determine the health characteristics of bears that feed on the fish in the river.

(H) The argument cites evidence that is insufficient to support a generalization about all wildlife.

(I) The company's financial relationship with researchers did not cause undue partiality to be introduced into the results.

(J) The proposed legislation will not damage the economy, a conclusion supported by a government study that found that the economy of a nearby community that passed nearly identical legislation was not damaged by that legislation, and in fact grew more rapidly after its passage.

(K) The fish in the lake are not subjected to any naturally occurring factors that would cause them to grow more slowly than fish in the river.

(L) The argument neglects to take into account the fact that many industrial chemicals have been conclusively proven to damage wildlife.

(M) The argument fails to consider the possibility that the company is harming wildlife in ways other than releasing chemicals into the river.

(N) Are the fish in the river of a different species than those in the lake?

(O) The rate of birth defects for the fish population in the river has doubled since the company began releasing chemicals into the river.

(P) The chemicals released by the factory quickly degrade into substances that can serve as nutrients for a number of species.

(Q) The comparison of the growth rate of fish in the river to that of fish in the lake has been proven to be the most accurate way to measure the overall well-being of all wildlife.

(R) The life expectancy of fish in the river is significantly lower than that of fish in the lake.

Explanations

The conclusion of the argument is the first sentence, since it is supported by the evidence in the second sentence. The argument works like this:

- The company commissioned a report to study the effects of the chemicals.
- The study found that fish in the river grow faster and produce more young than do fish in a nearby lake without industrial chemicals.

> **Therefore**, the chemicals released by the factory into the river do not damage wildlife.

There are many flaws in this argument, including some common flaws.

One common flaw committed here is a sampling flaw. Burns bases a conclusion about *all wildlife* on a study of *fish alone*. What about other species?

A second sampling flaw was committed when Burns bases a conclusion about *all kinds of damage* based on information about *growth rate and number of offspring alone*. Couldn't there be other types of damage?

Another common flaw committed here is an analogy flaw. Burns draws a conclusion based on a comparison of *fish in the river* to *fish in the lake*. But is the river analogous to the lake in every important way? Are the two populations of fish analogous in every important way? There is no evidence provided to confirm this.

Another flaw is that there may be some reason to doubt the study, since it was paid for by the company itself. How do you know the results are impartial?

Answers

1. **(B), (H)** Choices (B) and (H) both match the flaws found in the analysis of the passage.

   Choice (L) is **not a flaw** because Burns is not talking about all chemicals, just the ones released by this factory and studied by these researchers.

   Choice (M) is **not a flaw** because the scope of the argument is solely a discussion of the chemicals being released into the river. There is no conclusion drawn about other potential sources of harm.

2. **(O), (R)** Choices (O) and (R) both introduce other types of damage that wildlife may be experiencing due to the chemicals. These choices suggest that the chemicals do damage wildlife.

3. **(A), (I), (K), (P), (Q)** Choice (A) shows that other species in the river are flourishing as well, and choice (P) shows that the chemicals are not flowing down the river and potentially causing different damage to wildlife in different places. Both of these choices introduce new information to defend against potentially damaging possibilities, so both of them suggest that the chemicals do not damage wildlife.

   Choice (I) takes away the possibility that there was bias in the results of the study, and choice (K) strengthens the analogy between the lake and the river.

   Choice (Q) strengthens the argument so much that it actually guarantees that the conclusion is true. It says that the type of evidence found in the premises has been proven to show that the conclusion is true. (This is actually a sufficient assumption, which would not normally be found in the answer choices for a Strengthen question, but it does strengthen the argument, so it is correct in this case.)

4. **(N)** One of the assumptions made by Burns is that the fish in the two places are analogous. Choice (N) specifically addresses that assumption. If the fish are of different species, then comparisons of their growth and reproductive rates becomes meaningless.

   Choice (C) is irrelevant because the argument makes no assumptions about when the potential damage was studied, only whether or not it occurs.

5. **(I), (K)** Use the Negation Test. When choice (I) is negated, it destroys any credibility the evidence has, which destroys the argument. When choice (K) is negated, it destroys the relevance of the analogy upon which the argument is based, which leaves the conclusion without any support. Both of these are necessary to the argument.

Choices (A), (P), and (Q) all strengthen the argument, but the conclusion could still be true and supported by the given evidence even if these choices were not true. Thus, they are not necessary assumptions.

6. **(Q)** Choice (Q) says that the type of evidence found in the premises has been conclusively proven to show that the conclusion is true. This guarantees the validity of the conclusion.

7. **(E)** Choice (E) contains all the same flaws as the original argument. It bases a conclusion about *all students* in the school on a study of *ninth graders alone*. It bases a conclusion about *all kinds of cheating* only on information about *doing class assignments in groups*. It draws a conclusion based on a comparison of *the students in one school* to *the students in a different school*. Finally, there may be some reason to doubt the study, as it was done by students themselves.

Choice (J) is not parallel for several reasons. First, it is making a prediction about the future, whereas the original argument is talking about present damage. Second, the original comparison is between one place *with* the chemicals and one place *without* them, but choice (J) discusses the result of having the same legislation present in both places.

Other Choices:

Choice (D) is completely irrelevant to the argument because the argument makes no assumptions about the two populations not sharing any of the same food sources.

Choice (F) is irrelevant because the argument is about wildlife, not people.

Choice (G) can neither strengthen nor weaken the argument because the *results* of the study are not specified.

STOP. THIS IS THE END OF LECTURE 10. DO NOT PROCEED TO THE CORRESPONDING EXAM UNTIL INSTRUCTED TO DO SO IN CLASS.

LECTURE ⑪ CHAPTER ⑬

REVIEW OF FLAW-INDEPENDENT QUESTION TYPES

13.1 THE FLAW-INDEPENDENT QUESTION TYPES

Flaw-independent questions are not as closely related to each other as flaw-dependent questions are, but there are some very important things they have in common. Seeing these connections will save you tremendous amounts of time on the test.

The most important shared characteristic of these question types is what you *don't* have to do as part of your approach:

Don't waste any time looking for the flaw.

Even though many passages associated with flaw-independent questions actually contain flaws, spending time searching for and Prephrasing the flaw is completely unnecessary and will not gain you a single point. On flaw-independent questions, your work is focused on other tasks.

You can take this time-saving advice one step further. Some flaw-independent question types—Inference and Paradox—don't even contain a conclusion in the passage. The act of looking for the conclusion in every passage should be so ingrained in you by now that you may forget about the times when there is none. If you spend time looking for a conclusion in passages associated with these question types, you will just be wasting time and creating frustration for yourself. So the other major theme of flaw-independent questions is:

Don't waste any time looking for the conclusion when there is none.

Here's a list of the flaw-independent question types:

Passages with a conclusion:

- **Main Point** and its variation, Complete
- **Point at Issue** and its variation, Point of Agreement
- **Method** and its variation, Role
- **Conform** (the outcome of the principle is like a conclusion)
- **Parallel Reasoning**

Passages without a conclusion:

- **Inference** and its variation, Cannot Be True
- **Paradox** and its variation, Explain

13.2 A REVIEW OF EACH QUESTION TYPE

13.2.1 MAIN POINT QUESTIONS

Main Point questions present you with an argument and simply ask you to identify its conclusion.

Most tests contain one or two Main Point questions:

1. Identify

Here are some common Main Point question stems:

> Which one of the following most accurately expresses the main point of the argument above?

> Which one of the following best expresses the main conclusion of the bookkeeper's argument?

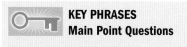

**KEY PHRASES
Main Point Questions**

Most accurately expresses
Main conclusion

2. Analyze

To analyze a Main Point passage, look for

- The premises
- The conclusion

The major tools to help you differentiate between the premises and the conclusion (in any argument) are:

- **Indicators.** Words such as *therefore, so, after all, since,* and *because* act as road signs to point out the different parts of the argument.

- **Facts and opinions.** Facts such as statistics, matters of historical record, and the results of simple observation are premises and should be accepted as true. Unproven opinions and sentences containing opinionated words such as *clearly* and *obviously* are conclusions and should be treated as debatable.

- **Suggestions.** Recommended courses of action, suggestions, and sentences with words like *should, ought to,* and *must* are usually conclusions.

- **Counterarguments.** When the author of the passage says that another person is wrong or that another viewpoint is mistaken, look at the so-called "wrong" viewpoint and negate it. The negated version is the author's conclusion. Since this is a good way to disguise a conclusion, this is a common feature on Main Point questions.

- The **Why Tool**. Here's how it works:

    1. Pick out a claim that might be the conclusion.

2. Ask, "Why _____?" and insert the potential conclusion into the blank.

3. The rest of the argument should provide evidence to answer the question.

If the rest of the argument provides evidence for the chosen claim, then you have correctly identified the conclusion. If not, you haven't identified the conclusion, and you should use the Why Tool on another claim.

3. Prephrase

When the conclusion is explicitly stated in the argument (as it usually is), don't bother trying to reword, simplify, or paraphrase it; it's already there for you. Just mark it in brackets and move on to the answer choices.

If the conclusion is not explicitly stated (as in a counterargument) you should always Prephrase a specific conclusion by negating the so-called "wrong" viewpoint.

4. Attack

The Real Question for Main Point questions is:

Is this the conclusion?

Remember that the correct answer choice will probably use different words to express the same conclusion. It is unlikely that it will simply restate the same sentence from the passage verbatim. However, if an answer choice *means* the same thing as the conclusion you identified, then it's correct.

Main Point questions have two common distracters:

Premises

Many wrong answers to Main Point questions are premises rather than conclusions. They sound familiar, because they come directly from the argument, but they don't match the conclusion.

Out of Scope

Most of the remaining wrong answers go beyond the scope of the argument in one way or another. These answers make claims that don't even appear in the passage.

13.2.2 COMPLETE QUESTIONS

Complete questions present an argument with the conclusion omitted from the passage. Your job is to provide the missing conclusion.

These questions are uncommon. Only about half of all tests contain a Complete question.

1. Identify

Most Complete questions contain a fill-in-the-blank at the end of the passage and feature a question stem like this:

> Which one of the following most logically completes the passage?

When there is no blank, another possible question stem is:

> The passage is structured to lead to which one of the following conclusions?

2. Analyze

Since the argument's conclusion is missing, you can't analyze Complete questions as you analyze Main Point questions. But you should still look for and understand the premises, and look carefully to see whether there is a counterargument.

> For every question type always mark the conclusion of the argument in brackets.

 KEY PHRASES
Complete Questions

Logically completes
Expresses the conclusion the argument is structured to establish

3. Prephrase

Prephrasing on a Complete question means predicting what the conclusion will be. This is usually easy when there is a counterargument. If there isn't one, just try to see where the author is leading and move on to the answer choices.

4. Attack

You can use the same Real Question as for Main Point questions:

Is this the conclusion?

If you Prephrased a conclusion, look for a match. If you couldn't, then use the Why Tool on each answer choice.

Also look out for these distracters:

Contradicts the Passage

The conclusion can never contradict the premises.

Out of Scope

These answers make claims that don't correspond to anything in the passage.

13.2.3 POINT AT ISSUE QUESTIONS

Point at Issue questions ask you to identify what two speakers disagree about. You should expect to see about two of these questions on your test.

1. Identify

There are two characteristics that help you identify a Point at Issue question:

- The passage has two speakers.
- The question stem asks about a *disagreement* or *point at issue*.

Here are some common Point at Issue question stems:

> The point at issue between Pedro and Napoleon is whether
>
> Their dialogue provides the most support for the claim that Jon and Mike disagree over whether

KEY PHRASES
Point at Issue Questions

Point at issue
Disagree

2. Analyze

Analyze Point at Issue questions by identifying which of the first speaker's claims is contradicted by the second speaker. This contradiction will come in one of two forms:

- **An explicit disagreement**. About half the time, the second speaker will say something that directly contradicts a statement made by the first speaker. When you see two statements that say opposite things, circle the statements.

- **An implicit disagreement**. If the disagreement is not readily apparent, look at each of the first speaker's claims, and decide which one the second speaker's statements work together to contradict. When you find it, circle that claim.

3. Prephrase

The answer to a Point at Issue question is nearly always contained in the passage. All you have to do is find it. Just mark the statement that the speakers disagree over so that you can move through the answers quickly and confidently.

Sometimes it helps to express the disagreement in your own words. You can use this phrase for stating the disagreement:

Disagreement: The speakers disagree over _____.

If you can't come up with a good Prephrased disagreement, don't worry. Just move on to the answer choices.

4. Attack

The Real Question for Point at Issue questions is:

Do the speakers voice disagreement about this?

In order for an answer choice to merit a "yes" to the Real Question, each speaker must have given some indication of (voiced) how she or he feels about the statement, and the speakers must have different opinions on it.

If these two conditions are met, then you have found the correct answer—something that the speakers disagree about.

Stay alert for these common distracters:

One-sided

These distracters make a claim that one of the speakers did not express an opinion on.

Point of Agreement

If both speakers would feel the same way about a statement in an answer choice—whether they would both agree or disagree with the statement—then the choice cannot be right.

The **Survey Tool** can help you identify a disagreement, especially in confusing answer choices. Here's how it works:

1. Create a T-Chart next to the answer choices.
2. Decide whether each speaker agrees or disagrees with the statement in the answer choice. Mark the response in the T-Chart:
   a. If the speaker agrees with the answer choice, put a plus (+).
   b. If the speaker disagrees with the answer choice, put a minus (–).
   c. If you don't know how the speaker feels about the answer choice, put a question mark (?).
3. The correct answer will have both a plus and a minus next to it.

> Just use the Survey Tool when you're not sure about a choice.

13.2.4 POINT OF AGREEMENT QUESTIONS

Point of Agreement questions are identical to Point at Issue questions, except that they ask you what the speakers *agree* about instead of what they *disagree* about. You can recognize these questions because they have the same question stem as Point at Issue questions, except that they use the word *agree* instead of *disagree*.

KEY WORD
Point of Agreement Q's

Agree

Point of Agreement questions are extremely rare.

Your approach to these questions is identical to your approach to Point at Issue questions. Simply reverse your tools to find something the speakers voice agreement about instead of disagreement.

The Real Question for Point of Agreement questions is:

Do the speakers voice agreement about this?

You can also use the **Survey Tool** on Point of Agreement questions. Instead of looking for an answer choice that merits a plus and a minus, look for one with two pluses.

13.2.5 METHOD QUESTIONS

Method questions ask you to identify *how* an author used the premises to support the conclusion. Most tests contain one or two Method questions.

1. Identify

Any question that asks you to describe a *method, technique, strategy of reasoning* , or how an argument *proceeds* is a Method question. Here are some Method question stems:

> The argument proceeds by
>
> The specialist's argument does which one of the following?
>
> Which one of the following is an argumentative strategy employed in the argument?
>
> Which one of the following most accurately describes a technique used in the banker's argument?

KEY PHRASES
Method Questions

Proceeds by

Argumentative strategy
Technique
Method

2. Analyze

To analyze a Method passage, look for:

- The conclusion
- The premises

3. Prephrase

Prephrasing on Method questions means telling the general story of the argument, divorced from the details. For example, an argument may reach its conclusion by drawing an analogy, introducing additional considerations, questioning an assumption, ruling out an alternative possible cause, or in many other ways.

4. Attack

The Real Question for Method Questions is:

> *Does this match the argument?*

If every part of an answer choice describes something that actually happened in the argument, then it's a good answer. Otherwise, get rid of it.

13.2.6 ROLE QUESTIONS

Role questions are a variation of Method questions that ask you about only **one claim** within an argument and what *role* the claim plays. Since arguments are made up of premises and conclusions, most claims are either premises or conclusions.

Role questions usually appear about once or twice per test.

1. Identify

Role questions are easy to identify because the question stem always repeats one of the claims from the argument. It then asks you to describe the *role* played by the claim or how the claim *figures in the argument*. Here's a typical Role question stem:

KEY PHRASES
Role Questions

Describes the role played
The claim that...figures in the argument in which way

> The claim that the methodology of the toxicology study was flawed plays which one of the following roles in the argument?

2. Analyze

To analyze a Role passage, identify:

- The premises
- The conclusion

In addition, focus on the claim in the question stem and figure out how it fits into the argument.

3. Prephrase

You should always come up with a general description of the role played by the claim in the question stem. Some common roles are:

- A premise
- The main conclusion
- A subsidiary or intermediate conclusion

- A counterexample
- A concession
- An illustration

> A subsidiary conclusion is based on evidence and features conclusion indicators, but it is used as a premise to support the main conclusion. It is often the correct answer to a Role questions.

4. Attack

The Real Question for Role questions is:

Does this match the role of the claim?

13.2.7 CONFORM QUESTIONS

On the LSAT, a "principle" is a general rule. Most principles on the LSAT tell you either:

- a rule of conduct in a particular circumstance, or
- how something should be judged, if it meets certain criteria

Conform questions ask you to match a general rule to a specific example in which that rule is followed.

Conform questions appear roughly three times per test.

1. Identify

Some Conform questions give you the general rule in the passage and a list of examples in the answer choices. These questions ask you to find the choice in which the principle is correctly applied. Here are some question stems that ask you to **apply a principle**:

> Which one of the following conforms most closely to the principle stated above?

> Which one of the following judgments best illustrates the proposition above?

> Which one of the following situations most closely conforms to the principle cited above?

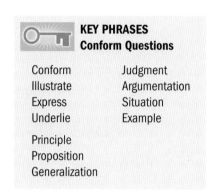

KEY PHRASES
Conform Questions

Conform	Judgment
Illustrate	Argumentation
Express	Situation
Underlie	Example
Principle	
Proposition	
Generalization	

Other Conform questions are backwards: they provide an example in the passage, and a list of general rules in the answer choices. Your job is to identify the principle that matches the example. Here are some question stems that ask you to **state a principle**:

> Which one of the following most closely conforms to the principle illustrated by the situation described above?

> The examples presented above best illustrate which one of the following propositions?

> Which one of the following generalizations most accurately expresses the principle underlying the argumentation above?

2. Analyze

Every principle is composed of two parts:

- **The circumstances.** This is the particular situation in which the rule applies or the particular criteria that must be met in order to pass judgment.

- **The outcome.** This is the action stipulated by the rule or the judgment to be passed on something.

If the principle is supplied for you in the passage, then your analysis consists of separating the general rule into its two parts, much like separating an argument into its premises and conclusion.

If the passage contains a specific example, then you should also identify the circumstances and the outcome in the example.

3. Prephrase

When the general rule is supplied for you and you are asked to **apply the principle**, you won't be able to Prephrase the specific example in the correct answer because there could be many examples in which the rule is followed. Just move on to the answer choices.

When you are asked to **state the principle** illustrated in the specific example in the passage, you can Prephrase an answer. To do this, tell the general story of the example that doesn't focus on the details of the passage.

4. Attack

The Real Question for all Conform questions is:

Does this match the principle in the passage?

For questions that ask you to **apply the principle**, you should look for an answer whose example matches the circumstances and the outcome stated in the principle in the passage.

For questions that ask you to **identify the principle**, you should look for an answer that matches your Prephrased general story of the circumstances and the outcome.

13.2.8 PARALLEL REASONING QUESTIONS

Parallel Reasoning questions require you to find the answer choice that uses the same method of reasoning that was used in the passage. You're looking for a good match.

You should expect to see two Parallel Reasoning questions on your test.

1. Identify

On Parallel Reasoning questions, each of the answer choices is an argument. The question stem asks you to choose the answer choice that *parallels* or is *most similar to* the reasoning in the passage.

Here are some Parallel Reasoning question stems:

> The reasoning in the argument above is most closely paralleled by that in which one of the following?

> Which one of the following arguments is most similar in its pattern of reasoning to the argument above?

Don't try to make the contrapositive of a principle.

When a Conform question asks you to apply the unstated principle, it starts to resemble a Parallel Reasoning question.

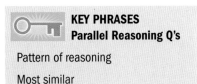

KEY PHRASES
Parallel Reasoning Q's

Pattern of reasoning

Most similar
Most closely parallel

2. Analyze

To analyze a Parallel Reasoning passage, look for the Parallel Pair:

- The number and types of premises
- The type of conclusion

3. Prephrase

Since there could be many possible arguments that are parallel to the one in the passage, you won't be able to Prephrase the specific argument in the correct answer. Just move on to the answer choices and look for a match for the Parallel Pair.

4. Attack

The Real Question for Parallel Reasoning questions is this:

Does this match the Parallel Pair in the passage?

If an answer matches the Parallel Pair, keep it. If not, cut it.

The vast majority of the time, the Parallel Pair can get you the correct answer right away, but sometimes matching the Parallel Pair leaves you with two possible answer choices. In this case:

- Compare the answer choices you have left and isolate a difference.
- Check the argument from the passage to see, based on the isolated difference, which answer is a better match.

There are three types of distracters that are especially common on Parallel Reasoning questions:

> Although you normally want to read every answer choice, if a Parallel Reasoning question is very long or if you are running out of time, you may wish to just pick the first answer that looks like it matches the Parallel Pair.

Topic Trap

Some answer choices have a topic similar to the topic in the passage. The writers of the LSAT hope that you will be distracted by the similarity in topic and will overlook the differences in reasoning.

Word Trap

The LSAT writers hope they can distract you with identical words and force you to ignore the differences in reasoning.

Mixed-Up Order

Order makes no difference when you are dealing with Parallel Reasoning questions. If you see an answer choice with the same reasoning in a mixed-up order, **keep it**.

13.2.9 INFERENCE QUESTIONS

Inference questions present you with a passage that contains only premises. You are then asked to draw your own valid conclusion. The correct answer choice is something that *is guaranteed to be true* based on the premises.

Inference questions are the second most common type of Logical Reasoning question. There are about six of them on every test.

1. Identify

Inference question stems often tell you to accept everything in the passage as true. The stem then asks you to choose an answer that:

- must be true
- can be inferred
- is supported by the passage
- can be properly concluded

Here are some typical Inference question stems:

> From the statements above, which one of the following can be properly inferred?
>
> If all of the statements above are true, which one of the following must be true?
>
> Which one of the following is most strongly supported by the information above?
>
> Which one of the following statements follows logically from the statements above?

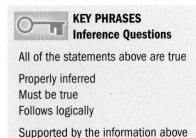

KEY PHRASES
Inference Questions

All of the statements above are true

Properly inferred
Must be true
Follows logically

Supported by the information above
Support which one of the following

2. Analyze

To analyze an Inference passage:

- Read each premise literally.

- Accept that the premises are true but that nothing beyond the premises is necessarily true.

- Watch out for repeated concepts.

In addition, if you see several conditional statements that may be linked together into a chain, you should diagram those statements.

3. Prephrase

If you can Prephrase an inference by combining repeated concepts or by following a linked chain of conditionals from one end to the other, you should do so.

However, since some correct answer choices to Inference questions are mere restatements of part of the passage, you won't always be able to Prephrase an inference. If you can't, just move on to the answer choices.

4. Attack

The Real Question for Inference questions is:

Is this guaranteed to be true?

Here are the most common distracters for Inference questions:

Out of Scope

If something in an answer choice did not appear at all in the passage, then it is probably out of scope. Be careful with this, however, since you can sometimes make inferences about seemingly new concepts by combining facts from the passage.

Extreme

Extreme distracters use much stronger language than is warranted by the passage. If the passage itself is extreme or leads to extreme inferences, however, an extreme answer choice can be correct.

Opposite

Opposite distracters change good inferences into bad ones.

Time Mismatch

Any answer choice that makes an inference about a time period other than one supported by the passage has a time mismatch.

13.2.10 CANNOT BE TRUE QUESTIONS

Cannot Be True questions are a variation of Inference questions that ask you to find, instead of what must be true, what cannot be true. You should approach these questions the same way that you approach Inference questions. The only difference is what counts as a good answer.

You will probably see no more than one of these on your test.

1. Identify

Here are some common Cannot Be True question stems:

> If all of the social critic's statements are true, each of the following could be true EXCEPT:

> If all of the statements above are true, then which one of the following must be false?

> If all of the statements above are true, which one of the following CANNOT be true?

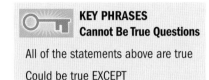

KEY PHRASES
Cannot Be True Questions

All of the statements above are true

Could be true EXCEPT
Must be false
CANNOT be true

2. Analyze

Your approach here is exactly the same as it is on Inference questions.

3. Prephrase

Again, this is the same as it is on Inference questions. If you have any conditionals, one possible Prephrased answer would be something that starts out the same as one of the conditionals but arrives at the opposite result.

4. Attack

The Real Question for Cannot Be True questions is:

Is this impossible?

13.2.11 PARADOX QUESTIONS

On the LSAT, a paradox is a set of two apparently contradictory facts.

On **Paradox** questions, your job is to resolve the paradox. You must find an answer to explain how both facts could simultaneously be true.

Paradox questions appear roughly three or four times per test.

1. Identify

All Paradox questions follow the same pattern:

- The question stem requires that you accept the truth of the answer choices.
- The question stem asks you to resolve the paradox.

Here are some Paradox question stems:

> Which one of the following, if true, most helps to resolve the apparent discrepancy above?

> Which one of the following, if true, contributes to a resolution of the apparent paradox?

> Which one of the following, if true, most helps to reconcile the activist's two claims?

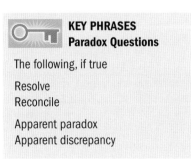

KEY PHRASES
Paradox Questions

The following, if true

Resolve
Reconcile

Apparent paradox
Apparent discrepancy

2. Analyze

To analyze a Paradox question, find the two apparently contradictory facts in the passage. A turnaround word usually appears immediately before one of the facts in the paradox. Here are some common turnaround words:

- However
- Yet
- But
- Despite
- Though
- Nevertheless
- Unlike

You can mark the paradox in the passage by circling each of the contradictory statements.

3. Prephrase

Prephrasing is not a major part of Paradox question strategy, since you can rarely Prephrase the specific correct answer. Just remember that the correct answer must explain how both facts could simultaneously be true.

> Prephrase: The correct answer must explain how it could be true that [Fact₁] even though [Fact₂].

4. Attack

The Real Question for Paradox questions:

> *Does this explain how both facts could be true?*

Three distracters are common on Paradox questions:

Incomplete

These answers explain how *one* but not *both* facts could be true.

Out of Scope

Out of scope answers explain neither fact. However, you should be careful about dismissing an answer as out of scope simply because it's unusual. Some correct answers are weird, but they provide the necessary explanation.

Opposite

Opposite answers exacerbate the paradox, making it harder to believe that both facts could simultaneously be true.

13.2.12 Explain Questions

Explain questions are like Paradox questions, but there is only one fact to be explained, rather than two contradictory facts.

Explain questions aren't very common. They appear on only about half of all tests.

1. Identify

Explain question stems always use the word *explain* or *explanation*. They refer you to the passage, asking you to explain a single particular fact or phenomenon. Here are some Explain question stems:

> Which one of the following, if true, most helps to explain the viewpoint of the economists described above?

> Which one of the following, if true, contributes most to an explanation of the patterns of erosion described above?

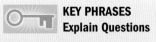
KEY PHRASES
Explain Questions

The following, if true

Most helps to explain

Contributes most to an explanation

Described above

2. Analyze

For Explain questions, just make sure you understand the one fact that you have to explain.

3. Prephrase

On Explain questions, there's no need to Prephrase a particular explanation of the fact from the passage. Just know that the correct answer must show how it could be true.

4. Attack

The Real Question for Explain questions is:

Does this explain how the fact could be true?

13.3 CONDITIONALS REVIEW

Conditionals are "all or nothing" statements that are usually expressed in the form of "If... then..." Sentences that talk about *some, many, most, sometimes,* or similar words cannot be expressed with conditional symbols.

- *If... Then...*
  When you see a sentence with *if*, the part of the sentence immediately following the *if* goes on the left-hand side of the conditional symbol:

Sentences:	If A, then B.
	If A, B.
	B if A.
Conditional Symbol:	A → B

- *Only if*
  The phrase *only if* works completely differently from the word *if*, so ignore the fact that they both contain the same word. Cross out the entire phrase *only if* and replace it with an arrow. Whatever the arrow points to goes on the right-hand side of the conditional symbol.

- *Unless*
  When you see a sentence with *unless*, cross that word out and replace it with *if not*. Remember, if the *if not* applies to two things linked with an AND or an OR, you'll have to negate both of them and turn the AND into an OR or vice versa.

- *All, Every, Whenever*
  Whatever follows one of these words goes on the left-hand side of the conditional symbol.

- *No, None, Never*
  When you see a sentence with one of these words, make sure the "~" is on the right-hand side of the conditional symbol.

- *Requires*
  When you see a sentence saying that one thing requires another, then put the thing that <u>is required</u> on the right-hand side of the conditional symbol.

- **The Contrapositive**
  You should construct the contrapositive of every conditional symbol. To do so, *Switch and Negate.* When negated, AND *becomes* OR, OR *becomes* AND.

Original Symbol:	A → B AND C
Contrapositive:	~B OR ~C → ~A

- **Making Chains**
  When you see something identical on the left-hand side of one conditional symbol and on the right-hand side of another conditional symbol, then you can link them together in a chain.

$$\begin{array}{ccc} B \rightarrow C & & A \rightarrow B & & A \rightarrow B \rightarrow C \\ \sim C \rightarrow \sim B & + & \sim B \rightarrow \sim A & = & \sim C \rightarrow \sim B \rightarrow \sim A \end{array}$$

If the identical thing is involved in an AND or OR, you can make a chain only when the AND is on the right-hand side and the OR is on the left-hand side:

$$\begin{array}{ccc} D \rightarrow F \text{ AND } G & & F \rightarrow H & & D \rightarrow F \text{ AND } G \\ \sim G \text{ OR } \sim F \rightarrow \sim D & + & \sim H \rightarrow \sim F & = & \searrow \\ & & & & H \\ & & & & \sim G \text{ OR } \sim F \rightarrow \sim D \\ & & & & \nearrow \\ & & & & \sim H \end{array}$$

Quantity statements can be symbolized with a dotted line. There are only two ways you can make a deduction using quantity statements: when you have the Most-Most Overlap, and when you have a quantity statement properly connected to the left-hand side of a conditional statement. Never try to negate or make the contrapositive of a quantity statement.

- **Conditionals within Inference Questions**
  When conditionals show up in Inference questions, there are two common situations. In one, you are given a collection of conditional statements that can be linked into a chain and you are told about something that is definitely true. Your job is to follow the chain and discover which other things must definitely be true.

  The other situation is that you are given a collection of conditional statements that can be linked into a chain but nothing else. In this case, the answer choices will also be conditionals, and your job is to find the one that matches the chain. It will usually start at the far left and end at the far right.

- **Conditionals within Sufficient Assumption Questions**
  These are flaw-dependent questions that often feature conditionals. In this case, you should *diagram the premises and the conclusion separately*. Then find the missing link that, if added to the premises, would result in the conclusion.

13.3.1 Drill: Conditionals

Symbolize each of the following conditional statements. Then make any chains that are possible.

1. Only if N participates will G participate.

    _____

2. F will not participate if G and H do.

    _____

3. If Q participates, then T does not.

    _____

4. S will not participate unless P or R participates.

    _____

5. T can participate only if R doesn't.

    _____

6. Unless Q participates, O cannot participate.

    _____

7. If J participates, then K and L must also participate.

    _____

8. U cannot participate unless N does.

    _____

9. M will participate if K participates.

    _____

10. Whenever U participates, V must as well.

    _____

Possible Chains

Answers & Explanations

1. Only if N participates will G participate.

$$G \rightarrow N$$
$$\sim N \rightarrow \sim G$$

2. F will not participate if G and H do.

$$G \text{ AND } H \rightarrow \sim F$$
$$F \rightarrow \sim H \text{ OR } \sim G$$

3. If Q participates, then T does not.

$$Q \rightarrow \sim T$$
$$T \rightarrow \sim Q$$

4. S will not participate unless P or R participates.

$$\sim P \text{ AND } \sim R \rightarrow \sim S$$
$$S \rightarrow R \text{ OR } P$$

5. T can participate only if R doesn't.

$$T \rightarrow \sim R$$
$$R \rightarrow \sim T$$

6. Unless Q participates, O cannot participate.

$$\sim Q \rightarrow \sim O$$
$$O \rightarrow Q$$

7. If J participates, then K and L must also participate.

$$J \rightarrow K \text{ AND } L$$
$$\sim L \text{ OR } \sim K \rightarrow \sim J$$

8. U cannot participate unless N does.

$$\sim N \rightarrow \sim U$$
$$U \rightarrow N$$

9. M will participate if K participates.

$$K \rightarrow M$$
$$\sim M \rightarrow \sim K$$

10. Whenever U participates, so does V.

$$U \rightarrow V$$
$$\sim V \rightarrow \sim U$$

Possible Chains

$$T \rightarrow \sim Q \rightarrow \sim O$$
$$O \rightarrow Q \rightarrow \sim T$$

$$J \rightarrow K \text{ AND } L$$
$$\searrow$$
$$M$$
$$\sim L \text{ OR } \sim K \rightarrow \sim J$$
$$\nearrow$$
$$\sim M$$

13.4 A LIST OF REAL QUESTIONS

These are the Real Questions for all the flaw-independent question types.

Inference	Is this guaranteed to be true?
Cannot Be True	Is this impossible?
Paradox	Does this explain how both facts could be true?
Explain	Does this explain how the fact could be true?
Main Point	Is this the conclusion?
Complete	Is this the conclusion?
Point at Issue	Do the speakers voice disagreement about this?
Point of Agreement	Do the speakers voice agreement about this?
Method	Does this match the argument?
Role	Does this match the role of the claim?
Conform	Does this match the principle in the passage?
Parallel Reasoning	Does this match the Parallel Pair in the passage?

13.5 Drill: Identifying Question Types

Look at each question stem and determine which question type it represents. Not all of the stems are flaw-independent questions.

1. Which one of the following is most strongly supported by the information above?

   _____

2. Cori uses which one of the following argumentative techniques in countering Hannah's argument?

   _____

3. Spruill's and Tozzi's statements most strongly support the view that they would disagree with each other about which one of the following?

   _____

4. Which one of the following judgments best illustrates the principle illustrated by the argument above?

   _____

5. Which one of the following most accurately expresses the main conclusion of the argument?

   _____

6. The claim that frequent caffeine users suffer from headaches more often plays which one of the following roles in the nutritionist's argument?

   _____

7. The situation described above most closely conforms to which one of the following propositions?

   _____

8. Leanna responds to Fritz's argument by

   _____

9. The reasoning in the argument above is most closely paralleled by that in which one of the following?

   _____

10. Which one of the following, if true, most helps to reconcile the poetry specialist's two claims?

    _____

11. If the statements above are true, each of the following cannot be true EXCEPT:

    _____

12. Which one of the following most accurately expresses the conclusion that the politician's argument, as it is stated above, is structured to establish?

    _____

13. If all of the herpetologist's statements are true, then which one of the following must be true?

    _____

14. Which one of the following principles, if accepted, does the most to justify the conclusion of the chemist's argument?

15. Which one of the following, if true, most helps to resolve the apparent conflict between Fenwick's statements?

16. If the statements above are true, which one of the following must be false?

17. Which one of the following, if true, most helps to explain the ability of newborn bats described above?

18. The statements above, if true, most strongly support which one of the following conclusions about the aurora borealis?

19. Which one of the following most accurately expresses the main point of the argument above?

20. Their dialogue provides the most support for the claim that Mark and Jeremy agree that their township

21. Which one of the following exhibits a pattern of reasoning most similar to that exhibited by the argument above?

22. If the statements above are true, each of the following could be true EXCEPT:

23. That the meaning of law is not fixed but fluid figures in the argument in which one of the following ways?

24. Which one of the following statements follows logically from the statements above?

25. Pae and Talia disagree about whether

26. Which one of the following principles, if valid, most helps to justify the essayist's reasoning?

27. Which one of the following, if true, most strongly supports the statements above?

28. If the statements above are true, which one of the following can be inferred on the basis of them?

29. Which one of the following best illustrates the proposition above?

30. If the statements above are true, each one of the following can be properly inferred EXCEPT:

Answers

1. Inference	11. Cannot Be True	21. Parallel Reasoning
2. Method	12. Complete	22. Cannot Be True
3. Point at Issue	13. Inference	23. Role
4. Conform	14. Justify	24. Inference
5. Main Point	15. Paradox	25. Point at Issue
6. Role	16. Cannot Be True	26. Justify
7. Conform	17. Explain	27. Strengthen
8. Method	18. Inference	28. Inference
9. Parallel Reasoning	19. Main Point	29. Conform
10. Paradox	20. Point of Agreement	30. Inference

STOP. THIS IS THE END OF LECTURE 11. DO NOT PROCEED TO THE CORRESPONDING EXAM UNTIL INSTRUCTED TO DO SO IN CLASS.

IN-CLASS EXAM ICE LECTURE 1

EXAMINATION

LECTURE 1 EXAM
Time—25 minutes

15 Questions

Directions: The questions in this section are based on the reasoning contained in brief statements or passages. For some questions, more than one of the choices could conceivably answer the question. However, you are to choose the best answer; that is, the response that most accurately and completely answers the question. You should not make assumptions that are by commonsense standards implausible, superfluous, or incompatible with the passage. After you have chosen the best answer, circle the answer choice.

1. Curator: If you have no familiarity with Italian, you will not be able to use the museum's guide. And without using the museum's guide, you will miss many of the nuances of the pieces on display.

   If the curator's statements are true, which one of the following must also be true?

   (A) If you miss many of the nuances of the exhibited works, you have no familiarity with Italian.
   (B) You will notice all of the nuances of the pieces on display if you are fluent in Italian.
   (C) If you are able to use the museum's guide, you will miss some of the details of the pieces on display.
   (D) You will fail to notice many of the details of the exhibited works if you lack any knowledge of Italian.
   (E) If you use the museum's guide, you have no knowledge of Italian.

2. Of the approximately 7,000 doctors in the United States who have passed the exams required for board certification for plastic surgery, only 600 are women, according to statistics published by the American Board of Plastic Surgery. But there were less than half as many female plastic surgeons just ten years ago, even though there was the same total number of certified plastic surgeons at that time, and a thorough Board analysis of current medical school and residency data shows that the changes in the gender distribution of plastic surgeons will continue to accelerate over the next decade. The changes may be attributable to the growing belief that female plastic surgeons are more understanding of the needs of female patients.

   If the above statements are true, which one of the following can be properly inferred from them?

   (A) A greater percentage of certified plastic surgeons will be female in five years.
   (B) A growing proportion of medical school students intend to become plastic surgeons.
   (C) Females pass the plastic surgery board certification exams at a lower rate than males.
   (D) Female plastic surgeons are superior to their male counterparts.
   (E) Plastic surgeons that operate without board certification are subject to severe fines.

3. American copyright law protects creative material such as novels and symphonies until seventy years after the death of the creator of the material. Clothing was not covered by initial copyright statutes, but fashion designers are currently asking for a three-year term of copyright protection for their clothing designs, citing a 1998 revision to copyright law that extended protection to boat hull designs for a period of ten years. Fashion designers assert that the duration of copyright protection they are seeking would suffice to eliminate the problem of retailers copying the designs and selling very similar clothes at a significant discount.

   If the statements above are true, which one of the following is most strongly supported by them?

   (A) Fashion designers do not get due credit for their creative output because it is so quickly copied by others.
   (B) Because of the similarity of their case to the boat hull case, fashion designers will win the copyright protection they are seeking.
   (C) Clothing designs are not widely considered to be creative material.
   (D) Clothing designs currently receive less than three years of copyright protection.
   (E) High-end fashion companies are unprofitable due to the unrestrained copying of their creative ideas.

GO ON TO THE NEXT PAGE.

4. Many of the condominium units in the new building offer a large balcony. Nearly ninety percent of the condominiums that lost value over the last five years are in old buildings, and none of them offers a large balcony.

   If the above statements are true, which one of the following must also be true?

   (A) Only new buildings have condominiums that offer large balconies.
   (B) None of the condominium units in the new building will lose value in the next five years.
   (C) All condominiums in old buildings lost value over the last five years.
   (D) Investors will profit on the condominium units in the new building.
   (E) Some condominiums that are not in old buildings lost value over the last five years.

5. Political scientist: Building an impenetrable wall is an extreme form of border control and is distinct from the policy sufficient for effectively managing immigration in peacetime. Policymakers sometimes react to changing population trends by building such walls, but only because they lack the creativity to react in any other manner.

   Each of the following can be logically inferred from the political scientist's statements EXCEPT:

   (A) Not all border control involves impenetrable walls.
   (B) The policy sufficient for effectively managing immigration does not include border control.
   (C) Some policies are affected by their makers' level of creativity.
   (D) In peacetime, immigration can be managed without impenetrable walls.
   (E) The construction of impenetrable walls is influenced by policymakers' level of creativity.

6. The recent increase in postage costs will have effects in many different industries and markets. One example is the magazine industry, whose costs of supply, particularly for subscriptions, are directly tied to postage costs. All of its other supply costs have remained steady for years, as have its two revenue sources, advertising and subscriptions. Magazine publishers will surely attempt to pass along the increased cost of supply in the near future, but it is unlikely that they will pass the cost on to their advertisers, as they have already raised advertising rates twice in the past year.

   If the statements in the above passage are true, which one of the following is most strongly supported by them?

   (A) Interest in magazines has dropped as use of the Internet has increased.
   (B) All costs of supply for magazine publishers will remain steady for years.
   (C) Magazine publishers will not raise advertising rates again for many years.
   (D) Magazine publishers are likely to increase the cost of subscriptions in the near future.
   (E) Magazine publishers will be unprofitable until postage rates are reduced.

7. To be eligible for the job, an applicant must be at least 25 years of age and must have at least 3 years of work experience in the field. Out of the five applicants whose applications were received today, exactly three are at least 25 years of age and exactly three have at least 3 years of work experience in the field.

   Which one of the statements below follows logically from the statements in the passage?

   (A) All five of the applicants whose applications were received today meet the two requirements of the job.
   (B) At least one of the five applicants whose applications were received today meets the two requirements for the job.
   (C) At least one of the five applicants whose applications were received today will be hired.
   (D) None of the five applicants whose applications were received today will be hired.
   (E) Three of the five applicants whose applications were received today meet the two requirements for the job.

GO ON TO THE NEXT PAGE.

8. The academic study of literature is largely occupied with deciphering the messages and lessons that the authors of the works studied intended to convey. But it is generally true that an author's intended message is directly applicable only within the broad socio-cultural conditions in which he or she wrote and decipherable only to those with a precise knowledge of the specific interpersonal interactions that influenced the author during the creative process. Particularly with respect to the study of older works, this tends to impede the academic endeavor to fully comprehend an author's intended message.

The information above most strongly supports which one of the following?

(A) Knowledge of an author's personal relationships is usually necessary to better understand the message of a work written by that author.

(B) Socio-cultural conditions always play an important role in influencing an author.

(C) Authors who lived in culturally interesting eras and places wrote books that are more widely studied today.

(D) The academic study of literature is questionable as it necessarily fails in its primary pursuit.

(E) Lack of knowledge of an author's surroundings impedes our understanding only of older works.

9. The work of Pierre Bonnard, a French painter who died in 1947, is experiencing a surge in value after being largely neglected following the artist's death. Bonnard's reputation was damaged by his equivocation on various social issues, which allowed his critics to attack his credibility as an artist. The value of Bonnard's work was also hurt by a number of poor business decisions he and his dealers made, allowing many of his paintings to be re-touched by others before sale and releasing many substandard pieces to market. New interpretations by several leading experts on early-twentieth-century European painting have precipitated the recent increase in interest in Bonnard's art.

Which one of the following is most reasonably supported by the information above?

(A) Bonnard was not considered a successful artist while he was alive.

(B) Bonnard's paintings are viewed as a good investment by many collectors.

(C) Bonnard has been more heavily criticized than most painters of his era.

(D) Bonnard is currently the most studied French painter of the twentieth century.

(E) Some paintings attributed to Bonnard are not entirely his own work.

10. Some people think that in the world of advertisements, there are only a few unethical ones. But if omitting certain truths is a quality of being unethical, I believe all advertisements that increase sales are unethical. They must omit certain truths in order to be efficacious. An advertisement that is meticulously candid about conveying all the positives and negatives of its product will never increase sales.

If the author's statements are accurate, each of the following statements could be true EXCEPT:

(A) Some people think all advertisements are unethical.

(B) Some advertisements are meticulously candid.

(C) Some people define an advertisement's function as conveying all the positives and negatives of its product.

(D) Some advertisements that omit certain truths do not increase sales.

(E) Some meticulously candid advertisements increase sales.

11. The beginning of the Late Bronze Age in the Aegean region has traditionally been dated to the 16th century B.C. This estimate was based on comparing Aegean pottery to pottery from civilizations whose dates were known with more certainty and noting the similarity of Late Bronze Age pottery to that of Egypt's New Kingdom, which began in the 16th century B.C. However, two independent radiocarbon-dating tests have confirmed beyond doubt that the Late Bronze Age began in the Aegean region at least a century earlier than previously thought. Both tests dated organic material preserved by a volcanic eruption on the island of Santorini.

If the above statements are true, which one of the following can be most reasonably inferred from them?

(A) No major volcanic eruptions occurred in the Aegean region after the Late Bronze Age.

(B) The beginning of the Late Bronze Age in the Aegean region predated the New Kingdom in Egypt.

(C) The pottery of Egypt's New Kingdom influenced the pottery of civilizations in the Aegean region.

(D) Radiocarbon-dating tests are the only reliable way to determine the exact date of volcanic eruptions.

(E) The Late Bronze Age in the Aegean region ended at least a century earlier than previously thought.

GO ON TO THE NEXT PAGE.

12. Softcover versions of American textbooks are often produced overseas and sold for a much lower price there than in America. According to a 1998 Supreme Court ruling, manufacturers who produce their goods cheaply abroad have no legal protection against having their products resold into the American market. But intellectual-property restrictions still apply to the books, so students who import foreign-made textbooks can only legally do so for personal and not commercial use. Many online distributors operating overseas have set up websites from which students can order the cheaper versions of the textbooks.

Which one of the following is most strongly supported by the information above?

(A) The online overseas textbook distributors are operating in violation of American law.

(B) The softcover versions of the textbooks produced overseas are not inferior to the hardcover versions produced domestically.

(C) Students cannot legally order the cheaper textbooks for the purpose of selling them at a profit.

(D) The Supreme Court ruling is not applicable to digital content.

(E) There are no tariffs on the import of foreign-made textbooks.

13. Manager: Staff members who have worked at the store for more than two years have some choice about which shifts they work. Among these staff members, those who have never been docked pay for misconduct get to choose their shifts before those who have been docked pay for misconduct. No other staff members have any choice about which shifts they work.

Which one of the following inferences is most strongly supported by the rules described above?

(A) Most staff members at the store do not have any choice about which shifts they work.

(B) Juan has never been docked pay before and has worked at the store for one year, so he has no choice about which shifts he works.

(C) Lau has worked at the store longer than any other staff member, so he will get to choose his shifts first.

(D) Rasheed has worked at the store for four years, but has been docked pay for misconduct on many occasions, so he does not have any choice about which shifts he works.

(E) Angela has worked at the store for three years and has never been docked pay for misconduct, so she gets to choose her shifts first.

14. According to census data, Country A had more schools per capita last year than Country B, while Country B had fewer people than Country A. Since the census data were accumulated, each country has closed 100 schools within its borders without opening any new schools.

If the above statements are true, which one of the following can be properly concluded from them?

(A) Country A presently has more schools than Country B.

(B) Country A and Country B both presently have fewer schools than they need.

(C) Country A presently has more schools per capita than Country B.

(D) Country A presently has more people than Country B.

(E) Country A and Country B presently have the same number of schools.

15. The price of gasoline is determined by a complex interaction of factors. One such factor is the demand for gasoline; as people decide to use more of it, its price increases. Another factor is the availability of the oil from which gasoline is produced; as any element of the oil supply chain is limited or threatened, the price of gasoline increases. The legislature has proposed lowering the current price of gasoline by reducing taxes applied to it by ten cents per gallon, and if passed this change will take effect within the next two weeks. The lower price resulting from the tax reduction would quickly encourage people to use more gasoline, but no other factors affecting the price of gasoline will change in the short term.

The statements above, if true, most strongly support which one of the following?

(A) Gasoline is currently too expensive for the average family.

(B) The current high price of gasoline is a detriment to overall economic productivity.

(C) The proposed gasoline tax cut would decrease the overall price of gasoline by less than ten cents per gallon.

(D) Taxes on gasoline are currently higher than they should be.

(E) Reducing gasoline taxes is the only way the legislature can help lower the price of gasoline.

STOP

IF YOU FINISH BEFORE TIME IS CALLED, YOU MAY CHECK YOUR WORK ON THIS EXAM ONLY.
DO NOT WORK ON ANY OTHER EXAM IN THE BOOK.

Answers

1. D
2. A
3. D
4. E
5. B
6. D
7. B
8. A
9. E
10. E
11. B
12. C
13. B
14. A
15. C

IN-CLASS EXAM   ICE   LECTURE   2

EXAMINATION

LECTURE 2 EXAM
Time—25 minutes
15 Questions

<u>Directions:</u> The questions in this section are based on the reasoning contained in brief statements or passages. For some questions, more than one of the choices could conceivably answer the question. However, you are to choose the <u>best</u> answer; that is, the response that most accurately and completely answers the question. You should not make assumptions that are by commonsense standards implausible, superfluous, or incompatible with the passage. After you have chosen the best answer, circle the answer choice.

1. Critics have argued that elementary schools should be designed to maximize the educational content they provide, and that physical education should therefore not be included in the curricula of elementary schools. But there is a clear link between physical health, which is indisputably enhanced and encouraged by physical education classes, and a student's ability to learn and retain information. Thus, _____.

   Which one of the following most logically completes the argument?

   (A) critics are wrong when they say physical education classes will be removed from the curricula of elementary schools
   (B) many of the subjects traditionally taught at elementary schools are not valuable
   (C) devoting some class time to physical education is not incompatible with the goal of maximizing the education of students
   (D) children who are physically unhealthy cannot be good students
   (E) schools should allocate more class time to physical education, even if it comes at the expense of standard academic subjects

2. John: In a game of poker, novices can have an advantage against experienced players. Because of their inexperience, they tend to make inadvisable betting decisions, which in turn mislead experienced players as they try to guess what cards the novices have. I've seen first-timers beat skilled players that way.

   Beth: I've also seen first-timers win plenty of games, but what you said is inaccurate. Any betting decision that helps a player win by confusing his opponents is obviously a good move, whether made by a novice or an expert.

   John and Beth disagree about whether

   (A) novices have an advantage against experienced poker players
   (B) first-time poker players win less often than experienced players
   (C) experienced players are good at guessing which cards a novice has
   (D) the betting decisions described by John are inadvisable
   (E) luck or skill plays a greater role in poker

3. One of the foundational principles of the ethics of Stoicism, a Hellenistic philosophy dating to the 3rd century B.C., is that nothing is good unless its possessor benefits from it under all circumstances. The Stoic definition is problematic in that it leaves open the possibility that nothing good exists. For instance, the Stoics believed that material wealth was not good, because it could drive someone to harmful indulgence. But while they claimed that the characteristic human virtues, such as courage, were truly good, even these virtues can be shown to be detrimental to their possessors in some cases. Courage can bring a man to harm when it compels him to intervene in a dangerous situation.

   Which one of the following most accurately states the main point of the argument?

   (A) Stoicism is the oldest known Hellenistic philosophy.
   (B) The Stoic definition of what is good is problematic.
   (C) Only objects or qualities that are always beneficial can be defined as good.
   (D) Material wealth can ultimately be harmful to a person.
   (E) Courage should not be considered one of the characteristic human virtues.

GO ON TO THE NEXT PAGE.

4. Tony: Most of today's most popular music is clearly inferior to the classical music produced in Europe in the 18th and 19th centuries. Today's music relies heavily on electronic instruments and electronically created audio effects, which Haydn never would have used, as he obviously did not need them to make his music sound good. And today's music is much simpler in structure and more repetitive than any of Haydn's pieces ever were.

    Fernandez: Haydn's music certainly sounded good, but he made use of every instrument available in his time, and there's no reason to believe that he would not have done the same had he been alive today. And many of his compositions were more repetitive than those of Beethoven, his successor.

    The dialogue most strongly supports the claim that Tony and Fernandez disagree with each other about whether

    (A)   popular music today is inferior to classical music produced in Europe in the 18th and 19th centuries
    (B)   Haydn's music is indisputably good
    (C)   Haydn's music is repetitive
    (D)   Haydn would have used electronic instruments had they been available to him
    (E)   Beethoven's music is superior to that of Haydn

5. Journalists and copy editors have traditionally written headlines with the intent of catching a reader's scanning eye and piquing a reader's curiosity. This has often been accomplished with double-entendres, puns, and subtle references to other stories or events. However, some readers have a new method of scanning for news stories and articles: using Internet search engines. Search engine programs return articles with the highest relevance scores, which are evaluated largely on the basis of the assessed relevance of the content of their headlines. The search programs recognize literal terms that indicate the content of the articles, but are unable to interpret the wordplay and general subtlety used to draw human readers' attention. Thus, _____.

    Which one of the following most logically completes the passage?

    (A)   to best attract readers using Internet search engines, headlines cannot be written in the traditional manner
    (B)   more readers are getting their news from the Internet today than from more traditional sources
    (C)   search engines represent the fastest-growing Internet-related industry
    (D)   despite technological advancements, the Internet remains a poor means of collecting information
    (E)   journalists and copy editors who received their training before the Internet was invented are now obsolete

6. Legislator: Although the proposed legislation to reduce the influence that monetary campaign contributions have in elections will benefit all citizens, the cost of enacting that legislation should be borne by large corporations alone. The undue advantages enjoyed by such contributors primarily benefit corporations, and indeed, the power that such donations bring is the reason that corporations are subject to a lower rate of taxation than they were a decade ago.

    Which one of the following most accurately states the main point of the argument?

    (A)   Legislation should be enacted to reduce the influence that monetary campaign contributions have in elections.
    (B)   Corporations are subject to a lower rate of taxation than they were a decade ago.
    (C)   The undue advantages enjoyed by such contributors primarily benefit corporations.
    (D)   The cost of enacting the proposed legislation should be borne by large corporations alone.
    (E)   A reduction in the influence that monetary campaign contributions have in elections will benefit all citizens.

GO ON TO THE NEXT PAGE.

7. Kernodle: There can be no doubt that many athletes from this era used illegal performance enhancers. To my mind, this makes them the worst kind of cheaters. All of the records set over the past decade should be considered invalid and none of the athletes from this era should be allowed into the hall of fame.

Ngobeh: It is probably true that many athletes used illegal performance-enhancing drugs. Many players also used other illegal substances, and they should have their records discounted as well, but we can only invalidate the records of those who have been proven to have broken the rules.

Kernodle and Ngobeh disagree about whether

(A) all of the records set over the past decade should be considered invalid

(B) users of performance-enhancing drugs are the worst kind of cheaters

(C) any players from this era should be eligible for induction into the hall of fame

(D) performance-enhancing drugs helped users set records

(E) many players used illegal drugs other than performance enhancers

8. The most widely accepted explanation for the extinction of the dinosaurs is that a massive meteor impact created sufficiently adverse conditions all over the earth. This is based primarily upon the observation that a large meteor impacted the earth around the same time that many dinosaur species began to disappear. Yet factors ignored by this theory must have played a role. Many similar impacts have failed to coincide with mass extinctions in the past, and many dinosaur populations were beginning to decline before the impact believed to have caused their extinction.

Which one of the following best expresses the main point of the passage?

(A) A massive meteor impact created the adverse conditions that led to the extinction of the dinosaurs.

(B) Many dinosaur species were beginning to go extinct before the impact that is thought to have caused their extinction.

(C) No meteor impact contributed to the extinction of the dinosaurs.

(D) Causes aside from a meteor impact must have contributed to the extinction of the dinosaurs.

(E) Large meteor impacts sometimes do not lead to mass extinctions.

9. Rebecca: Citizens have a right to know how their taxes are being spent. A government is obligated to spend tax revenue in the way that is most beneficial to its citizens, and only when the government keeps citizens informed can this obligation be met.

Miriam: It is true that a government should only spend tax revenue to the benefit of its citizens. But this can be achieved without informing the citizens of how tax revenues are allocated. All that is needed to ensure proper spending is a commitment by those in government to a general principle of justice.

Rebecca's and Miriam's statements commit them to disagreeing about which one of the following principles?

(A) Committing to a general principle of justice is necessary to bring about a just allocation of tax revenues.

(B) Informing citizens of tax revenue allocation is a necessary condition for allocating such revenue in the way most beneficial to citizens.

(C) A government has a duty to spend its tax revenues in a way most beneficial to its citizens.

(D) Allocating tax revenue in a way most beneficial to citizens is possible if citizens are made aware of how taxes are being spent.

(E) A government ought to keep its citizens informed of how it spends tax revenues.

GO ON TO THE NEXT PAGE.

10. Many professionals suggest that playing classical music for children, or even infants, can make those children more likely to excel in their academic careers, particularly as measured by graduation rates from postsecondary schools. Well-informed professionals are aware that there is even more support for the theory that educational television programs contribute to a child's likelihood of eventual academic success. There is only circumstantial evidence underpinning the belief in the benefits of classical music, whereas multiple studies, covering children in three different countries and accounting for the educational backgrounds of the parents, have served to increase professional acceptance of the link between educational television shows and academic achievement.

Which one of the following best expresses the main point of the argument?

(A) Playing classical music for children, in infancy or in later life, probably does not help them attain academic success.
(B) There is more reason to believe in the benefits of educational television programs than in those of classical music in improving children's academic success.
(C) Only theories backed by studies covering a variety of people and circumstances should be accepted.
(D) Showing educational television programs to children is recommended by more professionals than is any other method of improving children's academic capabilities.
(E) Even professionals are unable to suggest reliable methods to improve a child's likelihood of eventual academic success.

11. Historians have long known that Mozart was buried in a pauper's grave and was quite poor when he died. Many surviving letters also indicate that he frequently asked friends and associates for loans, strengthening the belief that he was poor throughout his life. Investigation of new documents has indicated that he earned about 10,000 florins per year. Many professionals of Mozart's time lived comfortably with incomes of 500 florins per year, and Mozart's income would have placed him in the top five percent, calling into question established notions about how he lived. Scholars continue to disagree about whether he squandered his wealth gambling or was simply too careless with his earnings.

Which one of the following best expresses the main point of the argument?

(A) Mozart earned 10,000 florins per year, which would have been in the top five percent of incomes in his time.
(B) New evidence demands a reconsideration of previously held beliefs about Mozart's wealth.
(C) Mozart was quite rich and lived his whole life much more comfortably than previously thought.
(D) Analysis of Mozart's grave and letters in which he requested loans indicate that Mozart was quite poor throughout his life.
(E) New evidence indicates that Mozart had a gambling problem and lost most of his wealth to gambling debts.

GO ON TO THE NEXT PAGE.

12. Barrett: Unlike most molecules, those of water
        experience between them a certain type of
        bond—the hydrogen bond—that causes water to
        be a liquid at unexpectedly high temperatures. We
        performed experiments using x-ray scattering, a
        technique that produces data based on the time-
        averaged behavior of the hydrogen bonds. From
        our research we have concluded that, contrary
        to what scientists previously assumed, water
        molecules, through their hydrogen bonds, form
        a network of large rings or chains, rather than
        tetrahedrons.

     Voigt: Although your discovery that nearly 80 percent
        of hydrogen bonds in water are broken at any
        one time contradicts the predictions of traditional
        models that presumed that water molecules
        form tetrahedrons, our research shows that a
        model based on ring and chain structures yields
        predictions inconsistent with the results of your
        own experiments, while predictions of our revised
        model, in which liquid water forms a tetrahedral
        structure, conform with your x-ray scattering data.

Their dialogue provides the most support for the claim
that Barrett and Voigt agree that

(A)   x-ray scattering is the most appropriate method
         by which to determine the structure of hydrogen
         bonds in water
(B)   if the molecules of water form rings and chains,
         nearly 80 percent of hydrogen bonds should be
         broken at any one time
(C)   the hydrogen bonds between water molecules
         form a network of large rings or chains
(D)   the fact that water is a liquid at unexpectedly high
         temperatures shows that its hydrogen bonds do
         not form tetrahedrons
(E)   previous models in which water molecules were
         thought to form tetrahedrons did not predict that
         nearly 80 percent of hydrogen bonds should be
         broken at any one time

13. Many people think that exercise is healthy regardless
     of how often one chooses to exercise. And recent
     research appears to confirm this view, since two separate
     independent research groups concluded that exercising
     every day has no appreciable negative impact on the
     overall health of an individual. But both studies relied
     on unrepresentative samples. In each case, the subjects
     were volunteers from local health clubs. The effect of
     exercising on health cannot be measured on only those
     who exercise regularly, just as the effect of secondhand
     smoke on health cannot be measured on only those who
     smoke regularly.

Of the following, which one most accurately expresses
the main point of the argument?

(A)   Proper studies of the effects of exercise should
         be conducted on those who do not exercise
         regularly as well as on those who do.
(B)   Measuring the effects of exercising on health by
         only testing those who exercise regularly is like
         measuring the effects of secondhand smoke only
         on those who smoke regularly.
(C)   The studies that denied appreciable negative
         effects of daily exercise were based on flawed
         sample groups.
(D)   Those people who frequent local health clubs
         are less likely to suffer negative effects of daily
         exercise than those who do not.
(E)   A study that included those people who do not
         exercise regularly would have shown that too
         much exercise can be unhealthy.

GO ON TO THE NEXT PAGE.

14. Umaru: The Moranese government's decision to forge ahead with its annual whale hunt is deplorable. The minke whale, the primary species targeted, will become extinct if it continues this practice, which is in violation of the moratorium on whaling agreed to by most international governments in 1986. Besides, demand for whale meat has diminished significantly since the moratorium, so the hunt will not even be very profitable for the government.

Celeste: But you have to consider that whale meat is very culturally significant in Morania, so the decades-old hunt can be valuable even if it is not profitable. And since the moratorium, minke populations have increased to numbers that can sustain pre-1986 whaling levels.

Umaru and Celeste's remarks provide the most support for holding that they disagree about whether

(A) the Moranese government's whale hunt will be profitable
(B) the Moranese government should continue the annual whale hunt indefinitely
(C) the Moranese government's whale hunt threatens to make the minke whales extinct
(D) the Moranese government's whale hunt is in violation of the moratorium on whaling
(E) hunting an animal is unethical when that animal faces the risk of extinction

15. Professor Ruehl: Although Professor Bollen correctly defends an artist's right to create any piece, regardless of how it may be perceived, his argument that artists should not accept government funds when they intend to create works that they know will, upon public display, cause community controversy is misguided. Almost no one would contend that public funds should not be used to support libraries, yet those same funds eventually benefit many authors whose works engender vehement disagreement. A divisive book is no different than a controversial painting.

The main conclusion drawn in Professor Ruehl's argument is that

(A) artists have the right to create any piece they choose
(B) a divisive book is no different than a controversial painting
(C) artists are justified in accepting government funds even in cases in which that money will be used to create controversial works
(D) Professor Bollen fails to consider ways in which public funding of art and that of libraries is similar
(E) both artists and authors should be given whatever public funding they request, regardless of whether the community will be offended by what they produce

STOP

IF YOU FINISH BEFORE TIME IS CALLED, YOU MAY CHECK YOUR WORK ON THIS EXAM ONLY.
DO NOT WORK ON ANY OTHER EXAM IN THE BOOK.

ANSWERS

1. C
2. D
3. B
4. D
5. A
6. D
7. A
8. D
9. B
10. B
11. B
12. E
13. C
14. C
15. C

IN-CLASS EXAM · ICE · LECTURE · 3

EXAMINATION

LECTURE 3 EXAM
Time—25 minutes
15 Questions

Directions: The questions in this section are based on the reasoning contained in brief statements or passages. For some questions, more than one of the choices could conceivably answer the question. However, you are to choose the <u>best</u> answer; that is, the response that most accurately and completely answers the question. You should not make assumptions that are by commonsense standards implausible, superfluous, or incompatible with the passage. After you have chosen the best answer, circle the answer choice.

1. In most people, consumption of ice cream is quickly followed by increased blood flow to the stomach, a condition that can last for up to thirty minutes. Careful analysis of available data reveals that on the days with the greatest number of drownings or near-drowning incidents at public beaches, there are typically large amounts of ice cream sold as well. Hence, increased ice cream consumption must lead to a greater risk of drowning.

    Which one of the following most accurately describes a flaw in the argument's reasoning?

    (A) It considers only a single factor in drawing its conclusion.
    (B) It postulates the existence of a causal relationship where the data support only the existence of a correlative relationship.
    (C) It establishes a broad conclusion on the basis of an insufficiently representative data set.
    (D) It takes for granted that if a statement must be true for the argument's conclusion to be true, then that statement's truth is sufficient for the truth of the conclusion.
    (E) It neglects to propose solutions to the problem presented.

2. Talk show host: Anyone who is president of this country should be able to respond quickly and decisively in crises, and our current president has proven that he is not capable of doing this. Hence, I believe that our current president is unfit for office.

    Guest: You have never held any position of power or responsibility, and you do not know what it is like to have to make decisions under pressure. So your criticism of the president is invalid.

    The guest's argument is most vulnerable to the criticism that it

    (A) presupposes the opposing argument to be invalid on the basis of previous reasoning errors made in unrelated arguments by the person presenting the opposing argument
    (B) addresses only the authority of the person making the opposing argument without addressing the opposing argument itself
    (C) neglects to take into account whether the person making the opposing argument has sufficient first-hand experience in the subject matter being debated
    (D) presumes, without providing justification, that anyone criticizing the president must have ulterior political motives for doing so
    (E) ignores the possibility that the qualities mentioned in the opposing argument are sufficient conditions for being a good president rather than necessary conditions for being a good president

GO ON TO THE NEXT PAGE.

3. A popular restaurant chain has announced that it will phase out its rewards program wherein customers receive a free sandwich with points earned from the purchase of ten sandwiches over any period at any of the restaurant's locations. The decision is a sensible one; since each sandwich served costs the chain a few dollars, and since the program resulted in the chain giving away many sandwiches for free, the chain was obviously losing money as a result of the program.

The argument is most vulnerable to the criticism that it

(A) overlooks the possibility that another program will be implemented to replace the program being phased out

(B) overlooks the possible benefit to the sandwich chain of exaggerating its own market data

(C) fails to consider whether any other retail food chains have opted to implement similar programs

(D) fails to consider whether the profit earned by the sandwich chain was sufficient to cover its losses from the program

(E) overlooks possible benefits of the program while considering only its costs

4. Editorialist: A new municipal government initiative will allocate nearly $1 million to improving the main parks in the city. While many residents enjoy the parks, it is hard to believe that anyone would prefer having improved parks over clean tap water and functioning traffic lights. So the allocation of the funds for the parks is a terrible misuse of public money.

The reasoning in the argument is flawed because the argument

(A) presumes, without providing justification, that the other services cited cannot be provided if the amount proposed is allocated to park improvement

(B) fails to consider whether some residents drink primarily bottled water and thus would not benefit from improvements to the city's water filtration system

(C) fails to consider the potential health benefits associated with the types of physical activity that are promoted and encouraged by the presence of parks

(D) presumes, without providing justification, that many residents will benefit from the improvements made to the parks with the allocated funds

(E) overlooks the fact that all budgets passed by fairly elected city council members are legally valid

5. Pete: I think produce at the grocery store should be labeled with the date it was harvested. That would give consumers a better idea of how fresh it is.

Nitsa: Your proposal doesn't make sense; there are many other factors that determine the freshness of produce, including the humidity at which it has been stored and any temperature extremes to which it may have been exposed during transport.

The dialogue above provides the most support to the view that Nitsa has most likely misinterpreted Pete's remarks to imply that

(A) produce is the only type of item at the grocery store that can spoil over time

(B) all consumers want to know how fresh their produce is

(C) labeling produce with the harvest date would tell consumers exactly how fresh it is

(D) labeling produce with the harvest date would be easy and inexpensive

(E) produce can be exposed to temperature extremes during transport

6. A recent study, conducted by transportation experts, concluded that the use of cellular phones while driving contributed to an increase in the rate of traffic accidents. Subsequently, a review board determined that there were numerous errors in the data upon which the study was based. Although many legislators and members of the public agree with the transportation experts, we must conclude that the use of cellular phones while driving does not contribute to an increase in the rate of traffic accidents.

The reasoning in the above argument is flawed because the argument

(A) fails to demonstrate that the review board knows more about cellular phones than do the transportation experts

(B) fails to elaborate on the specific nature of the errors in the data used for the study

(C) fails to provide evidence that the increase in the rate of traffic accidents is due to some cause other than the use of cellular phones

(D) presumes, without providing justification, that failure to prove a hypothesis constitutes proof that the hypothesis is false

(E) claims that because the study in question contained data errors, it is therefore impossible to devise a study that would be free of data errors

GO ON TO THE NEXT PAGE.

7. A respected polling agency questioned 1,000 adults in the province over a span of three days in March. With a margin of error of plus or minus three percentage points and a confidence level of 95 percent, the poll showed that nearly three-quarters of those questioned believed that road rage occurs much more frequently or somewhat more frequently than it did ten years ago. Thus, road rage is a greater problem in the province now than a decade ago.

The argument is most vulnerable to criticism on the grounds that it

(A) presumes, without providing justification, that the same percentage of all adults in the province believe road rage to be more frequent now than ten years ago

(B) presumes, without providing justification, that what people generally believe to be true is actually true

(C) draws an unequivocal conclusion based on data that only supports a conclusion drawn with 95 percent confidence

(D) fails to provide an adequate definition of the term "road rage"

(E) considers only a single province in discussing an issue with much broader implications

8. Columnist: It is an indisputable matter of historical fact that such culturally accepted forms of entertainment as the waltz and the novel were once thought to corrupt young people, and similar concerns were raised about technological innovations such as the telephone. Of course, all of these things are widely accepted today, and the concern that they might be harmful is now viewed by most people as absurd. So critics of violent television programs who contend that the programs are corrupting today's youth are making a claim that will eventually prove to be unfounded.

Which one of the following best describes a flaw in the columnist's reasoning?

(A) It treats as relevantly similar two cases that may differ in important respects.

(B) It overlooks the possibility that the telephone may have contributed to the corruption of some young people at the time it was invented.

(C) It purports to establish its conclusion by making a claim that, if true, would actually contradict that conclusion.

(D) It fails to consider the viewpoint of those who do not think violent television programs are harmful.

(E) It makes the questionable generalization that no one believes novels or the waltz to be harmful.

9. Essayist: The existence of a moral order in the universe—i.e., an order in which bad is always eventually punished and good rewarded—depends upon human souls being immortal. In some cultures this moral order is regarded as the result of a karma that controls how one is reincarnated, in others it results from the actions of a supreme being who metes out justice to people after their death. But however a moral order is represented, if human souls are immortal, then it follows that the bad will be punished.

Which one of the following most accurately describes a flaw in the essayist's reasoning?

(A) From the assertion that something is necessary to a moral order, the argument concludes that that thing is sufficient for an element of the moral order to be realized.

(B) The argument takes mere beliefs to be established facts.

(C) From the claim that the immortality of human souls implies that there is a moral order in the universe, the argument concludes that there being a moral order in the universe implies that human souls are immortal.

(D) The argument treats two fundamentally different conceptions of a moral order as essentially the same.

(E) The argument's conclusion is presupposed in the definition it gives of a moral order.

Test 24, Section 2, Question 23

10. A jury awarded a man more than $1 million for losing both legs in an attempt to outrun a subway train while intoxicated. The man's lawyer conducted a carefully controlled experiment to prove that the man was capable of running at speeds up to 8 miles per hour. The jury reasoned that, since the train operator should have had enough time to stop the train before hitting a man running that fast, the train company could be held partially at fault.

The jury's reasoning is flawed because it

(A) fails to consider whether the man could have done anything more to avoid being hit by the train

(B) relies on complicated calculations that were never verified by an expert

(C) presumes, without providing justification, that the train was functioning perfectly the night the man was hit

(D) takes for granted that the man was running his fastest when he was hit by the train

(E) presumes, without providing justification, that the train operator could not see the man

GO ON TO THE NEXT PAGE.

11. Inspired by London's Hyde Park and the Bois de Boulogne in Paris, landscape architect Andrew Jackson Downing began to assert New York City's need for a public park in 1844. His idea grew in popularity, until in 1853 the state legislature designated 700 acres for the creation of Central Park. Since Downing's efforts can be directly linked to the creation of the park, all those who have experienced Central Park would not have had the pleasure of doing so without the tremendous foresight of the brilliant landscape architect.

The argument above is most vulnerable to criticism on the grounds that it

(A) presumes, without providing justification, that Downing was the only person who played a large role in popularizing the project
(B) concludes that a claim about a causal connection must be true on the basis of a lack of evidence against that claim
(C) takes for granted the assertion that many people enjoy Central Park
(D) presumes, without providing justification, that something that resulted from a cause could only have resulted from that cause
(E) overlooks the fact that many other people have influenced the geography of New York City

12. Ten years ago, a law was enacted that required automakers to install an emissions control device on all new cars. Despite this, the total amount of harmful emissions released last year by cars equipped with this device actually exceeded the emissions released last year by older cars that lacked the device. Clearly, the law does not help to reduce harmful emissions.

This argument is most vulnerable to criticism on the grounds that it

(A) takes for granted that the device works properly when installed on new cars
(B) assumes, without providing justification, that the emissions released by cars equipped with the device have more serious long-term health effects than do the emissions released by cars that are not equipped with the device
(C) ignores the possibility that the owners of cars equipped with the device may have removed or disabled it
(D) overlooks the possibility that the number of cars equipped with the device exceeds the number of cars without the device
(E) takes for granted that the emissions released by cars equipped with the device are actually harmful

13. Professor: A colleague in my department recently conducted a computer simulation, based on some of his calculations and code he had written, that concluded that the local pigeon population will decrease over the next few years. His calculations have been verified as accurate, but, given that the pigeon population will in fact increase in the near future, there must have been some errors in the code that drove his simulation. Since my colleague's code was flawed, we cannot draw the conclusion that the pigeon population will decrease.

Which one of the following most accurately describes a flaw in the professor's argument?

(A) The professor inappropriately assumes that any prediction that does not consider all conditions must fail to consider all necessary conditions.
(B) The professor fails to identify the supposed flaw in the simulation code.
(C) The professor dismisses the value of all computer simulations without considering whether the simulation in question is useful.
(D) The professor presumes, without providing justification, that his colleague could not have made calculations and written code without committing any errors.
(E) The professor draws a conclusion that simply restates a claim presented in support of that conclusion.

GO ON TO THE NEXT PAGE.

14. A particular student suddenly began scoring much higher on his math tests. To confirm that he was not cheating, the teacher required him to take two additional tests. To ensure that the student was not getting help from classmates, the teacher had him take one test in a room alone. To ensure that he was not somehow getting the test questions in advance, the teacher administered, during class, a second test that she had created minutes beforehand with randomly chosen numbers. On both tests, the student matched his previous results, so the teacher concluded that the student must have been achieving his test scores without seeing the test questions beforehand or getting help from classmates.

Which one of the following most accurately describes a flaw in the teacher's reasoning?

(A) The teacher failed to recognize that the numbers she chose for the test questions may not have been truly random.

(B) The teacher inappropriately assumed that the student could have been cheating using only the two methods she considered.

(C) The teacher failed to consider that there are other ways to ensure that a student does not see the test questions before being given the test.

(D) The teacher overlooked the possibility that the student could have used different cheating methods on different tests.

(E) The teacher failed to consider whether other students had been cheating in some way.

15. A strong emphasis from parents on arts and arts education in early adolescence usually has a negative impact on a child's creative development. Children in their early adolescence tend to be rebellious, and as a result, they tend to resist those subjects emphasized by their parents. Parents who care about arts and arts education should be aware of this phenomenon. Parental emphasis on these subjects can only be effective once children reach early adulthood. At that age, parents can encourage certain activities without immediate resistance from their children.

The argument above is most vulnerable to which one of the following criticisms?

(A) It mistakes a correlation between resistance to parental guidance and age for a causal relationship between resistance and age.

(B) It fails to consider the possibility that children might be interested in arts and arts education without being guided toward these subjects by their parents.

(C) It ignores the fact that children in early adulthood are much more likely to respond positively to parental encouragement simply because they have a desire to please their parents.

(D) It makes crucial use of the term "creative development," yet it fails to properly specify what that entails.

(E) It fails to specify the effects of parental emphasis on arts during stages of childhood other than early adolescence.

STOP

IF YOU FINISH BEFORE TIME IS CALLED, YOU MAY CHECK YOUR WORK ON THIS EXAM ONLY.
DO NOT WORK ON ANY OTHER EXAM IN THE BOOK.

Answers

1. B
2. B
3. E
4. A
5. C
6. D
7. B
8. A
9. A
10. D
11. D
12. D
13. E
14. D
15. E

IN-CLASS EXAM · ICE · LECTURE 4

EXAMINATION

LECTURE 4 EXAM
Time—25 minutes
15 Questions

<u>Directions:</u> The questions in this section are based on the reasoning contained in brief statements or passages. For some questions, more than one of the choices could conceivably answer the question. However, you are to choose the <u>best</u> answer; that is, the response that most accurately and completely answers the question. You should not make assumptions that are by commonsense standards implausible, superfluous, or incompatible with the passage. After you have chosen the best answer, circle the answer choice.

1. NASA scientist: We know that for life to survive on a celestial body, there must be water, carbon-based molecules, and sufficient heat. We are extremely excited by new data collected on Saturn's moon Enceladus by the Cassini spacecraft, which, to our surprise, has detected water just below the surface and measured temperatures about 100 degrees warmer than expected. These findings, in addition to our prior knowledge of the presence of carbon-based molecules on Enceladus, suggest that this moon can support life.

   Which one of the following is an assumption required by the scientist's argument?

   (A) Life will always form on a celestial body with water, carbon, and heat.
   (B) The previously expected temperature on Enceladus was not more than 100 degrees lower than that needed to support life.
   (C) The water below the surface of Enceladus covers a significant proportion of the moon's area.
   (D) Scientists have equipment capable of detecting carbon-based molecules from a distance.
   (E) There are no other bodies in our solar system more likely than Enceladus to have life at the present time.

2. A new municipal program will test the city's wastewater for a byproduct of cocaine use. Since the method proposed can accurately measure the concentration of the byproduct in water, and a consistent relationship exists between the amount of cocaine used and the amount of the byproduct produced by users, this program will ascertain the amount of cocaine used by the population of the region.

   Which one of the following is an assumption required by the argument that the program will ascertain the amount of cocaine used by the population of the region?

   (A) There are no other common sources that might add the byproduct in question to the water.
   (B) Many people in the region use cocaine.
   (C) Cocaine is the only illicit drug used by many people in the region.
   (D) Similar programs undertaken by other municipalities have had good results.
   (E) There is no other means of determining the amount of cocaine used by the population of the region.

GO ON TO THE NEXT PAGE.

3. A professor of human physiology has recommended pushing back the standard start time of the work day to better fit with people's current sleep schedules. He reasons that since the biggest impediment to maximally productive functioning is an insufficient amount of sleep, productivity would increase if people did not have to begin their work day until one hour later than the current standard.

Which one of the following is an assumption required by the professor's argument?

(A) Well-rested people would be maximally productive at work.
(B) People would not adjust to the change in the work day by going to sleep and waking up one hour later.
(C) Most people are naturally inclined to go to bed and wake up much later than the standard work day allows.
(D) Nobody would choose to arrive at work at the current standard start time if the beginning of the work day were pushed back.
(E) There is no other way to help people get the sleep they require before work.

4. It is well known that over-exposure to radiation resulting from being subjected to too many CAT scans or simple x-rays can be harmful, with the most significant risk being increased risk of cancer as a result of the damage that radiation can cause to DNA. An MRI machine represents a radiation-free substitute for CAT scans and x-rays that functions by placing people in a chamber subject to powerful magnetic fields, which cannot damage DNA at all. Hence, MRIs are a harmless alternative to radiation-intensive imaging methods.

Which one of the following is an assumption on which the argument above relies?

(A) Many people choose to get a full-body MRI every year as an alternative to the traditional annual check-up.
(B) Function of the circulatory system is not compromised by exposure to powerful magnetic fields.
(C) The risk of sustaining DNA damage from a CAT scan is unacceptably high.
(D) MRI machines are not much more expensive than standard x-ray machines.
(E) People can also develop radiation sickness if they are subjected to a CAT scan or x-ray that is improperly conducted.

5. Archaeologist: No clothes or personal artifacts have survived at the site, but we have found a number of partially complete human skeletons. By comparing the sizes of certain bones found at the site to modern bone development charts, we have been able to ascertain that most of the skeletons found belonged to children between the ages of seven and ten.

Which one of the following is an assumption on which the archaeologist's argument depends?

(A) The most complete skeletons found at the site all clearly belonged to children.
(B) There is no way to determine the exact age at which a person died simply by analyzing skeletal remains.
(C) Human bone development from the period in question is comparable to modern human bone development.
(D) Any personal artifacts that will be found at the site are certain to be those that would have belonged to children.
(E) No adult bones have been found at the site in question.

GO ON TO THE NEXT PAGE.

6. Network executive: Many television networks have rushed into producing reality shows on the assumption that they will cost less in the long run, as they require no significant expenditure on writers or actors, which tend to be the greatest costs in the production of scripted shows. However, reality shows demand an incredible amount of editing, costing almost six times as much to edit as the average scripted show. Hence, reality shows will not be less expensive to produce than scripted shows, even in the long run.

    Which one of the following would it be most useful to know in evaluating the argument?

    (A) recent and projected ratings trends for the different types of shows
    (B) the difference between the extra cost of editing and the savings on actors and writers for reality shows
    (C) the number of reality shows that have been produced, year by year, since the genre became popular
    (D) the average per-season expenditure on the cast of a scripted show
    (E) the ratio of the cost of actors and writers for a reality show to the cost of actors and writers for a scripted show

7. Roberts: Without any surviving written accounts, we cannot possibly know for certain how many times a particular Genoese ship was used in exploratory voyages in the fifteenth and sixteenth centuries.

    Smith: That's not true. Because of the Genoese custom of etching lines around the circumference of a ship's mast in certain situations, we can determine precisely the number of exploratory expeditions even without written accounts from that period.

    Which one of the following is an assumption required by Smith's argument?

    (A) There are no adequate written accounts relating to fifteenth-century Genoese ships.
    (B) Only the Genoese partook in the etching ritual described during the period in question.
    (C) The Genoese etched exactly one line around a ship's mast for each expedition in which it was involved.
    (D) The Genoese did not etch lines around the circumference of a ship's mast after each rainstorm it endured.
    (E) The ships in question were not decorated in any other way following expeditions.

8. Companies in developed nations have long been in the practice of reducing labor costs by producing their goods in developing nations, where laborers often make less than one dollar per day. By requiring that companies pay any foreign laborers they hire nearly as much as they would have to pay domestic workers, the proposed "fair trade" legislation, if passed, would be a boon to the economies of developing countries.

    Which one of the following is an assumption on which the above argument depends?

    (A) All laborers should earn a similar wage for similar work, regardless of where they live.
    (B) Increasing the wages earned in a country always improves that country's economy.
    (C) Laborers in developed countries always earn higher wages than their counterparts in developing countries.
    (D) The legislation would not compel businesses in developed countries to replace foreign labor with domestic labor.
    (E) The tax rate on wage income in the developing countries is not excessively high.

9. It has long been suspected that drinking soda can increase alertness and concentration. Recent studies that used functional magnetic resonance imaging machines to observe the bodies of subjects have revealed that drinking soda increases blood flow to the brain without any physical or chemical results that can negatively affect alertness or concentration. Hence, there is now proof that drinking soda has a positive physiological effect on alertness and concentration.

    Which one of the following is an assumption on which the argument depends?

    (A) No other drinks increase alertness or concentration.
    (B) Drinking soda does not improve information retention.
    (C) Soda does not lead to excessive weight gain.
    (D) Increased blood flow to the brain improves alertness and concentration.
    (E) Drinking soda has a positive psychological effect on alertness and concentration.

GO ON TO THE NEXT PAGE.

10. An entertainment industry analyst released findings that parents of video-game-playing children are gaining awareness of the system of ratings symbols intended to warn them of content that is potentially inappropriate for children. Eighty-three percent claimed that they are aware of the ratings system, compared to seventy-eight percent last year, and seventy-four percent claimed that they take the ratings into account when purchasing games for their children, compared to seventy percent last year. Therefore, the video games ratings symbols are helping parents make more informed purchasing decisions.

Which one of the following is an assumption on which the argument relies?

(A) Parents purchasing video games understand the intended meaning of the ratings symbols.
(B) The number of children who play video games is increasing.
(C) There are no other indications on video game packaging to indicate potentially inappropriate content.
(D) There are at least some games with content too violent to be appropriate for young children.
(E) There were not more potentially inappropriate video games produced last year than in the year before.

11. Tom: Many people consume amounts of caffeine that can be quite harmful, a new study has shown. Luckily, the study may soon be picked up by major broadcast and print news distributors, so the study will surely inspire many people to decrease their caffeine intake.

Tom's argument requires assuming which one of the following?

(A) People who currently consume harmful amounts of caffeine can switch from regular coffee to decaffeinated coffee to reduce their caffeine intake.
(B) Many people are not aware that they consume harmful amounts of caffeine.
(C) Everyone who currently consumes harmful amounts of caffeine and learns of the results of the study will reduce caffeine intake to healthy levels.
(D) Everyone who currently consumes harmful amounts of caffeine reads or watches the news on a regular basis.
(E) Many people have a moderate chemical dependency on caffeine and would suffer withdrawal symptoms upon attempting to reduce caffeine intake.

12. In the year 2000, the government gave a private firm a large contract to develop a particular kind of defense system. An independent audit in 2002 revealed that the development proposal through which the private firm earned the contract had a number of glaring flaws that may render the proposed system unviable. Thus, the failure of the government bureaucrats responsible for the deal to adequately research the proposal is the reason that the government is now faced with a huge bill for a program that may never be fruitful.

Which one of the following is an assumption on which the argument relies?

(A) The glaring flaws in the proposed defense system cannot be fixed without redesigning the entire system.
(B) The firm that earned the development contract was the only firm to submit a proposal to the government for the defense system project.
(C) The government would not have made the same deal had the involved bureaucrats fully researched the proposal.
(D) The bureaucrats responsible for the deal did not have the technical background required to understand many elements of the proposal.
(E) No defense system with major flaws can ever be fruitful.

GO ON TO THE NEXT PAGE.

13. New findings indicate that the chemical cotinine can be traced in the fingerprints of people with this chemical in their system. Since cotinine is produced when someone metabolizes nicotine, which is found in cigarettes, finding cotinine in the suspect's fingerprints at a crime scene proves that the suspect is a cigarette smoker while the absence of cotinine proves that the suspect does not smoke.

The argument relies on each of the following assumptions EXCEPT:

(A) Cotinine is not produced by the metabolism of any chemicals not found in cigarettes.

(B) A person cannot get sufficient amounts of nicotine in his or her system by any means other than cigarette smoking.

(C) Cotinine remains detectable in skin secretions for at least several minutes after smoking a cigarette.

(D) Measurable amounts of cotinine cannot remain on someone's skin simply by making physical contact with a smoker.

(E) Authorities are always able to determine whether the fingerprints at a crime scene belong to the suspect or to someone else.

14. New evidence indicates that measuring blood pressure after a patient has been sitting with feet on the floor in a comfortable chair for five minutes can result in a reading that is lower by almost fifteen points on average. Yet most doctors persist in taking patients' blood pressures while they are sitting uncomfortably with their legs dangling over the edge of the exam table. Hence, high blood pressure is often diagnosed in patients who do not have high blood pressure.

The argument relies on which one of the following assumptions?

(A) Multiple blood pressure readings are required to confidently diagnosis high blood pressure to account for the possibility of an erroneous reading on any single test.

(B) The effect of sitting with feet planted on lowering blood pressure readings is more pronounced in elderly patients.

(C) Most patients diagnosed with high blood pressure are measured to have a blood pressure more than fifteen points above the threshold for the high blood pressure diagnosis.

(D) Blood pressure readings are not artificially elevated by the nervousness that many patients feel when they are undergoing medical tests.

(E) The standards against which high blood pressure is diagnosed are not based on blood pressure measurements from patients sitting on exam tables.

15. A recent analysis of hospital patient satisfaction surveys revealed that patient responses are much more highly influenced by the communication skills of their health providers than by the quality of the machines monitoring their conditions, as measured by the age of the machines, the cost of the machines, and the ratings given to the machines by physicians who use them regularly. The analysis also showed that patient responses are much more strongly influenced by the communication skills of their health providers than by the number of tests and procedures they undergo. Therefore, patient satisfaction surveys should not be taken into account in measures of overall quality of health care.

Which one of the following is an assumption on which the argument depends?

(A) The communication skills of health providers are not strongly correlated with the quality of care at their facilities.

(B) The machines monitoring the conditions of patients are the most important element of the overall quality of care.

(C) The surveys were not completed by a large enough sample of patients to provide meaningful results.

(D) Patient satisfaction surveys are always biased in favor of the health care facilities that provide the most pleasant accommodations.

(E) The patient satisfaction surveys analyzed failed to cover several important elements of patient care.

STOP

IF YOU FINISH BEFORE TIME IS CALLED, YOU MAY CHECK YOUR WORK ON THIS EXAM ONLY. DO NOT WORK ON ANY OTHER EXAM IN THE BOOK.

ANSWERS

1. B
2. A
3. B
4. B
5. C
6. B
7. D
8. D
9. D
10. A
11. B
12. C
13. E
14. E
15. A

IN-CLASS EXAM ICE LECTURE 5

EXAMINATION

LECTURE 5 EXAM
Time—25 minutes
15 Questions

Directions: The questions in this section are based on the reasoning contained in brief statements or passages. For some questions, more than one of the choices could conceivably answer the question. However, you are to choose the best answer; that is, the response that most accurately and completely answers the question. You should not make assumptions that are by commonsense standards implausible, superfluous, or incompatible with the passage. After you have chosen the best answer, circle the answer choice.

1. Geologist: The sporadic seismic activity we have observed in Greenland is confounding, as we are certain that it is not related to tectonic activity. But since these seismic episodes have been five times more frequent during the summer than the winter, we can conclude that they are somehow related to melting ice sheets impacting the bedrock.

Which one of the following, if true, most strengthens the geologist's argument?

(A) The instruments used to detect seismic activity are notoriously unreliable.
(B) There is no historical record of any significant earthquake in Greenland.
(C) During each of the two warmest years of the past decade, four times as many seismic episodes were observed as during an average year.
(D) Each year that geologists have studied the phenomenon, there have been at least twenty seismic episodes recorded.
(E) Computer programs used to simulate the response of Greenland's ice sheets to changing temperatures have produced contradictory results.

2. The region has had a very high incidence of lead poisoning, particularly in children, for more than a decade. A class-action lawsuit against the largest local paint manufacturer has been considered. The paint company has maintained that it cannot possibly be at fault for the poisonings, because although it once produced exclusively lead-based paint, it has made a long-standing commitment to reducing the health risks of its products and has not sold any lead-based paint in more than thirty years.

Which one of the following, if true, most undermines the paint company's claim that it cannot be at fault for the poisonings?

(A) The company's manufacturing process now releases a greater quantity of pollutants into the local river than it ever has in the past.
(B) Lead poisoning can lead to kidney failure and developmental disorders in children.
(C) Several other local paint manufacturers sold lead-based paint as recently as five years ago.
(D) The company's paint has been used in most of the schools in the area since the company was founded.
(E) Lead-based paint is only one of several potential causes of lead poisoning.

3. Politician: The lumber subsidy bill is very likely to pass. Prominent members of the four largest parties have pledged their support for the bill.

Which one of the following, if true, most strengthens the argument above?

(A) Most bills that have the support of at least some members from the largest parties pass.
(B) No bill can pass without the support of at least one prominent member of a large party.
(C) Only bills that have the support of prominent members of large parties pass.
(D) Bills that have the support of multiple large parties are usually viewed favorably by the public.
(E) Any bill that has the support of all parties is very likely to pass.

4. A domestic automobile manufacturer has perfected and patented a new technology that uses small radar sensors mounted on a car's bumper to sound a loud buzzer in the cabin as a warning to the driver that the car has come dangerously close to another vehicle or object. By alerting drivers whose attention to the road has briefly lapsed that a collision is possible, this technology will greatly reduce the number of accidents on the road.

Each of the following, if true, would strengthen the argument EXCEPT:

(A) The buzzer sounds early enough to allow drivers to react before an accident occurs.
(B) More accidents take place on highways than on city streets.
(C) A majority of accidents are the result of inattentive drivers colliding with other vehicles.
(D) The buzzer is sufficiently unobtrusive that it will not significantly distract drivers.
(E) The addition of the sensor technology to automobiles does not require the removal of any other safety features.

GO ON TO THE NEXT PAGE.

5. Biologist: Hyenas, which hunt in packs, exhibit more
    care for members of their packs than is necessary
    for hunting alone. It is clear, therefore, that
    hyenas have emotional ties that extend beyond
    evolutionary advantage, like the emotional ties
    that human families share.

    Which one of the following statements, if true, most
    seriously weakens the argument?

    (A) The amount of care that hyenas exhibit for
         members of their pack can be a disadvantage
         when hunting.
    (B) Caring for members of a pack can provide an
         evolutionary advantage.
    (C) Hyenas do not appear to exhibit certain human
         emotions, such as regret or envy.
    (D) Many species related to hyenas do not exhibit
         special care for members of their packs.
    (E) The extra care that hyenas share extends no
         further than protecting each other to allow for
         reproduction.

6. In 1999, an exhaustive study found that Brand H
    cigarettes exposed smokers to nearly two micrograms
    of formaldehyde, a highly poisonous embalming fluid,
    which is generated from the burning of certain sugars
    used as tobacco additives. Motivated by the study, the
    manufacturer of Brand H reformulated its blend of
    additives and succeeded in effectively eliminating all
    formaldehyde-producing components from its product.
    As a result of this endeavor, Brand H cigarettes are now
    clearly less harmful to smokers than they once were.

    Which one of the following, if true, would most weaken
    the argument?

    (A) Brand H has always contained an amount of
         ammonia, another injurious additive, that is
         nearly twice the average of other cigarette
         brands.
    (B) Some of the sugars previously used as additives
         came from natural sources such as honey and
         maple syrup.
    (C) Exposure to formaldehyde has been shown to
         be strongly correlated to respiratory, skin, and
         gastrointestinal ailments.
    (D) Since 1999, cigarettes have been discovered to be
         more harmful than previously believed.
    (E) Brand H's reformulated blend of additives has
         resulted in cigarettes that produce a greater
         concentration of acetaldehyde, a known
         carcinogen.

7. Researchers at a state university analyzed data on nearly
    100,000 annual check-ups at doctors' offices over a
    six-year span. They found that female physicians, on
    average, spent significantly more time with their patients
    at the annual visits. Therefore, in addition to performing
    the usual physical tests, female physicians must be more
    willing to spend time talking with their patients about
    healthy lifestyle choices.

    Which one of the following, if true, lends the most
    support to the argument?

    (A) Female physicians tend to perform a greater
         number of basic physical tests at annual check-
         ups.
    (B) A decreasing number of people schedule annual
         check-ups with their physicians.
    (C) The tests typically performed at annual check-
         ups rarely reveal signs of significant health
         problems, even when such problems are present.
    (D) Female physicians on average take no longer than
         male physicians to perform the usual physical
         tests.
    (E) Though the disparity is shrinking, there are
         still many more male physicians than female
         physicians.

8. An investigative journalist performed a series of tests
    on the model of radar gun used by police to measure the
    speed of a vehicle and determine whether a speeding
    ticket is warranted. In the tests, the journalist's co-
    workers drove vehicles at various known speeds while
    the journalist measured their speeds with the radar gun.
    The journalist's tests showed the radar gun to be quite
    unreliable, often misreporting the velocity of a vehicle
    by as much as ten miles per hour. On this basis, the
    journalist reported that the radar guns must have caused
    police to issue many erroneous speeding tickets.

    Which one of the following, if true, most seriously calls
    into question the journalist's report?

    (A) Many speeding tickets are issued to drivers who
         allegedly exceeded the speed limit by less than
         ten miles per hour.
    (B) Police rely exclusively on the radar gun in
         determining whether a vehicle is exceeding the
         speed limit.
    (C) Some of the tests conducted by the journalist
         were inconclusive.
    (D) Fewer speeding tickets have been issued since the
         journalist's report was publicized.
    (E) Traffic police receive training in the use of the
         radar gun that allows them to operate it without
         producing erroneous readings.

GO ON TO THE NEXT PAGE.

9. Surprising results compiled from a study following over two thousand people for many years clearly showed that those who slept less than seven hours per day on average tended to live longer than those who slept more than eight hours per day on average. Therefore, those who want to live longer should limit their sleep to seven hours per day at most.

Which one of the following, if true, most seriously weakens the argument?

(A) Some people who sleep an average of nine hours per day live beyond the typical expected lifespan of people who sleep an average of six hours per day.

(B) Those who slept less than six hours per day tended to live longer than those who slept between six and seven hours per day on average.

(C) Those who slept less than seven hours per day were less likely to contract ailments such as the common cold.

(D) There was no difference in socioeconomic status between those who slept less than seven hours and those who slept more than eight hours per day on average.

(E) Those who maintained the most unhealthy diets and exercise habits were also much more likely to sleep more than eight hours per day on average.

10. Early theories of the evolution of vision suggested that color vision evolved in primates to help them pick out colorful edible fruits among dense jungle foliage. Based upon observations of the defensive tactics of primates in the wild, which include making evasive movements as soon as hidden predators are spotted, a new theory claims that primates instead developed color vision to help detect hidden predators.

Which one of the following, if true, lends the most support to the new theory?

(A) Many predators have developed tremendous foot speed or flight speed that allows them to catch prey even when the predators are not hidden.

(B) Primates are not the only animals capable of perceiving color, as many birds and fish have color receptors in their eyes.

(C) Primates on the isolated island of Mentawai, which have few natural predators, developed color vision greatly inferior to that of most primates.

(D) In tests, chimps generally have a harder time spotting green tree-borne fruit than fruit of any other color.

(E) Another theory claims that humans developed color vision superior to that of other primates to better perceive emotion.

11. Producer: Only an hour after we aired our story about the illegal sports betting ring, local police launched a formal investigation, and they raided the ring's offices and made arrests by the end of the day. So citizens can thank our tireless, professional journalists for the elimination of this menace to the neighborhood.

Which one of the following, if true, lends the most support to the producer's claim?

(A) The operators of the betting ring had ties to other illegal operations.

(B) Local police were already informally investigating the sports betting ring before the story aired.

(C) Local police launch a formal investigation of any case only if a crime has been committed.

(D) No other news sources reported on the story until after the arrests were made.

(E) The journalists misreported the location of the betting ring's offices.

12. Architect: The new building on campus is full of open, accessible spaces that are perfect for casual meetings or socializing, so it is sure to increase the productivity of joint projects as well as the amount of socializing that goes on at this school.

Each of the following statements, if true, would weaken the architect's argument EXCEPT:

(A) The building is not well suited for holding classes.

(B) There are already many spaces on campus that are perfect for socializing yet are usually empty.

(C) The building is in an inconvenient location.

(D) Joint projects at the school, though rarely assigned, have been maximally productive for years.

(E) Many students will be deterred from visiting the building by its unsightliness.

GO ON TO THE NEXT PAGE.

13. A survey conducted on people from a wide range of age groups revealed that younger people tend to litter much more frequently than older people, with respondents seventy years of age and older littering the least and teenagers littering the most by far. Therefore, there must have been substantially less litter around in previous decades, when those who litter the least represented a larger proportion of the total population.

Which one of the following, if true, most calls into question the argument above?

(A) Because products are packaged differently today, the litter in previous generations looked very different.

(B) People tend to litter less as they age.

(C) Less than one-tenth of the population today is seventy years of age and older.

(D) Much of today's litter is composed of biodegradable wrappers, while in previous generations litter was generally more harmful to the environment.

(E) The study was conducted anonymously so as to increase the chances of obtaining honest responses.

14. New research has found that cells bearing the type of receptor favored by the avian influenza virus are only found deep in the human respiratory tract. Because of this, the avian influenza virus is less likely to be spread by coughing than the human influenza virus, whose receptors are usually found in the upper respiratory tract. We can therefore expect that it will be a long time before we see a widespread outbreak of avian influenza.

Which one of the following, if true, lends the most support to the argument?

(A) The avian influenza virus is resistant to most known vaccines, and attempts to create new vaccines for it have not been fruitful.

(B) The avian influenza virus tends to have much more severe, persistent symptoms than the human influenza virus.

(C) It would take decades for the avian influenza virus to accumulate the mutations necessary to allow it to settle in the upper respiratory tract.

(D) Influenza viruses can be spread by saliva and sneezing as well as by coughing.

(E) Influenza viruses are generally less contagious than some other viruses.

15. Maria was late to work one morning and was called into her boss's office. Her boss knew that if she had stayed out late the night before, her lateness would have a negative impact on her work. If her voice was weak, she could have been late because she spent too much time on the phone with a client the night before, and her work would probably not suffer. Since Maria's voice was not weak, her boss concluded that her work would suffer.

Which one of the following, if true, would undermine the boss's conclusion?

(A) The road from Maria's house to her office was closed due to construction.

(B) Maria's phone records indicate that she had had no long conversations the night before.

(C) Maria has a history of coming to work late after staying out late the night before.

(D) Maria has performed exceptionally well when she arrives to work on time.

(E) The quality of an employee's work can be affected by an employee's sleep habits.

STOP

IF YOU FINISH BEFORE TIME IS CALLED, YOU MAY CHECK YOUR WORK ON THIS EXAM ONLY.
DO NOT WORK ON ANY OTHER EXAM IN THE BOOK.

Answers

1. C
2. D
3. A
4. B
5. E
6. E
7. D
8. E
9. E
10. C
11. D
12. A
13. B
14. C
15. A

IN-CLASS EXAM ICE LECTURE 6

EXAMINATION

LECTURE 6   EXAM
Time—25 minutes
15 Questions

Directions: The questions in this section are based on the reasoning contained in brief statements or passages. For some questions, more than one of the choices could conceivably answer the question. However, you are to choose the best answer; that is, the response that most accurately and completely answers the question. You should not make assumptions that are by commonsense standards implausible, superfluous, or incompatible with the passage. After you have chosen the best answer, circle the answer choice.

1. The university's endowment, which is composed of donations that have been invested in various financial accounts, exceeded a total value of $1 billion for the first time last month. Curiously, the university has not received any donations in more than three months.

    Which one of the following, if true, most helps to resolve the apparent discrepancy?

    (A)   The university spent a significant sum of money on an upgrade to its computer network last month.
    (B)   The accounts in which the endowment's funds are invested are managed by several full-time employees.
    (C)   The university received several substantial donations six months ago.
    (D)   The accounts in which the endowment's funds are invested include a mixture of stocks and treasury bills.
    (E)   The accounts in which the endowment's funds are invested have increased in value over the last three months.

2. Millions of dollars have been spent on making commercial airplanes safer, and tests conducted by the manufacturers of the latest airplanes as well as by independent interests consistently confirm that modern planes are in fact much safer than the passenger planes used just twenty years ago. Yet there have been more casualties per plane crash among the latest passenger planes than there were in the average passenger plane crash twenty years ago.

    Which one of the following, if true, most helps reconcile the apparent conflict between the plane safety data and the crash casualty data?

    (A)   The latest passenger planes carry many more passengers than did those in use twenty years ago.
    (B)   There are many more overseas flights offered today than there were twenty years ago.
    (C)   The fuselages of the latest passenger planes are constructed with new materials that are nearly ten times stronger than those used twenty years ago.
    (D)   Because of their greater reliance on computers, there are more ways in which newer planes can malfunction.
    (E)   On a per-mile basis, flying is safer than driving, regardless of whether flight safety statistics from twenty years ago or from today are considered.

GO ON TO THE NEXT PAGE.

3. One year ago, the local tax on the sale of cigarettes was increased substantially, from 10 percent to 30 percent of the retail price. Survey data clearly indicates that, since the inception of the tax, there has been no decrease in the number of smokers in the area, nor has there been any decrease in the average number of cigarettes each smoker consumes per week. Yet the revenue collected by the local government from the cigarette tax has been lower over the last year than it was before the tax was increased.

   Which one of the following, if true, LEAST helps to resolve the apparent discrepancy described above?

   (A) There has been an increase in cigarette theft and subsequent sale of cigarettes on the black market.
   (B) To increase business, stores and vendors that sell cigarettes have stopped collecting sales tax on cash transactions.
   (C) The pre-tax retail price of a pack of cigarettes has decreased markedly since last year.
   (D) Revenue from income tax is down too, as is that from general local sales tax.
   (E) Because of the tax increase, many smokers have begun to buy their cigarettes in bulk from outside the area.

4. Alcohol's antiseptic properties allow it to kill some of the bacteria responsible for gum infections and toothaches. Yet people who treat such problems by applying alcohol to the affected area most often end up with worse infections than those who do not.

   Which one of the following, if true, would most help resolve the apparent paradox?

   (A) Some of the sugars in some alcohol solutions also help to kill bacteria.
   (B) Many toothaches are related to poor dental hygiene.
   (C) Most people who treat their own toothaches with alcohol do so as an alternative to going to the dentist, where superior treatment can be administered.
   (D) Certain sufficiently acidic juices and vinegars can also kill some of the bacteria responsible for gum infections and toothaches.
   (E) Consuming excessive amounts of alcohol can impair circulation, which in some cases can worsen gum infections and toothaches.

5. Doctors are now convinced that regularly drinking beer can actually reduce the risk of prostate cancer. This is significant because prostate cancer is the most common cancer in the United States among men, affecting one in six males in the country at some point in their lives. Despite this potential advantage, however, doctors do not suggest that men drink beer regularly, regardless of their risk factors for prostate cancer.

   Which one of the following, if true, most helps to resolve the apparent discrepancy above?

   (A) The amount of beer one would have to drink to reduce the risk of prostate cancer would cause significant liver damage.
   (B) Prostate cancer is not the leading cause of death among males in the United States, and beer has no appreciable effect on the most common cause of death.
   (C) Drinking beer regularly has been traditionally associated with negative stereotypes about men in the United States.
   (D) It took many years of research for doctors to become convinced that beer could have a positive effect on the risk of cancer.
   (E) Doctors are not yet sure whether the positive effects of regularly drinking beer extend beyond prostate cancer.

6. Nabeel: Jorge always goes to company headquarters if a meeting is scheduled, and if he goes to company headquarters, he always meets the project manager there. Earlier today Jorge mentioned that he did not see the project manager yesterday, but he did not say anything else about yesterday, so there is no way to know whether a meeting was scheduled yesterday.

   Which one of the following most accurately describes a flaw in Nabeel's reasoning?

   (A) The presumption is made, without providing justification, that Jorge's statements are necessarily reliable.
   (B) Jorge's statement represents a condition that is necessary but not sufficient for the argument's conclusion.
   (C) Nabeel assumes, without providing justification, that Jorge could not have met with the project manager anywhere other than company headquarters.
   (D) The argument bases its conclusion on the assumption that Jorge did go to company headquarters yesterday, which is inconsistent with Jorge's statement.
   (E) The argument claims as unknown information that is necessarily entailed by Jorge's statement.

GO ON TO THE NEXT PAGE.

7. Last week, mustard was on sale for half price at Murray's Grocery Store. Yet this week, even back at full price, mustard has sold at a much greater rate than it did last week.

Each of the following, if true, would help resolve the apparent paradox EXCEPT:

(A) Horseradish, which many people use instead of mustard, went on sale this week.

(B) A study was released this week indicating that mustard consumption can reduce blood pressure.

(C) Hot dogs, which many people like to eat with mustard, went on sale this week.

(D) A large condiment company began televising advertisements for mustard this week.

(E) Many people received their biweekly paycheck this Monday because it was the first day of the month.

8. Rigorous statistical analysis indicates that there is no such thing as a true clutch hitter—a player who hits better in more important situations—in professional baseball. However, more than half of the players on the Greenwood High School baseball team claimed during recent interviews with the local newspaper that they were certain that they are clutch hitters.

Which one of the following would most help explain the apparently inconsistent claims?

(A) The ability to perform better in more important situations is highly valued in many fields.

(B) Clutch hitting is a very rare talent, particularly among younger players.

(C) The players good enough to play professionally always play their best in any situation.

(D) Rigorous statistical analysis has also cast doubt on whether there are clutch shooters in professional basketball.

(E) The Greenwood High School baseball team won its league championship last year.

9. Certain kinds of fluorescent light bulbs have been confirmed to be by far the most common cause of mercury poisoning in children. Even though there has been no drop in the number of such fluorescent bulbs in production or in use in the country, there has been a sharp decline in recent years in the number of cases of mercury poisoning reported.

Which one of the following, if true, most helps explain the curious situation above?

(A) Techniques to detect symptoms of mercury poisoning have been improved in recent years.

(B) The hazardous fluorescent bulbs are now more commonly used in industrial settings instead of in homes or in busy retail centers.

(C) There has been no change in the use of mercury-based thermometers, which constitute the second leading cause of mercury poisoning.

(D) The general public has become much more aware of the need to be tested for mercury poisoning as soon as symptoms manifest themselves.

(E) Several new kinds of light bulbs have been developed that are more energy efficient than fluorescent bulbs.

10. Nutritionist: I advise strongly against the consumption of protein shakes. They commonly have around thirty grams of protein per serving, and with so much protein I suspect they can cause long-term kidney damage. I would instead recommend a quarter of a pound of chicken, which also has around thirty grams of protein, as a more kidney-healthy alternative.

Which one of the following, if true, most helps resolve the apparent contradiction in the nutritionist's remarks?

(A) Protein shakes cost more per serving than a quarter of a pound of chicken.

(B) Chicken also contains iron and several B vitamins, while containing a low amount of fat.

(C) Protein shakes are often unnecessarily high in simple sugars, which can lead to weight gain.

(D) Most professional body builders consume several protein shakes per day without showing signs of kidney damage.

(E) Consuming protein via a liquid causes a much higher concentration of protein to enter the kidneys.

GO ON TO THE NEXT PAGE.

11. Lying can involve a lot of different emotions and conditions, but all lies have a least one common characteristic: If someone tells a lie, then he must know in advance that his false statement is untrue. Not every lie is accompanied by remorse, however.

If the statements above are true, then each of the following could be true EXCEPT:

(A) People who tell the truth sometimes believe their true statements to be untrue.
(B) People who lie without feeling remorse sometimes believe their false statements to be true.
(C) Some statements that are accompanied by feelings of remorse are not lies.
(D) If a false statement is believed to be untrue, then it is a lie.
(E) No lies are ever accompanied by feelings of remorse.

12. Medical professionals are beginning to warn the public against the widespread use of a popular influenza vaccine, despite its continued efficacy and their certainty that it has no harmful side effects, even for the elderly or young children.

Which one of the following, if true, most helps resolve the apparent paradox indicated above?

(A) Children rarely suffer long-term harm as a result of contracting influenza.
(B) Overcoming influenza can strengthen the immune system of otherwise healthy people, improving their ability to combat more serious viruses.
(C) The vaccine is administered over three separate doses, and the elderly may be likely to forget one of the doses.
(D) The vaccine can be rendered ineffective by consumption of alcohol within several days of taking it.
(E) Many families cannot afford enough doses of the vaccine for all of their children.

13. In recent years, shrimp farmers have become increasingly concerned about the levels of a family of toxins known as PCBs in their shrimp. Two years ago, new regulations were instituted that required a 40-percent reduction of the PCB concentration in the water in which shrimp are raised. Despite regular, accurate testing and strict adherence to the new regulations, recently farmed shrimp have shown the same PCB levels as those farmed before the new standards took effect.

Which one of the following, if true, most helps to account for the unchanged PCB levels in the shrimp?

(A) PCBs have been determined to be less harmful to humans than previously thought.
(B) Non-farmed shrimp have shown a gradual increase in PCB levels over the last two years.
(C) Even at the lower PCB concentration enforced by the regulations, the shrimp are exposed to more PCBs than their bodies are capable of absorbing.
(D) When other creatures consume shrimp with high PCB levels, significant quantities of the toxin are absorbed by their own digestive systems, potentially leading to health complications.
(E) Adherence to the new regulations has turned out to be more costly than had initially been projected.

GO ON TO THE NEXT PAGE.

14. A new economic model for agriculture has recently come into practice. Called community-supported agriculture, or CSA farming, the concept is that consumers buy "shares" of a farm before growing season in return for regular shipments of a certain proportion of the farm's product once the harvesting begins. It was thought that this would increase crop yields, since farmers would have more funds available at the beginning of the season to pay for the necessary seeds and labor, and to invest in better machinery if needed. However, CSA farms have had much lower yields on average than normal farms every year since they came into existence.

Each of the following, if true, contributes to an explanation of the lower yields for CSA farms EXCEPT:

(A) Raising funds before the growing season does not allow CSA farmers to prepare for all possible weather-related setbacks.

(B) Traditional farms that are already high-yielding are less likely to become CSA farms than farms that are struggling.

(C) CSA farms tend primarily to be organic farms, which typically have lower yields than non-organic farms due to the avoidance of chemical pesticides and growth hormones.

(D) Farmers who are paid before the growing season begins have less incentive to be productive than farmers who are only paid for what they actually produce.

(E) CSA farmers are often compelled to grow lower-yield crops in accordance with the preferences and requests of their shareholders.

15. Analysis of psychiatric patient data shows that there is a fairly strong correlation between the development of schizophrenia and drug abuse. However, a number of reliable studies have proven that being schizophrenic does not cause a person to abuse drugs, nor does drug abuse contribute in any way to the development of schizophrenia.

Which one of the following, if true, most helps explain the correlation mentioned above?

(A) About one percent of the general population suffers from schizophrenia.

(B) Schizophrenia has been officially classified as a disease of the brain.

(C) Drug use has been identified as a cause of several other neurochemical disorders.

(D) The onset of schizophrenia most often occurs between the ages of 16 and 25, which is also the age range in which most drug users begin using drugs.

(E) Genetic inheritance plays a strong role in the likelihood that a person will develop schizophrenia, but it does not seem to play a strong role in determining drug-use habits.

STOP

IF YOU FINISH BEFORE TIME IS CALLED, YOU MAY CHECK YOUR WORK ON THIS EXAM ONLY. DO NOT WORK ON ANY OTHER EXAM IN THE BOOK.

Answers

1. E
2. A
3. D
4. C
5. A
6. E
7. A
8. C
9. B
10. E
11. B
12. B
13. C
14. A
15. D

IN-CLASS EXAM ICE LECTURE 7

EXAMINATION

LECTURE 7 EXAM
Time—25 minutes
15 Questions

<u>Directions:</u> The questions in this section are based on the reasoning contained in brief statements or passages. For some questions, more than one of the choices could conceivably answer the question. However, you are to choose the <u>best</u> answer; that is, the response that most accurately and completely answers the question. You should not make assumptions that are by commonsense standards implausible, superfluous, or incompatible with the passage. After you have chosen the best answer, circle the answer choice.

1. Any short story is worth reading if it has a protagonist that is neither too one-dimensional nor too complex, and a plot that is neither too predictable nor too convoluted. Millar's latest short story has an intriguing plot that is not at all predictable yet is easy to follow. Thus, it is worth reading Millar's latest short story.

   The conclusion of the argument above follows logically if which one of the following is added as a premise?

   (A) The quality of the plot is a much more important factor than the quality of the protagonist in evaluating short stories.

   (B) The supporting characters of Millar's latest short story are multidimensional without being too intricate to fully grasp.

   (C) Any short story that features a protagonist that is too simple or too complex is only worth reading if its plot does not have the same flaw.

   (D) The plot of Millar's latest short story is very original.

   (E) The protagonist of Millar's latest short story is neither overly complex nor too simple.

2. Editor: This magazine should not publish an article that disputes the potential benefits of genetic research. The scientific community is highly certain of these benefits, and the objections are misguided. By publishing the article, we would only offend our readers.

   Publisher: I disagree. By publishing the article, we can give members of the scientific community the opportunity to address the errors underlying these misguided objections. Our readers will see the case for genetic research reinforced by experts in a public forum.

   Which one of the following principles, if established, most contributes to the strength of the publisher's response?

   (A) The benefit of being exposed to several points of view outweighs the harm of being offended.

   (B) Opposition to scientific advancement is usually based in misunderstanding rather than a particular moral stance.

   (C) Readers are not often offended by views they consider to be plainly wrong.

   (D) The publication of offensive or widely discredited work should be avoided.

   (E) It is important to allow the general public to take part in scientific debate.

GO ON TO THE NEXT PAGE.

3. All major roads are divided by medians, and anything with a median is difficult to repair. It follows that all major roads are difficult to repair. Therefore, State Road 236 is not a major road.

    The final conclusion follows logically if which one of the following is assumed?

    (A) Every road that is difficult to repair is a major road.
    (B) Nothing difficult to repair lacks a median.
    (C) State Road 236 has a median.
    (D) State Road 236 is not difficult to repair.
    (E) State Road 236 either lacks a median or is difficult to repair.

4. When the teacher noticed that Mike was copying his answers from Jill's test, Mike immediately took full responsibility, claiming that Jill did not know that he had been copying her answers. However, the teacher decided that Jill should be punished almost as severely, since she had carelessly held her test in such a way that other students would be able and possibly even tempted to copy from her.

    Which one of the following principles, if valid, most helps justify the teacher's decision?

    (A) Anyone whose actions allow a transgression to occur shares some of the responsibility for it.
    (B) All students involved in cheating, knowingly or not, ought to be punished equally.
    (C) Anyone who makes it so easy for others to cheat must have intended to allow them to do so.
    (D) Cheating is a serious academic offense and thus should always be punished thoroughly as a deterrent.
    (E) Anyone who accepts full blame for something should not be punished as much as someone who does not admit to any wrongdoing.

5. In a countywide standardized test, a certificate of distinction was given to students who correctly answered over 50 percent of the questions. Fifteen females and seven males received this certificate. Hence, among the people who took the test, we can conclude that a randomly chosen female student is more likely than a randomly chosen male student to have correctly answered more than half of the questions on the test.

    The conclusion above can be properly drawn if which one of the following is assumed?

    (A) More males than females took the test.
    (B) The two highest scores on the test were both achieved by females.
    (C) The average score among females was slightly higher than the average score among males.
    (D) The test was composed of a math section and a vocabulary section.
    (E) Similar results were observed on last year's test.

6. The new gallery featuring Japanese sculpture of the Fujiwara period represents an excellent collection of pieces from this era. Unfortunately, there is limited information made available at the gallery regarding the political and social circumstances of Japan during the Fujiwara period. Since most visitors to the gallery will be unfamiliar with this history, the gallery will fail in its primary goal of instilling in the visitors a deep understanding of the sculptures.

    Which one of the following principles, if valid, most justifies the reasoning above?

    (A) Gallery directors should be as concerned with presenting historical information as with presenting the art itself.
    (B) One cannot attain a deep understanding of an artwork without familiarity with the culture in which it was created.
    (C) One cannot learn as much from a gallery with pieces from only a single period as from a gallery that covers a range of periods.
    (D) Everyone would benefit from a greater knowledge of Japanese history.
    (E) Galleries should be designed to instill a deep understanding of their art in all of their visitors.

GO ON TO THE NEXT PAGE.

7. The Chicago-bound plane was delayed due to inclement weather. Only planes that are delayed arrive late, though planes can be delayed for reasons other than inclement weather. Among planes that are delayed by inclement weather, only those delayed by mild rainfall do not arrive late. Therefore, the Chicago-bound plane must have arrived late.

The conclusion above follows logically if which one of the following is added as a premise to the argument?

(A) The Chicago-bound plane was not delayed for any additional reasons besides inclement weather.
(B) All flights on the day in question were delayed by the inclement weather.
(C) The Chicago-bound plane was not delayed by mild rainfall.
(D) The Chicago-bound plane was further delayed by the need to repair the landing gear.
(E) Both Chicago and the plane's city of departure experienced mild rainfall throughout the day in question.

8. All real estate loses value when nearby parks are replaced by buildings. The park near the Ascot condominium will be replaced by a new apartment building only if the developers are given approval, but the developers can be given approval only if they submit their designs before the deadline.

If the above statements are true, which one of the following must also be true?

(A) If the developers submit their designs before the deadline, the Ascot condominium will lose value.
(B) If the nearby park is not replaced by an apartment building, the Ascot will not lose value.
(C) The park near the Ascot will be replaced by an apartment building.
(D) If the developers fail to submit their designs before the deadline, the park near the Ascot will not be replaced by a new apartment building.
(E) If the developers are not given approval, the Ascot will not lose value.

9. Jasmine: Last week, a plumber replaced a valve under my sink that was preventing water from flowing normally. As a result of the increased flow, the pipe that leads to the faucet burst, flooding my kitchen. The plumber is liable for the damage to my kitchen, because if he had not replaced the valve, the pipe would not have burst.

Angela: The plumber is not liable for the damage. That pipe, which was installed by a different plumber, was defective and would have burst eventually. The only reason it had not done so already was that the faulty valve was preventing the water pressure from reaching its normal level.

A principle that, if established, justifies Angela's response to Jasmine is that a plumber is liable for damage to a customer's property

(A) if the damage was caused by either a part that the plumber installed or by a previously existing condition
(B) only if the damage was caused by a previously existing condition rather than a part the plumber installed
(C) only if the part that the plumber installed caused an already defective part to break
(D) if the damage was caused not by a part that the plumber failed to install properly, but rather by a part that was installed properly by a previous plumber
(E) only if the damage was caused by the malfunction of a part installed by that plumber

10. Rico competed in three events at the track meet and did not win any gold medals. Rico's school had only two fewer gold medals than the school with the most gold medals. Therefore, had Rico won gold medals in all of his events at the meet, his school would have had the most gold medals.

The argument's conclusion can be properly drawn if which one of the following is true?

(A) Other than the school with the most gold medals, no school won more gold medals than Rico's school.
(B) Rico was the only competitor from his school in the three events in which he competed.
(C) Rico did not win any silver or bronze medals in any of his three events.
(D) Rico's school has never won the most gold medals at a track meet before.
(E) The school with the most gold medals would have placed lower in the events in which Rico competed had Rico won three gold medals.

GO ON TO THE NEXT PAGE.

11. Physician: Our lives are better the more time we devote to the pursuits we truly enjoy. Future technologies that will be freely and universally available promise to eliminate our physiological need to sleep, allowing nearly a third of our time to be allocated to other activities. Hence, such technology will give us the chance to lead better lives.

The conclusion drawn by the physician follows logically if which one of the following is assumed?

(A)   People are always accurately aware of which pursuits they truly enjoy.
(B)   The technology to which the physician refers will be attainable within the next decade.
(C)   Sleep is not a pursuit that we truly enjoy.
(D)   Sleep is not physiologically necessary for human beings.
(E)   Future technologies will eliminate our physiological need to eat.

12. Professor: The metaphorical imagery of free verse poetry can in many cases be quite obscure and difficult to grasp. Many students become discouraged as they try to analyze these poems on the grounds that they cannot appreciate a poem's value when they can never be at all certain of the meaning the poet intended to convey with its imagery. However, most students would agree that the imagery succeeds in conjuring some sorts of meaningful ideas and emotions as they read, even if these may be divergent from the ideas and emotions the poet had in mind. Hence, the students' discouragement is unwarranted.

Which one of the following principles, if valid, most helps to justify the professor's reasoning?

(A)   Poets should never compose poetry with imagery too obscure to be easily understood.
(B)   Students should study poetry even if they are unable to appreciate its value.
(C)   One's own interpretation of poetic imagery is no less valuable than that of the author.
(D)   Readers who are certain of the intended meaning of poetic imagery will better appreciate a poem's value.
(E)   The study of poetry should not be compulsory in schools.

13. Attorney: An appeals court has upheld the decision that a Sun reporter endangered a suspect in a criminal case by publishing her name and several details about her. This decision will bring about even more lawsuits over legitimate journalism, and in so doing will restrict what journalists are able to write. The appeals court's decision is thus a terrible one, as it undermines a form of free speech, and free speech must always be protected to the maximum extent possible in any form in which it is beneficial to society as a whole.

Which one of the following principles, if established, provides the strongest justification for the attorney's characterization of the court's decision?

(A)   Freedom of journalistic expression benefits society as a whole.
(B)   Journalists have a responsibility to report personal details of people accused of crimes.
(C)   Criminals should have no right to sue those who endanger them.
(D)   The appeals process is inefficient and therefore does not benefit society as a whole.
(E)   Freedom of speech is the most important freedom to protect.

GO ON TO THE NEXT PAGE.

14. All true scientists are theoretical physicists, since theoretical physics is the only science that does not require relying on questionable empirical evidence, which can be deceiving. Also, most true scientists are deists. It follows, then, that at least one deist is a libertarian.

The argument follows logically if which one of the following is assumed?

(A) All libertarians are scientists.
(B) Many true scientists are libertarians.
(C) All theoretical physicists are libertarians.
(D) One cannot be a libertarian without eschewing empirical evidence, which can be deceiving.
(E) A scientist is a deist only if that person is also a theoretical physicist.

15. Some biologists are unconvinced that the pseudocopulation of the whiptail lizard serves a biological function. But until recently, their primary evidence for this claim was the lack of observations of pseudocopulation in the wild. Because it has since been observed in wild whiptail lizards, we should accept that pseudocopulation serves a biological function.

Which one of the following principles most helps to justify the reasoning above?

(A) When there is a lack of empirical evidence for a claim, that claim should be questioned.
(B) We should accept that a process serves a biological function only if that process occurs in the wild.
(C) Behaviors that occur in the wild often serve a biological function.
(D) We should accept that a behavior serves a biological function if it occurs in the wild.
(E) Behaviors that do not serve a biological function occur only in captivity.

STOP

IF YOU FINISH BEFORE TIME IS CALLED, YOU MAY CHECK YOUR WORK ON THIS EXAM ONLY.
DO NOT WORK ON ANY OTHER EXAM IN THE BOOK.

ANSWERS

1. E
2. A
3. D
4. A
5. A
6. B
7. C
8. D
9. E
10. B
11. C
12. C
13. A
14. C
15. D

IN-CLASS EXAM ICE LECTURE 8

EXAMINATION

LECTURE 8 EXAM

Time—25 minutes

15 Questions

Directions: The questions in this section are based on the reasoning contained in brief statements or passages. For some questions, more than one of the choices could conceivably answer the question. However, you are to choose the best answer; that is, the response that most accurately and completely answers the question. You should not make assumptions that are by commonsense standards implausible, superfluous, or incompatible with the passage. After you have chosen the best answer, circle the answer choice.

1. Alison: Hospitals in our area suffer from a shortage of nurses. We should seek government grants to allow us to raise nurses' wages. The higher wages will attract more applicants to nursing school, so in time our hospitals will no longer have to endure a lack of these essential professionals.

    Cahira: Many occupations that offer high wages still suffer from a shortage of qualified people to fill open positions. What is needed to avoid a shortfall is not only higher wages, but also an amelioration of the notoriously high-stress work environment in which nurses must perform.

    Cahira responds to Alison by

    (A) pointing out that something required for a certain result does not necessarily guarantee that result
    (B) showing that Alison's statements are self-contradictory
    (C) charging that Alison exaggerated the severity of a problem in order to defend a questionable proposal
    (D) suggesting that Alison's proposed solution could instead worsen the problem it is intended to solve
    (E) arguing that Alison fails to consider a strategy that could accomplish the same goal as the strategy that Alison considers

2. Law enforcement officials should not cite anyone for breaking a law in cases in which the illegal action cannot possibly lead to the harm the law is meant to prevent.

    Which one of the following judgments most closely conforms to the principle stated above?

    (A) Sue illegally ran a red light very late at night when she thought there were no other drivers on the road. Since there could have been vehicles or pedestrians that she was unable to see at night, she could have harmed someone, so the officer was right to cite her.
    (B) Heather illegally walked across the road during a red light at a busy intersection. Since she could have forced a car to swerve to avoid her and cause an accident, she should be heavily fined.
    (C) Maggie illegally chose not to signal while navigating the parking lot. Since it was clear that there were no other vehicles or pedestrians in the parking lot that could have been harmed, the officer was right not to cite her.
    (D) Julia exceeded the legal speed limit on a busy highway. Since she was in a hurry to get to an important meeting on time, the officer was right not to cite her.
    (E) Holly drove on the wrong side of the road for several blocks. Since she did not hurt anyone, the officer was right not to cite her.

GO ON TO THE NEXT PAGE.

3. Vishal: Smoking in bars and restaurants should not
     be banned. If smoking is forbidden at these
     establishments, people will stop going to them,
     and businesses will be forced to close for lack of
     customers. Government should not pass legislation
     that infringes upon a person's ability to earn a
     living.

    Samantha: The government's top priority is to ensure
     the health and safety of its citizens. The effects
     of second-hand smoke harm thousands of people
     every year. Enacting the ban would protect both
     workers and customers.

    Samantha responds to Vishal's argument using which
    one of the following argumentative techniques?

    (A) introducing a consideration that leads to a
         conclusion different from that of Vishal's
         argument
    (B) demonstrating that Vishal's conclusion is
         inconsistent with evidence advanced to support
         it
    (C) showing that Vishal's argument relies on citing
         an unrepresentative case
    (D) arguing that the health of customers is more
         important than the health of business owners
    (E) presenting a possible alternative method for
         preserving both public health and a person's
         ability to earn a living

4. Several well-publicized studies have presented evidence
    that drinking one or two glasses of red wine per day
    might help to reduce the likelihood of heart disease.
    The researchers responsible for the studies have
    suggested that these benefits may be due to certain
    organic compounds in red wine that act as antioxidants.
    However, it may well be that the people who have the
    self-control to drink in moderation exercise similar
    restraint in most areas of their lives. So it is possible that
    this capacity for restraint is the real factor that enables
    certain people to live longer and healthier lives.

    In disputing the researchers' conclusion, the author uses
    which one of the following techniques?

    (A) demonstrating that the original conclusion was
         based on false premises
    (B) suggesting an alternative explanation for the
         phenomenon observed by the researchers
    (C) showing that the researchers relied on an
         inaccurate understanding of the subjects' reasons
         for engaging in an activity
    (D) agreeing that a connection between the
         consumption of red wine and heart disease
         can be made, but questioning whether any
         conclusion about drinking guidelines can be
         drawn
    (E) challenging the validity of the statistical sample
         used by the researchers

5. Comptroller: The mayor has come under heavy criticism
     for hiring, at great public expense, a private firm
     to remove storm-damaged objects from the city
     streets. Critics are outraged because, since the deal
     was signed, other companies have come forward
     and claimed that they would have paid the city
     for the right to collect the scrap for reprocessing.
     However, the mayor should not be blamed, as he
     did not know about the alternative options that
     have since come to light, and he took the best
     offer available at the time.

    The comptroller's argument most closely conforms to
    which one of the following principles?

    (A) The mayor cannot be held responsible for every
         contract paid for with city funds.
    (B) Public officials are justified in making decisions
         quickly in order to bring about results rather than
         prolonging private bidding processes for too
         long.
    (C) It is unreasonable for citizens to complain about
         public administrators whom they voted into
         office.
    (D) It is acceptable for the mayor to overpay for a
         service from a private firm so long as the success
         of that firm benefits the city's economy.
    (E) Those who make the best choice from among the
         options of which they are aware should not be
         faulted for failing to choose the best course of
         action.

6. It is hard to determine exactly how prevalent a given
    psychosis actually is. For example, statistics reflecting
    a decrease in the reported incidence of a psychosis
    may reflect a lack of current public awareness of the
    psychosis rather than a decrease in its occurrence.
    We should therefore not treat a decrease in reported
    incidence of a psychosis to be indicative of an actual
    decrease.

    Which one of the following most closely conforms to the
    principle illustrated above?

    (A) Statistical data sometimes support a conclusion
         that is the opposite of the most obvious
         interpretation of the statistics.
    (B) Data indicating the reported frequency of a given
         event should not be treated as tantamount to data
         indicating the actual frequency of that event.
    (C) The reported incidence of a disorder tends to
         increase in proportion to the public awareness of
         the incidence of the disorder.
    (D) The incidence of an event can never be fully
         determined based on statistics alone.
    (E) Public health can be influenced by the awareness
         of a given psychosis or disorder.

GO ON TO THE NEXT PAGE.

7. Koji: The new regulations restricting online political campaign activity were long overdue. Unchecked freedom to advertise, solicit donations, or otherwise campaign represented an unacceptable loophole in our valuable system of campaign regulation.

Nobuo: But you're failing to see that the regulations are much broader than is acceptable. They will inevitably limit all citizens' freedom to express their political opinions, and it is more important to protect this freedom than it is to place restrictions on campaign activities.

Nobuo counters Koji's argument by

(A) refuting an assumption necessary to Koji's argument

(B) calling into question Koji's motives for supporting his claim

(C) undermining Koji's assertion that the system of campaign regulation is valuable

(D) challenging the main principle that Koji uses to justify his conclusion

(E) asserting that the benefit delineated by Koji is outweighed by a cost he did not consider

8. Professor: It is morally acceptable to steal if one is forced to do so in order to prevent severe physical or psychological harm, provided that the victim of the theft suffers only minor inconvenience or loss.

Which one of the following most closely conforms to the principle endorsed by the professor?

(A) Frank wanted to buy a new camera, but did not have enough money to make the purchase. He decided to steal the money from Greg, reasoning that since Greg was extremely wealthy, he would not notice that the money was gone.

(B) Emily, a janitor at a hospital, was prescribed antibiotics for her son, who had a serious infection. Since she could not afford the cost of the prescription, she decided it was acceptable to steal the antibiotics from the hospital storeroom, knowing that the hospital had a large supply and that no one would notice the missing antibiotics.

(C) David needed money to pay his rent, without which he would be evicted. He stole the money from Henry, thus causing Henry to be evicted. David argued that Henry was a disruptive tenant and deserved to be evicted.

(D) Carla, discovering that her father had embezzled millions of dollars from his employer, took the money from him and disbursed it to several well-known charities. She defended herself by saying that because she had taken the money from a criminal and given it to worthy causes, her actions were morally justified.

(E) Brad, when he noticed that the clerk was not watching, added a piece of fried chicken to his tray at the self-service buffet. He reasoned that since the chicken would probably be discarded at the end of the day, it was morally acceptable to take it.

9. Museum director: The French neoclassicism gallery must be cleared out so we can convert it into the showroom for our new photography exhibit. We must have the photography on display by the date advertised in our brochures, but we will be unable to obtain a permit in time to build a suitable new gallery. It is true that we have three other galleries, but our contracts with the lenders of the artwork preclude us from using those spaces for the photographs.

The museum director's argument proceeds by

(A) showing that the proposal recommended would be less expensive than any alternative

(B) proving a proposal to be superior by demonstrating that it has met certain necessary conditions

(C) supporting a proposal by disproving the feasibility of alternatives to that proposal

(D) assuming to be true that which it is ultimately trying to prove to be true

(E) supporting a proposal by proving that it would be the most popular of all possible options

10. The attorney general has investigated and uncovered many large-scale instances of illegal business practices, resulting in billions of dollars in fines and even prison sentences for some of the worst offenders. She has claimed that her actions have been an unmitigated success for her constituents. A claim this strong is not warranted when one considers the many innocent people who lost their jobs at the offending companies or who held stock that lost value when the businesses' misconduct was revealed.

Which one of the following best illustrates the principle illustrated by the argument above?

(A) Though the governor's tax initiative has had a positive impact on the economy, she has overstated the value of her program, because the favorable exchange rate played a role as well.

(B) Amir cannot reasonably claim that his home renovation project was successful, considering that it ran over budget and did not turn out as well as he had hoped.

(C) Biawa's self-help books have indeed helped many people improve their lives, but he should not take all of the credit when so many of his colleagues contributed ideas.

(D) As Mrs. Lee's fifth grade students showed continued improvement in their math scores, she has claimed total success for her new teaching methods. This claim is supported by the similarly improved reading scores.

(E) The mayor's redevelopment project fully achieved the desired effect of raising property values, but he cannot claim complete success, as it also displaced many residents.

GO ON TO THE NEXT PAGE.

11. Jean: To become a professional musician, one must become technically proficient at an instrument. In order to do so, aspiring musicians should only practice technical studies before moving to standard repertoire.

Alfonso: Technical proficiency is not enough to become a professional musician, and concentrating solely on technical studies may impede the development of musicianship. Aspiring musicians should practice both technical studies and standard repertoire throughout development.

Alfonso responds to Jean by

(A) citing an important consideration that Jean overlooks

(B) arguing that technical proficiency is unnecessary for musical development

(C) disputing the evidence on which Jean bases his claim

(D) offering a counterexample to undermine Jean's conclusion

(E) suggesting that not all aspiring musicians have developed musicianship

12. Managers in publicly traded companies must publish a yearly account of their companies' financial status and other affairs. As self-interested individuals, the managers must be expected to choose to publish only the information that will maximize their own wealth, to the point where they may choose to mislead competitors or even their own shareholders. Therefore, legislators should impose standards governing what information is reported and how it must be measured. However, enforcement of those standards will be at least as important as their imposition, since in some cases the measurement itself could be manipulated, which is especially dangerous because the misleading information would be lent credence by the appearance of compliance.

Which one of the following most accurately describes the role played in the argument by the claim that legislators should impose standards governing what information is reported and how it must be measured?

(A) It is used as a counterexample to the claim that managers will always publish the information that maximizes their own wealth.

(B) It is the conclusion that the argument as a whole is designed to support.

(C) It is cited as further evidence to support the conclusion that the manipulation of financial measurements is especially dangerous.

(D) It is a subsidiary conclusion used in turn to support the main conclusion that enforcement of standards is as important as their imposition.

(E) It is a premise used to support the claim that managers should not be required to publish a yearly account of their companies' financial status.

13. An advisor gave his student false information by telling her that she could not enroll in a class at any time other than in her first semester. However, by completing the class in her first semester, the student enjoyed it more than she would have had she taken it later. So the advisor should not be criticized for giving the student false information.

Which one of the following illustrates a principle most similar to that illustrated by the passage?

(A) The financial advisor encouraged his client to invest in several sectors that have since lost significant value. However, since the advisor cautioned his client that there was some risk in any investment, the advisor should not be criticized for giving bad advice.

(B) The consultant made a recommendation regarding a structural change to the bridge that resulted in some damage to the supports. The bad recommendation resulted from an erroneous calculation by the consultant, so the consultant is at fault for the damage to the bridge supports.

(C) The call center operator gave faulty instructions to the customer on how to fix the software problem. Because the instructions were ineffective, the customer was forced to devise her own solution and in the process gained better knowledge of the software. Since the operator is paid to give useful advice, he must be faulted for giving poor instructions.

(D) Thomas erroneously told his mother her car was handling poorly when the problem was actually due to his lack of skill at using a manual transmission. When she sent the car to be inspected, the mechanics noticed and repaired a potentially serious brake problem. Thus, Thomas cannot be criticized for misinforming his mother.

(E) The zookeeper fed the tigers food that is typically thought to be harmful to them. However, he knew that these tigers were able to digest the food without problem, and no harm came to them. So the zookeeper cannot be accused of endangering the tigers.

GO ON TO THE NEXT PAGE.

14. While employers have some responsibility to maintain a safe work environment, they should not be penalized for failing to do so when safety improvements are not logistically feasible and the employees are aware of and accept the risk.

Which one of the following judgments most closely conforms to the principle stated above?

(A)   All miners are aware of the many risks associated with their job, yet some mining companies could go to greater expense to ensure the safety of their workers. Therefore, mining companies should be penalized for failing to maintain a safe work environment.

(B)   The stairway leading up to the church's five hundred-year-old belfry is dangerously narrow and uneven, but renovation is not possible given the layout of the building, and the bell ringer happily navigates the stairway to perform his task, so no penalty should be assessed to the church for failing to maintain a safe work environment.

(C)   The chemical transportation trucks have a dangerous tendency to overturn at moderate speeds, but due to the specifics of their structure, they cannot be redesigned to be safer. However, since the trucking company has attracted enough job applicants that are unaware of the potential danger, it has a full crew of drivers and should not be penalized for failing to maintain a safe work environment.

(D)   The veterinarian's office is often visited by potentially dangerous animals, which sometimes carry communicable diseases. Since some of the office assistants are unaware of the potential risk from the animals, the office should be penalized in some way.

(E)   The deep fryer at the restaurant has a propensity to start dangerous grease fires, but the manager has trained his staff to put out the fires instead of replacing the appliance, so the restaurant should not be penalized for failing to maintain a safe work environment.

15. Sherry: In country S, everyone agrees that the privatization of the government's pension plan has been a success. Politicians in country T who oppose privatizing the government's pension plan are thus ignoring the available evidence.

   Al: One could just as easily point to the evidence that pension reform has failed in countries X and Y. Besides, the economic and social conditions in country S may not apply in country T.

Al responds to Sherry's argument in which one of the following ways?

(A)   He applies established general principles to a specific case.

(B)   He argues that two specific cases are analogous.

(C)   He cites specific cases in order to demonstrate the validity of a general law.

(D)   He offers counterexamples in order to show that a specific case may not always be generalized.

(E)   He states a conclusion without offering any supporting evidence.

STOP

IF YOU FINISH BEFORE TIME IS CALLED, YOU MAY CHECK YOUR WORK ON THIS EXAM ONLY.
DO NOT WORK ON ANY OTHER EXAM IN THE BOOK.

ANSWERS

1. A
2. C
3. A
4. B
5. E
6. B
7. E
8. B
9. C
10. E
11. A
12. D
13. D
14. B
15. D

IN-CLASS EXAM ICE LECTURE 9

EXAMINATION

LECTURE 9 EXAM
Time—25 minutes
15 Questions

Directions: The questions in this section are based on the reasoning contained in brief statements or passages. For some questions, more than one of the choices could conceivably answer the question. However, you are to choose the best answer; that is, the response that most accurately and completely answers the question. You should not make assumptions that are by commonsense standards implausible, superfluous, or incompatible with the passage. After you have chosen the best answer, circle the answer choice.

1. Yolanda promised that if it were cold she would wear a jacket when she went out. Since Yolanda never breaks her promises, and since she did not wear a jacket when she went out, it must not have been cold.

   Which one of the following is most similar in reasoning to the argument above?

   (A) The chef said that if no good beef was available, he would serve lamb instead. Since the chef is honest, and since he served fish, there must have been no good beef or lamb available.
   (B) The advertisement claimed that if a stain were still wet, the product could remove it. Since the product failed to remove the wet stain, the commercial must have been misleading.
   (C) The teacher said that if the weather was pleasant, he would hold class outside. Since he is always truthful, and it is nice out, he will certainly hold class outside.
   (D) The moderator promised that everyone who desired a chance to speak would get it, while still leaving time for the video presentation. Since she is a good moderator, everyone who wanted to must have spoken.
   (E) The makers of the alarm system guarantee that if a break-in is attempted the alarm will sound. Since they are always correct regarding their product, and since the alarm did not sound, there must not have been an attempted break-in.

2. Many engineers are well organized, and most well-organized people are punctual. Therefore, at least some engineers must be punctual.

   The flawed pattern of reasoning in the argument above is most similar to that in which one of the following?

   (A) Many agents are personable, and many agents are diligent. Therefore, some agents must be more popular than others.
   (B) Many football players are selfish, but no football players are cheaters. Therefore, no football players are selfish cheaters.
   (C) Many children are inquisitive, and most inquisitive people are well read. Therefore, at least some children must be well read.
   (D) Many students are hard working, and all hard-working people are thorough. Therefore, many students must be thorough.
   (E) Many doctors are creative problem solvers, and most creative problem solvers are intelligent. Therefore, it is possible that some doctors may be intelligent.

GO ON TO THE NEXT PAGE.

3. An artist's debut album usually does not draw much attention before its release unless the artist is already a celebrity from some other endeavor. Since Mark is not a celebrity, his debut album will likely not draw much attention before its release.

The reasoning in which one of the following is most similar to that in the argument above?

(A) New technology is usually hard to use unless it is derivative of older technology with which people are familiar. Since PFI devices are a new technology that is not derivative of any older technologies, no one will understand how to use them.

(B) Paintings are usually not popular unless they are truly original. Since Chen's most recent painting is truly original, he will sell it at a high price.

(C) Poets are usually not well known until after they have stopped writing. Since Ramesh has been published in many popular poetry journals, he is probably well known even though he has not stopped writing.

(D) Flat-panel monitors are usually not energy efficient unless they measure less than 21 inches across the diagonal. Since Ray's flat-panel monitor is greater than 21 inches across the diagonal, it is probably not energy efficient.

(E) Animals are not usually sought after by zoos unless they are rare or interesting to look at. Since pandas are both rare and interesting to look at, they are probably sought after by zoos.

4. If the new positive research regarding the health effects of chocolate is confirmed, it would benefit all chocolate companies. Since Harry's is the largest chocolate company, it stands to benefit the most.

The pattern of flawed reasoning displayed in the argument above most closely resembles that in which one of the following?

(A) If there is a downturn in overall television viewership this year, it will hurt the advertising industry. Since Taro Marketing operates differently from most other advertising firms, it may not be hurt as badly.

(B) If the food at Manny's gets a perfect score in the newspaper review, the restaurant will benefit greatly. Since Manny's is a new restaurant, it stands to benefit more from a good review than do large restaurants.

(C) If the new travel guide awards a top rating to Grenada's beaches, it will benefit all tourist resorts there. Since Naricosa Beach Resort is the biggest tourist resort in Grenada, it will likely benefit the most.

(D) If the new fertilizer is approved for sale, farmers across the country will benefit. Since grain farmers stand to benefit the most, they should invest the most in the new fertilizer.

(E) If, as expected, the city of Houston is unseated as the most overweight city in America, it would be a boon to the city. Since Roger was the heaviest man in Houston, he must have lost the most weight.

GO ON TO THE NEXT PAGE.

5. All master painters mix their own paint. No one who mixes his or her own paint can be insensitive to color. Therefore, anyone who is insensitive to color is not a master painter.

The pattern of reasoning displayed in the argument above is most similar to that displayed in which one of the following?

(A) All of the guests who appear on Celebrity Chef are amateurs. No amateur is eligible to win the Great American Chili Cook-off. Therefore, the winner of the Great American Chili Cook-off will not be a guest from Celebrity Chef.

(B) All of the guests who appear on Celebrity Chef will participate in the Great American Chili Cook-off. A celebrity often wins the Great American Chili Cook-off. Therefore, one of the guests from Celebrity Chef will win the Great American Chili Cook-off.

(C) All of the guests who appear on Celebrity Chef are excellent cooks. No excellent cook uses both food coloring and artificial flavors. Therefore, any guest on Celebrity Chef who uses food coloring does not use artificial flavors.

(D) All of the guests from Celebrity Chef who specialize in Creole cooking will participate in the Great American Chili Cook-off. None of the guests from Celebrity Chef who specialize in Tex-Mex cooking will participate in the Great American Chili Cook-off. Therefore, the winner of the Great American Chili Cook-off cannot be a specialist in Tex-Mex cooking.

(E) All of the guests who appear on Celebrity Chef are master chefs. It is impossible to objectively judge the work of a master chef. Therefore, it is impossible to evaluate the skills of the guests who appear on Celebrity Chef.

6. Studies have shown that there is a strong correlation between the practice of strict vegetarianism and a decreased risk of heart disease in those below the age of 50. However, it would be incorrect to conclude on the basis of this data that vegetarianism is the causative agent behind the decreased risk. After all, it may be that those who are most attracted to a vegetarian diet are also those who most frequently choose to exercise, an activity proven to reduce heart disease.

The pattern of reasoning in which one of the following arguments is most parallel to that in the argument above?

(A) Segments of highway on which drivers most often exceed the legal speed limit are also the segments of highway on which the most traffic accidents occur. However, it may be possible that increased law enforcement in these areas could lead to a reduced number of accidents, since drivers usually decrease their speed when they believe they may receive a citation.

(B) There is a strong link between cigarette smoking and an increased risk of heart disease in both men and women. Nevertheless, it would be erroneous to claim that heart disease is caused solely by cigarette smoking, since there are several other factors likely to contribute to a risk of heart disease, including obesity and hypertension.

(C) Dentists know that those who regularly consume large amounts of coffee are often afflicted with dental problems as they grow older. Although it is impossible to conclude from this observation alone that coffee consumption causes an increased risk of dental problems, government regulators should take proactive steps to limit citizens' access to coffee.

(D) Children who study music are more likely than their peers to perform well on tests of mathematics. However, it would be a mistake to conclude that the study of music brings about the improved performance on the tests. After all, it could be true that the children who have the best innate mathematical skills are also the same children who are drawn to the study of music.

(E) When a university installs floodlights on its campus, the action is usually followed by a drop in the number of robberies on campus. Yet it may be that the universities that choose to install floodlights are also likely to increase police presence on campus at the same time, so it would be wrong to conclude that the floodlights are responsible for the drop in robberies.

GO ON TO THE NEXT PAGE.

7. Critic: People agree that the most important thing about a movie is a good story. Thus, good actors, effects, and editing are only valuable to the extent that they can be used to augment a good story.

The pattern of reasoning in the critic's argument is most similar to that in which one of the following?

(A) One of the most important safety features a car can have is side airbags. Without side airbags, passengers remain largely unprotected in certain types of collisions.

(B) The most critical design feature for a building is its reflection of light. Uniqueness, fluidity of design, and contrast with the background are other critical design features.

(C) The most important quality for a boss to possess is a good understanding of social interactions. Some bosses are successful despite lacking this quality because they compensate with extra effort and dedication.

(D) The most important quality to have with respect to public speaking is the ability to communicate ideas clearly. Eye contact, body language, and humor are only helpful when they can enhance the audience's understanding of ideas that are already clear to them.

(E) The most valuable skill for a soccer player is good anticipation. Ball control, stamina, and selflessness are particularly important to master for those who lack good anticipation.

8. All dogs have a good sense of smell. Since pigs, like dogs, are mammalian quadrupeds, they must also have a good sense of smell.

Which one of the following most closely parallels the flawed reasoning of the argument above?

(A) All reptilian species lay eggs. Since marsupials are not reptiles, they must not lay eggs.

(B) No rabbits can digest meat, because they are herbivores. Since moose, like rabbits, are herbivores, they must also be unable to digest meat.

(C) All physicians have medical degrees. Since both pediatricians and dermatologists are physicians, both must have medical degrees.

(D) All old cars are unsafe. Since most unsafe cars are small cars, all old cars must be small cars.

(E) All of the buildings in Lendale are built to withstand hurricane-force winds. Since most of the buildings in Carlsville were built by the same construction company as those in Lendale, they must also be able to withstand hurricane-force winds.

9. The measles are only contagious for four days before the associated rash begins to show and for four days after. Ophelia contracted the measles, and her rash began five days ago, so she is no longer contagious.

Which one of the following arguments is most similar in logical features to the argument above?

(A) The warranty covering broken parts on this automobile lasts for three months. Nan bought the car six months ago, so his broken fuel pump is not covered by the warranty.

(B) Children must turn five years of age before they are eligible to attend kindergarten in this state. Bobby turned five last week, so he is eligible.

(C) The sanction against the basketball team for cheating was a reduction in scholarships from twelve to eight. Since then, it has regained one scholarship each year, and by next year it will be able to offer twelve scholarships again.

(D) Many students extend their loans beyond the original 180-month repayment term, at a lower rate of interest. Susan repaid her loans in only 150 months, and though she was assessed a higher interest rate, she paid less total money.

(E) An employee receives 20 percent of the company's stock options after every full year of employment, becoming fully vested only after five full years of employment. Only half the marketing team has been with the company for five years, so not all of them are fully vested.

GO ON TO THE NEXT PAGE.

10. To be successful, a basketball coach must keep players motivated throughout the entire season. In addition to building good relationships with players, a coach can foster motivation by occasionally rewarding the strongest performers with a day off from practice. Therefore, the more days off from practice a coach gives, the more successful he will be.

The flawed pattern of reasoning in the argument above is most similar to that in which one of the following?

(A) Successful advertising campaigns create memorable impressions in the largest possible number of people. Hence, any advertisement that is not seen by many people cannot be considered successful.

(B) To be effective, a teacher must hold the attention of a class. This can be accomplished with diversions such as quick games, as well as by clear and authoritative speaking. Hence, the more games a teacher plays during class, the more effective she will be.

(C) To be successful, an editorialist needs to keep readers from losing track of the argument. Besides communicating ideas unambiguously and concisely, the writer can use familiar examples to ensure that readers can follow the ideas. Therefore, learning to use examples effectively can make one a better editorialist.

(D) A company needs contented employees to function well. Employee satisfaction can be increased by giving raises as well as by giving more paid vacation days to the employees. Thus, companies that balance these perks well will function well.

(E) People appreciate the convenience of having a good variety of merchandise available in a store. Therefore, stores with good variety of merchandise will generally be more popular.

11. Marketer: Some managers are concerned about the discovery that the company's newest truck is unsafe. These managers fail to consider that the new truck is more popular than the older models. Because of the connection between the safety level of the new truck and its popularity, it would be foolish to attempt to make it safer.

The questionable pattern of reasoning in the argument above is most similar to that in which one of the following?

(A) Many customers have complained about the price increases on several popular items. These customers fail to realize that there has been an increase in the cost of delivering the items to stores. Because of the increased cost of delivery, the store should not reduce the cost of the popular items.

(B) Many voters feel that the current sales tax unfairly places a burden on average families. However, the revenue from the sales tax pays for several valuable programs. Because of the relationship between the sales tax and the programs it supports, voters should not call for changes to the sales tax unless they do not consider the programs valuable.

(C) Several consultants have pointed out that the advertisements fail to indicate which brand they are meant to represent. The consultants should recall that sales have increased since the advertisements began running. Because of this relationship, there is clearly no need to modify the advertisements.

(D) Parents of the students at Deerwood have been complaining about the lack of extracurricular activities. The parents have not complained about the lack of any art or music classes. Since art and music classes would be more beneficial, extracurricular programs should not be developed until art and music classes are in place.

(E) Some employees have complained about the decrease in hourly pay. These employees are neglecting to consider the corresponding increase in benefits. Because their pay has decreased while their benefits have increased, they should not be given an increase in pay unless their benefits are reduced.

GO ON TO THE NEXT PAGE.

12. If all great writers know the literary canon, and James is a great writer, then James must know the literary canon. But James is completely unfamiliar with the literary canon, so either James is not a great writer, or not all great writers know the literary canon.

The pattern of reasoning displayed in the argument above is most closely paralleled by that in which one of the following arguments?

(A) It is clear that either this is not a fun game or else not all fun games run quickly. This game has gone on much too long, and if all fun games run quickly and this is a fun game, then it should run quickly.

(B) One can become a great poet only by studying the great poets of the past. Jill claims to be a great poet, but since she has not studied the great poets of the past, Jill must not be great.

(C) If all hot dogs contain beef, and this is a hot dog, then it should have some beef in it. But this is not a hot dog, so either not all hot dogs contain beef, or this is not a beef product.

(D) Either Jim is a bad comedian or not all good comedians interact with the audience. Jim does not interact with the audience. And if only bad comedians avoid interaction, then he should try to interact more.

(E) This piece is composed by either Mozart or Haydn. If all great classical symphonies were written by Mozart, and this is a classical symphony, then this must be composed by Mozart rather than Haydn.

13. No children like to eat broccoli. And since most children like chicken nuggets, at least some people who like to eat broccoli must not like chicken nuggets.

The flawed reasoning in which one of the following is most similar to that in the argument above?

(A) No dogs can speak. And since most dogs can communicate, at least some animals that can communicate must not be able to speak.

(B) No teachers are disorganized. And since most teachers are affable, at least some teachers must be both affable and disorganized.

(C) No lemurs are color-blind. And since most lemurs are arboreal, there must be more lemurs that are arboreal than color-blind.

(D) No owls are diurnal. And since many animals that are diurnal are not omnivorous, all owls must be omnivorous.

(E) No bird gives birth to live young. And since most birds can fly, at least some animals that give birth to live young must be flightless.

GO ON TO THE NEXT PAGE.

14. Government spending during poor economic times softens the impact of recession on working families. Softening the impact of recession on working families leads to increased consumer confidence and can shorten the length of an economic downturn. Therefore, government spending during an economic downturn can shorten its duration.

Which one of the following most closely parallels the reasoning in the argument above?

(A) A steady regimen of exercise can reduce long-term heath-related costs. Additionally, it can lengthen one's lifespan such that those benefits are enjoyed longer. Thus, reducing long- term health-related costs is correlated with a longer lifespan.

(B) Intensive foreign-language study is an efficient way to increase professional skills. Increasing professional skills is a positive way to expand job opportunities and gain bargaining power. So intensive foreign-language study is an efficient way to increase bargaining power.

(C) Good preventative dental hygiene is the best way to avoid complicated dental surgery. Avoiding complicated dental surgery is the surest way to minimize dental costs. Clearly, good preventative dental hygiene is the surest way to minimize dental costs.

(D) Effective bargaining is a reliable way to reduce costs and increase competitiveness. Bargaining skills are also essential for increasing revenue when selling products and services. Thus, both reducing costs and increasing revenue when selling products and services increase competitiveness.

(E) Aerobic exercise increases the flow of oxygen to the brain. Studies show that aerobic exercise done as many as six hours before one takes a test can improve scores significantly. Therefore, increasing oxygen flow to the brain improves test scores significantly.

15. Researcher: An independent crash test analysis showed that cars using the new cab-reinforcement technology are one third less likely to sustain potentially fatal damage in a high-speed crash. Since most of the cab-reinforced cars used in the study were foreign, we can also conclude that foreign cars are less likely to be involved in a fatal crash.

The pattern of flawed reasoning in which one of the following is most similar to the pattern of flawed reasoning in the argument above?

(A) A statewide survey found that people with full-time jobs are 20 percent less likely to be smokers. Since the survey did not record gender data, we cannot say whether men or women are more likely to smoke.

(B) A recent study showed that people who drink more milk are at a lower risk of having a stroke. Since most of those in the study drank organic milk, we can also conclude that organic milk is better than non-organic milk at reducing the risk of stroke.

(C) A carefully controlled test showed that laptop computers running the new version of the operating system perform 40 percent faster than the same computers running the previous version. So we can conclude that computers are likely to run faster using the new version of the operating system.

(D) A recent study has shown that raw fish is much more likely to carry harmful bacteria than cooked fish. Since the fish used in the study was salmon, we can conclude that raw salmon is more likely to carry harmful bacteria than is cooked salmon.

(E) Available data indicate that four-engine jets are 70 percent less likely to crash than twin-engine planes. Since most of the four-engine jets used in the study were built within the last five years, we can also conclude that even the least-safe four-engine plane built within the last five years is safer than a twin-engine plane.

STOP

IF YOU FINISH BEFORE TIME IS CALLED, YOU MAY CHECK YOUR WORK ON THIS EXAM ONLY. DO NOT WORK ON ANY OTHER EXAM IN THE BOOK.

Answers

1. E
2. C
3. D
4. C
5. A
6. E
7. D
8. E
9. A
10. B
11. C
12. A
13. E
14. B
15. B

IN-CLASS EXAM ICE LECTURE 10

EXAMINATION

LECTURE 10 EXAM
Time—25 minutes
15 Questions

Directions: The questions in this section are based on the reasoning contained in brief statements or passages. For some questions, more than one of the choices could conceivably answer the question. However, you are to choose the best answer; that is, the response that most accurately and completely answers the question. You should not make assumptions that are by commonsense standards implausible, superfluous, or incompatible with the passage. After you have chosen the best answer, circle the answer choice.

1. Using two identical groups of 36 privately owned automobiles, engineers performed an experiment in which automobiles in one group received Brand X oil every three months, while those in the other received Brand Y oil according to the same schedule. After 15 years, exactly 35 automobiles from each group had experienced catastrophic engine failure. The engineers concluded that Brand X oil was no more effective at preventing engine failure than Brand Y.

   Which one of the following, if true, would most weaken the engineers' conclusion?

   (A) The automobiles that received Brand X oil avoided engine failure for an average of eighteen months longer than those that received Brand Y oil.
   (B) Some mechanics believe that the nature of Brand X's advertisements causes drivers who use it to drive more aggressively, putting added strain on their automobiles' engines.
   (C) Nearly every driver in the study whose automobile received Brand X oil reported that the automobile's engine ran more smoothly than it had before the experiment.
   (D) Of the two automobiles that lasted longer than 15 years, the one given Brand X oil avoided engine failure longer than the one given Brand Y oil.
   (E) The manufacturer of Brand X oil sells several other products proven to reduce the occurrence of other types of mechanical failure.

2. The executives discussed the advertising proposal too briefly to approve it, but too extensively to shelve it, so their discussion was insufficient to allow them to make a decision on the proposal.

   Which one of the following is an assumption on which the argument depends?

   (A) In order to discuss a proposal, the executives must be able to make a decision on it.
   (B) The advertising proposal can be neither approved nor shelved unless it is discussed to the proper extent by the executives.
   (C) If the executives discuss a proposal extensively, they will approve it.
   (D) If a proposal is discussed at length, it should be either approved or shelved.
   (E) In order for the discussion to allow the executives to make a decision on the advertising proposal, it must have led either to their approving it or to their shelving it.

3. Martial artist: All pressure-point attacks are effective because they temporarily cause the nervous system to transmit to the brain that the body is under far more dangerous attack than it actually is. This causes the body to reflexively react to protect itself in ways that can be compromising. Every skilled fighter uses pressure-point attacks, since all skilled fighters understand how to provoke and take advantage of this situation.

   The reasoning in the martial artist's argument is most vulnerable to criticism on the grounds that it

   (A) takes for granted that different people respond in predictable ways to pressure-point attacks
   (B) draws a general conclusion based only on a small sample of responses to pressure-point attacks
   (C) presumes, without providing justification, that the use of pressure-point attacks is necessary in order to be a skilled fighter
   (D) presumes, without providing justification, that fighters who use pressure-point attacks are always skillful
   (E) fails to quantify the nature of reflexive responses to pressure-point attacks and how they can be compromising

GO ON TO THE NEXT PAGE.

4. Last summer, legislators in the newly formed municipality of Chibaro relied for the first time on the testimony of academic experts in crafting tax regulations, which directly led to the new regulations being particularly effective. Thus, in order to ensure that future legislation is similarly effective, lawmakers should again call upon academic experts to testify.

Which one of the following principles, if established, would most help to justify the conclusion above?

(A) Legislatures that do not call upon academic experts in the crafting of regulations usually produce regulations that are not particularly effective.

(B) If a piece of legislation is effective because of expert testimony, future legislation will also be effective if aided by the same academic experts.

(C) Legislation is effective only if lawmakers call upon academic experts to testify as part of its creation.

(D) If a regulation is effective because of the testimony of academic experts, future legislation will be similarly effective if the legislature again calls upon academic experts to testify.

(E) Legislatures that utilize the testimony of academic experts and thoughtfully consider all sides of an issue stand a greater chance of crafting legislation that is particularly effective.

5. Past criminal trials are being reevaluated by examining DNA evidence. This evidence is usually stored by law enforcement officials, and can be easily accessed and evaluated even fifty years after a person has been convicted. Geneticists believe that by using DNA evidence they can overturn many mistaken criminal convictions.

Each of the following, if true, supports the geneticists' conclusion EXCEPT:

(A) Appeals courts are likely to accept the testimony of geneticists who present DNA evidence.

(B) DNA evidence can become corrupted in some cases without geneticists' knowledge.

(C) Genetic evidence loses none of its accuracy over long periods of time.

(D) In many criminal trials, the only evidence for conviction was unreliable eyewitness accounts.

(E) Though human witnesses may provide inconsistent accounts of a crime because of ulterior motives, DNA evidence is always consistent.

6. Council leader: Several council members claim that the public believes it is the responsibility of government to provide state-run day care programs and that it is irresponsible to leave children without sufficient supervision. However, these council members do not adequately capture the views of our constituents. In a survey conducted by a private day care center, only 12 percent of respondents thought that it was the responsibility of the state to provide a day care program, and only 7 percent thought that it was irresponsible of the state not to provide one. These numbers are a good measure of our constituents' opinions because those surveyed vote in every election.

The reasoning in the council leader's argument is flawed in that it

(A) presumes, without providing justification, that the people surveyed were not already participants in a day care program

(B) bases its conclusion on public opinion rather than on an objective standard for governmental responsibility

(C) fails to consider the possibility that state-run day care will cause an increase in voter turnout

(D) generalizes from a sample that is unlikely to be representative of public opinion

(E) attacks the credibility of the council members rather than addressing their concerns

7. A certain small freshwater animal called a tardigrade is the only animal that can survive extreme conditions by reducing its metabolism to zero activity, a state normally considered death, then reanimating itself when conditions improve. Because of this ability, tardigrades are better suited than any other animal to endure the rigors of long-distance space travel.

Which one of the following, if assumed, enables the argument's conclusion to be properly inferred?

(A) Long-distance space travel is impossible for any animal that cannot survive extreme conditions.

(B) An animal that can reduce its metabolism to zero activity and reanimate itself when conditions improve is always better suited than any other animal to endure the rigors of long-distance space travel.

(C) Animals other than tardigrades cannot survive extreme conditions.

(D) Enduring the rigors of long-distance space travel requires an animal to have the ability to reduce metabolism to zero activity and reanimate itself when conditions improve.

(E) In order to survive extreme conditions, all animals must reduce their metabolism at least to some extent.

GO ON TO THE NEXT PAGE.

8. If the new office security system were effective, it would not allow any unauthorized persons to access the building. Unfortunately, the system is ineffective, so it must allow unauthorized persons such access.

    The flawed reasoning in which one of the following is most similar to that in the argument above?

    (A) If intelligence is caused by the number of folds in the cerebral cortex, then those with the most folds should be the most intelligent. But those with the most folds are not the most intelligent, so there is clearly no relationship.
    (B) If a coffee product is labeled "decaffeinated," it must have had over 97.5 percent of its caffeine removed. This product has had 99 percent of its caffeine removed. Thus, it is labeled "decaffeinated."
    (C) The Middletown orchard will stage a fireworks display on its anniversary. There are no fireworks at the orchard now, so today is not the orchard's anniversary.
    (D) The city council will ratify Adler's proposal only if it is better than Burke's proposal. Since Adler's proposal is better than Burke's, the city council will ratify it.
    (E) If we have a moral obligation to improve the environment, then we will develop cleaner energy sources. But we have no such obligation, so we will not develop cleaner energy sources.

9. One supercomputer has a total of 100 processors, although on average, five are not functioning at any given time for a variety of reasons. The computer operates at its intended speed if precisely five processors are not functioning. Thus, it can be assumed that five processors could be removed from the supercomputer without any loss of speed.

    The argument is most vulnerable to criticism on the grounds that it

    (A) takes for granted that the speed of the supercomputer is not affected by how many processors its has
    (B) ignores the possibility that if five processors were removed, each of the other processors would function more quickly than before
    (C) fails to show that the proportion of nonfunctioning processors would decrease if five were removed
    (D) takes for granted that the intended speed of the supercomputer can be achieved only if at least ninety-five processors are functioning
    (E) overlooks the possibility that certain processors are a vital part of the supercomputer's infrastructure

10. Economist: Our field is working on a new picture of rationality that does not rely on game theory, and, indeed, we have developed alternatives to game theory that are more successful at predicting behavior in economic settings. No matter how influential the game-theory account of rationality may be, it is time to jettison it from economics.

    Which one of the following is an assumption on which the economist's argument depends?

    (A) An understanding of rationality that leads to more accurate predictions is preferable to one that is less successful.
    (B) Game theory cannot predict how non-rational agents will interact in experimental environments.
    (C) Economists measure the success of a theory by weighing it against the results given by other theories.
    (D) Economic theories are untenable when they provide experimental data that do not correspond to observations of actual people.
    (E) Game theory makes predictions that have been proven to be false through experimentation.

11. A study of young children found that the number of books present in their homes was a stronger indicator of their success on standardized tests than whether their parents read to them nightly. Those children who were read to nightly performed at the same level as those children who were read to between two and four times a week. Parents who care about their young child's success on tests should worry more about the number of books in their house and less about reading to their children.

    Which one of the following statements, if true, most seriously weakens the argument?

    (A) Children with a moderate number of books in the home who were read to frequently were outperformed by students with a larger book collection who were not read to at all.
    (B) The study also found that the number of books in a home has no positive effect if parents do not read to their children.
    (C) Children in homes with no books never become curious about school subjects.
    (D) The families in the study with more books in their homes also sent their children to better schools.
    (E) Studies of older children show no correlation between the number of books in the home and success on standardized tests.

GO ON TO THE NEXT PAGE.

12. Antonia: The raw information from which discoveries about human genetics are made is no more than the sequence of nucleotides in our cells. Since the data are obtained simply by "reading" something already present in our bodies, allowing researchers to patent this sequence would be absurd.

Jorge: I disagree. Patents have always played an important role in the field of genetics, and forbidding them would be disastrous, since if intellectual-property laws did not protect their work, scientists would have little incentive to develop and utilize their discoveries.

Jorge's statements can best be explained on the assumption that he has misinterpreted Antonia's remarks to be

(A) asserting that patents other than those on the sequence of nucleotides should be forbidden

(B) denying that researchers' discoveries should be protected by intellectual-property laws

(C) presuming that it is relatively easy for scientists to read the sequence of human nucleotides

(D) referring to the raw data from which the discoveries come rather than to the development and use of discoveries

(E) calling for the cessation of research on human genetics until patent laws are clarified

13. The arrowheads found at one burial ground were chipped, whereas those found at another one were not. Since arrowheads only become chipped when they are used in combat, this suggests that the arrowheads found at the first burial ground were made to be used in combat, whereas the arrowheads found at the second site were instead created to be buried with the dead.

Which one of the following, if shown to be true, would most support the argument?

(A) Arrowheads found at both burial grounds had cultural uses regardless of whether they were used in combat.

(B) Various other weapons that appear to have been used in combat were found at the second burial ground.

(C) The arrowheads found at the first burial ground appear to have been made by the same tribe that made the arrowheads at the second burial ground.

(D) Some arrowheads that have yet to be found at the first burial ground are not chipped and are adorned with markings characteristic of burial ceremonies.

(E) The arrowheads found at the second burial ground were made long enough before they were buried to allow ample time for potential use in combat.

GO ON TO THE NEXT PAGE.

14. Marine biologist: Many residents are concerned about the appearance of the non-indigenous New Zealand mud snail in local lakes. They worry that, because the mud snail has no natural predators in the area, its population will grow out of control and will negatively impact the local ecosystem. However, in the snail's original New Zealand habitat, its population is held in check by a particular water-borne parasite. So we can simply introduce the parasite in this area to control the mud snail population and prevent any negative impact to the local ecosystem.

The answer to which one of the following questions would be the most relevant in evaluating the validity of the marine biologist's conclusion?

(A) Will the mud snail displace native invertebrates that constitute an important part of the diet of local fish?

(B) Is the parasite that naturally controls the mud snail population edible to most species of local fish?

(C) Will the mud snail population explosion harm the local fishing economy if it is not controlled in some way?

(D) Will the parasite introduced to control the mud snail population have any negative impact on the local ecosystem?

(E) Has the mud snail caused irreversible damage to ecosystems in the other areas in which it has suddenly appeared?

15. A scientist who believes that a measurement is inaccurate will not bother to record it, and thus will not ask colleagues to review it. Additionally, any scientist who is sure that a measurement is accurate will record it without colleague review. Thus, review by colleagues is not a useful part of recording a measurement.

The reasoning in this argument is flawed because the argument

(A) presumes, without providing justification, that a scientist's only possible responses to a measurement are belief in its inaccuracy and surety of its accuracy

(B) infers, from the claim that colleague review of measurements is useless, that a scientist who is recording a measurement will not request it regardless

(C) concludes, on the basis that a scientist does not erroneously believe that a measurement is inaccurate, that the scientist will be sure that the measurement is accurate

(D) ignores the possibility that review of measurements by colleagues can be useful for those who are not scientists

(E) takes for granted that colleagues cannot contribute to scientific work in other useful ways

STOP

IF YOU FINISH BEFORE TIME IS CALLED, YOU MAY CHECK YOUR WORK ON THIS EXAM ONLY. DO NOT WORK ON ANY OTHER EXAM IN THE BOOK.

Answers

1. A
2. E
3. C
4. D
5. B
6. D
7. B
8. E
9. C
10. A
11. B
12. A
13. E
14. D
15. A

IN-CLASS EXAM ICE LECTURE 11

EXAMINATION

LECTURE 11 EXAM
Time—25 minutes
15 Questions

<u>Directions:</u> The questions in this section are based on the reasoning contained in brief statements or passages. For some questions, more than one of the choices could conceivably answer the question. However, you are to choose the <u>best</u> answer; that is, the response that most accurately and completely answers the question. You should not make assumptions that are by commonsense standards implausible, superfluous, or incompatible with the passage. After you have chosen the best answer, circle the answer choice.

1. Bites from the same insect trigger different levels of immune response in different people. Flea bites, for example, do not cause most people anything more than mild annoyance or itching, but some people—those with particularly responsive antibodies—suffer large blotchy rashes and severe itchiness because their immune systems enter an elevated state in order to isolate and eliminate the toxins introduced by a flea bite. Other people's immune systems barely respond at all because their antibodies do not detect the poisons introduced by the flea.

    Which one of the following is most strongly supported by the information above?

    (A) A person's immune system can be induced into a course of action by an insect bite.
    (B) People with particularly responsive antibodies are healthier than other people since their bodies more readily eliminate toxins.
    (C) People tend to suffer more severe immune response from flea bites than from other kinds of insect bites.
    (D) People with responsive antibodies more quickly isolate and eliminate from their bodies the toxins from an insect bite.
    (E) Anyone who is bitten by a flea undergoes either an elevated immune response or barely any immune response as a result.

2. Ashwagandha is a tonic herb grown in southwest Asia. Local residents have long taken the herb orally to cure certain debilitating conditions. In addition to this use, Ashwagandha can be made into a salve, applied directly to the skin, that is extremely effective at disinfecting wounds. Yet European scientists who studied this herb and tested it on numerous people found that it was poisonous and actually caused a severe debilitating condition.

    Which one of the following, if true, most helps to resolve the apparent paradox described above?

    (A) Europeans produce an enzyme that interacts with and destroys the chemical in Ashwagandha that disinfects wounds.
    (B) The poison in Ashwagandha is not lethal, and the herb can be applied as a salve with a small amount of preparation.
    (C) Without preparation as a salve, the herb is not poisonous but also does not act to cure debilitating conditions.
    (D) In light of the scientists' findings, the herb is very rarely consumed in Europe.
    (E) The people of southwest Asia have developed immunity to the poison in Ashwagandha.

GO ON TO THE NEXT PAGE.

3. Heidi: A famous editor, who, in denouncing "fledgling writers who pour out unauthorized biographies on movie stars," wrote that, "This brand of 'me-too' publishing only drives the focus of moviegoers away from more important issues and fuels pointless rumor mongering." These remarks are unprofessional.

   Alain: You're mistaken. Movie stars only attained their positions because they lead fascinating lives, but unauthorized biographies punish those stars for being interesting people, and editors are employed to make fair points like this one.

   The point at issue between Heidi and Alain is whether

   (A) the editor's criticism of the writers is unprofessional
   (B) publishing a biography about a movie star leads to pointless rumor mongering
   (C) fledgling writers have a responsibility to publish works that avoid rumor mongering and protect the privacy of stars
   (D) it is expected that fledgling writers would produce works about interesting people
   (E) fledgling writers present significant dangers to the careers of movie stars

4. Emma: You cannot write effectively about the civil rights movement since you are not a member of an affected group. You may care about the issues involved in the movement, but you will never have the same motivation to explore those issues as someone who is directly affected by them.

   Madison: Your point is grossly inaccurate. There are many men who write insightfully about the feminist movement. These men are sufficiently motivated by their sense of justice, even though they are not women. In a field as compelling as civil rights, what would preclude me from having ample motivation to explore important issues?

   Madison responds to Emma's criticism by

   (A) citing the case of the feminist movement in order to demonstrate that the civil rights movement is worthy of attentive writing
   (B) providing an analogy that contradicts an important premise in Emma's argument
   (C) questioning whether Emma is qualified to judge whether Madison's writing will be effective
   (D) providing evidence against Emma's assertion that Madison is not a member of an affected group
   (E) elucidating Emma's unstated premise about what it means to be considered part of an affected group

5. An athlete is not a leader unless he or she is more skilled than the average athlete on the team and motivates others to perform well; an athlete is a detriment to the team if he or she criticizes teammates or is less skilled than is typical for that team.

   Which one of the following judgments most closely conforms to the principle stated above?

   (A) Carmen has played her sport longer than the other players on her team and has thus become more skilled. But since her team usually loses, she is not a leader, even though she motivates her teammates to perform well by encouraging them.
   (B) Geraldine is a detriment to the team because although she is skilled, it comes not from hard work but from her unusual physical size, and her bad practice habits set a bad example for her teammates.
   (C) Ira sees that his teammate has poor technique and gives him advice on how to perform better in competition. However, Ira is a detriment to the team because his teammate misinterprets the advice as criticism.
   (D) Marcia practices and trains with such dedication that she has become the most skilled player on her team. Marcia is a leader because her skill has led to numerous team victories.
   (E) Craig scores an average of 25 points in every game, which helps his team win often. Since all the athletes on Craig's team display a similar degree of skill, Craig is not a leader.

6. Researchers have discovered that ginseng is no more effective at improving memory than any other dietary supplement. Tests also confirm that people who take ginseng performed no better at tasks involving memorization and recollection than a control group of people who did not take ginseng. This is significant since most people only consume ginseng in order to improve their memory.

   Which one of the following can be logically concluded from the information above?

   (A) It is unusual for a person's performance on memorization tasks to improve as a result of taking a dietary supplement.
   (B) There is no dietary supplement that is more effective than ginseng at improving memory.
   (C) The dietary supplement St. John's Wort cannot be less effective than ginseng at improving memory.
   (D) A dietary supplement may be less effective than ginseng at improving memory.
   (E) The majority of people who consume ginseng would cease to do so if they knew that it did not improve their memory.

GO ON TO THE NEXT PAGE.

7. Most people who place wagers on horse races do so without studying the horses' records. Of those people, some use intuition or superstition, while others rely completely on advice from friends. Other people occasionally study the horses' records but are just as likely to fall back on intuition or advice. Few people unfailingly study the horses' records before placing a wager, and most people who place wagers on horse races lose money.

If the statements above are true, which one of the following must also be true?

(A)   Most people who do not study the horses' records lose money from placing wagers on horse races.

(B)   Most people who use intuition or superstition rather than relying completely on advice from friends lose money from placing wagers on horse races.

(C)   Some people who lose money from placing wagers on horse races do not study the horses' records.

(D)   Most people who place wagers on horse races either use intuition or rely completely on advice from friends.

(E)   At least one person who sometimes studies the horses' records while other times falling back on intuition or advice has lost money from placing a wager on a horse race.

8. Some scientists believe that life on Earth is the result of extraterrestrial intervention, asserting that it is incredibly unlikely that the nucleic acids present in early unicellular life could have formed spontaneously due to their extreme complexity and the hostile conditions of the planet at the time. These scientists hypothesize that billions of years ago, matter from outer space entered Earth's atmosphere carrying extraterrestrial cells. Yet these same scientists also believe that any foreign object entering the atmosphere would burn up before it hit the surface of the earth.

Which one of the following beliefs, if shown to be held by these scientists, most helps to resolve the apparent discrepancy described above?

(A)   The burnt debris from the extraterrestrial matter stimulated common elements to combine and form the nucleic acids in early life.

(B)   The nucleic acids found in early life were formed over heat vents deep within the ocean.

(C)   No part of the extraterrestrial object hit the surface of the earth because it burned up before it could do so.

(D)   Extraterrestrial cells developed on other planets under vastly more favorable conditions than those on Earth at the time.

(E)   The nucleic acids found in the extraterrestrial object were destroyed when the object entered Earth's atmosphere.

9. Manager: The decision on the proposal to shut down the manufacturing plant is clearly fraught with emotion, but we are additionally uncertain as to whether it will make our company more profitable in the long run. Certain computer models provide evidence that it will not, but conventional economic theory supplies equally convincing evidence to the contrary. Since neither body of evidence can conclusively prove what will happen, we should heed conventional economic theory and shut down the manufacturing plant.

Which one of the following principles underlies the manager's argument?

(A)   One should abide by conventional theory only if there is unconventional evidence that suggests the theory is correct.

(B)   One should heed conventional theory only in the process of making a decision fraught with emotion.

(C)   When no body of evidence can prove the outcome of a decision, one should delay action until such evidence is available.

(D)   When a computer model contradicts conventional theory, one ought not act upon it unless there is conclusive proof it is correct.

(E)   When there is uncertainty as to what the eventual outcome of an action will be, one should take that action.

10. A person's metabolic rate is determined by more than just level of physical activity. A research study found that students who regularly attended a gym had similarly low metabolic rates to those students who did not attend a gym. Both groups experienced high levels of stress, leading researchers to conclude that the similar results were attributable to stress. It seems that metabolic rates can be affected by psychological states as much as by activity.

The claim that a person's rate of metabolism depends on more than just level of physical activity figures into the argument in which one of the following ways?

(A)   It is support for the conclusion that the similar results were attributable to stress.

(B)   It is evidence for the position the argument is designed to discredit.

(C)   It is the conclusion for which the argument is presenting a case.

(D)   It is an assumption upon which the conclusion relies.

(E)   It is a premise that undermines one of the argument's other premises.

GO ON TO THE NEXT PAGE.

11. Calling an argument "fallacious" is not necessarily the same thing as calling it "unconvincing" or "unimportant." While the first term denotes something about the logical composition of the argument, the other two terms denote something about the argument's impact. It is not, however, mere coincidence that many unconvincing arguments are fallacious. When people find an argument specious, they are unlikely to be swayed by it.

Which one of the following best expresses the main point of the passage?

(A) Not all descriptions of an argument denote the same thing.

(B) An argument that is fallacious can be distinguished from other arguments by studying its impact.

(C) When people find an argument specious, it is due to the argument's logical composition.

(D) The fact that an argument is fallacious often contributes to its unpersuasiveness.

(E) An unconvincing argument is also likely to be unimportant.

12. Unless a political candidate receives generous donations from a number of donors, that candidate cannot win the election. Only those candidates who are believed by donors to have a strong chance of winning the election receive generous donations. If a candidate performs strongly in a nationally televised debate, then donors will believe that the candidate has a good chance of winning. A candidate who either appears nervous and unprepared or who gives unpopular answers cannot win televised debates.

If all the statements in the passage are true which one of the following CANNOT be true?

(A) A candidate who gives unpopular answers in a televised debate may still receive generous donations from a number of donors.

(B) Given that donors do not believe this candidate has a good chance of winning, it is certain that the candidate did not perform strongly in the nationally televised debates.

(C) If a candidate does not perform strongly in the nationally televised debates, then donors will not believe that the candidate has a good chance of winning.

(D) Donors may believe that a candidate has a strong chance of winning the election even though that candidate did not perform strongly in the nationally televised debates.

(E) A candidate who is not believed to have a good chance of winning, but who performs strongly in a televised debate, may still receive the donations needed to win an election.

13. Executive officer: Next fiscal year, only those companies with innovative technological initiatives will experience significant profit growth. These companies will require their employees to adapt to pervasive changes to their work environment. This course of events will force companies to spend resources training their employees in order to ensure a smooth transition. Therefore, in the next fiscal year, the workforce of a given company will probably _____.

Which one of the following most logically completes the executive officer's argument?

(A) increase in size if the business is innovative enough to invest its profits in expansion

(B) become more skilled if the company is undergoing a period of significant profit growth

(C) decrease in size through the dismissal of those employees who cannot adapt to pervasive changes

(D) become more skilled in order to adapt to pervasive changes in the work environment

(E) be best served through intense training sessions that rapidly instill in employees the skills they need to succeed

GO ON TO THE NEXT PAGE.

14. To be eye-catching, a Latin dancer must use exaggerated facial expressions. Whether or not the dancer has superior footwork, exhibits striking lines in his or her body with poses, or wears flashy costumes, if a Latin dancer is eye-catching then he or she uses dramatic expressions. In fact, even a dancer with average technique can be eye-catching if he or she demonstrates a great deal of personality.

Which one of the following logically follows from the statements above?

(A) A Latin dancer who uses dramatic expressions but does not demonstrate a great deal of personality is not eye-catching.

(B) If a Latin dancer wears flashy costumes but does not demonstrate a great deal of personality, then she is not eye-catching.

(C) Only if a Latin dancer is eye-catching does he or she use dramatic expressions.

(D) All Latin dancers who do not use dramatic expressions but exhibit superior footwork and a great deal of personality are eye-catching.

(E) If a Latin dancer does not use dramatic expressions but exhibits striking lines in his body, then he is not eye-catching.

15. The fact that cities with higher crime rates have more police officers does not prove that a greater number of officers causes crime, since the number of police officers a city hires depends on the level of crime in the city.

The reasoning in which one of the following arguments is most similar to that in the argument above?

(A) Since a person's taste in music greatly depends on the taste in music of his or her friends, the fact that a person listens to one kind of music does not demonstrate that the person prefers that kind of music.

(B) The fact that youths with smaller frames tend to outshine other youths in gymnastics does not show that a particular body type is necessary for gymnastics, for smaller-framed individuals tend to do gymnastics more often than others.

(C) The fact that two medical treatments cause similar side effects does not mean that those treatments affect the same part of the body, since a particular side effect can be the result of any number of different causes.

(D) Having a low income often forces a person to consume a diet of low nutritional quality, so the fact that people who consume nutritionally poor diets have lower incomes does not prove that a poor diet leads to a lower income.

(E) Superior attention to detail is not necessary for success in business if one has creative ideas. The fact that some businesspeople are successful but cannot generate original ideas proves that they must have superior attention to detail.

STOP

IF YOU FINISH BEFORE TIME IS CALLED, YOU MAY CHECK YOUR WORK ON THIS EXAM ONLY.
DO NOT WORK ON ANY OTHER EXAM IN THE BOOK.

Lecture 11 Examination

ANSWERS

1. A
2. E
3. A
4. B
5. E
6. C
7. C
8. A
9. D
10. C
11. D
12. E
13. B
14. E
15. D

IN-CLASS EXAM **ICE** LECTURE **1**

EXPLANATIONS

1. **Choice (D) is the correct answer.**

This is an Inference question since the stem asks you to find something that must be true. You can combine repeated concepts in the two given statements and Prephrase an inference: *if you have no familiarity with Italian, then you will miss many of the nuances of the pieces on display.* The correct answer choice is likely to be close to this Prephrased answer.

(A)   If you miss many of the nuances of the exhibited works, you have no familiarity with Italian.

Is it guaranteed that if you miss many of the nuances of the pieces, you have no familiarity with Italian?

No. This gets the Prephrased inference backwards. Even someone familiar with Italian could miss the nuances for another reason, such as not paying close attention.

(B)   You will notice all of the nuances of the pieces on display if you are fluent in Italian.

Is it guaranteed that you will notice all of the nuances of the pieces if you are fluent in Italian?

No. Again, even someone familiar with Italian could miss the nuances for another reason, such as not paying close attention. Also, the passage only mentions familiarity, never fluency, so this choice is **out of scope**.

(C)   If you are able to use the museum's guide, you will miss some of the details of the pieces on display.

Is it guaranteed that if you are able to use the museum's guide, you will miss some of the details?

No. This doesn't make much sense at all. It seems like the guide would help you catch the details, not miss them.

(D)   You will fail to notice many of the details of the exhibited works if you lack any knowledge of Italian.

Is it guaranteed that you will fail to notice many of the details if you lack any knowledge of Italian?

Yes. Even though the wording has been rearranged, this means precisely the same thing as the Prephrased answer. Don't be fooled by paraphrasing; if an answer choice has the same meaning as what you predicted, pick it.

(E)   If you use the museum's guide, you have no knowledge of Italian.

Is it guaranteed that if you use the museum's guide, you have no knowledge of Italian?

No. Those using the museum's guide are familiar with Italian. This is an **opposite** distracter.

2. **Choice (A) is the correct answer.**

This is an Inference question since the stem asks you to find something that can be inferred. There are no obvious Prephrased inferences to come up with here, so move on and attack the answer choices using the **Real Question**.

(A)   A greater percentage of certified plastic surgeons will be female in five years.

Is it guaranteed that a greater percentage of certified plastic surgeons will be female in five years?

Yes. This is simply a restatement of information from the passage. The percentage of plastic surgeons who are female is higher than it used to be, and the change in this percentage will continue over the next decade. So there will certainly be a higher percentage of female plastic surgeons in five years.

(B)   A growing proportion of medical school students intend to become plastic surgeons.

Is it guaranteed that a growing proportion of medical school students intend to become plastic surgeons?

No. The passage gives no information about trends within the group of all medical students. This is **out of scope**.

(C)   Females pass the plastic surgery board certification exams at a lower rate than males.

Is it guaranteed that females pass the plastic surgery board certification exams at a lower rate than males?

No. Even though many more men have passed the exam, it may simply be because many more men take the exam. The passage does not give any information about rates of passing the exam.

(D)   Female plastic surgeons are superior to their male counterparts.

Is it guaranteed that female plastic surgeons are superior to their male counterparts?

No. The passage mentions one way in which female surgeons are believed to have an advantage, but it does not mention any way to determine overall superiority.

(E)   Plastic surgeons that operate without board certification are subject to severe fines.

Is it guaranteed that plastic surgeons that operate without board certification are subject to severe fines?

No. The passage doesn't mention anything about what happens to those who operate without board certification. This is **out of scope**.

3. **Choice (D) is the correct answer.**

This is an Inference question because the stem asks you to find an answer choice *supported by* the passage. There are no obvious Prephrased inferences to come up with here, so move on and attack the answer choices using the **Real Question**.

(A)   Fashion designers do not get due credit for their creative output because it is so quickly copied by others.

Is it guaranteed that fashion designers do not get credit for their output?

No. The passage mentions nothing about getting credit for anything. This is **out of scope**.

(B)   Because of the similarity of their case to the boat hull case, fashion designers will win the copyright protection they are seeking.

Is it guaranteed that fashion designers will win the copyright protection they are seeking?

No. The passage give no information that would help predict the future of the case. This is a **time mismatch**.

(C)   Clothing designs are not widely considered to be creative material.

Is it guaranteed that clothing designs are not widely considered to be creative material?

No. The passage gives some information about clothing's legal status, but there is no information about how it is widely viewed by the general public.

(D)   Clothing designs currently receive less than three years of copyright protection.

Is it guaranteed that clothing designs currently receive less than three years of copyright protection?

Yes. Even though the passage does not reveal the current length of protection, it says that designers are seeking the three-year term of copyright protection in order to eliminate the problem of stores copying their designs. In order for the requested term to eliminate the problem, it must be longer, not shorter, than the current term.

(E)   High-end fashion companies are unprofitable due to the unrestrained copying of their creative ideas.

Is it guaranteed that high-end fashion companies are unprofitable?

No. Perhaps they are losing some revenue due to copying, but there is not enough information to say that they are unprofitable overall.

4. **Choice (E) is the correct answer.**

This is an Inference question since the stem asks you to find something that must be true. There are no obvious Prephrased inferences to come up with here, but it is worth noticing that the passage talks only about the past, so answer choices that predict the future will be wrong.

(A)   Only new buildings have condominiums that offer large balconies.

Is it guaranteed that only new buildings have condominiums that offer large balconies?

No. The passage doesn't mention anything about what types of buildings generally offer large balconies.

(B)   None of the condominium units in the new building will lose value in the next five years.

Is it guaranteed that none of the condominiums in the new building will lose value in the next five years?

No. Past trends may not continue into the future. This is a **time mismatch**.

(C)   All condominiums in old buildings lost value over the last five years.

Is it guaranteed that all condominiums in old buildings lost value over the last five years?

No. You know that most losers were located in old buildings, but that doesn't mean that every condo in an old building was a loser.

(D)   Investors will profit on the condominium units in the new building.

Is it guaranteed that investors will profit on the condominium units in the new building?

No. Again, past trends may not continue into the future. This is a **time mismatch**.

(E)   Some condominiums that are not in old buildings lost value over the last five years.

Is it guaranteed that some condominiums that are not in old buildings lost value over the last five years?

Yes. Only ninety percent of the condos that lost value over the last five years are in old buildings. Hence, at least some must not be in old buildings.

5. **Choice (B) is the correct answer.**

This is an Inference EXCEPT question. Use the normal **Real Question** (*"Is this guaranteed to be true?"*) and mark **G** next to the four answer choices that are guaranteed. Pick the answer choice that is different—it will be the only one without a **G**.

(A)   Not all border control involves impenetrable walls.

Lecture 1 Explanations

Is it guaranteed that not all border control involves impenetrable walls?

This is guaranteed. The author asserts that building such walls is just one form of border control, so there must be other forms. Put a *G*.

(B)   The policy sufficient for effectively managing immigration does not include border control.

Is it guaranteed that good immigration policy does not include border control?

This is not guaranteed. You know there is an effective immigration policy and that it doesn't employ impenetrable walls, but you don't know whether it includes border control. Don't put a *G*.

(C)   Some policies are affected by their makers' level of creativity.

Is it guaranteed that some policies are affected by their makers' level of creativity?

This is guaranteed. The passage mentions one such policy: building impenetrable walls. Put a *G*.

(D)   In peacetime, immigration can be managed without impenetrable walls.

Is it guaranteed that in peacetime immigration can be managed without impenetrable walls?

This is guaranteed. The passage says that the effective policy is distinct, or different, from the one that uses walls. Put a *G*.

(E)   The construction of impenetrable walls is influenced by policymakers' level of creativity.

Is it guaranteed that the construction of walls is influenced by policymakers' level of creativity?

This is guaranteed. When policymakers react by building walls, it is because they lacked the creativity to come up with a different policy. Put a *G*.

Choice (B) is different from the rest, since it is the only choice without a *G*.

6. **Choice (D) is the correct answer.**

This is an Inference question because the stem asks you to find an answer choice *supported by* the passage. This passage lends itself strongly to a good Prephrased answer. If magazines will attempt to pass on the new cost, yet it's *unlikely* that they'll pass on the cost to their advertisers, then it's *likely* that they'll pass on the cost to subscribers, their only other revenue source.

(A)   Interest in magazines has dropped as use of the Internet has increased.

Is it guaranteed that interest in magazines has dropped as use of the Internet has increased?

No. You have no information about interest in magazines or about the Internet. This is **out of scope**.

(B)   All costs of supply for magazine publishers will remain steady for years.

Is it guaranteed that all costs of supply for magazine publishers will remain steady for years?

No. You are given no information about future supply costs, only past trends. This is a **time mismatch**.

(C)   Magazine publishers will not raise advertising rates again for many years.

Is it guaranteed that magazine publishers will not raise advertising rates again for many years?

No. The passage discusses what may happen to ad rates in the near future, but not what can be expected for many years. This is a **time mismatch**.

(D)   Magazine publishers are likely to increase the cost of subscriptions in the near future.

Is it guaranteed that magazine publishers are likely to increase the cost of subscriptions in the near future?

Yes. This is a close match for the Prephrased inference and is well supported by the passage.

(E)   Magazine publishers will be unprofitable until postage rates are reduced.

Is it guaranteed that magazine publishers will be unprofitable until postage rates are reduced?

No. The passage does not discuss profitability in any way. This is **out of scope**.

7. **Choice (B) is the correct answer.**

This is an Inference question since the stem asks you to find an answer choice that *follows logically*. This passage contains a common feature on the LSAT. It's called the *Most-Most Overlap*. If most (over 50%) of a group has a certain characteristic, and most of the same group also has a second characteristic, there MUST be some members of the group that have both characteristics. The correct answer will likely refer to this.

(A)   All five of the applicants whose applications were received today meet the two requirements of the job.

Is it guaranteed that all five of the applicants meet the two requirements of the job?

No. In fact, you know for certain that some applicants do not meet the requirements, since two of them aren't old enough, and two don't have enough experience. This is an **opposite** distracter.

(B)   At least one of the five applicants whose applications were received today meets the two requirements for the job.

Is it guaranteed that at least one of the applicants meets the two requirements for the job?

Yes. This matches the Prephrased inference. Essentially, there are six qualifications to distribute among only five people, so at least one person has to have more than one qualification.

(C)   At least one of the five applicants whose applications were received today will be hired.

Is it guaranteed that at least one of the applicants will be hired?

No. The passage does not discuss who will be hired.

(D)   None of the five applicants whose applications were received today will be hired.

Is it guaranteed that none of the five applicants will be hired?

No. Since at least one person does meet both requirements, it's at least possible that someone will be hired.

(E)   Three of the five applicants whose applications were received today meet the two requirements for the job.

Is it guaranteed that three of the applicants meet the two requirements for the job?

No. It's possible that one or two of the applicants meet the first but not the second requirement, and another one or two meet the second but not the first.

8. **Choice (A) is the correct answer.**

This is an Inference question since the stem asks you to find an answer choice *supported by* the passage. There are no obvious Prephrased inferences to come up with here, so just make sure you understand what was said and move on to the answer choices.

(A)   Knowledge of an author's personal relationships is usually necessary to better understand the message of a work written by that author.

Is it guaranteed that knowledge of an author's personal relationships is usually necessary to better understand the message of a work?

Yes. The passage states that an author's message can generally be deciphered only with knowledge of his or her interpersonal interactions. This answer choice simply restates the same idea and uses appropriately qualified language.

(B)   Socio-cultural conditions always play an important role in influencing an author.

Is it guaranteed that socio-cultural conditions always play an important role in influencing an author?

No. The passage merely says it is generally (not always) true that these factors play a role. This answer choice is **extreme**.

(C)   Authors who lived in culturally interesting eras and places wrote books that are more widely studied today.

Is it guaranteed that those authors wrote books that are more widely studied today?

No. The passage contains no discussion of what types of books are studied more. This is **out of scope**.

(D)   The academic study of literature is questionable as it necessarily fails in its primary pursuit.

Is it guaranteed that such study will necessarily fail in its primary pursuit?

No. The passage says that it is impeded by the factors being discussed, but not guaranteed to fail. This is **extreme**.

(E)   Lack of knowledge of an author's surroundings impedes our understanding only of older works.

Is it guaranteed that lack of knowledge of an author's surroundings impedes our understanding only of older works?

No. The passage says the point being made applies particularly to older works, but not exclusively to them. This is **extreme**.

9. **Choice (E) is the correct answer.**

This is an Inference question since the stem asks you to find an answer choice *supported by* the passage. There are no obvious Prephrased inferences to come up with here, so just make sure you understand what was said and move on to the answer choices.

(A)   Bonnard was not considered a successful artist while he was alive.

Is it guaranteed that Bonnard was not considered a successful artist while he was alive?

No. The passage says his reputation was damaged, but it does not say whether he was viewed as successful.

(B)   Bonnard's paintings are viewed as a good investment by many collectors.

Is it guaranteed that Bonnard's paintings are viewed as a good investment by many collectors?

No. You are told about a recent surge in value, but you don't know whether collectors think it will continue.

(C)   Bonnard has been more heavily criticized than most painters of his era.

Is it guaranteed that Bonnard has been more heavily criticized than most painters of his era?

No. The passage makes no comparison between him and other painters. This is **out of scope.**

(D)   Bonnard is currently the most studied French painter of the twentieth century.

Is it guaranteed that Bonnard is currently the most studied French painter of the twentieth century?

No. The passage does not mention how much other painters are studied. This is **out of scope.**

(E)   Some paintings attributed to Bonnard are not entirely his own work.

Is it guaranteed that some paintings attributed to Bonnard are not entirely his own work?

Yes. This follows from the claim that many of his paintings were re-touched by others before sale.

10.   **Choice (E) is the correct answer.**

This is a Cannot Be True question. Remember to use the correct **Real Question** for this question type: *"Is this impossible?"*

(A)   Some people think all advertisements are unethical.

Is it impossible that some people think all advertisements are unethical?

No. This could be true. You might be able to find some people who indeed think this.

(B)   Some advertisements are meticulously candid.

Is it impossible that some advertisements are meticulously candid?

No. This could be true. The passage suggests that there could indeed be some meticulously candid ads.

(C)   Some people define an advertisement's function as conveying all the positives and negatives of its product.

Is it impossible that some people define an advertisement's function that way?

No. This could be true. You might be able to find some people who indeed agree with this.

(D)   Some advertisements that omit certain truths do not increase sales.

Is it impossible that some truth-omitting advertisements do not increase sales?

No. This could be true. Even though omitting truths is necessary for increasing sales, there might be other things that are necessary too, such as a good price on the item. So an ad that leaves out some truths might not increase sales if the price on the item is too high.

(E)   Some meticulously candid advertisements increase sales.

Is it impossible that some meticulously candid advertisements increase sales?

Yes. You know this is impossible from the last sentence in the passage, which says that a meticulously candid ad will never increase sales.

11.   **Choice (B) is the correct answer.**

This is an Inference question because the stem asks you to find an answer choice that can be *inferred.* There are no obvious Prephrased inferences to come up with here, so move on and attack the answer choices using the **Real Question**.

(A)   No major volcanic eruptions occurred in the Aegean region after the Late Bronze Age.

Is it guaranteed that no major volcanic eruptions occurred in the region after the Late Bronze Age?

No. The passage mentions nothing about later eruptions. This is a **time mismatch.**

(B)   The beginning of the Late Bronze Age in the Aegean region predated the New Kingdom in Egypt.

Is it guaranteed that the Late Bronze Age in the Aegean predated the New Kingdom in Egypt?

Yes. Since the Late Bronze Age in the Aegean region was thought to have begun in the 16th century B.C., but is now known beyond doubt to have begun at least a century earlier, then it must have begun before Egypt's New Kingdom, which began in the 16th century B.C.

(C)   The pottery of Egypt's New Kingdom influenced the pottery of civilizations in the Aegean region.

Is it guaranteed that the pottery of Egypt's New Kingdom influenced that in the Aegean region?

No. The passage says that the styles are similar, but that doesn't guarantee that one influenced the other.

(D)   Radiocarbon-dating tests are the only reliable way to determine the exact date of volcanic eruptions.

Is it guaranteed that radiocarbon dating is the only reliable way to determine the date of eruptions?

No. Clearly, these tests are one reliable way to determine dates, but calling them the only reliable way is **extreme.**

(E)   The Late Bronze Age in the Aegean region ended at least a century earlier than previously thought.

Is it guaranteed that the Aegean Late Bronze Age ended a century earlier than previously thought?

No. The passage does not discuss anything about the supposed duration or end date of the period.

12.   **Choice (C) is the correct answer.**

This is an Inference question since the stem asks you to find an answer choice *supported by* the passage. There are no obvious Prephrased inferences to come up with here, so just make sure you understand what was said and move on to the answer choices.

(A)   The online overseas textbook distributors are operating in violation of American law.

Is it guaranteed that the online overseas textbook distributors are violating American law?

No. The information given suggests that the online distributors are probably operating legally, though you can't say with total certainty.

(B)   The softcover versions of the textbooks produced overseas are not inferior to the hardcover versions produced domestically.

Is it guaranteed that the softcover versions are not inferior to the domestic hardcover versions?

No. The passage tells you nothing about the quality of the books. This is **out of scope**.

(C)   Students cannot legally order the cheaper textbooks for the purpose of selling them at a profit.

Is it guaranteed that students cannot legally order the cheaper textbooks to sell them at a profit?

Yes. You are told that students who buy the foreign books can only legally do so for personal use, so this answer choice, which describes a non-personal, commercial use of the books, must be true.

(D)   The Supreme Court ruling is not applicable to digital content.

Is it guaranteed that the Supreme Court ruling is not applicable to digital content?

No. The passage only talks about manufactured goods and doesn't mention digital content. This is **out of scope**.

(E)   There are no tariffs on the import of foreign-made textbooks.

Is it guaranteed that there are no tariffs on the import of foreign-made textbooks?

No. The passage tells you nothing about tariffs on the books. This is **out of scope**.

13.   **Choice (B) is the correct answer.**

This is an Inference question since the stem asks you to find an answer choice *supported by* the passage. This passage puts forth a set of rules but does not lead to any obvious Prephrased inferences, so just make sure you understand the rules and move on to the answer choices.

(A)   Most staff members at the store do not have any choice about which shifts they work.

Is it guaranteed that most staff members at the store do not have any choice about which shifts they work?

No. You don't know anything about how many staff members fall into each category.

(B)   Juan has never been docked pay before and has worked at the store for one year, so he has no choice about which shifts he works.

Is it guaranteed that Juan has no choice about which shifts he works?

Yes. The only employees that get a choice of shifts are those who have worked there for more than two years, and Juan is not in that group. Thus, Juan doesn't get a choice.

(C)   Lau has worked at the store longer than any other staff member, so he will get to choose his shifts first.

Is it guaranteed that Lau will get to choose his shifts first?

No. Perhaps he had his pay docked for misconduct. Also, the passage doesn't say that tenure determines the order of choosing.

(D)   Rasheed has worked at the store for four years, but has been docked pay for misconduct on many occasions, so he does not have any choice about which shifts he works.

Is it guaranteed that Rasheed does not have any choice about which shifts he works?

No. Rasheed will have to choose after anyone who hasn't had docked pay, but since he has been there for over two years, he will have a choice. This is an **opposite** distracter.

(E)   Angela has worked at the store for three years and has never been docked pay for misconduct, so she gets to choose her shifts first.

Is it guaranteed that Angela gets to choose her shifts first?

No. She'll be ahead of those who have been docked, but you can't say she'll be first.

14. Choice (A) is the correct answer.

This is an Inference question because the stem asks you to find an answer choice that can be *properly concluded.* You can do a little inferring and Prephrasing here. If Country A had more schools *per person* and more *people,* then Country A must have had more schools overall. What's more, if each country closed the same number of schools, then Country A must still have more schools.

(A)   Country A presently has more schools than Country B.

Is it guaranteed that Country A presently has more schools than Country B?

Yes. This is a perfect match for the Prephrased inference.

(B)   Country A and Country B both presently have fewer schools than they need.

Is it guaranteed that Country A and Country B both presently have fewer schools than they need?

No. The passage never mentions what the countries need. This is **out of scope.**

(C)   Country A presently has more schools per capita than Country B.

Is it guaranteed that Country A presently has more schools per capita than Country B?

No. If the populations of the countries changed drastically, then the per capita numbers may have changed as well.

(D)   Country A presently has more people than Country B.

Is it guaranteed that Country A presently has more people than Country B?

No. This was true last year, but you don't know if it's still true. This is a **time mismatch.**

(E)   Country A and Country B presently have the same number of schools.

Is it guaranteed that Country A and Country B presently have the same number of schools?

No. This is definitely false, according to the Prephrased inference. This is an **opposite** distracter.

15. Choice (C) is the correct answer.

This is an Inference question since the stem asks you to find an answer choice *supported by* the passage. There is a Prephrased inference lurking in here. You're told that the tax cut will encourage people to use more gasoline, and that as people decide to use more gasoline, its price increases. Since no other factors will change, it follows that the tax cut will be accompanied by a base price *increase* as people decide to use more of the cheaper gasoline.

(A)   Gasoline is currently too expensive for the average family.

Is it guaranteed that gasoline is currently too expensive for the average family?

No. The passage doesn't mention average families or what they can afford. This is **out of scope.**

(B)   The current high price of gasoline is a detriment to overall economic productivity.

Is it guaranteed that the current high price of gasoline is a detriment to overall economic productivity?

No. The passage doesn't mention economic productivity. This is **out of scope.**

(C)   The proposed gasoline tax cut would decrease the overall price of gasoline by less than ten cents per gallon.

Is it guaranteed that the tax cut would decrease the price of gasoline by less than ten cents per gallon?

Yes. Taxes go down by ten cents, but the base price rises because of increased demand. The overall price will be reduced by less than ten cents.

(D)   Taxes on gasoline are currently higher than they should be.

Is it guaranteed that taxes on gasoline are currently higher than they should be?

No. The passage doesn't discuss what taxes should be. This is **out of scope.**

(E)   Reducing gasoline taxes is the only way the legislature can help lower the price of gasoline.

Is it guaranteed that reducing gasoline taxes is the only way the legislature can help lower the price of gasoline?

No. Perhaps the legislature could do something to decrease demand.

IN-CLASS EXAM ICE LECTURE 2

EXPLANATIONS

1. **Choice (C) is the correct answer.**

   This is a Complete question, so you are looking for the answer choice that contains the conclusion. In this case, you can Prephrase an answer because the passage contains a counterargument. The critics say that physical education should not be included in the curricula. The author's conclusion must be the negation of that: [Physical education *should* be included in the curricula.]

   For each answer choice, the **Real Question** is, "*Is this the conclusion?*"

   (A) critics are wrong when they say physical education classes will be removed from the curricula of elementary schools

   No. Although the author thinks the critics are wrong, this misrepresents the critics' position. They don't predict the future.

   (B) many of the subjects traditionally taught at elementary schools are not valuable

   No. The argument is about physical education, not many subjects. This is **extreme**.

   (C) devoting some class time to physical education is not incompatible with the goal of maximizing the education of students

   Yes. This is a little more complicated than the Prephrased answer, but it does suggest that physical education has value, and it refutes the critics' position.

   (D) children who are physically unhealthy cannot be good students

   No. You know there is a link between health and learning ability, but this answer choice is **extreme**.

   (E) schools should allocate more class time to physical education, even if it comes at the expense of standard academic subjects

   No. This is **extreme**. The author advocates including it in the curricula, but says nothing to support the idea that it should take the place of other subjects.

2. **Choice (D) is the correct answer.**

   This Point at Issue question contains an explicit disagreement. John says novices win by making "inadvisable betting decisions." Beth contradicts him by saying that any decision that leads to winning is a "good move." Look for an answer choice that expresses this disagreement.

   For each answer choice, the **Real Question** is, "*Do the speakers voice disagreement about this?*"

   (A) novices have an advantage against experienced poker players

   No. Both speakers state that novices can beat experienced players. This is a **point of agreement**.

   (B) first-time poker players win less often than experienced players

   No. Both say that novices can beat experienced players, but neither addresses which group wins more or less often. This is **out of scope**.

   (C) experienced players are good at guessing which cards a novice has

   No. Beth does not mention this topic at all, so this is **one-sided**.

   (D) the betting decisions described by John are inadvisable

   Yes. John says they are inadvisable, while Beth describes them as a good move.

   (E) luck or skill plays a greater role in poker

   No. Neither speaker mentions luck. This is **out of scope**.

3. **Choice (B) is the correct answer.**

   This is a Main Point question. The conclusion of the argument is: [The Stoic definition (of what is good) is problematic.] You know this is the conclusion because it sounds more like an opinion that anything else in the argument, and you can also use the Why Tool. The rest of the argument provides evidence as to why the definition is problematic.

   For each answer choice, the **Real Question** is, "*Is this the conclusion?*"

   (A) Stoicism is the oldest known Hellenistic philosophy.

   No. You know it's old, but the claim that it's the oldest is **extreme**.

   (B) The Stoic definition of what is good is problematic.

   Yes. This is a perfect match for the Prephrased answer.

   (C) Only objects or qualities that are always beneficial can be defined as good.

   No. This matches the Stoic philosophy, but not the author's conclusion.

   (D) Material wealth can ultimately be harmful to a person.

   No. This again matches the Stoic philosophy, but not the author's conclusion.

   (E) Courage should not be considered one of the characteristic human virtues.

No. This is **incomplete**. The discussion of courage is only one example designed to support the larger point about the Stoic definition as a whole.

4. **Choice (D) is the correct answer.**

This Point at Issue question contains an explicit disagreement. Tony says that Haydn "never would have used" electronic instruments and effects, but Fernandez says "there is no reason to believe he would not have" used every available instrument. Look for an answer choice that expresses this disagreement.

For each answer choice, the **Real Question** is, "*Do the speakers voice disagreement about this?*"

(A)   popular music today is inferior to classical music produced in Europe in the 18th and 19th centuries

No. Fernandez does not address popular music today. This is **one-sided**.

(B)   Haydn's music is indisputably good

No. This is a **point of agreement**, since both speakers explicitly call Haydn's music good.

(C)   Haydn's music is repetitive

No. Both speakers compare the repetitiveness of Haydn's music to others, with Tony citing music more repetitive than Haydn's and Fernandez citing music less repetitive than Haydn's, but you don't know for sure whether either of them would classify Haydn's music as repetitive in general.

(D)   Haydn would have used electronic instruments had they been available to him

Yes. Tony says he would not have, while Fernandez says he would have.

(E)   Beethoven's music is superior to that of Haydn

No. Tony never mentions Beethoven, so this is **one-sided**.

5. **Choice (A) is the correct answer.**

This Complete question does not contain a counterargument, but it still provides you with some clues as to where it is leading. It starts by describing the traditional manner of writing headlines, then uses the word *however* to show this technique isn't fully compatible with the new method of looking for news, suggesting a weakness. Look for an answer choice that captures this context.

For each answer choice, the **Real Question** is, "*Is this the conclusion?*"

(A)   to best attract readers using Internet search engines, headlines cannot be written in the traditional manner

Yes. If the traditional manner isn't compatible with Internet search engines, then it can't be the best way to attract readers. This choice also works with the **Why Tool**. The entire passage provides an answer as to why this answer choice is true.

(B)   more readers are getting their news from the Internet today than from more traditional sources

No. The number of readers using the various methods is not mentioned and is **out of scope**.

(C)   search engines represent the fastest-growing Internet-related industry

No. Other Internet-related industries are not mentioned. This is **out of scope**.

(D)   despite technological advancements, the Internet remains a poor means of collecting information

No. One particular weakness of search engines is discussed, but that's a long way from saying that the Internet is a poor means of collecting information. This choice is **extreme**.

(E)   journalists and copy editors who received their training before the Internet was invented are now obsolete

No. Calling a whole class of people obsolete is certainly more **extreme** that anything the passage supports.

6. **Choice (D) is the correct answer.**

This is a Main Point question. The passage contains a suggestion, which is almost always the conclusion. If you use the **Why Tool** on it, the rest of the passage provides an explanation as to why the author believes it. So the suggestion that [the cost of enacting that legislation should be borne by large corporations alone] is the conclusion.

For each answer choice, the **Real Question** is, "*Is this the conclusion?*"

(A)   Legislation should be enacted to reduce the influence that monetary campaign contributions have in elections.

No. The author states that the legislation would be beneficial, but the conclusion is about who should bear the cost.

(B)   Corporations are subject to a lower rate of taxation than they were a decade ago.

No. This was stated in the argument, but it's a **premise**.

(C)   The undue advantages enjoyed by such contributors primarily benefit corporations.

No. This is another **premise**.

(D)   The cost of enacting the proposed legislation should be borne by large corporations alone.

Yes. This is a perfect match for the Prephrased conclusion.

(E)   A reduction in the influence that monetary campaign contributions have in elections will benefit all citizens.

No. This is another **premise**.

7.   **Choice (A) is the correct answer.**

This Point at Issue question contains an explicit disagreement. Kernodle says, "All the records… should be considered invalid," but Ngobeh says, "We can only invalidate the records of those who have been proven to have broken the rules." Look for an answer choice that expresses this disagreement.

For each answer choice, the **Real Question** is, *"Do the speakers voice disagreement about this?"*

(A)   all of the records set over the past decade should be considered invalid

Yes. Kernodle says they all should be invalidated, but Ngobeh advocates this action for only some.

(B)   users of performance-enhancing drugs are the worst kind of cheaters

No. Ngobeh does not mention what kind of cheating is the worst, so this is **one-sided**.

(C)   any players from this era should be eligible for induction into the Hall of Fame

No. Kernodle mentions the Hall of Fame, but Ngobeh never does, so this is **one-sided**.

(D)   performance-enhancing drugs helped users set records

No. Neither speaker says anything about the effects of using the drugs. This is **out of scope**.

(E)   many players used illegal drugs other than performance enhancers

No. Ngobeh mentions other illegal substances, but Kernodle never does, so this is **one-sided**.

8.   **Choice (D) is the correct answer.**

This Main Point contains a counterargument of sorts against the most widely accepted explanation for dinosaur extinction. That counterargument is presented when the author states that [facts ignored by this theory must have played a role.] The last sentence is the **premise** that explains why the author believes this conclusion to be true.

For each answer choice, the **Real Question** is, *"Is this the conclusion?"*

(A)   A massive meteor impact created the adverse conditions that led to the extinction of the dinosaurs.

No. This is the claim the author is arguing against.

(B)   Many dinosaur species were beginning to go extinct before the impact that is thought to have caused their extinction.

No. This is a **premise** that supports the conclusion.

(C)   No meteor impact contributed to the extinction of the dinosaurs.

No. This is **extreme**. The author thinks there were other factors as well, not that the meteor had nothing to do with it.

(D)   Causes aside from a meteor impact must have contributed to the extinction of the dinosaurs.

Yes. This is a good match for the Prephrased answer.

(E)   Large meteor impacts sometimes do not lead to mass extinctions.

No. You know this is true, but it basically just restates part of the **premise** in the last sentence.

9.   **Choice (B) is the correct answer.**

This is a Point at Issue question. Regarding the issue of spending tax revenue in the most beneficial manner for citizens, Rebecca states, "Only when the government keeps citizens informed can this obligation be met." Miriam contradicts this by saying, "This can be achieved without informing the citizens." Look for an answer choice that expresses this disagreement.

For each answer choice, the **Real Question** is, *"Do the speakers voice disagreement about this?"*

(A)   Committing to a general principle of justice is necessary to bring about a just allocation of tax revenues.

No. Rebecca doesn't mention a general principle of justice, so this is **one-sided**.

(B)   Informing citizens of tax revenue allocation is a necessary condition for allocating such revenue in the way most beneficial to citizens.

Yes. Rebecca states that it is necessary, while Miriam says it's not.

(C)   A government has a duty to spend its tax revenues in a way most beneficial to its citizens.

No. Both speakers confirm this, so this is a **point of agreement**.

(D)   Allocating tax revenue in a way most beneficial to citizens is possible if citizens are made aware of how taxes are being spent.

No. Although Rebecca says informing the citizens is necessary, you don't know if she thinks anything else is necessary as well, so you don't know if she thinks the most beneficial allocation is made possible simply by making citizens aware. Since you don't know if Rebecca agrees with this choice, it's **one-sided**.

(E)   A government ought to keep its citizens informed of how it spends tax revenues.

No. Miriam says keeping citizens informed is not necessary, but you don't know if she thinks the government ought to do it anyway. This is also **one-sided**.

10.   **Choice (B) is the correct answer.**

This is a Main Point question, but you need to do a little work to express the conclusion in a concise way. Two theories are presented. The author says the first is supported by circumstantial evidence, but the second has much more convincing evidence behind it. A good Prephrased conclusion is: [the theory about educational television has stronger evidence than the theory about classical music.] The entire passage works together to support this conclusion.

For each answer choice, the **Real Question** is, "*Is this the conclusion?*"

(A)   Playing classical music for children, in infancy or in later life, probably does not help them attain academic success.

No. This is **extreme**. The author says the theory about classical music has less support, not that it's wrong.

(B)   There is more reason to believe in the benefits of educational television programs than in those of classical music in improving children's academic success.

Yes. This means the same thing as the Prephrased answer.

(C)   Only theories backed by studies covering a variety of people and circumstances should be accepted.

No. The passage makes no mention of which theories should be accepted, and it makes no blanket statements covering all theories. This is **out of scope**.

(D)   Showing educational television programs to children is recommended by more professionals than is any other method of improving children's academic capabilities.

No. The passage compares only two methods, and does not provide any evidence to say how often they are recommended. This is **out of scope**.

(E)   Even professionals are unable to suggest reliable methods to improve a child's likelihood of eventual academic success.

No. This is **extreme** and doesn't match the Prephrased answer at all.

11.   **Choice (B) is the correct answer.**

The passage for this Main Point question consists almost entirely of things that sound like facts. The only thing that sounds remotely like an opinion is the statement that the [new documents…call into question established notions of how he lived.] This also sounds a little like a counterargument, and the rest of the passage provides an explanation as to why the author believes this claim, so this is the conclusion.

For each answer choice, the **Real Question** is, "*Is this the conclusion?*"

(A)   Mozart earned 10,000 florins per year, which would have been in the top five percent of incomes in his time.

No. This is a **premise**. You can tell because it is simply a calculation, which is factual—not really debatable.

(B)   New evidence demands a reconsideration of previously held beliefs about Mozart's wealth.

Yes. This matches the meaning of the Prephrased conclusion.

(C)   Mozart was quite rich and lived his whole life much more comfortably than previously thought.

No. The conclusion calls for a reconsideration, but this answer choice makes a definitive statement.

(D)   Analysis of Mozart's grave and letters in which he requested loans indicate that Mozart was quite poor throughout his life.

No. The conclusion is that views about Mozart's financial situation should be questioned, but this answer choice makes a definitive statement.

(E)   New evidence indicates that Mozart had a gambling problem and lost most of his wealth to gambling debts.

No. Again, this choice makes a definitive statement about Mozart, which the conclusion didn't do.

12.   **Choice (E) is the correct answer.**

This is a Point of Agreement question—you have to pay close attention to the question stem to keep from confusing this type of question with Point at Issue questions. The passage here is very complex, and it is difficult to Prephrase any immediately obvious point of agreement. When this happens, just move on to the answer choices.

For each answer choice, the **Real Question** is, *"Do the speakers voice agreement about this?"*

(A)   x-ray scattering is the most appropriate method by which to determine the structure of hydrogen bonds in water

No. Neither speaker compares x-ray scattering to any other method. This is **out of scope**.

(B)   if the molecules of water form rings and chains, nearly 80 percent of hydrogen bonds should be broken at any one time

No. Barrett would agree with this, but Voigt says that ring-and-chain models yield predictions inconsistent with the discovery that 80 percent are broken at any one time. This is a **point of disagreement**.

(C)   the hydrogen bonds between water molecules form a network of large rings or chains

No. This is a **point of disagreement**. Barrett says they form rings, but Voigt says they form tetrahedrons.

(D)   the fact that water is a liquid at unexpectedly high temperatures shows that its hydrogen bonds do not form tetrahedrons

No. Neither scientist uses the fact that water is a liquid to conclude anything—they use the x-ray scattering data and model predictions. In addition, they disagree about whether water forms tetrahedrons.

(E)   previous models in which water molecules were thought to form tetrahedrons did not predict that nearly 80 percent of hydrogen bonds should be broken at any one time

Yes. When presented with the discovery that nearly 80 percent of the bonds are broken, Barrett rejects the previous model, and Voigt revises the previous model. Thus, they are both showing that previous models did not predict that nearly 80 percent of the bonds should be broken.

13. **Choice (C) is the correct answer.**

This Main Point question starts out looking like it contains a counterargument when it says, "Many people think…" You would expect the conclusion to be the opposite of what many people think, namely that exercise is *not* healthy regardless of frequency. However, the author stops short of saying this, instead concluding that [both studies relied on unrepresentative samples.] The author doesn't conclude anything about the effects of exercise, just that the studies were problematic. The second half of the passage provides premises to explain why the samples were unrepresentative.

For each answer choice, the **Real Question** is, *"Is this the conclusion?"*

(A)   Proper studies of the effects of exercise should be conducted on those who do not exercise regularly as well as on those who do.

No. The conclusion is just about the two studies mentioned. The author never makes any suggestions.

(B)   Measuring the effects of exercising on health by only testing those who exercise regularly is like measuring the effects of secondhand smoke only on those who smoke regularly.

No. This analogy is a **premise**, not the main conclusion.

(C)   The studies that denied appreciable negative effects of daily exercise were based on flawed sample groups.

Yes. This means the same thing as the Prephrased answer.

(D)   Those people who frequent local health clubs are less likely to suffer negative effects of daily exercise than those who do not.

No. This claim never appeared in the argument. It's **out of scope**.

(E)   A study that included those people who do not exercise regularly would have shown that too much exercise can be unhealthy.

No. This choice predicts what would have happened in a hypothetical case, but there was no prediction in the passage.

14. **Choice (C) is the correct answer.**

In this Point at Issue question, Umaru says that the whale species "will become extinct" if the hunt continues, but Celeste says the population "can sustain" pre-1986 whaling levels, which necessarily includes the decades-old annual hunt. Look for an answer choice that expresses this disagreement.

For each answer choice, the **Real Question** is, *"Do the speakers voice disagreement about this?"*

(A)   the Moranese government's whale hunt will be profitable

No. Celeste acknowledges the possibility that the hunt may not be profitable, but she does not predict whether or not it will be, so you don't know whether she would agree with this choice. This is **one-sided**.

(B)   the Moranese government should continue the annual whale hunt indefinitely

No. Umaru definitely disagrees with this choice, but you can't say based on Celeste's comments that she thinks the hunt should be continued "indefinitely."

(C)   the Moranese government's whale hunt threatens to make the minke whales extinct

Yes. This is a good match for the Prephrased answer. Umaru says it does, but Celeste says it doesn't.

(D)   the Moranese government's whale hunt is in violation of the moratorium on whaling

No. Celeste, though she seems to support the hunt in general, doesn't say anything to indicate whether she believes it to be in violation of the moratorium. This is **one-sided**.

(E)   hunting an animal is unethical when that animal faces the risk of extinction

No. Since Celeste does not think the whale faces the risk of extinction, she provides no evidence for what she thinks in the case of an animal that does face that risk. This is **one-sided**.

15.   **Choice (C) is the correct answer.**

This Main Point question has a counterargument. When Ruehl says Bollen's argument is "misguided," you can Prephrase Ruehl's conclusion by negating Bollen's argument. In this case, the conclusion is: [artists *can* accept government funds when they intend to create works that they know will cause community controversy.] The rest of the passage provides premises to support this.

For each answer choice, the **Real Question** is, "*Is this the conclusion?*"

(A)   artists have the right to create any piece they choose

No. Ruehl's conclusion is about accepting funding, not about what artists have a right to create.

(B)   a divisive book is no different than a controversial painting

No. This is an analogy used as a **premise**.

(C)   artists are justified in accepting government funds even in cases in which that money will be used to create controversial works

Yes. This is a good match for the Prephrased answer.

(D)   Professor Bollen fails to consider ways in which public funding of art and that of libraries is similar

No. Ruehl is concerned with Bollen's stance on art funding, not his stance on library funding.

(E)   both artists and authors should be given whatever public funding they request, regardless of whether the community will be offended by what they produce

No. Ruehl's conclusion is about whether artists should accept public funds, not whether requests for funds should be granted.

IN-CLASS EXAM ICE LECTURE 3

EXPLANATIONS

1. **Choice (B) is the correct answer.**

    In this Flaw question, the conclusion is that [increased ice cream consumption must lead to a greater risk of drowning.] The flaw is one of the common flaws: the premises provide data showing a *correlation*, but the argument draws the conclusion that one thing *causes* the other. This is a *causal* flaw. It fails to consider that there could be a different cause—such as hot weather—that explains both the increased drownings and the increased ice cream sales.

    For each answer choice, the **Real Question** is, *"Is this a flaw in the argument?"*

    (A) It considers only a single factor in drawing its conclusion.

    No. Although this matches the argument, this is **not a flaw.** Since the conclusion is only about a single factor, considering a single factor is not a logical error.

    (B) It postulates the existence of a causal relationship where the data support only the existence of a correlative relationship.

    Yes. This is a good match for the Prephrased flaw.

    (C) It establishes a broad conclusion on the basis of an insufficiently representative data set.

    No. This **doesn't match** what happened in the argument. The data set and the conclusion are appropriately matched.

    (D) It takes for granted that if a statement must be true for the argument's conclusion to be true, then that statement's truth is sufficient for the truth of the conclusion.

    No. This answer choice describes a necessary vs. sufficient flaw, which is a real flaw, but it **doesn't match** what occurred in this argument.

    (E) It neglects to propose solutions to the problem presented.

    No. Although this matches what happened in the argument, this is not the reason the logic was questionable. This is **not a flaw.**

2. **Choice (B) is the correct answer.**

    This Flaw question asks you about the guest's logic, but make sure you understand both speakers. The guest's conclusion is that [the criticism is invalid,] but her premises concern only the qualifications of the talk show host, not the president or the logic of the criticism. This is a common flaw: a *personal attack.*

    For each answer choice, the **Real Question** is, *"Is this a flaw in the argument?"*

    (A) presupposes the opposing argument to be invalid on the basis of previous reasoning errors made in unrelated arguments by the person presenting the opposing argument

    No. The guest never mentions previous arguments made by the talk show host, so this **doesn't match** the argument.

    (B) addresses only the authority of the person making the opposing argument without addressing opposing argument itself

    Yes. This is a good match for the Prephrased flaw.

    (C) neglects to take into account whether the person making the opposing argument has sufficient first-hand experience in the subject matter being debated

    No. The guest does take into account the host's first-hand experience—in fact that's the whole reason the argument is flawed. This **doesn't match.**

    (D) presumes, without providing justification, that anyone criticizing the president must have ulterior political motives for doing so

    No. The guest never comes close to suggesting anything about ulterior motives. This **doesn't match.**

    (E) ignores the possibility that the qualities mentioned in the opposing argument are sufficient conditions for being a good president rather than necessary conditions for being a good president

    No. This describes a necessary vs. sufficient flaw, which is a real flaw when it occurs, but it **doesn't match** what occurred in this argument.

3. **Choice (E) is the correct answer.**

    This Flaw question contains the conclusion that [the restaurant chain was losing money as a result of the program.] The premises do establish *one cost* of the program—giving away free sandwiches—but there is a Concept Shift when the author jumps to drawing a conclusion about the *overall* profitability of the program. He neglected to consider any potential revenue the program generated, such as increased business.

    For each answer choice, the **Real Question** is, *"Is this a flaw in the argument?"*

    (A) overlooks the possibility that another program will be implemented to replace the program being phased out

    No. While the argument didn't consider any other programs, that's not the reason the argument was logically problematic. This is **not a flaw.**

(B)   overlooks the possible benefit to the sandwich chain of exaggerating its own market data

No. It's true that the argument didn't consider this possible benefit, but this is **not a flaw**. The problem was the overlooked benefits of the rewards program.

(C)   fails to consider whether any other retail food chains have opted to implement similar programs

No. The argument is not concerned with other food chains, so failing to consider them is **not a flaw**.

(D)   fails to consider whether the profit earned by the sandwich chain was sufficient to cover its losses from the program

No. This is tricky, but the conclusion is about the profitability of the rewards program, not the profitability of the restaurant chain overall.

(E)   overlooks possible benefits of the program while considering only its costs

Yes. This correctly describes what happened in the argument, and it correctly points to the reason why the argument is flawed.

4. **Choice (A) is the correct answer.**

The premises in this Flaw question establish that clean tap water and functioning traffic lights are *more important* than improvements to the park. But a Concept Shift occurs when the author draws the conclusion that [spending money on parks is a *misuse* of public money.] The flaw is that the author failed to consider the possibility that the municipality has enough money to accomplish all these goals simultaneously.

For each answer choice, the **Real Question** is, *"Is this a flaw in the argument?"*

(A)   presumes, without providing justification, that the other services cited cannot be provided if the amount proposed is allocated to park improvement

Yes. This correctly describes what happened in the argument, and it correctly points to the reason the argument is flawed. The author assumed that the government has to choose one or the other, when it may be possible to provide both.

(B)   fails to consider whether some residents drink primarily bottled water and thus would not benefit from improvements to the city's water filtration system

No. Although the argument really did fail to consider this possibility, this is **not a flaw** in the argument.

(C)   fails to consider the potential health benefits associated with the types of physical activity that are promoted and encouraged by the presence of parks

No. The premises established, regardless of health benefits, that residents prefer clean water and functioning traffic lights. This is **not a flaw** in the argument.

(D)   presumes, without providing justification, that many residents will benefit from the improvements made to the parks with the allocated funds

No. The argument never made this presumption. It said that people enjoy the parks, but it never implied anything about benefits. This **doesn't match** what happened in the argument.

(E)   overlooks the fact that all budgets passed by fairly elected city council members are legally valid

No. The argument is concerned with whether the spending is a poor use of public money, so there is no consideration of the legal validity of anything, nor should there be. This **doesn't match** the argument.

5. **Choice (C) is the correct answer.**

This is a Misinterpretation question, so look for the Concept Shift between the two speakers. Pete mentions giving consumers "a better idea" of the freshness of the produce, while Nitsa refers to factors that "determine" the freshness. In other words, Pete is just talking about *additional information* about the freshness, while Nitsa is talking about a *complete determination* of precisely the level of freshness. This is the Concept Shift, so look for an answer choice that expresses this.

For each answer choice, the **Real Question** is, *"Is this a misinterpretation in the passage?"*

(A)   produce is the only type of item at the grocery store that can spoil over time

No. Neither speaker mentions or alludes to other types of items that can spoil.

(B)   all consumers want to know how fresh their produce is

No. Nitsa doesn't mention anything about consumers, so she must have misinterpreted something else.

(C)   labeling produce with the harvest date would tell consumers exactly how fresh it is

Yes. Nitsa rebuts this point, but this is not the point that Pete was trying to make. This matches the Prephrased answer.

(D)   labeling produce with the harvest date would be
        easy and inexpensive

No. Neither speaker has anything to say about the ease or the cost of the idea.

(E)   produce can be exposed to temperature extremes
        during transport

No. This is something found in Nitsa's remarks, but the question stem asks for something that Nitsa thought was in Pete's remarks.

6. **Choice (D) is the correct answer.**

This Flaw question concludes that [the use of cellular phones while driving does not contribute to an increase in the rate of traffic accidents.] The premises begin by citing a study that reaches the opposite conclusion. The argument then goes on to show the study to be full of errors. The flaw in this argument is an *absence of evidence* flaw. By showing the study to be flawed, the author takes away support for the opposing position, but that alone is not enough to prove that his own position is true.

For each answer choice, the **Real Question** is, "*Is this a flaw in the argument?*"

(A)   fails to demonstrate that the review board
        knows more about cellular phones than do the
        transportation experts

No. It's true that the argument failed to demonstrate this, but this is not the reason the argument is faulty. This is **not a flaw**.

(B)   fails to elaborate on the specific nature of the
        errors in the data used for the study

No. Since the statement about the presence of errors is part of the premises, you must accept it as true. You don't need to know the specific nature of the errors. This is **not a flaw**.

(C)   fails to provide evidence that the increase in the
        rate of traffic accidents is due to some cause
        other than the use of cellular phones

No. The author concludes that there is no increase in the rate of traffic accidents, so he has no obligation to provide evidence of some other cause for a rate increase. This is **not a flaw**.

(D)   presumes, without providing justification, that
        failure to prove a hypothesis constitutes proof
        that the hypothesis is false

Yes. This matches what happened in the argument, and it is a flaw. It's also a good match for the Prephrased answer.

(E)   claims that because the study in question
        contained data errors, it is therefore impossible to
        devise a study that would be free of data errors

No. The argument never made any claim about it being impossible to devise a good study, so this **doesn't match** the argument.

7. **Choice (B) is the correct answer.**

The conclusion in this Flaw question is that [road rage is a greater problem,] but the only evidence to support that conclusion is that people think it occurs more frequently. The argument *appeals to the authority* of the general population, but there is no good reason to believe that the general population is a credible authority on the statistical frequency of the problem. Simply put, they may not know what they're talking about.

For each answer choice, the **Real Question** is, "*Is this a flaw in the argument?*"

(A)   presumes, without providing justification, that
        the same percentage of all adults in the province
        believe road rage to be more frequent now than
        ten years ago

No. There actually is some justification for presuming this, since the study was conducted by a "respected polling agency." This **doesn't match** the argument.

(B)   presumes, without providing justification, that
        what people generally believe to be true is
        actually true

Yes. This is a good match for the Prephrased answer.

(C)   draws an unequivocal conclusion based on data
        that only supports a conclusion drawn with 95
        percent confidence

No. The statement about 95 percent confidence is a reference to how small the margin of error is. Even if you're not familiar with statistics, think about it this way: if the confidence level had been 100 percent, would this be a good argument? No. It would still draw a conclusion based on the opinion of people who are not experts. So this is **not a flaw**.

(D)   fails to provide an adequate definition of the term
        "road rage"

No. This matches the argument, since road rage was indeed never defined, but this is **not a flaw**. Failing to provide a definition is never a flaw, so you can always confidently eliminate any answer choice that mentions this.

(E)   considers only a single province in discussing an
        issue with much broader implications

No. The premises are about just the province, and the conclusion is about just the province, so there is no need to consider any broader implications.

8. **Choice (A) is the correct answer.**

The feature of this Flaw question that you should notice first is the Concept Shift between the premises, which concern the waltz, the novel, and the telephone, and the conclusion, which says that [violent television programs are not corrupting today's youth.] What does the waltz have to do with violent TV? In fact, this argument tries to draw an analogy between the past situations and the current one, when the two situations may not in fact be analogous. That's the flaw.

For each answer choice, the **Real Question** is, "*Is this a flaw in the argument?*"

(A)   It treats as relevantly similar two cases that may differ in important respects.

Yes. This answer choice uses LSAT-speak to describe a bad analogy, which is indeed the flaw in this argument.

(B)   It overlooks the possibility that the telephone may have contributed to the corruption of some young people at the time it was invented.

No. Even if some young people were corrupted at the time, the argument still draws its conclusion about violent TV using premises about something completely different. The analogy flaw would still exist. This is **not a flaw**.

(C)   It purports to establish its conclusion by making a claim that, if true, would actually contradict that conclusion.

No. This describes a circular flaw, which is a real flaw when it occurs, but it did not happen in this argument. This **doesn't match**.

(D)   It fails to consider the viewpoint of those who do not think violent television programs are harmful.

No. The author didn't talk about those who like violent TV, but that's not the reason the argument is flawed. This is **not a flaw**.

(E)   It makes the questionable generalization that no one believes novels or the waltz to be harmful.

No. This **doesn't match** the argument. The argument said that most people think they are not harmful, not that no one thinks they are harmful.

9. **Choice (A) is the correct answer.**

This Flaw question starts out with the premise that the presence of a moral order depends on human souls being immortal—that is, immortal souls are *necessary* in order for there to be a moral order. But the conclusion says that [if souls are immortal, then there is a moral order]—that is,

immortal souls are *sufficient* to guarantee a moral order. This is a *necessary vs. sufficient* flaw.

For each answer choice, the **Real Question** is, "*Is this a flaw in the argument?*"

(A)   From the assertion that something is necessary to a moral order, the argument concludes that that thing is sufficient for an element of the moral order to be realized.

Yes. This is a perfect match for the Prephrased answer.

(B)   The argument takes mere beliefs to be established facts.

No. This **doesn't match** the argument, which never concluded that something is a fact simply because it is believed.

(C)   From the claim that the immortality of human souls implies that there is a moral order in the universe, the argument concludes that there being a moral order in the universe implies that human souls are immortal.

No. This **doesn't match** the argument because it gets things backwards. It mixes up which idea is the claim used to draw the conclusion and which idea is the conclusion itself.

(D)   The argument treats two fundamentally different conceptions of a moral order as essentially the same.

No. This describes an analogy flaw, which is a real flaw when it occurs, but it **doesn't match** what occurred in this argument.

(E)   The argument's conclusion is presupposed in the definition it gives of a moral order.

No. This describes a circular flaw, which is a real flaw when it occurs, but it did not happen in this argument. This **doesn't match**.

10. **Choice (D) is the correct answer.**

In this Flaw question, the conclusion is that [the train company could be held partially at fault.] There is a Concept Shift here, which occurs between two of the premises. The lawyer established that the man was *capable of running that fast*, but the jury considered the case of what should have happened to a man who *was running that fast*. Since he was intoxicated, there is good reason to believe he may not have been running at his top speed, and the jury's reasoning is flawed because it fails to consider that.

For each answer choice, the **Real Question** is, "*Is this a flaw in the argument?*"

Lecture 3 Explanations

(A)   fails to consider whether the man could have done anything more to avoid being hit by the train

No. The flaw in the argument was that the jury drew its conclusion on the presumption that the man was running 8 miles per hour. This choice does not describe where the reasoning went wrong.

(B)   relies on complicated calculations that were never verified by an expert

No. While it's true that there was no expert, the argument would still be flawed even if there had been. This is **not a flaw**.

(C)   presumes, without providing justification, that the train was functioning perfectly the night the man was hit

No. There is no evidence in the passage to indicate that the jury made this presumption. This **doesn't match** the argument.

(D)   takes for granted that the man was running his fastest when he was hit by the train

Yes. This correctly describes what happened in the argument, and it correctly points to the reason why the argument is flawed.

(E)   presumes, without providing justification, that the train operator could not see the man

No. If anything, the jury presumed that the train operator could see the man. This **doesn't match** the argument.

11. **Choice (D) is the correct answer.**

This Flaw question establishes in its premises that Downing's efforts led to the creation of Central Park, then concludes that [without him there would be no Central Park.] This is basically a *necessary vs. sufficient* flaw. You know that what he did was sufficient to bring about the park, but perhaps the park would still have been created even if he hadn't gotten involved. Perhaps he wasn't necessary, as there could have been other people who would have advocated a park.

For each answer choice, the **Real Question** is, "*Is this a flaw in the argument?*"

(A)   presumes, without providing justification, that Downing was the only person who played a large role in popularizing the project

No. The argument never made this presumption. In fact, it mentions the important role played by the legislature as well. This **doesn't match**

(B)   concludes that a claim about a causal connection must be true on the basis of a lack of evidence against that claim

No. This describes an absence of evidence flaw, which is a real flaw when it occurs, but it **doesn't match** what occurred in this argument.

(C)   takes for granted the assertion that many people enjoy Central Park

No. The argument never asserts that many people enjoy Central Park, so this **doesn't match**.

(D)   presumes, without providing justification, that something that resulted from a cause could only have resulted from that cause

Yes. In convoluted LSAT-speak, this choice describes a necessary vs. sufficient flaw, which is what happened in this argument.

(E)   overlooks the fact that many other people have influenced the geography of New York City

No. This argument is about the park, not about the geography of the entire city, and it also mentions other people (the legislature) who had an influence, so this **doesn't match** what happened in the argument.

12. **Choice (D) is the correct answer.**

This Flaw question concludes that [the law does not help to reduce harmful emissions,] based on a comparison of the amount of emissions released by older cars and newer cars. The flaw here is based on bad statistics. In comparing the two groups, no consideration is given to their respective sizes. What if there were only ten old cars without the device? Then you would expect the amount of emissions from the millions of newer cars to exceed the pollution from the older cars, even if the device worked magnificently. The flaw is the failure to consider the relative sizes of the groups.

For each answer choice, the **Real Question** is, "*Is this a flaw in the argument?*"

(A)   takes for granted that the device works properly when installed on new cars

No. The argument concluded that the law doesn't reduce emissions, but didn't make any statements about why not. This **doesn't match**.

(B)   assumes, without providing justification, that the emissions released by cars equipped with the device have more serious long-term health effects than do the emissions released by cars that are not equipped with the device

No. This **doesn't match**, since the argument never made presumptions about health effects.

(C)   ignores the possibility that the owners of cars equipped with the device may have removed or disabled it

Lecture 3 Explanations

No. Again, the argument concluded that the law doesn't reduce emissions, but didn't make any statements about why not. This **doesn't match**.

(D)   overlooks the possibility that the number of cars equipped with the device exceeds the number of cars without the device

Yes. The argument indeed overlooks this possibility, and considering this possibility might lead one to conclude that the law does reduce emissions.

(E)   takes for granted that the emissions released by cars equipped with the device are actually harmful

No. The argument makes no statements about harm. This **doesn't match**.

13.   **Choice (E) is the correct answer.**

This Flaw question contains the conclusion that [the pigeon population will not decrease.] But one of the professor's premises is that the pigeon population will increase. When an argument's conclusion is basically the same as one of the premises, then the argument has a *circular* flaw.

For each answer choice, the **Real Question** is, "*Is this a flaw in the argument?*"

(A)   The professor inappropriately assumes that any prediction that does not consider all conditions must fail to consider all necessary conditions.

No. This sounds fancy but **doesn't match** anything that actually happened in the argument.

(B)   The professor fails to identify the supposed flaw in the simulation code.

No. This is similar to the "fails to provide a definition" distracter, which is never correct. This is **not a flaw**.

(C)   The professor dismisses the value of all computer simulations without considering whether the simulation in question is useful.

No. The professor never dismisses all computer simulations, so this **doesn't match**.

(D)   The professor presumes, without providing justification, that his colleague could not have made calculations and written code without committing any errors.

No. The professor never says anything about his colleague being unable to produce flawless work. This **doesn't match**.

(E)   The professor draws a conclusion that simply restates a claim presented in support of that conclusion.

Yes. This describes a circular flaw, which is the problem in this argument.

14.   **Choice (D) is the correct answer.**

The conclusion in this Flaw question is that [the student is achieving the high scores without seeing the questions beforehand or getting help.] In the premises, one of her experiments ruled out the possibility that he was getting help—*on that test only*. Her other experiment ruled out the possibility that he was getting the questions in advance—again on that test only. But she didn't perform any experiment to rule out both at the same time. Thus, her flaw was failing to consider that the student could be using those two methods at different times.

For each answer choice, the **Real Question** is, "*Is this a flaw in the argument?*"

(A)   The teacher failed to recognize that the numbers she chose for the test questions may not have been truly random.

No. Even if they weren't random, her experiment still ruled out the possibility that he was getting the answers to that test in advance. This is **not a flaw**.

(B)   The teacher inappropriately assumed that the student could have been cheating using only the two methods she investigated.

No. The teacher's conclusion was restricted to the two methods she tested, so this **doesn't match** an assumption she made.

(C)   The teacher failed to consider that there are other ways to ensure that a student does not see the test questions before being given the test.

No. Any experiment in which the student couldn't see the answers beforehand would have been good enough. There's no reason for her to consider every method. This is **not a flaw**.

(D)   The teacher overlooked the possibility that the student could have used different cheating methods on different tests.

Yes. This correctly describes what happened in the argument, and it correctly points to the reason the argument is flawed.

(E)   The teacher failed to consider whether other students had been cheating in some way.

No. Maybe she did fail to consider this, but that's not why her reasoning is flawed. This is **not a flaw**

15. Choice (E) is the correct answer.

The conclusion in this Flaw question is that [parental emphasis on the arts can only be effective once children reach early adulthood.] The author reaches this conclusion by establishing that parental emphasis doesn't work during early adolescence. But this is a *false dichotomy*. Aren't there other phases of childhood besides early adolescence and early adulthood? Why couldn't parental emphasis be effective then?

For each answer choice, the **Real Question** is, "*Is this a flaw in the argument?*"

(A)   It mistakes a correlation between resistance to parental guidance and age for a causal relationship between resistance and age.

No. This describes a causal flaw, which is a real flaw when it occurs, but it **doesn't match** what occurred in this argument.

(B)   It fails to consider the possibility that children might be interested in arts and arts education without being guided toward those subjects by their parents.

No. The argument is concerned with the effectiveness of parental emphasis, so failing to consider this possibility is **not a flaw**.

(C)   It ignores the fact that children in early adulthood are much more likely to respond positively to parental encouragement simply because they have a desire to please their parents.

No. The argument doesn't mention this fact, but that's **not a flaw**.

(D)   It makes crucial use of the term "creative development," yet it fails to properly specify what that entails.

No. Failing to define a term is **not a flaw**. Never choose this kind of answer choice.

(E)   It fails to specify the effects of parental emphasis on arts during stages of childhood other than early adolescence.

Yes. This points out the false dichotomy. It says the argument failed to consider the other stages of childhood.

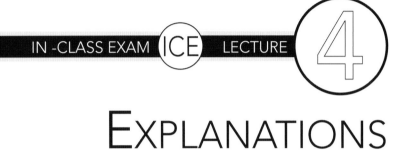

IN -CLASS EXAM ICE LECTURE 4

EXPLANATIONS

1. **Choice (B) is the correct answer.**

This is a Necessary Assumption question because it asks for a *required assumption*. The Concept Shift in this argument occurred between *sufficient heat* and *100 degrees warmer than expected*. Okay, so it's warmer, but is that enough to be sufficient? The scientist assumed that 100 degrees warmer than expected is sufficient.

For each answer choice, the **Real Question** is, *"Does the argument depend on this being true?"*

(A)   Life will always form on a celestial body with water, carbon, and heat.

No. The conclusion is that the moon can support life, not that there actually is life.

(B)   The previously expected temperature on Enceladus was not more than 100 degrees lower than that needed to support life.

Yes. This is a good match for the Prephrased answer. If the expected temperature were 200 degrees colder than what is sufficient, then the newly measured temperature would still not be sufficient, so the argument depends on this answer choice being true.

(C)   The water below the surface of Enceladus covers a significant proportion of the moon's area.

No. The premises make no mention of how much water is necessary.

(D)   Scientists have equipment capable of detecting carbon-based molecules from a distance.

No. This can't be an assumption because it is already stated as a premise. The scientist says there is prior knowledge of carbon-based molecules.

(E)   There are no other bodies in our solar system more likely than Enceladus to have life at the present time.

No. The argument is not concerned with other planets. This is **out of scope**.

2. **Choice (A) is the correct answer.**

This is a Necessary Assumption question since it asks for a *required assumption*. The Concept Shift in this argument occurred between *the amount of the byproduct produced by users* and *the concentration of the byproduct in the city's wastewater*. The author assumed that those two amounts are the same, and that nothing added or took away any of the byproduct between the users and the wastewater testing facility.

For each answer choice, the **Real Question** is, *"Does the argument depend on this being true?"*

(A)   There are no other common sources that might add the byproduct in question to the water.

Yes. This is a good match for the Prephrased answer. If there were other common sources, then the test would not be able to tell how much was from cocaine use and how much was from the other source, and the results would not be accurate. So the argument depends on this answer choice being true.

(B)   Many people in the region use cocaine.

No. The program is designed to find out how much use there is. It doesn't depend on there being a high number.

(C)   Cocaine is the only illicit drug used by many people in the region.

No. Other drugs are **out of scope**.

(D)   Similar programs undertaken by other municipalities have had good results.

No. This argument doesn't depend on what happened in other municipalities. Even if no one else has tried this program, it might still work.

(E)   There is no other means of determining the amount of cocaine used by the population of the region.

No. Even if there were other means, that would have no impact on whether this program will work.

3. **Choice (B) is the correct answer.**

This is a Necessary Assumption question since it asks for a *required assumption*. The Concept Shift here is between *the current standard work day* and *an insufficient amount of sleep*. The physiologist assumed that by changing the standard work day, it will fit better with people's sleep schedules—that is, she assumed that people's sleep schedules would stay the same, not also change, thus keeping the people tired.

For each answer choice, the **Real Question** is, *"Does the argument depend on this being true?"*

(A)   Well-rested people would be maximally productive at work.

No. The professor's conclusion is about being more productive, not maximally productive. This is **extreme**.

(B)   People would not adjust to the change in the work day by going to sleep and waking up one hour later.

Yes. This is a good match for the Prephrased answer. If people just started going to bed later, then they would still be getting an insufficient amount of sleep, so the argument depends on this answer choice being true.

Lecture 4 Explanations

(C)   Most people are naturally inclined to go to bed and wake up much later than the standard work day allows.

No. If this were true, it might actually weaken the argument, since it would suggest people would just start going to bed later.

(D)   Nobody would choose to arrive at work at the current standard start time if the beginning of the work day were pushed back.

No. Even if a few early birds still showed up early, it could still be true that general productivity would increase, so the argument does not depend on everybody coming to work one hour later.

(E)   There is no other way to help people get the sleep they require before work.

No. Even if there were other ways, that would have no impact on the effectiveness of this program. This is **out of scope**

4. **Choice (B) is the correct answer.**

This is a Necessary Assumption question, because it asks for an *assumption* on which the argument *relies*. The Concept Shift in this argument is between *cannot damage DNA* and *harmless*. Couldn't there be other types of harm besides harm to DNA? The author assumed that the powerful magnetic fields can't cause any other type of harm.

For each answer choice, the **Real Question** is, "*Does the argument depend on this being true?*"

(A)   Many people choose to get a full-body MRI every year as an alternative to the traditional annual check-up.

No. The argument is about whether MRIs are harmful, but the number of people who get one is irrelevant.

(B)   Function of the circulatory system is not compromised by exposure to powerful magnetic fields.

Yes. This is a good match for the Prephrased answer. If magnetic fields hurt the circulatory system, then MRIs might not be so harmless after all, so the argument depends on this answer choice being true. This is a shielding assumption.

(C)   The risk of sustaining DNA damage from a CAT scan is unacceptably high.

No. The conclusion is about MRIs, not CAT scans.

(D)   MRI machines are not much more expensive than standard x-ray machines.

No. The cost is irrelevant to whether or not the procedure is harmless.

(E)   People can also develop radiation sickness if they are subjected to a CAT scan or x-ray that is improperly conducted.

No. This is already somewhat implied by the argument, and in any case it has nothing to do with MRIs.

5. **Choice (C) is the correct answer.**

This is a Necessary Assumption question since it asks for an *assumption* on which the argument *depends*. The Concept Shift in this argument occurred between *bones found at the site* and *modern bone development charts*. But couldn't there be differences, due to a different diet, for example? The archaeologist assumed that the ancient humans' bones developed in the same way as those of modern humans.

For each answer choice, the **Real Question** is, "*Does the argument depend on this being true?*"

(A)   The most complete skeletons found at the site all clearly belonged to children.

No. This doesn't address the Concept Shift.

(B)   There is no way to determine the exact age at which a person died simply by analyzing skeletal remains.

No. If this were true, it would actually weaken the conclusion, so the argument certainly doesn't depend on this.

(C)   Human bone development from the period in question is comparable to modern human bone development.

Yes. This is a good match for the Prephrased answer.

(D)   Any personal artifacts that will be found at the site are certain to be those that would have belonged to children.

No. The conclusion has nothing to do with the ancient people's belongings, only their age.

(E)   No adult bones have been found at the site in question.

No. Even if there were some adult bones, that wouldn't hurt the conclusion, since the archaeologist only asserted that most of the skeletons were those of children, not all.

6. **Choice (B) is the correct answer.**

This is an Evaluate question. You should still look for the Concept Shift and determine what the author assumed. Here, the Concept Shift occurred between *costing six times as much to edit* and *not less expensive to produce*. But couldn't there be other cost savings to offset the increased editing cost? In fact, the executive even mentions one—no writer and actor costs. The executive assumed that no savings will offset the increased editing cost.

For each answer choice, the **Real Question** is, *"Does this address an assumption?"*

(A)   recent and projected ratings trends for the different types of shows

No. Ratings don't affect production cost.

(B)   the difference between the extra cost of editing and the savings on actors and writers for reality shows

Yes. This choice addresses the executive's assumption.

(C)   the number of reality shows that have been produced, year by year, since the genre became popular

No. The number of shows doesn't affect their production cost.

(D)   the average per-season expenditure on the cast of a scripted show

No. This alone would not be useful to know because it doesn't allow you to compare the various costs and decide which is cheaper.

(E)   the ratio of the cost of actors and writers for a reality show to the cost of actors and writers for a scripted show

No. This doesn't provide any information about the actual editing costs, which you'd need to know.

7.   **Choice (D) is the correct answer.**

This is a Necessary Assumption question since it asks for a *required assumption*. The Concept Shift in this argument is between *certain situations* and *the number of exploratory expeditions*. How do you know those situations have anything to do with the number of expeditions? Smith assumed that the number of lines etched somehow corresponds to the number of expeditions.

For each answer choice, the **Real Question** is, *"Does the argument depend on this being true?"*

(A)   There are no adequate written accounts relating to fifteenth-century Genoese ships.

No. Smith's argument does not depend on an absence of written accounts. He's just saying they aren't necessary.

(B)   Only the Genoese partook in the etching ritual described during the period in question.

No. Even if other people used the same ritual, that wouldn't destroy Smith's argument.

(C)   The Genoese etched exactly one line around a ship's mast for each expedition in which it was involved.

No. This is tricky, but this choice is more **extreme** than Smith's argument requires. He simply assumed some correspondence, not a 1:1 correspondence. If they etched two lines for every expedition, his conclusion could still be true.

(D)   The Genoese did not etch lines around the circumference of a ship's mast after each rainstorm it endured.

Yes. If the ship got a new line after every rainstorm, that would destroy the correspondence between the number of lines and the number of expeditions, so the argument depends on this choice being true. This is a classic shielding assumption.

(E)   The ships in question were not decorated in any other way following expeditions.

No. Other methods of decoration don't impact Smith's argument.

8.   **Choice (D) is the correct answer.**

This is a Necessary Assumption question because it asks for an *assumption* on which the argument *depends*. The Concept Shift in this argument is between *requiring companies to pay more* and *boon to the economy*. You may have heard some arguments attempting to undermine this connection every time a minimum wage hike is proposed. How do you know that companies won't eliminate jobs or ignore the law? How do you know the higher wages won't lead to inflation? The author assumed that none of these things will occur and have a detrimental effect on the economy.

For each answer choice, the **Real Question** is, *"Does the argument depend on this being true?"*

(A)   All laborers should earn a similar wage for similar work, regardless of where they live.

No. This is beyond the scope of the conclusion, which is just about whether the law will benefit the local economies.

(B)   Increasing the wages earned in a country always improves that country's economy.

No. This is more **extreme** than the argument requires. The argument is about only this law and only developing countries, so even if there are some cases, for example in developed countries, when wage increases do nothing, the conclusion to this argument could still be true.

(C)   Laborers in developed countries always earn higher wages than their counterparts in developing countries.

No. This is again more **extreme** than the argument requires. Even if there is one developed country with exceptionally low wages, that wouldn't affect whether this law will benefit these local economies.

(D)   The legislation would not compel businesses in developed countries to replace foreign labor with domestic labor.

Yes. This matches the Prephrased answer. If the law compels businesses to bring the jobs back home, then the loss of jobs in the developing countries might actually hurt the local economy, so the argument depends on this choice being true.

(E)   The tax rate on wage income in the developing countries is not excessively high.

No. Even with an excessive tax rate, more money in the pockets of workers might still help the local economy.

9.   **Choice (D) is the correct answer.**

This is a Necessary Assumption question since it asks for an *assumption* on which the argument *depends*. The premises establish that there are no negative effects on concentration, but then the argument makes a Concept Shift between *increased blood flow to the brain* and *a positive effect on alertness*. The author assumed increased blood flow has some kind of effect on alertness. If that weren't true, then there would be no evidence to support the conclusion.

For each answer choice, the **Real Question** is, *"Does the argument depend on this being true?"*

(A)   No other drinks increase alertness or concentration.

No. The conclusion is about soda, so other drinks are **out of scope**.

(B)   Drinking soda does not improve information retention.

No. The conclusion concerns alertness and concentration, not information retention.

(C)   Soda does not lead to excessive weight gain.

No. The conclusion concerns alertness and concentration, not weight.

(D)   Increased blood flow to the brain improves alertness and concentration.

Yes. This is a good match for the Prephrased answer.

(E)   Drinking soda has a positive psychological effect on alertness and concentration.

No. The conclusion concerns the physiological effects, not the psychological effects.

10.   **Choice (A) is the correct answer.**

This is a Necessary Assumption question since it asks for an *assumption* on which the argument *relies*. The Concept Shift in this argument is between parents *being more aware of/taking into account the system* and *making more informed purchasing decisions*. How do you know parents are properly interpreting the symbols? The author assumed that better awareness leads to more informed decision-making.

For each answer choice, the **Real Question** is, *"Does the argument depend on this being true?"*

(A)   Parents purchasing video games understand the intended meaning of the ratings symbols.

Yes. If they don't understand the intended meanings, then their decisions are misinformed, so the argument depends on this choice being true.

(B)   The number of children who play video games is increasing.

No. The conclusion concerns the parents being informed, not the number of children playing the games.

(C)   There are no other indications on video game packaging to indicate potentially inappropriate content.

No. If this were true, it would make it less likely that parents are making informed decisions, so the argument does not depend on this.

(D)   There are at least some games with content too violent to be appropriate for young children.

No. Even if there were no games like this, perhaps there could be some other things parents need to be informed about, and perhaps the symbols could still be doing a good job of informing them.

(E)   There were not more potentially inappropriate video games produced last year than in the year before.

No. The number of inappropriate games is irrelevant.

11.   **Choice (B) is the correct answer.**

This is a Necessary Assumption question since it asks for a *required assumption*. The Concept Shift here is between *picked up by news distributors* and *inspire people to decrease*. How do you know people will take any action as a result of the news? There could be many reasons people choose not to react to the broadcast.

For each answer choice, the **Real Question** is, *"Does the argument depend on this being true?"*

(A) People who currently consume harmful amounts of caffeine can switch from regular coffee to decaffeinated coffee to reduce their caffeine intake.

No. Even if they can't switch to decaf, these people could still decrease their caffeine intake, perhaps by drinking less regular coffee.

(B) Many people are not aware that they consume harmful amounts of caffeine.

Yes. If everyone is already aware of his or her excessive consumption, then the broadcast of the study would not give them any new information, and there would be no grounds to draw a conclusion about widespread action based on the broadcast. In order for the premises to be relevant to this conclusion, this answer choice must be true.

(C) Everyone who currently consumes harmful amounts of caffeine and learns of the results of the study will reduce caffeine intake to healthy levels.

No. This is more **extreme** than the argument requires. Even if a few people ignore the study, there could still be many people who take action.

(D) Everyone who currently consumes harmful amounts of caffeine reads or watches the news on a regular basis.

No. Again, this is more **extreme** than necessary. Even if a few caffeine freaks skip the news, the conclusion could still be true.

(E) Many people have a moderate chemical dependency on caffeine and would suffer withdrawal symptoms upon attempting to reduce caffeine intake.

No. If this were true, it would actually weaken the conclusion, because it would give you reason to think that people would ignore the study in order to avoid the withdrawal symptoms. The argument certainly doesn't depend on this.

12. **Choice (C) is the correct answer.**

This is a Necessary Assumption question because it asks for an *assumption* on which the argument *relies*. This argument has a common flaw. You know the bureaucrats didn't adequately check the proposal, and you know there is now a huge bill for a bad program. But then the author concludes that one caused the other. This is a causal flaw. Every author who commits a causal flaw assumes that there is no other cause. In this case the author assumed that it wasn't for some other reason

that the firm got the contract—favoritism, for example.

For each answer choice, the **Real Question** is, *"Does the argument depend on this being true?"*

(A) The glaring flaws in the proposed defense system cannot be fixed without redesigning the entire system.

No. The conclusion is about the cause of the awarding of the contract, not the fix.

(B) The firm that earned the development contract was the only firm to submit a proposal to the government for the defense system project.

No. The author didn't assume this. In fact, if this were true, it would weaken the argument by suggesting some other reason why the firm got the contract—they were the only option.

(C) The government would not have made the same deal had the involved bureaucrats fully researched the proposal.

Yes. If the government would have made the same deal, then it shows that the missing research was irrelevant and not the cause of the suspicious awarding. The argument depends on this choice being true.

(D) The bureaucrats responsible for the deal did not have the technical background required to understand many elements of the proposal.

No. The author seems to think that they could have understood if they had researched it, and that they would have made a different decision. If this choice is true, it weakens the argument because it suggests that the bad decision was based on lack of technical background, not lack of adequate research.

(E) No defense system with major flaws can ever be fruitful.

No. The conclusion is concerned with the cause of the problem, not the possible outcome.

13. **Choice (E) is the correct answer.**

This is a Necessary Assumption question because it asks for *assumptions* on which the argument *relies*. There are lots of assumptions here. The author made a large Concept Shift by connecting *cotinine produced by nicotine metabolism* and *presence/absence in fingerprints proves smoker/nonsmoker*. Couldn't cotinine get in the system some other way besides nicotine? Couldn't nicotine get in the system some other way besides smoking? Does the cotinine persist indefinitely in the fingerprints? Is cotinine present in a smoker even when he isn't smoking?

This is also an EXCEPT question. Four of the

Lecture 4 Explanations

choices will be something the argument *depends on*, so put a D next to those choices, and pick the one that looks different.

For each answer choice, you can still use the same **Real Question**: *"Does the argument depend on this being true?"*

(A)   Cotinine is not produced by the metabolism of any chemicals not found in cigarettes.

The argument depends on this being true. If cotinine could come from something else, then there's no way to tell if it came from smoking or not. Put a D.

(B)   A person cannot get sufficient amounts of nicotine in his or her system by any means other than cigarette smoking.

The argument depends on this being true. If nicotine could come from gum or a patch, then cotinine wouldn't prove someone was a smoker. Put a D.

(C)   Cotinine remains detectable in skin secretions for at least several minutes after smoking a cigarette.

The argument depends on this being true. If cotinine disappeared after 10 seconds, then the fingerprints of smokers and nonsmokers could appear the same. Put a D.

(D)   Measurable amounts of cotinine cannot remain on someone's skin simply by making physical contact with a smoker.

The argument depends on this being true. If shaking hands with a smoker gives you "smoker's" fingerprints, then the test can't distinguish between the two. Put a D.

(E)   Authorities are always able to determine whether the fingerprints at a crime scene belong to the suspect or to someone else.

The argument does not depend on this. The conclusion limits itself to what you can tell about a suspect's fingerprints, so any prior difficulty in determining which prints are the suspect's is beyond the scope of this argument. Don't put a D.

Since choice (E) looks different from the rest, pick it.

14.   **Choice (E) is the correct answer.**

This is a Necessary Assumption question since it asks for an *assumption* on which the argument *relies*. This Concept Shift is a little hard to see but it's there. You know that blood pressure is *different* depending on whether you're sitting with your feet dangling or on the floor. But the conclusion says that taking a reading with dangling feet is a *misdiagnosis*. Look for something that addresses this connection.

For each answer choice, the **Real Question** is, *"Does the argument depend on this being true?"*

(A)   Multiple blood pressure readings are required to confidently diagnosis high blood pressure to account for the possibility of an erroneous reading on any single test.

No. The argument doesn't depend on a need for multiple readings.

(B)   The effect of sitting with feet planted on lowering blood pressure readings is more pronounced in elderly patients.

No. The argument doesn't depend on a difference based on age.

(C)   Most patients diagnosed with high blood pressure are measured to have a blood pressure more than fifteen points above the threshold for the high blood pressure diagnosis.

No. This is stronger than what the argument requires. The argument concludes that misdiagnosis often (=sometimes) occurs, but this choice says most patients. That's **extreme**.

(D)   Blood pressure readings are not artificially elevated by the nervousness that many patients feel when they are undergoing medical tests.

No. If you negate this and say readings are artificially elevated, that might even strengthen the conclusion that there is misdiagnosis, not destroy it.

(E)   The standards against which high blood pressure is diagnosed are not based on blood pressure measurements from patients sitting on exam tables.

Yes. Negate this. If all the blood pressure charts come from people on exam tables, then doing it that way would lead to the correct diagnosis, and doing it differently, with feet on the floor, would be the misdiagnosis. This negated version destroys the argument, so this is the necessary assumption.

15.   **Choice (A) is the correct answer.**

This is a Necessary Assumption question since it asks for an *assumption* on which the argument *depends*. To summarize, the premises tell you that satisfaction scores are correlated with health providers' communication skills, not the machines and number of tests. The conclusion says surveys should be ignored as a measure of quality of care. Thus, the author tried to establish a connection between *machines/tests* and *quality of care*, and assumed that there is no connection between communication and quality.

For each answer choice, the **Real Question** is, *"Does the argument depend on this being true?"*

(A)   The communication skills of health providers are not strongly correlated with the quality of care at their facilities.

Yes. This is a good match for the Prephrased answer. If there is a connection, then maybe we shouldn't ignore the surveys after all, so the argument depends on this being true.

(B)   The machines monitoring the conditions of patients are the most important element of the overall quality of care.

No. This is more **extreme** than the argument requires. The author assumed some connection between the two, not that machines are the most important thing.

(C)   The surveys were not completed by a large enough sample of patients to provide meaningful results.

No. The author drew her conclusion using the surveys, so she didn't assume they were meaningless.

(D)   Patient satisfaction surveys are always biased in favor of the health care facilities that provide the most pleasant accommodations.

No. Pleasant accommodations are **out of scope**.

(E)   The patient satisfaction surveys failed to cover several important elements of patient care.

No. Again, the author drew her conclusion using the surveys, so she didn't assume they were flawed.

IN-CLASS EXAM (ICE) LECTURE 5

EXPLANATIONS

1. **Choice (C) is the correct answer.**

In this Strengthen question, the conclusion is that [the seismic activity is related to melting ice sheets,] based on its correlation with the seasons. The flaw here is a causal flaw—the evidence merely supports a correlation. To strengthen this conclusion, look for an answer choice that rules out other potential causes or provides a stronger suggestion of a causal relationship.

For each answer choice, the **Real Question** is, *"Does this suggest that the seismic episodes are related to melting ice sheets impacting the bedrock?"*

(A)   The instruments used to detect seismic activity are notoriously unreliable.

No. This choice might even weaken the argument by casting doubt on whether there is even a correlation. This is an **opposite** distracter.

(B)   There is no historical record of any significant earthquake in Greenland.

No. The presence or absence of a "significant" earthquake has no impact on the cause of the sporadic seismic activity.

(C)   During each of the two warmest years of the past decade, four times as many seismic episodes were observed as during an average year.

Yes. This doesn't prove a causal link, but it does strengthen the correlation (and thus the argument) by showing that when there is more melting (the warmest years) there is more seismic activity.

(D)   Each year that geologists have studied the phenomenon, there have been at least twenty seismic episodes recorded.

No. The number of episodes says nothing about their cause. This is **out of scope**.

(E)   Computer programs used to simulate the response of Greenland's ice sheets to changing temperatures have produced contradictory results.

No. This choice has no link to seismic activity, and contradictory results can do nothing to support one hypothesis over another.

2. **Choice (D) is the correct answer.**

In this Weaken question, the company's conclusion is that [it is not at fault for the lead poisoning.] The claim is based on the premise that the company has not sold any lead-based paint in over thirty years. But perhaps the company could still be responsible, either in some way other than selling lead-based paint, or due to the paint it sold over thirty years ago.

For each answer choice, the **Real Question** is, *"Does this suggest that the paint supplier is at fault for the poisonings?"*

(A)   The company's manufacturing process now releases a greater quantity of pollutants into the local river than it ever has in the past.

No. Although this reflects badly on the company, there is no evidence in this answer choice that the pollutants released into the river contain any lead, so this can't suggest a connection to the lead poisonings.

(B)   Lead poisoning can lead to kidney failure and developmental disorders in children.

No. This choice tells you that lead poisoning is bad, but it has nothing to do with the company.

(C)   Several other local paint manufacturers sold lead-based paint as recently as five years ago.

No. This strengthens the argument because it suggests that the other companies are responsible. This is an **opposite** distracter.

(D)   The company's paint has been used in most of the schools in the area since the company was founded.

Yes. This choice shows how the lead-based paint sold by the company over thirty years ago could still be impacting children, since it may still be on the walls in local schools.

(E)   Lead-based paint is only one of several potential causes of lead poisoning.

No. This would also strengthen the company's conclusion, since it suggests the cause of the poisonings could be coming from something other than the company's old paint. This is an **opposite** distracter.

3. **Choice (A) is the correct answer.**

In this Strengthen question, the conclusion is the politician's judgment that [the bill is likely to pass.] This is based on the factual observation that certain people have pledged support. The flaw here is the Concept Shift between *pledged support* and *likely passage*. You don't know whether the prominent members will do what they pledge to do, and you don't know how the other people will vote.

For each answer choice, the **Real Question** is, *"Does this suggest that the lumber subsidy bill is very likely to pass?"*

(A)   Most bills that have the support of at least some members from the largest parties pass.

Yes. This doesn't prove that the bill will pass, but if most bills (more than half) with some support from the largest parties pass, then, since you know this bill fits into that category, you can say that it's likely (more than a 50% chance) this bill will pass.

(B)   No bill can pass without the support of at least one prominent member of a large party.

No. If this choice is true, then the premises establish that the bill has one necessary base covered, but that isn't enough to tell you whether the bill's passage is likely.

(C)   Only bills that have the support of prominent members of large parties pass.

No. Again, if this choice is true, then the premises establish that the bill has one necessary base covered, but that isn't enough to tell you whether the bill's passage is likely.

(D)   Bills that have the support of multiple large parties are usually viewed favorably by the public.

No. Public opinion is **out of scope**, since it has nothing to do with whether the bill will pass.

(E)   Any bill that has the support of all parties is very likely to pass.

No. You don't know if the lumber bill has the support of all parties, so this choice tells you nothing about the likelihood of its passage.

4. **Choice (B) is the correct answer.**

The conclusion here is that [the number of accidents will be greatly reduced,] based on a description of the technology. There are a number of flaws here. How do you know there are a "great" number of accidents that could be averted with this technology? How do you know people will be able to take action sufficient to avoid an accident when they hear the buzzer? Since this is a Strengthen EXCEPT question, use the EXCEPT Tool. Four of the choices will strengthen the argument. Put an **S** next to those that do, and pick the choice that doesn't have an **S**.

For each answer choice, the **Real Question** is, *"Does this suggest that the new technology will greatly reduce the number of accidents on the road?"*

(A)   The buzzer sounds early enough to allow drivers to react before an accident occurs.

This suggests that the buzzer will help people avoid accidents. Put an **S**.

(B)   More accidents take place on highways than on city streets.

The passage gives you no reason to think that the buzzer would be any more or less effective on highways, so this doesn't really affect the argument in any way. Don't put an **S**.

(C)   A majority of accidents are the result of inattentive drivers colliding with other vehicles.

This suggests that there are a lot of accidents that would be addressed by the buzzer technology, so this supports the conclusion that a "great" number of accidents will be avoided. Put an **S**.

(D)   The buzzer is sufficiently unobtrusive that it will not significantly distract drivers.

This rules out a potential danger from the buzzer, so it helps the case that the buzzer will allow drivers to take action to avoid an accident. Put an **S**.

(E)   The addition of the sensor technology does not require the removal of any other safety features.

Like choice (D), this also rules out a potential drawback of the new technology. Put an **S**.

Since choice (B) is different from all the rest, pick it.

5. **Choice (E) is the correct answer.**

In this Weaken question, the biologist is talking about the care hyenas exhibit for each other. But she commits a Concept Shift between *more than is necessary for hunting alone* and *beyond evolutionary advantage*. Maybe there could be other kinds of care that still confer an evolutionary advantage, so maybe the care they exhibit goes beyond what's needed for hunting but does *not* go beyond an evolutionary advantage.

For each answer choice, the **Real Question** is, *"Does this suggest that hyenas' emotional ties do not extend beyond evolutionary advantage?"*

(A)   The amount of care that hyenas exhibit for members of their pack can be a disadvantage when hunting.

No. This is an **opposite** distracter, since it suggests that hyenas do go beyond evolutionary advantage and into the realm of evolutionary disadvantage.

(B)   Caring for members of a pack can provide an evolutionary advantage.

No. This does no more than restate something the premises already told you was true. Effective hunting is an evolutionary advantage, and you already know that the hyenas' care covers at least enough to confer this advantage.

(C)   Hyenas do not appear to exhibit certain human emotions, such as regret or envy.

No. The passage provides you no information to judge whether regret and envy confer an evolutionary advantage, so you can't use statements about them to judge whether hyenas' care is restricted to or goes beyond evolutionary advantage.

(D)   Many species related to hyenas do not exhibit special care for members of their packs.

No. The conclusion is about hyenas, not other species. This is **out of scope**.

(E)   The extra care that hyenas share extends no further than protecting each other to allow for reproduction.

Yes. This gives an example of a kind of care unrelated to hunting that still confers an evolutionary advantage (reproduction), so this suggests that perhaps the hyenas' extra care is still confined to evolutionary advantage and doesn't extend beyond that.

6. **Choice (E) is the correct answer.**

This Weaken question establishes that Brand H got rid of the formaldehyde and concludes that [the cigarettes are now less harmful than they used to be.] The author tries to equate *no formaldehyde* and *less harmful*, but you don't know whether anything else changed in the same time period, whether there was an increase in some other harmful component, for example.

For each answer choice, the **Real Question** is, *"Does this suggest that Brand H cigarettes are not less harmful than they once were?"*

(A)   Brand H has always contained an amount of ammonia, another injurious additive, that is nearly twice the average of other cigarette brands.

No. Even though the ammonia is harmful, if the ammonia content is the same, then there is no reason to believe they are just as harmful as they used to be, given that the formaldehyde has been eliminated.

(B)   Some of the sugars previously used as additives came from natural sources such as honey and maple syrup.

No. The source of the sugars is **out of scope**. Perhaps the new additives also come from natural sources. You can't draw any conclusions about harmfulness.

(C)   Exposure to formaldehyde has been shown to be strongly correlated to respiratory, skin, and gastrointestinal ailments.

No. The argument already told you that formaldehyde is bad, so this choice doesn't add anything new.

(D)   Since 1999, cigarettes have been discovered to be more harmful than previously believed.

No. This choice suggests that some new dangers of cigarettes were discovered, but if the only thing about Brand H that changed was the elimination

of one risk (formaldehyde), then they would still be safer than they once were.

(E)   Brand H's reformulated blend of additives has resulted in cigarettes that produce a greater concentration of acetaldehyde, a known carcinogen.

Yes. If formaldehyde went down but some other harmful agent went up, that suggests (even though it doesn't prove) that Brand H might not be less harmful than it used to be.

7. **Choice (D) is the correct answer.**

This Strengthen question has a Concept Shift between *spent more time at visits* and *spend more time talking about lifestyle choices*. To strengthen this flawed argument, look for a choice that suggests the additional time was indeed spent on lifestyle chats and not on something else.

For each answer choice, the **Real Question** is, *"Does this suggest that female physicians are more willing to spend time talking with their patients about healthy lifestyle choices?"*

(A)   Female physicians tend to perform a greater number of basic physical tests at annual check-ups.

No. This is an **opposite** distracter, since it suggests that the additional time is spent on tests.

(B)   A decreasing number of people schedule annual check-ups with their physicians.

No. The number of people going to the doctor is **out of scope**.

(C)   The tests typically performed at annual check-ups rarely reveal signs of significant health problems, even when such problems are present.

No. This argument is all about how female physicians spend time during check-ups, not about the results of check-ups.

(D)   Female physicians on average take no longer than male physicians to perform the usual physical tests.

Yes. This suggests that the additional time is not being spent on the usual tests, which is a good match for the Prephrased answer.

(E)   Though the disparity is shrinking, there are still many more male physicians than female physicians.

No. The argument is about how female physicians spend their time, not about how many of them there are.

8. **Choice (E) is the correct answer.**

The premises in this Weaken question establish that *the journalist* got erroneous results from the radar gun and concludes that [the police must be getting erroneous results as well.] To weaken this argument, look for an answer choice that shows some difference between the journalist and police.

For each answer choice, the **Real Question** is, *"Does this suggest that the radar guns have not caused police to issue many erroneous speeding tickets?"*

(A)   Many speeding tickets are issued to drivers claimed to be exceeding the speed limit by less than ten miles per hour.

No. This is an **opposite** distracter. If the typical radar gun error is 10 mph, and if many tickets fall within this error, then it suggests that police really are giving erroneous tickets.

(B)   Police rely exclusively on the radar gun in determining whether a vehicle is exceeding the speed limit.

No. This is also an **opposite** distracter. If the gun is unreliable and there is no other tool used, then there is ample opportunity for bad tickets.

(C)   Some of the tests conducted by the journalist were inconclusive.

No. Maybe some tests were inconclusive, but the premises tell you that he did obtain some final results. This answer choice doesn't do anything to the argument.

(D)   Fewer speeding tickets have been issued since the journalist's report was publicized.

No. The conclusion is about what police did before the report, so anything that occurred afterward is **out of scope**.

(E)   Traffic police receive training in the use of the radar gun that allows them to operate it without producing erroneous readings.

Yes. This suggests a difference between the journalist and the police, and suggests that police may be giving accurate tickets even though the journalist got erroneous results.

9. **Choice (E) is the correct answer.**

This Weaken question establishes a *correlation* between less sleep and a longer lifespan but concludes that switching to less sleep will *cause* people to have a longer lifespan. To weaken this argument, look for an answer choice that suggests that there is a different cause for the longer lifespan, that the causation is reversed, or that some third factor is causing both phenomena.

For each answer choice, the **Real Question** is, *"Does this suggest that limiting sleep to seven hours per day will not cause one to live longer?"*

(A)   Some people who sleep an average of nine hours per day live beyond the typical expected lifespan of people who sleep an average of six hours per day.

No. This argument is all about averages. When you're considering an average lifespan, it's understood that not everyone will live exactly the average number of years. Some people will be below that number, while others will be above. This choice simply tells you that a few nine-hour sleepers live longer than normal, but that doesn't tell you anything new, and it doesn't impact the reasoning. This is a common LSAT trick, but remember: the presence of a few statistical outliers never strengthens or weakens an argument.

(B)   Those who slept less than six hours per day tended to live longer than those who slept between six and seven hours per day on average.

No. This is an **opposite** distracter because it **strengthens** the connection between less sleep and longer life.

(C)   Those who slept less than seven hours per day were less likely to contract ailments such as the common cold.

No. Even if you assume that having fewer common ailments will lead to a longer lifespan, this again **strengthens** the argument by showing how less sleep eventually leads to a longer lifespan.

(D)   There was no difference in socioeconomic status between those who slept less than seven hours and those who slept more than eight hours per day on average.

No. This **strengthens** the argument by showing that the study did not contain certain methodological flaws.

(E)   Those who maintained the most unhealthy diets and exercise habits were also much more likely to sleep more than eight hours per day on average.

Yes. This suggests a third factor (bad diet and exercise habits) that may be causing both the increased amount of sleep and the shorter lifespan. Thus, the causal connection between sleep and lifespan is weakened.

10. **Choice (C) is the correct answer.**

The new theory concludes that [primates developed color vision to help detect hidden predators.] The supporting premises are not that strong—they just tell you that people developed the new theory by observing defensive tactics. Look for an answer choice that discredits the old theory or provides any evidence at all to support the new theory.

For each answer choice, the **Real Question** is, *"Does this suggest that primates developed color vision to help detect hidden predators?"*

(A)   Many predators have developed tremendous foot speed or flight speed that allows them to catch prey even when the predators are not hidden.

No. This suggests that color vision would not be useful against predators since they don't need to gain an advantage by hiding.

(B)   Primates are not the only animals capable of perceiving color, as many birds and fish have color receptors in their eyes.

No. Other animals that can see color are **out of scope**, and this choice has nothing to do with the reason the color vision developed.

(C)   Primates on the isolated island of Mentawai, which have few natural predators, developed color vision greatly inferior to that of most primates.

Yes. If the reason for color vision were to avoid predators, then primates without predators would have no reason to develop it. This choice fits with the new theory.

(D)   In tests, chimps generally have a harder time spotting green tree-borne fruit than fruit of any other color.

No. At best, this choice tells you that perhaps one way in which primates now use color vision is to help them pick out colorful fruits, but it doesn't illuminate anything new about the development of color vision.

(E)   Another theory claims that humans developed color vision superior to that of other primates to better perceive emotion.

No. So there's another theory. So what?

11.   **Choice (D) is the correct answer.**

This Strengthen question establishes a *correlation* between *airing the story* and *the police action* but concludes that one *caused* the other. To strengthen this argument, look for an answer choice that rules out a different possible cause for the police action or rules out the possibility that it was merely a coincidence.

For each answer choice, the **Real Question** is, *"Does this suggest that the journalists deserve the credit for the elimination of the betting ring?"*

(A)   The operators of the betting ring had ties to other illegal operations.

No. This does nothing to tie the story to the police action.

(B)   Local police were already informally investigating the sports betting ring before the story aired.

No. This **weakens** the argument by suggesting that the timing was just a coincidence.

(C)   Local police only launch a formal investigation of any case if a crime has been committed.

No. This suggests that the presence of a crime caused the investigation, but does nothing to tie the journalists to the police action.

(D)   No other news sources reported on the story until after the arrests were made.

Yes. This rules out another potential cause for the police action—reporting by rival news sources.

(E)   The journalists misreported the location of the betting ring's offices.

No. If anything, this would **weaken** the argument by suggesting that the police were able to raid the offices based on some other information besides the journalists' work.

12.   **Choice (A) is the correct answer.**

The passage for this question has a major Concept Shift between *full of open, accessible spaces* and *sure to increase productivity and socializing*. Since this is a Weaken EXCEPT question, put a **W** next to the four choices that show a disconnect between the two sides of the Concept Shift.

For each answer choice, the **Real Question** is, *"Does this suggest that the new building will not increase the productivity of joint projects or the amount of socializing?"*

(A)   The building is not well suited for holding classes.

The conclusion is about joint projects and socializing, so holding classes is **out of scope**. Don't put a **W**.

(B)   There are already many spaces on campus that are perfect for socializing yet are usually empty.

This suggests that people don't care about perfect socializing spaces, so this weakens the conclusion. Put a **W**.

(C)   The building is in an inconvenient location.

Even if the building is perfect, maybe no one will use it if it's in a bad location. This weakens the conclusion. Put a **W**.

(D)   Joint projects at the school, though rarely assigned, have been maximally productive for years.

You can't increase the productivity of something that's "maximally productive." Put a **W**.

(E)   Many students will be deterred from visiting the building by its unsightliness.

The building won't have any effect if no one uses it. Put a **W**.

Since choice (A) looks different from the rest, pick it.

13. **Choice (B) is the correct answer.**

The premises in this Weaken question establish a difference in the tendency to litter between two groups of people, made up of different individuals of different ages. The conclusion suggests that it is a permanent personality trait of the individuals that is responsible for the difference. The flaw is that the author ignores the possibility that it is the age of the people that is responsible. If youth is what causes people to litter, then the current old people must have littered more when they were young, and there is no reason to believe there would have been less litter in the past. Look for an answer choice that addresses this flaw.

For each answer choice, the **Real Question** is, *"Does this suggest that there was not substantially less litter around in previous decades?"*

(A)   Because products are packaged differently today, the litter in previous generations looked very different.

No. The conclusion is about the amount of litter, not its appearance. This is **out of scope**.

(B)   People tend to litter less as they age.

Yes. This is a good match for the Prephrased answer.

(C)   Less than one-tenth of the population today is seventy years of age and older.

No. The precise proportion of old people in the population is irrelevant.

(D)   Much of today's litter is composed of biodegradable wrappers, while in previous generations litter was generally more harmful to the environment.

No. Again, the argument is about the amount of litter, not its characteristics.

(E)   The study was conducted anonymously so as to increase the chances of obtaining honest responses.

No. This choice does nothing but strengthen the credibility of the premises, which you already accepted as true.

14. **Choice (C) is the correct answer.**

In this Strengthen question, there is a Concept Shift between *less likely to be spread by coughing* and *a long time before an outbreak*. Look for an answer choice that reinforces this connection or rules out any other possible mechanism that would increase the probability of an outbreak.

For each answer choice, the **Real Question** is, *"Does this suggest that it will be a long time before we see a widespread outbreak of avian influenza?"*

(A)   The avian influenza virus is resistant to most known vaccines, and attempts to create new vaccines for it have not been fruitful.

No. This is an **opposite** distracter. It weakens the argument by suggesting that the virus is harder for us to control and thus more likely to cause an outbreak.

(B)   The avian influenza virus tends to have much more severe, persistent symptoms than the human influenza virus.

No. The conclusion is about the transmission of the disease, not its symptoms. This is **out of scope**.

(C)   It would take decades for the avian influenza virus to accumulate the mutations necessary to allow it to settle in the upper respiratory tract.

Yes. This choice rules out one possible mechanism that would increase the probability of an outbreak in the short term.

(D)   Influenza viruses can be spread by saliva and sneezing as well as by coughing.

No. This is another **opposite** distracter, since it suggests a way the virus could cause an outbreak in the near future.

(E)   Influenza viruses are generally less contagious than some other viruses.

No. The existence of other contagious diseases out there has no impact on the likelihood of an influenza outbreak.

15. **Choice (A) is the correct answer.**

In this Weaken question, the only thing that you know for sure would cause Maria's work to suffer is *staying out late*, but the boss concludes that her work would suffer based on her *lack of a weak voice*. Although this lack of a weak voice establishes that she was not on the phone too long with a client, there could still be lots of reasons she was late other than staying out late. To weaken the boss's conclusion, look for a choice that suggests another reason for her lateness. If there is another reason, then there is no evidence from which to conclude that her work will suffer.

For each answer choice, the **Real Question** is, *"Does this suggest that Maria's lateness was not due to her staying out late the night before?"*

(A)   The road from Maria's house to her office was closed due to construction.

Yes. This suggests that she was late due to travel delays.

(B)   Maria's phone records indicate that she had had no long conversations the night before.

No. The premises already established that she was not on the phone too long with a client, so this choice adds nothing new.

(C)   Maria has a history of coming to work late after staying out late the night before.

No. This is an **opposite** distracter, since it suggests she really might have been out late.

(D)   Maria has performed exceptionally well when she arrives to work on time.

No. Since the argument is about a day when she was not on time, this choice is **out of scope**.

(E)   The quality of an employee's work can be affected by an employee's sleep habits.

No. This does nothing to establish another cause for Maria's lateness.

IN-CLASS EXAM ICE LECTURE 6

EXPLANATIONS

1. **Choice (E) is the correct answer.**

You can identify this as a Paradox question by the phrase *apparent discrepancy* in the question stem. The two facts in need of explanation are separated by the turnaround word *curiously*. The correct answer must explain how it could be true that the endowment exceeded $1 billion for the first time last month, even though the university has not received any donations in more than three months.

For each answer choice, the **Real Question** is, *"Does this explain how both facts could be true?"*

(A) The university spent a significant sum of money on an upgrade to its computer network last month.

No. If they're spending a lot of money, you'd expect the amount of cash they have to go down, not up. This is an **opposite** distracter.

(B) The accounts in which the endowment's funds are invested are managed by several full-time employees.

No. You'd expect someone to be managing the endowment, but their number and work schedule are **out of scope** since that doesn't explain how the endowment went up without new donations.

(C) The university received several substantial donations six months ago.

No. The time frame in question is the last three months, in which there were no donations but the endowment went up. Six months ago is **out of scope**.

(D) The accounts in which the endowment's funds are invested include a mixture of stocks and treasury bills.

No. You already know the endowment is invested, but the specifics of the type of investments is **out of scope**.

(E) The accounts in which the endowment's funds are invested have increased in value over the last three months.

Yes. This explains how the endowment could have gone up without donations. The investments started getting a good monetary return.

2. **Choice (A) is the correct answer.**

You can identify this as a Paradox question by the phrase *apparent conflict*. The two facts that form the paradox are separated by the turnaround word *yet*. The correct answer must explain how it could be true that there are more casualties per plane crash than twenty years ago, even though modern planes are much safer than they were twenty years ago.

For each answer choice, the **Real Question** is, *"Does this explain how both facts could be true?"*

(A) The latest passenger planes carry many more passengers than did those in use twenty years ago.

Yes. If there are many more people per plane, then you'd expect there to be more casualties per individual crash, even if there are fewer crashes due to the safer planes.

(B) There are many more overseas flights offered today than there were twenty years ago.

No. You have no reason to think overseas flights vs. overland flights would have anything to do with casualties per crash.

(C) The fuselages of the latest passenger planes are constructed with new materials that are nearly ten times stronger than those used twenty years ago.

No. Even if this explains why the planes are much safer, this answer choice is **incomplete** since it gives no explanation for why there are more casualties per crash.

(D) Because of their greater reliance on computers, there are more ways in which newer planes can malfunction.

No. This is also **incomplete**, since it doesn't address why planes are considered much safer today. The choice seems to suggest they are more dangerous.

(E) On a per-mile basis, flying is safer than driving, regardless of whether flight safety statistics from twenty years ago or from today are considered.

No. A comparison to driving is **out of scope**. You're trying to explain a comparison between planes now and planes twenty years ago.

3. **Choice (D) is the correct answer.**

This is a Paradox EXCEPT question, as identified by the phrase *apparent discrepancy* and the word *LEAST*. The two facts are separated by the turnaround word *yet*. You can use the EXCEPT Tool here. The four incorrect answer choices must explain how it could be true that the tax revenue is lower, even though the tax rate went up and smokers are still consuming the same amount.

For each answer choice, the **Real Question** is, *"Does this explain how both facts could be true?"* If a choice explains both facts, write an **E** next to the choice.

(A) There has been an increase in cigarette theft and subsequent sale of cigarettes on the black market.

Lecture 6 Explanations

This explains both facts. People are still smoking, but they're avoiding the higher taxes by going through the black market. Put an E.

(B)   To increase business, stores and vendors that sell cigarettes have stopped collecting sales tax on cash transactions.

This explains both facts. People aren't paying the higher tax rate because vendors aren't charging them. Put an E.

(C)   The pre-tax retail price of a pack of cigarettes has decreased markedly since last year.

This explains both facts. The higher tax rate is defined as a higher percentage of the price. If the price dropped dramatically, then the higher percentage might still result in a lower actual amount of tax being charged per pack. Put an E.

(D)   Revenue from income tax is down too, as is that from general local sales tax.

This doesn't explain both facts. Just because other tax revenues are down too doesn't show why cigarette taxes are down—with the same number of cigarettes being smoked, you'd think the higher tax rate would lead to higher tax revenues, regardless of what's happening with other taxes. Don't put an E.

(E)   Because of the tax increase, many smokers have begun to buy their cigarettes in bulk from outside the area.

This explains both facts. Residents are avoiding the tax by going somewhere else to buy their cigarettes. Put an E.

Choice (D) is different from the rest because it lacks an E. Thus, it must be correct.

4. **Choice (C) is the correct answer.**

You can identify this as a Paradox question by the phrase *apparent paradox*. The two facts are separated by the turnaround word *yet*. The correct answer must explain how it could be true that alcohol kills some of the gum-infection bacteria, while people who use it to do so most often end up with worse infections than those who don't.

For each answer choice, the **Real Question** is, *"Does this explain how both facts could be true?"*

(A)   Some of the sugars in some alcohol solutions also help to kill bacteria.

No. This is an **opposite** distracter, since if this were true you'd expect people who use alcohol to have more success against infections.

(B)   Many toothaches are related to poor dental hygiene.

No. This is **out of scope** because it addresses the cause of toothaches, while the passage is concerned with the outcome of a certain treatment.

(C)   Most people who treat their own toothaches with alcohol do so as an alternative to going to the dentist, where superior treatment can be administered.

Yes. If alcohol is somewhat effective but the dentist is better, then you'd expect people who skip the dentist to have worse infections than those who go.

(D)   Certain sufficiently acidic juices and vinegars can also kill some of the bacteria responsible for gum infections and toothaches.

No. The passage is concerned with people who use alcohol as a treatment. The existence of other home remedies is **out of scope**.

(E)   Consuming excessive amounts of alcohol can impair circulation, which in some cases can worsen gum infections and toothaches.

No. This is tricky, but it talks about something different from the passage. The passage mentions "applying alcohol to the affected area," which is not the same as "consuming excessive amounts of alcohol." This choice is **out of scope**.

5. **Choice (A) is the correct answer.**

The phrase *apparent discrepancy* identifies this as a Paradox question. The two facts are separated by the turnaround work *despite*. The correct answer must explain how it could be true that doctors do not advise men to drink beer regularly, even though beer can reduce the risk of prostate cancer.

For each answer choice, the **Real Question** is, *"Does this explain how both facts could be true?"*

(A)   The amount of beer one would have to drink to reduce the risk of prostate cancer would cause significant liver damage.

Yes. If the benefit is outweighed by some detrimental factor, then it makes sense that doctors wouldn't recommend beer.

(B)   Prostate cancer is not the leading cause of death among males in the United States, and beer has no appreciable effect on the most common cause of death.

No. Doctors are not solely concerned with the most common cause of death. You would expect them to recommend something beneficial even if it doesn't address the biggest problem.

(C)   Drinking beer regularly has been traditionally associated with negative stereotypes about men in the United States.

No. Regardless of traditional stereotypes, the passage establishes that beer reduces prostate cancer risk, so you'd expect doctors to recommend it. This choice doesn't explain why they don't.

(D)   It took many years of research for doctors to become convinced that beer could have a positive effect on the risk of cancer.

No. Regardless of the time it took to make the discovery, doctors now know that beer works. This choice doesn't explain why doctors don't recommend it.

(E)   Doctors are not yet sure whether the positive effects of regularly drinking beer extend beyond prostate cancer.

No. Even if it has no other benefits, you'd still expect doctors to recommend it, and this choice doesn't explain why they don't.

6.   **Choice (E) is the correct answer.**

This is a Flaw question since you are asked to describe a flaw. There are a couple of conditional statements here, so it's helpful to diagram them out.

MS → CH   CH → MPM
~CH → ~MS   ~MPM → ~CH

You can link them into a chain, and the passage also tells you one thing that's true: Jorge did not meet the project manager. Thus you can infer that he didn't go to company headquarters and that there was no meeting scheduled.

MS → CH → MPM
~MPM → ~CH → ~MS
     ✔   ✔   ✔

However, Nabeel concludes that there is no way to know anything about a meeting. His flaw is that he's just plain wrong. There *is* a way to know something about a meeting—the premises prove there was no meeting scheduled.

For each answer choice, the **Real Question** is, "*Is this a flaw in the argument?*"

(A)   The presumption is made, without providing justification, that Jorge's statements are necessarily reliable.

No. Nabeel did assume this, but that's not the reason his argument is flawed. This is **not a flaw**.

(B)   Jorge's statement represents a condition that is necessary but not sufficient for the argument's conclusion.

No. This **doesn't match** the argument. Nabeel did not commit a necessary vs. sufficient flaw.

(C)   Nabeel assumes, without providing justification, that Jorge could not have met with the project manager anywhere other than company headquarters.

No. There *is* justification for presuming that Jorge didn't meet the manager anywhere: Jorge's statement in the premises. This **doesn't match** the argument.

(D)   The argument bases its conclusion on the assumption that Jorge did go to company headquarters yesterday, which is inconsistent with Jorge's statement.

No. The argument bases its conclusion on the presumption that the only thing known about Jorge is that he didn't see the manager. This **doesn't match** the argument.

(E)   The argument claims as unknown information that is necessarily entailed by Jorge's statement.

Yes. This matches what happened in the argument, and it is a flaw.

7.   **Choice (A) is the correct answer.**

This is a Paradox EXCEPT question, as identified by the phrase *apparent paradox* and the word *EXCEPT*. The two facts are separated by the turnaround word *yet*. You can use the EXCEPT Tool here. The four incorrect answer choices must explain how it could be true that mustard sold at a much greater rate this week, even though it was on sale last week.

For each answer choice, the **Real Question** is, "*Does this explain how both facts could be true?*" If a choice explains both facts, write an E next to the choice.

(A)   Horseradish, which many people use instead of mustard, went on sale this week.

This doesn't explain both facts. If this were true, you'd expect mustard sales this week to be down, not up. Don't put an E.

(B)   A study was released this week indicating that mustard consumption can reduce blood pressure.

This explains both facts. If the study came out this week, you'd expect the sales to surge this week too. Put an E.

(C)   Hot dogs, which many people like to eat with mustard, went on sale this week.

This explains both facts. It gives a reason why people would buy a lot of mustard even though it's no longer on sale. Put an E.

(D)   A large condiment company began televising advertisements for mustard this week.

This explains both facts. If the ad campaign started this week, you'd expect sales to go up this week too. Put an E.

(E) Many people received their biweekly paycheck this Monday because it was the first day of the month.

This explains both facts. If people had a lot more money this week compared to last, then sales of everything would rise, including mustard. Put an **E**.

Choice (A) is different from the rest because it lacks an **E**. Thus, it must be correct.

8. **Choice (C) is the correct answer.**

This is a Paradox question, as you can tell by the phrase *apparently inconsistent claims*. The two facts are separated by the turnaround word *however*. The correct answer must explain how it could be true that there is no such thing as a clutch hitter in pro baseball, even though half the local high school players claim to be clutch hitters.

For each answer choice, the **Real Question** is, *"Does this explain how both facts could be true?"*

(A) The ability to perform better in more important situations is highly valued in many fields.

No. The passage is concerned with why there's a difference in clutch hitting between the pros and the high schoolers. The value placed on abilities is **out of scope**.

(B) Clutch hitting is a very rare talent, particularly among younger players.

No. This is **incomplete**. It explains why there are no clutch hitters in the pros, but not why half the high school players claim to be clutch hitters.

(C) The players good enough to play professionally always play their best in any situation.

Yes. This explains why there are no clutch hitters in the pros—they have to be good at *all* times, not just at important times. It also explains how it could be true that half the local high school players could be clutch hitters—they're not pros, so there's no reason to expect what's true of pros to be true of them.

(D) Rigorous statistical analysis has also cast doubt on whether there are clutch shooters in professional basketball.

No. The passage is about baseball. Basketball is completely **out of scope**.

(E) The Greenwood High School baseball team won its league championship last year.

No. This is **incomplete** because it does nothing to address the discrepancy between the high schoolers and the pros.

9. **Choice (B) is the correct answer.**

This is a Paradox question, as indicated by the phrase *curious situation*. The two facts to be explained are in the last sentence, as evidenced by the turnaround phrase *even though*. The correct answer must explain how it could be true that there has been a sharp decline in reported cases of mercury poisoning, even though there has been no drop in the number of fluorescent bulbs in production or in use.

For each answer choice, the **Real Question** is, *"Does this explain how both facts could be true?"*

(A) Techniques to detect symptoms of mercury poisoning have been improved in recent years.

No. If anything, this would cause you to think the number of reported cases would rise, not fall. This is an **opposite** distracter.

(B) The hazardous fluorescent bulbs are now more commonly used in industrial settings instead of in homes or in busy retail centers.

Yes. If the bulbs are now being used more in industrial settings, then they are being used less around children. That would explain the drop in mercury poisoning of kids.

(C) There has been no change in the use of mercury-based thermometers, which constitute the second leading cause of mercury poisoning.

No. This would make you think the number of reported cases of poisoning should be the same— it doesn't explain why it dropped.

(D) The general public has become much more aware of the need to be tested for mercury poisoning as soon as symptoms manifest themselves.

No. Again, this would make you think the number of reported cases would rise, since more people are being tested. This is another **opposite** distracter.

(E) Several new kinds of light bulbs have been developed that are more energy efficient than fluorescent bulbs.

No. This would make you think that people would move away from the fluorescent bulbs, but the passage tells you that the number of bulbs in use is the same. This choice does nothing to explain the paradox.

10. **Choice (E) is the correct answer.**

You can identify this as a Paradox question because of the phrase *apparent contradiction* in the question stem. The two facts are separated by the turnaround word *instead*. The correct answer must explain how it could be true that the nutritionist

Lecture 6 Explanations

thinks chicken is healthier than a protein shake, even though they contain the same amount of kidney-damaging protein.

For each answer choice, the **Real Question** is, *"Does this explain how both facts could be true?"*

(A)   Protein shakes cost more per serving than a quarter of a pound of chicken.

No. Cost is completely **out of scope**. The nutritionist's claim is about health.

(B)   Chicken also contains iron and several B vitamins, while containing a low amount of fat.

No. This is **incomplete**. It addresses why the chicken might be good, but not why the thirty grams of protein is harmful in the shake but not so in the chicken.

(C)   Protein shakes are often unnecessarily high in simple sugars, which can lead to weight gain.

No. This is also **incomplete**. It gives additional reasons why the shake might be bad, but it again fails to explain why the thirty grams of protein is harmful in the shake but not so in the chicken.

(D)   Most professional body builders consume several protein shakes per day without showing signs of kidney damage.

No. This seems to contradict what the nutritionist says about kidney damage, but it doesn't resolve the paradox.

(E)   Consuming protein via a liquid causes a much higher concentration of protein to enter the kidneys.

Yes. This explains why the same amount of protein could be healthier in one form than another.

11.   **Choice (B) is the correct answer.**

This is a Cannot Be True question. There is one conditional statement in the passage, and it can be diagrammed like this:

$$Lie \rightarrow KIAFSU$$
$$\sim KIAFSU \rightarrow \sim Lie$$

(Where **KIAFSU** stands for *know in advance that a false statement is untrue*.) When you have a conditional statement, you can always predict something that must be false by creating a statement that *matches* the left side of the symbol but *contradicts* the right side. Two good Prephrased answers in this case would be "Someone who lies does not know in advance that the false statement is untrue" and "Someone who does not know in advance that a false statement is untrue is lying." These two statements are impossible, so look for something like one of these.

For each answer choice, the **Real Question** is, *"Is this impossible?"*

(A)   People who tell the truth sometimes believe their true statements to be untrue.

No. The passage doesn't allow you to conclude anything for sure about people who are telling the truth. The conditional only allows you to draw a conclusion about someone you know is lying. You can't say for sure whether this is possible or impossible.

(B)   People who lie without feeling remorse sometimes believe their false statements to be true.

Yes. Ignore the remorse part, and this choice matches the first Prephrased answer.

(C)   Some statements that are accompanied by feelings of remorse are not lies.

No. You can only judge something to be a lie when you know something about the beliefs of the person saying the statement. Since you don't know that information here, you can't judge if this choice is possible or impossible.

(D)   If a false statement is believed to be untrue, then it is a lie.

No. Although this goes backwards against the arrow of the conditional, that just means you can't be sure whether it's true or not. It doesn't mean it's impossible.

(E)   No lies are ever accompanied by feelings of remorse.

No. The passage says not all lies are accompanied by remorse, and this choice just takes that one step further. It's certainly not impossible.

12.   **Choice (B) is the correct answer.**

This is a Paradox question, as evidenced by the phrase *apparent paradox*. The two facts to be explained are separated by the turnaround word *despite*. The correct answer must explain how it could be true that professionals are warning against the use of the vaccine, even though it's effective and has no side effects.

For each answer choice, the **Real Question** is, *"Does this explain how both facts could be true?"*

(A)   Children rarely suffer long-term harm as a result of contracting influenza.

No. This might make the professionals not care about whether kids take the vaccine, but it doesn't explain why they'd be concerned.

(B)   Overcoming influenza can strengthen the immune system of otherwise healthy people, improving their ability to combat more serious viruses.

Yes. Even though the vaccine doesn't harm anyone, this explains why the avoidance of influenza might be harmful, and thus, why professionals might be concerned about widespread use of the vaccine.

(C)   The vaccine is administered over three separate doses, and the elderly may be likely to forget one of the doses.

No. Even if the elderly forget, it seems that this would just make the vaccine ineffective, not dangerous or alarming.

(D)   The vaccine can be rendered ineffective by consumption of alcohol within several days of taking it.

No. Again, just because there are ways the vaccine could become ineffective doesn't explain why professionals would be concerned about its widespread use.

(E)   Many families cannot afford enough doses of the vaccine for all of their children.

No. Health professionals are concerned about too many people taking the vaccine, but this does nothing to explain why. This is **out of scope**.

13.   **Choice (C) is the correct answer.**

You can identify this as a Paradox question since the stem asks you to account for a strange situation, and because there are two apparently contradictory facts in the passage separated by the turnaround word *despite*. The correct answer must explain how it could be true that the PCB levels in the shrimp are unchanged, even though the PCB levels in their water have dropped by 40 percent.

For each answer choice, the **Real Question** is, *"Does this explain how both facts could be true?"*

(A)   PCBs have been determined to be less harmful to humans than previously thought.

No. You need to explain why the levels didn't change. The harmfulness of PCBs is **out of scope**.

(B)   Non-farmed shrimp have shown a gradual increase in PCB levels over the last two years.

No. The passage is about farmed shrimp. Non-farmed shrimp are **out of scope**.

(C)   Even at the lower PCB concentration enforced by the regulations, the shrimp are exposed to more PCBs than their bodies are capable of absorbing.

Yes. Both before and after the regulations, the shrimp's absorption of PCB was determined not by the amount in the water but by the maximum amount their bodies could absorb. If this were true, you'd expect their levels to be the same in both cases.

(D)   When other creatures consume shrimp with high PCB levels, significant quantities of the toxin are absorbed by their own digestive systems, potentially leading to health complications.

No. Again, you're concerned with the levels in the shrimp, not the ramifications of those levels in other creatures.

(E)   Adherence to the new regulations has turned out to be more costly than had initially been projected.

No. Since the passage tells you that the farmers have strictly adhered to the regulations, the cost is irrelevant.

14.   **Choice (A) is the correct answer.**

This is an Explain question since you are asked to *explain* the lower yield of the CSA farms. It's also an EXCEPT question, so you should use the EXCEPT Tool. The four incorrect answers must explain how it could be true that CSA farms have consistently had much lower yields than normal farms.

For each answer choice, the **Real Question** is, *"Does this explain the fact from the passage?"* If a choice explains the lower yield, write an E next to the choice.

(A)   Raising funds before the growing season does not allow CSA farmers to prepare for all possible weather-related setbacks.

This does not explain why CSA farms should be any different from normal farms, as it seems that normal farms would also be in the same situation—they would not be able to prepare for all possible weather-related setbacks either. Don't put an E.

(B)   Traditional farms that are already high-yielding are less likely to become CSA farms than farms that are struggling.

This explains the fact. CSA farms do worse because it's only the bad farms that decide to become CSA farms. Put an E.

(C)   CSA farms tend primarily to be organic farms, which typically have lower yields than non-organic farms due to the avoidance of chemical pesticides and growth hormones.

This explains the fact. CSA farms have lower yields because they use less efficient methods. Put an E.

(D)   Farmers who are paid before the growing season begins have less incentive to be productive than farmers who are only paid for what they actually produce.

This explains the fact. CSA farms have lower yields because the farmers don't work as hard. Put an **E**.

(E)   CSA farmers are often compelled to grow lower-yield crops in accordance with the preferences and requests of their shareholders.

This explains the fact. CSA farms have lower yields because of their crop choices. Put an **E**.

Choice (A) is different from the rest because it lacks an **E**. Thus, it must be correct.

15. **Choice (D) is the correct answer.**

This is an Explain question, as you can tell from the word *explain* in the question stem and from the fact that you're asked to explain a single fact. You should be very familiar with correlation and causation from your study of common flaws. How could there be a correlation between two things when neither causes the other? One explanation would be that it's merely a coincidence. A more likely explanation would be that there is a third factor that causes both.

For each answer choice, the **Real Question** is, *"Does this explain the fact from the passage?"*

(A)   About one percent of the general population suffers from schizophrenia.

No. The exact number of people with schizophrenia does nothing to explain the correlation.

(B)   Schizophrenia has been officially classified as a disease of the brain.

No. The classification of schizophrenia also does nothing to explain the correlation.

(C)   Drug use has been identified as a cause of several other neurochemical disorders.

No. Other things that drug use can cause are **out of scope**.

(D)   The onset of schizophrenia most often occurs between the ages of 16 and 25, which is also the age range in which most drug users begin using drugs.

Yes. This is the third factor you're looking for. Being a certain age causes an increase in both schizophrenia and drug use, which is enough to create a correlation.

(E)   Genetic inheritance plays a strong role in the likelihood that a person will develop schizophrenia, but it does not seem to play a strong role in determining drug-use habits.

No. This is **incomplete**. It gives a third factor, but genetic inheritance causes only one part of the correlation, not both.

IN-CLASS EXAM   ICE   LECTURE   7

EXPLANATIONS

Lecture 7 Explanations

1. **Choice (E) is the correct answer.**

This is a Sufficient Assumption question since the question stem asks you to add a premise that would make the conclusion *follow logically*. The premises give you two criteria—good protagonist, good plot—that make a short story worth reading, and tell you that Millar's meets one of them. But the author jumps to the conclusion that [Millar's story is worth reading.] The missing piece here is the second criterion. The correct answer should establish that Millar's story has a good protagonist.

For each answer choice, the **Real Question** is, *"Does this guarantee the conclusion?"*

(A)   The quality of the plot is a much more important factor than the quality of the protagonist in evaluating short stories.

No. Measuring the relative weight of the two criteria does nothing to guarantee the conclusion.

(B)   The supporting characters of Millar's latest short story are multidimensional without being too intricate to fully grasp.

No. The supporting characters were never mentioned in the passage and are **out of scope**.

(C)   Any short story that features a protagonist that is too simple or too complex is only worth reading if its plot does not have the same flaw.

No. The missing piece is about Millar's story, but this choice establishes nothing new about Millar.

(D)   The plot of Millar's latest short story is very original.

No. You already know the plot is good enough. You need to establish that the protagonist is good too.

(E)   The protagonist of Millar's latest short story is neither overly complex nor too simple.

Yes. This is a good match for the Prephrased answer.

2. **Choice (A) is the correct answer.**

This is a Justify question since it asks for a *principle* that strengthens the publisher's conclusion. You have to do a little work to determine what that conclusion is. Her comments are a counterargument against the editor's, so her conclusion must be the negation of the editor's. Since the editor concludes that the magazine should not publish the article, the publisher must be arguing that [the magazine *should* publish the article.]

In the publisher's premises, she doesn't argue against the fact that the objections are misguided or even that the readers would be offended. But she does point out that readers would get to see the article rebutted by experts in a public forum. This is her only evidence. So her argument works like this:

- The article is misguided.

- Publishing it would offend readers.

- Publishing it would give readers the chance to see the article rebutted by experts.

Therefore, the magazine should publish the article.

Since the premises include something good and something bad about the article, the correct answer must establish that the reason *to* publish is more important than the reason *not* to publish. That's the missing piece in this argument.

For each answer choice, the **Real Question** is, *"Does this guarantee the conclusion?"*

(A)   The benefit of being exposed to several points of view outweighs the harm of being offended.

Yes. This is a good match for the Prephrased answer.

(B)   Opposition to scientific advancement is usually based in misunderstanding rather than a particular moral stance.

No. This doesn't add any new information, since the editor already established that "the objections are misguided."

(C)   Readers are not often offended by views they consider to be plainly wrong.

No. This misconstrues the publisher's conclusion. She is not arguing about whether readers will be offended. She is arguing about whether the article should be published.

(D)   The publication of offensive or widely discredited work should be avoided.

No. This supports the editor's conclusion, not the publisher's.

(E)   It is important to allow the general public to take part in scientific debate.

No. This is wrong because the experts, not the general public, will be engaging in the debate.

3. **Choice (D) is the correct answer.**

This is a Sufficient Assumption question because the question stem asks you to add a premise that would make the conclusion *follow logically*. The conclusion, which is that [State Road 236 is not a major road], contains a new concept—*State Road 236*—that was not mentioned anywhere else in the argument. Thus, you can eliminate choices (A) and (B), which don't contain this new concept.

The premises contain this conditional chain:

$$MR \rightarrow DBM \rightarrow DTR$$
$$\sim DTR \rightarrow \sim DBM \rightarrow \sim MR$$

The far right end of the second chain has the thing you want to be able to say about SR 236. Since the LSAT writers love long chains, the best Prephrased answer is to say that the far *left* end of the chain is true for SR 236. If it were true that SR 236 was not difficult to repair, then you could follow the chain and logically conclude that it was not a major road.

For each answer choice, the **Real Question** is, *"Does this guarantee the conclusion?"*

(A)   Every road that is difficult to repair is a major road.

No. This was eliminated by the New Concept Tool.

(B)   Nothing difficult to repair lacks a median.

No. This was eliminated by the New Concept Tool.

(C)   State Road 236 has a median.

No. This would simply establish that it is difficult to repair, which is not the conclusion.

(D)   State Road 236 is not difficult to repair.

Yes. A perfect match for the Prephrased answer.

(E)   State Road 236 either lacks a median or is difficult to repair.

No. The part about lacking a median is good, but being difficult to repair does nothing, so this choice is not good enough to guarantee the conclusion.

4.   **Choice (A) is the correct answer.**

This is a Justify question since it asks for a *principle* that *justifies* the teacher's conclusion. The teacher concludes that [Jill should be punished almost as severely], but the premises simply establish that Jill held her test in such a way as to facilitate the cheating, even though she didn't know it was happening. That's a definite Concept Shift. The correct answer must establish that facilitating cheating is an action that deserves punishment.

You can also use the New Concept Tool to eliminate any answer choice that fails to mention punishment, as that's a new concept that appears only in the conclusion.

For each answer choice, the **Real Question** is, *"Does this guarantee the conclusion?"*

(A)   Anyone whose actions allow a transgression to occur shares some of the responsibility for it.

Yes. Jill's actions "allowed a transgression to occur," so this choice, if true, establishes that she shares some responsibility and should thus be punished along with others who are responsible.

(B)   All students involved in cheating, knowingly or not, ought to be punished equally.

No. This doesn't match the conclusion, since Jill is not punished "equally." She is punished "almost as severely."

(C)   Anyone who makes it so easy for others to cheat must have intended to allow them to do so.

No. You can eliminate this choice using the New Concept Tool, since it doesn't mention punishment.

(D)   Cheating is a serious academic offense and thus should always be punished thoroughly as a deterrent.

No. This choice has nothing to do with Jill, since she didn't cheat. It was Mike that cheated, so this choice doesn't justify the punishment of Jill.

(E)   Anyone who accepts full blame for something should not be punished as much as someone who does not admit to any wrongdoing.

No. This doesn't match the argument, since Mike, who accepted full blame, was punished more than Jill.

5.   **Choice (A) is the correct answer.**

This is a Sufficient Assumption question as the question stem asks you to add a premise that would allow the conclusion to be *properly drawn*. The premises establish that a higher *number* of females got the certificate. But the author jumps to the conclusion that [females had a higher *probability* of getting the certificate]—that is, that a larger *percentage* of females got the certificate.

You should recognize this as a statistics flaw, one of the common flaws. The missing piece in this argument is something that establishes that the two populations are appropriately sized to make the math work out. The size of the female population must be the same or smaller.

For each answer choice, the **Real Question** is, *"Does this guarantee the conclusion?"*

(A)   More males than females took the test.

Yes. This is what you're looking for. For example, if 35 males took the test, then 1 in 5 of them (20%) got a certificate. If the female population was smaller, say 30, then 1 in 2 of them (50%) got the certificate. That guarantees that a random female is more likely than a random male to have received the certificate.

(B)   The two highest scores on the test were both achieved by females.

No. You care only about those who received the certificate, not about who got the top score.

(C)   The average score among females was slightly higher than the average score among males.

No. You only care only about those who received the certificate, not about the averages.

(D)   The test was composed of a math section and a vocabulary section.

No. The composition of the test is completely irrelevant.

(E)   Similar results were observed on last year's test.

No. The argument is about this year's test. Last year's is **out of scope**.

6. **Choice (B) is the correct answer.**

This is a Justify question as it asks for a *principle* that *justifies* the reasoning. The premises establish that the gallery provides little information about the political and social circumstances surrounding the sculpture and that visitors won't already have this knowledge. But the author jumps to the conclusion that [the gallery will fail to instill a deep understanding of the sculptures.]

First, use the New Concept Tool to eliminate any answer choice that fails to mention a "deep understanding," since that idea appears for the first time in the conclusion. That gets rid of choices (A), (C), and (D). Next, look for a choice that connects the premises and conclusion. It should establish that knowledge of the political and social circumstances surrounding something is necessary for a deep understanding of that thing.

For each answer choice, the **Real Question** is, *"Does this guarantee the conclusion?"*

(A)   Gallery directors should be as concerned with presenting historical information as with presenting the art itself.

No. This was eliminated by the New Concept Tool.

(B)   One cannot attain a deep understanding of an artwork without familiarity with the culture in which it was created.

Yes. This matches the Prephrased answer perfectly.

(C)   One cannot learn as much from a gallery with pieces from only a single period as from a gallery that covers a range of periods.

No. This was eliminated by the New Concept Tool.

(D)   Everyone would benefit from a greater knowledge of Japanese history.

No. This was eliminated by the New Concept Tool.

(E)   Galleries should be designed to instill a deep understanding of their art in all of their visitors.

No. Even if this is true, it doesn't guarantee that the gallery will fail to establish a deep understanding in visitors, since it doesn't mention historical knowledge.

7. **Choice (C) is the correct answer.**

This is a Sufficient Assumption question since the question stem asks you to add a premise that would make the conclusion *follow logically*. The passage is full of conditionals, so start diagramming them. The second sentence has the word *only*, which you should turn into an arrow and diagram like this:

$$AL \rightarrow D$$
$$\sim D \rightarrow \sim AL$$

The next sentence if a little trickier. Again, turn *only those* into an arrow. Put **DIW** on the left side of the conditional too, because the conditional only applies to those planes delayed by inclement weather.

$$DIW \text{ and } \sim AL \rightarrow DMR$$
$$\sim DMR \rightarrow \sim DIW \text{ or } AL$$

You could try to combine the two conditionals into a branching chain, but that seems confusing because of all the different types of D's. See if you can answer the question without a chain.

The conclusion is that [the Chicago plane arrived late.] The contrapositive of the second conditional ends with **AL** on the right-hand side, so you'd like to be able to trigger that conditional for the Chicago plane. You could do so by establishing that it was not delayed by mild rainfall. However, the or is troubling. Couldn't the alternate conclusion be that the Chicago plane was not delayed by inclement weather? No. The first sentence of the passage tells you it was delayed by inclement weather. Thus, your Prephrased answer should be that the Chicago plane was not delayed by mild rainfall. That would guarantee that it arrived late.

For each answer choice, the **Real Question** is, *"Does this guarantee the conclusion?"*

(A)   The Chicago-bound plane was not delayed for any additional reasons besides inclement weather.

No. This doesn't necessarily trigger the last conditional because the inclement weather could have been mild rainfall.

(B)   All flights on the day in question were delayed by the inclement weather.

No. Other flights are irrelevant.

(C)   The Chicago-bound plane was not delayed by mild rainfall.

Yes. A perfect match for the Prephrased answer.

(D)   The Chicago-bound plane was further delayed by the need to repair the landing gear.

No. Don't try to go backwards against the arrow in the first conditional.

(E)   Both Chicago and the plane's city of departure experienced mild rainfall throughout the day in question.

No. This is the opposite of what you're looking for.

8.   **Choice (D) is the correct answer.**

This is an Inference question because the question stem asks you for something that *must be true*. The passage is full of conditionals, so start diagramming. A quick skim of the passage and answer choices reveals that you can keep everything in terms of the Ascot for simplicity.

$$NPRBB \longrightarrow LV$$
$$\sim LV \longrightarrow \sim NPRBB$$

$$NPRBB \longrightarrow DGA \longrightarrow SDBD$$
$$\sim SDBD \longrightarrow \sim DGA \longrightarrow \sim NPRBB$$

The two conditionals in the second sentence can be combined into a chain, but they cannot be combined with the conditional in the first sentence, since they both start with **NPRBB** (nearby parks replaced by buildings).

Since you're not told anything that is certain about the Ascot, you can't conclude anything definite from the passage alone. The correct answer choice must give you a conditional that follows the ones you diagrammed.

For each answer choice, the **Real Question** is, "*Is this guaranteed to be true?*"

(A)   If the developers submit their designs before the deadline, the Ascot condominium will lose value.

No. You can't conclude anything from **SDBD** because you can't go backwards against the arrow.

(B)   If the nearby park is not replaced by an apartment building, the Ascot will not lose value.

No. This also tries to go backwards.

(C)   The park near the Ascot will be replaced by an apartment building.

No. You can't conclude anything definite from the passage alone.

(D)   If the developers fail to submit their designs before the deadline, the park near the Ascot will not be replaced by a new apartment building.

Yes. This follows the contrapositive chain from left to right.

(E)   If the developers are not given approval, the Ascot will not lose value.

No. You can conclude that the nearby park will not be replaced by buildings, but you can't go backwards against the arrow and say the Ascot will not lose value.

9.   **Choice (E) is the correct answer.**

This is a Justify question since the stem asks you to find a *principle* that *justifies* Angela's response. The premises are the details of Jasmine's situation, which both people agree on. Angela's conclusion is that [the plumber is not liable.] This is a new concept, but the New Concept Tool is not of much use here because the question stem is written in such a way that every answer choice relates to plumber liability.

However, the answer choices all involve conditional language, so a rough diagram can help. The correct direction for an answer choice that guarantees the conclusion is:

if premises ⟶ then conclusion

So in this case, you'd be looking for

Jasmine's situation ⟶ plumber not liable
plumber liable ⟶ not Jasmine's situation

Look for an answer choice that, combined with the grammar in the question stem, yields one of these two conditionals.

For each answer choice, the **Real Question** is, "*Does this guarantee the conclusion?*"

(A)   if the damage was caused by either a part that the plumber installed or by a previously existing condition

No. Jasmine's damage was caused by a previously existing condition, so this matches Jasmine's situation and yields the conditional:

Jasmine's situation ⟶ plumber liable

That's not what you're looking for.

Lecture 7 Explanations

(B)   only if the damage was caused by a previously existing condition rather than a part the plumber installed

No. The damage was caused by a previously existing condition, so this matches Jasmine's situation. Because the *only if* acts like an arrow, this answer choice yields:

plumber liable ⟶ Jasmine's situation

That's also not what you're looking for.

(C)   only if the part that the plumber installed caused an already defective part to break

No. This matches Jasmine's situation, so this choice produces:

plumber liable ⟶ Jasmine's situation

That's not what you're looking for.

(D)   if the damage was caused not by a part that the plumber failed to install properly, but rather by a part that was installed properly by a previous plumber

No. The previous part was not installed properly, so this does not match Jasmine's situation. The answer choice produces:

not Jasmine's situation ⟶ plumber liable

That's not what you're looking for.

(E)   only if the damage was caused by the malfunction of a part installed by that plumber

Yes. The damage was not caused by a malfunction of a part installed by the new plumber, so this doesn't match Jasmine's situation. If you combine the *only if* with the grammar of the question stem, this choice yields:

plumber liable ⟶ not Jasmine's situation

This matches the conditional you're looking for.

10. **Choice (B) is the correct answer.**

This is a Sufficient Assumption question since the question stem asks you to add a premise that would allow the conclusion to be *properly drawn*. The argument sounds like it makes sense; Rico's school was two gold medals behind the leading school, so if Rico had won three gold medals for his school instead of none, his school would have had the most.

This sounds pretty good, except it overlooks the possibility that some other competitors from Rico's school won gold medals in Rico's events. In such a case, Rico's winning a gold medal would remove a gold medal from another competitor from his school, and thus would not add any new gold medals to his school's total. Basically, there's a concept shift between *Rico* getting more

gold medals and *Rico's school* getting more gold medals. Look for an answer choice that eliminates this problem.

For each answer choice, the **Real Question** is, *"Does this guarantee the conclusion?"*

(A)   Other than the school with the most gold medals, no school won more gold medals than Rico's school.

No. This does not solve the problem of Rico potentially taking medals away from his classmates.

(B)   Rico was the only competitor from his school in the three events in which he competed.

Yes. This matches the Prephrased answer.

(C)   Rico did not win any silver or bronze medals in any of his three events.

No. The argument concerns only gold medals, so this is **out of scope**.

(D)   Rico's school has never won the most gold medals at a track meet before.

No. The argument concerns the current meet, so past performance is **out of scope**.

(E)   The school with the most gold medals would have placed lower in the events in which Rico competed had Rico won three gold medals.

No. You don't know whether any of the leading school's gold medals came from Rico's events, so this does not necessarily guarantee any fewer gold medals for the leading school, and it still allows for the problem of Rico taking gold medals away from his classmates, so this does not guarantee the conclusion.

11. **Choice (C) is the correct answer.**

This is a Sufficient Assumption question since the question stem asks you to add a premise that would make the conclusion *follow logically*. The premises establish that the new technology will give us the chance to devote more time to activities other than sleep, but the author jumps to the conclusion that [the new technology will give us the chance to lead better lives.]

The **Concept Shift** in this argument occurs when the author treats as equal the concepts of *devoting more time to activities other than sleep* and *devoting more time to the pursuits we truly enjoy*. If we truly enjoy sleep, then this argument falls apart. If we don't, then the argument is sound—we would indeed have at least the chance to lead better lives.

For each answer choice, the **Real Question** is, *"Does this guarantee the conclusion?"*

(A)   People are always accurately aware of which pursuits they truly enjoy.

No. This doesn't fix the Concept Shift or guarantee the conclusion.

(B)   The technology to which the physician refers will be attainable within the next decade.

No. Even if it arrives soon, the physician's conclusion is not guaranteed.

(C)   Sleep is not a pursuit that we truly enjoy.

Yes. This matches the Prephrased answer.

(D)   Sleep is not physiologically necessary for human beings.

No. This doesn't fix the Concept Shift.

(E)   Future technologies will eliminate our physiological need to eat.

No. Eating is not mentioned and is **out of scope**.

12.   **Choice (C) is the correct answer.**

This is a Justify question since the question stem asks you for a *principle* that *justifies* the professor's reasoning. The students' discouragement comes from their perceived inability to appreciate a poem's value, but the professor concludes that [the students' discouragement is unwarranted]—that is, they *do* have an ability to appreciate a poem's value. He reaches this conclusion based on the premise that they can get some sorts of meaningful ideas and emotions as they read. The Concept Shift occurs between the students' perceptions of imagery and the poet's intended imagery. If an answer choice shows these are equally valid, then either can be used to appreciate a poem's value, and the professor's conclusion is guaranteed.

For each answer choice, the **Real Question** is, *"Does this guarantee the conclusion?"*

(A)   Poets should never compose poetry with imagery too obscure to be easily understood.

No. The argument is not about what poets should do.

(B)   Students should study poetry even if they are unable to appreciate its value.

No. The conclusion is about whether they can appreciate the value, not whether they should study poetry.

(C)   One's own interpretation of poetic imagery is no less valuable than that of the author.

Yes. This matches the Prephrased answer.

(D)   Readers who are certain of the intended meaning of poetic imagery will better appreciate a poem's value.

No. The argument only makes a distinction between whether or not someone can appreciate a poem's value, not different degrees of appreciation.

(E)   The study of poetry should not be compulsory in schools.

No. This is completely **out of scope**.

13.   **Choice (A) is the correct answer.**

This is a Justify question because the question stem asks for a *principle* that *justifies* the attorney's judgment. The premises establish that free speech must always be protected to the maximum extent possible in any form in which it is beneficial to society as a whole. The premises also establish that the appeals court's decision undermined a type of free speech, but the attorney jumps to the conclusion that [the decision is a terrible one.] The missing piece here is whether the free speech being restricted (what journalists are able to write) is beneficial to society as a whole. Look for an answer choice that establishes this.

For each answer choice, the **Real Question** is, *"Does this guarantee the conclusion?"*

(A)   Freedom of journalistic expression benefits society as a whole.

Yes. This is a perfect match for the Prephrased answer.

(B)   Journalists have a responsibility to report personal details of people accused of crimes.

No. Even if they have such a responsibility, that doesn't guarantee that it benefits society as a whole, so the attorney's conclusion is not guaranteed.

(C)   Criminals should have no right to sue those who endanger them.

No. The right to sue is not the relevant issue.

(D)   The appeals process is inefficient and therefore does not benefit society as a whole.

No. This mentions society as a whole, but it does not provide the missing piece in the attorney's logic.

(E)   Freedom of speech is the most important freedom to protect.

No. Even if this is true, it doesn't establish that journalistic expression is beneficial to society as a whole.

14. **Choice (C) is the correct answer.**

This is a Sufficient Assumption question as it asks for a premise to be added that allows the conclusion to *follow logically*. The passage is also crawling with conditional and quantity statements. Diagram the premises and the conclusion separately.

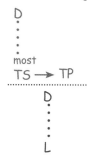

First, notice that libertarianism is an entirely new concept that appears only in the conclusion, so use the New Concept Tool to eliminate any answer choice that lacks this idea. That gets rid of choice (E).

Next, think about how you can link libertarianism into the premises in such a way as to be able to conclude that at least one deist is a libertarian. One way would be to use the Most-Most Overlap and say that most true scientists are libertarians. The other way would be to link libertarianism to the end of the conditional chain and say that all theoretical physicists are libertarians.

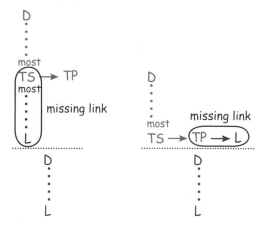

Either of these missing links would guarantee the conclusion.

For each answer choice, the **Real Question** is, *"Does this guarantee the conclusion?"*

(A)   All libertarians are scientists.

No. You need something more specific—you need to know about true scientists.

(B)   Many true scientists are libertarians.

No. This comes close to using the Most-Most Overlap, but it falls short by using *many* instead of *most*.

(C)   All theoretical physicists are libertarians.

Yes. This matches the Prephrased answer.

(D)   One cannot be a libertarian without eschewing empirical evidence, which can be deceiving.

No. This can be simplified to say that if you are a libertarian, you eschew empirical evidence, but that doesn't provide the link you need.

(E)   A scientist is a deist only if that person is also a theoretical physicist.

No. This was eliminated using the New Concept Tool.

15. **Choice (D) is the correct answer.**

This is a Justify question. The author jumps to the conclusion that [we should accept that pseudocopulation serves a biological function] based on the premise that pseudocopulation has been observed in wild whiptail lizards. This is a pretty big Concept Shift. Look for an answer choice that says if something has been observed in the wild, we should accept that it serves a biological function.

For each answer choice, the **Real Question** is, *"Does this guarantee the conclusion?"*

(A)   When there is a lack of empirical evidence for a claim, that claim should be questioned.

No. You're looking for a choice that justifies something being accepted, not questioned.

(B)   We should accept that a process serves a biological function only if that process occurs in the wild.

No. This choice is close, but the *only if* instead of an *if* means it gets the pieces backwards.

(C)   Behaviors that occur in the wild often serve a biological function.

No. You need something that guarantees the conclusion, but *often* is not strong enough.

(D)   We should accept that a behavior serves a biological function if it occurs in the wild.

Yes. This is a perfect match for the Prephrased answer.

(E)   Behaviors that do not serve a biological function occur only in captivity.

No. The argument is about behaviors that *do* serve a biological function.

IN-CLASS EXAM ICE LECTURE 8

EXPLANATIONS

Lecture 8 Explanations

1. **Choice (A) is the correct answer.**

This is a Method question since the stem asks you *how* Cahira responds. Alison argues that raising wages can solve the problem of the nurse shortage. In Cahira's first sentence she shows that shortages can still exist even in a profession with high wages. In her second sentence, she says, "We need *not only* better wages *but also* less stress." That is, she doesn't disagree with the idea that Alison's proposal is necessary, but she thinks something else is *also* necessary to solve the problem. Look for a choice that matches this.

For each answer choice, the **Real Question** is, *"Does this match the argument?"*

(A)   pointing out that something required for a certain result does not necessarily guarantee that result

Yes. This is a good match for the Prephrased answer. She thinks higher wages are necessary, but that they can't single-handedly solve the shortage.

(B)   showing that Alison's statements are self-contradictory

No. This didn't happen. There is no contradiction.

(C)   charging that Alison exaggerated the severity of a problem in order to defend a questionable proposal

No. This doesn't match the argument. There is no accusation of exaggeration.

(D)   suggesting that Alison's proposed solution could instead worsen the problem it is intended to solve

No. Cahira's objection to Alison's solution is that it's incomplete, not that it will make things worse.

(E)   arguing that Alison fails to consider a strategy that could accomplish the same goal as the strategy that Alison considers

No. Cahira argues that Alison failed to consider something, but she thinks the two strategies are both necessary, not that either could accomplish the goal by itself.

2. **Choice (C) is the correct answer.**

This is a Conform question since the question stem uses the words *principle* and *conform*. In this case, you are asked to apply the principle. The principle pertains to these **circumstances**: when an illegal action cannot possibly lead to the harm the law is meant to prevent. The **outcome** is: law enforcement officials should not cite.

For each answer choice, the **Real Question** is, *"Does this match the principle in the passage?"*

(A)   Sue illegally ran a red light very late at night when she thought there were no other drivers on the road. Since there could have been vehicles or pedestrians that she was unable to see at night, she could have harmed someone, so the officer was right to cite her.

No. This doesn't match the circumstances, since she could have harmed people, and it doesn't match the outcome, since the officer did cite her.

(B)   Heather illegally walked across the road during a red light at a busy intersection. Since she could have forced a car to swerve to avoid her and cause an accident, she should be heavily fined.

No. This doesn't match the circumstances, since she could have harmed people, and it doesn't match the outcome, since the judgment is that she should be cited.

(C)   Maggie illegally chose not to signal while navigating the parking lot. Since it was clear that there were no other vehicles or pedestrians in the parking lot that could have been harmed, the officer was right not to cite her.

Yes. This matches the circumstances, since she could not have harmed anyone, and it matches the outcome, since it judges that the officer should not cite her.

(D)   Julia exceeded the legal speed limit on a busy highway. Since she was in a hurry to get to an important meeting on time, the officer was right not to cite her.

No. This doesn't match the circumstances, since her speeding could have caused an accident and harmed people.

(E)   Holly drove on the wrong side of the road for several blocks. Since she did not hurt anyone, the officer was right not to cite her.

No. This doesn't match the circumstances, since her driving on the wrong side of the road could have caused an accident and harmed people.

3. **Choice (A) is the correct answer.**

This is a Method question because it asks you *how* ("using which technique") Samantha responds. Vishal argues on the basis of a principle: government should not pass legislation that infringes upon a person's ability to earn a living. Samantha does not dispute his principle, but she introduces another principle: government's priority is to ensure the health and safety of its citizens. Using this principle she reaches an opposite conclusion, that [the ban should be enacted.] She deals with the contradictory conclusions by saying her principle is more important that Vishal's—she says it's government's "top priority."

For each answer choice, the **Real Question** is, *"Does this match the argument?"*

(A)   introducing a consideration that leads to a conclusion different from that of Vishal's argument

Yes. This matches her first sentence, in which she introduces a new consideration, and her conclusion, which contradicts his.

(B)   demonstrating that Vishal's conclusion is inconsistent with evidence advanced to support it

No. Vishal's conclusion follows logically from his premises, and Samantha doesn't try to point out any contradiction within his argument.

(C)   showing that Vishal's argument relies on citing an unrepresentative case

No. This simply doesn't match what happened.

(D)   arguing that the health of customers is more important than the health of business owners

No. Samantha argues that the health of everyone should be protected.

(E)   presenting a possible alternative method for preserving both public health and a person's ability to earn a living

No. Samantha does not address anyone's ability to earn a living.

4.   **Choice (B) is the correct answer.**

This is a Method question since it asks you *how* ("using which technique") the author reaches his conclusion. The author disagrees with the researchers, but it's important to notice what exactly is in dispute. The researchers found that moderate wine drinkers are healthier, and they attributed this phenomenon to the wine. The author *does not* dispute the data, but he *does* dispute their explanation for it. He suggests that the better health might come from the moderation, not from the wine. His method is to offer a different reason.

For each answer choice, the **Real Question** is, *"Does this match the argument?"*

(A)   demonstrating that the original conclusion was based on false premises

No. This doesn't match the argument.

(B)   suggesting an alternative explanation for the phenomenon observed by the researchers

Yes. This is a good match for the Prephrased answer.

(C)   showing that the researchers relied on an inaccurate understanding of the subjects' reasons for engaging in an activity

No. You're never told what the researchers think about why people drink moderate amounts of wine, and the author never speculates on this either.

(D)   agreeing that a connection between the consumption of red wine and heart disease can be made, but questioning whether any conclusion about drinking guidelines can be drawn

No. The author never mentions drinking guidelines at all.

(E)   challenging the validity of the statistical sample used by the researchers

No. The author agrees with the raw data. He just disagrees with the interpretation of it.

5.   **Choice (E) is the correct answer.**

This is a Conform question because the question stem uses the words *conform* and *principle*. In this case, you are asked to state the principle. The first two sentences in the passage give you the background of the situation, and the third conveys the comptroller's principle. In general terms, her principle is that: someone should not be blamed if they made the best decision using the information available at the time.

For each answer choice, the **Real Question** is, *"Does this match the principle in the passage?"*

(A)   The mayor cannot be held responsible for every contract paid for with city funds.

No. This doesn't mention making the best decision.

(B)   Public officials are justified in making decisions quickly in order to bring about results rather than prolonging private bidding processes for too long.

No. This choice argues on the basis of making quick decisions, but the principle in the passage is concerned with making the best decision with the given information.

(C)   It is unreasonable for citizens to complain about public administrators whom they voted into office.

No. This doesn't mention good decision-making.

(D)   It is acceptable for the mayor to overpay for a service from a private firm so long as the success of that firm benefits the city's economy.

No. The principle in the passage is not based on benefiting the local economy.

(E)   Those who make the best choice from among the options of which they are aware should not be faulted for failing to choose the best course of action.

Yes. This is a good match for the Prephrased answer.

6.   **Choice (B) is the correct answer.**

This is a Conform question since the question stem uses the words *conform* and *principle*. As the principle is "illustrated" in the passage and the answer choices are composed of general rules, you are being asked to state the principle. A good general story of the situation presented in this passage can be based on the last sentence: statistics about the reported incidence of something don't necessarily correspond to the actual incidence of that thing.

For each answer choice, the **Real Question** is, *"Does this match the principle in the passage?"*

(A)   Statistical data sometimes support a conclusion that is the opposite of the most obvious interpretation of the statistics.

No. The principle in the passage is not about drawing the opposite of the conclusion that the stats would suggest—it's just about not blindly believing the stats.

(B)   Data indicating the reported frequency of a given event should not be treated as tantamount to data indicating the actual frequency of that event.

Yes. This is a fancy way of saying the same thing as the Prephrased answer.

(C)   The reported incidence of a disorder tends to increase in proportion to the public awareness of the incidence of the disorder.

No. In the passage, public awareness was just one example offered to show how there could be a disconnect between actual and reported incidence. However, the actual principle was not about public awareness.

(D)   The incidence of an event can never be fully determined based on statistics alone.

No. This is too extreme. The principle in the passage is that statistics may not always tell the whole story, not that statistics could never tell the whole story in any situation.

(E)   Public health can be influenced by the awareness of a given psychosis or disorder.

No. In the passage, awareness influenced reported incidence of a psychosis, not public health itself.

7.   **Choice (E) is the correct answer.**

This is a Method question since it asks *how* Nobuo responds. Koji argues that there was a problem, that the legislation fixed it, and that the legislation is therefore good. Nobuo doesn't argue that the first problem was solved, but says that a "more important" problem was created by the legislation, so it is therefore bad.

For each answer choice, the **Real Question** is, *"Does this match the argument?"*

(A)   refuting an assumption necessary to Koji's argument

No. Nobuo does not refute Koji's assumption but rather introduces additional considerations.

(B)   calling into question Koji's motives for supporting his claim

No. Koji's motives are never mentioned.

(C)   undermining Koji's assertion that the system of campaign regulation is valuable

No. Nobuo seems to think campaign regulation is valuable, just not as valuable as the freedom to express political opinions.

(D)   challenging the main principle that Koji uses to justify his conclusion

No. Nobuo doesn't challenge Koji's principle. He instead introduces a "more important" principle.

(E)   asserting that the benefit delineated by Koji is outweighed by a cost he did not consider

Yes. This is a good match for the Prephrased answer.

8.   **Choice (B) is the correct answer.**

This is a Conform question because the question stem uses the words *principle* and *conform*. In this case, you are asked to apply the principle. The principle pertains to these **circumstances**: if one is forced to steal in order to prevent severe physical or psychological harm and the victim suffers only minor inconvenience or loss. The **outcome** is: it is morally acceptable.

For each answer choice, the **Real Question** is, *"Does this match the principle in the passage?"*

(A)   Frank wanted to buy a new camera, but did not have enough money to make the purchase. He decided to steal the money from Greg, reasoning that since Greg was extremely wealthy, he would not notice that the money was gone.

No. This doesn't match the circumstances, since Frank's getting a new camera didn't prevent severe physical or psychological harm.

(B)   Emily, a janitor at a hospital, was prescribed antibiotics for her son, who had a serious infection. Since she could not afford the cost of the prescription, she decided it was acceptable to steal the antibiotics from the hospital storeroom, knowing that the hospital had a large supply and that no one would notice the missing antibiotics.

Yes. The antibiotics prevented severe physical harm (the serious infection) and caused only minor loss (no one noticed the theft). Thus, the theft was acceptable.

(C)   David needed money to pay his rent, without which he would be evicted. He stole the money from Henry, thus causing Henry to be evicted. David argued that Henry was a disruptive tenant and deserved to be evicted.

No. This doesn't match the circumstances since the victim was evicted—certainly more than a minor inconvenience.

(D)   Carla, discovering that her father had embezzled millions of dollars from his employer, took the money from him and disbursed it to several well-known charities. She defended herself by saying that because she had taken the money from a criminal and given it to worthy causes, her actions were morally justified.

No. There is no prevention of severe physical or psychological harm, and since millions of dollars were stolen, it's highly debatable whether the loss was a "minor inconvenience."

(E)   Brad, when he noticed that the clerk was not watching, added a piece of fried chicken to his tray at the self-service buffet. He reasoned that since the chicken would probably be discarded at the end of the day, it was morally acceptable to take it.

No. The piece of chicken did not prevent severe physical or psychological harm.

9.   **Choice (C) is the correct answer.**

This is a Method question since it asks you *how* the argument proceeds. You can use the Why Tool to determine that the director's conclusion is [the French neoclassicism gallery must be cleared out so we can convert it into the showroom for our new photography exhibit.] How does the director get to that conclusion? He rules out the possibility of not displaying the photos. He mentions building a new gallery but shows that option is impossible. Then he mentions the other existing galleries, but shows that option is also impossible. In short, he rules out the other alternatives.

For each answer choice, the **Real Question** is, *"Does this match the argument?"*

(A)   showing that the proposal recommended would be less expensive than any alternative

No. Cost is never mentioned.

(B)   proving a proposal to be superior by demonstrating that it has met certain necessary conditions

No. There is no mention of necessary conditions that the director's proposal meets.

(C)   supporting a proposal by disproving the feasibility of alternatives to that proposal

Yes. This is a good match for the Prephrased answer.

(D)   assuming to be true that which it is ultimately trying to prove to be true

No. This describes a circular argument, which the director's is not.

(E)   supporting a proposal by proving that it would be the most popular of all possible options

No. Popularity is never mentioned.

10.   **Choice (E) is the correct answer.**

This is a Conform question since the question stem uses the word *principle* and asks you to match the answer choice to the passage. In this question, you have to apply the unstated principle, since the principle is "illustrated" in both the passage and the answer choices—it's never stated.

Start by telling a general story of what happened in the passage. Your version should be something like this: even if it accomplished considerable good, something should not be claimed to be an unmitigated success if it had any significant negative consequences.

Next, think about the circumstances and outcome that the correct answer should have. The principle pertains to these **circumstances**: when something has both positive and negative consequences. The **outcome** is: that thing should not be judged an unmitigated success.

For each answer choice, the **Real Question** is, *"Does this match the principle in the passage?"*

(A)   Though the governor's tax initiative has had a positive impact on the economy, she has overstated the value of her program, because the favorable exchange rate played a role as well.

No. This doesn't match the circumstances because there are no negative consequences.

(B)   Amir cannot reasonably claim that his home renovation project was successful, considering that it ran over budget and did not turn out as well as he had hoped.

Lecture 8 Explanations

No. This doesn't match the circumstances because there is no mention of any positive outcome.

(C) Biawa's self-help books have indeed helped many people improve their lives, but he should not take all of the credit when so many of his colleagues contributed ideas.

No. This doesn't match the circumstances because there are no negative consequences.

(D) As Mrs. Lee's fifth grade students showed continued improvement in their math scores, she has claimed total success for her new teaching methods. This claim is supported by the similarly improved reading scores.

No. This doesn't match the circumstances because there are no negative consequences.

(E) The mayor's redevelopment project fully achieved the desired effect of raising property values, but he cannot claim complete success, as it also displaced many residents.

Yes. The positive consequences are the higher property values, and the negative consequences are the displaced residents. The outcome also matches since the project is called "not a complete success."

11. **Choice (A) is the correct answer.**

This is a Method question since it asks *how* Alfonso responds. Both speakers mention technical studies and repertoire, and both acknowledge that technical proficiency is necessary for a professional musician. Jean concludes from this that technical studies should come first. Alfonso disagrees. He brings up the additional consideration that "concentrating solely on technical studies may impede the development of musicianship." Based on this he concludes that musicians should focus on both at the same time. In other words, Alfonso brings up an additional issue that Jean didn't consider.

For each answer choice, the **Real Question** is, *"Does this match the argument?"*

(A) citing an important consideration that Jean overlooks

Yes. This is a good match for the Prephrased answer.

(B) arguing that technical proficiency is unnecessary for musical development

No. Alfonso said it's "not enough." He doesn't think it's unnecessary.

(C) disputing the evidence on which Jean bases his claim

No. Alfonso agrees that a musician must become technically proficient at an instrument. That's Jean's evidence.

(D) offering a counterexample to undermine Jean's conclusion

No. Alfonso does not offer any specific examples.

(E) suggesting that not all aspiring musicians have developed musicianship

No. This doesn't match anything that Alfonso suggested.

12. **Choice (D) is the correct answer.**

This is a Role question because the question stem uses the word *role* and repeats a claim from the passage. Start by breaking the argument into premises and conclusion. There are several things in this passage that sound like conclusions. The claim in the question stem sounds like a conclusion because it suggests a course of action using the word *should*. The claim that "enforcement is as important as imposition" sounds like a conclusion because it predicts the future and precedes the indicator word *since*. The claim that "manipulation of measurements is especially dangerous" sounds like a conclusion because it precedes the indicator word *because*.

But only one of these can be the real conclusion. If you use the Why Tool, you'll find that the real conclusion is this: [enforcement of those standards will be at least as important as their imposition.] The first half of the argument contains the premises that explain why the imposition of standards is important; the second half of the argument contains the premises that explain why their enforcement is equally important. The whole argument works together to support this statement.

So what about the claim in the question stem? It is indeed a conclusion, as it sounds like an opinion, suggests a course of action, and is supported by the sentences before it. But it's not the main conclusion. Rather it's an **intermediate conclusion** that supports the main conclusion.

For each answer choice, the **Real Question** is, *"Does this match the role of the claim?"*

(A) It is used as a counterexample to the claim that managers will always publish the information that maximizes their own wealth.

No. It's supported by the claim about the managers; it is not a counterexample to that claim.

Lecture 8 Explanations

(B)   It is the conclusion that the argument as a whole is designed to support.

No. It's an intermediate conclusion, not the main conclusion.

(C)   It is cited as further evidence to support the conclusion that the manipulation of financial measurements is especially dangerous.

No. It supports the main conclusion, not this.

(D)   It is a subsidiary conclusion used in turn to support the main conclusion that enforcement of standards is as important as their imposition.

Yes. This is a perfect match for the Prephrased answer.

(E)   It is a premise used to support the claim that managers should not be required to publish a yearly account of their companies' financial status.

No. Such a claim is never even made in the argument.

13.   **Choice (D) is the correct answer.**

This is a Conform question since the question stem uses the word *principle* and asks you to match the answer choice to the passage. In this question, you have to apply the unstated principle, since the principle is "illustrated" in both the passage and the answer choices—it's never stated.

Start by telling a general story of what happened in the passage. Your version should be something like this: someone should not be criticized for giving false information if the person who acted on it benefited from doing so.

Next, think about the circumstances and outcome that the correct answer should have. The principle pertains to these **circumstances**: someone gave false information, and the person who acted on it benefited from it. The **outcome** is: the person who gave false information should not be criticized.

For each answer choice, the **Real Question** is, *"Does this match the principle in the passage?"*

(A)   The financial advisor encouraged his client to invest in several sectors that have since lost significant value. However, since the advisor cautioned his client that there was some risk in any investment, the advisor should not be criticized for giving bad advice.

No. This doesn't match the circumstances. The person who acted on the information did not benefit from it, as the investments lost significant value.

(B)   The consultant made a recommendation regarding a structural change to the bridge that resulted in some damage to the supports. The bad recommendation resulted from an erroneous calculation by the consultant, so the consultant is at fault for the damage to the bridge supports.

No. This doesn't match the circumstances. There was no benefit from the false information.

(C)   The call center operator gave faulty instructions to the customer on how to fix the software problem. Because the instructions were ineffective, the customer was forced to devise her own solution and in the process gained better knowledge of the software. Since the operator is paid to give useful advice, he must be faulted for giving poor instructions.

No. This matches the circumstances, since there was false information and the person receiving it actually benefited. However, this doesn't match the outcome, since the operator is judged to be deserving of criticism.

(D)   Thomas erroneously told his mother her car was handling poorly when the problem was actually due to his lack of skill at using a manual transmission. When she sent the car to be inspected, the mechanics noticed and repaired a potentially serious brake problem. Thus, Thomas cannot be criticized for misinforming his mother.

Yes. This matches the circumstances—Thomas gave false information, but when his mother acted on it, she benefited from the repaired brake problem. It also matches the outcome, since the choice says Thomas should not be criticized.

(E)   The zookeeper fed the tigers food that is typically thought to be harmful to them. However, he knew that these tigers were able to digest the food without problem, and no harm came to them. So the zookeeper cannot be accused of endangering the tigers.

No. This doesn't match the circumstances since the zookeeper never gave false information. He knew all along the food would be acceptable. Also, there was no unforeseen benefit from the food.

14.   **Choice (B) is the correct answer.**

This is a Conform question since the question stem uses the words *principle* and *conform*. In this case, you are asked to apply the principle. The principle pertains to these **circumstances**: when there is an unsafe work environment but safety improvements are not logistically feasible and the employees are aware of and accept the risk. The **outcome** is: employers should not be penalized.

For each answer choice, the **Real Question** is, *"Does this match the principle in the passage?"*

(A)   All miners are aware of the many risks associated with their job, yet some mining companies could go to greater expense to ensure the safety of their workers. Therefore, mining companies should be penalized for failing to maintain a safe work environment.

No. This doesn't match the outcome, since the choice says that the mining companies should be penalized.

(B)   The stairway leading up to the church's five hundred-year-old belfry is dangerously narrow and uneven, but renovation is not possible given the layout of the building, and the bell ringer happily navigates the stairway to perform his task, so no penalty should be assessed to the church for failing to maintain a safe work environment.

Yes. This matches the circumstances, since the safety improvements are not logistically feasible and the bell ringer is aware of and accepts the risk. This also matches the outcome, since the choice says the church should not be penalized.

(C)   The chemical transportation trucks have a dangerous tendency to overturn at moderate speeds, but due to the specifics of their structure, they cannot be redesigned to be safer. However, since the trucking company has attracted enough job applicants that are unaware of the potential danger, it has a full crew of drivers and should not be penalized for failing to maintain a safe work environment.

No. This doesn't match the circumstances, since the employees are unaware of the risk.

(D)   The veterinarian's office is often visited by potentially dangerous animals, which sometimes carry communicable diseases. Since some of the office assistants are unaware of the potential risk from the animals, the office should be penalized in some way.

No. This doesn't match the circumstances, since some of the employees are unaware of the risk.

(E)   The deep fryer at the restaurant has a propensity to start dangerous grease fires, but the manager has trained his staff to put out the fires instead of replacing the appliance, so the restaurant should not be penalized for failing to maintain a safe work environment.

No. This doesn't match the circumstances, since the safety improvements are logistically feasible. The manager could feasibly replace the appliance.

15. **Choice (D) is the correct answer.**

This is a Method question since it asks *how* ("in which way") Al responds. Sherry tries to prove her conclusion about country T using an analogy to country S. Al responds by pointing out that S and T may not be analogous, especially given the fact that countries X and Y did *not* experience the same outcome as country S.

For each answer choice, the **Real Question** is, *"Does this match the argument?"*

(A)   He applies established general principles to a specific case.

No. Al refers to specific cases, not general principles.

(B)   He argues that two specific cases are analogous.

No. That's what Sherry tries to do.

(C)   He cites specific cases in order to demonstrate the validity of a general law.

No. Al argues against the validity of a general law. He thinks it "may not apply in country T."

(D)   He offers counterexamples in order to show that a specific case may not always be generalized.

Yes. His counterexamples are countries X and Y, and he thinks what happened in country S may not generally apply to every country.

(E)   He states a conclusion without offering any supporting evidence.

No. His evidence is made up of the specific examples he cites.

EXPLANATIONS

Lecture 9 Explanations

1. **Choice (E) is the correct answer.**

   This is a Parallel Reasoning question since it asks for the choice *most similar* to the passage. Take note of the Parallel Pair. There are three premises: a promised conditional and two facts, one of which is negative. The conclusion is a negative speculation: [it must not have been cold.]

   For each answer choice, the **Real Question** is, *"Does this match the Parallel Pair from the passage?"*

   (A)   The chef said that if no good beef was available, he would serve lamb instead. Since the chef is honest, and since he served fish, there must have been no good beef or lamb available.

   No. The conclusion has an OR, which doesn't match the passage.

   (B)   The advertisement claimed that if a stain were still wet, the product could remove it. Since the product failed to remove the wet stain, the commercial must have been misleading.

   No. There are only two premises, not three.

   (C)   The teacher said that if the weather was pleasant, he would hold class outside. Since he is always truthful, and it is nice out, he will certainly hold class outside.

   No. The conclusion is a positive speculation, not negative.

   (D)   The moderator promised that everyone who desired a chance to speak would get it, while still leaving time for the video presentation. Since she is a good moderator, everyone who wanted to must have spoken.

   No. There are only two premises, not three.

   (E)   The makers of the alarm system guarantee that if a break-in is attempted the alarm will sound. Since they are always correct regarding their product, and since the alarm did not sound, there must not have been an attempted break-in.

   Yes. There are three premises: a promised conditional and two facts, one of which is negative. The conclusion is a negative speculation. This matches.

2. **Choice (C) is the correct answer.**

   This is a Parallel Flaw question because it asks for the *flawed* choice *most similar* to the passage. Look for the flaw in the passage. The premises have a *many* and a *most* statement, but the author jumps to the conclusion that there is some overlap. The flaw here is that the author tried to use the Most-Most Overlap when one of the statements only had a *many*. That's a flaw.

   For each answer choice, the **Real Question** is, *"Does this match the flaw in the passage?"*

   (A)   Many agents are personable, and many agents are diligent. Therefore, some agents must be more popular than others.

   No. This has two *manys* in the premises.

   (B)   Many football players are selfish, but no football players are cheaters. Therefore, no football players are selfish cheaters.

   No. There is no *most* statement.

   (C)   Many children are inquisitive, and most inquisitive people are well read. Therefore, at least some children must be well read.

   Yes. This has the same flaw as the original passage.

   (D)   Many students are hard working, and all hard-working people are thorough. Therefore, many students must be thorough.

   No. One of the premises here is an *all* statement. That doesn't match the passage.

   (E)   Many doctors are creative problem solvers, and most creative problem solvers are intelligent. Therefore, it is possible that some doctors may be intelligent.

   No. The conclusion doesn't match. The original said there "must be" some overlap, but this choice says "it is possible" there is some overlap.

3. **Choice (D) is the correct answer.**

   This is a Parallel Reasoning question since it asks for the choice *most similar* to the passage. Take note of the Parallel Pair. There are two premises: an *unless* statement talking about what is usually the case, and a negative fact. The conclusion is a negative statement about what is likely: [his debut album will likely not draw much attention before its release.]

   For each answer choice, the **Real Question** is, *"Does this match the Parallel Pair from the passage?"*

   (A)   New technology is usually hard to use unless it is derivative of older technology with which people are familiar. Since PFI devices are a new technology that is not derivative of any older technologies, no one will understand how to use them.

   No. This is close, but the conclusion is a definite prediction, not a prediction about what is likely.

   (B)   Paintings are usually not popular unless they are truly original. Since Chen's most recent painting is truly original, he will sell it at a high price.

   No. The second premise is a positive fact, not a negative one.

(C)   Poets are usually not well known until after they have stopped writing. Since Ramesh has been published in many popular poetry journals, he is probably well known even though he has not stopped writing.

No. The second premise is a positive fact, not a negative one, and the conclusion is positive.

(D)   Flat-panel monitors are usually not energy efficient unless they measure less than 21 inches across the diagonal. Since Ray's flat-panel monitor is greater than 21 inches across the diagonal, it is probably not energy efficient.

Yes. There are two premises: an *unless* statement talking about what is usually the case, and a negative fact. (It may be a little hard to see, but by saying it's "greater than 21 inches across," the second premise is indeed negative because that's like saying it's *not* "less than 21 inches across," which is the criterion that appeared in the *unless* statement.) The conclusion is a negative statement about what is likely.

(E)   Animals are not usually sought after by zoos unless they are rare or interesting to look at. Since pandas are both rare and interesting to look at, they are probably sought after by zoos.

No. The premises here have ANDs and ORs, which is not the same as the original passage.

4. **Choice (C) is the correct answer.**

This is a Parallel Flaw question since it asks for the *flawed* choice that *most resembles* the passage. Look for the flaw in the passage. The premises establish that if there's some positive development, it will benefit all members of some group, but the author erroneously concludes that it would benefit the biggest member of that group the most. That's a flaw.

For each answer choice, the **Real Question** is, *"Does this match the flaw in the passage?"*

(A)   If there is a downturn in overall television viewership this year, it will hurt the advertising industry. Since Taro Marketing operates differently from most other advertising firms, it may not be hurt as badly.

No. The conclusion in this choice is not about the biggest marketer. It's about one that's "different."

(B)   If the food at Manny's gets a perfect score in the newspaper review, the restaurant will benefit greatly. Since Manny's is a new restaurant, it stands to benefit more from a good review than do large restaurants.

No. The premises aren't about all members of a group benefiting.

(C)   If the new travel guide awards a top rating to Grenada's beaches, it will benefit all tourist resorts there. Since Naricosa Beach Resort is the biggest tourist resort in Grenada, it will likely benefit the most.

Yes. This choice says all resorts will benefit, thus the biggest will benefit the most.

(D)   If the new fertilizer is approved for sale, farmers across the country will benefit. Since grain farmers stand to benefit the most, they should invest the most in the new fertilizer.

No. The statement about who will benefit the most is a premise here, not the conclusion.

(E)   If, as expected, the city of Houston is unseated as the most overweight city in America, it would be a boon to the city. Since Roger was the heaviest man in Houston, he must have lost the most weight.

No. The premises talk about *one* city benefiting, not all cities in a group.

5. **Choice (A) is the correct answer.**

This is a Parallel Reasoning question since the stem asks for the choice that is *most similar* to the passage. Take note of the Parallel Pair. There are two premises: an *all* conditional, and a *no* conditional. The conclusion is also a conditional involving the same three ideas, with a *not* on the right-hand side: [anyone who is insensitive to color is not a master painter.]

For each answer choice, the **Real Question** is, *"Does this match the Parallel Pair from the passage?"*

(A)   All of the guests who appear on Celebrity Chef are amateurs. No amateur is eligible to win the Great American Chili Cook-off. Therefore, the winner of the Great American Chili Cook-off will not be a guest from Celebrity Chef.

Yes. This is a perfect match for the Parallel Pair.

(B)   All of the guests who appear on Celebrity Chef will participate in the Great American Chili Cook-off. A celebrity often wins the Great American Chili Cook-off. Therefore, one of the guests from Celebrity Chef will win the Great American Chili Cook-off.

No. This choice uses the word *often* instead of a second conditional premise.

(C)   All of the guests who appear on Celebrity Chef are excellent cooks. No excellent cook uses both food coloring and artificial flavors. Therefore, any guest on Celebrity Chef who uses food coloring does not use artificial flavors.

No. This choice contains ANDs and ORs, which were not used in the passage.

(D)   All of the guests from Celebrity Chef who specialize in Creole cooking will participate in the Great American Chili Cook-off. None of the guests from Celebrity Chef who specialize in Tex-Mex cooking will participate in the Great American Chili Cook-off. Therefore, the winner of the Great American Chili Cook-off cannot be a specialist in Tex-Mex cooking.

No. There are way too many logical elements involved here. The original passage had three, but this has six.

(E)   All of the guests who appear on Celebrity Chef are master chefs. It is impossible to objectively judge the work of a master chef. Therefore, it is impossible to evaluate the skills of the guests who appear on Celebrity Chef.

No. The premises in this choice refer to "objectively judging" chefs, but the conclusion refers to "evaluating the skills" of the chefs. A Concept Shift like this did not appear in the original argument.

6.   **Choice (E) is the correct answer.**

This is a Parallel Reasoning question since the stem asks for the choice that is *most parallel* to the passage. Take note of the Parallel Pair. There are two premises: a statement of a correlation, and a statement that a third factor may be responsible for the correlation. The conclusion says that the correlation doesn't prove causation: [it would be incorrect to conclude on the basis of this data that vegetarianism is the causative agent behind the decreased risk.]

For each answer choice, the **Real Question** is, *"Does this match the Parallel Pair from the passage?"*

(A)   Segments of highway on which drivers most often exceed the legal speed limit are also the segments of highway on which the most traffic accidents occur. However, it may be possible that increased law enforcement in these areas could lead to a reduced number of accidents, since drivers usually decrease their speed when they believe they may receive a citation.

No. The conclusion here suggests a possible solution to a problem, which doesn't match the Parallel Pair.

(B)   There is a strong link between cigarette smoking and an increased risk of heart disease in both men and women. Nevertheless, it would be erroneous to claim that heart disease is caused solely by cigarette smoking, since there are several other factors likely to contribute to a risk of heart disease, including obesity and hypertension.

No. This conclusion says the correlation doesn't prove cigarette smoking is the *sole* cause, but the conclusion in the passage says the correlation doesn't prove there is *any* causal link. Since it's about heart disease, this is also a **topic trap**.

(C)   Dentists know that those who regularly consume large amounts of coffee are often afflicted with dental problems as they grow older. Although it is impossible to conclude from this observation alone that coffee consumption causes an increased risk of dental problems, government regulators should take proactive steps to limit citizens' access to coffee.

No. This conclusion calls for a certain action to be taken, which didn't occur in the original argument.

(D)   Children who study music are also more likely than their peers to perform well on tests of mathematics. However, it would be a mistake to conclude that the study of music brings about the improved performance on the tests. After all, it could be true that the children who have the best innate mathematical skills are also the same children who are drawn to the study of music.

No. The second premise doesn't introduce a third factor that may be responsible for both things in the correlation. Instead, it suggests that the causal relationship between the two things may be reversed.

(E)   When a university installs floodlights on its campus, the action is usually followed by a drop in the number of robberies on campus. Yet it may be that the universities that choose to install floodlights are also likely to increase police presence on campus at the same time, so it would be wrong to conclude that the floodlights are responsible for the drop in robberies.

Yes. There is a statement of correlation between floodlights and fewer robberies, and a statement that a third factor (police presence) is responsible for the correlation. The conclusion is that the correlation doesn't prove that floodlights cause fewer robberies.

7.   **Choice (D) is the correct answer.**

This is a Parallel Reasoning question because the stem asks for the choice that is *most similar* to the passage. Take note of the Parallel Pair. There is one premise: a statement asserting that one element is the most important in some area. The conclusion brings up other elements and says they only matter insofar as they support the main element: [good actors, effects, and editing are only valuable to the extent that they can be used to augment a good story.]

For each answer choice, the **Real Question** is, *"Does this match the Parallel Pair from the passage?"*

(A)   One of the most important safety features a car can have is side airbags. Without side airbags, passengers remain largely unprotected in certain types of collisions.

No. The statement about which property is the most important seems to be the conclusion here, and the argument fails to mention other safety features in cars.

(B)   The most critical design feature for a building is its reflection of light. Uniqueness, fluidity of design, and contrast with the background are other critical design features.

No. The conclusion says the other properties are also critical, not that they only matter insofar as they support the main property.

(C)   The most important quality for a boss to possess is a good understanding of social interactions. Some bosses are successful despite lacking this quality because they compensate with extra effort and dedication.

No. The original argument never mentions things that *lack* the most important property.

(D)   The most important quality to have with respect to public speaking is the ability to communicate ideas clearly. Eye contact, body language, and humor are only helpful when they can enhance the audience's understanding of ideas that are already clear to them.

Yes. The premise asserts that clear communication is the most important property. The conclusion mentions other properties and says they only matter insofar as they support the main property.

(E)   The most valuable skill for a soccer player is good anticipation. Ball control, stamina, and selflessness are particularly important to master for those who lack good anticipation.

No. Again, the original argument never mentions things that *lack* the most important property.

8.   **Choice (E) is the correct answer.**

This is a Parallel Flaw question because it asks for the *flawed* choice that *most closely parallels* the passage. Look for the flaw in the passage. One premise establishes a conditional: dog → good sense of smell. But the author jumps to the conclusion that an animal with *something in common with dogs* (being a mammalian quadruped) must also follow the same conditional. That's a flaw.

For each answer choice, the **Real Question** is, *"Does this match the flaw in the passage?"*

(A)   All reptilian species lay eggs. Since marsupials are not reptiles, they must not lay eggs.

No. This introduces a couple of negatives, and it doesn't say marsupials have anything in common with reptiles.

(B)   No rabbits can digest meat, because they are herbivores. Since moose, like rabbits, are herbivores, they must also be unable to digest meat.

No. This is tricky, but the thing both animals have in common (being herbivores) is established in an additional premise to be the *cause* of the inability to digest meat. That wasn't present in the original argument (being a mammalian quadruped is not the *cause* of having a good sense of smell), and it actually makes the reasoning here valid, not flawed.

(C)   All physicians have medical degrees. Since both pediatricians and dermatologists are physicians, both must have medical degrees.

No. There is no flaw in this argument.

(D)   All old cars are unsafe. Since most unsafe cars are small cars, all old cars must be small cars.

No. The flaw in this choice is that it tries to build a chain using a single *most* statement. That's a flaw, but not the same one as in the passage.

(E)   All of the buildings in Lendale are built to withstand hurricane-force winds. Since most of the buildings in Carlsville were built by the same construction company as those in Lendale, they must also be able to withstand hurricane-force winds.

Yes. The first premise establishes a conditional: building in Lendale → withstand winds. But the author jumps to the conclusion that buildings with *something in common with the buildings in Lendale* (being built by the same construction company) must also follow the same conditional.

9.   **Choice (A) is the correct answer.**

This is a Parallel Reasoning question because the question stem asks for the choice *most similar* to the passage. Look for the Parallel Pair. There are two premises: one establishes that something (contagiousness) only happens within a certain window of time. The second establishes that a particular case falls outside of that window of time. The conclusion says the thing won't occur: [she is no longer contagious.]

For each answer choice, the **Real Question** is, *"Does this match the Parallel Pair from the passage?"*

(A)   The warranty covering broken parts on this automobile lasts for three months. Nan bought the car six months ago, so his broken fuel pump is not covered by the warranty.

Yes. One premise establishes that warranty coverage only occurs within a certain window of time. The next premise establishes that Nan's case falls outside that window of time. The conclusion says there is no warranty coverage for Nan.

(B)   Children must turn five years of age before they are eligible to attend kindergarten in this state. Bobby turned five last week, so he is eligible.

No. In this case, Bobby is *within* the time window.

(C)   The sanction against the basketball team for cheating was a reduction in scholarships from twelve to eight. Since then, it has regained one scholarship each year, and by next year it will be able to offer twelve scholarships again.

No. Even if you consider the sanction as being the window of time, the team is within that window, not outside it. Also, the original argument has no mention of gradual gain or loss; you're either contagious or you're not.

(D)   Many students extend their loans beyond the original 180-month repayment term, at a lower rate of interest. Susan repaid her loans in only 150 months, and though she was assessed a higher interest rate, she paid less total money.

No. The premise doesn't establish that something occurs only within a certain window of time. Also, there's really no conclusion here.

(E)   An employee receives 20 percent of the company's stock options after every full year of employment, becoming fully vested only after five full years of employment. Only half the marketing team has been with the company for five years, so not all of them are fully vested.

No. This choice features more than one case, some of which are within the window while others are not.

10.   **Choice (B) is the correct answer.**

This is a Parallel Flaw question since the question stem asks for the choice *most similar* to the *flawed* reasoning in the passage. Look for the flaw. The premises establish that two things can help a coach be more successful, including "occasionally rewarding the strongest performers with a day off from practice." But the author jumps to the conclusion that [the more days off from practice a coach gives, the more successful he will be.] The author overlooks the possibility that there can be too much of a good thing (if the coach gives too

many days off, they won't be "occasional" any more), and the author forgets about the other beneficial factor (building good relationships.)

For each answer choice, the **Real Question** is, *"Does this match the flaw in the passage?"*

(A)   Successful advertising campaigns create memorable impressions in the largest possible number of people. Hence, any advertisement that is not seen by many people cannot be considered successful.

No. This conclusion is about not enough of a good thing, not too much.

(B)   To be effective, a teacher must hold the attention of a class. This can be accomplished with diversions such as quick games, as well as by clear and authoritative speaking. Hence, the more games a teacher plays during class, the more effective she will be.

Yes. This is another case of too much of a good thing. If all the teacher does is play games, the children won't learn anything. This choice also forgets about the other beneficial factor, which is clear and authoritative speaking.

(C)   To be successful, an editorialist needs to keep readers from losing track of the argument. Besides communicating ideas unambiguously and concisely, the writer can use familiar examples to ensure that readers can follow the ideas. Therefore, learning to use examples effectively can make one a better editorialist.

No. The conclusion in this choice doesn't follow the form of "the more, the better."

(D)   A company needs contented employees to function well. Employee satisfaction can be increased by giving raises as well as by giving more paid vacation days to the employees. Thus, companies that balance these perks well will function well.

No. This calls for a balance of the two factors, which is not what happens in the original passage.

(E)   People appreciate the convenience of having a good variety of merchandise available in a store. Therefore, stores with good variety of merchandise will generally be more popular.

No. The premises here fail to mention two things that can both be beneficial. There is only one—good variety.

11.   **Choice (C) is the correct answer.**

This is a Parallel Flaw question since the question stem asks for the choice *most similar* to the *flawed* reasoning in the passage. Look for the flaw. The premises establish that the new truck is both less safe and more popular. But the marketer's conclusion, [it would be foolish to attempt to make it safer], mistakes that correlation for causation. That is, he thinks the decreased safety has caused the greater popularity, so increasing the safety would decrease the popularity. That's a common flaw: correlation vs. causation.

For each answer choice, the **Real Question** is, *"Does this match the flaw in the passage?"*

(A)   Many customers have complained about the price increases on several popular items. These customers fail to realize that there has been an increase in the cost of delivering the items to stores. Because of the increased cost of delivery, the store should not reduce the cost of the popular items.

No. The causal link (between delivery cost and retail price) is established here by the premises. It's not erroneously assumed by the author.

(B)   Many voters feel that the current sales tax unfairly places a burden on average families. However, the revenue from the sales tax pays for several valuable programs. Because of the relationship between the sales tax and the programs it supports, voters should not call for changes to the sales tax unless they do not consider the programs valuable.

No. Again the premises establish that there is no mere correlation—the sales tax actually supports the programs.

(C)   Several consultants have pointed out that the advertisements fail to indicate which brand they are meant to represent. The consultants should recall that sales have increased since the advertisements began running. Because of this relationship, there is clearly no need to modify the advertisements.

Yes. There is a correlation between the vague ads and the increased sales, but the conclusion in this choice is built on the idea that the vague ads are causing the increased sales. That's the same correlation vs. causation flaw that occurred in the original argument.

(D)   Parents of the students at Deerwood have been complaining about the lack of extracurricular activities. The parents have not complained about the lack of any art or music classes. Since art and music classes would be more beneficial, extracurricular programs should not be developed until art and music classes are in place.

No. The conclusion is fairly well supported by the premise that art and music classes would be more beneficial. There is no correlation vs. causation flaw here.

(E)   Some employees have complained about the decrease in hourly pay. These employees are neglecting to consider the corresponding increase in benefits. Because their pay has decreased while their benefits have increased, they should not be given an increase in pay unless their benefits are reduced.

No. This is not a good match, especially since the conclusion has an *unless* that doesn't match the original argument.

12.   **Choice (A) is the correct answer.**

This is a Parallel Reasoning question because the question stem asks for the choice that *most closely parallels* the passage. Look for the Parallel Pair. There are two premises: The first is a big conditional with an AND on the left-hand side. The second is the negation of the right-hand side of the conditional. The conclusion takes the form of *not one thing or not another*: [either James is not a great writer, or not all great writers know the literary canon.]

For each answer choice, the **Real Question** is, *"Does this match the Parallel Pair from the passage?"*

(A)   It is clear that either this is not a fun game or else not all fun games run quickly. This game has gone on much too long, and if all fun games run quickly and this is a fun game, then it should run quickly.

Yes. This is in a mixed-up order but notice the Parallel Pair. There is a big conditional with an AND on the left-hand side: "if all fun games run quickly and this is a fun game, then it should run quickly." There is a second premise with the negation of the right-hand side of the conditional: "this game has gone on much too long." The conclusion takes the form of *not one thing or not another*: "either this is not a fun game or else not all fun games run quickly." Everything matches the original argument.

(B)   One can become a great poet only by studying the great poets of the past. Jill claims to be a great poet, but since she has not studied the great poets of the past, Jill must not be great.

No. There are three premises here, and the conclusion doesn't feature an OR.

(C)   If all hot dogs contain beef, and this is a hot dog, then it should have some beef in it. But this is not a hot dog, so either not all hot dogs contain beef, or this is not a beef product.

No. The second premise contains the negation of the *left-hand* side of the big conditional, not the right-hand side.

(D)   Either Jim is a bad comedian or not all good comedians interact with the audience. Jim does not interact with the audience. And if only bad comedians avoid interaction, then he should try to interact more.

No. The *either/or* statement is in the premises, not the conclusion, and the conclusion gives a suggestion. This is a bad match.

(E)   This piece is composed by either Mozart or Haydn. If all great classical symphonies were written by Mozart, and this is a classical symphony, then this must be composed by Mozart rather than Haydn.

No. Again the *either/or* statement is in the premises, not the conclusion.

13.   **Choice (E) is the correct answer.**

This is a Parallel Flaw question because the question stem asks you to find the choice *most similar* to the *flawed* reasoning in the passage. Look for the flaw. The premises do allow you to infer that some people who do not like broccoli do like chicken nuggets. However, the conclusion tries to negate both things and make the contrapositive of that inferred *some* statement: [some people who like to eat broccoli must not like chicken nuggets.] That's a flaw. You absolutely cannot negate or make the contrapositive of a *some* statement.

For each answer choice, the **Real Question** is, *"Does this match the flaw in the passage?"*

(A)   No dogs can speak. And since most dogs can communicate, at least some animals that can communicate must not be able to speak.

No. There is no flaw in this choice.

(B)   No teachers are disorganized. And since most teachers are affable, at least some teachers must be both affable and disorganized.

No. There is a flaw here, but not the right one. You can infer that some affable people are not disorganized, and the conclusion here erroneously negates part of that *some* statement, but it only negates one half of it. In the original argument, both sides were negated.

(C)   No lemurs are color-blind. And since most lemurs are arboreal, there must be more lemurs that are arboreal than color-blind.

No. There is no flaw in this choice.

(D)   No owls are diurnal. And since many animals that are diurnal are not omnivorous, all owls must be omnivorous.

No. There is a flaw here, but not the right one. The most obvious problem is that the conclusion is an *all* statement, not a *some* statement.

(E)   No bird gives birth to live young. And since most birds can fly, at least some animals that give birth to live young must be flightless.

Yes. The premises here allow you to infer that some animals that do not give birth to live young can fly. But the conclusion negates both of these and says, "some animals that give birth to live young must be flightless." That's the same flaw as in the original argument.

14.   **Choice (B) is the correct answer.**

This is a Parallel Reasoning question since the question stem asks for the choice that *most closely parallels* the passage. Look for the Parallel Pair. There are two premises: The first says that one thing (government spending) causes another (softened impact). The next premise says the second thing causes a third (increased confidence) and a fourth (possibly shortened downturn). The conclusion is that the first thing causes the fourth: [government spending during an economic downturn can shorten its duration.]

For each answer choice, the **Real Question** is, *"Does this match the Parallel Pair from the passage?"*

(A)   A steady regimen of exercise can reduce long-term heath-related costs. Additionally, it can lengthen one's lifespan such that those benefits are enjoyed longer. Thus, reducing long-term health-related costs is correlated with a longer lifespan.

No. The conclusion here is about a correlation, not a causal relationship.

(B)   Intensive foreign-language study is an efficient way to increase professional skills. Increasing professional skills is a positive way to expand job opportunities and gain bargaining power. So intensive foreign-language study is an efficient way to increase bargaining power.

Yes. This follows the same kind of causal chain.

(C)   Good preventative dental hygiene is the best way to avoid complicated dental surgery. Avoiding complicated dental surgery is the surest way to minimize dental costs. Clearly, good preventative dental hygiene is the surest way to minimize dental costs.

No. There are only three factors here, not four, and the relationships are about the "best way" to do something, which doesn't match the original argument.

(D)   Effective bargaining is a reliable way to reduce costs and increase competitiveness. Bargaining skills are also essential for increasing revenue when selling products and services. Thus, both reducing costs and increasing revenue when selling products and services increase competitiveness.

No. The conclusion is about two things (*both* reducing costs and increasing revenue) not just one. This doesn't match the original argument.

(E)   Aerobic exercise increases the flow of oxygen to the brain. Studies show that aerobic exercise done as many as six hours before one takes a test can improve scores significantly. Therefore, increasing oxygen flow to the brain improves test scores significantly.

No. There are only three factors, not four. Furthermore, one thing (aerobic exercise) causes both a second (oxygen flow) and a third (increased test scores), but the conclusion says the second thing causes the third. That doesn't match the original argument.

15.   **Choice (B) is the correct answer.**

This is a Parallel Flaw question since the question stem asks you to find the choice *most similar* to the *flawed* reasoning in the passage. Look for the flaw. The study established that one factor (the new technology) had a certain effect (fewer fatal crashes). But the author jumps to the conclusion that something completely incidental to the study (being a foreign car) also has that same effect, even thought the study was not designed to test that hypothesis. That's a flaw.

For each answer choice, the **Real Question** is, *"Does this match the flaw in the passage?"*

(A)   A statewide survey found that people with full-time jobs are 20 percent less likely to be smokers. Since the survey did not record gender data, we cannot say whether men or women are more likely to smoke.

No. This logic is not flawed.

(B)   A recent study showed that people who drink more milk are at a lower risk of having a stroke. Since most of those in the study drank organic milk, we can also conclude that organic milk is better than non-organic milk at reducing the risk of stroke.

Yes. The study was designed to test the effect of milk. The fact that most of it was organic was incidental, so it's a flaw to conclude that organic milk shares the same effect.

(C)   A carefully controlled test showed that laptop computers running the new version of the operating system perform 40 percent faster than the same computers running the previous version. So we can conclude that computers are likely to run faster using the new version of the operating system.

No. This is good logic.

(D)   A recent study has shown that raw fish is much more likely to carry harmful bacteria than cooked fish. Since the fish used in the study was salmon, we can conclude that raw salmon is more likely to carry harmful bacteria than is cooked salmon.

No. This logic is not flawed.

(E)   Available data indicate that four-engine jets are 70 percent less likely to crash than twin-engine planes. Since most of the four-engine jets used in the study were built within the last five years, we can also conclude that even the least-safe four-engine plane built within the last five years is safer than a twin-engine plane.

No. This has a different kind of conclusion, since it compares individual planes, not the safety of an overall category.

IN-CLASS EXAM ICE LECTURE 10

EXPLANATIONS

1. **Choice (A) is the correct answer.**

This is a Weaken question, as you can tell from the word *weaken* in the question stem. The author concludes that [Brand X oil was no more effective at preventing engine failure than Brand Y], based on the premise that, with one exception, cars in neither group lasted more than 15 years. But the flaw is that you don't know exactly *when* the 34 cars that failed did so. Perhaps the cars using Brand Y all failed after two weeks, and the cars using Brand X lasted fourteen years.

For each answer choice, the **Real Question** is, *"Does this suggest that Brand X oil is more effective at preventing engine failure than Brand Y?"*

(A) The automobiles that received Brand X oil avoided engine failure for an average of eighteen months longer than those that received Brand Y oil.

Yes. Even though almost none of the cars lasted more than 15 years, this suggests that Brand X made a difference, since the cars using it did last longer.

(B) Some mechanics believe that the nature of Brand X's advertisements causes drivers who use it to drive more aggressively, putting added strain on their automobiles' engines.

No. What mechanics believe has nothing to do with whether one brand is or is not more effective than the other. That's **out of scope**.

(C) Nearly every driver in the study whose automobile received Brand X oil reported that the automobile's engine ran more smoothly than it had before the experiment.

No. The conclusion is about avoiding engine failure, not about what people believe or about engines running smoothly. That's also **out of scope**.

(D) Of the two automobiles that lasted longer than 15 years, the one given Brand X oil avoided engine failure longer than the one given Brand Y oil.

No. This is a small piece of good news for Brand X, but it doesn't address the argument's main flaw, and it doesn't weaken the engineers' conclusion nearly as much as choice (A), so it's not the choice that "most weakens" the argument.

(E) The manufacturer of Brand X oil sells several other products proven to reduce the occurrence of other types of mechanical failure.

No. The argument is only about the oils, not other products made by the same manufacturers. Those would be **out of scope**.

2. **Choice (E) is the correct answer.**

This is a Necessary Assumption question since the stem asks you for an *assumption* on which the argument *depends*. The Concept Shift here occurs when the author jumps from *can't allow approval or shelving* to concluding that the discussion was *insufficient to allow them to make a decision*. Couldn't there be other types of decisions besides approving or shelving, such as rejecting or calling for revision? The author assumed that a discussion that allows them to make a decision must have allowed the executives to either approve or shelve the proposal.

For each answer choice, the **Real Question** is, *"Does the argument depend on this being true?"*

(A) In order to discuss a proposal, the executives must be able to make a decision on it.

No. This would weaken the argument by suggesting that any discussion must lead to their ability to decide, but the conclusion here is that even after some discussion they *weren't* able to decide. Since this weakens the conclusion, the argument certainly doesn't depend on this being true.

(B) The advertising proposal can be neither approved nor shelved unless it is discussed to the proper extent by the executives.

No. The argument doesn't depend on there being no one else who can approve it or shelve it or on there being no other way that could happen. The conclusion is only about whether the discussion allowed the executives to make a decision.

(C) If the executives discuss a proposal extensively, they will approve it.

No. The premises assert that they won't approve it without extensive discussion, but that doesn't mean they *must* approve it *with* extensive discussion, nor does the argument depend on this being true.

(D) If a proposal is discussed at length, it should be either approved or shelved.

No. The argument is not about what *should* happen to proposals, only about whether the discussion allowed the executives to make a decision.

(E) In order for the discussion to allow the executives to make a decision on the advertising proposal, it must have led either to their approving it or to their shelving it.

Yes. This is a good match for the Prephrased answer.

3. **Choice (C) is the correct answer.**

This is a Flaw question since the question stem asks you to pick out a *criticism* that the argument is *vulnerable to*. The premises establish that all skilled fighters *know how* to use pressure-point attacks, but the author jumps to the conclusion that [every skilled fighter *uses* pressure-point attacks.] The flaw is that the author failed to consider the possibility that some skilled fighters might not necessarily use that knowledge.

For each answer choice, the **Real Question** is, "*Is this a flaw in the argument?*"

(A) takes for granted that different people respond in predictable ways to pressure-point attacks

No. This **doesn't match** the argument. The premises say people respond compromisingly, but they never say people respond predictably.

(B) draws a general conclusion based only on a small sample of responses to pressure-point attacks

No. There is no small sample. The premises are worded in such a way as to establish that pressure point attacks have the same effect on all people. This **doesn't match** the argument.

(C) presumes, without providing justification, that the use of pressure-point attacks is necessary in order to be a skilled fighter

Yes. This is a good match for the Prephrased answer.

(D) presumes, without providing justification, that fighters who use pressure-point attacks are always skillful

No. This distracter is tricky because it looks a lot like the conclusion, but the two ideas are backwards. That means it **doesn't match** the argument.

(E) fails to quantify the nature of reflexive responses to pressure-point attacks and how they can be compromising

No. Although the argument really did fail to quantify the nature of the reflexive responses, that's **not a flaw** in this argument. Even if the author had described the responses in more detail, the same flaw you identified earlier would still exist. This choice is a little like the common "fails to provide a definition" answer choice, which is *never* correct.

4. **Choice (D) is the correct answer.**

This is a Justify question since the stem asks you for a *principle* that *justifies* the reasoning. Look for the Concept Shift. The premises are concerned with what happened with the past tax regulations,

but the conclusion is that [in order to ensure that future legislation is similarly effective, lawmakers should again call upon academic experts to testify.] The switch between past and future is the Concept Shift. Look for a choice that connects the two, and use the New Concept Tool to eliminate any choice that doesn't mention using experts for future legislation.

For each answer choice, the **Real Question** is, "*Does this guarantee the conclusion?*"

(A) Legislatures that do not call upon academic experts in the crafting of regulations usually produce regulations that are not particularly effective.

No. This doesn't connect the past and the future. Furthermore, the word *usually* makes it weaker than the conclusion you're trying to guarantee, which said experts would *ensure* effectiveness.

(B) If a piece of legislation is effective because of expert testimony, future legislation will also be effective if aided by the same academic experts.

No. This comes very close, but it doesn't match the conclusion because it calls for *the same* experts, while the conclusion only called for more collaboration, not necessarily the same experts.

(C) Legislation is effective only if lawmakers call upon academic experts to testify as part of its creation.

No. This doesn't connect the past and the future, and the *only if* makes it backwards. Reworded, this choice says if legislation is effective, experts must have been consulted, which flows in the wrong direction from conclusion to premises.

(D) If a regulation is effective because of the testimony of academic experts, future legislation will be similarly effective if the legislature again calls upon academic experts to testify.

Yes. This connects the two sides of the Concept Shift, and it flows neatly from premises to conclusion.

(E) Legislatures that utilize the testimony of academic experts and thoughtfully consider all sides of an issue stand a greater chance of crafting legislation that is particularly effective.

No. This lacks the past-future connection, brings in the **out of scope** idea of considering all sides of an issue, and is too weak because it talks about a *greater chance* rather than an assured outcome.

5. **Choice (B) is the correct answer.**

This is a Strengthen question because the question stem refers to answer choices that *support* the argument. The geneticists' conclusion is that [by using DNA evidence they can overturn many mistaken criminal convictions.] This is based on the premises that the evidence can be stored, easily accessed, and evaluated as much as fifty years later. There are many flaws in this argument. How do you know the evidence will be accurate, properly evaluated, accepted, and properly understood? How do you know courts will react to it by overturning convictions? Since this is a Strengthen EXCEPT question, use the **EXCEPT Tool**. Four of the choices will strengthen the argument. Put an **S** next to those that do, and pick the choice that doesn't have an **S**.

For each answer choice, the **Real Question** is, *"Does this suggest that geneticists can overturn many mistaken criminal convictions using DNA evidence?"*

(A)   Appeals courts are likely to accept the testimony of geneticists who present DNA evidence.

This strengthens the conclusion, since if courts accept these testimonies, then DNA evidence can be used to overturn wrongful convictions. Put an **S**.

(B)   DNA evidence can become corrupted in some cases without geneticists' knowledge.

This weakens the conclusion. If geneticists can't tell when DNA evidence has become corrupt, then appeals courts have a good reason not to rely on this evidence. Don't put an **S**.

(C)   Genetic evidence loses none of its accuracy over long periods of time.

This strengthens the conclusion by ruling out a potential flaw in the argument. Put an **S**.

(D)   In many criminal trials, the only evidence for conviction was unreliable eyewitness accounts.

This strengthens the conclusion. If the only evidence in a trial was an unreliable eyewitness account, then appeals courts are likely to welcome and utilize additional testimony using more reliable DNA evidence. Put an **S**.

(E)   Though human witnesses may provide inconsistent accounts of a crime because of ulterior motives, DNA evidence is always consistent.

This strengthens the conclusion. If DNA is consistent while other forms of evidence are not, then the court is much more likely to use DNA evidence to overturn a conviction. Put an **S**.

Since choice (B) is different from all the rest, pick it.

6.   **Choice (D) is the correct answer.**

This is a Flaw question because the question stem asks you to identify a flaw in the argument. The

council leader concludes that [these numbers are a good measure of our constituents' opinions] based on the fact that those surveyed vote in every election. The two most obvious flaws in this argument are both statistical flaws. First, the study is conducted by a private day care center, which might be biased against the idea of state-run day care, so there might be methodological errors. Second, the respondents of the survey were only people who vote in every election, which is likely to be a small fraction of the council's actual constituency, and is probably unrepresentative.

For each answer choice, the **Real Question** is, *"Is this a flaw in the argument?"*

(A)   presumes, without providing justification, that the people surveyed were not already participants in a day care program

No. The leader only makes a claim about people's opinions of state-run day care, never about whether those surveyed participated in any day care. This choice **doesn't match** the argument.

(B)   bases its conclusion on public opinion rather than on an objective standard for governmental responsibility

No. This answer choice correctly describes the argument, but this is **not a flaw** in the argument. A conclusion about public opinion must rely on public opinion. The flaw is the way in which the opinion was measured.

(C)   fails to consider the possibility that state-run day care will cause an increase in voter turnout.

No. Even though the leader did fail to consider that possibility, this is **not a flaw**. Potential effect on voter turnout has nothing to do with whether the survey numbers accurately represent constituents' opinions.

(D)   generalizes from a sample that is unlikely to be representative of public opinion

Yes. This is a good match for the Prephrased answer.

(E)   attacks the credibility of the council members rather than addressing their concerns

No. This **doesn't match** the argument at all since the latter never talks about the other council members or their credibility.

7.   **Choice (B) is the correct answer.**

This is a Sufficient Assumption question since the question stem asks you for something that allows the conclusion to be *properly inferred*. The Concept Shift is basically the argument itself. Based on the premises that describe the tardigrade's ability, the author concludes that [tardigrades are better suited than any other animal to endure the rigors of long-distance space travel.] These are two completely different concepts. First, you can use the New Concept Tool to eliminate any choices that don't mention space travel. That gets rid of choices (C) and (E). Next, look for a choice that equates the two sides of the Concept Shift.

For each answer choice, the **Real Question** is, *"Does this guarantee the conclusion?"*

(A) Long-distance space travel is impossible for any animal that cannot survive extreme conditions.

No. This doesn't mention being *better suited* to space travel than other animals, which is an important part of the conclusion that needs to be guaranteed.

(B) An animal that can reduce its metabolism to zero activity and reanimate itself when conditions improve is always better suited than any other animal to endure the rigors of long-distance space travel.

Yes. This provides a link between the premises and conclusion ("is *always* better suited") that's strong enough to guarantee the conclusion.

(C) Animals other than tardigrades cannot survive extreme conditions.

No. This can be eliminated using the New Concept Tool.

(D) Enduring the rigors of long-distance space travel requires an animal to have the ability to reduce metabolism to zero activity and reanimate itself when conditions improve.

No. This doesn't mention being *better suited* to space travel than other animals.

(E) In order to survive extreme conditions, all animals must reduce their metabolism at least to some extent.

No. This can be eliminated using the New Concept Tool.

8. **Choice (E) is the correct answer.**

This is a Parallel Flaw question since you are asked to find the *flawed* choice *most similar* to the passage. The flaw in this argument is that it misuses a conditional. The first premise is a conditional, the second premise negates the left-hand side, and the conclusion negates the right. Basically, the author negated the conditional without switching it. (If you want to get technical, this argument commits the common flaw of confusing a sufficient condition for a necessary one.)

For each answer choice, the **Real Question** is, *"Does this match the flaw in the passage?"*

(A) If intelligence is caused by the number of folds in the cerebral cortex, then those with the most folds should be the most intelligent. But those with the most folds are not the most intelligent, so there is clearly no relationship.

No. This negates both parts, but it also switches them, so this doesn't match.

(B) If a coffee product is labeled "decaffeinated," it must have had over 97.5 percent of its caffeine removed. This product has had 99 percent of its caffeine removed. Thus, it is labeled "decaffeinated."

No. This choice switches, but it doesn't negate, which is a flaw, but not the same one.

(C) The Middletown orchard will stage a fireworks display on its anniversary. There are no fireworks at the orchard now, so today is not the orchard's anniversary.

No. This starts introducing extra terms by shifting from a discussion of staging a fireworks display to a discussion of whether the fireworks are currently at the orchard.

(D) The city council will ratify Adler's proposal only if it is better than Burke's proposal. Since Adler's proposal is better than Burke's, the city council will ratify it.

No. There's no negation here.

(E) If we have a moral obligation to improve the environment, then we will develop cleaner energy sources. But we have no such obligation, so we will not develop cleaner energy sources.

Yes. This choice negates both parts but doesn't switch them, so it commits the same flaw as the passage.

9. **Choice (C) is the correct answer.**

This is a Flaw question because it asks you to find where the argument is *vulnerable to criticism*. The premises establish that when there are 95 processors *functioning*, the computer operates at its designed speed, but it concludes that [the computer would operate at its designed speed if there were only 95 processors *present*.] The author assumes that all 95 of those present would be functioning, which is especially dubious given that he mentions elsewhere in the argument that there is a certain average rate of nonfunctioning processors. How do you know that rate of nonfunctioning processors would suddenly disappear if you removed five?

(A) takes for granted that the speed of the supercomputer is not affected by how many processors its has

No. This **doesn't match** the argument, since the author seems to imply that the speed of the computer *is* affected by the number of processors, at least to some extent.

(B) ignores the possibility that if five processors were removed, each of the other processors would function more quickly than before

No. This is **not a flaw**. The problem in this argument is that the author ignored the rate of nonfunctioning processors.

(C) fails to show that the proportion of nonfunctioning processors would decrease if five were removed

Yes. The author makes the dubious assumption that the proportion (rate) of nonfunctioning processors would go to zero, but there is no evidence to support this.

(D) takes for granted that the intended speed of the supercomputer can be achieved only if at least ninety-five processors are functioning

No. It's a premise that the computer functions at its intended speed when 95 processors are functioning, but the conclusion is not based on the idea that this is the *only* time the computer can function at its designed speed. This **doesn't match** the argument.

(E) overlooks the possibility that certain processors are a vital part of the supercomputer's infrastructure

No. Although the argument indeed overlooked this possibility, that's not what went wrong in the argument's logic. This is **not a flaw**.

10. **Choice (A) is the correct answer**

This is a Necessary Assumption question because it asks you to find an *assumption* on which the economist's argument *depends*. This argument does not have a conclusion indicator, but the entire passage builds up to the suggested course of action in the last sentence: [it is time to jettison game theory from economics.] This is based on the premise that there are more successful predictive models of behavior than game theory, which is a major Concept Shift. The economist assumes that the accuracy of a model's predictions is an important part of whether or not it should be involved in economics.

For each answer choice, the **Real Question** is, *"Does the argument depend on this being true?"*

(A) An understanding of rationality that leads to more accurate predictions is preferable to one that is less successful.

Yes. If one theory is less preferable to another, then the other should not be included.

(B) Game theory cannot predict how non-rational agents will interact in experimental environments.

No. The passage is based on predictive success in economic settings. Experimental environments are **out of scope**.

(C) Economists measure the success of a theory by weighing it against the results given by other theories.

No. The argument doesn't depend on this. You're looking for something to support the idea that game theory should be jettisoned.

(D) Economic theories are untenable when they provide experimental data that do not correspond to observations of actual people.

No. The argument doesn't depend on this being true. In fact, it's completely **out of scope**, since you're told that game theory is less successful at predicting behavior in economic settings, not that it provides experimental data that do not correspond to observations of actual people

(E) Game theory makes predictions that have been proven to be false through experimentation.

No. This is **extreme**. The conclusion rests in part on the premise that game theory's predictions are "less successful," not that they have been proven false.

11. **Choice (B) is the correct answer.**

This is a Weaken question since it asks you which answer choice *weakens* the argument. The author concludes that [parents should worry more about the number of books and less about reading to their children] based on the premise that nightly reading had the same effect as less frequent reading. The flaw is that the author never really established that reading to kids makes no difference. What's the effect of *no* reading? Could there be some kind of synergy between reading and the number of books?

For each answer choice, the **Real Question** is, *"Does this suggest that parents should still be concerned with reading to their children?"*

(A) Children with a moderate number of books in the home who were read to frequently were outperformed by students with a larger book collection who were not read to at all.

No. This is an **opposite** distracter. It strengthens the conclusion by suggesting that the number of books is more important than whether or not parents read to children.

(B)   The study also found that the number of books in a home has no positive effect if parents do not read to their children.

Yes. This suggests that reading to kids *really is* important, since without it, a house full of books is irrelevant.

(C)   Children in homes with no books never become curious about school subjects.

No. This potentially strengthens the conclusion, making it an **opposite** distracter. If the number of books increases curiosity, it might also increase interest in school subjects and performance. The choice also fails to mention reading to kids.

(D)   The families in the study with more books in their homes also sent their children to better schools.

No. This answer choice fails to mention anything that suggests parents should still be concerned with reading to their children.

(E)   Studies of older children show no correlation between the number of books in the home and success on standardized tests.

No. This answer choice is **out of scope**. The claim in the passage is not about older children, so this answer choice neither strengthens nor weakens the argument.

12.   **Choice (A) is the correct answer.**

This is a Misinterpretation question since the stem asks you about how Jorge *misinterpreted* Antonia's remarks. Look for the Concept Shift between the two speakers. Antonia argues against patenting *this sequence (of nucleotides)*, but Jorge argues in favor of patents *in the field of genetics*. His argument revolves around a different concept—a different type of patent—so he must have misinterpreted her to be talking about patents in the entire field of genetics instead of those just on the sequence of nucleotides.

For each answer choice, the **Real Question** is, *"Is this a misinterpretation in the passage?"*

(A)   asserting that patents other than those on the sequence of nucleotides should be forbidden

Yes. This is a good match for the Prephrased answer.

(B)   denying that researchers' discoveries should be protected by intellectual-property laws

No. This is too broad. He is arguing with her about patents in the field of genetics, not about those on all researchers' discoveries.

(C)   presuming that it is relatively easy for scientists to read the sequence of human nucleotides

No. Nothing in his argument addresses ease or difficulty.

(D)   referring to the raw data from which the discoveries come rather than to the development and use of discoveries

No. She *really is* talking about the raw data, but he misinterpreted her to be talking about something else. This is backwards.

(E)   calling for the cessation of research on human genetics until patent laws are clarified

No. Neither of them refers to the continuation or cessation of research.

13.   **Choice (E) is the correct answer.**

This is a Strengthen question since it asks you to pick the answer that would *most support* the argument. The last sentence of the passage uses the phrase *this suggests*, which indicates a conclusion. The conclusion is that [the arrowheads found at the first burial ground were made to be used in combat, whereas the arrowheads found at the second site were instead created to be buried with the dead.] The first part of the conclusion is well supported, since arrowheads can only be chipped in combat, but the second part is definitely flawed. How do you know the arrowheads weren't used in combat without getting chipped? (Remember, they *only* get chipped in combat, but you don't know that they *always* get chipped in combat.) How do you know that they weren't created for combat but never got a chance to be used? How do you know that they weren't created for some completely different third purpose?

For each answer choice, the **Real Question** is, *"Does this suggest that the arrowheads found at the second site were created to be buried with the dead?"*

(A)   Arrowheads found at both burial grounds had cultural uses regardless of whether they were used in combat.

No. This neither strengthens nor weakens the argument. If this is true it provides no additional support for the conclusion. It's **out of scope**.

(B)   Various other weapons that appear to have been used in combat were found at the second burial ground.

No. The conclusion is about the arrowheads. Other weapons are **out of scope**.

(C)   The arrowheads found at the first burial ground appear to have been made by the same tribe who made the arrowheads at the second burial ground.

No. The conclusion is about the purpose of the arrowheads. Which tribe made them is **out of scope**.

(D)   Some arrowheads that have yet to be found at the first burial ground are not chipped and are adorned with markings characteristic of burial ceremonies.

No. The conclusion is about the arrowheads that were already found. Undiscovered arrowheads are **out of scope**.

(E)   The arrowheads found at the second burial ground were made long enough before they were buried to allow ample time for potential use in combat.

Yes. This certainly doesn't *prove* the conclusion, but it does strengthen it by ruling out the potential flaw that they were created for combat but never got a chance to be used.

14.   **Choice (D) is the correct answer.**

This is an Evaluate question. The author concludes that [we can simply introduce the parasite in this area to control the mud snail population and prevent any negative impact to the local ecosystem.] This is based on the premise that the parasite controls the snail's population in New Zealand. But even if the snail's population really is controlled, the author assumes that the introduction of the parasite will not itself cause any negative impact. That might be true, or perhaps the parasite could attack other species as well, causing damage. Look for an answer choice that addresses this assumption.

For each answer choice, the **Real Question** is, *"Does this address an assumption?"*

(A)   Will the mud snail displace native invertebrates that constitute an important part of the diet of local fish?

No. The assumption is about the harmlessness of the parasite, not anything about the snail.

(B)   Is the parasite that naturally controls the mud snail population edible to most species of local fish?

No. The author didn't assume that the parasite was edible to local fish, and even knowing whether it is or isn't will not help you determine whether introducing it will prevent any negative impact to the local ecosystem.

(C)   Will the mud snail population explosion harm the local fishing economy if it is not controlled in some way?

No. Same problem. The assumption is about the harmlessness of the parasite, not anything about the snail.

(D)   Will the parasite introduced to control the mud snail population have any negative impact on the local ecosystem?

Yes. This is a good match for the Prephrased answer.

(E)   Has the mud snail caused irreversible damage to ecosystems in the other areas in which it has suddenly appeared?

No. The assumption is about the harmlessness of the parasite, not anything about the snail.

15.   **Choice (A) is the correct answer.**

This is a Flaw question since it asks you to find the flaw in the argument. The conclusion is that [review by colleagues is not a useful part of recording a measurement], based on premises that show it's not useful in two cases. But this argument is guilty of a false dichotomy. It talks about only two possibilities in regard to a measurement—the scientist either believes it's inaccurate or is sure it's accurate—but there could be other reactions. For example, maybe the scientist simply isn't sure whether it's accurate or inaccurate, in which case consulting a colleague could be very useful.

For each answer choice, the **Real Question** is, *"Is this a flaw in the argument?"*

(A)   presumes, without providing justification, that a scientist's only possible responses to a measurement are belief in its inaccuracy and surety of its accuracy

Yes. This matches the flaw in the Prephrased answer.

(B)   infers, from the claim that colleague review of measurements is useless, that a scientist who is recording a measurement will not request it regardless

No. This answer choice **doesn't match** anything that happened in the argument. The passage is about whether consulting colleagues is useful, not about whether scientists will choose to do it.

(C)   concludes, on the basis that a scientist does not erroneously believe that a measurement is inaccurate, that the scientist will be sure that the measurement is accurate

No. First, the passage never mentions anything about the correctness of beliefs, so another possibility is consistent with the passage: the scientist *correctly* believes that a measurement is inaccurate. A worse problem with this answer choice is that the argument's conclusion is about the usefulness of consulting colleagues, so the argument certainly doesn't *conclude* anything about the beliefs of scientists, as this choice suggests. That **doesn't match** the argument.

(D)   ignores the possibility that review of
         measurements by colleagues can be useful for
         those who are not scientists

No. Although the argument indeed overlooked this possibility, that's not what went wrong in the argument's logic. This is **not a flaw**.

(E)   takes for granted that colleagues cannot
         contribute to scientific work in other useful ways

No. This **doesn't match** the argument. It made no such assumption, since it had nothing to do with other ways colleagues could contribute.

IN-CLASS EXAM **ICE** LECTURE **11**

EXPLANATIONS

424 • Examkrackers LSAT Logical Reasoning

1. **Choice (A) is the correct answer.**

   This is an Inference question since it asks you what is *most strongly supported* by the passage. There is no obvious way to Prephrase an answer because the passage does not build on repeated concepts. Instead, move on to the answer choices and examine each one in light of the Real Question.

   (A)   A person's immune system can be induced into a course of action by an insect bite.

   Is it guaranteed that a person's immune system can be induced into a course of action by an insect bite?

   Yes. The passage states that there are some people who suffer from an elevated immune response because of flea bites. Fleas are insects, and therefore an insect bite can affect a person's immune system.

   (B)   People with particularly responsive antibodies are healthier than other people since their bodies more readily eliminate toxins.

   Is it guaranteed that people with responsive antibodies are healthier than other people?

   No. This answer choice is **out of scope** because the passage never talks about comparing the relative health of a person due to the responsiveness of his or her immune system.

   (C)   People tend to suffer more severe immune response from flea bites than from other kinds of insect bites.

   Is it guaranteed that people tend to suffer more severe immune responses from flea bites than from other kinds of insect bites?

   No. This answer choice is also **out of scope** since the passage does not mention any other kind of insect bite.

   (D)   People with responsive antibodies more quickly isolate and eliminate from their bodies the toxins from an insect bite.

   Is it guaranteed that people with responsive antibodies more quickly isolate and eliminate toxins from an insect bite?

   No. This answer choice is also **out of scope**. While the passage suggests that some people's antibodies respond to isolate and eliminate these toxins, it says nothing about how quick or effective this increased response is.

   (E)   Anyone who is bitten by a flea undergoes either an elevated immune response or barely any immune response as a result.

   Is it guaranteed that anyone who has been bitten by a flea has one of these two responses?

   No. The passage does not say that everyone falls into one of these two designations. There could be, for example, some people whose immune systems respond somewhere between the two examples mentioned in the passage.

2. **Choice (E) is the correct answer.**

   This is a Paradox question because the question stem asks you to choose the answer that *resolves* the *apparent paradox* in the passage. The two apparently contradictory facts in the passage are separated by the turnaround word *yet*. The correct answer must explain how it could be true that southwest Asians take this herb to cure debilitating conditions, even though Europeans found it to be a poison that causes a debilitating condition.

   For each answer choice, the **Real Question** is, *"Does this explain how both facts could be true?"*

   (A)   Europeans produce an enzyme that interacts with and destroys the chemical in Ashwagandha that disinfects wounds.

   No. This provides no explanation for why the herb poisons Europeans but not southwest Asians.

   (B)   The poison in Ashwagandha is not lethal, and the herb can be applied as a salve with a small amount of preparation.

   No. Even if the poison is nonlethal and the salve is easy to prepare, this does not show how something that causes a condition in some people could cure it in others.

   (C)   Without preparation as a salve, the herb is not poisonous but also does not act to cure debilitating conditions.

   No. This shows how the herb could be *neither* poisonous nor curative, but you're looking for an answer choice that shows how it could be *both* poisonous to some but curative to others.

   (D)   In light of the scientists' findings, the herb is very rarely consumed in Europe.

   No. This answer choice describes a possible European response to the findings, but it does not explain why southwest Asians are cured by the herb.

   (E)   The people of southwest Asia have developed immunity to the poison in Ashwagandha.

   Yes. The fact that there is a poison explains why the herb hurt the Europeans; the fact that the southwest Asians developed immunity explains why they weren't hurt by it.

3. **Choice (A) is the correct answer.**

This is a Point at Issue question since the question stem asks you to find the *point at issue* between the two speakers. In this passage, there is an explicit disagreement. Heidi says the editor's remarks are unprofessional, but Alain says that editors are employed to make comments like this—that is, they're professional. Look for an answer choice that expresses this disagreement.

For each answer, the **Real Question** is, *"Do the speakers voice disagreement about this?"*

(A)   the editor's criticism of the writers is unprofessional

Yes. This matches the Prephrased answer well.

(B)   publishing a biography about a movie star leads to pointless rumor mongering

No. This answer choice is **one-sided**. The only thing you know about Heidi's viewpoint is that she thinks the editor's remarks were unprofessional. She never reveals her own opinion of movie stars or writers—she only repeats the editor's comments on that topic. Thus, there is no way to know how she would feel about this choice.

(C)   fledgling writers have a responsibility to publish works that avoid rumor mongering and protect the privacy of stars

No. This answer choice brings in **out of scope** ideas that are not present in either speaker's comments.

(D)   it is expected that fledgling writers would produce works about interesting people

No. This answer choice also brings in **out of scope** ideas that are not present in either speaker's comments.

(E)   fledgling writers present significant dangers to the careers of movie stars

No. This answer choice is **one-sided** for the same reason as choice (B).

4. **Choice (B) is the correct answer.**

This is a Method question because the question stem asks you *how* Madison responds to Emma. Emma concludes that Madison [cannot write effectively about the civil rights movement], based on the premise that, not being a member of an affected group, she doesn't have the sufficient motivation. Madison reaches the opposite conclusion, but her premises have to do with a *different* movement. She uses the analogy to show that there's no reason she couldn't have the proper motivation.

For each answer choice, the **Real Question** is, *"Does this match the argument?"*

(A)   citing the case of the feminist movement in order to demonstrate that the civil rights movement is worthy of attentive writing

No. While Madison does cite the case of the feminist movement, it is not in order to demonstrate anything about the civil rights movement. She's trying to make a point about her ability to write.

(B)   providing an analogy that contradicts an important premise in Emma's argument

Yes. This matches the Prephrased answer. Madison cites the example of men writing about the feminist movement to contradict the premise in Emma's argument that you need to be a member of an affected group in order to be motivated to explore that group's concerns.

(C)   questioning whether Emma is qualified to judge whether Madison's writing will be effective

No. While Madison does call Emma's point "grossly inaccurate," Madison is not questioning Emma's qualifications to judge, but instead is attacking a premise in her argument.

(D)   providing evidence against Emma's assertion that Madison is not a member of an affected group

No. Madison never claims to be a part of an affected group. In fact, with her counterargument, Madison implies that Emma's assertion is true.

(E)   elucidating Emma's unstated premise about what it means to be considered part of an affected group

No. Madison does not talk about what it means to be a part of an affected group.

5. **Choice (E) is the correct answer.**

This is a Conform question, as you can tell from the words *conform* and *principle* in the question stem. In this case, you are asked to apply the principle, and the passage actually contains two related but distinct principles. In the first one, turn the *unless* into *if not*, and you can see that the principle pertains to these **circumstances**: when an athlete is not more skilled than average or doesn't motivate others. The **outcome** is: the athlete is not a leader. The second principle pertains to these **circumstances**: when an athlete is less skilled than typical or criticizes teammates. The **outcome** in that case is: the athlete is a detriment.

For each answer choice, the **Real Question** is, *"Does this match the principle in the passage?"*

(A) Carmen has played her sport longer than the other players on her team and has thus become more skilled. But since her team usually loses, she is not a leader, even though she motivates her teammates to perform well by encouraging them.

No. This doesn't match the circumstances of either principle, since she *is* more skilled than average, and she *does* motivate her teammates.

(B) Geraldine is a detriment to the team because although she is skilled, it comes not from hard work but from her unusual physical size, and her bad practice habits set a bad example for her teammates.

No. Even if you construe setting a bad example to be the same as failing to motivate, the outcome should be that she is not a leader. But this choice doesn't match the outcome, because it says she is a detriment.

(C) Ira sees that his teammate has poor technique and gives him advice on how to perform better in competition. However, Ira is a detriment to the team because his teammate misinterprets the advice as criticism.

No. To conclude that someone is a detriment, you need the person to criticize (which Ira doesn't) or be less skilled. Since you don't know anything about Ira's skills, this doesn't match the circumstances.

(D) Marcia practices and trains with such dedication that she has become the most skilled player on her team. Marcia is a leader because her skill has led to numerous team victories.

No. Neither principle discusses how to judge someone who is *more* skilled than average, and neither principle has an outcome in which someone is judged to be a leader. This doesn't match anything.

(E) Craig scores an average of 25 points in every game, which helps his team win often. Since all the athletes on Craig's team display a similar degree of skill, Craig is not a leader.

Yes. If everyone is similarly skilled, then Craig is not more skilled than average. That matches the circumstances of the first principle. This also matches the outcome, since it judges that Craig is not a leader.

6. **Choice (C) is the correct answer.**

This is an Inference question because it asks you what can be *logically concluded* from the passage. In this case there is no obvious way to Prephrase an answer, so move on and attack each answer choice.

(A) It is unusual for a person's performance on memorization tasks to increase as a result of taking a dietary supplement.

Is it guaranteed that it is unusual for a person's performance on memorization tasks to increase after taking a dietary supplement?

No. This answer choice is **out of scope** since the passage never says anything about performance on memorization tasks when people take other dietary supplements.

(B) There is no dietary supplement that is more effective than ginseng at improving memory.

Is it guaranteed that there is no dietary supplement more effective than ginseng?

No. The passage says that ginseng is no more effective than any other dietary supplement, implying that there are dietary supplements that could be more effective. This answer choice is an **opposite** distracter.

(C) The dietary supplement St. John's Wort cannot be less effective than ginseng at improving memory.

Is it guaranteed that St. John's Wort cannot be less effective than ginseng?

Yes. The first line of the passage states that ginseng is no more effective than any other dietary supplement at improving memory, which means that every other dietary supplement is at least as effective as ginseng is, which necessarily includes St. John's Wort.

(D) A dietary supplement may be less effective than ginseng at improving memory.

Is it guaranteed that a dietary supplement may be less effective than ginseng at improving memory?

No. Ginseng is no more effective than any dietary supplement, which means that there is no dietary supplement less effective than it. This answer choice is also an **opposite** distracter.

(E) The majority of people who consume ginseng would cease to do so if they knew that it did not improve their memory.

Is it guaranteed that the majority of people would cease to consume ginseng if they knew it did not improve their memory?

No. The passage says that most people only consume ginseng because they believe that it improves their memory, but the passage never says anything about what they would do if they knew it was ineffective at improving memory. This is **out of scope.**

7. **Choice (C) is the correct answer.**

This is an Inference question because it asks you what *must be true* given the statements in the passage. This passage is loaded with *some* and *most* statements, and you might be tempted to diagram each one out. However, remember that you can only make an inference using quantity statements in two cases: when one is properly connected to a conditional (of which there are none here), and when you have the Most-Most Overlap. Do you see that here? Yes. *Most* bettors do so without studying the horses' records, and *most* bettors lose money, which means that *some* people bet without studying the horses' records and lose money. That's a good Prephrased inference.

(A)   Most people who do not study the horses' records lose money from placing wagers on horse races.

Is it guaranteed that most people who bet without studying the records lose money?

No. This is very close to the Prephrased inference, but the word *most* makes it **extreme**. You can only say such a thing about *some* bettors.

(B)   Most people who use intuition or superstition rather than relying completely on advice from friends lose money from placing wagers on horse races.

Is it guaranteed that these people lose money betting on horse races?

No. Again, while there is information about the majorities of the groups, there is no information about the breakdown of the groups, so it is possible that everyone who uses intuition or superstition makes money betting on horse races.

(C)   Some people who lose money from placing wagers on horse races do not study the horses' records.

Is it guaranteed that some people who lose money on horse racing do not study the horses' records?

Yes. This is a perfect match for the Prephrased answer.

(D)   Most people who place wagers on horse races either use intuition or rely completely on advice from friends.

Is it guaranteed that most people who bet on horse races either use intuition or rely completely on advice from friends?

No. The passage does not tell you what proportion of people fall into the categories it puts forth, so you have no information that guarantees this to be true.

(E)   At least one person who sometimes studies the horses' records while other times falling back on intuition or advice has lost money from placing a wager on a horse race.

Is it guaranteed that at least one person using that technique has lost money?

No. Since only *some* people use that technique, it could be as few as one or two people, and maybe they've never lost.

8. **Choice (A) is the correct answer.**

This is a Paradox question because it asks you to choose the answer that *resolves* the *apparent discrepancy* in the passage. The two facts that form the paradox are separated by the turnaround word *yet*. The correct answer must explain how it could be true that the scientists believe matter from outer space resulted in life on Earth, even though they also believe that any foreign object entering the atmosphere would burn up before it hit the surface of the earth.

For each answer choice, the **Real Question** is, *"Does this explain how both facts could be true?"*

(A)   The burnt debris from the extraterrestrial matter stimulated common elements to combine and form the nucleic acids in early life.

Yes. This answer choice recognizes that the object from outer space would be burnt up and describes how this debris could still influence life on Earth.

(B)   The nucleic acids found in early life were formed over heat vents deep within the ocean.

No. This answer choice gives an alternative explanation about how life on Earth formed but does not address the paradox in the passage. This is **out of scope**.

(C)   No part of the extraterrestrial object hit the surface of the earth because it burned up before it could do so.

No. This does not explain how the extraterrestrial object could influence life, and it only casts more doubt on the scientists' argument. This is an **opposite** distracter.

(D)   Extraterrestrial cells developed on other planets under vastly more favorable conditions than those on Earth at the time.

No. This explains how alien matter capable of producing life came to be, but it does not account for how this life could come to influence life on Earth. At best, it's **incomplete**.

(E)   The nucleic acids found in the extraterrestrial object were destroyed when the object entered Earth's atmosphere.

No. This does not explain how the extraterrestrial object could influence life, and it only casts more doubt on the scientists' argument. This is another **opposite** distracter.

9. **Choice (D) is the correct answer.**

This is a Conform question since the question stem asks for the *principle* that *underlies* the argument. Since the answer choices are composed of general rules, you are being asked to state the principle. A good general story of the situation presented in this passage is this: when neither the computer model nor the conventional theory provides conclusive proof of an outcome, one should reject the computer model and act on the conventional theory.

For each answer choice, the **Real Question** is, *"Does this match the principle in the passage?"*

(A) One should abide by conventional theory only if there is unconventional evidence that suggests the theory is correct.

No. This doesn't match because there is no mention of unconventional evidence in the passage.

(B) One should heed conventional theory only in the process of making a decision fraught with emotion.

No. The manager says they should heed the conventional theory in this case, but she never says they should do so *only* in this case.

(C) When no body of evidence can prove the outcome of a decision, one should delay action until such evidence is available.

No. This doesn't match because the manager calls for action, not delay.

(D) When a computer model contradicts conventional theory, one ought not act upon it unless there is conclusive proof it is correct.

Yes. The computer model contradicts conventional theory in this passage, and there is no conclusive proof it is correct, so the manager suggests they do not act on the computer model. Everything here matches.

(E) When there is uncertainty as to what the eventual outcome of an action will be, one should take that action.

No. There is uncertainty about *both* actions (closing the plant or not), but the manager doesn't suggest taking both actions—that would be impossible.

10. **Choice (C) is the correct answer.**

This is a Role question since the question stem asks you to judge what *role* a particular part of the passage plays in the argument. Break the argument into its parts. The research study is factual data, so that's certainly a premise. That premise supports the researchers' conclusion, which in turn supports the last sentence. Finally, the last sentence explains why the author thinks you should believe the first sentence. So the first sentence is the main conclusion: [a person's metabolic rate is determined by more than just level of physical activity.] This also happens to be the claim repeated in the question stem, so your Prephrased answer is that it's the main conclusion. By the way, notice that the researchers' conclusion is a subsidiary or intermediate conclusion. You're not being asked about it in this case, but a fair number of Role questions do ask you about subsidiary conclusions.

For each answer choice, the **Real Question** is, *"Does this match the role of the claim?"*

(A) It is support for the conclusion that the similar results were attributable to stress.

No. The claim in the question stem is the main conclusion, not support for any other conclusion.

(B) It is evidence for the position the argument is designed to discredit.

No. The author of the passage does not seem to be directly discrediting any particular position.

(C) It is the conclusion for which the argument is presenting a case.

Yes. This matches the Prephrased answer.

(D) It is an assumption upon which the conclusion relies.

No. Assumptions are always unstated. Something written in the passage can never be an assumption.

(E) It is a premise that undermines one of the argument's other premises.

No. The claim in question is the main conclusion, not a premise. Also, nothing in the argument undermines anything else.

11. **Choice (D) is the correct answer.**

This is a Main Point question as the question stem asks you to identify the *main point* of the passage. This passage contains a little bit of a counterargument: the author thinks that "it is *not* a coincidence that many unconvincing arguments are fallacious." So what does he think? The negation of this, and thus the conclusion, is that [fallaciousness can have something to do with an argument being unconvincing.] This conclusion is additionally supported by the premise in the last sentence.

For each answer choice, the **Real Question** is, "*Is this the conclusion?*"

(A)   Not all descriptions of an argument denote the same thing.

No. This looks like the first sentence, which is a **premise**.

(B)   An argument that is fallacious can be distinguished from other arguments by studying its impact.

No. This answer choice **contradicts the passage**. You cannot tell that an argument is fallacious by its impact because in the second sentence you learn that fallaciousness has something to do with the *structure* of an argument rather than its impact.

(C)   When people find an argument specious, it is due to the argument's logical composition.

No. This is something of a restatement of the second sentence, which is a **premise**.

(D)   The fact that an argument is fallacious often contributes to its unpersuasiveness.

Yes. This closely matches the Prephrased answer.

(E)   An unconvincing argument is also likely to be unimportant.

No. This doesn't really match anything the argument said.

12. **Choice (E) is the correct answer.**

This is a Cannot Be True question. The passage has a lot of conditional statements. The first two sentences can be combined to form a chain:

$$\sim\text{BSCW} \longrightarrow \sim\text{RGD} \longrightarrow \sim\text{WE}$$
$$\text{WE} \longrightarrow \text{RGD} \longrightarrow \text{BSCW}$$

The next sentence is also a conditional, but it can't be added to the chain:

$$\text{PSTD} \longrightarrow \text{BSCW}$$
$$\sim\text{BSCW} \longrightarrow \sim\text{PSTD}$$

The final sentence must also stand alone:

$$\text{ANUUA} \longrightarrow \sim\text{WTD}$$
$$\text{WTD} \longrightarrow \sim\text{ANUUA}$$

Anything that matches the left side of a conditional but contradicts the right side is impossible, so look for an answer choice that does that. As always, keep a particularly close eye on the chain.

(A)   A candidate who gives unpopular answers in a televised debate may still receive generous donations from a number of donors.

Is it impossible that a candidate who gives unpopular answers may still receive generous donations?

No. This is possible. You know such a candidate would not win the debate, but you can't conclude anything else.

(B)   Given that donors do not believe this candidate has a good chance of winning, it is certain that the candidate did not perform strongly in the nationally televised debates.

Is it impossible that the candidate did not perform strongly in the debates, given that the donors do not believe the candidate can win?

No. This is possible. In fact, it perfectly matches the second conditional.

(C)   If a candidate does not perform strongly in the nationally televised debates, then donors will not believe that the candidate has a good chance of winning.

Is it impossible that if a candidate does not perform strongly in the nationally televised debates, donors will not believe that the candidate can win?

No. You can't conclude anything about someone who does not perform strongly in the debates. Thus, anything is possible.

(D)   Donors may believe that a candidate has a strong chance of winning the election even though that candidate did not perform strongly in the nationally televised debates.

Is it impossible that donors may believe that a candidate can win even though he did not perform strongly in the debates?

No. Again, you can't conclude anything about someone who does not perform strongly in the debates, so anything is possible.

(E)   A candidate who is not believed to have a good chance of winning, but who performs strongly in a televised debate, may still receive the donations needed to win an election.

Is it impossible that a candidate who is not believed to have a good chance of winning, but who performs strongly in a televised debate, will still receive donations needed to win an election?

Yes. The first conditional tells you that someone who isn't believed to have a good chance at winning will *not* receive generous donations and will *not* win the election. This answer choice directly contradicts that, so it must be impossible.

13. **Choice (B) is the correct answer.**

This is a Complete question because the stem asks you to pick the answer that *completes* the argument. The executive mentions two things that will happen to employees: they will have to adapt to change, and they will have to be trained. But keep in mind the first sentence: this only applies at companies experiencing significant profit growth. A good Prephrased conclusion is that [the workforce will have to adapt to change and be trained if the company is experiencing significant profit growth.]

For each answer choice, the **Real Question** is, "*Is this the conclusion?*"

(A)   increase in size if the business is innovative enough to invest its profits in expansion

No. Size is never mentioned and is completely **out of scope**.

(B)   become more skilled if the company is undergoing a period of significant profit growth

Yes. This answer choice is very close to the Prephrased answer. You know they'll be trained, so it is "probably" true that they'll become more skilled.

(C)   decrease in size through the dismissal of those employees who cannot adapt to pervasive changes

No. Size is never mentioned and is completely **out of scope**.

(D)   become more skilled in order to adapt to pervasive changes in the work environment.

No. This matches the line of reasoning in the second two premises, but it does not use the first premise at all. The executive never said this would happen at *any* given company, only at those experiencing significant profit growth.

(E)   be best served through intense training sessions that rapidly instill in employees the skills they need to succeed

No. The executive mentions training sessions but never anything about their nature. That's **out of scope**.

14. **Choice (E) is the correct answer.**

This is an Inference question since it asks you what *logically follows* from the passage. Most of the statements tell you what could be true or isn't necessarily true, which doesn't usually help you make inferences. One thing for sure is that if a dancer is eye-catching, then he or she definitely uses dramatic or exaggerated facial expressions. You can't combine any repeated concepts to come up with anything else that is certain.

(A)   A Latin dancer who uses dramatic expressions but does not demonstrate a great deal of personality is not eye-catching.

Is it guaranteed that any Latin dancer who uses dramatic expressions but does not demonstrate a great deal of personality is not eye-catching?

No. This doesn't match the one conditional in the passage.

(B)   If a Latin dancer wears flashy costumes but does not demonstrate a great deal of personality, then she is not eye-catching.

Is it guaranteed that if a dancer wears flashy costumes but does not demonstrate personality that he or she is not eye-catching?

No. The last sentence says that a Latin dancer with personality can get away with average technique, but it does not suggest that demonstrating personality is required to be eye-catching.

(C)   Only if a Latin dancer is eye-catching does he or she use dramatic expressions.

Is it guaranteed that only if a Latin dancer is eye-catching does he or she use dramatic expressions?

No. Because of the *only if*, this gets the conditional in the passage **backwards**.

(D)   All Latin dancers who do not use dramatic expressions but exhibit superior footwork and a great deal of personality are eye-catching.

Is it guaranteed that all Latin dancers who do not use dramatic expressions but exhibit superior footwork and personality are eye-catching?

No. This is an **opposite** distracter. The contrapositive of the information in the passage says that any Latin dancer who does not use exaggerated facial expressions *cannot* be eye-catching.

(E)   If a Latin dancer does not use dramatic expressions but exhibits striking lines in his body, then he is not eye-catching.

Is it guaranteed that a Latin dancer who does not use dramatic expressions but exhibits striking lines is not eye-catching?

Yes. The contrapositive of the information in the passage says that any Latin dancer who does not use exaggerated facial expressions cannot be eye-catching, and this answer choice matches that statement.

15. **Choice (D) is the correct answer.**

This is a Parallel Reasoning question as the question stem asks you to pick the answer choice that is *most similar* to the passage. Look for the Parallel Pair. This passage has only one sentence, but in that sentence there is one premise and a conclusion. The premise shows that one thing can affect another. The conclusion cautions against looking at the correlation and getting the causal relationship backwards: [the fact that cities with higher crime rates have more police officers does not prove that a greater number of officers causes crime.] Also notice that only two factors are mentioned in this passage: police numbers and crime rates.

For each answer choice, the **Real Question** is, *"Does this match the Parallel Pair from the passage?"*

(A)   Since a person's taste in music greatly depends on the taste in music of his or her friends, the fact that a person listens to one kind of music does not demonstrate that the person prefers that kind of music.

No. There are too many factors here: a person's preference, the friends' taste, what the person listens to, etc.

(B)   The fact that youths with smaller frames tend to outshine other youths in gymnastics does not show that a particular body type is necessary for gymnastics, for smaller-framed individuals tend to do gymnastics more often than others.

No. This answer choice has one premise, but its conclusion does not refer to a causal relationship— it instead refutes a necessary relationship.

(C)   The fact that two medical treatments cause similar side effects does not mean that those treatments affect the same part of the body, since a particular side effect can be the result of any number of different causes.

No. This has the wrong type of premise. Instead of showing that one thing can affect another, this shows that *many* things could all cause the same side effect.

(D)   Having a low income often forces a person to consume a diet of low nutritional quality, so the fact that people who consume nutritionally poor diets have lower incomes does not prove that a poor diet leads to a lower income.

Yes. The premise shows that low income can cause bad diet. The conclusion cautions against looking at the correlation and getting the causal relationship backwards, and it restricts the discussion to the same two factors.

(E)   Superior attention to detail is not necessary for success in business if one has creative ideas. The fact that some businesspeople are successful but cannot generate original ideas proves that they must have superior attention to detail.

No. This has the wrong type of premise. Instead of showing that one thing can affect another, this shows that one thing is not necessary if you have a different thing.

About the Author

David Lynch has been teaching test preparation since 2001. He achieved 99th percentile scores on the LSAT, GMAT, SAT, and GRE and enjoys turning his abilities into unique and powerful materials that can help others achieve their career goals. He has won several awards for his teaching and has authored all the books in the Examkrackers LSAT series. He currently resides in Philadelphia with his wife.